BIBLIOGRAPHICAL GUIDE TO IRAN

BIBLIOGRAPHICAL GUIDE TO IRAN

The Middle East Library Committee Guide

EDITED BY

L. P. ELWELL-SUTTON

THE HARVESTER PRESS · SUSSEX

BARNES & NOBLE BOOKS · NEW JERSEY

First published in Great Britain in 1983 by
THE HARVESTER PRESS LIMITED
Publisher: John Spiers
16 Ship Street, Brighton, Sussex

and in the USA by
BARNES & NOBLE BOOKS
81 Adams Drive, Totowa, New Jersey 07512

British Library Cataloguing in Publication Data
Bibliographical guide to Iran.
1. Iran—Bibliography
I. Elwell-Sutton, L. P.
016.955 Z3366.A6

ISBN 0-7108-0412-1

Library of Congress Cataloging in Publication Data
Main entry under title:

Bibliographical guide to Iran.
1. Iran—Bibliography. I. Elwell-Sutton, L. P.
(Lawrence Paul)
Z3366.B5 1983 016.955 82-22748
[DS254.5]
ISBN 0-389-20339-4

Printed in Great Britain by
St Edmundsbury Press, Bury St Edmunds, Suffolk

CONTENTS

FOREWORD

Following on the success of the *Arabic Islamic Bibliography*, published in 1977, the decision was taken to produce a companion volume on Iran, and the work now in the reader's hands is the result. In the course of time the original scope of the book was modified; pre-Islamic Iran was included (in recognition of the continuity of Iranian culture), and while Islam naturally figures very prominently, non-Islamic aspects are given due coverage, especially in the chapters on Religion, History, and Language. Moreover the structure of the book has been based on a thematic classification, rather than dealing primarily with types of material.

In the past scholars aimed to produce encyclopaedic works in which all existing knowledge of the particular field was contained. An outstanding example of this genre was the monumental *Grundriss der iranischen Philologie*, published in 1895-1904, while the two editions of the *Encyclopaedia of Islam*, and the recently launched *Encyclopaedia Iranica*, mark the furthest point that such projects can successfully attain. The accumulation of knowledge is now so great that it cannot be covered in a shelf-ful of books, let alone in a single volume. The present work therefore has a different aim; like the others, it is encyclopaedic, but instead of itself containing the knowledge sought, it is designed rather to point out where it is to be found, to signpost the road for the student, scholar and research worker. It does not seek to be an exhaustive bibliography (even this is now impossible within the confines of a single volume), but rather to list the most useful and significant books and articles in each of the fields with which it deals, and as far as possible to indicate the scope and usefulness of each. The intention is that the senior undergraduate student, the postgraduate researcher, and even the established scholar in any field related to the civilization and culture of Iran, should have a guide to lead him through the maze of available scholarship, and to help him to build up his own specialized bibliography.

The *Guide* is the cooperative product of a team of more than thirty scholars specializing in different aspects of Iran and the Middle East.

This has helped to ensure that the coverage of each subject is as balanced, accurate and up to date as human endeavour can make it. Each contributor was given as free a hand as he wished, and editorial control has been confined to standardizing, avoiding unnecessary duplication, and ensuring that roughly equivalent depth of coverage has been maintained throughout. At the same time it has been accepted that somewhat more attention should be paid to areas of interest that have been neglected bibliographically in the past. While inevitably the main emphasis has been on material in the English language, the hope is that the *Guide* will be found useful by scholars throughout the world, and consequently no linguistic restriction was placed on choice of citations. Relevant material is listed in French, German, Russian, Italian and other European languages, as well of course as in Persian and Arabic. To save space, bibliographical details are reduced to a minimum; names of publishers are generally omitted, page-length of books is not given, and publication dates are quoted only in the European (AD) form. Moreover bibliographical details are given only on the item's first appearance; where it is repeated, a short title is followed by a cross-reference to the first citation.

The editor's thanks go to the many contributors whose names are listed on pp.xvi-xvii, and also to Miss Caroline McCanna of the Open University, who patiently typed and retyped a seemingly unending series of redrafts of Chapter XIV, and above all to Mrs Grace Young, who out of a bafflingly miscellaneous collection of contributions both typed and handwritten in a variety of styles and formats produced a homogeneous and intelligible first draft, and followed that by successfully completing the difficult task of making an error-free 'camera-ready' typescript for the printers.

Financial assistance towards the publication of this volume is gratefully acknowledged from the University of Edinburgh, the Manchester University Egyptian and Oriental Society, and the British Society for Middle Eastern Studies.

In a work such as this there can never be full and final agreement on what should be included and what omitted. Everyone will have his private complaint, his outrage at the omission of a favourite piece of work. But if the *Guide* succeeds in no more than pointing the enquirer in the right direction, it will have achieved its purpose.

L.P. E-S.

LIST OF CONTRIBUTORS

In a composite work such as the present one, it is difficult to allocate credit freely and fairly. While some chapters are almost entirely the work of one individual, others have been put together from contributions and suggestions made by a number of specialists in different fields, though under the direction of an editor who indeed may in the end have done the lion's share of the work. For this reason it was thought best not to provide each chapter or section with its own byline, but rather to compile a general list of contributors together with an indication of the contributions they have made.

AUCHTERLONIE, J P C (Exeter University Library), VIII Muslim Geographers and Travellers. XIII Film (non-Iranian).

AVERY, P W (University of Cambridge), IX Modern History.

BAGLEY, F R C (School of Oriental Studies, University of Durham), VIII Geography. XIV Education and Law.

BAILY, John (Queen's University of Belfast), XIII Music.

*BEELEY, Brian W (Open University), XIV Social Sciences.

*BEHN, Wolfgang H (Staatsbibliothek, Berlin), II Bibliographies and Reference Works. V Official Publications. XV Epilogue. Also contributions to III Libraries. IV Press. IX Archaeology, Epigraphy and Palaeography. XIV Social Sciences.

BLEANEY, C Heather (University of Durham), XIV General works.

BOSWORTH, C E (University of Manchester), IX Islamic Iran up to the Mongol Period, Martial Arts and Sports.

CHELKOWSKI, Peter (New York University), XIII Ta^{c}ziya.

*COOK, Andrew S (India Office Library and Records), VIII Geography and Topography, Maps.

DARKE, Hubert S G (University of Cambridge), X New Persian.

FARHAT, Hormoz (Queen's University of Belfast), XIII Music.

GAFFARY, Farrokh (Paris), XIII Theatre, Dance, Film, Radio and Television, Zūrkhāna.

*HANAWAY, William L (University of Pennsylvania), XI Literature.

LIST OF CONTRIBUTORS

*HILLENBRAND, Robert (University of Edinburgh), XII Arts and Crafts.

JACKSON, Peter (University of Keele), IX From the Mongol invasion to the rise of the Ṣafavids.

LAWLESS, Richard I (University of Durham), XIV General works.

MacEOIN, Denis M (University of Newcastle), VI Shaikhism, Babism, Baha'ism.

McLACHLAN, Keith S (School of Oriental and African Studies, University of London), XIV Economy.

MOJTAHEDI, Ahmad (University of Isfahan), VIII Geography (Persian titles).

NERSESSIAN, V (British Library), X Armenian.

PEARSON, J D (School of Oriental and African Studies, University of London), III Manuscripts, Libraries and Archives. IX Archaeology.

*SALIBA, George (Columbia University), VII Science and Technology.

SAVORY, R M (Trinity College, Toronto), IX Iran under the Ṣafavids.

SCARCE, Jennifer M (Royal Scottish Museum Edinburgh), VIII European Travel Accounts, Guide Books, XII Carpets, Textiles and Costume.

SIMS-WILLIAMS, Nicholas (School of Oriental and African Studies, University of London), X Old, Middle and Modern Iranian languages.

*SIMS-WILLIAMS, Ursula (India Office Library and Records), X Languages.

TAPPER, Richard (School of Oriental and African Studies, University of London), XIV Social Groups, Villages and Rural Change.

TEYMOURI, Morteza (University of Isfahan), VI Islamic Law (Persian titles). XIV Education and Law (Persian Titles).

*WALEY, Muhammad Isa (British Library), VI Religion, Philosophy and Ethics. Also suggestions for X Languages.

*The names starred had overall responsibility for their chapters. Sections not otherwise attributed were provided by the General Editor.

Suggestions for Chapter X were also received from J ELFENBEIN, T O GANDJEI, B INGHAM, and J RUSSELL, and for Chapter XIV from W O BEEMAN, Hamid ENAYAT, R W FERRIER, and D J MARSDEN.

ABBREVIATIONS

AA	Asian Affairs
AARP	Art and Archaeology Research Papers
AeI	Athār-é Īrān
AI	Ars Islamica
AIA	Art in Iran and Anatolia
AIB	Arab Islamic Bibliography
AION	Annali dell'Instituto Orientale di Napoli
AJA	American Journal of Archaeology
AMI	Archäologische Mitteilungen aus Iran
AO	Ars Orientalis
AQ	Art Quarterly
AUFS	American Universities Field Staff
BAO bull.	Bulletin of the British Association of Orientalists
BBRAS	Bombay Branch of the Royal Asiatic Society
BM	Burlington Magazine
BMMA	Bulletin of the Metropolitan Museum of Art
BMML	Bulletin des Musées et Monuments Lyonnais
BSMES bull.	Bulletin of the British Society for Middle Eastern Studies
BSOAS	Bulletin of the School of Oriental and African Studies
CAH	Cambridge Ancient History
CAJ	Central Asian Journal
CH	Current History
CHI	Cambridge History of Iran
CHIs	Cambridge History of Islam
DSB	Dictionary of Scientific Biography
EI.1	Encyclopaedia of Islam - 1st edition
EI.2	Encyclopaedia of Islam - 2nd edition
EW	East and West
GAL	Geschichte der Arabischen Litteratur
GAS	Geschichte der Arabischen Schrifttums
GIP	Grundriss der Iranischen Philologie

GJ	Geographical Journal
GMS	E J W Gibb Memorial Series
GR	Geographical Review
HdO	Handbuch der Orientalistik
HJAS	Harvard Journal of Asian Studies
IAMMA	Islamic Art in the Metropolitan Museum of Art
IC	Islamic Culture
ICLQ	International and Comparative Law Quarterly
IDERIC	Institut d'Études et de Recherches Intertechniques et Interculturelles
IQ	Islamic Quarterly
I.stud.	Iranian Studies
ISMEO	Istituto per il Medio ed Estremo Oriente
IJMES	International Journal of Middle Eastern Studies
I.rev.int.rel.	Iranian Review of International Relations
JA	Journal Asiatique
JAH	Journal of Asian History
JAOS	Journal of the American Oriental Society
JAS Pakistan	Journal of the Asiatic Society of Pakistan
JCH	Journal of Contemporary History
JESHO	Journal of the Economic and Social History of the Orient
JHAS	Journal for the History of Arabic Science
JNES	Journal of Near Eastern Studies
JOR Madras	Journal of Oriental Research, Madras
JRCAS	Journal of the Royal Central Asian Society
JRAS	Journal of the Royal Asiatic Society
KdO	Kunst des Orients
MEA	Middle Eastern Affairs
MEJ	Middle East Journal
MELA notes	Notes of the Middle East Libraries Association
MERIP Reports	Middle East Research and Information Project
MES	Middle Eastern Studies
MESA bull.	Bulletin of the Middle East Studies Association
MW	Moslem/Muslim World
NTS	Norsk Tidskrift for Sprogvidenskap
PL	Persian Literature: a Bio-bibliographical Survey
RAS	Royal Asiatic Society
RCAJ	Royal Central Asian Journal
REA	Revue des Études Arméniennes

REI	Revue des Études Islamiques
Rev.géog.Est	Revue Géographique de l'Est
Rev.géog.Lyon	Revue de Géographie de Lyon
RIPEH	Review of Iranian Political Economy and History
RMM	Revue du Monde Musulman
SI	Studia Iranica
SPA	Survey of Persian Art
TESG	Tijdschrift voor Economische en Sociale Geografie
TOCS	Transactions of the Oriental Ceramic Society
UNRCAFE	UN Regional Cartographic Conferences for Asia and the Far East
ZDMG	Zeitschrift der Deutschen Morgenländischen Gesellschaft
ZII	Zeitschrift für Indologie und Iranistik

TRANSLITERATION

Methods of transliterating and transcribing Persian are legion. In making one's choice one must be guided first of all by the purpose for which the 'latinization' is required. In the preparation of grammars, linguistic studies, and so on, a *transcription* is needed that represents to a limited degree the pronunciation of the original language; the spelling in the original script is of secondary importance, and may even be irrelevant. On the other hand, historical, literary, philosophical or scientific works call for a *transliteration* that will enable the specialist reader easily to convert names and words back into their original spelling; pronunciation is of minor importance, though for the benefit of non-specialist readers it may be desirable that deviation from the actual sounds should not be too great. A further complication in the case of Persian is that many of the names and words are of Arabic origin, and book titles indeed may be in pure Arabic; it is probably preferable for that reason to adopt a transliteration system that is based strictly on the original script, and so can be applied to any language written in that script, regardless of pronunciation. The effect of this is of course to produce 'latin' spellings that may often look unfamiliar, but nevertheless are easily interpreted.

A second consideration is that, when transliteration systems, especially for Persian, are already legion, it is undesirable to invent yet another. It was natural therefore for the editorial working party to decide that one of the better-known existing systems should be adopted, and faced with the choice between those used by the *Cambridge History of Iran*, the *Encyclopaedia of Islam*, and the *Encyclopaedia Iranica*, they opted for the first.

In compiling a bibliography, a particular problem concerns the names of Iranian or Arab writers who frequently or solely use European languages, and latinize their names for this purpose according to some conception of their own. In the present work the policy adopted has been,

(a) when the author has written only in European languages, to use his own spelling;

(b) when he has written in both Persian or Arabic and in a European language, to use the properly transliterated form for his Persian or Arabic works and his own spelling for his European-language works, and in the index to cross-reference from the second to the first. In certain cases the transliterated form has been included in brackets after the European spelling of the name.

The *CHI* version of the Arabo-Persian alphabet, as adopted for the present work, is as follows:

Consonants

ʾ b p t s̱ (Pers.) ṯẖ (Ar.) j c̱ẖ ḥ ḵẖ ḵẖw̱ d ẕ (Pers.) ḏẖ (Ar.) r z ẕẖ s s̱ẖ
ṣ ż (Pers.) ḍ (Ar.) ṭ ẓ ᶜ g̱ẖ f q k g l m n v (Pers.) w (Ar.) y

Vowels

a i u ā ī ū ai au

DATE CONVERSION TABLES

Exact conversion from the Islamic lunar calendar to the Christian solar calendar and vice-versa can only be done with the use of tables such as Wolseley HAIG, *Comparative tables of Muhammadan and Christian dates*, London, 1932; G S P FREEMAN-GRENVILLE, *The Muslim and Christian calendars*, London, 1963, and others listed on pp.56-57 of the *Arabic Islamic Bibliography* (see II 2.3). For quick reference the following table shows those Islamic years that fall wholly within the corresponding Christian year. This will enable the intervening overlapping years to be ascertained without too much difficulty. Thus AH 18 = AD 638/9, AH 20 = AD 640/1, AH 30 = AD 650/1, etc; AD 649 = AH 28/9, AD 659 = AH 38/9, etc.

AH 19 falls wholly within	AD 640	AH 723 falls wholly within	AD 1323
52	672	757	1356
86	705	790	1388
119	737	824	1421
153	770	858	1454
186	802	891	1486
221	836	925	1519
254	868	958	1551
287	900	993	1585
321	933	1026	1617
354	965	1060	1650
388	998	1093	1682
421	1030	1127	1715
455	1063	1161	1748
488	1095	1194	1780
522	1128	1228	1813
555	1160	1261	1845
589	1193	1295	1878
623	1226	1329	1911
656	1258	1362	1943
690	1291	1396	1976

In Iran an Islamic solar calendar was introduced in 1924, the months being based on the zodiacal signs but bearing the names of the pre-Islamic Iranian months.

The following table will enable the corresponding Persian and Christian dates to be determined for any year between AD 1897 and 1029 (1276 and 1407 AHS).

Persian leap years

A	B	C	D
1276	1309	1342	1375
1280	1313	1346	1379
1284	1317	1350	1383
1288	1321	1354	1387
1292	1325	1358	1391
1296	1329	1362	1395
1300	1333	1366	1399
1304	1337	1370	1403

	1276 D 1407	All other years	A + 1 (excl. 1277) A + 2 (excl. 1278 B + 1
I Farvardin 1st (31) iv Apr.1st (30)	20.iii 13.I	21.iii 12.I	22.iii 11.I
II Ordibehesht 1st (31) v May 1st (31)	20.iv 12.II	21.iv 11.II	22.iv 10.II
III Khordad 1st (31) vi June 1st (30)	21.v 12.III	22.v 11.III	23.v 10.III
IV Tir 1st (31) vii July 1st (31)	21.vi 11.IV	22.vi 10.IV	23.vi 9.IV
V Mordad 1st (31) viii Aug.1st (31)	22.vii 11.V	23.vii 10.V	24.vii 9.V
VI Shahrivar 1st (31) ix Sept.1st (30)	22.viii 11.VI	23.viii 10.VI	24.viii 9.VI
VII Mehr 1st (30) x Oct.1st (31)	22.ix 10.VII	23.ix 9.VII	24.ix 8.VII
VIII Aban 1st (30) xi Nov.1st (30)	22.x 11.VIII	23.x 10.VIII	24.x 9.VIII
IX Azar 1st (30) xii Dec.1st (31)	21.xi 11.IX	22.xi 10.IX	23.xi 9.IX
X Dey 1st (30) i Jan.1st (31)	21.xii 12.X	22.xii 11.X	23.xii 10.X
XI Bahman 1st (30) ii Feb.1st (28/29)	20.i 13.XI	21.i 12.XI	22.i 11.XI
XII Esfand 1st (29/30) iii Mar.1st (31)	19.ii 11.XII	20.ii 10.XII 11.XII[1]	21.ii 9.XII 10.XII[2]

[1] In Christian leap years 1964-2028
[2] In Christian leap years 1904-1960

(Reprinted by permission from L P ELWELL-SUTTON, *Elementary Persian Grammar*, Cambridge University Press, 1963 and reprints.)

On Farvardīn 1st, 1355 (March 21, 1976) the Imperial (Shāhanshāhī) calendar was officially introduced, a solar calendar reckoned from the putative date of the foundation of the Persian Empire by Cyrus the Great. Under this reckoning the year 1355 became 2535. This calendar was abandoned in Mihr 2537.

It is not clear whether the Islamic solar calendar has been discontinued by the Islamic regime in Iran; most propaganda publications carry the Islamic lunar date.

I

THE STUDY OF IRAN

1. *WESTERN TRAVELLERS AND SCHOLARS*

Although the scholarly study of Iran and Iranian history, literature and culture did not begin in the western world until the 17th and 18th centuries, western knowledge of Iran dates back to the dawn of history, and specifically to the 5th century BC, when HERODOTUS wrote his account of the early history of the Achaemenid dynasty. The most convenient text and English translation is that by A D GODLEY, published in four volumes in London in 1921-24 (and reprints).

Other classical writers from whom more or less reliable accounts of aspects of Iran can be gleaned include

THUCYDIDES (5th cent. BC), text and English tr. C F SMITH, 4 vols, London 1919-23 (and reprints). French tr. *La guerre du Péloponnèse*, ed. and tr. J de ROMILLY, R WEIL, L BODIN, 8 vols in 6, Paris 1953-72.

The relevant part is contained in Book I, pp.93-112.

CTESIAS (5th cent. BC), *La Perse, l'Inde: les sommaires de Photius*, Greek text: R HENRY (ed), Brussels 1947; *The fragments of the Persika*, John GILMORE (ed), London 1888; *Die Persika des Ktesias von Knidos*, K W KOENIG (ed), Graz 1972.

XENOPHON (c.430-354 BC), *Anabase*, ed. and French tr. P MASQUERAY, 2 vols, Paris 1949; English tr. *The Persian expedition*, tr. R WARNER, Harmondsworth 1949.

—— *Cyropaedia*, text and English tr. Walter MILLER, 2 vols, London 1914. French tr. Marcel BIZOS, 3 vols, Paris 1971-78.

DIODORUS (1st cent. BC) Siculus, *Bibliotheca Historica*, with English tr. C H OLDFATHER *et al.*, 12 vols, London 1933-57; French tr. Michel CASEVITZ *et al.*, Paris 1972- (in progress).

References to Iran throughout, but Book 11 is especially relevant.

STRABO (c.63 BC - 21 AD), *Geographia*, English tr. H L JONES, *The Geography of Strabo*, London 1917-32, repr. Cambridge, Mass, 1949-54; French tr.

G AUJAC, Paris 1966-75.

Book 15 on India and Persia is of particular relevance.

JUSTINUS (3rd cent. AD epitome of) POMPEIUS TROGUS, *Historiae Philippicae*, F RUEHL (ed), Leipzig 1886, also J JEEP (ed), Leipzig 1885; French tr. E CHAMBRY et L THELY-CHAMBRY, *Abrégé des histoires philippiques de Trogue Pompée*, 2 vols, Paris 1936; English tr. J S WATSON, *Justin, Cornelius Nepos, and Eutropius*, London 1882.

The original work, no longer extant, was written between 63 BC and 14 AD.

CURTIUS RUFUS, Quintus (1st cent. AD), *History of Alexander*, with an English tr. J C ROLFE, 2 vols, London 1946 (repr. 1962); French tr. H BARDON, 2 vols, Paris 1947-48.

PLUTARCH (c.46-120 AD), *Lives*, English tr. B PERRIN, 11 vols, London 1914-26 (and reprints).

The lives of Alexander (Vol.IV) and Artaxerxes (Vol.VIII) are relevant.

ARRIANUS, Flavius (2nd cent. AD), *Arriani anabasis*, English tr. E Iliffe ROBSON, 2 vols, London 1929, 1933; also by P A BRUNT, 2 vols, London 1976.

Volumes I-VII deal with Alexander, Volume VIII with India.

The next important sources are the accounts of travellers from Marco Polo onwards, for details of whom reference should be made to Chapter VIII of the present work.

By the 17th century, and more especially after the middle of the 18th century, travellers' accounts (though they continue to be of importance as primary sources) begin to be superseded by scholars applying the methods of western scholarship to the study of Iran. A comprehensive account of Iranian studies as so understood appears in

DRESDEN, M J, 'Survey of the history of Iranian studies', *HdO*, Abt.I, iv.2/1, Leiden/Cologne 1968 :168-90.

The following notes supplement and bring up to date the information in Dresden's article, which was completed in 1962.

AFSHĀR, Īraj, *Rāhnumā-yi taḥqīqāt-i Īrānī*, Tehran 1970.

This work devotes separate sections to the history of Iranian studies in the main languages of Europe and the rest of the world, together with lists of institutions and societies, individual Iranologists, journals, congresses, libraries and publishers concerned with Iranian studies.

A much more comprehensive work, of which unfortunately only the first volume has been published, is

SHAFĀ, Shujāᶜ al-dīn, *Jahān-i Īrānshināsī*, Pahlavi Library, Tehran 1969.

The first volume covers Argentina, Albania, Germany, Austria and the USSR.

The complete manuscript was deposited in the Pahlavi Library in Tehran, but its present fate is unknown.

Surveys of Iranian or oriental studies in individual countries include:

ARBERRY, Arthur J, *British orientalists*, London 1943.

—— *British contributions to Persian studies*, London 1942.

An entirely different publication with the same title is

BRITISH INSTITUTE OF PERSIAN STUDIES, *British contributions to Persian studies*, Tehran 1971.

AFSHĀR, Īraj, 'Communication au Premier Congrès National sur les études iraniennes', *Studia Iranica*, I/1, 1972 :147-54.

KARA, G, 'Recherches hongroises sur les langues orientales 1945-1970', *Acta Linguistica Academiae Scientiarum Hungaricae*, XXI/1-2, 1971 :165-71.

ZBAVITEL, Dušan, *Die Orientalistik in der Tschechoslovakei*, Prague 1959. English tr. Iris URWIN, *Oriental studies in Czechoslavakia*, Prague 1959.

Ocherki po istorii russkogo vostokovedeniya, 5 vols, Moscow 1953-60.

Ocherki po istorii izucheniya iranskikh yazykov, Moscow 1962.

Biographies of selected Russian orientalists.

MILIBAND, S D, *Bibliograficheskii slovar' sovetskikh vostokovedov*, Moscow 1975.

DANDEKAR, R N, and V RAGHAVAN (ed), *Oriental studies in India*, New Delhi 1964.

Iranian studies are dealt with on pp.137-56.

AFSHĀR, Īraj, 'Īrānshināsī dar Īrān-i imrūz', *Rahnumā-yi kitāb*, XIV, 4-6, 1971 :195-205.

GIŪNASHVĪLĪ, Jamshīd, *Bānuvān-i Īrānshinās-i Gurjī*, Tbilissi 1978.

Bio-bibliographic details on Georgian Iranists.

—— 'Īrānshināsī dar Gurjistān', *Rahnumā-yi kitāb*, XIV, 7-8, 1971 :480-84.

HONDA, Minobu, 'Īrānshināsī dar Zhāpun', *Rahnumā-yi kitāb*, XXI, 5-7, 1978 :486-92. English tr. 'Iranian studies in Japan', *Acta Iranica*, 2 :5.

KUROYANAGI, Tsuneo, 'Īrānshināsī dar Zhāpun', *Rahnumā-yi kitāb*, XIV, 4-6, 1971 :205-17.

2. *RESEARCH CENTRES IN UNIVERSITIES*

2.1 *Research facilities in Iran*

Research facilities in Iran itself (prior to the revolution) were described in a series of articles:

RAMAZANI, R K, 'Research facilities in Iran', *MESA bull.* 3 iii (1969),

6 i, ii, iii (1972), 7 i, iii (1973), 10 i (1976- by Īraj AFSHĀR), and also in

IRANIAN DOCUMENTATION CENTRE, INSTITUTE FOR RESEARCH AND PLANNING IN SCIENCE, *Scientific and technical research institutions in Iran*, Tehran 1972.

CENTRE FOR EAST ASIAN CULTURAL STUDIES, *Iran studies in Iran*, Tokyo 1978. Lists universities, research institutes, libraries, periodicals and scholars.

2.2 *Research facilities outside Iran*

A comprehensive list of centres of Iranian and Persian studies throughout the world appeared in AFSHĀR, *Rahnumā*, *op.cit.*, pp.130-55. Reference may also be made to the one available volume of SHAFĀ, *op.cit.* Information is also available in the standard handbooks.

Internationales Universitäts-Handbuch, 4 vols, Munich 1976-77.

The world of learning, London, annual.

World list of universities : Liste mondiale des universités, 1979-81, Paris 1979 (14th ed).

International handbook of universities, Paris 1977 (7th ed).

Commonwealth universities yearbook, London, annual.

Minerva, Internationales Verzeichnis wissenschaftlicher Institutionen, Berlin/New York 1972 (33rd ed).

The disadvantage of these works is that they are not classified according to subject, and so it is not easy to locate references to Iranian and Persian studies. Books and articles with special reference to the Middle East and Iran include the following:

LJUNGGREN, Florence, and Charles L GEDDES (ed), *An international directory of institutes and societies interested in the Middle East*, Djambatan/ Amsterdam 1962.

Based mainly on information provided by the institutions themselves, there are many entries where no information was available. The directory was therefore incomplete even when it was published, and is now twenty years out of date. Within these limitations it is a valuable guide.

BOLTON, A R C, *Soviet Middle East studies*, an analysis and bibliography, Chatham House Memoranda, 8 parts, Oxford 1959.

Part 1 carries an introduction and indices listing institutions past and present, periodicals and series in the USSR concerned with Middle Eastern studies. The other parts deal only with the Arab countries. 'Les études islamiques dans le monde', *REI*, 33, 1965 to 41, 1973.

A series of contributions by various authors on individual institutions. A complete list of these contributions is given in

PEARSON, J D, 'Institutions', Diana GRIMWOOD-JONES, Derek HOPWOOD, J D PEARSON (ed), *Arab Islamic Bibliography*, (see II 2.3) :157-59,

except for the last, by J WAARDENBURG on the various departments of the University of California, *REI*, 41, 1973, pp.297-305.

GIGNOUX, Philippe, 'L'Iran ancien', Charles-Henri de FOUCHÉCOUR, 'L'Iran moderne', *JA*, 261, 1973 :117-33.

Two of a series of contributions on Asiatic studies in France during the past fifty years, in a special number of the Journal to celebrate the 150th anniversary of the Société Asiatique.

A comprehensive survey of German institutions is

BÜREN, Rainer, *Gegenwartsbezogene Orientwissenschaft in der Bundesrepublik Deutschland*. Mit Verzeichnis von Institutionen mit gegenwartsbezogener Forschung zu der Region Vorderer und Mittlerer Orient, Göttingen 1974.

PIEMONTESE, Angelo M, 'Cinquant'anni di persianologia', *Gli studi sul Vicino Oriente in Italia dal 1921 al 1970*, Istituto per l'Oriente, Rome 1971 :307-408.

NURUDINOVIĆ, Bisera, 'Iranistike : Persian Studies', *Bibliografija Jugoslovenske Orijentalistike : Bibliography of Yugoslav Orientalistics, 1945-1960*, Sarajevo, Orijentalni Institut, 1968 :96-108.

Some 160-odd universities are listed and described in

EICKELMAN, Christine, *Directory of graduate and undergraduate programs and courses in Middle East studies in the United States, Canada and abroad, with* [a] *Directory of library collections on the Middle East in the United States and Canada*, by James W POLLOCK, Middle East Studies Association bulletin, vol.X, 1976, special issue, New York 1976.

An exhaustive list, based primarly on SHAFĀ's complete manuscript and with numerous additions, has been prepared by J D PEARSON, but not so far published.

3. *CONGRESSES*

A list of international orientalist congresses appears in

GRIMWOOD-JONES, Diana, *et al.*, *AIB, op.cit.*, :155-56.

It may be noted that the Mexico Congress was postponed to 1978, and that the next meeting (renamed the International Congress of Human Sciences in Asia and North Africa) is scheduled for September 1983 in Tokyo and Kyoto.

Congresses of the European Union of Arabic and Islamic Studies were held in Ghent in 1978, in Edinburgh in 1980, and in Portugal in 1982. To these lists should be added

International Congress of Iranian Art and Archaeology, Philadelphia 1926, London 1931, Leningrad 1935, New York 1960, Tehran 1968, Munich 1972, Oxford 1976.

4. *ORIENTALISTS*

A recent publication lists more than one hundred scholars concerned primarily with Iranian and linguistic studies:

'Bio-bibliographies de 134 savants', *Acta Iranica* 20, Leiden 1979.

A directory of British orientalists was published in 1969:

'Directory of British orientalists', *Bulletin of the Association of British Orientalists*, NS, vol.4/2, 1969.

See also AFSHĀR, *Rahnumā*, *op.cit.*

BOSWORTH, C E, 'Orientalism and orientalists', *AIB* :148-56.

II

REFERENCE WORKS AND BIBLIOGRAPHIES

1. *GENERAL REFERENCE WORKS AND ENCYCLOPAEDIAS*

It is difficult to decide where to draw the line between Iranian and Islamic civilization, particularly in the period up to the 19th century. At its height the Iranian civilization stretched from Turkey to India far into Central Asia. For this reason most of the works dealing with the whole of the Islamic civilization include material relating to greater Iran.

A selection of reference works from the countries bordering on Iran has been supplied so as to remind readers that valuable information might be found there.

ĀL ṢĀḤIB JAVĀHIR, ʿAbd al-ʿazīz, *Dā'irat al-maʿārif al-Islāmiyya-yi Īrān va hamajī-yi maʿārif-i Shīʿa-yi imāmiyya-yi Isnā-ʿasharīyya*, 3rd ed. 8 parts, Tehran 1953-60.

AMĪN, Ḥasan, *Dā'irat al-maʿārif-i Shīʿa*, (tr) Kamāl MŪSAVĪ, vol.1-, Tehran 1966. English tr. *Islamic Shiʿite encyclopaedia*.

ASADĪZĀDA, P, *et al*. *Dā'irat al-maʿārif yā farhang-i dānish va hunar*, Tehran 1966.

BACHARACH, J L, *A Near East studies handbook, 570-1974*, Seattle/London 1974.

Dā'irat al-maʿārif-i Āryānā, 6 vols, Kabul 1949-69.

Dānishnāma-i Īrān va Islām, I YĀRSHĀṬIR (ed), fasc.1-8, Tehran 1976-78.

In progress. Translations of items on Iran from the *Encyclopaedia of Islam* together with specially written articles. See also *Encyclopaedia Iranica*.

Encyclopaedia Iranica, Iḥsān YĀR-SHĀṬIR (ed), New York/London 1982-. The first fascicule was published in May.

Encyclopaedia of Islam, 1st ed. and suppl. Leiden 1913-38; 2nd ed. Leiden 1960-.

First edition published in three versions - English, French and German; second edition published in English and French. The second edition completed the letter K in 1981.

UNITED KINGDOM, NAVAL INTELLIGENCE DIVISION, *Persia*, Geographical Handbooks Series, London 1945.

Great Soviet encyclopedia: a translation of the third edition, New York/London 1973-.

HERAVI, M (ed), *Concise encyclopedia of the Middle East*, Washington DC 1973.

HUGHES, T P, *A dictionary of Islam, being a cyclopedia of the doctrines, rites, ceremonies and customs ... of the Muhammadan religion*, London 1896, repr. Karachi 1964.

Iran: a country study, 3rd ed. by R F NYROP, DA Pamphlet; 550, 68, Washington DC 1978.

Iran: Natur, Bevolkerung, Geschichte, Kultur, Staat, Wirtschaft, 2, rev. Aufl. hrsg. von U GEHRKE and H MEHNER, Tübingen/Basel 1976.

Īrānshahr, 2 vols, Tehran 1963-64.

A survey of Iran's land, people, culture, government and economy.

Islām ansiklopedisi, Istanbul 1940-.

Fascicule 135 (ʿUbayd Allāh-Utarid) was published in 1979.

JANJŪʿA, ʿAbd al-razzāq, *Modern Iran in the 20th century; Īrān-i jadīd dar qarn-i bīstum*, Tehran 1966.

JAUHARĪZĀDA, Muḥammad Riẓā, *Dā'irat al-maʿārif-i shīʿa*, Tehran 1975.

KHWĀNSĀRĪ, Jaʿfar Mūsavī, *Manāhij al-maʿārif dar bayān-i uṣūl-i dīn yā farhang-i ʿaqā'id-i shīʿa : Encyclopaedia of Shiite opinions and beliefs*, Tehran 1972.

The Middle East and Islam: a bibliographical introduction, (rev.enl.ed.) D GRIMWOOD-JONES, Bibliotheca asiatica: 15, Zug 1979.

The Middle East and North Africa, Europa Publications, London 1948-; 28th ed. 1981.

PAREJA CASAÑAS, F M, *Islamología*, en collaboración con A BAUSANI, L v HERTLING, Madrid 1952-54, 2 vols. French ed. *Islamologie*, Beyrouth 1957-63, 2 vols.

SAʿĪDIYĀN, ʿAbd al-ḥusain, *Dā'irat al-maʿārif yā majmūʿa-i iṭṭilāʿāt-i ʿumūmī*, 2nd ed. Tehran 1965.

Sālnāma-i kishvar-i Īrān, V, 21, Tehran 1966.

Sovremennyi Iran: spravochnik, Otv. redaktor S M ALIEV, Moscow 1975.

Statistical yearbook of Iran, (ed) Plan and Budget Organisation, vol.5 (1352), Tehran 1976.

Türk ansiklopedisi, Cilt 1-, Istanbul 1968-.

1.1 *Handbuch der Orientalistik*

The *HdO* was begun in 1952 as a project to cover the whole of the Asian world in all its aspects - linguistic, historical, religious, literary, and so on. So far as Iran is concerned, the relevant sections are contained mainly in

Handbuch der Orientalistik, B SPULER (ed), *et al.*, Erste Abteilung: Der nahe und der mittlerer Osten, Leiden 1952-.

Band II, *Keilschriftforschung und alte Geschichte Vorderasiens.*

Abschnitt 3, H SCHMÖKEL, *Geschichte des alten Vorderasien*, 1957, repr. 1979.

Abschnitt 4, E VISSER, *et al.*, *Orientalische Geschichte von Kyros bis Mohammed*, 1966, 1971.

Band IV, *Iranistik*

Abschnitt 1, K HOFFMANN, *et al.*, *Linguistik*, 1958, repr. 1967.

Abschnitt 2, I GERSHEVITCH, *et al.*, *Literatur*, Lieferung 1, 1968.

Lieferung 2, G MORRISON, *et al.*, *History of Persian literature from the beginning of the Islamic period to the present day*, 1981.

Abschnitt 3, W KRAUSE, *Tocharisch*, 1955, repr. 1971.

Band VI, *Geschichte der islamischen Länder.*

Abschnitt 1, B SPULER, *Die Chalifenzeit*, 1952.

Abschnitt 2, —— *Die Mongolenzeit*, 1953.

Abschnitt 3, H J KISSLING, *et al.*, *Neuzeit*, 1959. English tr. and rev. F R C BAGLEY, vol.I, *The age of the Caliphs*, 1960, repr. 1968; vol.II, *The Mongol period*, 1960, repr. 1969; vol.III, *The last great Muslim empires*; vol.IV, *Modern times*, 1981.

Band VII, B DEETERS, *et al.*, *Armenisch und Kaukasische Sprachen*, 1963.

Band VIII, *Religion.*

Abschnitt 1, *Religionsgeschichte des alten Orients*, Lieferung 1, O EISSFELDT, *et al.*, 1964. Lieferung 2, Heft 2A, Mary BOYCE, *A history of Zoroastrianism*, vol.I, 1975; vol.II (in preparation).

Abschnitt 2, *Religionsgeschichte des Orients in der Zeit der Weltreligionen*, A ADAM, *et al.*, 1961.

Ergänzungband I, Heft 1, W HINZ, *Islamische Masse und Gewichte*, 1955, repr. 1970.

Ergänzungband III, E SEIDL, *et al.*, *Orientalisches Recht*, 1964.

Ergänzungsband IV, H HICKMANN and W STAUDER, *Orientalische Musik*, 1970.

Ergänzungsband VI, M ULLMANN, Abschn. 1, *Die Medizin in Islam*, 1970; Abschn. 2, *Die Natur- und Geheimwissenschaften im Islam*, 1972.

Ergänzungsband VII, I GOMAA, *A historical chart of the Muslim world*, 1972.

1.2 *Introductory works*

ARBERRY, A J (ed), *The legacy of Persia*, Oxford 1953, repr. 1963, 1968.

ELWELL-SUTTON, L P, *Modern Iran*, London 1941 and reprints.

FRYE, Richard N, *Iran*, London 1954, 2nd ed. 1960, 3rd ed. (as *Persia*) 1968.

FURON, Raymond, *L'Iran. Perse et Afghanistan*, Paris 1951.

IMHOFF, Christoph von, *Iran. Persien*, Heroldsberg 1977.

MONTEIL, Vincent, *Iran*, Paris 1957, repr. 1959. English tr. *Iran*, London 1965.

PETROV, M P, *Iran: fiziko-geograficheskii ocherk*, Moscow 1955.

WILBER, Donald N, *Iran. Past and present*, Princeton 1948 and rev. repr. (8th ed. 1976).

2. *BIBLIOGRAPHIES*

2.1 *Books published in Iran or in Persian*

ALAVI, Bozorg, 'Die ersten persischen Bibliographien', *Forschen und Wirken. Festschrift zur 150-Jahr-Feier der Humboldt-Universität zu Berlin*, Band III, Berlin 1960 :401-13.

ANJUMAN-I KITĀB, *Kitābhā-yi Īrān*, annual, Tehran 1954-66.

Classified national bibliography, with subject and title indices.

BANĪ ĀDAM, Ḥusain, *Kitābshināsī-yi mauzūʿī-yi Īrān, 1343-1348 : An index of Persian printed books according to subject for the years 1964-1969*, Tehran 1974.

Fihrist-i kitābhā-yi chāpī-yi Fārsī : A bibliography of Persian printed books, 1808-1967. Intishārāt-i Bunyād-i Tarjama va Nashr-i Kitāb, 409, 3 vols, Tehran 1973.

IRAN DOCUMENTATION CENTRE, *Bibliography of Persian printed law books up to 1345*, Tehran 1967.

—— *Bibliography of Persian books on economics up to 1349*, Tehran 1971.

—— *Bibliography of Iranian scientific publications*, Tehran 1971.

KARĪMĪ, Kh, and P ISTAKHRĪ, *Fihrist-i mauẓūʿī-yi kitāb-hā-yi maujūd dar bāzār-i Īrān :* Subject guide to books in print in Iran, Tehran 1975.

KITĀBKHĀNA-YI MILLĪ, *Kitābshināsī-yi Īrān* (later *Kitābshināsī-yi millī-yi Īrān*), Tehran 1954-.

The first Iranian national bibliography was published in 1954. The title was changed in 1966. More information on the history as well as the content and frequency of the national bibliography can be found in

BEHN, W, 'Book production in Iran', *MELA notes*, no.6, Oct. 1975 :10-13.

MAẒĀHIRĪ, Nāṣir, *Kitābnāma-yi nukhustīn-i daha-yi inqilāb*, Tehran 1972.

MUSHĀR, Khānbābā, *Fihrist-i kitābhā-yi chāpī-i ᶜArabī-yi Īrān az āghāz-i chāp ta kunūn*, Tehran 1965.

Contains many books not listed in BROCKELMANN (see 2.3.1 below).

—— *Fihrist-i kitābhā-yi chāpī-yi Fārsī : A bibliography of books printed in Persian*, 2 vols, Tehran 1958-63.

—— *Fihrist-i kitābhā-yi chāpī-yi Fārsī*, Tehran 1971.

Volumes 1-2, letters A-ZH; no more published.

NĀYIL, Ḥusain, *Fihrist-i kutub-i chāpī-yi darī-yi Afghānistān : Catalogue of Dari printed books in Afghanistan*, Kabul 1977.

Arranged alphabetically by author with title index; translations have been entered under the translator without reference from the author's name.

RAᶜNĀ ḤUSAINĪ, Karāmat, *Fihrist-i kitābhā-yi chāpī-yi Fārsī: zail-i Fihrist-i Mushār : Bibliography of Persian printed books, the Supplement of Mushar's Bibliography*, Tehran 1970.

REGIONAL COOPERATION FOR DEVELOPMENT, Tehran, *Bibliography of publications on public administration and management*, Tehran 1967.

SHCHEGLOVA, O P, *Iranskaya litografirovannaya kniga*. Iz istorii knizhnogo dela v 19 i pervom desyatiletii 20 v, Moscow 1979.

TEHRAN BOOK PROCESSING CENTRE, *Books cataloged by TBPC*, Annual cumulation, Tehran 1970-.

ZAMĀNĪ, Maḥmūd, *Kitābshināsī-yi farhang-i ᶜāmma va mardumshināsī-yi Īrān*, Tehran 1972.

The monthly quarterly publication *Rahnumā-yi Kitāb* (Tehran 1958-78; from 1979 published as *Āyanda*, vol.V-) contains a listing of new Persian publications. In 1967 the editor published a cumulative listing.

AFSHĀR, Īraj, *Kitābshināsī-yi dah-sāla-yi 1333-1342*, Tehran 1967.

2.1.1 *Persian literature: a bio-bibliographical survey*

Charles Ambrose STOREY devoted many years of his life to the compilation of this work. Intended as the Persian counterpart of BROCKELMANN's *Geschichte der arabischen Literatur* (see 2.3.1 below), its author was, unfortunately, not able to complete it. All of the materials collected for the remaining part of the work were bequeathed to the Royal Asiatic Society, which has subsequently arranged for the publication of the sections on Medicine and Miscellaneous arts and crafts, which appeared to be ready for the press. It is to be hoped that further parts will appear in the not too distant future.

The chapters on biography and mathematics have been translated into Persian, and the Russian version makes use of some hundred catalogues not available to STOREY, enabling the compilers to describe some 850 additional works, and to signal the existence of about 5000 further codices.

STOREY, C A, *Persian literature: a bio-bibliographical survey*, i. Qur'anic literature, London 1927; ii.1. A. General history. B. The Prophets and early Islam, 1935; ii.2. C-L. Special histories of Persia, Central Asia, and the remaining parts of the world except India, 1936; ii.3. M. History of India, 1939; II.i. A. Mathematics. B. Weights and measures. C. Astronomy and astrology. D. Geography, 1958.

These sections were reprinted and published in two volumes in 1970 and 1972.

II.ii. E. Medicine, 1971; II.iii. F. Encyclopaedias and miscellanies. G. Arts and crafts. H. Science. J. Occult arts, 1977.

These sections were published posthumously from the materials in the Royal Asiatic Society.

Persian tr. Taqī BĪNISH, 'Tazkira-yi shuᶜarā', *Majalla-yi Dānishkada-yi Adabiyāt va ᶜUlūm-i Insānī-yi Dānishgāh-i Mashhad*, 3 (1346) :88-109, 240-54, 323-26; 4 (1347) :81-102, 269-81; 5 (1348) :98-111, 698-711; 6 (1349) :253-67, 497-512, 706-20, 889-99; 7 (1350) :232-47, 680-705; 8 (1351) :193-207, 579-92, Tehran 1967-72. 'Kitābhā-yi fārsī-yi riyāẓī', *Nuskha-hā-yi khaṭṭī*, 4, Tehran 1965 :13-51.

Russian tr. Yu E BREGEL, Yu E BORSHCHEVSKII (ed), *Persidskaya literatura; bio-bibliograficheskiy obzor*, rev. with additions and corrections, 3 vols, Moscow 1972.

TASBĪḤĪ, G H, *The problems of bringing Storey's 'Persian literature' up to date: Persian lexicography*, Ph.D. thesis, London 1979.

In this thesis G H TASBĪḤĪ tackles the problem of bringing STOREY up to date. In the special field of lexicography, he was able to record from 62 catalogues not known to STOREY, some 1900 extra MSS and printed books, slightly more than half of which related to additional works. He demonstrates what a colossal task lies ahead of any scholar making so bold as to bring this essential *Hilfsmittel* up to date.

2.1.2 *Books in Kurdish and Afghan (Darī) Persian*

The contemporary Kurdish minority in Iran profits from the post-war history, culminating in the short-lived Mahābād Republic of 1945/46, as well as from the proximity of the Bārzānī Kurds in the oil-rich northern part of Iraq. There is considerable literature on what is generally referred to as the Kurdish question.

Some 300 Kurdish works published anywhere are contained in
NARĪMĀN, Muṣṭafā Sayyid Aḥmad, *Kitēbkhānay kurdī*, Kirkuk 1960.
Mainly literary texts and translations but some religious and ethnographic works are included.

By the same author is
Bibliyūghrāfiyā al-kutub al-kurdiyya, 1787-1975, Baghdad 1977.
Lists 1254 items arranged chronologically according to the years of the Christian era (introduction in Kurdish as well as Arabic).

A classified list of the Kurdish books in the Central Library of the University of Sulaimāniyya is entitled *Līstay bibliyōgrāfiyāy kitēba kurdiyakānī kitēbkhānay Zānkōy Silēmānī* (Sulaimāniyya 1977, v.1-).

The Afghan national bibliography does not seem to be published regularly. Only one issue has appeared so far.

SUTŪDA, M I, and A Żiyā MUDARRISĪ, *Kitābshināsī-i millī-i Afghānistān-i maużuᶜī-i tauṣīfī, 26 Saraṭān 2352 tā imrūz*, Kabul University Library series, 11, Kabul 1977.

An annotated bibliography of Persian and English publications only.

2.2 *Books on Iran*

ABŪ AL-ḤAMD, ᶜAbd al-Ḥamīd, and Nāṣir PĀKDAMĀN, *Kitābshināsī-yi tamaddun-i īrānī dar firānsa : Bibliographie française de civilisation iranienne*, 3 vols, Tehran 1972-74.

ARAKI, Shigeru, and Otoya TANAKA, *A catalogue of books relating to Persia*, Tokyo 1934.

BARTSCH, William H, and Julian BHARIER, *The economy of Iran, 1940-1970. A bibliography*. University of Durham Centre for Middle Eastern and Islamic Studies, Publ.no.2, Durham 1971.

'Bibliographie der deutschen Veröffentlichungen über Iran', *Festschrift aus Anlass der Gründung des iranischen Kaiserreiches vor 2500 Jahren durch Kyros den Grossen*, Köln 1971 :63-220.

To be used with caution.

DJALILI, Mohammad Reza, *Le Golfe persique: introduction bibliographique*, Genève 1979.

EHLERS, E, *Iran: ein bibliographischer Forschungsbericht mit Kommentaren und Annotationen : Iran: a bibliographical research survey with comments and annotations*. Bibliographien zur regionalen Geographie und Landeskunde, 2, Munich 1980.

The literal translations at times defy comprehension; to be used with caution.

ELWELL-SUTTON, L P, *Guide to Iranian area study*, Ann Arbor, Mich. 1952.

FARMAN, H F, *Iran: a selected and annotated bibliography*, US Library of Congress, Washington 1951, repr. New York 1968.

412 titles in classified order.

GEHRKE, U, *Deutsche Beiträge zur Kenntnis Irans im 20. Jahrhundert: eine Bibliographie*, Hamburg 1968.

—— 'Deutsche Beiträge zur Kenntnis Irans im 20. Jahrhundert', *Orient*, Heft 5/6 (Dez. 1971) :167-77.

HANDLEY-TAYLOR, G, *Bibliography of Iran*, 5th ed. Chicago/London 1969.

HAZEN, Wm E, *Iran: a selected list of references*, Library of Congress, Washington DC 1964.

KAZEMI, Asghar, *Iran Bibliographie: deutschsprachige Abhandlungen, Beiträge, Aufsätze, Bücher, Dissertationen*, Intishārāt-i Dānishgāh-i Tihrān, 1303, Tehran 1970.

MĀHYĀR NAVĀBĪ, Yaḥyā, *A bibliography of Iran: a list of books and articles on Iranian subjects, mainly in European languages. Kitābshināsī-i Īrān*. Iranian Culture Foundation; 75, 106, 261, 271, 175, Tehran 1969-78, 5 vols.

NEW YORK PUBLIC LIBRARY, *List of works in the New York Public Library relating to Persia*, compiled by Ida PRATT, under direction of R GOTTHEIL, New York 1915.

Annotated list of approximately 2000 books in western languages.

OECD, *Bibliography on Iran*, Paris 1965.

PEARSON, J D, *A bibliography of pre-Islamic Persia*, Persian Studies Series no.2, London 1975.

RICKS, Thomas, Thomas GOUTTIERRE, and Denis EGAN, *Persian studies: a selected bibliography of works in English*, Bloomington, Ind. 1969.

ṢABA, Moḥsen, *Bibliographie française de l'Īrān*, Paris 1933, rev. Tehran 1951, 1966.

About 3000 French titles published since 1560, classified under subject headings.

—— *English bibliography of Iran*, Tehran 1968.

SCHWAB, Moïse, *Bibliographie de la Perse*, Paris 1875, repr. Amsterdam 1962.

1332 titles classified under subject headings.

SVERCHEVSKAYA, A K, *Bibliografiya Irana: literatura na russkom yazyka. (1917-1965 gg)*, N A KUZNETSOVA (ed), Moscow 1967.

WERYHO, J W, *A guide to Persian reference sources available at McGill Islamics Library*, Montreal 1973.

WICKENS, G M, and R M SAVORY, *Persia in Islamic times: a practical bibliography of its history, culture and language*, W J WATSON (ed), Montreal 1964.

WILSON, A T, *A bibliography of Persia*, Oxford 1930.

Approximately 5000 titles in European languages, arranged in alphabetical order of authors but otherwise unclassified.

2.3 *General bibliographies on the Middle East, Asia and the Islamic World.*

An exhaustive list of bibliographies on the Arab world and Islam is given in

GRIMWOOD-JONES, Diana, Derek HOPWOOD, and J D PEARSON, *Arabic Islamic bibliography*, The Middle East Library Committee Guide, Hassocks, Sussex/Atlantic Highland, NJ 1977 :1-150.

The same book contains many other references to works of Iranian interest.

Other general bibliographies, not mentioned in the above listing but worthy of note, include

E J BRILL LONDON, *Bibliography of books in print in European languages on the Middle East, North Africa and Islam*, London 1980.

Lists 4306 titles.

ETTINGHAUSEN, Richard (ed), *A selected and annotated bibliography of books and periodicals in Western languages dealing with the Near and Middle East*, Washington 1952.

LITTLEFIELD, David W, *The Islamic Middle East and North Africa: an annotated guide to books in English for non-specialists*, Littleton, Col. 1977.

MEISELES, Gustav, *Reference literature to Arabic studies: a bibliographical guide*, Tel Aviv 1978.

PEARSON, J D, *Oriental and Asian bibliography*, London 1966.

The quarterly *Middle East Journal* (Washington 1947-) publishes a regular listing of new books and articles on the Middle East (for the latter, see also the cumulative index listed below under 3.).

A useful directory of libraries, booksellers, commercial and institutional publishers, newspapers and periodicals in the Middle East is

RUDKIN, Anthony, and Irene BUTCHER, *A book world directory of the Arab countries, Turkey and Iran*, London 1981.

Sluglett, Peter. Theses on Islam, M.E., + N.W. Africa, 1880-1978. N.Y., Mansell, 1983.
Theses submitted to British + Irish universities.

2.3.1 *BROCKELMAN and SEZGIN*

BROCKELMANN, Carl, *Geschichte der arabischen Literatur*, 2 vols, Weimar 1898-1902. Suppl. 1-3, Leiden 1937-42. Zweite, den Supplementbänden angepasste Aufl. 2 vols, Leiden 1943-49. Arabic tr. ᶜAbd al-Ḥalīm

NAJJĀR, *Ta'rīkh al-adab al-ᶜarabī*, 3 vols, Cairo 1960-62.

Carl BROCKELMANN's pioneering survey of writers and writing in Arabic from the earliest times to the present day naturally includes many works by authors of Iranian provenance or domicile. The piecemeal method of its completion and publication makes it somewhat difficult to use, but in spite of this, as well as of the progress of its modern rival (see SEZGIN below), it is still an indispensable tool for the Islamist.

SEZGIN, Fuat, *Geschichte des arabischen Schrifttums*, Leiden 1967-. Band I. Qur'ānwissenschaften, Ḥadīṯ, Geschichte, Fiqh, Dogmatik, Mystik, 1967; Band II. Poesie, 1975; Band III. Medizin-Pharmazie, Zoologie-Tierheilkunde, 1970; Band IV. Alchimie-Chemie, Botanik-Agrikultur, 1971; Band V. Mathematik, 1974; Band VI. Astronomie. Mit Gesamtverzeichnis der Bibliotheken und Sammlungen arabischer Handschriften, 1978; Band VII. Astrologie-Meteorologie und Verwandten, 1979.

The first series, of which another seven volumes are planned, covers the period up to c.430/1040. A further series is planned for the period up to the 11/17th century.

2.4 *Bibliographies of bibliographies*

AFSHĀR, Īraj, *Fihristnāma-i kitābshināsīhā-yi Īrān : A bibliography of bibliographies on Iranian studies*, Tehran 1963.

AHMED, M D, 'Iranbibliographien: eine Übersicht', *Iranistische Mitteilungen*, vol.8, 1974 :2-21.

ALLAMEH, Manijeh, and Lila MORTEZAIE, *List of current bibliographies available in the Library of IRANDOC*, Tehran 1975.

BESTERMAN, Th, *A world bibliography of oriental bibliographies*, rev. by J D PEARSON, Totowa, NJ/Oxford 1975.

SHEVCHENKO, Z M, and D S LEIVI, *Bibliografiya bibliografii Tadzhikistana*, Dushanbe 1966.

Analytical bibliography of Tājīk bibliographies in Russian, Tājīk and Uzbek, 1920-1964.

3. *PERIODICAL INDICES AND COLLECTIVE WORKS*

AFSHĀR, Īraj, *Fihrist-i maqālāt-i Fārsī: Index iranicus*; répertoire méthodique des articles persans concernant les études iranologiques, publiés dans les périodiques et publications collectives, Tehran 1961-. Vol.1 covers the period 1910-58; Vol.2, 1959-66; Vol.3, 1967-71; Vol.4, forthcoming in 1982.

—— *Fihrist-i maqālāt-i īrānshināsī dar zabān-i ᶜarabī : An index of*

Arabic articles concerning Iranian studies, Majmūʿa-i kitābshināsīhā-yi Fārsī va Īrān, Tehran 1977.

ASIAN CULTURAL DOCUMENTATION CENTRE, *Index of cultural articles in Iranian periodicals*, annual, Tehran 1976-.

BERLIN, Ch, *Index to Festschriften in Jewish studies*, Cambridge, Mass; New York, NY 1971.

CHAKĪDA, *Irandoc science and social science abstract bulletin*, Tehran 1970-.

FAṢĪḤ, Yūsuf Mūsavīzāda, *Fihrist-i dah-sāla-i Rāhnamā-yi kitāb, 1337-1348: Index of Rāhnemā-ye ketāb, vols 1-10*, Tehran 1971.

Fihrist-i guzīda-yi maqālāt-i rūznāmahā-yi Īrān: Iranian newspapers: (Āyandagān, Iṭṭilāʿāt, Kaihān), vols.1-, Tehran 1974-.

Volume 1 (1352); volume 2 (1353). No more published?

Fihrist-i maqālahā-yi majallahā-yi Īrān dar zamīna-yi ʿulūm va ʿulūm-i ijtimāʿī, Tehran 1971-.

Fihrist-i maqālāt-i farhangī dar maṭbūʿāt-i Īrān, Asian Cultural Documentation Center for UNESCO, Daura 1-, quarterly, Tehran 1976-.

Fihrist-i mundarijāt-i majallahā-yi ʿilmī va ʿulūm-i ijtimāʿī, no.1-, Tehran 1969-.

This journal merely reproduces the title pages of the periodicals covered.

Index to papers in commemoration volumes, Bhandarkar Oriental Research Institut, Post-graduate and Research Dept. series 4, Poona 1963, 2 vols.

Index to papers read at the Indian Historical Records Commission Sessions, 1920-1956, New Delhi, c.1956.

The Middle East: abstracts and index, A C LOWENSTEIN (ed), vol.1-, Pittsburg, Pa, 1978-.

LEISTNER, O, *Internationale Bibliographie der Festschriften mit Sachregister*, Osnabrück 1976.

PEARSON, J D, *Index islamicus:* a catalogue of articles on Islamic subjects in periodicals and other collective works, Cambridge/London 1958-.

The original work covers the period from 1906 to 1955. Since then the *Index* has been published annually with five-year cumulations entitled *Supplement*. The 5th *Supplement* is to be published in 1982.

Starting in 1977 the *Index* has been published quarterly entitled *Quarterly index islamicus*. Under the new title the index also lists monographs, but for the period from 1976 to 1980 only. The cumulation of the monographs is to be published separately from the periodical articles but simultaneously in 1982.

NEW YORK PUBLIC LIBRARY, *Guide to Festschriften*, 2 vols, New York 1977.

ROSSI, Peter M, and Wayne E WHITE, *Articles on the Middle East 1947-1971*, a cumulation of the bibliographies from the Middle East Journal, Ann Arbor 1975.

SARMA, K V, *Index of papers submitted to the All-India Oriental Conference*, Poona 1949-.

Sessions 1-12 (1949); 13-17 (1959); 18-22 (1967).

3.1 *Book reviews*

Most periodicals devoted to Islamic studies in general or to Iranian studies in particular publish book reviews. There are two periodicals in this context which publish book reviews only. *Orientalische Literaturzeitung*, published since 1898 in Berlin, covers the whole range of oriental studies. It currently takes three to four years before reviews are published. More up-to-date is

Abstracta iranica, vol.1-, (Suppl. to *Studia iranica*), Leiden 1978-.

Periodical publishing nothing but reviews of Iran-related monographs as well as articles without restriction of language.

Rāhnumā-yi kitāb, vols 1-20, Tehran 1958-78. The journal of the Book Society of Persia.

Āyanda, vol.5-, Tehran 1979-.

It covers the full range of Iranian studies and publishes book reviews of Persian as well as foreign books on Iran. In its section 'Muᶜarrifī-yi kitāb-hā-yi tāza' it lists the 300-odd important Iranian publications annually.

There is one bibliography of Persian book reviews:

MUᶜĀẒID, M, *Kitābshināsī-yi naqd-i kitāb*, Majmūᶜa-yi kitābshināsī-hā-yi Fārsī va Īrānī, 9, Tehran 1976.

4. *BIOGRAPHICAL DICTIONARIES*

ĀDAMĪYAT, Muḥammad Ḥusain, *Dānishmandān va sukhan-sarāyān-i Fārs*, 4 vols, Tehran 1958-61.

BAMDĀD, Mahdī, *Sharh-i hāl-i rijāl-i Īrān dar qarn-i 12 va 13 va 14 hijrī*, 6 vols, Tehran 1968-72.

BERENGIAN, S, *Poets and writers from the Iranian Azerbaijan in the twentieth century*, Ph.D. thesis, Columbia University, NY 1965.

BURQAᶜĪ, ᶜAlī Akbar, *Rāhnumā-yi dānishvarān*, 2 vols, Qum 1949-50.

—— *Sukhanvarān-i nāmī-yi muᶜāsir*, 3 vols, Tehran 1950-57.

Chihrahā-yi āshnā, 2nd ed, Tehran 1965.

DAULATĀBĀDĪ, ᶜAzīz, *Sukhanvarān-i Āzabāyjān: Poètes d'Azarbaidjan*.

Intishārāt-i Dānishgāh-i Tabrīz, 200, Tabriz 1976.

DIRAKHSHĀN, Mahdī, *Buzurgān va sukhansarāyān-i Hamadān*, 2 vols, Tehran 1963-64.

Biographies of famous men from Hamadān.

Iran who's who, 3rd ed. Tehran 1976.

JĀMĪ, ^{c}Abd al-Raḥmān, *Nafaḥāt al-uns min ḥaḍarāt al-quds*, Mahdī TAUḤĪDĪ-PŪR (ed), Tehran 1957.

KHĀẒI^{c}, Ardashīr, *Tazkīra-i sukhanvarān-i Yazd : Biographies of ancient, modern and contemporary poets of Yazd*, 2 vols, Bombay 1963.

LEWIN, M, *et al.*, *Pisateli Tadzhikistana*, 2nd ed. Dushanbe 1976.

MIHRĀZ, Raḥmatallāh, *Buzurgāni Shīrāz*, Tahran 1969.

MUSHĀR, Khānbābā, *Mu'allifīn-i kutub-i chāpī-yi fārsī va ^{c}arabī az āghāz-i chāp tā kunūn*, 6 vols, Tehran 1969-65.

NADĪM, Abu'l-faraj Muḥammad al-, *al-Fihrist*, G FLÜGEL (ed), 2 vols, Leipzig 1871-72, repr. Cairo 1930. English tr. Bayard DODGE, 2 vols, New York 1970.

NĪRŪMAND, Karīm, *Sukhanvarān va khaṭṭāṭān-i Zanjān az qarn-i chahārum tā ^{c}aṣr-i ḥāẓir*, Zanjān 1968.

RĀMIYĀN, Mahmūd, Muhammad TAMADDUN, and ^{c}Alā' al-dīn TAKISH, *Buzurgān va sukhan-sarāyān-i Āzarbāyjān-i gharbī*, n.p. 1965.

SĀDĀT NĀSIRĪ, Saiyid Hasan, *Sar-āmadān-i farhang va tārīkh-i Īrān dar daura-yi Islāmī : Great figures in Iranian culture*, Part I (A-S), Tehran 1974. No more published?

ṬĀLIQĀNĪ, Mīrzā Ḥasan, *et al.* *Nāma-yi dānishvarān*, 7 vols, Tehran 1879-1906.

ZIRIKLĪ, Khayr al-dīn, *al-A^{c}lām: qāmūs tarājim li-ashhar al-rijāl wa-al-nisā' min al-^{c}Arab wa-al-musta^{c}ribīn wa-al-mustashriqīn*, 3rd rev.ed. 11 vols in 12, Beirut c.1970.

More specialised biographical dictionaries are listed in the appropriate chapters, especially VI.

III

MANUSCRIPTS, LIBRARIES AND ARCHIVES

1. *IRANIAN MANUSCRIPTS*

1.1 *The earliest manuscripts*

The oldest extant written materials in any Iranian language are the Old Persian inscriptions of Pasargadae, Persepolis and other sites, the earliest of which date back to the 6th century BC. By contrast, the surviving portions of the Avestan scriptures, though in a form of the language at least as old as that of the Achaemenian inscriptions, exist only in manuscripts written no earlier than the 14th century AD.

The oldest extant Iranian manuscripts proper, however, are the *Soghdian* letters and other fragments discovered by Sir Aurel STEIN in 1907 in a watch-tower on the Great Wall of China and preserved in the British Museum. These were dated originally to the 2nd century AD, but according to HENNING must be assigned to 312/3 AD.

REICHELT, Hans, *Die Soghdischen Handschriftenreste des Britischen Museums in Umschrift und Übersetzung*, 2 vols, Heidelberg 1928, 1931, vol.II :1-56.

PELLIOT, Paul, 'Review of Reichelt, *Die Soghdischen Handschriftenreste ...*'. *Toung Pao*, xxviii, 1931 :457-63.

HENNING, W B, 'The date of the Soghdian ancient letters', *BSOAS*, xii, 1947-48 :601-15.

From the 7th century AD comes a psalter fragment in Pahlavi.

ANDREAS, F C, 'Bruchstücke einer Pehlevi-Übersetzung der Psalmen'. Aus dem Nachlass herausgegeben von Kaj BARR. *Sitzungsberichte der Preuss. Akad. Wiss.*, Berlin 1933, i :91-152.

A letter fragment in Hebrew script, found by Sir Aurel STEIN in Dandan-Uiliq (Khotan), and dating from the 8th century AD, is probably the oldest manuscript in *Persian*, though possibly not as early as the Tang-i Azao inscription, also Persian in Hebrew letters, which is dated 752 AD.

STEIN, Aurel, 'The early Sogdian documents from T.XII.A and their paper',

Serindia, ii, :671-7, 776-7, 924.

p.924 is a list of Sogdian manuscripts from Ch'ien-Fo-Tung.

HENNING, W B, 'The inscription of Tang-i Azao', *BSOAS*, xx, 1957 :335-42.

The richest source of early Iranian and Persian manuscripts is the collection discovered between 1902 and 1914 in the Turfan basin in Chinese Turkistan by a series of expeditions sent out by the Museum für Völkerkunde, Berlin. Most of these are in the Institut für Orientforschung in Berlin, about a quarter in the Akademie der Wissenschaften und der Literatur in Mainz, and some fragments in Leningrad, Paris and London. The following catalogue has been published.

BOYCE, Mary, *A catalogue of the Iranian manuscripts in Manichaean script in the German Turfan collection*, Berlin 1960.

Details of the publication of this material are contained in

LENTZ, Wolfgang, 'Funfzig jahre Arbeit an den iranischen Handschriften der deutschen Turfan-Sammlung', *ZDMG*, 176/ii, 1956 *3*.

Dating from the 10th century AD are a number of Christian manuscripts in Syriac script, of which an account was published by

MÜLLER, F W K, 'Handschriften-Reste in Estrangelo-Schrift aus Turfan, Chinesisch-Turkistan'. 1 Teil, *Sitzungsber. K. Preuss. Akad. Wiss.*, 1904 :348-52. 2 Teil, *Abh. K. Preuss. Akad. Wiss.*, phil.-hist. Abh., 1904/Abh. II :1-117.

—— 'Ein syrisch-neupersisches Psalmenbruchstück aus Chinesisch-Turkistan'. *Festschrift E. Sachau*, 1915 :215-22.

Manichaean manuscripts in the same collection, also dating from the 10th century AD, include what have been described as 'the oldest written literary works in the Persian language'. They include 27 couplets of a poem on Bilauhar and Būdāsaf (N581), apparently contemporary with the poet RŪDAKĪ though probably not by him, and a fragment of a qaṣīda without attribution (M786).

BOYCE, Mary, 'The Manichaean literature in Middle Iranian', *HdO*, Abt.I, iv/2/1 :67-76.

HENNING, W B, 'Die älteste persische Gedichthandschrift: eine neue Version von Barlaam und Joasaph'. *Akten des XXIV Int. Orientalisten-Kongress München 1957*, Wiesbaden 1959 :305-6.

—— 'Persian poetical manuscripts from the time of Rudaki', *A Locust's Leg*, W B HENNING and E YARSHATER (eds), London 1962 :89-104; Persian tr. with full text of poems: Iḥsān YĀR-SHĀṬIR, *Qadīmtarīn nuskha-yi shi^{c}r-i fārsī*, Tehran 1958; also in *Majalla-yi Dānishkada-yi Adabīyāt-i Tihrān*, vol.IV.

Possibly older than these however is a Persian manuscript in Arabic script recently discovered in the Shrine of Imām Riẓā in Mashhad, which may be as early as the beginning of the 4th/10th century. This is a semi-metrical translation of part of the Qur'ān.

RAJĀ'Ī, Aḥmad ᶜAlī, *Pulī miyān-i shiᶜr-i hijā'ī va ᶜarūẓī-yi fārsī*, Tehran 1974.

If the dating of this is correct, it pre-dates by more than a century what has long been regarded as the earliest New Persian manuscript in Arabic script:

MUVAFFAQ AL-DĪN Abū Manṣūr ᶜAlī al-Haravī, *Al-abniya ᶜan ḥaqā'iq al-adviya*, F R SELIGMANN (ed), *Codex Vindobonensis ... Liber fundamentorum pharmocologiae*, Vienna 1859; facsimile: Mujtabā MĪNUVĪ (ed), Intishārāt-i Bunyād-i Farhang-i Īrān, Tehran 1965; Aḥmad BAHMANYĀR and Ḥusain Maḥbūbī ARDAKĀNĪ (eds), University of Tehran, no.1163, Tehran 1967; German tr. Abdul-Chalig ACHUNDOW, Die pharmakologischen Grundsätze (Liber fundamentorum pharmakologiae) des Abu Mansur Muwaffak ... Halle 1893, repr: Introduction by C H TALBOT and F R SELIGMANN, *Historische Studien zur Pharmakologie der Griechen, Römer und Araber*, 1972.

See also:

QAZVĪNĪ, Muḥammad, 'Qadīmtarīn kitāb dar zabān-i fārsī-yi ḥāliya'. *Bist maqāla-yi Qazvīnī*, Tehran 1953 (2nd ed), vol.I :62-70, vol.II :264-7.

Composed c.360/970, the extant manuscript was written by the poet ᶜAlī b. Aḥmad Ṭūsī ASADĪ in 447/1055, and is preserved in the Nationalbibliothek in Vienna (AF340).

FLUGEL, Gustav, *Die arabische, persische und türkische Handschriften der Kaiserliche-Königliche Hofbibliothek zu Wien*, 3 vols, Vienna 1865-7, vol.II, no.1465.

It thus ranks also as one of the earliest prose works in New Persian, together with the Persian translations of ṬABARĪ's *History* by Abu ᶜAlī Muḥammad BALᶜAMĪ, and an anonymous translation of the same author's *Tafsīr*, both of which date from the same period but survive only in manuscripts of the 7th/13th century. Other Persian manuscripts from the 5th/11th century include the *Sharḥ-i Taᶜarruf* (473/1080, preserved in Peshawar), Abū Ibrāhīm Ismāᶜīl al-MUSTAMLĪ's commentary on the *Kitāb al-taᶜarruf* of Abū Bakr al-KALĀBĀDHĪ, and the *Hidāyat al-mutaᶜallimīn fīᶜl-ṭibb* (478/1085, preserved in the Bodleian Library in Oxford, BEESTON (see 3.2.2 below), vol.III, p.92, no.2841) by the 4th/10th century physician Abū Bakr Rabīᶜ b. Aḥmad al-Akhavain al-BUKHĀRĪ.

For other accounts of early Iranian and Persian manuscripts see

MARGOLIOUTH, David S, 'An early Judaeo-Persian document from Khotan, in the Stein collection, with other early Persian documents', *JRAS*, 1903 :735-60.

—— 'Early documents in the Persian language', *JRAS*, 1903 :760-70.

SALEMANN, Carl, review of Margoliouth's articles, *Zapiski Vostochnago Otdeleniya*, xvi, 1904 :046-057.

HOERNLE, A F Rudolf, 'The "unknown languages" of eastern Turkistan', *JRAS*, 1910 :1283-1300, 1911 :447-77.

COWLEY, A, 'Another unknown language from eastern Turkistan', *JRAS*, 1911 :159-66.

GAUTHIOT, R, 'Notes sur la langue et l'écriture inconnues des documents Stein-Cowley', *JRAS*, 1911 :497-507.

MINORSKY, Vladimir, 'Some early documents in Persian', *JRAS*, 1942 :181-94, 1943 :80.99.

1.2 *Manuscript collections in Europe*

Persian manuscripts began to arrive in Europe in the late 16th and early 17th centuries. Pietro della VALLE (1586-1652) brought back manuscripts from his travels in the Middle East; 26 of these are now in the Vatican, to which they were given by Clement I in 1718.

LEVI DELLA VIDA, G, *Ricerche sulla formazione del piu antico fondo dei manoscritti della Biblioteca Vaticana*. Studi e testi, 92, Città del Vaticano 1939.

But the first Persian MS to be placed in that library, a Persian translation of the Gospel of St Matthew (Vat.pers.4) was already there in 1570.

The Dutch scholar Thomas ERPENIUS (1584-1624) amassed at considerable expense to himself a fine collection of MSS in Arabic, Persian and Turkish, though he personally never visited the East. These MSS were acquired by the Duke of Buckingham and presented to Cambridge University by the Duchess in 1632.

OATES, J C T, 'The manuscripts of Thomas Erpenius', *Occasional Publ. Bibliogr. Soc. Australia and New Zealand* 1, 1974 :1-17.

Though the University of Leiden failed to acquire the collections of its first two professors of Arabic, ERPENIUS and Jacobus GOLIUS, many of whose books were bought by Archbishop Narcissus Marsh and presented by him to the Bodleian Library in Oxford, the great glory of Leiden's oriental collections, in fact *the* oriental collection of the Library, is the Legatum Warnerium, bequeathed by Levinus WARNER, Dutch Resident in Constantinople

1644-5, among which are to be found 224 Persian texts.

Levinus Warner and his legacy: three centuries of Legatum Warnerium in the Leiden University Library. Catalogue of the commemorative exhibition held in the Bibliotheca Thysiana, Leiden 1970.

In 1632 Archbishop Laud procured a letter from Charles I to the Turkey Company requiring that each of its ships returning from the east bring back one manuscript in Arabic or Persian (S.P.Dom.Car.I, 260, no.16).

BEESTON, A F L, 'The oriental manuscript collections of the Bodleian Library', *Bodleian Library Record* 5, 2, 1954 :73-79.

A similar letter to the East India Company ensured that its factors overseas 'endeavour their utmost' to search for Arabic and Persian MSS, and we hear of a consignment of ten books sent, though the despatcher felt that 'few in England will understand them' (S.P.Col., East Indies and Persia, 1630-1634, pp.523, 598, 623). Ambassadors of other nations were instructed in similar terms, for there is preserved in the Library of Lincoln's Inn apparently from about the same date, a 'catalogue of oriental manuscripts then lately sent to Paris by the French Ambassador at Constantinople, which catalogue was then transmitted to Selden by Lord Herbert of Cherbury, then the English Ambassador at Paris'.

MATTHEWS, Noel, and Mary D WAINWRIGHT, *A Guide to manuscripts and documents in the British Isles relating to the Middle East and North Africa*, J D PEARSON (ed), Oxford 1980 :133.

LINCOLN'S INN LIBRARY, Vol.XII, *Collectanea Seldeni*, no.61.

2. *LIBRARIES*

2.1 *Libraries in Iran*

Libraries in Iran have a long history, of which the best account is to be found in

HUMĀYŪN-FARRUKH, Rukn al-dīn, *Kitāb va kitābkhānahā-yi shāhanshāhī-yi Īrān* vol.I, Tehran 1966; vol.II, Tārīkhcha-yi kitābkhānahā-yi Īrān az ṣadr-i Islām tā ᶜaṣr-i kunūnī, Tehran 1968. English tr. Abū Ṭālib ṢĀRIMĪ, *History of books and the imperial libraries of Iran*, Tehran 1968.

Volume I deals with the history of bookcraft in Iran, while volume II gives details of 623 libraries of the past and 180 of the present day.

Also valuable are

FREYTAG, M E, *Das Bibliothekswesen und die Bibliographie in Iran: historische Voraussetzungen und gegenwärtiger Stand*, Ph.D. thesis, Humboldt University, Berlin 1976.

PŪR AHMAD JAKTĀJĪ, M T, *Tārīkhcha-yi kitābkhāna-yi millī-yi Īrān*, Tehran 1978.

A useful introduction to the subject is afforded by

EBRAMI, Hooshang, 'Iran, libraries in', *Encyclopaedia of library and information sources*, vol.13, New York 1975 :15-53.

This is followed by a description by Ali SINAI of the Iranian Documentation Center (pp.53-60), which caters largely for the documentation needs of modern Iranian libraries. Two volumes of directories have been published by the institution:

SIPIHRĪ, Abāzar, *Rāhnumā-yi kitābkhānahā-yi Īrān*, vol.I: West Āzarbāyjān, East Āzarbāyjān, Kurdistān, Kirmānshāhān, Gīlān, Hamadān, Tehran 1970.

RAŻAVI, Firishta, *Rāhnumā-yi kītabkhānahā-yi shimāl-i sharq-i Īrān*, vol.II, Khurāsān, Māzandarān, Samnān, Tehran 1970.

Another important production is

Iranian National Union Catalog. A cumulative author list. Compiled by the Tehran Book Processing Centre, Tehran 1973-.

The catalogue was planned to be published in three sections:

1. Latin section: foreign books in Iranian libraries which are not in the Arabic alphabet. Entries for non-western languages have been romanized. A-F (1973); G-H (1974); I-L (1974).
2. Persian-Arabic section: Arabic, Ottoman-Turkish and Persian books in Iranian libraries.
3. International section: books on Iran regardless of language in selected libraries abroad.

A list of 383 libraries throughout the world, including 84 in Iran, that have significant collections of Persian manuscripts, is given in AFSHĀR, *Rāhnumā*, *op.cit.*, (I.1) :325-48. See also SHAFĀ, *op.cit*.

2.2 *Libraries outside Iran*

Outside Iran, the libraries with important collections of Persian printed books are, naturally enough, those with collections of Persian manuscripts. Noteworthy in the United Kingdom are the British Library, the India Office Library and Records, and the Library of SOAS, all of which have published catalogues of their printed books in Persian, and, so far as the last-named is concerned, of works about Iran as well. The Library of Harvard University in the United States has done likewise.

DĀNISHPUZHŪH, Muḥammad Taqī, *Nuskhahā-yi khaṭṭī*, 10, 1979.

A list of libraries in the USSR, Europe and America with Islamic collections.

SUTTON, S C, *A guide to the India Office Library*, 2nd ed. London 1971.

INDIA OFFICE LIBRARY AND RECORDS, *Guide to the Persian collections*, London, n.d. (1980?)

KOZYREVA, L G, *Biblioteki Tadzhikistana: spravochnik*, Dushanbe 1978.

A handbook of libraries in Tājīkistān.

2.3 *Catalogues of printed books*

ARBERRY, Arthur J, *Catalogue of the India Office Library*, vol.2, part 6, 'Persian books', London 1937.

BROWNE, Edward G, *A hand-list of the Turkish and other printed and lithographed books presented by Mrs E J W Gibb to the Cambridge University Library (and Persian, Arabic and Urdu books from the Cowell collection)*, Cambridge 1906.

CENTER FOR RESEARCH LIBRARIES, *Catalogue: monographs*, 5 vols, Chicago 1969-70; suppl. no.1, 2 vols, Chicago 1974.

—— *Catalogue: newspapers*, Chicago 1969.

A list of newspapers catalogued by the Center up to 1 January 1969. Cross-references from variant transliterations or spellings in the case of Islamic titles are not always supplied (e.g. Ettala^{c}at).

—— *Catalogue: serials*, 2 vols, Chicago 1972.

Contains entries for all serials, including newspapers, catalogued by the Center from its foundation up to April 1971.

CHICAGO UNIVERSITY ORIENTAL INSTITUTE, *Catalog of the Oriental Institute Library*, 16 vols, Boston 1970; 1st suppl. *Catalog of the Middle Eastern collection*, 1 vol, Boston 1977.

EDWARDS, E, *A catalogue of the Persian printed books in the British Museum*, London 1922.

HALL, David E, *Union Catalogue of Asian publications*, compiled under the auspices of the Orientalists' Group, Standing Conference of National and University Libraries, 4 vols, London 1971. 1971 suppl. 1 vol, London 1973.

HARVARD UNIVERSITY LIBRARY, *Catalogue of Arabic, Persian and Ottoman Turkish books*, 5 vols, Cambridge, Mass. 1968.

HOOVER INSTITUTE, *The library catalogs of the Hoover Institution on War, Revolution, and Peace, Stanford University. Catalogs of the Turkish and Persian collections*, Boston 1969.

The National union catalog: pre-1956 imprints and suppls, London/Totowa, NJ/Ann Arbor, Mich. 1968-.

An increasing amount of Persian material has been included in the catalogues since 1968.

NEW YORK PUBLIC LIBRARY, *Dictionary catalog of the oriental collection*, 16 vols, Boston 1960; 1st suppl. 8 vols, Boston 1976.

SCHOOL OF ORIENTAL AND AFRICAN STUDIES, *Library catalogue*, vol.16, Subject catalogue, Middle East, A-Iran, esp. :661-844; vol.17, Middle East, Iraq-Z, Boston, Mass. 1963.

—— *Library Catalogue*, 1st suppl. vol.9, Middle East, Boston 1968.

—— *Library Catalogue*, 2nd suppl. vols 9 and 10, Near and Middle East, Boston 1973.

—— *Library Catalogue*, 3rd suppl. vols 12 and 13, Near and Middle East, Boston 1979.

SHCHEGLOVA, O P, *Katalog litografirovannykh knig na persidskom jazyke v sobranii Leningradskogo otdelenija*, Yu E BORSHCHEVSKII (ed), 2 vols, Moscow 1975.

Analytical catalogue of the Persian lithographs in the Leningrad section of the Oriental Institute of the USSR Academy of Sciences, with references to the standard bibliographies.

TEHRAN UNIVERSITY LIBRARY, *Fihrist-i alifbā'ī-yi ᶜunvān-i kitābhā-yi chāpī-yi sharqī az badv-i ta'sīs tā pāyān-i nīma-yi avval 1340*, Tehran 1961.

TOKYO. AJIA KEIZAI KENKYŪJO, *Union list of materials on Islamic studies*, Isuramo kankei shiryō sōgō mokuroku, Tokyo 1961.

UNIVERSITY OF MICHIGAN LIBRARY, *Arabic script union list. 1974*, Ann Arbor 1975. Cumulation through 1977, Ann Arbor 1978.

3. *CATALOGUES AND MANUSCRIPTS*

3.1 *Bibliographies of catalogues*

A complete inventory of catalogues of Persian manuscripts, similar to that for Arabic to be found in the pages of

SEZGIN, Fuat, *GAS*, *op.cit.*, II 2.3.1, vol.I :706-69, Bibliothekan und Sammlungen arabischer Handschriften; vol.III :392-420, Nachträge,

remains a desideratum. Some 450 titles published to 1962 were listed in

AKIMUSHKIN, O F, and Yu E BORSHCHEVSKII, 'Materialy dlya bibliografii rabot o persidskikh rukopisakh', *Narody Azii i Afriki*, 1963(3) :165-74, 1973(6) :228-41.

AFSHĀR, Īraj, *Kitābshināsī-yi fihristhā-yi nuskhahā-yi khaṭṭī-yi fārsī dar kitābkhanahā-yi dunyā*, Tehran 1958,

lists 222 catalogues published in 17 countries.

PEARSON, J D, *Oriental manuscripts in Europe and North America*, Bibliotheca Asiatica, 7, Zug 1971.

An attempt to list the collections of Oriental manuscripts in Europe and

North America, recording all catalogues available at the time, whether published or not. Persian, together with Arabic and Ottoman Turkish MSS, are treated on pp.189-345.

Supplementary information on various collections, mainly in Asia, may be found in

UTAS, Bo, 'Notes on some public and semi-public libraries in the Near and Middle East containing Persian and other Moslem manuscripts', *Acta Orientalia* 33, 1971 :169-92.

—— 'Manuscript collections in the USSR, Iran, Afghanistan and Germany', *Annual vol. Scand. Inst. Asian Stud.* 8, 1974 :33-40.

BESTERMAN, T N D, *A world bibliography of oriental bibliographies*, *op.cit.*, 2.4.

Enumerates catalogues in chronological order from 1814 (O FRANK, *Ueber die morgenländischen Handschriften der königlichen Hof- und Central-Bibliothek in München*, Munich 1814), the first catalogue devoted solely to Persian MSS, to 1973 (cols.203-18), but earlier descriptions will be found in the list of oriental manuscript collections in cols.71-78. In neither of these places are given titles in oriental languages or periodical articles, which may be sought in *Index Iranicus* and *Index Islamicus* (*op.cit.*).

List of catalogues consulted by STOREY, *PL*, *op.cit.*, II 2.1.1, are given in volume I, pp.ix-xxiii, xxix-xxxv, xliv, xlviii, liii-liv; volume II, pp.iv-vii, 193. A much expanded version of STOREY's list is to be found in the Russian edition on pp.55-96 and 1325-27.

AUCHTERLONIE, Paul (ed), 'British library collections in Middle Eastern and Islamic Studies', Durham Centre for Middle Eastern and Islamic Studies, Occasional Papers, Durham 1982.

3.2 *Catalogues of individual collections*

3.2.1 *Collections in Iran*

The following list includes some of the major collections in Tehran.

(a) Royal Library

ĀTĀBĀY, Badrī, *Fihrist-i Qur'ānhā-yi khaṭṭī-yi kitābkhāna-yi salṭanatī*, Tehran 1972.

222 items.

—— *Fihrist-i kutub-i dīnī va mazhabī-yi kitābkhāna-yi salṭanatī*, Tehran 1974.

—— *Fihrist-i muraqqaʿāt-i kitābkhāna-yi salṭanatī*, Tehran 1974.

—— *Fihrist-i dīvānhā-yi khaṭṭī va kitāb-i hazār u yak-shab*, 2 vols, Tehran 1976.

—— *Fihrist-i tārīkh, safarnāma, siyāḥatnāma, rūznāma va jughrāfiyā-yi khaṭṭī-yi kitābkhāna-yi salṭanatī*, Tehran 1977.

—— *Fihrist-i ālbūmhā-yi kitābkhāna-yi salṭanatī*, Tehran 1978.

BAYĀNĪ, Mahdī, *Fihrist-i namūna-yi khuṭūṭ-i khwush-i kitābkhāna-yi shāhanshāhī-yi Īrān*, Tehran 1950.

—— *Fihrist-i nā-tamām-i tiᶜdādī az kitābhā-yi kitābkhāna-yi salṭanatī*, Tehran, n.d.

460 items.

(b) Tehran University

DĀNISHPUZHŪH, Muhammad Taqī, *Fihrist-i nuskhahā-yi khaṭṭī Dānishkada-yi Ḥuqūq va ᶜUlūm-i Siyāsī va Iqtiṣādī*, Tehran 1960.

—— *Fihrist-i nuskhahā-yi khaṭṭī-yi kitābkhāna-yi Dānishkada-yi Adabīyāt* Tehran 1960-.

In progress; 16 volumes published up to 1979.

—— *Fihrist-i mīkrūfīlmhā-yi kitābkhāna-yi markazī-yi Dānishgāh-i Tihrān*, Tehran 1969. Persian MSS :1-275.

ḤUJJATĪ, Muḥammad Bāqir, and Muḥammad Taqī DĀNISHPUZHŪH, *Fihrist-i nuskhahā-yi khaṭṭī-yi kitābkhāna-yi Dānishkada-yi Ilāhīyāt va Maᶜārif-i Islāmī*, Tehran 1966.

IBN YŪSIF SHĪRĀZĪ, *Fihrist-i kitābkhāna-yi Dānishkada-yi Maᶜqūl va Manqūl* (Madrasa-yi ᶜĀlī-yi Sipahsālār), Tehran vol.I, 1934-5; vol.II, 1937-9.

MUNZAVĪ TIHRĀNĪ, ᶜAlī Naqī (cont. by Muḥammad Taqī DĀNISHPUZHŪH), *Fihrist-i kitābkhāna-yi ihdā'ī-yi Āqā-yi Sayyid Muḥammad Mishkāt*, Tehran vol.I, 1951; vol.II, 1953; vol.III (in 5 parts) 1953-59. Cont. as *Fihrist-i kitābkhāna-yi markazī-yi Dānishgāh-i Tihrān*, vols VIII-XVI, 1960-78.

8000 items.

RAHĀVARD, Ḥasan, *Fihrist-i kutub-i khaṭṭī-yi kitābkhāna-yi Dānishkada-yi Pizishkī*, Tehran 1954.

Many other catalogues with details of accessions and other matters of library interest are published in the annual

Nuskhahāyi khaṭṭī. Nashrīya-yi kitābkhāna-yi markazī-yi Dānishgāh-i Tihrān, Tehran 1961-79.

3.2.2 *Collections outside Iran*

The following list is limited to libraries with substantial collections of Persian manuscripts.

Bankipore

ORIENTAL PUBLIC LIBRARY, *Catalogue of the Arabic and Persian manuscripts in the Oriental Public Library at Bankipore*. Under the supervision of Sir E D ROSS, Patna, various dates.

Persian manuscripts are the subject of volumes 7 (1921), 8 (1925), 9 (1925), 11 (1927), 14 (1928), 16 (1929), 17 (1930), and the *Supplement to the Catalogue of the Persian manuscripts* (1932). All these were prepared by Maulavi ABDUL MUQTADIR, who was also responsible for the *Index to the catalogue raisonée*, Patna 1939.

Berlin

Institut für Orientforschung

BOYCE, Mary, *A catalogue of the Iranian manuscripts ..., op.cit.* 1.1.

Königliche Bibliothek

PERTSCH, Wilhelm, *Die Handschriften-Verzeichnisse der Königlichen Bibliothek zu Berlin*, vol.IV, Verzeichnis der persischen Handschriften, Berlin 1888.

1117 items.

Calcutta

Buhar Library

RAZAVI, Kāsim Hasīr, *Catalogue of the Persian manuscripts in the Buhar Library*, Calcutta 1921 (500 MSS).

Asiatic Society

IVANOV, W, *Concise descriptive catalogue of the Persian manuscripts in the Curzon collection*, Asiatic Society of Bengal, Calcutta 1926.

Cambridge

University Library

BROWNE, Edward G, *Catalogue of the Persian manuscripts in the Library of the University of Cambridge*, Cambridge 1896.

—— *A hand-list of the Muhammadan manuscripts ... in the library of the University of Cambridge*, Cambridge 1900.

—— *A supplementary hand-list of the Muhammadan manuscripts in the libraries of the University and Colleges of Cambridge*, Cambridge 1922.

—— *A descriptive catalogue of the oriental MSS belonging to the late E G Browne*. Completed and ed. ... by R A NICHOLSON, Cambridge 1932.

ARBERRY, Arthur J, *A second supplementary hand-list of the Muhammadan manuscripts in the University and Colleges of Cambridge*, Cambridge 1952.

Copenhagen

Royal Library

WESTERGAARD, N L, *Codices orientales Bibliothecae Regiae Havniensis*, Copenhagen 1846.

CHRISTENSEN, Arthur E, *Codices Avestici et Pahlavici Bibliothecae Hafniensis*, 12 vols, Copenhagen 1931-44.

Dublin

CHESTER BEATTY LIBRARY, *A catalogue of the Persian manuscripts and miniatures*, 3 vols, Dublin 1959-62.

The compilers include A J ARBERRY, M MINOVI, E BLOCHET, J V S WILKINSON, B W ROBINSON, and J WATSON.

—— *Manichaische Handschriften der Sammlung A Chester Beatty*, H J POLOTSKY, C R C ALLBERRY, and H IBSCHER (eds), 2 vols, Stuttgart 1934-38.

Edinburgh

HUKK, Mohammed Ashraful, Hermann ETHÉ, and Edward ROBERTSON, *A descriptive catalogue of the Arabic and Persian manuscripts in Edinburgh University Library*, Edinburgh 1925.

SERJEANT, Robert B, *A handlist of the Arabic, Persian and Hindustani MSS of New College, Edinburgh*, London 1942.

Istanbul

Topkapi Saray Museum

KARATAY, Fehmi Edhem, *Topkapi Sarayi Müzesi kütüphanesi farsca yazmalar katalogu*, Istanbul 1961.

940 items.

Leningrad

Institut Narodov Azii (Institut Vostokovedeniya)

MIKLUKHO-MAKLAI, N D, *Opisaniye Tadzhikshikh i Persidskikh rukopisei Instituta Vostokovedeniya (Narodov Azii)*, Moscow/Leningrad, vol.I, 1955; Moscow, vol.II, 1961; vol.III, 1975. Continued by

BAEVSKII, S I, vol.IV, 1962; vol.V, 1968; vol.VI, ?

VOROZHEIKINA, Z N, vol.VII, 1980.

AKIMUSHKIN, O F, *et al.*, *Instituta Narodov Azii: Persidkii i Tadzhikskii rukopisi*. Kratkii alfabitnyi katalog, 2 vols, Moscow 1964.

4790 items.

London

British Library

REICHELT, Hans, *Die soghdische Handschriftenreste*, *op.cit.*, 1.1, Teil I, Die buddhistische Texte; Teil II, Die nicht-buddhistische Texte und Nachtrag zu den buddhistischen Texten.

RIEU, Charles, *Catalogue of the Persian manuscripts in the British Museum*, London, vol.I, 1879; vol.II, 1881; vol.III, 1888; suppl. 1895; repr. 1966, 1968.

3000 items.

MEREDITH-OWENS, G M, *Handlist of Persian manuscripts, 1895-1966*, London 1968.

India Office Library and Records.

ETHÉ, Hermann, *Catalogue of the Persian manuscripts in the Library of the India Office*, Oxford, vol.I, 1903; vol.II (completed by Edward EDWARDS), 1937.

3650 items.

DHALLA, M N, 'Iranian manuscripts in the Library of the India Office', *JRAS*, 1912 :387-98.

ROSS, E Denison, and Edward G BROWNE, *Catalogue of two collections of Persian and Arabic MSS ... in the India Office Library*, London 1902.

Munich

AUMER, J, *Die persischen Handschriften der K Hof- und Staatsbibliothek in München*, Munich 1866.

BARTHOLOMAE, C, *Die Zend-Handschrifte der K Hof- und Staatsbibliothek in München*, Munich 1915.

Oxford

Bodleian Library

SACHAU, Ed. and Hermann ETHÉ, *Catalogue of the Persian, Turkish, Hindustani and Pushtu manuscripts in the Bodleian Library*, Oxford, vol.I (Persian) 1889; vol.II (Turkish, Pushtu, Urdu and additional Persian) 1930; vol.III (by A F L BEESTON, Additional Persian) 1954.

1519 items.

Paris

Bibliothèque Nationale

BLOCHET, E, *Bibliothèque Nationale: Catalogue des manuscrits persans*, 4 vols, Paris 1905-34.

—— *Catalogue des manuscrits mazdéens ... de la Bibliothèque Nationale*, Paris 1905.

Vatican City

ROSSI, E, *Elenco dei manoscritti persiani della Biblioteca Vaticana*, Vatican City 1948.

Vienna

FLUEGEL, Gustav, *Die arabische, persische und türkische Handschriften* *op.cit.* 1.1.

Now known as the Nationalbibliothek.

3.3 *Union catalogues*

Comparatively few union catalogues of Persian manuscripts have appeared so far, though STOREY, *PL* (*op.cit.* II.2.1.1) in both the English and Russian editions to some extent fulfils that function. Notice may also be taken of

MUNZAVĪ, Aḥmad, *Fihrist-i nuskhahā-yi khaṭṭī-yi fārsī*, 6 vols, Tehran 1969-n.d.

A cumulative bibliography of 85 published catalogues of Persian MSS (73 from Iran and 12 from other countries).

DĀNISHPUZHŪH, Muḥammad Taqī, *Majmūʿa-yi fihrist-i nuskhahā-yi khaṭṭī-yi kitābkhānahā-yi shahristānhāyi Īrān*, vol.1-, Tehran 1972-.

HEINZ, Wilhelm, *Persische Handschriften*, Teil 1, Verzeichnis der orientalischen Handschriften in Deutschland, Band XIV, 1, Wiesbaden 1968.

DIVSHALI, S H, and Paul LUFT, *Persische Handschriften*, Teil 2, Verzeichnis der orientalischen Handschriften in Deutschland, Band XIV, 2, Wiesbaden 1980.

FUAD, Kamal, *Kurdische Handschriften*. Verzeichnis der orientalischen Handschriften, Band XXX, Wiesbaden 1970.

UNVALA, J M, *Collection of colophons of MSS bearing on Zoroastrianism in some libraries of Europe*, Bombay 1940.

MAJDA, T, *Katalog rekopisów tureckich i perskich*, Catalogue des manuscrits orientaux des collections polonaises, V, 2, Warsaw 1967.

3.4 *Cataloguing aids*

ʿALĪ, Āqā Sayyid Muḥammad, *Khaṭṭ-i Lātīn barā-yi Fārsī*, Hyderabad 1968.

The romanization of Persian written in Arabic, Hebrew, and Pahlavi characters.

DEWEY, M, *Decimal classification and relative index: Islam*, Tehran Book Processing Centre, 174, Tehran 1975.

—— *Radabandī-i dahdahī-i Diyū'ī va fihrist-i nasbī: gustarish-i adab-i Īrānī : Dewey decimal classification and relative index: Iranian literature*, Tehran 1973.

—— *Tabaqa-bandī-i dahdahī-i Diyū'ī va fihrist-i nasbī: gustarish-i zabānhā-yi Īrānī : Dewey Decimal Classification and relative index: Iranian languages expanded by Tehran Book Processing Centre*, Tehran 1971.

GUSHTĀSB-PŪR PĀRSĪ, Mihrabān, *Ganjīna-i nāmhā-yi Īrānī*, 2nd ed. Tehran 1978.

JALĀLĪ, Tahmūras, *Farhang-i pāya*, Tehran 1975.

Vowelled dictionary of neologisms and idioms.

MARKAZ-I ĀMĀDA-SĀZĪ-YI KITĀB, *Ṣūrat-i kitābhā-yi fihrist shuda dar Markaz : Books cataloged by Tehran Book Processing Centre*, Tehran 1971-. no.1-.

—— *Fihrist-i mustanad-i asāmī-i mashāhīr va mu'allifān : The name authority file of authors and famous people*, Tehran 1977.

Qavāᶜid-i fihristnavīsī-i anglū āmrīkan, Tehran 1975-, part 1-. Translation of *Anglo-American cataloging rules.*

SHARIFY, Nasser, *Cataloging of Persian works, including rules for transliteration, entry and description : Fihrist kardan-i āsār-i Fārsī*, Chicago 1959.

4. *ARCHIVES*

4.1 *Documents in Persian*

Historical documents relating to the various dynasties that have ruled Iran will be found scattered among the various manuscript collections, archive depositories, and in private ownership in Iran and many other countries. A total of 595 records and letters of rulers from the beginning of the 7th/13th century to the end of the reign of the Qājār Muḥammad Shāh which have been published are recorded in

FRAGNER, B G, *Repertorium persischer Herrscherurkunden*. Publizierte Originalurkunde (bis 1848). Islamkundliche Materialien 4, Freiburg im Breisgau 1980.

4.1.1 *Iran*

Little is known of the National Archives in Iran, which even before the revolution of 1979 were difficult of access even to Iranian scholars, and even when accessible were found to be in considerable disorder and inadequately catalogued if at all. A law promulgated on May 7, 1970, established the Iranian Archives Organization, with responsibility for records of all Ministries (save that of War), but omitting also the records of the Imperial Court and the National Archives. Details of the activities of this organization are given in the very useful list of owners of archives, public and private, included, with a bibliography, in

AFSHĀR, Īraj, 'Neuere Archivstudien in Iran. Übersicht und Bibliographie', *Die islamische Welt zwischen Mittelalter und Neuzeit. Festschrift für H R Roemer*, Beirut 1979 :20-34.

In 1975 a special organization was set up under the Imperial Court to collect and photocopy documents relevant to the celebration of the 50th anniversary of the Pahlavi dynasty. These were classified under the headings Political, Social, Economic, and Legal. During 1975 the issue of four separate roneo'd catalogues was begun; it is not known whether any further lists were issued. The catalogues give full summaries of most of the documents listed.

DARBĀR-I SHĀHANSHĀHĪ, Sāzmān-i bar-guzar-kunanda-yi āyīn-i millī-yi buzurgdāsht-i panjāh sāl-i shāhanshāhī-yi Pahlavī. Markaz-i taḥqīqāt. *Fihrist-i asnād va madārik*, Tehran 1975.

Siyāsī: vols 1-2, 1451 documents; Ijtimāʿī: vols 1-2, 1656 documents; Iqtiṣādī: vols 1-2, 586 documents; Qużā'ī: vol.1, 52 documents.

4.1.2 *Turkey*

Vast collections of Persian documents exist in the archives and libraries of Turkey. A start was made on the cataloguing of those relating to Iranian history.

GHARAVĪ, Maḥmūd, *Fihrist-i asnād-i tārīkhī-yi Īrān dar ārshīv-i Ṣidārat-i ʿUsmānī dar Istanbūl*, vol.I, Tehran 1978.

4.1.3 *Indian Subcontinent*

A wealth of documentation exists in the central government and regional archives in India, Pakistan and Bangladesh, especially the National Archives, the Secretariat Record Office in Bombay, and many other record offices. The published calendars available and press-lists for these documents, as well as other information on the collections, will readily be found in

LOW, D A, J C ILTIS, and M D WAINWRIGHT, *Government archives in South Asia, a guide to national and state archives in Ceylon, India and Pakistan*, Cambridge 1969.

4.1.4 *Europe*

Italy

TIEPOLO, M F, *La Persia e la repubblica di Venezia*. Mostra di documenti dell'Archivio di Stato e della Biblioteca Marciana di Venezia ... Biblioteca Centrale dell'Università di Tehran, 26 aprile 1973. Introduzione e catalog, Tehran 1973.

Portugal

QĀ'IM-MAQĀMĪ, Jahāngīr, 'Asnād-i fārsī, ʿarabī va turkī dar ārshīv-i millī-yi Purtūghāl dar bāra-yi Hurmuz va Khalīj-i Fārs', *Barrasīhā-yi tārīkhī*, Tehran 1977-78, XII, 2 :123-164; 3 :161-208; 4 :193-214; 5 :221-254; 6 :189-224; XIII, 1 :191-218.

Spain

FĀKHIR, Ḥusain, *Kutub va asnād-i tārīkhī rājiʿ bi-Īrān dar Ispāniyā*, Tehran 1961.

Sweden

ZETTERSTEEN, K V, *Türkische, tatarische und persische Urkunden im schwedischen Reichsarchiv*, Uppsala 1945.

USSR

SMIRNOV, K N, and Dzh GAIBOV, *Nakhichevanskiye rukopisnye dokumenty XVII-XIX vv*, Persian text ed. tr. and comm. Yu N MARR, Tiflis 1936.

ROSTOPCHIN, F, *Ukazye kubinshikh khanov*, Tiflis 1936.

KHUBUA, Makar, *Persidskiye firmany i ukazy Muzeya Gruzii*, I, Tiflis 1949.

PUTURIDZE, V S, *Gruzino-persidskiye istoricheskiye dokumenty*, Persian text, Georgian tr. and comm., Tiflis 1955.

PAPAZYAN, A D, *Persidskiye dokumenty Matenadarana*, I, 1, XV-XVI vv, Erevan 1959.

Persian text with translations into Armenian and Russian.

PUTURIDZE, V S, *Persidskiye istoricheskiye dokumenty v knigokhranilishchakh Gruzii*, I, 1, 1541-1664 gg, Tiflis 1966.

Persian text, Georgian translation and introduction.

4.2 *Documents in western languages*

Much information relating to Persia will be found in

TUSON, Penelope, *The records of the British Residency and agencies in the Persian Gulf*, India Office Records, Guides to Archive Groups, London 1979.

This is a guide to Archive Group R/15 of the Persian Gulf records in the India Office Library and Records. Factories were opened by the East India Company at Shīrāz and Iṣfahān in 1617, and at Bandar ᶜAbbās (Gombroon) in 1623. Between 1763 and 1947 a Political Residency was maintained at Bushire; its surviving records are calendared at R/15/1 (pp.1-10). Though the records of the early factories as a whole have disappeared, some documents which have endured are enumerated in the Appendices, and those embodied in the Gulf records may be located from the index.

The same writer contributed the section on the India Office records in

MATTHEWS, N, and M D WAINWRIGHT, *Guide to manuscripts*, *op.cit.*, 1.2.

The editors visited all the principal record offices, libraries, and military offices in the British Isles and the Republic of Ireland, and collected also an enormous amount of data from the catalogues published by the Royal Commission on Historical Manuscripts and the National Register of Archives.

An important series of guides to archive collections is in course of publication:

INTERNATIONAL COUNCIL ON ARCHIVES/CONSEIL INTERNATIONAL DES ARCHIVES, *Guides to the sources for the history of nations*. 3rd series: North Africa, Asia and Oceania, vol.I, Guide des sources de l'histoire d'Afrique du Nord, d'Asie et d'Océanie conservées en Belgique, Munich 1972; vol.II, Sources de l'histoire de l'Asie et de l'Océanie dans les archives et bibliothèques françaises, part 1, Archives; part 2, Bibliothèque Nationale, Munich 1981; vol.III, Sources of the history of North Africa, Asia and Oceania in Scandinavia, part 1, Denmark; part 2, Finland, Norway, Sweden, Munich 1980, 1981; vol.IV, Sources of the history of Asia and Oceania in the Netherlands, part 1, Sources up to 1796; part 2, Sources 1796-1949, Munich (forthcoming).

5. *THESES*

General guides to theses may be found in

REYNOLDS, Michael M, *Guide to theses and dissertations*. An annotated bibliography of bibliographies, Detroit 1975.

Also of a general nature, but written with an eye to Middle Eastern interests, is

COLVIN, Peter, 'Bibliographies of theses', *BSMES Bull.*, 5/1, 1978 :61-5.

No general catalogue of theses relating specifically to Iran exists, but a few lists of theses on specific subjects submitted to universities in Iran have been published.

SHĪRĀZĪ, Khalīl, and Mahīn MAḤJŪB, *Fihrist-i pāyānnāmaha-yi dukturī-yi dāmpizishkī az Dānishgāh-i Tihrān*, Tehran 1972.

BASHĀRAT, Mihrī-dukht, *Fihrist-i risālahā-yi taḥṣīlī-yi Dānishgāh-i Tihrān*, Central Library Publications, 14, Tehran 1977.

FARNIYĀ, Farānīk, *Fihrist-i Pāyānnāmahā-yi ᶜulūm-i ijtimāᶜī*, Tehran 1974.

Iran as a subject is of course included in lists of theses relating to Asia or more specifically the Middle East.

BLOOMFIELD, B C, *Theses on Asia accepted by universities in the United Kingdom and Ireland, 1877-1964*, London 1967. Supplemented in Bull. Assoc. British Orientalists, NS4, 1968 :56-65; NS5, 1970 :19-40; NS7, 1972 :9-18; NS8, 1973-76 :26-80; NS10, 1978 :74-109.

—— 'Theses', *South Asian Bibliography*, J D PEARSON (ed), Hassocks 1979 :54-64.

Lists of current theses on the Middle East are included regularly in reports from individual universities under the heading

'Work in progress in British Universities', *BSMES Bull.*, six-monthly, 1975-.

A register of current research on the Middle East is also kept at Durham University:

DURHAM UNIVERSITY. CENTRE FOR MIDDLE EASTERN AND ISLAMIC STUDIES, *Register of current research in Middle Eastern and Islamic studies*, Durham 1969, rev.ed. 1971, 1977.

Information on American theses on Iran can be found in

EELLS, Walter Crosby, *American doctoral dissertations on education in countries of the Middle East*, The Middle East Institute, Washington 1955.

HART, Donn V, *An annotated bibliography of theses and dissertations on Asia accepted at Syracuse University, 1907-1963*, Syracuse 1964.

Many American dissertations are listed (and microfilmed or xeroxed on demand) by UNIVERSITY MICROFILMS INTERNATIONAL, with offices in Ann Arbor, Michigan, and London. *The Comprehensive Dissertation Index* is claimed to list 600,000 North American dissertations published since 1861, to which are added annually 30,000 new dissertaions. What proportion of them are relevant to Iran is of course not indicated, but selected lists are issued from time to time under such headings as 'Islam', 'The Middle East', 'Religion and Theology', 'Fine Arts', etc., that frequently contain Iranian material. It must be stressed however that this is a commercial rather than an academic undertaking.

A list of Australian theses is to be found in

BISHOP, Enid, *Australian theses on Asia*, Australian National University Canberra, Faculty of Asian Studies, Occasional Paper no.12, Canberra 1972.

Theses from German-speaking countries are listed in

FINKE, Detlev, *et al.*, *Deutsche Hochschulschriften über den modernen islamischen Orient*. Deutsches Orient-Institut, Dokumentationsdienst Moderner Orient, Reihe A,1. Hamburg 1973.

GEHRKE, U, *Beitrage zur Kenntnis Irans im 20. Jahrhundert*, *op.cit.*, II 2.2.

SCHWARZ, Klaus, *Der vordere Orient in den Hochschulschriften Deutschlands, Oesterreichs und der Schweiz*. Eine Bibliographie von Dissertationen und Habilitationsschriften (1885-1978). Freiburg in Breisgau 1980.

For a list of Russian theses see

INSTITUT VOSTOKOVEDENIYA, *Doktorskiye i kandidatskiye dissertatsii, zashchishchennye v Institute Vostokovedeniya Akad Nauk SSR s 1950 po 1970*, Moscow 1970.

SHEVCHENKO, Z M, and Nikolaeva, *Katalog kandidatskikh i doktorskikh dissertatsii, zashchishchennykh na materialakh Tadzhikskoi SSR, 1934-1959*, Stalinabad 1960.

—— *Katalog kandidatskikh i doktorskikh dissertatsii, zashchishchennykh na materialakh Tadzhikskoi SSR, 1960-1965*, Dushanbe 1970.

For other Asian countries see

List of theses approved for the D.Sc., Ph.D., M.Sc. and M.A. degrees in the Aligarh Muslim University, 1920-1969, Aligarh 1969.

STWODAH, M I, and ᶜAbd al-Raḥmān PAHWAL, *Index to theses and monographs, holdings of Kabul University Library*, Kabul 1974.

IV

NEWSPAPERS, PERIODICALS, AND SERIES

1. *HISTORY OF THE PERSIAN PRESS*

Persian printing in Europe and India pre-dates the introduction of printing in Iran. The first typographical works to come out of Iran were Armenian works. Conventional Persian printing did not start in Iran until the early nineteenth century.

RĀ'ĪN, I, *Avvalīn chāpkhāna-yi Īrān*, Intishārāt-i rūznāma-yi Ālīk, 11, Tehran 1968.

A brief history of Armenian printing in Iran.

The first Persian newspaper was published in 1837 in Tehran but, with the exception of the brief notice in the Cairo journal *al-Hilāl* of February 1900, no account of the Persian periodical press appeared until H L RABINO's pamphlet *Ṣūrat-i jarāyid-i Īrān va jarāyidī ki dar khārij-i Īrān bi-zabān-i fārsī ṭabᶜ shuda ast* was published at Rasht in 1911. This was translated into French by L BOUVAT in the *Revue du monde musulman*, 1913, and was also incorporated into the larger work by Mīrzā Muḥammad ᶜAlī Khān TARBIYAT which, translated and annotated by E G BROWNE, appeared as the first half of the latter's work on the press and poetry of Iran.

BROWNE, E G, *The press and poetry of modern Persia*, Cambridge 1914.

L BOUVAT published a further short article on the Iranian press: 'La presse à Téhéran en 1915', *RMM* 30, 1915 :274 sqq.

Subsequent articles of a similar nature included

NOROUZÉ, Ali, 'Registre analytique de la presse persane', *RMM* 60, 1925 :35-62.

LESCOT, R, 'Notes sur la presse iranienne', *REI* 12, 1938 :261-77.

BROWNE's book, but not the subsequent articles, were used by M ṢADR HĀSHIMĪ in compiling the most exhaustive account of the Iranian press up to 1941 to have appeared hitherto.

SADR HĀSHIMĪ, M, *Tārīkh-i jarāyid va majallāt-i Īrān*, 4 vols, Iṣfahān 1948-53.

This work lists 1186 Persian periodicals, with in most cases full bibliographical details, quotations from leading articles, biographies of editors, etc.

For the period after 1941 the information is in inverse proportion to the number of periodicals published.

MACHALSKI, F, 'La presse en Iran sous la régime des alliés, 1942-1946', *Acta orientalia* 30, 1966 :141-50.

Particulars of about 40 Persian newspapers and magazines published in Iran.

ELWELL-SUTTON, L P, 'The Iranian press, 1941-1947', *Iran* 6, 1968 :65-104.

Details of 433 newspapers and periodicals in Persian, and 31 in other languages with notes on editors and contributors, political leanings, publishing history, etc.

KANUS-CREDÉ, H, 'Die Presse der Ära Mossadegh', *Iranistische Mitteilungen*, vol.2, no.1, 1968 :2-85.

A list of 341 newspapers and periodicals from Iran and abroad.

A comprehensive account of the history and organization of a large Iranian publishing house is to be found in the 25th anniversary volume published by the newspaper Iṭṭilāᶜāt.

Iṭṭilāᶜāt dar yak rubᶜ qarn, Tehran 1950.

Lists of newspapers and magazines, together with other general information on the Iranian press, appear in the following.

ABUZIA, P, and N MORADI, *A directory of Iranian newspapers*, 21 March 1973 - 20 March 1974 (i.e. 1352), Tehran Book Processing Centre, 26, Tehran 1974. Persian ed. Parvīn ABŪ AL-ŻIYĀ, *Rāhnumā-yi rūznāmahā-yi Īrān*.

An annual publication listing approximately 125 titles.

ĀL-I AḤMAD, Jalāl, 'Varshikastagī-yi maṭbūᶜāt', *Raushanfikr*, no.284, Bahman 1337 (Jan.-Feb. 1959), repr. in *Sih maqāla-yi dīgar*, Tehran 1960.

A scathing criticism of the contemporary press by one of Iran's leading writers.

BARZĪN, Masᶜūd, *Sairī dar maṭbūᶜāt-i Īrān*, Tehran 1966.

—— *Maṭbūᶜāt-i Īrān, 1343-1353*, Tehran 1976.

BEHN, W H, and W FLOOR, *Twenty years of power struggle in Iran: a bibliography of political periodicals from 1341/1962 to 1360/1981*, Berlin 1982.

Alphabetical list of some 700 dissident periodicals published in Iran and abroad with complete bibliographic data as well as subject index.

HAI'AT, F, *Rūznāma-nigārī va tārīkh-i ān dar jahān*, 2nd ed, Tehran 1954.

HARAVĪ, Gh R Māyil, *Muᶜarrifī-yi rūznāma-hā, jarāyid, majallāt-i Afghānistān*, Kabul 1962.

POURHADI, I V, *Persian and Afghan newspapers in the Library of Congress, 1871-1978*, Washington DC 1979.

An annotated bibliography of 326 Iranian and 23 Afghan periodicals with exact holdings and complete bibliographic data.

RIŻVĀNĪ, M I, *Tārīkhcha-yi rūznāma-nigārī dar Īrān*.

ṢĀBIR, ᶜAlī A, and ᶜAbd al-Ghaffūr MARDUMĪ, *Rāhnamā-yi majallāt, jarāyid va rūznāma-hā-yi Afghānistān, 1252-1356*, Kabul 1977.

A bibliography of 174 Persian periodicals with bibliographic description.

ṢĀLIḤYĀR, Gh H, *Chashm-andāz-i jahānī va vīzhagī-ha-yi īrānī-i maṭbūᶜāt*, Tehran 1977.

—— *Chihra-i maṭbūᶜāt-i muᶜāṣir*, Tehran 1973.

The latter work contains biographies of editors, journalists and other personalities associated with the Iranian press.

SARTĪPZĀDA, B, and K KHUDĀPARAST, *Fihrist-i rūznāma-hā-yi maujūd dar Kitābkhāna-yi Millī-i Īrān*, Tehran 1977.

A list of 479 Persian newspapers with full bibliographic data.

SULṬĀNĪ, Murtażā, *Fihrist-i rūznāma-hā-yi Fārsī dar majmūᶜa-yi Kitābkhāna-yi Markazī va Markaz-i Asnād-i Dānishgāh-i Tihrān, 1267 q. - 1320 sh*, Intishārāt-i Kitābkhāna-i Markazī va Markaz-i Asnād, 60, Tehran 1975.

—— *Fihrist-i majalla-hā-yi fārsī az ibtidā ta sāl-i 1320 shamsī*, Tehran University Library, Tehran 1977.

SULTĀNĪ, Pūrī (SOLTANI, Poori), *A directory of Iranian periodicals, 21st March 1979 - 20th March 1980*, Tehran Book Processing Centre, no.25, Tehran 1980.

The most recent up-dated edition of the standard bibliography which has been published since 1969. The simultaneously published Persian edition is entitled *Rāhnamā-yi majalla-hā-yi Īrān, 1358*.

Taḥqīqāt-i rūznāma-nigārī, vol.1-, Tehran 1345 (1965/66) -.

This quarterly journal devoted to journalism in general also lists current publications. Number 10 appeared in Farvardīn 1347 (March-April 1968). It is not known whether any issues were published after that.

2. *PERIODICALS CONCERNED WITH IRANIAN STUDIES*

An exhaustive list of periodicals dealing with Islam, the Middle East, and the Orient in general is to be found in *AIB*, pp.118-22. Reference may also be made to

LJUNGGREN, F, and M HAMDY, *Annotated guide to journals dealing with the*

Middle East and North Africa, Cairo 1964.

A useful guide of 360 items.

RUDKIN, Anthony, and Irene BUTCHER, *A Book World directory*, *op.cit.* II 2.3.

The following list includes periodicals dealing specifically with Iranian affairs, as well as a few additions to the *AIB* list. Other journals specializing in particular fields are mentioned in the appropriate chapters.

Āyanda, monthly, Tehran, vol.I, 1925-26; vol.II, 1926-28; vol.III, 1944-46; vol.IV, 1959-60; vol.V, 1979-80; vol.VI, 1980-.

British Society for Middle Eastern Studies Bulletin, six-monthly, London 1975-77, Oxford 1977-.

Central Asiatic Journal, The Hague 1955-.

Central Asian Review, London 1953-.

Farhang-i Īrān-zamīn, quarterly, Tehran 1953-.

Harvard Journal of Asiatic Studies, Cambridge, Mass. 1936-.

Hunar va Mardum, monthly, Tehran 1962-78.

Iran, annually, Journal of the British Institute of Persian Studies, London 1963-.

Iranica Antiqua, Leiden 1961-.

Iranian Studies, quarterly, Bulletin of the Society for Iranian Studies, Newhaven, Los Angeles, Chestnut Hill, Mass. 1967-.

Kāva, monthly, Munich 1963-.

Middle East Studies Association Bulletin, New York.

Mihr, monthly, Tehran 1933-43.

Persica, Annuaire de la Société Néerlando-Iranienne, Amsterdam 1963-.

Rahnumā-yi Kitāb, monthly, Tehran 1958-78.

Review of Iranian Political Economy and History, six-monthly, Washington 1976-.

Studia Iranica, six-monthly, Leiden 1972-.

Sukhan, monthly, Tehran 1943-78.

Yādgār, monthly, Tehran 1944-.

3. *PUBLICATIONS OF ACADEMIES AND LEARNED INSTITUTIONS*

Many universities and learned societies publish works of Iranian and orientalist interest as part of a more general series, most items in which are irrelevant to the present study. Among such institutions may be mentioned the Iranian universities - Tehran, Tabrīz/Āzarbādigān, Mashhad/Firdausī, Iṣfahān, and Pahlavī (Shīrāz); the Anjuman-i Ās̱ār-i Millī, Bungāh-i Tarjama va Nashr-i Kitāb, Bunyād-i Farhang-i Īrān, Farhang-i Īrān-zamīn, and the Markaz-i Mardum-shināsī-yi Īrān (formerly Idāra-yi

Farhang-i ʿĀmma, and Markaz-i Puzhūhish-hā-yi Mardum-shināsī va Farhang-i ʿĀmma), all of Tehran; the Institut Franco-Iranien de Recherche of Tehran and Paris; the Institut d'Études Iraniennes de l'Université de la Sorbonne Nouvelle, and the École des Langues Orientales Vivantes, both in Paris; the Royal Asiatic Society, London; the Akademien der Wissenschaften in Göttingen, Mainz, Marburg, Munich and Wiesbaden, and the Deutsche Orient-Institut in Opladen; the Österreichische Akademie der Wissenschaften in Vienna; the Societas Orientalis Fennica in Helsinki; the Koninglijke Nederlandse Akademie van Wetenschappen in Amsterdam; the Istituto per il Medio ed Estremo Oriente in Rome; the Kgl. Danske Videnskabernes Selskab and the Scandinavian Institute of Asian Studies in Copenhagen; and the Türk Tarih Kurumu in Ankara.

3.1 *Other series*

Among series that include a substantial number of works relevant to Iran may be mentioned the following (many of these are no longer active):

Abhandlungen für die Kunde des Morgenlandes, Wiesbaden.
Acta Iranica, Tehran/Liège 1971-77.
Asiatische Forschungen, Wiesbaden.
Beiruter Texte und Studien, Beirut/Wiesbaden 1964-.
Bibliographien zur regionalen Geographie und Landeskunde, Munich 1980-.
Bibliotheca Asiatica, Zug.
Bibliotheca Geographorum Arabicorum, Leiden 1870-89, repr. 1967.
Bibliotheca Indica, Calcutta 1853-.
Bibliotheca Islamica, Minneapolis/Chicago.
Bibliothek Arabische Historiker und Geographen, Leipzig 1928-.
Bibliothéque des Géographes Arabes, Paris 1927-.
Bibliothéque des Oeuvres Classiques Persanes, Paris 1968-.
Bonner Orientalische Studien, Bonn.
Broadway Travellers Series, London 1926-.
E G Browne Memorial Series, Berlin 1928-.
E J W Gibb Memorial Publications, Old Series, 1905-28. New Series, 1921-.
Gaekwad's Oriental Series, Baroda 1916-53.
Hakluyt Society Publications, London 1847-98; 2nd Series 1899-.
Harvard Iranian Series, Cambridge, Mass.
Harvard Middle East Monographs, Cambridge, Mass.
Harvard Oriental Series, Cambridge, Mass. 1891-.
Iranica Antiqua, Leiden 1961-.
Islamkundliche Materialien, Freiburg.

Islamkundliche Untersuchungen, Freiburg.

Memoirs of the Archaeological Survey of India, Calcutta 1919-36, Delhi 1934-.

Oriental Translation Fund, London 1824-.

Pamyatniki Pis'mennosti Vostoka, Moscow.

Papers on Islamic History, Oxford.

Persian Heritage Series, various, 1968-.

Persian Studies Monographs, various, 1971-.

Studies in Middle Eastern History, Minneapolis/Chicago.

Teksty po Istorii Srednei Azii, Petrograd 1915-.

Textes et Traductions d'Auteurs orientaux, Cairo 1937-.

Wiener Beiträge zur Kunst und Kulturgeschichte, Vienna.

V

OFFICIAL PUBLICATIONS

1. *GENERAL*

Persian book production, both private and official, has been on the increase since the nineteen-sixties. In the seventies the volume and the direction of publishing underwent changes. Commercial publishers were hard hit by rising costs and inflation; the political situation created an atmosphere of uncertainty so that publishers no longer produced at full capacity. While the output became somewhat stablized there was a marked shift towards government publishing. The ministries as well as old and new institutions (Iranian Culture Foundation, Literacy Corps, Health Corps, Pahlavi Foundation, etc.) involved in the implementation of the White Revolution poured out statistics, surveys, and studies.

Iranian commercial publishing figures in general can be determined with a reasonable degree of accuracy on the basis of the United Nations as well as the Unesco *Statistical yearbook* or the *Iranian national bibliography*. The situation is quite different with respect to official publications. It is futile to look for a complete repertoire of government documents to the *Iranian national bibliography* because legal deposit in Iran does not apply to this type of publication. They are listed haphazardly in the national bibliography. The percentage varies from 1.56 in 1975 to 14.9 in 1966. Accepting the total book production as reported in the *Iran almanac and book of facts*, 1978, and considering that approximately ten percent of all Iranian publications are official publications of some sort, one is faced with the bibliographic control of some 4,000 items.

In such circumstances the Library of Congress' *National union catalog* with approximately two thousand Iranian official publications represents the most easily accessible source of such documents. A useful guide to this material is

SEPEHRI, (SIPIHRI), Abazar, *Iranian corporate headings with references*, New York 1976.

The Persian equivalent is

BIHNĀM, Mahvash, *Fihrist-i mustanad-i asāmī-yi mu'assasāt-i sāzmānhā-yi daulatī-yi Īrān*, Tehran 1977.

Basically a print-out of the authority file of Iranian corporate headings used by the Markaz-i Asnād va Farhangī-yi Āsiyā.

Material of a general nature comes from the Ministry of Information (Vizārat-i Iṭṭilāᶜāt) as well as from the information and press departments of the various ministries. The publications range from glossy descriptions of the country to documentary surveys of Iran's foreign policy, press conferences of the Shah, and addresses by the prime minister. The material is published not only in Persian but also in English, French or other western languages. An annotated list with selective locations of 220 official publications of the various ministries (mainly from the period 1970 to 1975) has been published by Deutsches Orient-Institut, Hamburg, in its irregular publication *Neuerwerbungen der Instituts-Bibliothek* 5, Jahrgang, no.2, 1976.

2. *LAW*

The laws passed by the Iranian parliament since 1906 have been published under the title *Majmūᶜa-yi qavānīn-i mauẓūᶜa va muṣavvabāt*. Since 1961 this collection of laws is entitled *Majmūᶜa-yi qavānīn-i ... daura-yi qānūn-guzārī-yi Majlis-i Shūrā-yi Millī*. An index to volumes 1 to 22 (1906-1971) was published in 1972. The *Iran almanac and book of facts* publishes an annually cumulated bibliography of laws in its section 'Documents'. In addition, the *Iran almanac and book of facts* lists those that are available from the Echo of Iran publishers. The *National union catalog* lists 153 laws under the entry 'Iran. Laws, statutes, etc.'. Ordinances and local laws are entered in the *National union catalog* under the name of the municipality.
A list of 45 titles appears in

BANĪ ĀDAM, Ḥusain, *Kitābshināsī-yi mauẓūᶜī-yi Īrān*, *op.cit.*, II 2.1 :209-13.

ḤUJJATĪ ASHRAFĪ, Ghulam Riża, *Majmūᶜa-yi kāmil-i qavānīn va muqarrarāt-i ḥuqūqī*, Tehran 1976.

3. *INTERNAL AFFAIRS*

The prime source for domestic politics are the parliamentary debates which were first recorded in 1906 in *Majlis*, the first newspaper to report them among other current events. The debates of the National Assembly are now being published separately as *Muẕākarāt*. The official gazette, *Rūznāma-i rasmī-yi Īrān*, has been published by the Ministry of Justice since 1945; it is continued under the republican government.

4. *EXTERNAL AFFAIRS*

The country's foreign relations are systematically surveyed since 1967 in the annual publication *Ravābiṭ-i khāriji-yi Īrān* as well as in *Akhbār va asnād* by the Ministry of Foreign Affairs. From 1970 to 1971 this Ministry issued a collection of bilateral treaties in two volumes entitled *Majmūᶜa-yi muᶜāhadāt-i dū jāniba-yi muᶜtabar ... tā sāl-i 1349*. From time to time the Information and Press Department of the Ministry of Foreign Affairs published surveys of Iran's foreign policy in western languages.

5. *ECONOMIC AFFAIRS*

The most authoritative reports of economic development come from the Statistical Centre and the Plan Organization, both of which publish a *Sālnāma* and its English edition, the *Statistical yearbook*. Other regular publications by the Plan Organization are the national development plans as well as their outline, amendments, reviews, and summaries in both Persian and English. A bibliography of publications from the Statistical Centre is *Fihrist-i nashriyyāt-i markaz-i āmār-i Īrān tā pāyān-i sāl-i 1353*, Tehran 1974.

ĀZĀDIYĀN, Ānūsh Huvsipiyān, *Fihrist-i nashriyyāt-i Sāzmān-i Barnāma*, Tehran 1972.

A bibliography of publications received from the Plan Organization at the Iranian Documentation Centre, Tehran.

—— *Fihrist-i nashriyyāt-i Vizārat-i Iqtiṣād*, Tehran 1973.

Two hundred publications of the Ministry of Economics can be found in BANĪ ĀDAM, *op.cit.*, :182-96.

It must be remembered that many ministries and institutions have statistical sections that publish independently of the Statistical Centre.

Most Iranian banks publish regularly reports, annual reports, and balance sheets in both Persian and English. But the activities of the banks are not restricted to the collection of statistical material; many of the following banks carry out research which they publish irregularly in the form of guides, studies, and economic surveys in English: Bank ᶜUmrān, Bank Rahnī, Bank of Iran and the Middle East, Central Bank, Industrial and Mines Development Bank, Industrial Credit Bank, National Bank of Iran.

Some economic reports are to be found in the periodical publications of the Regional Cooperation for Development, Tehran: *Economic report*, *RCD magazine*, *RCD newsletter*.

6. *SOCIAL AND CULTURAL AFFAIRS*

The Ministry of Labour and Social Services, the Ministry of Arts and

Culture, and the Ministry of Science and Higher Education are mainly responsible for social and cultural services. A comprehensive description of cultural organizations is

SAᶜĪDLŪ, Parvīz, *Sāzmānhā-yi farhangī-yi Īrān: tārīkhcha, mabānī, faᶜᶜāliyyat*, Tehran 1975.

The Imperial Organization for Social Services published c.1970 a brief survey of its activities from 1946 to 1971 entitled *Yak rubᶜ-i qarn dar khidmat-i mardum*. Similar publications covering shorter periods are issued annually or occasionally by many institutions, e.g. the High Council of Culture and Art, the Iranian Culture Foundation, the Literacy Corps, the Organization of Iranian Women, and usually entitled *faᶜᶜāliyyat, guzārish-i faᶜᶜāliyyat*, or *sālgard-i sāzmān*. The Iranian Culture Foundation which endeavoured to balance indiscriminate westernization by emphasizing the Iranian heritage issued a bibliography of its publications entitled

Kārnāma-i Bunyād-i Farhang-i Īrān, Tehran 1971.

The Institute for Research and Planning in Science and Education supports the compilation of bibliographical handbooks as well as reference works. An annotated bibliography of the publications of its Iranian Documentation Centre is entitled

Intishārāt-i Markaz-i Madārik-i ᶜIlmī, Tehran 1974.

A bibliography of publications from the Ministry of Health received at the Iranian Documentation Centre is entitled

ĀZĀDIYĀN, Ānūsh Huvsipiyān, *Fihrist-i nashriyyāt-i Vizārat-i Bihdārī*, Tehran 1974.

Iranian institutions of post-primary education entered the publishing field in 1935 with the first *sālnāma* of the Īrānshahr High School, Tehran, and the Shāh Riżā High School, Mashhad. The custom spread to the universities, all of which now have their own presses and issue directories, annual reports, yearbooks, reports, etc. Some of such publications are listed in BANĪ ĀDAM, *op.cit.*, pp.225-30. Some fifty can be found in

Kitābshināsī-yi dah sāla-i Kitābhā-yi Īrān, Tehran 1967 :166-70.

A bibliography of publications from the Ministry of Education received by the Iranian Documentation Centre is

ĀZĀDIYĀN, Ānūsh Huvsipiyān, *Ṣūrat-i nashriyyāt-i Vizārat-i Āmūzish va Parvarish*, Tehran c.1974.

For post-revolution developments see chapter XV.

VI

RELIGION, PHILOSOPHY, ETHICS AND LAW

1. *GENERAL*

1.1 *Reference works and bibliographies*

ARBERRY, Arthur John, *et al.* (ed), *Religion in the Middle East*. Three religions in concord and conflict, 2 vols, Cambridge 1969.

ASMUSSEN, Jes Peter, and J LAESSE, with C COLPE (ed), *Handbuch der Religionsgeschichte*, 3 vols, Göttingen 1971-5.

BARROW, John Graves, *Bibliography of bibliographies in religion*, Ann Arbor 1955.

By subject, with annotations and locations.

BLEECKER, Jouco, and Geo. WIDENGREN (ed), *Historia Religionum*. Handbook for the history of religions, 2 vols, Leiden 1969-71.

Volume I covers religions of the past; volume II religions of the present.

BRANDON, Samuel George Frederick (ed), *Dictionary of comparative religion*, New York 1970.

EDWARDS, Paul (ed), *The encyclopaedia of philosophy*, 8 vols, New York/London 1967.

EHLERS, Eckart, *Iran: ein bibliographischer Forschungsbericht*, *op.cit.* II 2.2.

See section 6.1.2 (pp.229-35), 'Race, language, religion'.

FĀRŪQĪ, Ismaᶜīl Rāgī, and David E SOPHER (ed), *Historical atlas of the religions of the world*, New York/London 1974.

HASTINGS, James (ed), *Encyclopaedia of religion and ethics*, 12 vols, Edinburgh 1908-26.

PFEIFFER, Martin, *Minderheiten in Asien (Auswahlbibliographie) : Minorities in Asia (a select bibliography)*, Hamburg 1977.

Reference should also be made to the general bibliographies listed in Chapter Two.

1.2 *General works on religion in Iran*

ALGAR, Hamid, 'An introduction to the history of freemasonry in Iran',

Middle East Studies VI, 1970 :276-96.

BAUSANI, Alessandro, *La persia religiosa, da Zaratustra a Bahâ'u'llâh*, Milan 1959.

FISCHER, Michael M J, *Zoroastrian Iran between myth and praxis*, Ph.D. thesis, 2 vols, Chicago University 1973.

FRYE, Richard Nelson, 'Problems in the study of Iranian religions', *Religions in antiquity, studies in memory of Erwin Ramsdell Goodenough*, Leiden 1968 :583-9.

GABRIEL, Alfons, *Religionsgeographie von Persien*, Vienna 1971.

—— *Die religiöse Welt des Iran. Entstehung und Schicksal von Glaubensformen auf persischem Boden*, Vienna/Cologne/Graz 1974.

ḤAQĪQAT, ᶜAbd al-rafīᶜ, *Tārīkh-i nihżat-hā-yi fikrī-yi Īrāniyān*, 3 vols, Tehran 1977-78.

MINORSKY, V, 'Ahl-i Ḥaḳḳ', *EI.2*, vol.I :260-63.

SPOONER, Brian J, 'The function of religion in Persian society', *Iran, Journal of the British Institute for Persian Studies* I, 1963 :83-95.

STATE UNIVERSITY OF NEW YORK, STONY BROOK. INSTITUTE FOR ADVANCED STUDY OF WORLD RELIGIONS, *Iranian religious studies information*, Stony Brook, New York.

Issued at irregular intervals.

2. *ISLAM*

2.1 *General bibliographies*

ADAMS, Charles J (ed), *A reader's guide to the great religions*, chap.8 'Islam', New York 1965.

—— 'The state of the art, VIII: Islamic religion', *MESA bull.* IV, 1970 :3, and V, 1971 :1.

GRIMWOOD-JONES, Diana (ed), *The Middle East and Islam*, *op.cit.* II 1.

See particularly the following sections: P JOHNSTONE, D A KERR, and J B TAYLOR, 'Islamic religion', pp.105-14; J D LATHAM, 'Islamic theology', pp.115-22.

Abstracta Islamica. Bibliographie sélective des études islamiques, Paris 1927-.

'Abstracta Islamica' appeared as an integral part of the journal *Revue des études islamiques* from 1927 to 1964; since that date it is published annually as a supplement.

ISLAMIC COUNCIL OF EUROPE, LONDON, *New books quarterly, on Islam and the Muslim world*, London, autumn 1980-.

GEDDES, C L, *Books in English on Islām, Muhammad, and the Qur'ān: a selected and annotated bibliography*, Denver 1976.

—— *An analytical guide to the bibliographies on Islam, Muhammad, and the Qur'an*, Denver 1973.

BOOKS ON ISLAM LTD, NEW YORK, *Catalogue and guide to books on Islam*, 2nd ed. and suppl., New York 1976-8.

PEARSON, James Douglas, *Index Islamicus*, *op.cit.*

—— *Quarterly Index Islamicus*, *op.cit.* Section III: *Religion, Theology.*

Abstracta Iranica, *op.cit.* II 3.1.

Relevant sections are: *Islam (sauf Soufisme); Soufisme.*

FIDĀ'Ī, G͟hulām-Riżā, *Guzīda-yi kitāb͟shināsī-yi tauṣīfī-yi islāmī*, Tehran n.d. [c.1979].

A select bibliography of about 900 works written in or translated into Persian. Very much favours recent publications at the expense of older, sometimes more important, ones.

PFANMÜLLER, G, *Handbuch der Islamliteratur*, Berlin/Leipzig 1923.

See also Chapter Two, *General Bibliographies.*

2.2 *General studies*

AHMAD, Khurshid (ed), *Islam - its meaning and message*, London 1975.

ARBERRY, A J, *et al.* (ed), *Religion in the Middle East*, *op.cit.*, vol.2.

FARAH, Caesar E, *Islam: beliefs and observances*, New York 1968.

GIBB, H A R, *Mohammedanism: a historical survey*, London 1950.

—— and J H KRAMERS, *Shorter Encyclopaedia of Islam*, Leiden 1953, repr. 1969.

Contains the articles relating to religion in the original edition of the *Encyclopaedia of Islam*. Many are now very dated.

HAMIDULLAH, Muhammad, *Introduction to Islam*, Paris 1959.

HUGHES, Thomas Patrick, *A dictionary of Islam*, *op.cit.* II 1.

LĀRĪ, Sayyid Mujtabā Ruknī Mūsavī, *Western civilisation through Muslim eyes*, tr. F J GOULDING, Worthing 1977. German tr. R H SENGLER, *Westliche Zivilisation und Islam: muslimische Kritik und Selbstkritik.*

MAḤMŪD, ᶜAbd al-Ḥalīm, *The Creed of Islam*, foreword by Martin LINGS, London 1978.

NASR, Seyyed Hossein, *Ideals and realities of Islam*, London 1966.

—— *Islamic life and thought*, Albany 1981.

RAHMAN, F [FAḌL AL-RAḤMĀN], *Islam*, London 1966.

SCHUON, Frithjof, *Understanding Islam*, London 1963.

SCHIMMEL, Annemarie, 'Islam', C J BLEECKER and G WIDENGREN (eds), *Historia religionum*, vol.II, Leiden 1971 :124-210.

MAUDŪDĪ, Abū 'l-ᶜAlā, Sayyid *Towards understanding Islam*, tr. and ed. Khurshid AHMAD, Karachi 1960, 6th ed.

WADDY, Charis, *The Muslim mind*, London 1976.

WATT, W Montgomery, *What is Islam?* 2nd ed., London 1979.

2.3 *Islam in Iran*

CORBIN, Henry, *En Islam iranien*, 4 vols. vol.I, Le shî^{c}isme duodécimain; vol.II, Sohrawardî et les Platoniciens de Perse; vol.III, Les Fidèles d'amour. Shī^{c}isme et soufisme; vol.IV, L'École d'Ispahan. L'Ecole shaykhie. Le Douzième Imâm, Paris 1971-72, repr. 1978.

MASSIGNON, Louis, *Salmân Pak et les prémices spirituelles de l'Islam iranien*, Tours 1934. English tr. J M UNVALA, *Salman Pak and the spiritual beginnings of Iranian Islam*, Bombay 1955.

MUṬAHHARĪ, Murtaẓā, *Khadamāt-i mutaqābil-i Islām va Īrān*, 8th ed., Qum 1978.

NETZER, Amnon, 'Islam in Iran', R ISRAELI (ed), *The Crescent in the East*, London 1981.

SADIGHI, Gholam Hossein (ṢADĪQĪ, Ghulām Ḥusain), *Les mouvements religieux iraniens au IIe et au IIIe siècle de l'hégire*, Paris 1938.

2.4 *Shī'a: General and Isnā-^{c}asharī ("Twelver")*

Bibliographical works

AMĪNĪ, Muḥammad Hādī, *Mu^{c}jam al-maṭbū^{c}āt al-Najafīya*, Najaf 1966.

ĀQĀ BUZURG, Muḥammad Muḥsin, al-Ṭihrānī, *al-Dharī^{c}a ilā taṣānīf al-Shī^{c}a*, 27 vols, Najaf (vols 1-3), Tehran 1936-78.

The bio-bibliography, in Arabic, of Shī^{c}ī literature. Over 50,000 entries.

IBN SHAHRĀSHŪB, M b ^{c}Alī, *Ma^{c}ālim al-^{c}ulamā' fī fihrist kutub al-shī^{c}a : Bibliography of the Shy'ahs, Supplement to Tusy's Fihrist*, A EGHBAL (ed), Tehran 1934.

JAVĀHIR AL-KALĀM, ^{c}Abd al-^{c}Azīz, *Āthār al-Shī^{c}at al-Imāmiya*, etc. 20 vols.

For the full title and description of this work, of which only part has been published, see STOREY, *PL*, *op.cit.*, volume I, part 2, pp.135-36.

KANTŪRĪ, I^{c}jāz Ḥasan al-, *Kashf al-ḥujūb wa-al-astār ^{c}an asmā' al-kutub wa-al-asfār : The bibliography of Shi'a literature*, M Hidāyat ḤUSAIN (ed), Bibliotheca Indica, 203, 2 vols, Calcutta 1912-35.

Kitābnāma-yi Imām-i Mahdī, Tehran 1977.

A bibliography of writings concerning the Twelfth Imam.

MUNZAVĪ, Aḥmad, *Fihrist-i nuskha-hā-yi khaṭṭī-i fārsī* *op.cit.* III 3.3, vol.II, part 1.

See the section *Kalām*, *^{c}aqā'id*, pp.868-1008, in which a large number of Shī^{c}a texts in manuscript are listed. Despite the merits of MUNZAVĪ's great compilation, it cannot be assumed that all Shī^{c}ī doctrinal MSS in Persian are included: other catalogues should also be consulted.

NAJĀSHĪ, Muhammad b ^{c}Alī al-, *Kitāb al-rijāl*, Bombay 1899.

PEARSON, J D, *Index Islamicus*, and *Quarterly Index Islamicus*, *op.cit*. II 3, 'II (Religion and theology) b. viii: Shī^{c}ites'.

STOREY, *PL*, *op.cit*. II 2.1.1, vol.I, part 2.

See particularly section N. 'Biography: (n) Shī^{c}ites', pp.1126-36.

ṬŪSĪ, Abū Ja^{c}far Muḥammad ibn al-Ḥasan al-, *Túsy's list of Shy'ah books and 'Alam al-Hoda's notes on Shy'ah biography*. Ed. by A SPRENGER and Mawlawy ^{c}ABD AL-ḤAQQ (and Mawlawy Gholam QADIR), Bibliotheca Indica 19, Calcutta 1853-55.

Text in Arabic.

—— *al-Fihrist*, M B al-KARSĀN (ed), 2nd ed., Najaf 1961.

Studies

AMINE, Hassan ul-, *Islamic Shi^{c}ite Encyclopaedia*, vols I, II, III, Beirut 1968-74.

—— *Shorter Islamic Shi^{c}ite Encyclopaedia*, Beirut 1969.

See bio-bibliographical chapter on Shī^{c}ite authors and scholars, pp.84-262.

—— *Dā'irat al-ma^{c}ārif al-islāmīyat al-shī^{c}īya*, 8 vols, 2nd ed., Beirut 1973.

AYOUB, Mahmoud (AYYŪB, Maḥmūd), *Redemptive suffering in Islam: a study of the devotional aspects of ^{c}Āshūrā in Twelver Shī^{c}ism*, The Hague 1978.

BRASWELL, George W, Jr, *A mosaic of mullas and mosques: religion and politics in Iranian Shī^{c}ah Islam*, Ph.D. thesis, London University 1975.

CORBIN, Henry, 'Le shī'isme iranien', *En islam iranien*, *op.cit*., tome 4.

This study, by the most - if not the only - understanding western scholar of the subject, emphasizes the esoteric and philosophical aspects of Shī^{c}ism. Some readers, however, will be put off by CORBIN's unswervingly phenomenological and anti-historicist stance.

DONALDSON, Dwight M, *The Shi^{c}ite religion: a history of Islam in Persia and Irak*, London 1933.

Rather uneven and in some respects dated, but still worth perusing.

Encyclopaedia of Islam, 2nd edition.

Many articles; among the most important to have appeared to date are those on the '^{c}Alids' (B LEWIS), 'Imāma' (W MADELUNG), 'Imāmzāda' (A K S LAMBTON) and 'Iran. Religions' (J T P De BRUIJN).

HOLLISTER, John Norman, *The Shi^{c}a of India*, London 1953.

Informative on Shī^{c}ism generally.

JAFRI, S H M, [JA^{c}FARĪ, Ḥusain Muḥammad, Sayyid], *Origins and early development of Shi^{c}a Islam*, London 1979. Pirated edition, Qom 1980.

An important work from the historical point of view. The fact that the Persians are not within the scope of the book, except in the context of Kūfah, does not greatly lessen its value for the student of later Iranian manifestations of the Shīᶜa.

KHODAYAR MOHEBBI, M, [KHUDĀYĀR-I MUḤIBBĪ, Murtaża], 'Les principes essentiels de la théologie chiite'. *Ex orbe religionum: studia Geo Widengren oblata*, Leiden 1978, vol.II :126-33.

Lists the basic sources for Shīᶜa law and doctrine.

RICHARD, Yann, *Le shi'isme en Iran. Imam et révolution*, Paris 1980.

An excellent concise account of the history of Shīᶜism in Iran. Despite the sub-title, the book does not unduly emphasize recent events at the expense of earlier ones. Useful bibliography, pp.120-26.

NASR, Seyyed Hossein, [NAṢR, Ḥusain, Sayyid], ᶜIthnā-ᶜasharī Shīᶜism and Iranian Islam', A J ARBERRY *et al.* (eds), *Religion in the Middle East*, *op.cit.*, vol.II :96-118.

SACHEDINA, Abdulaziz Abdulhussein, *Islamic Messianism: the idea of the Mahdi in Twelver Shiᶜism*, Albany 1981.

ṬABĀṬABĀ'Ī, Muḥammad Ḥusain, Sayyid, *Shīᶜa dar Islām*, Tehran 1969-70.

Written in Persian, by an eminent traditional authority, but with the westerner as much as the easterner in mind.

—— *Shiᶜite Islam*. Tr. from the Persian and ed. with an introduction and notes by S H NASR, London 1975. Pirated ed. Karachi, n.d.

This book, a translation with introduction, notes and appendix of *Shīᶜa dar Islām*, is the best available general study in English. With a bibliography of Arabic and Persian sources, pp.239-44, and of the author's other writings.

—— *A Shīᶜite anthology*. Selected and with a foreword by ᶜAllāmah ... ṬABĀṬABĀ'Ī. Tr. and with explanatory notes by William C CHITTICK. Introduction by Seyyed Hossein NASR, London 1980.

Technically an anthology of Shīᶜa ḥadīth literature, this book merits inclusion here both on account of the introductory and explanatory matter and as providing what is almost the only available source material in English on the teachings of the Imāms.

—— *Shīᶜa: majmūᶜa-yi muzākarāt bā prufisūr Hānrī Kurban*, Qum 1977.

The following two organizations produce and publish works on various aspects of Shīᶜism.

PEERMOHAMED EBRAHIM TRUST.

MUHAMMADI TRUST.

2.5 *Ismāʿīliyya*

Bibliographies

POONAWALA, Ismail K, *Biobibliography of Ismāʿīlī literature*, Malibu, Cal. 1977.

Indispensable. A most thorough and comprehensive work, which almost completely supersedes the other bibliographical works listed here. Amongst the appendices is a long list of references to published writings on (and by) Ismāʿīlīs.

IVANOW, Vladimir, *Ismaili literature: a bibliographical survey*, Tehran 1963.

A revised edition of IVANOW's *A guide to Ismaili literature*, London 1933. The primary reference work until the appearance of the *Biobibliography*. On pp.413-14 of the latter, POONAWALA lists other writings by IVANOW, almost all of which are concerned with the Ismāʿīliyya.

FYZEE, A A A, [FAIŻI, A A A], 'Materials for an Ismaili bibliography, 1920-34', *Journal of the Bombay Branch of the Royal Asiatic Society, New Series* XII, Bombay 1935 :59-65.

—— 'Additional notes for an Ismaili bibliography', *Journal of the B.B.R.A.S., New series* XII, Bombay 1936 :107-09.

—— 'Materials for an Ismaili bibliography, 1936-1938', *Journal of the B.B.R.A.S., New series* XVI, Bombay 1940 :99-101.

ḤAMDĀNĪ, Ḥusain F al-, 'Some unknown Ismāʿīlī authors and their works', *JRAS*, 1933 :359-78.

MAJDŪʿ, Ismāʿīl ibn ʿAbd al-rasūl al-, *Fihrist al-kutub va 'l-rasā'il*, Tehran 1966.

Edited by ʿAlī Naqī MUNZAVĪ. An 18th century compilation upon which IVANOW's survey was largely based.

MASSIGNON, Louis, 'Esquisse d'une bibliographie Qarmaṭe', *ʿAjab-nāmah: a volume of oriental studies presented to E G Browne*, Cambridge 1922 :329-38.

With a list of the then known doctrinal texts, historical or legendary texts, and studies by orientalists, of the Qarāmiṭa.

PEARSON, J D (ed), *Index Islamicus*, *op.cit.*

46 items listed on pp.89-90.

General works

MADELUNG, Wilfred, 'Isma iliyya', *EI.2*, vol.IV :198-206. With bibliography.

MAKAREM, Sami Naseb [MAKĀRIM, Sāmī Nasīb], *The doctrine of the Ismāʿīlīs*, Beirut 1972.

Useful short introduction despite its limitations.

CORBIN, Henry, with Seyyed Hossein NASR, and Osman YAHIA [ᶜUthmān YAḤYĀ], *Histoire de la philosophie islamique*, I: Des origines jusqu'à la mort d'Averroes (1198), Paris 1964.

Includes a masterly account of Ismāᶜīlī esoteric doctrine by CORBIN, pp.110-51.

Some important studies

ALGAR, Hamid, 'The revolt of Āghā Khān Maḥallātī and the transference of the Ismāᶜīlī Imamate to India', *Studia Islamica* XXIX, Paris 1969 :55-81.

CORBIN, Henry, 'Nāṣir-i Khusrau and Iranian Ismāᶜīlism', *CHI*, vol.IV :520-42.

Includes on pp.689-90 a list of NĀṢIR-I KHUSRAU's writings. CORBIN's numerous and weighty contributions to Ismāᶜīlī studies are detailed in the 'Liste des travaux et publications d'H. Corbin' included in S H NASR (ed), *Mélanges offerts à Henry Corbin*, Tehran 1977, pp.iii, xxxii.

HALM, Heinz, *Kosmologie und Heilslehre der frühen Ismāᶜīlīya*, Wiesbaden 1978.

IMPERIAL IRANIAN ACADEMY OF PHILOSOPHY, *Series on Ismaili thought*, Seyyed Hossein NASR (General editor), Tehran 1977, 5 vols.

Titles published: *Nasir-i Khusrau, Forty poems from the Divān*, tr. by P L WILSON and Gh R AAVANI; *Wajh-i Din*, by NĀṢIR-I KHUSRAU, (ed) AAVANI; *Aᶜlām al-nubuwwah*, by Abu Ḥātim al-RĀZĪ, (ed) S al-SAWY; *al-Aqwāl al-dhahabiyyah*, by Ḥamīd al-Dīn KIRMĀNĪ, (ed) SAWY; *Ismaᶜīlī contributions to Islamic culture*, (ed) NASR.

IVANOW, Wladimir, *Studies in early Persian Ismailism*, Leiden 1948, repr. Bombay 1955.

LEWIS, Bernard, *The origins of Ismailism*, Cambridge 1940.

MADELUNG, Wilfred, 'Das Imamat in der frühen ismailitischen Lehre', *Der Islam* XXXVII, Berlin 1961 :43-135.

POURJAVADI, N [PŪR-I JAVĀDĪ, N], and Peter Lamborn WILSON, 'Ismailis and Nimatullahis', *Studia Islamica* XLI, Paris 1975 :113-36.

The Nizari 'Assassins'

HODGSON, Marshall G S, 'The Ismāᶜīlī State', *CHI*, vol.V :422-82.

---- *The Order of Assassins: the struggle of the early Nizari Ismaᶜilis against the Islamic world*, The Hague 1955.

LEIWS, Bernard, *The Assassins: a radical sect in Islam*, London [1967].

2.6 *Shīᶜa biographies and hagiographies*

ᶜĀMILĪ, Muḥsin al-Amīn al-, *Aᶜyān al-Shīᶜa*, Beirut 1948.

—— *al-Majālis al-sanīya*, 2 vols, 6th ed., Beirut 1978.

AMĪNĪ, ʿAbd al-Ḥusain ibn Aḥmad, Tabrīzī, *al-Ghadīr*, 4 parts, Najaf 1945.

On the episode of Ghadīr Khumm, where according to Shīʿites the Prophet proclaimed ʿAlī to be his successor.

ĀQĀ BUZURG, Muḥammad Muḥsin, al-Ṭihrānī, *Ṭabaqāt aʿlām al-Shīʿa*, ʿAlī Naqī MUNZAVI (ed), Najaf/Beirut 1953- (in progress).

IBN RUSTAM, al-Tabarī, *Dalā'il al-imāma*, Najaf 1949.

IBN SHAHRĀSHŪB, Muḥammad ibn ʿAlī, *Manāqib Āl Abī Ṭālib*, Najaf 1956.

ʿIMĀDZĀDA, ʿImād al-Dīn Ḥusain, Iṣfahānī, *Majmūʿa-yi zindagānī-yi Chahārdah Maʿṣūm*, Tehran 1951-3.

IṢFAHĀNĪ, Abū 'l-Faraj al-, *Maqātil al-Ṭālibiyyīn*, Cairo 1949.

MAJLISI, Muḥammad Bāqir, *Ḥayāt al-qulūb*, Lucknow 1883-4 (and other editions listed in STOREY, *PL*, *op.cit.*, vol.I :197).

MUṬAHHARĪ, Murtaẓā, *Jāẕiba va dāfiʿa-yi ʿAlī, ʿalaih al-salām*, Tehran 1971.

MUNSHĪ, Maḥmūd, *Ṣādiq-i Āl-i Muḥammad*, Tehran 1969.

A biography of the sixth Imām, Jaʿfar al-Ṣādiq.

MUFĪD, Muḥammad b Muḥammad al-Shaikh al-, *Al-Irshād*, Najaf 1962. Persian tr. Sayyid Hāshim RASŪLĪ, Tehran 1967. English tr. I K A HOWARD, *Kitāb al-Irshād. The book of guidance into the lives of the Twelve Imams*, London 1981.

This is the earliest extant work on the lives of the Imāms.

NIʿMA, ʿAbdallāh, *Falāsifat al-shīʿa: ḥayātuhum wa ārā'uhum: Les philosophes Che'ites: biographies et pensées*, Beirut c.1961. Persian tr. Tabrīz 1968.

RAHNUMĀ, Zain al-ʿĀbidīn, *Payāmbar*, vol.I, Damascus 1937; vol.II, Tehran 1953; vol.III (with rev.ed. of vols 1 and II), Tehran 1957. At least twenty re-issues, some with revised text. French tr. Henri MASSÉ, *Le Prophète*, Paris 1957. English tr. L P ELWELL-SUTTON, *Payambar. The Messenger*, Lahore 1964-66.

Somewhat romanticized biography of the Prophet Muhammad based on traditional sources, with slight Shīʿī leanings.

—— *Zandagānī-yi Imām Ḥusain*, Tehran 1966, and reprints.

SHARĪF RĀZĪ, Muḥammad, *Ganjīna-i dānishmandān*, 7 vols, Qum 1973-75.

Bio-bibliographical dictionary of Shi'ites.

See also *AIB*, pp.86-87.

2.7 *Qur'ānic literature*

Bibliographies

BROCKELMANN, C, *GAL*, *op.cit.*, vol.I :188-92 and 406-18; Suppl. vol.I :327-36.

MUNZAVĪ, Aḥmad, *Fihrist-i nuskha-hā-yi khaṭṭī-yi fārsī*, vol.I, Tehran 1969.

Union catalogue by subject and title of Persian MSS. Volume I lists MSS on *Tafsīr* pp.1-68, Recitation pp.69-104, Works on the Qur'ān pp.105-211.

SEZGİN, F, *GAS*, *op.cit.*, vol.I :1-49: 'Qur'ānwissenschaften'.

STOREY, *PL*, *op.cit.*, vol.I, part 1, section 1: 'Qur'ānic literature', London 1927.

Divided into eight sections: A, Translations and commentaries; B, Glossaries; C, Pronunciation and variant readings; D, Orthography; E, Indices, concordances, etc.; F, The talismanic virtues of the Qur'ān; G, Fal-nāmahs; H, Miscellaneous works.

—— *Persidskaya literature: bio-bibliograficheskii obzor*. Chast' I: Koranicheskaya literatura, Moscow 1972.

See pp.99-276.

GEDDES, C L, *Books in English*, *op.cit.*

PEARSON, J D, *Index Islamicus*, 'Section II. Religion. Theology. v: The Koran'.

Recent studies etc. of Persian interest

ABUL QUASEM, Muhammad, *The recitation and interpretation of the Qur'ān: al-Ghazali's theory*, Selanger 1979.

ḤIJĀZĪ, Sayyid ᶜAbd al-rasūl, *Nidāhā-yi Qur'ān*, Tehran 1969.

ḤIKMAT, ᶜAlī Aṣghar, *Amsāl-i Qur'ān*, Tehran 1954.

KHAZĀ'ILĪ, Muḥammad, *Aᶜlām al-Qur'ān*, Tehran 1962.

Study of proper names in the Qur'ān.

MAᶜṢŪMĪ LĀRĪ, Sayyid Ḥusain, *Miftāḥ al-tafāsīr va kashf al-āyāt*, Tehran 1953.

13,124 verses in alphabetical order of first word, with references to nine classical *tafāsīr*.

RĀMYĀR, Maḥmūd, *Tārīkh al-Qur'ān*, Tehran 1967.

SALMĀSĪ-ZĀDA, Javād, *Tārīkh-i sair-i tarjama-yi Qur'ān dar Urūpā va Āsiyā*, Tehran 1963.

SHAFīᶜĪ, Muḥammad, *Mufassirān-i Shīᶜa*, Shīrāz 1970.

ṬABĀṬABĀ'Ī, Sayyid Muḥammad Ḥusain, *Qur'ān dar Islām*, Tehran 1974.

ŻARGHĀMFAR, Murtażā, *Ḥāfiẓ va Qur'ān*, Tehran 1966.

Qur'ān commentaries, concordances, etc.

The following list includes only recent works of special Persian interest.

ᶜAṢṢĀR, Sayyid Muḥammad Kāẓim, *Tafsīr al-Qur'ān al-Karīm*, Sayyid J ĀSHTIYANI (ed), Mashhad 1971.

FARĀHĀNĪ, Mu'assasa-yi intishārāt-i, *Qur'ān karīm fi lawḥ maḥfūẓ*, Tehran 1977.

Partly calligraphed in Kufic script. With concordances, etc.

NAJAFĪ, Muḥammad Javād, *Tafsīr-i āsān*, muntakhab az tafāsīr-i muᶜtabar, 5 vols, Tehran 1978.

QUMSHA'Ī, Mahdī Ilāhī, *al-Qur'ān al-karīm*. Persian tr. and comm., Tehran 1980.

RAHNUMĀ, Zain al-ᶜabidīn, *Qur'ān-i majīd*, bā tarjama va jamᶜ-āvarī-yi tafsīr, Tehran, vol.I 1967, repr. 1973; vol.II, 1970; vol.III 1974, vol.IV 1975.

Text reproduced from Cairo Royal Edition. Extensive commentary in Persian drawn from Muslim and western sources.

RĀZĪ, Abu'l-futūḥ, *Tafsīr-i rauḥ al-jinān va rūḥ al-janān*, ed. with notes by Abu'l-ḥasan SHAᶜRĀNĪ and ᶜAlī Akbar GHAFFĀRĪ, 13 vols, Tehran 1977-78.

ṬABĀṬABĀ'Ī, Sayyid Muḥammad Ḥusain, *al-Mīzān*, 20 vols, Qum n.d. Persian tr. and comm. Iḥsānallāh ᶜAlī ISTAKHRĪ, *Kalima-yi ᶜulyā*, Tehran 1967.

A monumental Arabic commentary.

ṬĀLIQĀNĪ, Sayyid Maḥmūd, *Partavī az Qur'ān*, 2nd ed., 4 vols, n.p. 1977.

Commentary on Sūras I, II, LXXVIII-CXII.

2.8 *Shīᶜa dogmatic theology (kalām)*

ANTES, P, *Zur Theologie des Schia*. Eine Untersuchung des Ǧāmiᶜ al-asrâr wa-manbaᶜ al-anwâr von Sayyid Ḥaidar Âmolî. Freiburg 1971.

ḤURR al-ᶜĀMILĪ, Muḥammad ibn Ḥasan al-, *Vaṣā'il al-Shīᶜa*, 20 vols, Tehran 1956-69.

A massive compendium on Shīᶜite theology.

IBN BĀBŪYA, Muḥammad ᶜAlī al-Qummī, called Shaikh ṢADŪQ, *Risāla fī'l-iᶜtiqādāt*, Tehran n.d. (c.1865), 28 folios. English tr. Asaf A A FYZEE, *A Shiᶜite creed*, London 1942. Persian tr. Sayyid Muḥammad ᶜAlī AL-ḤASANĪ, *Tarjama-yi iᶜtiqādāt*, Tehran 1959, 3rd ed.

—— *Kitāb al-tawḥīd*, Sayyid H al-ḤUSAINĪ (ed), Beirut 1967. Persian tr. M ᶜA ARDAKĀNĪ, *Asrār-i tauḥīd*, n.p., c.1974.

CHARANDĀBĪ, ᶜAbbās Qulī (ed), *Sharḥ ᶜaqā'id al-Ṣadūq, aw Taṣḥīḥ al-iᶜtiqād*, Tabrīz 1951, 2nd ed.

CORBIN, Henry, 'La philosophie islamique depuis la mort d'Averroës jusqu'à nos jours', Y BELAVAL (ed), *Histoire de la philosophie*, vol.III, Paris 1974 :1067-188.

—— 'Le douzième Imam', *En Islam iranien*, vol.IV, Paris 1971 :302-37.

IBN AL-MUṬAHHAR, Ḥasan b Yūsuf al-Ḥillī, *Al-bāb al-ḥādī-ᶜashar*, Tehran 1865. English tr. W McE MILLER, *Al-Bâbu'l-ḥâdî ᶜashar*. A treatise on the principles of Shiᶜite theology ... with commentary by Miqdâd-i Fâḍil al-ḤILLÎ, London 1928.

—— *Kashf al-murād fī sharḥ Tajrīd al-iʿtiqād*, Qum n.d.

—— *Minhaj al-karāma fī maʿrifat al-imāma*, Cairo 1962.

MADELUNG, Wilfred, 'Imāma', *EI.2*, vol.III :1163-69.

MCDERMOTT, M J, *The theology of Al-Shaikh Al-Mufīd (d.413/1022)*, Beirut 1978.

This fine study includes a comparison of al-MUFĪD with his teacher IBN BĀBŪYA and pupil al-SHARĪF al-MURTAḌĀ.

MUFĪD, Muḥammad b Muḥammad al-Shaikh al-, *Awā'il al-maqālāt*, ʿAbbās Qulī CHARANDĀBĪ (ed), Tabrīz 1951, 2nd ed. French tr. D SOURDEL, *L'imamisme vu par le Cheykh al-Mofid*.

—— *Al-nukat al-iʿtiqādiyya*, ed. with Persian tr. by M T DĀNISHPUZHŪH, Tehran 1945.

NAṢĪR AL-DĪN, Ṭūsī, *Risāla-yi imāmat*, M T DĀNISHPUZHŪH (ed), Tehran 1956-57.

NAUBAKHTĪ, Al-Ḥasan b Mūsā, *Firaq al-Shīʿa*, H RITTER (ed), Istanbul 1931.

2.9 *Ḥadīth (Tradition) and Sīra (Life of the Prophet)*

Bibliographies

ANEES, Munawar Aḥmad, and ʿĀlia Nasreen AṬHAR, *Ḥadīth and Sīra literature in western languages: a bibliographic study*, n.p. (USA) 1980.

BROCKELMANN, *GAL*, *op.cit.*, vol.I :163-75.

DENFFER, Ahmad von, *Hadith: a select and annotated guide to materials in the English language*, Leicester 1979.

GEDDES, C L, *Books in English*, *op.cit.*

HAMADEH, M M, *Muhammad the Prophet: a selected bibliography*, thesis (microfilm), Ann Arbor.

SEZGİN, *GAS*, *op.cit.*, vol.I :51-234.

Sīra

HAMIDULLAH, Muhammad, *Le Prophète de l'Islam*, 2 vols, Paris 1959.

IBN ISḤĀQ, Muḥammad, *Sīrat al-Nabī*, M al-ṬAHṬAWI (ed), 2 vols, Cairo 1928. English tr. A GUILLAUME, *The Life of Muhammad*, Oxford 1955.

The translation is not wholly reliable.

ISḤAQ B MUḤAMMAD, Rafiʿ al-dīn, Hamadānī, *Sīrat-i Rasūl Allāh, mashhūr ba Sīrat al-Nabī*, A MAHDAVĪ (ed), 2 vols, Tehran 1981.

LINGS, Martin, *Muhammad: his life, based on the earliest sources*, forthcoming.

MAJLISĪ, Muḥammad Bāqir, *Ḥayāt al-qulūb*, part English tr. J L MERRICK, *The life and religion of Mohammad, as contained in the Sheeah traditions of the Hyat-ul-Kuloob*, Boston 1850.

MIHRĪN SHŪSHTARĪ, ^{c}Abbās, *Khātim al-nabiyīn*, 3rd ed., Tehran 1970.

MUIR, William, *The life of Muhammad and history of Islam, to the end of the Hegira*, 4 vols, London 1858-61.

Very thoroughly researched; extremely hostile in its approach!

RĀHNUMĀ, Zain al-^{c}Ābidīn, *Payāmbar*, *op.cit.* 2.6.

SHARĪ^{c}ATĪ, ^{c}Alī, *Sīmā-yi Muḥammad : The visage of Mohammed*, English tr. ^{c}A ^{c}A SĀSHĀDĪN, Tehran 1971.

ṬABARĪ, Muḥammad b Jarīr al-, *Mohammed, sceau des prophètes: une biographie traditionelle, extraite de la Chronique de Tabari*, French tr. Hermann ZOTENBERG, Paris 1980.

ṬABĀṬABĀ'Ī, Sayyid Muḥammad Ḥusayn, *Muḥammad in the mirror of Islam*, English tr. W C CHITTICK, Tehran 1970.

WATT, W Montgomery, *Muhammad at Mecca*, London 1953.

—— *Muhammad at Medīna*, London 1956.

Studies

A^{c}ẒAMĪ, Muḥammad Muṣṭafā, *Studies in early Ḥadith literature, with a critical edition of some early texts*, Indianapolis 1978.

—— *Studies in Ḥadīth methodology and literature*, Indianapolis 1977.

An excellent introduction to *^{c}Īlm al-Ḥadīth*.

—— 'Isnād and its significance', *The place of Ḥadīth in Islam*, Plainfield 1977 :41-53.

GUILLAUME, Alfred, *The Traditions of Islām: an introduction to the study of the Ḥadīth literature*, London 1924.

ḤĀKIM AL-NĪSHĀPŪRĪ, Abū ^{c}Abdallāh Muḥammad b ^{c}Abdallāh al-, *An Introduction to the Science of Tradition, being al-Madkhal ilā ma^{c}rifat al-Iklīl*, ed. with introduction and tr. J ROBSON, London 1953.

HAMIDULLAH, Muhammad, *The earliest extant work on the Ḥadīth: Ṣahīfah Hammām ibn Munabbih*, English tr. Muḥammad RAḤĪMUDDĪN, 5th rev.ed., Paris 1961.

IBN ḤAJAR AL-^{c}ASQALĀNĪ, Aḥmad b ^{c}Alī, *al-Iṣāba fī tamyīz al-Ṣaḥāba*, 4 vols, Cairo 1910.

IBN AL-ṢALĀḤ AL-SHAHRAZŪRĪ, ^{c}Uthmān b ^{c}Abd al-Raḥmān, *Muqaddimat Ibn al-Ṣalāḥ wa Maḥāsin al-iṣṭilāḥ*, ^{c}A ^{c}A BINT AL-SHĀṬI^{c} (ed), Cairo 1974.

DAHSURKHĪ AL-IṢFAHĀNĪ, Maḥmūd al-, *Miftāḥ al-kutub al-arba^{c}a*, vols 1-, Najaf 1967-.

IBN FŪRAK, Muḥammad b al-Ḥasan, *Bayān mushkil al-aḥādīth*, ed. and German tr. R KÖBERT, Rome 1941.

IBN QUTAIBA, ^{c}Abdallāh b Muslim, *Ta'wīl mukhtalif al-ḥadīth*, I al-IS^{c}IRDĪ (ed), Cairo 1908. French tr. G LECOMTE, *Le traité des divergences du Ḥadīt*, Damascus 1962.

JUYNBOLL, G H A, *The authenticity of the Tradition literature: discussions in modern Egypt*, Leiden 1969.

LECOMTE, Gerard, 'Aspets de la litterature du Hadīṯ chez les Imāmites', *Le shīᶜisme imāmite*, Paris 1968 :91-103.

MĪR-KHĀNĪ, Aḥmad, *Sair-i ḥadīs̲ dar Islām*, Tehran 1978.

MIZZĪ, Yūsuf b ᶜAbd al-raḥmān al-, *Tuḥfat al-ashrāf bi-maᶜrifat al-aṭrāf*, ᶜA SHARAF AL-DĪN (ed), vol.I-, Bombay 1965-.

MUHAMMAD ᶜALĪ, *A manual of Hadith*, Lahore 1951.

NAWAWĪ, Yaḥyā ibn Sharaf al-, *al-Taqrīb wa'l-taisīr*, with *Tadrīb al-rāwī*, comm. ᶜAbd al-raḥmān al-SUYUṬĪ, Cairo 1899. French tr. M MARÇAIS, 'Le Taqrīb de En-Nawawī', *Journal Asiatique*, neuvième série, XVI, 1900 :315-46 and 478-531; XVII, 1901 :101-49, 193-232, 524-40; XVIII 1901 :61-146.

RAHMAN, Fazlur, 'Sunna and Ḥadīth', *Islamic Studies* I, 2, 1962 :1-36.

ROBSON, James, 'Ḥadīth', *EI.2*, vol.III :23-28.

With bibliography.

—— 'A Shīᶜa collection of Divine Traditions', *Glasgow University Oriental Society. Transactions* XXII, 1970 :1-13.

SA'EED, Ahmad, *Ḥadees-e-Qudsi*, English tr. from Urdu by R ᶜAlī al-HĀSHIMĪ, New Delhi 1972.

ṢĀLIḤĪ, Muḥyī'l-dīn, *Aṣḥāb-i ṣiḥaḥ-i sitta, bā muqaddima va khātima dar tārīkh-i fiqh va ḥadīs̲*, Tehran 1975.

SCARCIA AMORETTI, B, 'ᶜIlm al-ridjāl', *EI.2*, vol.III :1150-52.

ṢIDDĪQĪ, Muḥammad Zubair, *Ḥadith literature: its origin, development, special features and criticism*, Calcutta 1961.

—— 'ᶜUlūm al-Ḥadīth', *Studies in Islam* V, 4, 1968 :197-211.

WENSINCK, Arent Jan, *A handbook of early Muḥammadan tradition, alphabetically arranged*, Leiden 1927.

—— *et al. Concordance et indices de la tradition musulmane: les Six Livres, le Musnad d'al-Dārimī, le Muwaṭṭa' de Mālik, le Musnad de Aḥmad ibn Ḥanbal*, 7 vols, Leiden 1936-69.

YUSUF, 3 M, *An essay on the Sunnah: its importance, transmission, development and revision*, 2nd rev.ed., Lahore 1977.

YUSUFUDDIN, M, 'Pre-Bukhārī Ḥadīth literature', *Proceedings of the 26th International Congress of Orientalists*, vol.IV, Poona 1970 :357-61.

Texts - Sunnī

BUKHĀRĪ, Muḥammad b Ismaᶜīl al-, *al-Jāmiᶜ al-ṣaḥīḥ*, ed. with English tr. M M KHAN, *The translation of the meanings of Ṣaḥīḥ al-Bukhārī*, rev. 3rd ed., Chicago 1979, 8 vols.

MUSLIM B ḤAJJĀJ, al-Qushairī, *Ṣaḥīḥ Muslim*, ed. with abr. of al-NAWAWĪ's comm. by M F ^{c}ABD AL-BĀQĪ, 5 vols, Cairo 1955-56. English tr. Abdul Hameed SIDDIQUI, *Ṣaḥīḥ Muslim, being Traditions of the sayings and doings of the Prophet Muḥammad*, 4 vols, Lahore 1972-76.

ABŪ DĀ'ŪD, Sulaimān b Ash^{c}ath al-Sijistānī, *Sunan*, ed. and ann. A S ^{c}ALĪ, 2 vols, Cairo 1952.

TIRMIDHĪ, Muḥammad b ^{c}Īsa al-, *Ṣaḥīḥ al-Tirmidhī*, with comm. of Ibn al-^{c}Arabī al-MĀLIKĪ, 13 parts, Cairo 1931-34.

IBN MĀJA, Muhammad b Yazīd, *Sunan*, ed. and ann. M F ^{c}ABD AL-BĀQĪ, 2 vols, Cairo 1952-53.

NASĀ'Ī, Aḥmad b Shu^{c}aib al-, *al-Sunan al-kubrā*. Selection from this work, by the compiler: *al-Mujtabā*, with comms of al-SUYŪṬĪ and al-SINDĪ, ed. H M al-MAS^{c}ŪDĪ, 8 vols, Cairo 1930.

MĀLIK B ANAS, al-Muwaṭṭa', with comm. of al-ZARQĀNĪ, *Sharḥ al-Zarqānī ^{c}alā Muwaṭṭa' al-Imām Mālik*, 4 vols, Cairo 1936.

IBN ḤANBAL, Aḥmad b Muḥammad, *al-Musnad*, with *Muntakhab Kanz al-^{c}ummāl* of al-MUTTAQĪ, ed. M al-ZUHRĪ al-Ghamrāwī, 6 vols, Cairo 1895.

DĀRIMĪ, ^{c}Abdallāh b ^{c}Abd al-raḥmān al-, *al-Musnad al-jāmi^{c}*, M ^{c}A KASHMĪRĪ (ed), *Sunan al-Dārimī*, Kanpur 1876.

SUYŪṬĪ, Jalāl al-Dīn ^{c}Abd al-raḥmān al-, *al-Jāmi^{c} al-ṣaghīr*, Cairo 1967.

NAWAWĪ, Yaḥyā b Sharaf al-, *Riyāḍ al-ṣāliḥīn*, ed. and ann. R M RIḌWĀN, Cairo 1939. English tr. Muhammad ZAFRULLA KHAN, *Gardens of the righteous*, London 1975.

KHAṬĪB AL-TABRĪZĪ, Muḥammad b ^{c}Abdallāh al-, *Mishkāt al-maṣābīḥ*, M N al-ALBĀNĪ (ed), Beirut 1961-62. English tr. J ROBSON, *Mishkāt-al-maṣābīḥ : English translation with explanatory notes*, 4 vols, Lahore 1963-66.

Texts - Shī^{c}ite

ṬABĀṬABĀ'Ī, Sayyid Muḥammad Ḥusain (ed), *A Shi^{c}ite anthology*, ed. and tr. W C CHITTICK, London 1980.

Valuable introduction to the corpus of Shī^{c}a Tradition, at last. Introduction by S H NASR and W C CHITTICK list and describe the principal sources.

KULAINĪ, Muḥammad b Ya^{c}qūb al-, *al-Kāfī fī ^{c}ilm al-dīn*. Compete ed. but for *Kitāb al-rauḍa: al-Kāfī*, with *^{c}Ain al-ghazāl* (on KULAINĪ) of Faḍlallāh al-ILĀHĪ, 2 vols in one, Tehran 1898. *Uṣūl al-kāfī*, ed. Persian tr. and comm. Sayyid J MUṢṬAFAVĪ KHURĀSĀNĪ, 4 vols, Tehran 1965. Text with English tr. of Book I, Sayyid M Ḥ RIŻVĪ, *al-Kāfī, vol.I al-Uṣūl*, part 1, *The book of reason and ignorance*, Tehran 1978. *al-Furū^{c} min al-Kāfī*, ^{c}A A GHAFFĀRĪ (ed), vols 1-, Tehran 1958-.

IBN BĀBŪYA, Muḥammad, al-Shaikh al-Ṣaduq, *Kitāb man la yaḥḍuruh al-faqīh*, 4 vols, Jucknow 1889-90.

—— *^{c}Uyūn Akhbār al-Riḍā*, M Ḥusainī LĀJAVARDĪ (ed), Qum 1976.

ṬŪSĪ, Abū Ja^{c}far Muḥammad al-, *al-Istibṣār fī mā ukhtulif fīh min al-akhbār*, 3 vols, Lucknow 1890.

—— *Tahdhīb al-aḥkām*, comm. on *al-Muqni^{c}a* of al-Shaikh al-MUFĪD, in margin of *al-Muqni^{c}a*, 2 vols, n.p., Iran 1898-1901.

SHARĪF AL-RAḌĪ, Muḥammad b Ḥusain al-, *Nahj al-balāgha*, ed. M M ^{c}ABD AL-ḤAMĪD, comm. by Muḥammad ^{c}ABDUH, 3 vols, Cairo, n.d. Persian tr. and comm. M T JA^{c}FARĪ, *Tarjama va tafsīr-i Nahj al-balāgha*, 2 vols, Tehran 1978. English tr. S M A JAFERY, *Nahjul Balagha*, 2nd ed., Karachi 1971.

Collected discourses, sermons, dicta and writings of ^{c}Ali. Many other commentaries exist, in Arabic and in Persian.

MAJLISĪ, Muḥammad Bāqir al-, *Biḥār al-anwār*, 110 vols, Tehran 1960-70.

QUMMĪ, ^{c}Abbās al-, *Mafātīḥ al-jinān*, Tehran 1961.

^{c}ALĪ ZAIN AL-^{c}ĀBIDĪN, *al-Ṣaḥīfat al-Sajjādīya*, with Persian tr. by J FĀẒIL, Tehran 1969.

2.10 *Sufism (Taṣavvuf), Gnosis (^{c}Irfān)*

Bibliographies

Abstracta Iranica, s.v. 'Soufisme'.

MUNZAVĪ, Aḥmad, *Fihrist-i nuskha-hā-yi khaṭṭī-yi fārsī*, vol.II, part 1, Tehran 1970.

Manuscripts on *^{c}Irfān* are listed on pp.1009-1489.

PEARSON, J D, *Index Islamicus. Quarterly Index Islamicus*, *op.cit.*, II c ii-vi. ii Sufism, iii Sufi Orders, iv Saints, v Religious communities, vi Convents [sic].

STOREY, *PL*, *op.cit.*, 'N. Biography: (b) Saints, mystics, etc.' :923-1066.

BROCKELMANN, C, *GAL*, *op.cit.*, I. 10. Kapitel. 'Die Mystik', :212-18.

SEZGİN, F, *GAS*, *op.cit.*, I. 6, 'Mystik', :629-76.

See also under 4. *Philosophy*.

Introductory works

ARBERRY, A J, *Sufism*, London 1950.

BAKHTIAR, Laleh, *Sufi: expressions of the mystic quest*, London 1976.

BURCKHARDT, Titus, *An introduction to Sufi doctrine*, tr. D M MATHESON, Lahore 1959, repr. London 1968 etc.

LINGS, Martin, *What is Sufism?* London 1975, repr. 1981.

MOLÉ, Marijan, *Les mystiques musulmans*, Paris 1965.

RICE, Cyprian, *The Persian Sufis*, London 1964.

STODDART, William, *Sufism: the doctrines and methods of Islam*, London 1976.

Studies

ANAWATI, G C, [QANAWĀTĪ, Jūrj], and Louis GARDET, *Mystique musulmane*, Paris 1961.

BALĀGHĪ, ᶜAbd al-ḥujjat, *Maqālāt al-ḥunafā' fī maqāmāt Shams al-ᶜurafā'*, Tehran 1948.

BALDICK, Julian, 'Medieval Ṣūfī literature in Persian prose', and 'Persian Ṣūfī poetry up to the fifteenth century', *HdO*, Bd.IV, Abs.2, Lief.2 :83-132.

BERTEL'S, E E, *Ṣufizm i sufiiskaya literatura*, Moscow 1965. Persian tr. S ĪZADĪ, *Taṣavvuf va adabīyāt-i taṣavvuf*, Tehran 1977.

CHABBI, J, [SHĀBBĪ, J], 'Reflexions sur le soufisme iranien primitif', *Journal Asiatique* 266, 1-2, 1978 :37-55.

—— 'Remarques sur le développement historique des mouvements ascétiques et mystiques au Khorasan, IIIe/IXe siècle-IVe/Xe siècle', *Studia Islamica* 46, 1977 :5-72.

CHITTICK, William C, *The Sufi doctrine of Rumi: an introduction*, Tehran 1974.

CORBIN, Henry, *Avicenne et le récit visionnaire*, 2 vols, Paris 1952-54. English tr. W R TRASK, *Avicenna and the Visionary Recital*, London 1960.

—— 'L'intériorisation du sens et herméneutique soufie iranienne', *Eranos-Jahrbuch* XXVI, 1957 :57-187.

—— *L'imagination créatice dans le soufisme d'Ibn ᶜArabî*, Paris 1958. English tr. R MANHEIM, *Creative imagination in the Sufism of Ibn ᶜArabī*, Princeton 1969.

—— *Les Fidèles d'Amour: Shiᶜisme et Soufisme*, Paris 1972, repr. 1978.

—— *L'homme de lumière dans le soufisme iranien*. English tr. N PEARSON, *The man of light in Iranian Sufism*, Boulder 1978.

CORDT, H, *Die Sitzungen des ᶜAlā' ad-dawla as-Simnānī*, Zürich 1977.

FURŪZĀNFAR, Badīᶜ al-zamān, *Risāla dar taḥqīq-i aḥvāl va zindagānī-yi Maulānā Jalāl al-dīn Muḥammad mashhūr ba-Maulavī*, 2nd ed., Tehran 1954.

—— *Sharḥ-i aḥval va naqd va taḥlil-i asar-i Shaikh Farīd al-Dīn Muḥammad ᶜAṭṭār*, Tehran 1961.

GHANĪ, Qāsim, *Baḥs dar āsār va afkār va aḥvāl-i Ḥāfiz*, 2 vols, Tehran 1942-43, 2nd ed. 1951. vol.II, *Tārīkh-i taṣavvuf dar Īrān*.

GRAMLICH, Richard, *Die schiitischen Derwischorden Persiens*, 3 vols,

Wiesbaden, 1965-80, vol.I, Die Affiliationen; II, Glaube und Lehre; III, Brauchtum und Riten.

HUMĀ'Ī, Jalāl al-dīn, *Maulavī-nāma: Maulavī chi mīgūyad?* 2 vols, Tehran 1976-77.

IMĀM, Muḥammad Kāẓim, *Māhīyat va maẓāhir-i taṣavvuf*, Tehran n.d.

KAIVĀN, ᶜAbbās, *Ustuvār-nāma*, Tehran n.d.

KEDDIE, Nikki R (ed), *Scholars, saints and Sufis*, Berkeley 1972.

LANDOLT, H, 'Two types of mystical thought in Muslim Iran: an essay on Suhrawardī Shaykh al-Ishrāq and ᶜAynalquẓāt-i Hamadānī', *The Muslim World* 88, no.3, 1978 :187-204.

LAUGIER DE BEAURECUEIL, Serge de, *Khwādja ᶜAbdullāh Anṣārī (396-481 H./ 1006-1089), mystique hanbalite*, Beirut 1965.

MABLAGH, Muḥammad Ismāᶜīl, *Jāmī va Ibn-i ᶜArabī*, Kabul 1963.

MASSIGNON, Louis, *La passion d'al-Ḥosayn Ibn Manṣour al-Ḥallâj*, 2 vols, Paris 1922.

—— *Recueil de textes inédits concernant l'histoire de la mystique en pays d'Islam*, Paris 1929.

—— *Essai sur les origines du lexique technique de la mystique musulmane*, Paris 1954, new ed. 1968.

MEYEROVITCH, Eva de Vitray, *Mystique et poésie en Islam: Djalâl-ud-Dîn Rûmî et l'ordre des derviches tourneurs*, Bruges 1972.

—— *Anthologie du soufisme*, Paris 1978.

MILLER, W McElwee, 'Shīᶜah mysticism: the Ṣūfīs of Gunabad', *Muslim World* 13, 1923 :343-63.

MIRAS, M de, *Le méthode spirituelle d'un maître du soufisme iranien. Nur ᶜAli-Shah*, Paris 1973.

MIR VALIUDDIN, *Love of God: the Sufi approach*, Hyderabad (Deccan) 1958.

— *The Quranic Sufism*, Delhi 1959.

MOLÉ, Marijan, 'Les Kubrawiya entre sunnisme et shiisme aux huitième et neuvième siècles de l'hégire', *Revue des Études Islamiques* 29, 1961 :61-142.

MUDARRISĪ CHAHĀRDIHĪ, Nūr al-Dīn, *Sairī dar taṣavvuf*, Tehran 1980.

NAFĪSĪ, Saᶜīd, *Sar-chashma-yi taṣavvuf dar Īrān*, Tehran 1964.

NASR, Seyyed Hossein, *Sufi essays*, London 1972, repr. as *Living Sufism*, 1982.

NICHOLSON, R A, *Studies in Islamic mysticism*, Cambridge 1921.

—— *The idea of personality in Sufism*, Cambridge 1923.

NŪR ᶜALĪ ILĀHĪ, *Burhān al-ḥaqq*, 3rd ed., Tehran 1975.

NŪRBAKHSH, Javād, *Gulistān-i jāvīd*, 9 vols, Tehran 1956-64.

—— *Masters of the Path: a history of the Masters of the Nimatullahi Sufi Order.*

—— *Zindigī va āsār-i janāb-i Shāh Niʿmatallāh Valī Kirmānī*, Tehran 1959.

—— *Iṣṭilāhāt-i ʿirfānī / Taʿbīrāt-i ʿirfānī*, Tehran 1979.

NWYIA, Paul, *Exégèse coranique et langage mystique*, Beirut 1970.

PADWICK, Constance, *Muslim devotions*, London 1961.

PALMER, E H, *Oriental mysticism*, London 1967, repr. 1968.

POURJAVADY, Nasrollah, and Peter Lamborn WILSON, *Kings of Love: the history and poetry of the Niʿmatullāhī Sufi Order of Iran*, Tehran 1978.

PŪR-JAVĀDĪ, Naṣrallāh, *Sulṭān-i ṭarīqat: savāniḥ-i zindigī va sharḥ-i āsār-i Khvāja Aḥmad-i Ghazālī*

RASHĀD, Muḥammad, *Khafīf-i Shīrāzī, ʿārif-i buzurg-i qarn-i-chahārum-i hijrī*, Tehran 1973.

RITTER, Helmut, *Das Meer der Seele: Mensch, Welt und Gott in den Geschichten des Farīduddīn ʿAṭṭār*, Leiden 1955, rev.ed. 1978.

SAJJĀDĪ, Sayyid Jaʿfar, *Farhang-i lughāt va iṣṭilāḥāt va taʿbīrāt-i ʿirfānī*, Tehran 1971.

SCHIMMEL, Annemarie, *Mystical dimensions of Islam*, Chapel Hill 1975, repr. 1978.

—— *The Triumphal Sun: a study of the works of Jalāloddin Rumi*, London 1978, rev.ed. 1980.

SCHUON, Frithjof, *Dimensions of Islam*, London 1970.

SHAIBĪ, Kāmil Muṣṭafā al-, *al-Ṣila bain al-taṣawwuf wa'l-tashayyuʿ*, Baghdad 1963.

ṢŪRATGAR, Luṭf ʿAlī, *Tajallīyāt-i ʿirfān dar adabīyāt-i fārsī*, Tehran 1966.

TAVAKKULĪ, Muḥammad Ra'ūf, *Tārīkh-i taṣavvuf dar Kurdistān ...*, n.p. 1975.

TIHRĀNĪ, Javād, *ʿĀrif va Ṣūfī chi mīgūyand?* 4th ed., Tehran 1973.

TRIMINGHAM, J Spencer, *The Sufi orders in Islam*, Oxford 1971.

Useful on organizational and social aspects; excellent bibliography.

ZAEHNER, R C, *Hindu and Muslim mysticism*, London 1960.

ZARRĪN-KŪB, ʿAbd al-Ḥusain, *Arzish-i mīrās-i Ṣūfīya*, Tehran 1965.

—— *Az kūcha-yi rindān: dar bāra-yi zindigī va andīsha-yi Ḥāfiẓ*, Tehran 1970.

—— *Firār az madrasa: dar bāra-yi zindigī va andīsha-yi Abū Ḥāmid-i Ghazālī*, Tehran 1974.

—— *Justujū dar taṣavvuf-i Īrān*, Tehran 1978.

ZHUKOVSKY, V A, 'Persian Sufism', *Bulletin of the School of Oriental and African Studies* 5, 1928-30 :475-88.

Texts

ʿABBĀDĪ, Quṭb al-dīn Manṣūr al-, *al-Taṣfiya fī aḥvāl al-mutaṣavvifa*, Gh

YŪSIFĪ, Tehran 1968.

^{c}AIN AL-QUŻĀT, ^{c}Abdallāh, *Nāma-hā*, ^{c}A MUNZAVĪ and ^{c}A ^{c}UṢAIRĀN (eds), Tehran 1969.

—— *A Sufi martyr: the apologia of Ain al-Qudat al-Hamadhani*, tr. A J ARBERRY, London 1969.

ANṢĀRĪ, ^{c}Abdallāh, *Manāzil al-sā'irīn*, ed. and French tr. S de LAUGIER DE BEAURECUEIL, Cairo 1962.

—— *Ṭabaqāt al-Ṣūfīya*, ^{c}A ḤABĪBĪ (ed), Kabul 1962.

^{c}AṬṬĀR, Farīd al-Dīn, *Tazkirat al-auliyā*, R A NICHOLSON (ed), 2 vols, London 1905-07, abr. English tr. A J ARBERRY, *Muslim saints and mystics*, London 1966.

—— *Ilāhī-nāma*, H RITTER (ed), Istanbul 1940. English tr. J A BOYLE, *The Ilāhī-nāma or Book of God*, Manchester 1977.

—— *Dīvān*, T TAFAẒẒULI (ed), Tehran 1962.

—— *Manṭiq al-ṭair*, Sayyid Ṣ GAUHARĪN (ed), Tehran 1963. French tr. J GARCIN DE TASSY, *Le langage des oiseaux*, Paris 1963. Partial English tr. C S NOTT, *The conference of the birds*, London 1954, repr. 1961.

BĀKHARZĪ, Abū 'l-mafākhir Yaḥyā, *Aurād al-aḥbāb va fuṣūṣ al-ādāb*, Ī AFSHĀR (ed), 2 vols, Tehran 1966.

DĀYA, Najm al-Dīn, *Mirṣād al-^{c}ibād*, M A RIYĀḤĪ (ed), Tehran 1973.

GHAZĀLĪ, Aḥmad al-, *Majmū^{c}a-yi āsār*, A MUJĀHID (ed), Tehran 1979.

ḤAFIẒ, Shams al-Dīn Muḥammad, *Dīvān*, Q GHANĪ and M QAZVĪNĪ (eds), Tehran 1941.

HUJVĪRĪ, ^{c}Alī b ^{c}Usmān, *Kashf al-maḥjūb*, V A ZHUKOVSKII (ed), Leningrad 1926, repr. Tehran 1957 etc. English abr. R A NICHOLSON, *The Kashf al-Maḥjub, the oldest Persian treatise on Sufism*, London 1911, repr. 1959.

IBN ^{c}ARABĪ, Muhyī 'l-dīn, *Fuṣūṣ al-ḥikam*, A ^{c}AFĪFĪ (ed), Cairo 1946. English tr. R W J AUSTIN, *The Bezels of Wisdom*, London 1980.

—— *al-Futūḥāt al-Makkīya*, ^{c}U YAḤYA (ed), Cairo.

IṢBAHĀNĪ, Abū Nu^{c}aim, *Ḥilyat al-auliyā wa ṭabaqāt al-aṣfiyā'*, ^{c}U YAḤYĀ (ed), 10 vols, Cairo 1932-38.

JĀMĪ, ^{c}Abd al-Raḥmān, *Lavā'iḥ*, ed. and tr. E H WHINFIELD and M QAZVĪNĪ, London 1906.

—— *Nafaḥāt al-uns*, M TAUḤĪDĪ-PŪR (ed), Tehran 1939.

KALĀBĀDHĪ, Abū Bakr Muḥammad al-, *al-Ta^{c}arruf li-madhhab ahl al-taṣawwuf*, M A al-NAWAWĪ (ed), Cairo 1969. English tr. A J ARBERRY, *The doctrine of the Ṣūfīs*, Cambridge 1935, repr. Lahore 1966 etc.

KHARAQĀNĪ, Abū'l-ḥasan, *Nur al-^{c}ulūm*, selections in *Aḥvāl va aqvāl*, M MĪNUVĪ (ed), Tehran 1975.

MAIHANĪ, Muḥammad ibn Munavvar, *Asrār al-tauḥīd fī maqāmāt Shaikh Abī Sa^{c}īd*, Ż ṢAFA (ed), Tehran 1953. French tr. M ACHENA, *Les étapes mystiques du shaykh Abu Sa^{c}id*, Bruges 1974.

MAKKĪ, Abū Ṭālib al-, *Qūt al-qulūb*, 2 vols, Cairo 1892.

PĀRSĀ, Muḥammad ibn Muḥammad, *Qudsīya*, A ṬĀHIRĪ ^{c}IRĀQĪ (ed), Tehran 1975.

QUSHAIRĪ, Abu'l-qāsim al-, *al-Risālat al-Qushairīya*, 2nd ed., Cairo 1959.

RŪMĪ, Jalāl al-dīn, *Fīh mā fīh*, B FURŪZĀNFAR (ed), 2nd ed., Tehran 1969. English tr. A J ARBERRY, *Discourses of Rumi*, London 1961. French tr. Eva de Vitray MEYEROVITCH, *Le livre du dedans*, Paris 1975.

The French translation includes passages not found in the Persian edition.

—— *The Mathnawī of Jalālu'ddin Rūmī*, ed. tr. and comm. R A NICHOLSON, 8 vols, Leiden 1925-40, repr. 1960, 1968, 1977.

—— *Kullīyāt-i Shams yā Dīvān-i kabīr*, B FURŪZĀNFAR (ed), 10 vols in 9, Tehran 1963-66.

RŪZBIHĀN BAQLĪ, *^{c}Abhar al-^{c}āshiqīn*, H CORBIN and M MU^{c}ĪN (eds), Tehran/Paris 1958.

SANĀ'Ī, Abu'l-majd, *Ḥadīqat al-ḥaqīqa*, Sayyid M T MUDARRIS RAŻAVĪ (ed), Tehran 1950.

—— *Dīvān*, M MUṢAFFĀ (ed), Tehran 1957.

—— *Masnavīhā*, MUDARRIS RAŻAVĪ (ed), Tehran 1969.

SARRĀJ, Abū Naṣr al-, *Kitāb al-luma^c*, ed. and English summ. R A NICHOLSON, London 1914.

SHABISTARĪ, Maḥmūd, *Gulshan-i rāz*, ed. and tr. E H WHINFIELD, London 1880.

SUHRAVARDĪ, Shihāb al-dīn ^{c}Umar, *^{c}Awārif al-ma^{c}ārif*, Cairo 1939.

SULAMĪ, Abū ^{c}Abd al-raḥmān al-, *Ṭabaqāt al-Ṣūfiya*, J PEDERSEN (ed), Leiden 1960.

For contemporary Islamic movements and theories in Iran see chapter XV.

3. *OTHER RELIGIONS*

3.1 *Pre-Zoroastrian*

All those bibliographies and studies containing bibliographies which are listed in the section on *Zoroastrianism* are also useful for sources on pre-Zoroastrian Iranian religion; careful study of the latter is a prerequisite for the correct understanding of the former. Particularly important are the works given below.

Bibliographies

PEARSON, J D (ed), *A bibliography of pre-Islamic Persia*, *op.cit.* II 2.2. Most of the relevant works are in: 'Religion; general', pp.149-53; 'Comparative religion', pp.215-21; 'Indo-Iranian religion and the pre-

Zoroastrian religion of Iran', pp.221-4; 'Folklore and the Iranian epic', pp.224-30.

OXTOBY, W G, *Ancient Iran and Zoroastrianism in Festschriften: an index*, Waterloo, Ont./Shiraz 1973.

See particularly the sections: 'Ahura Mazda', p.133; 'Mithra, Anahita, Verethragna', pp.133-34; 'Spirits and divine beings', pp.135-37; 'Cosmology, eschatology, soteriology', pp.137-38; 'Heroes and legendary figures', pp.138-39; 'Fire', pp.146-47; 'Zoroastrian-Hindu religious parallels and comparisons', pp.156-57.

Monograph

BOYCE, Mary, *A history of Zoroastrianism*, 2 vols, Leiden 1975, 1981. vol.I, The early period.

Chapters 1-6 provide what is certainly now the best account of the pre-Zoroastrian background of Zoroastrianism. Mithra, Verethragna and other divinities are discussed in detail.

3.2 *Zoroastrianism*

Bibliographies

PEARSON, James Douglas (ed), *A bibliography of pre-Islamic Persia*, *op.cit.* II 2.2.

This invaluable work was compiled in collaboration with a committee of Iranologists. Soviet material is not included (see below, SVERCHEVSKAYA). Incorporated is a selection of Persian-language studies. Rather few post-1970 publications are cited in this bibliography. Coverage of journals is extensive, that of Festschriften less so (see below, OXTOBY). Nearly 1200 items concerned with Zoroastrianism are listed, pp.153-95, and Zoroastrian texts are found under the language headings *Old Iranian* and *Middle Iranian*.

OXTOBY, Willard G, *op.cit.*

This very thorough bibliography lists 1808 articles in 18 languages which appeared in 421 collective publications between 1875 and 1973. Items are arranged according to subject and indexed by author. Contains interesting introductory matter on the problematical position of Zoroastrian studies in North America; the merits and uses of the Festschrift; and Iran and Zoroastrianisn in Festschriften.

NAWABI, Y M, [MĀHYĀR-I NAVVĀBĪ, Yaḥyā], *A bibliography of Iran*, *op.cit.* II 2.2, vol.I, containing studies on Avesta, Mani and Manichaeism, Old Persian, Pahlavi (Parsik and Parthian), Parsis of India, and Zoroaster and Zoroastrianism.

Does not claim to be either complete or up-to-date; does, however, mention a few items not found in the two above works besides Gujerati Parsi literature. Parsis, pp.161-79; Zoroastrianism, including Zurvanism, pp.180-244; a total of roughly 1500 works in these chapters. Translations and studies of texts are found in the appropriate language sections.

Abstracta Iranica, *op.cit.*, 'Religions: Zoroastrisme'.

HINNELLS, J R, 'Parsis: a bibliographical survey', *Journal of Mithraic Studies* III, Oxford 1980.

NEW YORK STATE UNIVERSITY, *Iranian religious studies information*, *op.cit.* 1.2.

Provides cumulative bibliographic information for the study of Manichaeanism, Mithraism, and Zoroastrianism, and lists enquiries and reports on research planned, in progress, or completed. Compiled in cooperation with the Religionswissenschaftliches Seminar der Universität Bonn.

KULKE, Eckehard, *Die Parsen: Bibliographie über eine indische Minorität : The Parsees: bibliography on an Indian minority*, Freiburg im Breisgau 1968.

Not totally superseded, at least as regards the Parsis themselves. Marred by errors and deficient entries. Includes some Festschriften without detailing the contents. Lists 25 periodicals of Parsi interest.

SVERCHEVSKAYA, Antonina Karlovna, *Bibliografiya Irana*, *op.cit.* I 2.2.

It appears that there have been very few Russian contributions to the study of Zoroastrianism. Scattered entries on pp.68-69 and 237. None under 'Religion'.

IFTIKHĀRZĀDA, Ḥasan, Sayyid, *Fihrist-i maqalāt va kutub-i falsafī dar sāl-i 2533 [2534, 2535]*, Tehran 1975-77, 3 annual issues.

Covers the modest number of studies - many of them translations from western originals - published in Iran in Persian during (approximately) 1974-76.

Major studies, and monographs containing useful bibliographies

BOYCE, Mary, *A history of Zoroastrianism*, *op.cit.*, vol.I, The early period; vol.II, Under the Achaemenians.

The most authoritative monograph study to date, thanks to the author's knowledge and sympathetic understanding of Zoroastrian traditions and practices as well as to recent advances in scholarship. The work is to be completed in four volumes as *HdO*, Abt.I, Band VIII, Abs 1, Lief 2, Heft 2 A-D. An appendix will assess the diverse interpretations of Zoroastrianism advanced during recent decades.

—— *Zoroastrians: their religious beliefs and practices*, London 1979.

Designed primarily for the student of religions. Guide to the main sources and secondary literature, pp.229-36.

DUCHESNE-GUILLEMIN, Jacques, *The western response to Zoroaster*, Oxford 1958, repr. 1973.

A critical survey of western scholarship on Zoroaster. Later chapters examine the highly contentious questions of the possible links between Zoroastrianism and both ancient Greek religion and Judaism.

—— *La religion de l'Iran ancien*, Paris 1962.

This important study contains a 'bibliographie générale', pp.17-19, as well as an 'histoire des études', pp.384-99, a critique of scholarship down to 1961. English translation K M Jamasp ASA, *Religion of ancient Iran*, Bombay 1973.

—— 'The religion of ancient Iran', *Historia religionum* I :323-76.

Useful as a short introduction, with select bibliography.

WIDENGREN, Geo, *Die Religionen Irans*, Stuttgart 1975.

Surveys pre-Islamic religion in Iran. To be used (like most writing on the subject) with caution. The 'Literaturverzeichnis', pp.360-75, is worth perusing. French translation *Les religions de l'Iran*, Paris 1974.

ZAEHNER, Robert Charles, *The dawn and twilight of Zoroastrianism*, London 1961, repr. 1975.

The bibliography, pp.339-48, furnishes a lengthy annotated list of source material and western studies. The text of the book is useful mainly where it concentrates on the texts themselves.

—— *The teachings of the Magi*, London 1956, repr. 1976.

A selection of Sasanian and later texts in translation, with commentary.

Some noteworthy recent publications

Series

Acta Iranica, Tehran/Liège 1971-77, 18 vols.

This series includes some important studies and bulky Festschriften.

The Pahlavi Codices and Iranian Researches, Shiraz 1976, 54 vols.

Devoted mainly to facsimiles of Pahlavi MSS, but includes some collected studies.

Text editions and translations

Ardā Wirāz Nāmag. The Pahlavi book of the righteous Viraz, ed. and tr. with comm. Walter BELARDI. Chapter I-II, Rome 1979.

ĒMĒTĀN, Aturpāt Ī, *The Wisdom of the Sages*, (Dēnkart VI), tr. Shaul SHAKED, Boulder, Col. 1979.

With introduction, critical text, commentary and glossary.

BORDEAUX, E S (tr), *The Zend Avesta of Zarathustra*, San Diego 1973.

INSLER, S (ed and tr), *The Gāthās of Zarathustra*, *Acta Iranica* 8, Tehran/

Liege 1977.

MONNA, M C, *The Gathas of Zarathustra:* a reconstruction of the text, Amsterdam 1978.

Studies

BAUER, J, *Symbolik des Parsismus: Tafelband*, Stuttgart 1973.

Plates to complement J DUCHESNE-GUILLEMIN's text volume, Stuttgart 1961.

BELARDI, Walter, *Studi mithraci e mazdei*, Rome 1977.

BOYCE, Mary, *A Persian stronghold of Zoroastrianism*, Oxford 1977.

On the faith as practised today in the strongly traditional village of Sharīfābād.

BREUIL, Paul du, *Zarathoustra et la transfiguration du monde*, Paris 1978.

CORBIN, Henry, *Terre céleste et corps de résurrection d'après quelques traditions iraniennes*, Paris 1961. English tr. Nancy PEARSON, *Spiritual body and celestial earth; from Mazdean Iran to Shīᶜite Iran*, Princeton 1977.

On the continuity of certain Iranian cosmological and angelogical doctrines.

DOROSHENKO, E A, *Zoroastriitsy v Irane: istorichesko-etnograficheskii ocherk*, Moscow 1981.

DUCHESNE-GUILLEMIN, J, *Opera minora*, 3 vols, Tehran 1974-78.

FRYE, Richard Nelson, *Opera minora*, vol.1, Shiraz 1976.

Reprinted articles, some of which relate to Zoroastrianism.

GNOLI, G, and A V ROSSI (eds), *Iranica III: Zoroastrisme*, Naples 1979.

HARTMAN, Sven S, *Parsism, the religion of Zoroaster*, Iconography of Religions Series, Leiden 1980.

MENASCE, Jean de (Festschrift), *Mémorial Jean de Menasce*, P GIGNOUX et A TAFAZZOLI (eds), Tehran/Liège 1974.

NYBERG, Henrik Samuel (Festschrift), *Monumentum H S Nyberg*, 4 vols, Tehran/Liège 1975.

3.3 *Zurvanism*

Bibliographies

PEARSON, J D (ed), *A bibliography of pre-Islamic Persia*, *op.cit.*

Lists 28 works, pp.195-96.

MĀHYĀR-I NAVVĀBĪ, Yaḥyā, *op.cit.* II 2.2.

Writings on Zurvanism are dispersed throughout the section *Zoroaster and Zoroastrianism (including: Zurvanism)*, volume I, pp.180-244.

OXTOBY, W G, *op.cit.*

Lists eight articles on p.134.

The monograph by ZAEHNER (see below) also contains a useful bibliography.

Monograph study and two critiques

ZAEHNER, Robert Charles, *Zurvan: a Zoroastrian dilemma*, Oxford 1955, repr. with new intr., New York 1972.

The only full-length study of the subject. Includes most of the surviving texts relating to Zurvanism, with (in most cases) translations. ZAEHNER's interpretations have been challenged by other scholars and revised by himself to a considerable extent. Two important critiques are listed below.

BOYCE, Mary, 'Some reflections on Zurvanism', *BSOAS* XIX, 1957 :304-16.

DUCHESNE-GUILLEMIN, Jacques, 'Notes on Zervanism in the light of Zaehner's "Zurvan", with additional references', *JNES* XV, 1956 :108-12.

3.4 *Mithra and Mithraism in Iran*

Bibliographies

PEARSON, J D (ed), *A bibliography of pre-Islamic Persia*, *op.cit*.

Of the 164 works listed under the heading 'Divine and mythical beings' on pp.189-95, many are concerned with Mithra.

NEW YORK STATE UNIVERSITY, STONY BROOK, INSTITUTE FOR ADVANCED STUDIES OF WORLD RELIGIONS, *Iranian religious studies information*, *op.cit*.

Concerned with Mithraism, Zoroastrianism and Manichaeanism.

Abstracta Iranica, *op.cit*., 'Religions (sauf Islam): Mithraisme'.

OXTOBY, W G, *op.cit*.

Includes nine articles on Mithra, pp.133-34.

There seems to be no satisfactory bibliography on Mithraism.

Studies

ASMUSSEN, Jes Peter, 'Der Mithraskult', *Handbuch der Religionsgeschichte* III :301-08.

Summary account of Mithraism in general; with a short bibliography.

BOYCE, Mary, *A history of Zoroastrianism*, *op.cit*., *I*, *The early period*.

An authoritative discussion of Mithra in pre-Zoroastrian Iran is to be found in the chapter on 'The gods of pagan Iran', pp.22-84.

—— 'On Mithra's part in Zoroastrianism', *BSOAS* XXXII, part 1, 1969 :10-34.

CAMPBELL, Leroy A, *Mithraic iconography and ideology*, Leiden 1968.

A wide-ranging study of aspects of Mithraism, partly concerned with the Iranian cult of Mithra.

GERSHEVITCH, Ilya (ed and tr), *The Avestan Hymn to Mithra*, Cambridge 1959.

With an introduction, concerned mainly with the question of Mithra's functions in the Avesta and earlier.

HINNELLS, John R, *Persian mythology*, London 1973.

This well-written and -illustrated book contains a useful summary account of Mithra and his cult, from the Indo-Iranian Mitra to Roman times.

—— (ed), *Mithraic studies*. Proceedings of the First International Congress of Mithraic Studies, 2 vols, Manchester 1975.

—— (ed), *Études mithriaques*. Actes du 2e Congrès International, Téhéran, du ler au 8 septembre 1975, Tehran/Liège 1978.

A relatively small number of the contributions to these Congresses were concerned with Iranian Mithraism.

The periodicals *Journal of Mithraic Studies* and *Mithras: Journal of the Society* publish some articles on Iranian aspects of the subject.

3.5 *Iranian gnosticism (excluding Manichaeism)*

Bibliographies

MACUCH, R, *Handbook of classical and modern Mandaic*, Berlin 1965.

Contains a copious bibliography of writings on Mandaeism. See pp.467-77.

PALLIS, Svend Aage Frederik Dichmann, *Essay on Mandaean bibliography, 1560-1930*, London/Copenhagen 1933.

Arranged according to date of publication, with an author index. With an introduction discussing the history of scholarship on the Mandaeans.

RUDOLPH, K, 'Die Religion der Mandäer', H GESE, M HÖFNER, and K RUDOLPH, *Die Religionen Altsyriens, Altarabiens und der Mandäer*, Stuttgart 1970 :403-62. 'Literaturverzeichnis', see pp.459-62.

OXTOBY, W G, *op.cit.*

Lists on pp.114-15 twelve articles on the subject of Zoroastrian influences in Iranian gnosticism.

Studies and surveys

DORESSE, J, 'Gnosticism', *Historia religionum*, vol.I :533-79.

One of the few available surveys in English. Select bibliography, pp.578-79.

DROWER, E S, *The Mandaeans of Iraq and Iran: their cults, customs, magic, legends and folklore*, Oxford 1937, repr. Leiden 1972.

The classic study of Mandaeans.

LAYTON, Bentley (ed), *The rediscovery of Gnosticism: proceedings of the Conference at Yale, March 1978*, 2 vols, Leiden 1981.

Articles on aspects of Gnosticism; up to date scholarship in the light of recent work and discoveries.

PUECH, Henri-Charles, 'Le Mandéisme', M GOREC, and R MORTIER (eds), *Histoire générale des religions*, vol.III, Paris 1948 :67-83.

Still a useful summary.

RUDOLPH, K, *Die Mandäer*, 2 vols; vol.I, Prolegomena, Die Mandäerproblem; vol.II, Der Kult, Göttingen 1960-61.

—— *Mandaeism*, Leiden 1978.

In the series *Iconography of religions*.

TIJDENS, E F, 'Der mythologisch-gnostische Hintergrund der "Umm al-Kitāb"', *Acta Iranica*, XVI: *Varia 1977*, Leiden 1977 :141-525.

WIDENGREN, Geo, 'Der iranische Hintergrund der Gnosis', *Zeitschrift für Religions- und Geistesgeschichte*, IV, 1952 :97-114.

3.6 *Manichaeism*

Bibliographies

NAWABI [MĀHYĀR-I NAVVĀBĪ], *op.cit.* :58-92.

About 520 works listed.

OXTOBY, W R, *op.cit.* :118-20.

Lists 39 articles.

PEARSON, J D, *op.cit.* :196-212.

Abstracta Iranica, *op.cit.*, 'Manichéisme'.

The following monograph also contains a lengthy bibliography, pp.261-77.

ORT, L J R, *Mani: a religio-historical description of his personality*, Leiden 1967.

The progress of studies in Manichaeism is surveyed in

RIES, J, 'Introduction aux études manichéennes: quatre siècles de recherches', [part I] *Ephemerides Theologicae Lovanienses*, XXIII, Louvain 1957 :453-82; [part II] *Analecta Biblica et Orientalia*, série II, Louvain 1959 :362-409.

Some important monographs and introductory surveys

ASMUSSEN, Jes Peter, 'Manichaeism', *Historia religionum*, Leiden 1969, I :580-610.

Summary account in English; with select bibliography.

KLÍMA, Otakar, *Manis Zeit und Leben*, Prague 1962.

Useful for historical and sociological aspects.

POLOTSKY, H J, 'Manichäismus', A F von PAULY, and Georg WISSOWA (eds), *Real-encyclopädie der classischen Altertumswissenschaft*, Supplementband VI, Stuttgart 1935, cols 240-71.

Perhaps still the best concise account of Manichaean doctrine.

PUECH, Henri-Charles, *Le manichéisme: son fondateur, sa doctrine*, Paris 1949.

The classic study; has not been superseded.

TAQĪZĀDA, Ḥasan, Sayyid, *Mānī va dīn-i ū*, A AFSHĀR SHĪRĀZĪ (ed), Tehran 1335/1956.

Includes interesting quotations from mediaeval Islamic texts regarding Manichaeism.

The Mani Codex

CAMERON, Ron, and Arthur J DEWEY (ed and tr), *The Cologne Mani Codex* (P. Colon. inv. no.4780) 'Concerning the Origin of his Body', Missoula, Montana 1979.

HENRICHS, A, and L KOENEN (eds), 'Der Kölner Mani-Kodex. Edition', *Zeitschrift für Papyrologie und Epigrafik* XIX, Cologne 1975 :1-85, and XXXII, 1978 :87-199.

—— 'Ein griechischer Mani-Codex', *Zeitschrift für Papyrologie und Epigrafik* V, Cologne 1970 :97-216.

KOENEN, L, 'From Baptism to the Gnosis of Manichaeism', B LAYTON (ed), *The rediscovery of Gnosticism* II, *op.cit.* 3.5, :734-56.

An account of Mānī's life and the background of his teachings in the light of the recent discoveries.

Middle Iranian Manichaean texts

ASMUSSEN, Jes P (sel and tr), *Manichaean literature: representative texts chiefly from Middle Persian and Parthian writings*, Delmar, NY 1975, 2nd ed. 1977.

BOYCE, Mary (ed and tr), *The Manichaean hymn-cycles in Parthian*, London 1954.

—— *A reader in Manichaean Middle Persian and Parthian:* texts with notes, Tehran/Liège 1975.

Includes nearly all significant texts in the languages concerned. A complementary word-list with reverse index is available separately (Tehran/ Liège 1977).

SUNDERMANN, W (ed), *Mittelpersische und parthische Kosmogonische und Parabeltexte der Manichäer*, Berlin 1973.

—— (ed), *Mitteliranische manichäische Texte kirchengeschichtlichen Inhalts*, Berlin 1981.

3.7 *Mazdakism*

KLÍMA, Otakar, *Mazdak: Geschichte einer sozialen Bewegung im sassanidischen Persien*, Prague 1957, repr. 1979.

The most substantial study to date. Source materials are surveyed in the opening chapter, 'Uber die Quellen der mazdakitischen Geschichte' and its notes, pp.7-20.

—— *Beiträge zur Geschichte des Mazdakismus*, Prague 1977.

In these articles on various aspects of Mazdakism a good deal of space is devoted to observations on the views of other scholars: in particular, see the *Vorwort*, pp.5-15, and Chapter X: 'Der Mazdakismus in den Werken neuzeitlicher europäischer Geschichtsschreiber', pp.136-48. In fact, with this book KLÍMA has performed an invaluable service not only to scholarship but also to bibliography. Listed on pp.5-6 are all the significant references in western languages, excluding Russian, published concerning Mazdakism since KLÍMA's *Mazdak*, 1957; on pp.147-48 are references to all the Russian contributions from the Soviet period.

CHRISTENSEN, Arthur, *Le règne du roi Kavadh I et le communisme Mazdakite*, Copenhagen 1925.

Much historical writing on the Sasanian period inevitably touches on the subject of Mazdak, see especially IX 2.5.5.

3.8 *Shaikhism, Bābism, Bahā'ism*

3.8.1 *Shaikhism*

Materials for the study of Shaikhism are unusually abundant. The various shaikhs of the school were prolific writers, while the controversy concerning Shaikhī teachings provoked a sizeable body of polemic from orthodox Shīᶜī authors. An invaluable bibliographical work is

IBRĀHĪMĪ, Abu'l-qāsim, *Fihrist-i kutub-i marḥūm Shaikh Aḥmad Aḥsā'ī va sāyir-i mashāyikh-i ᶜiẓām*, Kirman 1958, repr. 1977.

Reference may also be made to

ĀQĀ BUZURG al-Ṭihrānī, *al-dharīᶜa*, *op.cit.*

Biographical material on Shaikh Aḥsā'ī is contained in

AḤSĀ'Ī, Shaikh ᶜAbdallāh al-, *Sharḥ-i ḥālāt-i Shaikh Aḥmad al-Aḥsā'ī*, Bombay 1892, repr. Kirman.

MUDARRISĪ CHAHĀRDIHĪ, Murtaẓā, *Shaikh Aḥmad Aḥsā'ī*, Tehran 1955.

Al-AḤSĀ'Ī's most important works include

AḤSĀ'Ī, Shaikh Aḥmad al-, *Jawāmiᶜ al-kalām*, 2 vols, Tabriz 1856, 1860.

94 treatises of varying length.

—— *Sharḥ al-ziyāra al-jāmiᶜa al-kabīra*, Tehran 1850.

—— *Sharḥ al-ᶜarshīya*, Tabriz 1861.

—— *Sharḥ al-mashāᶜir*, Tabriz 1861.

The last two are commentaries on works by Mullā Ṣadrā.

—— *Ḥayāt al-nafs*, Persian tr. Sayyid Kāẓim RASHTĪ, 2nd ed. Kirmān 1974.

The original text is printed in *Jawāmiᶜ al-kalām*, *op.cit.* It is valuable for the basic Shīᶜī beliefs of the Shaikh.

General studies of Shaikhism, for the most part insubstantial, include

NICOLAS, A L M, *Essais sur le Cheikhisme*, vol.I, Cheikh Ahmed Lahçahi,

Paris 1910; vol.II, Sayyed Kazem Rechti, Paris 1914; vol.III, La doctrine, Paris 1911; vol.IV, La science de Dieu, Paris 1911.

Directly based on Persian sources without commentary or analysis.

CORBIN, Henry, 'L'école Shaykhie en théologie shī^{c}ite', *Annuaire de l'École Pratique des Hautes Études. Section des Sciences Religieuses*, Paris 1960-61. Persian tr. Farīdūn BAHMANYĀR, *Maktab-i Shaikhī az ḥikmat-i ilāhī-yi Shī^{c}ī*, Tehran 1967.

—— 'L'école shaykhie', *En Islam iranien, op.cit.*, vol.4 :205-300.

—— *Terre céleste et corps de résurrection ..., op.cit.*

Contains extensive and useful references to Shaikhī doctrine, as well as translations of some important passages.

MACEOIN, Denis M, *From Shaykhism to Babism: a study in charismatic renewal in Shī^{c}ī Islam*, Ph.D. thesis, Cambridge 1979.

Critical and analytical study of the early period.

3.8.2 *Bābism*

The literature on Bābism is vast and extremely uneven. Much of it is dated, although little has been written in the modern period to replace older materials adequately. The main bibliographical sources are:

BROWNE, Edward G (ed and tr), *A traveller's narrative written to illustrate the episode of the Bāb*, 2 vols, Cambridge 1891, repr. Amsterdam 1975.

—— (ed), *Materials for the study of the Bābī religion*, Cambridge 1918 :173-211.

—— 'The Bābīs of Persia. II: their literature and doctrines', *JRAS* 21, 1889 :881-1009.

—— 'A catalogue and description of 27 Bābī manuscripts', *JRAS* 24, 1892 :433-99.

—— and Reynold A NICHOLSON, *A descriptive catalogue, op.cit.* III 3.2.2.

Useful introductory articles are

BAUSANI, Alessandro, 'Bāb', *EI.2*, vol.I :833-35; 'Bābīs', *ibid.* :846-47.

DIHKHUDĀ, ^{c}Alī Akbar, 'Bāb', *Lughatnāma*, Bā', :32-64.

MACEOIN, Denis M, 'Bāb', 'Babism', 'Bayān', *Encyclopaedia Iranica* (forthcoming).

A number of works of the BĀB have been published by the Azalīs of Tehran, but all are undated and extremely rare. The Bahā'īs of Tehran have published:

Muntakhabāt-i āyāt az āsār-i hazrat-i Nuqṭa-yi Ūlā, Tehran 1977. English tr. Habib TAHERZADEH, *Selections from the writings of the Bāb*, Haifa 1976.

French translations of works by the BĀB include

al-Bayān al-ᶜarabī: NICOLAS, A L M, *Le Beyan Arabe*, Paris 1905.

Bayān-i Fārsī: —— *Le Bayan persan*, 4 vols, Paris 1911-14.

Dalā'il-i sabᶜa: —— *Le Livre des Sept Preuves*, Paris 1902.

The most up-to-date summary and analysis of the early history of Babism is MACEOIN, D M, *From Shaykhism to Babism*, *op.cit.*

The two earliest Muslim accounts appear in

LISĀN AL-MULK, Muḥammad Taqī Sipihr, *Nāsikh al-tavārīkh*, Tehran 1886-87.

HIDĀYAT, Riżā Qulī Khān, *Raużat al-ṣafā-yi Nāṣirī*, 2 vols, Tehran 1853-56.

For details see BROWNE, *A traveller's narrative*, *op.cit.*

IᶜTIŻĀD AL-SALṬANA, ᶜAlī Qulī Mīrzā, *Fitna-yi Bāb*, ᶜAbd al-Ḥusain NAVĀ'Ī (ed), Tehran 1954, repr. 1972.

The section on Bābism from the author's *Al-Mutanabbi'ūn*.

Also based on these court histories is the seminal European work on the subject

GOBINEAU, Arthur Comte de, *Les religions et les philosophies dans l'Asie centrale*, Paris 1865, and reprints.

Although this work was the basis for most later European and North American accounts of Bābism, it is extremely dated and should only be used with the greatest caution.

Also based on the official accounts is

KAZEM BEG, Mirza, *Bab i Babidy*, St Petersburg 1865. French tr. 'Bab et les Babis', *JA*, 1866, vol.VII, 6th series :329-84, 457-522; vol.VIII :196-252, 357-400, 473-507.

Bābī accounts include

BROWNE, Edward G (ed), *Nuqṭatu'l-kāf*, London 1910.

—— *A traveller's narrative*, *op.cit.*

—— *The Tārīkh-i-Jadīd or New History of Mīrzā ᶜAlī Muḥammad the Bāb*, Cambridge 1893.

Among European studies may be mentioned

NICOLAS, A L M, *Séyyèd Ali Mohamed dit le Bab*, Paris 1905.

IVANOV, Mikhail, *Babidskiye Vosstaniya v Irane*, Leningrad 1939.

Among a number of Bahā'ī histories the following are useful:

ZARANDĪ, Mīrzā Muḥammad Nabīl, *The Dawn-breakers: Nabil's narrative of the early days of the Baha'i revelation*, Wilmette, III, 1932.

FĀŻIL-I MĀZANDARĀNĪ, Mīrzā Asadallāh, *Kitāb-i ẓuhūr al-ḥaqq*, vol.3, Cairo n.d.

Arranged alphabetically under place-names, then by individuals within each section, this work is exceedingly useful, especially for its extensive quotations from original documents.

BALYUZI, H M, *The Báb*, Oxford 1973.

MOMEN, Moojan (ed), *The Bábí and Bahá'í religions, 1844-1944. Some contemporary western accounts*, Oxford 1981.

A comprehensive compilation of original source materials with detailed notes.

3.8.3 *Bahā'ism*

Bahā'ī literature is extensive, being published, according to Bahā'ī sources, in over 500 languages. Much of this however is devotional or polemical in nature, and most is translated or derivative. Since Bahā'īs have conflated their religion with Bābism, out of which it developed, a number of the titles mentioned in the section on Bābism also deal with Bahā'ism (notably ZARANDĪ, *The Dawn-Breakers*; BROWNE, *Materials*). Manuscripts are listed in the catalogues for the Bibliothèque Nationale and the British Library, as well as in

BROWNE, E G, and R A NICHOLSON, *A descriptive catalogue*, *op.cit.* III 3.2.2.

The largest collections are in the central Bahā'ī Archives in Tehran and the Bahā'ī World Centre Archives in Haifa, Israel; no published catalogues for these exist. Early western manuscript materials may be located in the US Bahā'ī Archives in Wilmette, Illinois. For early published literature BROWNE, *Materials*, *op.cit.*, pp.175-98, is useful, while early material in English may be found listed in

NEW YORK PUBLIC LIBRARY, *List of works relating to Persia*, *op.cit.* II 2.2, :103-07,

and the hand-list for the Cattanach Collection in the National Library of Scotland.

A comprehensive list of M.A. and doctoral theses on the subject is

SMITH, Peter, 'Doctoral and Masters theses on Bahā'ī subjects 1923-77', *BSMES Bull.* vol.6, no.2 :129-30.

Bahā'ī scriptures consist of the writings of Mīrzā Ḥusain ʿAlī Nūrī BAHĀ'ALLĀH and his son ʿAbbās Effendi ʿABD AL-BAHĀ', in Persian and Arabic. The principal works of BAHĀ'ALLĀH are described in

K͟HĀVARĪ, ʿAbd al-ḥamīd Is͟hrāq, *Ganj-i s͟hāyigān*, Tehran 1967-68.

TAHERZADEH, Adib, *The revelation of Bahā Allāh*, 2 vols, Oxford 1974, 1977.

The most important published works of BAHĀ'ALLĀH include

Kitāb-i mustaṭāb-i Īqān, Cairo 1933. English tr. SHOGHI EFFENDI, *The book of certitude*, Wilmette 1931.

Majmūʿa-yi alvāḥ-i mubāraka, Cairo 1920.

Al-kitāb al-aqdas, Bombay 1890 1st ed; 1896 2nd ed. English tr. Earl E ELDER, *The most holy book*, London 1961.

Other translations and free renderings were published by SHOGHI EFFENDI.

French translations of several works are also available.

DREYFUS, Hippolyte, *L'oeuvre de Bahaou'llah*, 3 vols, Paris 1923-28.

Published works of ᶜABD AL-BAHĀ' include

Makātīb-i ᶜAbd al-bahā', 3 vols, Cairo 1910, 1912, 1921. A further four volumes, Tehran ?, 1976, 1977, 1978.

Risāla-yi madaniya, Cairo 1911. English tr. Marzieh GAIL, *The secret of divine civilization*, Wilmette 1957.

Risāla-yi siyāsiyya, n.p., n.d.

Several important compilations of Bahā'ī scriptures exist.

KHĀVARĪ, ᶜAbd al-ḥamīd Ishrāq (ed), *Mā'ida-yi āsmānī*, 9 vols, Tehran 1971-73. Index vol., Tehran 1972-73.

—— *Ganjīna-yi ḥudūd va aḥkām*, Tehran 1972-73.

A comprehensive collection of texts on Bahā'ī law.

—— *Risāla-yi tasbīḥ va taḥlīl*, Tehran 1972-73.

Devotional texts for special purposes, such as *ṣalāt*, fasting, etc.

—— *Ayyām-i tisᶜa*, Tehran 1964-65.

Devotional texts for Bahā'ī holy days.

Bahā'ī world faith, Wilmette 1956, 2nd ed. In English.

The Bahá'í revelation, London 1970, 2nd ed. In English.

A full bibliography of SHOGHI EFFENDI's works is available in

GIACHERY, Ugo, *Shoghi Effendi*, Oxford 1973, app.III :199-205.

The following should be particularly noted:

God passes by, Wilmette 1944.

The standard authoritative history of the movement.

The world order of Bahá'u'lláh, Wilmette 1936.

The advent of divine justice, Wilmette 1939.

The promised day is come, Wilmette 1941.

Letters of the 'Universal House of Justice' are valuable for the light they shed on the contemporary phase of the religion.

Wellspring of divine guidance, Wilmette 1969.

Messages from the Universal House of Justice 1968-1973, Wilmette 1976.

The Constitution of the Universal House of Justice, Haifa 1972.

For the history of the movement, reference may be made to

NUQABĀ'Ī, Ḥisām, *Manābiᶜ-i tārīkh-i amr-i Bahā'ī*, Tehran 1977.

An uncritical but comprehensive guide to the main sources.

The first attempt at a comprehensive history is

ĀVĀRA, Mīrzā ᶜAbd al-Ḥusain, *Al-kawākib al-durriyya fī tārīkh ẓuhūr al-Bābiyya wa'l-Bahā'iyya*, 2 vols, Cairo 1923.

Two authoritative works are

BALYUZI, H M, *Bahá'u'lláh. King of glory*, Oxford 1980.

—— *ᶜAbd al-Bahá*, London 1971,

and reference should also be made to MOMEN, *op.cit.*

3.9 *Judaism*

Bibliographies

COHEN, Hayyim J, and Zvi YEHUDA, *Yehūdhē Asyāh ve-Aphriḳāh bam-mizrāḥ hat-tīkhōn*. Asian and African Jews in the Middle East, 1860-1971: annotated bibliography, Jerusalem 1976.

FISCHEL, Walter Joseph, 'Israel in Iran. A survey of Judeo-Persian literature', Louis FINKELSTEIN (ed), *The Jews*, New York 1949 :1149-90.

Covers both religious and secular literature. FISCHEL is the leading authority on the history and culture of the Jews in Iran. Most of his writings on the subject are enumerated in the bibliographical section of the above, p.1189.

NEW YORK PUBLIC LIBRARY, *List of works ...*, *op.cit.* II 2.2.

Includes a chapter, compiled by A S FREIDUS, on 'Jews in Persia', pp.107-18. The chapter is sub-divided and some entries are annotated.

OXTOBY, W G, *op.cit.*

Lists 34 articles under the heading 'Judaism and Iran', pp.112-14.

Studies

ADLER, Elkan Nathan, *The Persian Jews. Their books and rituals*, London 1899.

DUCHESNE-GUILLEMIN, Jacques, *The western response to Zoroaster*, Oxford 1958, repr. 1973.

Includes one chapter assessing western scholarship on the question of possible Zoroastrian influences upon Judaism. This question is also discussed in the same author's book, *La religion de l'Iran ancien*, Paris 1962, and in some of the other works listed in the section *Zoroastrianism*.

Encyclopaedia Judaica, 16 vols, Jerusalem 1972.

See particularly the articles 'Iran' (vol.VIII, cols 1439-43) and 'Persia' (vol.XIII, cols 302-19) by various hands. Both have appended bibliographies.

HIRSCHBERG, H Z (formerly J W), 'The Oriental Jewish communities', A J ARBERRY, *et al.* (eds), *Religion in the Middle East*, *op.cit.*, vol.I :119-225.

Bibliography in the same work, pp.659-63 of volume II.

LIVĪ, Ḥabīb, *Tārīkh-i Yahūd-i Īrān*, 3 vols, Tehran 1956-60.

A substantial history of the Jews of Iran.

LOEB, Laurence D, *Outcaste: Jewish life in southern Iran*, New York 1977.

Based on 1970 Ph.D. thesis at Columbia University, New York, on *The Jews of south-west Iran: a study of cultural persistence*. Social-scientific study of Jews in Shīrāz. Useful bibliography on pp.307-13.

MIZRĀḤĪ, Ḥanīnā, *Tōledoth Yehūdhe Phāras ū-meshōrerēhem*, Jerusalem 1966.

Mainly concerned with history and poetry.

NEUSNER, Jacob, *Aphrahat and Judaism: the Christian-Jewish argument in fourth century Iran*, Leiden 1971.

—— *A history of the Jews of Babylonia*, 5 vols, Leiden 1965-70.

ROSENTHAL, Erwin Isak Jakob, *Judaism and Islam*, London 1961.

SPICEHANDLER, Ezra, *Yahaduth ᶜIrān, ḳiyyumah u-veᶜayoteha*, Jerusalem 1970.

On the present situation and future prospects for Jews in Iran.

WIDENGREN, Geo, 'The status of the Jews in the Sassanian Empire', *Iranica Antiqua* I, Leiden 1961 :117-62.

SPECTOR, Earl Daniel, *A history of the Persian Jews*, Ph.D. thesis, University of Texas, Austin 1975.

3.10 *Christianity*

Bibliographies

CHURCH OF ROME. CONGREGAZIONE ORIENTALE, *Oriente cattolico: cenni storici e statistichi*, Vatican City 1962.

Contains copious bibliographical and other information on each of the eastern Churches.

OXTOBY, W G, *op.cit.*

Lists 18 articles under the heading Christian communities in Iran, pp.115-16.

PEARSON, J D (ed), *A bibliography of pre-Islamic Persia*, *op.cit.*

References to 61 works; see pp.212-14.

SAUGET, J M, *Bibliographie des liturgies orientales (1900-1960)*, Rome 1962.

A bibliography of published liturgies.

Studies: general

ARBERRY, A J, *et al.* (eds), *Religion in the Middle East*, *op.cit.*

Volume I includes chapters on Christianity, on the individual Churches, and on relations with Islam and Judaism. Volume II has bibliographies, pp.663-71.

ATIYAH, Aziz Suryal (ᶜAṬIYYA, ᶜAzīz Suryal), *A history of eastern Christianity*, London 1968.

Religionsgeschichte des Orients in der Zeit der Weltreligionen, *HdO*, Abt.I,

Bd.VIII, Abs.2, Leiden/Cologne 1961.
Includes articles and bibliographical lists for the various Churches.

HORNER, Norman A, *A handbook on the Christian communities in Iran*, Tehran n.d.

LATOURETTE, Kenneth Scott, *A history of the expansion of Christianity*, 7 vols, London 1947.
There are relevant sections in volumes I-III as well as the whole of volume VI. Each volume contains a lengthy bibliography.

NAFĪSĪ, Saᶜīd, *Masīḥiyyat dar Īrān tā ṣadr-i Islām*, Tehran 1964.
Apparently the only work of any length on the subject published in Persian.

SCHWARTZ, Richard Merrill, *The structure of Christian-Muslim relations in contemporary Iran*, Ann Arbor 1973.
A thesis based on fieldwork in Urūmīya.

WATERFIELD, Robin E, *Christians in Persia: Armenians, Roman Catholics and Protestants*, London 1973.
A lively, readable account; interesting on missions. There is a good bibliography on pp.182-88, in which the author mentions the possibility of his publishing in full the comprehensive bibliographical materials he has amassed.

Armenian Church

HEYER, Friedrich (ed), *Die Kirche Armeniens: eine Volkskirche zwischen Ost und West*, Frankfurt 1982.

KASSARDJIAN, Bedros, *L'église arménienne et sa doctrine*, Paris 1943.

NERSESSIAN, Rev Verej, *An index of articles on Armenian studies in western journals*, London 1976.
See in particular section 8: 'The Armenian dispersion', pp.91-95.

ORMANIAN, Malachia, Patriarch, *The Church of Armenia*, tr. G M GREGORY, rev. second ed. London 1955.

SARKISSIAN, Rev K V, 'The Armenian Church', *Religion in the Middle East*, *op.cit.*, vol.I :482-520.

—— *The Armenian Christian tradition in Iran*, Isfahan 1975.

SPULER, Bertold, 'Die armenische Kirche', *HdO*, Abt.1, Bd.VIII, Abs.2 :120-69.

Nestorian and Assyrian Churches

BADGER, Rev George Percy, *The Nestorians and their rituals*, 2 vols, London 1852.
Volume II contains the study, volume I being an entertaining travelogue.

BRAUN, Oskar (ed and tr), *Ausgewählte Akten persischer Märtyrer, aus dem Syrischen übersetzt*, 2 vols, Kempten/Munich 1915.

FIEY, Maurice, *Communautés syriaques en Iran et Irak, des origines à 1552*, London 1979.
Authoritative articles, mostly concerning Iran, reprinted together.
GERO, Stephen, *Barṣauma of Nisibis and Persian Christianity in the fifth century*, Louvain 1981.
JOSEPH, John, *The Nestorians and their Muslim neighbours: a study of Western influences on their relations*, Princeton 1961.
LABOURT, Jérôme, *Le christianisme dans l'Empire Perse sous la dynastie sassanide (224-632)*, Paris 1904.
MAUROY, Hubert de, *Les Assyro-Chaldéens dans l'Iran d'aujourd'hui*, Paris 1978.
SELB, W, *Orientalisches Kirchenrecht*. Vol.I, *Die Geschichte der Nestorianer (von den Anfangen bis zur Mongolenzeit)*, Vienna 1981.
SPULER, Bertold, 'Die nestorianische Kirche', *HdO*, Abt.1, Bd.VIII, Abs.2 :240-68.
Good bibliography included.
WIGRAM, William Ainger, *Introduction to the history of the Assyrian Church or the Church of the Sassanid Persian Empire 100-640 A.D.*, London 1910.

Protestant Churches

CRAGG, Rev Kenneth, 'The Anglican Church', *Religion in the Middle East*, vol.I :570-95.
ELDER, John, *History of the American Presbyterian Mission to Iran, 1834-1960*, Tehran 1960.
HORNUS, Pasteur Jean-Michel, 'The Lutheran and Reformed Churches', *Religion in the Middle East*, op.cit., vol.I :534-69.
LYKO, Dieter, *Gründung, Wachstum und Leben der evangelischen christlichen Kirchen in Iran*, Leiden 1964.
RICHTER, Julius, *A history of Protestant missions in the Near East*, Edinburgh/London 1910.
USA PRESBYTERIAN CHURCH. BOARD OF FOREIGN MISSIONS, *Iran Mission: a century of mission work in Iran (Persia) 1834-1934*, Beirut [1936].

Roman Catholic Church

ANAWATI, Rev Fr G C. 'The Roman Catholic Church and Churches in communion with Rome', *Religion in the Middle East*, op.cit., vol.I :347-422.
CHURCH OF ROME. CONGREGAZIONE ORIENTALE, *Oriente cattolico:* op.cit.
OUSSANI, Gabriel, 'Persia', *Catholic Encyclopaedia. Universe edition*, London 1913, vol.XIII, cols 722-5.
Covers the Catholic and other Churches. Bibliography includes a list of

main sources on Catholicism in Iran.

CARMELITE ORDER, *A chronicle of the Carmelites in Persia and the Papal Mission of the XVIIth and XVIIIth centuries*, 2 vols, London 1939.

An important source not cited in some bibliographies.

4. *PHILOSOPHY*

4.1 *Bibliographies*

Abstracta Iranica, 'Philosophie', vol.1-, Paris 1978-.

ANAWATI, G C, *Essai de bibliographie avicennienne*, Cairo 1950.

BADAWĪ, ^{c}Abd al-raḥmān, *Mu'allafāt al-Ghazālī*, Cairo 1961.

BOILOT, D J, 'L'oeuvre d'al-Biruni: essai bibliographique', *MIDEO* II, 1955 :161-256; III, 1956 :391-96.

BOUYGES, Maurice, *Essai de chronologie des oeuvres de al-Ghazali (Algazel)*, ed. and rev. M ALLARD, Beirut 1959.

BRADY, David, 'Islamic philosophy', D GRIMWOOD-JONES (ed), *Middle East and Islam*, *op.cit.* :123-38.

BROCKELMANN, Carl, *GAL*, vol.I, *Die Philosophie* :229-38.

CORBIN, Henry, *Histoire de la philosophie islamique*, tome I :348-63.

List of works wholly or partly in Western languages.

ERGİN, O, *İbni Sina (Bibliyografyası)*, Istanbul 1956.

IFTIKHĀRZĀDA, Sayyid Ḥasan, *Fihrist-i maqālāt-i falsafī* : Annual bibliography of philosophical works published in Iran, 3 vols, Tehran 1975-77.

LATHAM, J D, 'Islamic theology', D GRIMWOOD-JONES (ed), *Middle East and Islam*, *op.cit.* :115-22.

MAHDAVĪ, Yaḥyā, *Fihrist-i nuskha-hā-yi muṣannafāt-i Ibn Sīnā*, Tehran 1954.

MENASCE, Jean Pierre de, *Arabische Philosophie*, Bern 1948.

MUNZAVĪ, Aḥmad, *Fihrist-i nuskha-hā-yi khaṭṭī-yi fārsī*, vol.II, part 1 :721-867, *Falsafa*; vol.II, part 2 :1490-512, *Manṭiq* (logic), :1513-719, *Falsafa-yi ^{c}amali* (practical philosophy).

Lists, arranged by title, of Persian works extant in MSS described in published catalogues.

NAFĪSĪ, Sa^{c}īd, *Bibliographie des principaux travaux européens sur Avicenne*, Tehran 1953.

NAJMĀBĀDĪ, Maḥmūd, *Mu'allafāt va muṣannafāt-i Abū Bakr Muḥammad bin Zakariyyā-yi Rāzī*, Tehran 1960.

NASR, Seyyed Hossein, *An introduction to Islamic cosmological doctrines*, rev.ed. London 1978.

This invaluable study boasts a copious 'Selected bibliography' and

'Supplementary bibliography', pp.287-308, special sections of which are devoted to al-Bīrūnī, Ibn Sīnā and the *Ikhwān al-ṣafā*.

—— with W C CHITTICK and P ZIRNIS, *An annotated bibliography of Islamic science*, 2 vols, Tehran 1975-78.

Wide-ranging work containing various sections relevant to philosophy. Several additional volumes were compiled but remain unpublished.

—— *Kitābshināsī-yi tauṣīfī-yi Abū Raiḥān-i Bīrūnī*, Tehran 1973.

—— (ed), 'Bibliography of the writings of Henry Corbin', *Mélanges offerts à Henry Corbin*, Tehran 1977.

PEARSON, J D, *Index Islamicus op.cit.*, IV(a) Philosophy, IV(b) Individual scientists and philosophers.

4.2 *Islamic philosophy: general works*

AFNĀN, Suhail Muḥsin, *Vāzha-nāma-yi falsafī* : A philosophical lexicon in Persian and Arabic, Beirut 1969.

Includes English, French and Greek equivalents.

—— *Philosophical terminology in Arabic and Persian*, Leiden 1964.

ANAWATI, G C, *Études de philosophie musulmane*, Paris 1974.

ARBERRY, A J, *Revelation and reason in Islam*, London 1957.

ARKOUN, Mohammed (ARKŪN, Muḥammad), 'Introduction à la pensèe islamique', *ibid.*, *Essais sur la pensée islamique*, tome I, Paris 1973 :13-49.

ARNALDEZ, R, 'Falsafa', *EI.2*, II :769-75.

BADAWĪ, ᶜAbd al-raḥmān, *Histoire de la philosophie en Islam*, 2 vols, Paris 1972.

CORBIN, Henry, *Histoire de la philosophie islamique*, *op.cit.* 2.5.

Essential (almost), although the firmly anti-historicist approach antagonizes some readers. Emphasizes the importance of the Shīᶜī and Iranian contributions.

—— 'La philosophie islamique', *op.cit.* 2.8.

Continuation in more summary form of the preceding work.

DĀVARĪ, Riẓā, *Maqām-i falsafa dar tārīkh-i daura-yi islāmī-yi Īrān*, Tehran 1977-78.

Examines the role of philosophy, and attitudes towards it, in Islamic Iran.

FAKHRY, Majid (FAKHRĪ, Majīd), *A history of Islamic philosophy*, New York/ London 1970.

—— *Islamic occasionalism and its critique by Averroes and Aquinas*, London 1958.

GARDET, L, and G C ANAWATĪ, *Introduction à la théologie musulmane*, 2nd ed. Paris 1970.

ḤALABĪ, ʿAlī Aṣghar, *Tārīkh-i falsafa-yi īrānī az āghāz-i islām tā imrūz*, Tehran 1972.

The best of the few general accounts to have appeared in Persian.

ḤAQĪQAT, ʿAbd al-rafīʿ, *Tārīkh-i nihżat-hā-yi fikrī*, *op.cit.* 1.2.

HORTEN, N von, *Die Philosophie des Islam*, Munich 1923.

HUMĀ'Ī, Jalāl al-Dīn, *Ghazālī-nāma*, Tehran 1936.

IBRĀHĪMĪ DĪNĀNĪ, Ghulām Ḥusain, *Qavāʿid-i kullī-yi falsafī dar falsafa-yi islāmī*, 2 vols, Tehran 1978-79.

MARQUET, Y, *La philosophie des Ikhwan al-Safa*, Lille 1973.

MUḤAQQIQ, Mahdī, *Failasūf-i Rayy, Muḥammad ibn Zakarīyā-yi Rāzī*, Tehran 1970.

NASR, S H, *Three Muslim sages: Avicenna, Suhrawardī, Ibn ʿArabī*, Cambridge, Mass. 1964.

—— *Islamic life and thought*, Albany 1981.

RAHMAN, Fazlur, *Prophecy in Islam: philosophy and orthodoxy*, London 1958.

ROSENTHAL, Franz, *Knowledge triumphant*, Leiden 1970.

—— *The classical heritage in Islam*, London 1975.

SHAIKH, M Saeed, *Studies in Muslim philosophy*, Lahore 1962.

SHARIF, M M (ed), *A history of Islamic philosophy*, 2 vols, Wiesbaden 1963-66.

Contributions by distinguished authorities.

ṬABĀṬABĀ'Ī, Sayyid M H, *Uṣūl-i falsafa va ravish-i ri'ālism*, 2nd ed., 5 vols, Qum 1978.

WALZER, Richard, 'Early Islamic philosophy', A H ARMSTRONG (ed), *The Cambridge History of later Greek and early medieval philosophy*, Cambridge 1967.

WATT, William Montgomery, *Islamic philosophy and theology*, Edinburgh 1962.

Good introductory account, for earlier periods.

—— *The formative period of Islamic thought*, Edinburgh 1973.

WOLFSON, H, *The philosophy of the kalām*, London 1976.

For Political Philosophy and Theory, see IX 9.3.

4.3 *Metaphysics and 'theosophy'*

ʿAFĪFĪ, Abū'l-ʿAlā', *The mystical philosophy of Muḥyi'-d Dīn Ibn ul-ʿArabī*, Cambridge 1939.

ASHTIYÂNÎ, Sayyed Jalâloddin, *Anthologie des philosophes iraniens*. Introduction analytique par Henry CORBIN, 2 vols, Tehran/Paris 1972.

BURCKHARDT, Titus, *Introduction to Sufi doctrine*, tr. D M MATHESON, Lahore 1959.

CHRISTENSEN, Arthur, 'Un traité de métaphysique de ʿOmar Khayyām', *Le Monde Oriental* I, Uppsala 1906 :1-16.

CORBIN, H, *Sohrawardî et les Platoniciens de Perse*, Paris 1971, repr. 1978.

—— *En Islam iranien, op.cit.*

HAYDAR AMOLI, Sayyed, *La philosophie Shiʿite*. 1. Somme des doctrines (Jāmiʿ al-asrār). 2. Traité de la connaissance de l'être (Fī maʿrifat al-vujūd), Henry CORBIN and Osman YAHIA (eds), Paris 1963.

IBN ʿARABĪ, Muḥyī'l-dīn, *Fuṣuṣ al-ḥikam : The bezels of wisdom*, tr. R W J AUSTIN, London 1980.

IBN SĪNĀ, *La metaphysique du Shifā'*, Livres I a V, tr. and ed. G C ANAWATI, Paris 1978.

—— (*al-Shifā'*), I *al-Manṭiq*. 1 al-Madkhal, Cairo 1952.

ILĀHĪ QUMSHA'Ī, Mahdī, *Ḥikmat-i ilāhī*, 2 vols, Tehran 1956-57.

IQBAL, Muhammad, *The development of metaphysics in Persia*, London 1908.

IZUTSU, T, *The key philosophical concepts in Sufism and Taoism*, 2 vols, Tokyo 1966-67.

—— *The concept and reality of existence*, Tokyo 1971.

—— *An outline of Islamic metaphysics*, (in preparation).

JĀMĪ, ʿAbd al-raḥmān, *The precious pearl : Jāmī's al-Durra al-fākhira*, tr. N HEER, Albany 1972.

MOREWEDGE, Parviz, *The Metaphysica of Avicenna (Ibn Sīnā)*. A critical translation, commentary and analysis of the fundamental arguments in the *Dānish Nāma-i ʿalā'ī* (The Book of Scientific Knowledge), London 1973.

NASR, Seyyed Hossein, *Sadr al-Din Shirazi and his transcendent theosophy*, Tehran 1978.

On Ṣadr al-dīn's intellectual background, bio-bibliography, study of Asfār, note on the expression *al-ḥikmat al-mutaʿāliyya*.

SABZAVĀRĪ, Mullā Hādī, *Sharḥ ghurar al-fawā'id*. Also *Sharḥ-i manẓūma-yi ḥikmat*, Mahdī MUḤAQQIQ and T IZUTSU (eds), Tehran 1969.

A basic text for madrasa students, including commentary by the author on his own Arabic philosophical poem *Ghurar al-fawā'id*.

—— *Rasā'il-i Ḥakīm Sabzavārī*, Sayyid J ASHTIYĀNĪ (ed), Mashhad 1970.

—— *The metaphysics of Sabzavārī*, tr. from the Arabic by M MOHAGHEGH and T IZUTSU, Delmar, NY 1977.

ṢADRĀ, Mullā, *Kitāb al-mashāʿir*, Arabic text with Persian tr. of ʿIMĀD AL-DAULA, ed. with French tr. H CORBIN, Tehran 1963.

—— *Kitāb al-asfār*, abr. Persian tr. J MUṢLIḤ, 2nd ed. Tehran 1974.

—— *al-Mabda' wa'l-maʿād*, Sayyid J ĀSHTIYĀNĪ (ed), Tehran 1976.

—— *Wisdom of the throne: an introduction to the philosophy of Mulla Sadra*, tr. J W MORRIS, Princeton 1981.

SUHRAWARDĪ, S̲h̲ihāb al-dīn ᶜUmar b Muḥammad al-, *Opera metaphysica et mystica*, H CORBIN (ed), 3 vols, Istanbul 1954, Tehran 1952-70.

Serial publications

Jāvidān k̲h̲irad : Sophia Perennis, Bulletin of the Imperial Iranian Academy of Philosophy, published twice annually, Tehran 1975-77.

Intis̲h̲ārāt-i Anjuman-i islāmī-yi ḥikmat va falsafa-yi Īrān, previously *Intis̲h̲ārāt-i Anjuman-i s̲h̲ahans̲h̲ahi-yi falsafa-yi Īrān*, various other nomenclatures, Tehran 1975-.

Over 60 important texts, commentaries and studies have now appeared in this series; it would be difficult to single out particular volumes here. The accent is on *ḥikmat* rather than *falsafa*. Many texts are in Arabic.

Silsila-yi Dānis̲h̲-i Īrānī : Wisdom of Persia series, of texts and studies published by the Institute of Islamic Studies, McGill University, Tehran Branch in collaboration with Tehran University, Tehran 1969-.

Edited by Mahdī MUḤAQQIQ, first with T IZUTSU and subsequently with C J ADAMS. 36 texts, studies and translations published to date, including a few works in verse. This series also has a somewhat esoteric emphasis.

5. *ETHICS*

5.1 *Studies*

ABUL QUASEM, Muhammad (ABŪ 'L-QĀSIM, Muḥammad), *The ethics of al-Ghazālī: a composite ethics in Islam*, Selangor 1975.

ANSARI, M A H, *The ethical philosophy of Miskawaih*, Aligarh 1964.

ARKOUN, Mohammed, *Essais sur la pensée islamique*, op.cit.

Reprinted studies, several of which are devoted to ethics.

BOER, T J de, 'Ethics and morality (Moslem)', *Hasting's Encyclopaedia of Religion and Ethics*, vol.V, London 1912.

The same reservations apply to this article as to the following one.

DONALDSON, Dwight M, *Studies in Muslim ethics*, London 1953.

While not altogether reliable this is one of the few general works on the subject.

FĀRŪQĪ, Ismāᶜīl Rajī, 'On the ethics of the Brethren of Purity', *Muslim World*, L, 1960 :109-21, 193-98, 252-58; LI, 1961 :18-24.

IBN BĀJJA, Abū Bakr Muḥammad, ᶜIlm al-nafs, English tr. M Ṣ Ḥ MAᶜṢŪMĪ, Karachi 1961.

IBN SĪNĀ, *Avicenna's psychology: an English translation of Kitāb al-najāt, Book II, chapter VI*, tr. F RAHMAN, London 1952.

IZUTSU, Toshihiko, *The structure of the ethical terms in the Koran*, Tokyo 1959.

—— *Ethico-religious concepts in the Qur'ān*, Montreal 1966.

KULMATOV, N A, *Eticheskie vzglady Saadi*, Dushanbe 1968.

MUBĀRAK, Zakī, *al-akhlāq ᶜind al-Ghazzālī*, Cairo 1968.

RATSCHOW, C H (ed), *Ethik der Religionen: ein Handbuch. Primitive. Hinduismus, Buddhismus, Islam*, Stuttgart 1980.

SHERIF, Mohamed Ahmed (SHARĪF, Muḥammad Aḥmad), *Ghazali's theory of virtue*, Albany 1975.

ᶜUMARUDDĪN, M, *The ethical philosophy of Al-Ghazzali*, Lahore 1962, 2nd ed. 1970.

WALZER, Richard, 'Some aspects of Miskawaih's Tahdhīb al-Akhlāq', *Melanges Levi della Vida*, Rome 1956.

—— and Sir Hamilton A R GIBB, 'Akhlāḳ', *EI.2*, vol.I :325-29.

5.2 *Texts*

BADIE, B, 'La philosophie politique de l'héllenisme musulman. L'oeuvre de Nasired-Din Tusi', *Revue française de Science Politique* 27, 2, Paris 1977 :190-304.

DAVĀNĪ, Jalāl al-dīn, *Akhlāq-i Jalālī*, M K SHIRAZI and W GREY (eds), Calcutta 1911. English tr. W F THOMPSON, *Practical philosophy of the Muhammadan people*, London 1839.

GHAZĀLĪ, Muhammad, *Iḥyā' ᶜulūm al-din*, 4 vols, Cairo 1916. English tr. (part) M HOLLANDER, *Al-Ghazali on the duties of brotherhood*, London 1973. *Book XX of Al-Ghazālī's Iḥyā' ᶜulūm al-dīn*, tr. L ZOLONDEK, Leiden 1963.

—— *Mīzān al-ᶜamal*, Cairo 1910. French tr. Hikmat HACHEM, *Critère de l'action*. Traité d'éthique psychologique et mystique d'Abu Ḥamid al-Ghazzālī, Paris 1954.

—— *Kīmiyā-yi saᶜādat*, Ahmad ĀRĀM (ed), 2 vols, Tehran 1942. Ḥusain KHADĪVJAM (ed), vol.i, Tehran 1975. German tr. Helmut RITTER, *Das Elixir der Glückseligkeit*, Jena 1925, Dusseldorf 1959.

IBN MISKAWAIH, Aḥmad b Muḥammad, *al-Ḥikmat al-khālida*, Persian tr. Taqī al-dīn Muḥammad al-ARRAJĀNĪ, *Jāvīdān-i khirad*, Bihrūz SARVATIYĀN (ed), French intro. M ARKŪN, Tehran 1974.

—— *Tahdhīb al-akhlāq*, Q ZURAIK (ed), Beirut 1967. English tr. C K ZURAYK, *The refinement of character*, Beirut 1968.

JĀMĪ, ᶜAbd al-Raḥmān, *Bahāristān*, Lucknow 1870, many other eds. English tr. E REHATSEK, *The Beharistan. Abode of Spring*, Benares 1887.

MĀWARDĪ, ᶜAlī b Muḥammad, *Kitāb al-bughyat al-ᶜulyā fī adab al-dunyā wa'l-dīn*, Būlāq 1922 (as well as many other eds). German tr. O RESCHER, Stuttgart 1932-33.

RĀZĪ, Abū Bakr Muḥammad b Zakarīyā al-, *al-Ṭibb al-rūḥānī*, *Opera philosophica*, P KRAUS (ed), Cairo 1939 :15-96. English tr. A J ARBERRY, *The spiritual physic of Rhazes*, London 1950.

RĀZĪ, Fakhr al-dīn Muḥammad al-, *Kitāb al-nafs wa'l-rūh*, M Ṣ Ḥ MAᶜṢŪMĪ (ed), Karachi 1968.

SAᶜDĪ, Muṣliḥ al-dīn, *Gulistān*. Many eds, e.g. Muḥammad ᶜAlī FURŪGHĪ, Tehran 1937 and reprs; Rustam ALIEV, Moscow 1959; Nūrallāh ĪRĀNPARAST, Tehran 1970. English tr. E B EASTWICK, London 1852; J T PLATTS, London 1873; A J ARBERRY, *Kings and beggars* (first two books), London 1945. For tr. in other languages see XI 9.1.2, 9.1.4.

—— *Būstān*. Many eds, e.g. Muḥammad ᶜAlī FURŪGHĪ, Tehran 1937; Rustam ALIEV, Moscow 1968; Nūrallāh ĪRĀNPARAST, Tehran 1973. English tr. G M WICKENS, *Morals pointed and tales adorned*, Toronto 1974.

SAMARQANDĪ, Abu'l-laith al-, *Tanbīh al-ghāfilīn*, ᶜA M al-WAKĪL (ed), 2 vols, Jidda 1980.

ṢARRĀF, Murtaẓā (ed), *Traités des compagnons-chevaliers. Rasā'il-i javānmardān*, Intro. Henry CORBIN, Tehran/Paris 1973.

TŪSĪ, Naṣīr al-dīn Muḥammad b Muḥammad, *Akhlāq-i Nāsirī*, M MĪNUVĪ and ᶜAlī Riẓā ḤAIDARĪ (eds), Tehran 1978. English tr. G M WICKENS, *The Nasirean ethics*, London 1964.

Excellent, well-annotated translation.

6. *LAW*

6.1 *Zoroastrian law*

AḤMADĪ, Ashraf, *Qānūn va dādgostarī dar shāhanshāhī-yi Īrān-i bāstān*, Tehran 1970.

Covers all aspects of Achaemenid and Sasanid justice and legal practice.

BARTHOLOMAE, Ch, *Zum sasanidischen Recht*, 5 vols, Heidelberg 1918-23.

Contains fragments of the Pahlavī law-book *Mātighān-i hazār dādistān* and other sources.

BULSARA, Sohrab Jamshedji, *The laws of the ancient Persians as found in the Mātīkān ē Hazār Dādastān*, Bombay 1937.

CHRISTENSEN, Arthur, 'Introduction bibliographique à l'histoire du droit de l'Iran ancien', *Archives d'histoire du droit oriental* II, Brussels 1938 :243-57.

ṢAFĀ-IṢFAHĀNĪ, Nezhat, *Rivāyat-i hēmīt-i ašawahistan*. A study in Zoroastrian law, Harvard University 1980.

ṢALIḤ, ᶜAlī Pāshā, *Mabāḥisī az tārīkh-i ḥuqūq: dūrnamā ī az rūzgārān-i pīsh tā imrūz*, Tehran University Publications 1235, Tehran 1969.

6.2 *Islamic law - general*

The Sunnī mazhabs prevailed in Iran before the Ṣafavid period, and the Isnaᶜasharī mazhab thereafter.

Bibliographies

BROCKELMANN, Carl, *GAL*, *op.cit.*, vol.II, chap.7, 'Al-Fiqh'.

MŪSĀZĀDA, Yūsuf, and Ibrāhīm ṢAMDĀNĪ, *Fihrist-i maqālāt-i huqūqī tā ākhir-i sāl-i 1345*, Tehran 1969.

The articles listed in this bibliography relate mainly to secular law.

PEARSON, J D, *Index Islamicus*. *Quarterly Index Islamicus*, section III, 'Law'.

PRATT, Ida Augusta, *List of works in the New York Public Library relating to Muhammadan law*, New York 1907.

SEZGİN, Fuat, *GAS*, *op.cit.*, vol.I, chap.4, 'Fiqh'.

Studies

ABŪ ZAHRA, Muḥammad, *Ta'rīkh al-madhāhib al-Islāmīya*, vol.II, Cairo 1976.

ANDERSON, J N D, *Islamic law in the modern world*, New York 1959.

BASHIR, Muhammad, *The manual of auqaf laws*, Lahore 1977.

COULSON, N J, *A history of Islamic law*, Edinburgh 1964.

Brief indications of differences between Sunnī and Shīᶜī law.

FAKIR, Abu Bakr, *A manual of prayer and fasting*, Capetown 1978.

FARUKI, Kemal, *Islamic jurisprudence*, Karachi 1962.

FYZEE, A A A, *Outlines of Muhammadan law*, London 1955.

GIBB, Hamilton A R, 'Law and religion in Islam', E I J ROSENTHAL (ed), *Judaism and Christianity*, vol.III, London 1938 :145-70.

HAMIDULLAH, Muhammad, *The Muslim conduct of state*, rev. 7th ed. Lahore 1977.

On Sunnī international law.

JAᶜFARĪ LANGARŪDĪ, Muḥammad, *Maktabhā-yi ḥuqūqī dar ḥuqūq-i islāmī*, Tehran n.d. (c.1974).

—— *Farhang-i ḥuqūqī*, Tehran c.1958.

With French equivalents of Persian legal terms.

—— *Tārīkh-i ḥuqūq-i Īrān az inqirāż-i Sāsāniyān tā āghāz-i Mashrūṭa*, Tehran 1960.

JAᶜFARĪ, Muhammad Taqī, *Manābiᶜ-i fiqh*, Tehran 1970.

JAZĪRĪ, ʿAbd al-raḥmān, *al-Fiqh ʿalā'l-madhāhib al-arbaʿa*, 4 vols, Cairo c.1935.

LINANT DE BELLEFONDS, Y, *Traité de droit musulman comparé*, 3 vols, The Hague 1965-73.

MAḤMAṢĀNĪ, Ṣubḥī, *Falsafat al-tashrīʿ fī l-islām*, Beirut 1946. English tr. Farhat J ZIADEH, *The philosophy of jurisprudence in Islam*, Leiden 1961. Persian tr. Ismāʿīl GULISTĀNĪ, *Falsafa-yi qānūnguzārī dar Islām*, Tabriz 1967.

Compares the sharīʿa system with modern legal systems.

MAUDŪDĪ, Sayyid Abū'l-ʿalā', *The Islamic law and constitution*, tr. Khursh-id AHMAD, 4th ed, Lahore 1969.

MERCHANT, Muhammad Valibhai, *A book of Quranic laws*, Lahore 1960.

MUGHANĪYA, Muḥammad Jawād, *al-Fiqh ʿalā'l-madhāhib al-khamsa*, Beirut 1960.

MUSLEHUDDIN, Muhammad, *Philosophy of Islamic law and the orientalists*, Lahore n.d.

PEARL, David, *A textbook on Muslim law*, London 1979.

SCHACHT, Joseph, 'Fiqh', *Encyclopaedia of Islam*, 2nd ed.

—— *An introduction to Islamic law*, Oxford 1964.

Recommended more for the copious bibliography than for the approach adopted.

—— *The origins of Muhammadan jurisprudence*, Oxford 1950.

TĀRĀ, Javād, *Falsafa-yi ḥuqūq va aḥkām dar Islām az naẓar-i tajziya va taḥlīl-i ʿaqlī*, Tehran 1966.

6.3 *Islamic law ; Shīʿite*

The fundamental sources of Shīʿa law are the Qur'ān and the Hadīth collections.

Bibliographies

BROCKELMANN, Carl, *GAL*, *op.cit.*, vol.1 :195-201.

SEZGİN, Fuat, *GAS*, *op.cit.*, 4. Kapitel. B. Abbasidische Zeit. 3. Šīʿa. vol.I :525-86.

Studies and collections

ʿABDUH BURŪJIRDĪ, Aḥmad, *Kullīyāt-i ḥuqūq-i islāmī*, Tehran University, Dānishkada-yi Maʿqūl va Manqūl, Tehran 1956.

—— *Mabānī-yi ḥuqūq-i islāmī*, Tehran 1962.

Chapters on *Sharʿī* proofs, rational proofs, *ijtihād*, *taqlīd*, *taʿādul*, and *tarjīḥ*.

BAḤR AL-ʿULŪM, Muḥammad ʿAlī, *Maṣdar al-tashrīʿ li-niẓām al-ḥukm fi'l-Islām*, Beirut 1977.

BAILLIE, Niel Benjamin Edmonstone, *A digest of Moohummudan law*, 2 vols, London 1865.

Volume II is based upon the *Sharāʾiᶜ al-islām* (see below).

BRUNSCHVIG, R, 'Les uṣûl al-fiqh imâmites à leur stade ancien (Xe et XIe siècles)', *Le Shîᶜisme Imamite, Colloque de Strasbourg*, Paris 1970 :201-13.

ELIASH, J, 'The Ithnā ᶜasharī-Shīᶜī juristic theory of political and legal authority', *Studia Islamica* XXIX, 1969 :17-30.

FĀRSĪ, Jalāl al-dīn, *Ḥuqūq-i bain-al-milalī-yi Islām*, Tehran 1965.

FYZEE, A A A (FAYẒĪ, Āṣaf A A), *Compendium of Fatimid law*, Simla 1969.

ḤAQQĀNĪ ZANJĀNĪ, Ḥusain, *Ḥuqūq-i khānvāda dar Islām*, Qum 1972.

Hazāra-yi Shaikh-i Ṭūsī, ᶜAli DAVĀNĪ (ed), vol.1, Tehran 1970.

ḤIJĀZĪ, Qudsiya, *Izdivāj dar Islām*, Tehran 1966.

ḤILLĪ, Najm al-dīn Jaᶜfar al-Muḥaqqiq al-, *Sharāʾiᶜ al-islām fī masāʾil al-ḥalāl wa l-ḥarām*, Calcutta 1839, various other eds. French tr. A QUERRY, *Droit musulman. Recueil de lois concernant les Musulmans schyites*, C A C BARBIER DE MEYNARD (ed), 2 vols, Paris 1871-72. Persian tr. Abu'l-qāsim YAZDĪ, M T DĀNISHPUZHŪH (ed), 4 vols, Tehran 1967-79.

IBN al-MUṬAHHAR, Ḥasan ibn Yūsuf, *Taḥrīr al-aḥkām al-sharᶜīya*, 2 vols, Tehran 1896.

KHWĀNSARĪ, Muḥammad Bāqir (compiler), *al-Jawāmiᶜ al-fiqhīya*, Tehran 1860. 400 folios.

A compilation of twelve important works on Shīᶜite *fiqh*, including treatises by IBN BĀBŪYA, al-ḤILLĪ and al-ṬŪSĪ.

LINANT DE BELLEFONDS, Yves, 'Le droit imâmite', *Le Shîᶜisme Imâmite. Colloque de Strasbourg*, Paris 1970 :183-99.

LÖSCHNER, H, *Die dogmatischen Grundlagen des šiᶜitischen Rechts*, Erlangen/ Nuremberg 1971.

MUFĪD, Muḥammad b Muḥammad al-Shaikh al-, *al-Muqniᶜa fī masāʾil al-ḥalal wa'l-ḥarām*, Tehran 1858.

MŪSĀ, Sharaf al-Dīn, *al-Naṣṣ wa'l-ijtihād*, Najaf 1955-56.

MUṬAHHARĪ, Murtaẓā, *Niẓām va ḥuqūq-i zan dar islām*, Qum n.d.

—— *Mas'ala-yi ḥijāb*, Tehran n.d.

NĀṢIR AMĪNĪ, Ẓiyā al-dīn, *Ḥuqūq-i idāri-yi zamān-i Ṣafavīya*, Mashhad 1970.

NŪRĪ, Yaḥyā, *Ḥuqūq-i zan dar Islām va jahān*, 2nd ed., Tehran 1969.

ṢADR, Riẓā Sayyid, *Nigāhī bi-āṣār-i fiqhī-yi Shaikh-i Ṭūsī*, Qum 1970.

SANGALAJĪ, Muḥammad, *Āyīn-i dādrasī dar Islām*, Tehran 1956.

A useful study of rules, conventions, qualifications to be a qāẓī, etc.

—— *Qaẓā dar Islām*, Tehran 1963.

ṬĀLIQĀNĪ, Maḥmūd, *Islām va mālikiyyat*, 4th ed., Tehran 1965.

ṬŪSĪ, Abū Ja^cfar Muḥammad ibn al-Ḥasan al-, *al-Mabsuṭ fī 'l-fiqh al-imāmīya*, Tehran 1855.

—— *al-Nihāya fī mujarrad al-fiqh wa 'l-fatāwā*, 2 vols, Tehran 1963-65. Arabic text edited with Persian translation by M T DĀNISHPUZHŪH.

*Yādnāma-yi Shaikh al-Ṭā'ifa Abū Ja*ᶜ*far Muḥammad b Ḥasan Ṭūsī*, 2 vols, Mashhad 1970-72.

VII

SCIENCE AND TECHNOLOGY

1. *INTRODUCTION*

To separate Iranian (or Persian) science and technology from Islamic science and technology would be somewhat arbitrary, and in a sense ahistorical. The only condition under which such an arbitrary separation may make some sense is at the time when linguistic considerations are given exclusive priority. But even then most Persian mediaeval scientists who wrote in Persian wrote in Arabic also, as did Avicenna and Ṭūsī, for example, and it would be absurd to separate the works of the same scientist as partly Persian and partly Islamic/Arabic. It was thought advisable, then, to prepare the following bibliographical outline with only an 'intended bias' towards Persian science and technology, and no real attempt was made to separate that from its general context - which is Islamic science and technology.

2. *GENERAL WORKS AND BIBLIOGRAPHIES*

Primary tools for the study of Persian science and technology may be divided into the following categories:

2.1 *Basic works*

Encyclopedia of Islam, *op.cit.*, both editions.

Dictionary of scientific biography (DSB), New York 1970-78.

Contains over ninety biographies of Islamic scientists with a most up-to-date evaluation of their works and a guide to the secondary literature. A good number of these scientists either lived or worked in Iran, and some of them wrote extensively in Persian. Names of scientists like Avicenna (Ibn Sīnā), Bīrūnī, Ṭūsī, Quṭb al-dīn al-Shīrāzī, Kāshī, Qāzī-zāda Rūmī, to name only a few, have extensive entries in this *Dictionary*.

PEARSON, J D, *Index Islamicus*, *op.cit.*

One must remember that since most articles written by historians of Islamic science are published in journals that are not usually covered by

PEARSON, the *Index* is not always comprehensive in this regard. Most times it can be supplemented by

'Critical Bibliography', *Isis*, History of Science Society, annually, Brussels 1913-; Washington 1941-; repr. New York 1965-.

Published in the spring of each year. But since Islamic science itself is not in the mainstream of the history of science in general, that *Bibliography* too is often wanting.

Journal for the History of Arabic Science, Inst. for the History of Arabic Science, Aleppo University, Alleppo, Syria 1977-.

NASR, S M, *et al.*, *An annotated bibliography of Islamic science*, 2 vols, Tehran 1975-77.

Especially rich in secondary literature devoted to Persian science and technology.

2.2 *Manuscripts and bibliographies*

Since most of the sources of Persian science and technology are still in manuscript form, this category of general sources is of the utmost importance. The main source is still

STOREY, *PL*, *op.cit.*, vol.II, part 1, 1958 (Mathematics, Weights and Measures, Astronomy and Astrology, Geography); vol.II, part 2, 1971 (Medicine).

Other sources, although mainly devoted to Arabic manuscripts, are especially significant in this regard, for they contain references to Persian scientists as well. These include

BROCKELMANN, Carl, *GAL*, *op.cit.*, II 2.3.1.

SEZGİN, F, *GAS*, *op.cit.*, II 2.3.1.

Volumes III-VII are devoted to scientific manuscripts but unfortunately stop at the middle of the 5th/11th century.

SUTER, H, *Die Mathematiker und Astronomen der Araber und ihre Werke*, Leipzig 1900.

Still the most comprehensive source for manuscripts in these two disciplines.

SARTON, G, *Introduction to the history of science*, 3 vols, Baltimore, Md. 1927-58.

Especially important for European literature on the subject and for editions, translations, and criticisms of texts.

2.3 *Surveys*

There are several surveys, of different lengths and levels.

ELGOOD, Cyril L, 'Persian science', A J ARBERRY (ed), *Legacy of Persia*, *op.cit.*, II 1.2 :292-317.

To be read very critically on account of its heavy attempt to draw ethnic lines.

HARROW, Len, and P L WILSON, *Science and technology in Islam*. Preface by S H NASR. An exhibition at the Science Museum, London, 7 April - 29 August 1976, London 1976

KENNEDY, E S, 'The sciences in Iran under the Saljuqs and the Mongols', *CHI*, vol.5 :659-79. *CHI*, vol.6 (forthcoming).

—— 'The Arabic heritage in the exact sciences', *al-Abḥāth* 23, 1970 :327-44.

—— 'The history of trigonometry, an overview', *21st Yearbook of the National Council of Teachers of Mathematics*, Washington DC 1969 :333-59.

—— 'A survey of Islamic astronomical tables (zījes)', *Transactions of the American Philosophical Society*, 46(2), 1956 :123-77.

All of KENNEDY's surveys include very important manuscript and bibliographical material for Persian science.

MIÉLI, A, *La science Arabe et son role dans l'évolution scientifique mondiale*, Leiden 1966.

Extensive bibliography by A MAZAHERI of some 1110 entries, pp.341-461.

NASR, S H, *Science and civilization in Islam*, Cambridge, Mass. 1968, repr. New York 1970, Persian tr. Aḥmad ĀRĀM, *ᶜIlm va tamaddun dar Islam*, Tehran 1971.

ṢAFĀ, Ẕabiḥallāh, *Tārīkh-i ᶜulūm-i ᶜaqlī dar tamaddun-i Islāmī*, University Press, Tehran 1952.

SHARIF, M M, *A history of Muslim philosophy*, *op.cit.*, VI 4.2, vol.II, book 5, part 4: 'The sciences', Nafis AHMAD, 'Geography' :1244-77; M R SIDDIQI, 'Mathematics and astronomy' :1277-92; Muhammad Abdur Rahman KHAN, 'Physics and mineralogy' :1292-96; S SIDDIQI and S MAHDIHASSAN, 'Chemistry' :1296-1316; S H NASR, 'Natural history' :1316-32; K S SHAH, 'Medicine' :1332-48.

WINTER, H J J, 'Science in medieval Persia', *Journal of the Iran Society*, vol.1, 1951 :55-70.

Historical surveys by modern Iranian scholars include:

IRAN, MINISTRY OF SCIENCE AND HIGHER EDUCATION (ᶜULŪM VA ĀMŪZĪSH-Ī ᶜĀLI), *Gūsha-ī az sīmā-yi tārīkh-i taḥavvul-i ᶜulūm dar Īrān*, Tehran 1971.

Contains essays on medicine, history, geography, navigation, mathematics, philosophy, and music.

SADRĪ AFSHĀR, Ghulām Ḥusain, *Sarguzasht-i sāzmānhā va nihādhā-yi ᶜilmī va āmūzishī dar Īrān*, Tehran 1971.

Contents: before Islam, from Islam to the Mongols, on the ruins, modern times. Sources are listed at end of each chapter.

ZARRINKŪB, ᶜAbd al-ḥusain, *Kārnāma-yi Islām*, Tehran 1969.

Main contents: madrasas, academies, hospitals, etc., mathematics, astronomy, chemistry, medicine, pharmacology, arts and crafts, mysticism, and relevant methods of education in Islamic Iran.

2.4 *Mediaeval biographical dictionaries*

NADĪM, al-, *al-Fihrist*, *op.cit.*, II 4.

Chapter VII is devoted to science, pp.571-711.

IBN KHALLIKĀN, Aḥmad b Muḥammad, *Biographical Dictionary*, tr. M de SLANE, Paris 1842-71.

2.5 *Technical terminology*

KHWĀRIZMĪ, Abū ᶜAbdallāh, al-, *Mafātīḥ al-ᶜulūm*, G van VLOTEN (ed), Leiden 1895. German tr. (part) E WIEDEMANN, 'Stücke aus dem *mafātīḥ al-ᶜulūm*', *Sitz. Phys.-Med.Soz. Erlangen*, Bd.42, 1910, 303f.

A very useful text for technical terminology used in most of the sciences, crafts, and technological disciplines.

Farhang-i iṣṭilāḥāt-i ᶜilmī, Bunyād-i farhang-i Īrān, Tehran 1970.

2.6 *General Festschrifts*

Several distinguished historians of Persian science and Islamic science in general have across the years published articles that are relevant to Persian science. These articles are now collected in festschrifts and available in book-form. They include:

WIEDEMANN, E, *Aufsätze zur arabischen Wissenschaftsgeschichte*, 2 vols, Hildesheim/New York 1970.

HARTNER, W, *Oriens Occidens*, Hildesheim 1968.

A similar Festschrift is announced to appear among the publications of the Institute for the History of Arabic Science in Aleppo, Syria, to include most of the articles of E S KENNEDY.

A locust's leg, London 1962.

Festschrift for the Persian historian of science, S H TAQĪZĀDA.

3. *NATURAL HISTORY*

Classical works on natural history include:

AVICENNA (IBN SĪNĀ), *Dānishnāma-yi ᶜAlā'ī*, Aḥmad KHURĀSĀNĪ (ed), Tehran

1936, French tr. M ACHENA and H MASSÉ, *Le livre de science*, 2 vols, Paris 1955, 1958.

A more philosophically oriented survey of the sciences, which also contains a clear simple exposition of Ibn Sīnā's position on natural philosophy.

BAUSANI, Alessandro, 'Some considerations on three problems of the anti-Aristotelian controversy between Al-Bīrūnī and Ibn Sīnā', *Akten des VII. Kongresses für Arabistik und Islamwissenschaft. Abhand. Akad. Wiss. in Gott. Phil. Hist. Klasse*, 3, Folge, no.98, Göttingen 1975 :74-85.

KOPF, L, and Fr BODENHEIMER, *The natural history section from a 9th century 'Book of useful knowledge', the ᶜUyūn al-Akhbār of Ibn Qutayba*. Collection de travaux de l'académie internationale d'histoire des sciences, no.4, Paris/Leiden 1949.

NIẒĀMĪ ᶜARUẒĪ, *Chahār maqāla*, Muhammad QAZVĪNĪ (ed), *GMS* XI/1, Leiden 1910. *ibid.*, revised Muhammad MUᶜĪN, Tehran University 292, Tehran 1954. English tr. E G BROWNE, *GMS* XI/2, London 1921. French tr. Isabelle de GASTINES, *Les quatre discours*, Paris 1968.

A very lucid description of the interrelationships among the sciences in general and their status in mediaeval Iran.

STEPHENSON, J, *The zoological section of the Nuzhatu-l-Qulūb of Ḥamdullah al-Mustaufī al-Qazwīnī*, Royal Asiatic Society, London 1926.

Several physical problems that are dealt with by E WIEDEMANN (*op.cit.*, 2.6) are related to natural history. Moreover, the specific weights of select minerals and precious stones and metals have been studied by BĪRŪNĪ and KHĀZINĪ, and compared with modern values by E WIEDEMANN, and MIÉLI. cf. NASR, *Science and civilization*, (*op.cit.*, 2.3) p.140.

To these must be added the studies dealing with optics, mainly by WIEDEMANN, and others referred to by R RASHED in *DSB*, s.v. 'Kamāl al-Dīn al-Fārisī'.

A somewhat different subject is covered by

ISFIZĀRĪ, Abū Ḥātim Muẓaffar, *Risāla-yi āsār-i ᶜulvī*, MUDARRIS RAẒAVĪ (ed), Tehran 1940.

Work on meteorology composed c.500/1100.

4. *ASTRONOMY, ASTRONOMICAL INSTRUMENTS AND OBSERVATORIES*

NALLINO, C A, 'Sun, moon, and stars (Muhammadan)', *Encyclopedia of Religion and Ethics*, Edinburgh 1921.

A very useful survey.

SALIBA, George, 'Astronomy/astrology, Islamic', *Dictionary of the Middle Ages*, vol.I, New York 1982.

Includes an extensive bibliography.

For the special class of *zījes* see KENNEDY, *Survey*, (*op.cit.*, 2.3).

There are two documents dealing with work at an observatory, one by ᶜURDĪ (d.1266 A.D.) from Marāgha and the other, more personal, from Samarqand by Jamshīd b Ghiyās al-dīn al-KĀSHĪ (c.1420 A.D.).

SEEMAN, H J, 'Die Instrumente der Sternwarte zu Maragha ...', *Sitz. Phys. Med. Soz. Erlangen* 60, 1928 :15-126.

Contains a German translation of ᶜURDĪ's text on the scientific instruments that were built at Marāgha in A.D. 1259-1261.

KĀSHĪ's letter to his father about work at the Samarqand Observatory is published by

SAYILI, A, *Ulugh Bey ve Semerkandeki İlim Faaliyeti Hakkında Giyasuddin-i Kaşi'inin mektubu*, Ankara 1960.

Contains the original Persian, with a Turkish and an English translation; see also S H NASR, *Science and civilization*, (*op.cit.*, 2.3) pp.81-87.

Other studies dealing specifically with instruments, and dealing with the astrolabe, an instrument perfected by Muslim astronomers and made a work of art mainly by Persian artisans, are:

HARTNER, W, 'The principle and use of the Astrolabe', *SPA*, vol.3 :2530-54, repr. in *Oriens Occidens*, *op.cit.*, 2.6, and summarized in *EI.2* 'asṭurlab'.

Still the best brief survey of the working of the instrument, any student aspiring to construct one for him/herself should begin by consulting this article.

GUNTHER, R, *The astrolabes of the world*, Oxford 1932, includes facsimile of: William H MORLEY, *Description of a planispheric astrolabe, constructed for Sháh Sultán Husain Safavi*, London 1856.

To be read very carefully on the inscriptions. This attempted to be a full listing of all the astrolabes known to have existed at the time of publication. It soon became outdated by the continuously updated work of

PRICE, D J, 'An international checklist of astrolabes', *Archives Internationales d'Histoire des Sciences* 32-33, 1955 :343-63, 363-81.

A similar attempt to list all the works of Persian astrolabists was completed, and quickly outdated, by

MAYER, L A, *Islamic astrolabists and their works*, Geneva 1956.

On the general topic of instruments add the work of

SOKOLOVSKAYA, Z K, 'Classification of pre-telescopic astronomic instruments using an example of al-Bīrūnī's instruments', *Proc. XIVth Int.Cong. Hist. of Sc.*, 1974 (pub.1975), 2 :83-86.

For transmission, foreign influences on Islamic astronomy, and the status of Persian astrology, including the pre-Islamic period, see:

PINGREE, D, 'Indian influence on early Sassanian and Arabic astronomy', *J.O.R. Madras* 33, 1963-64 :1-8.

—— 'The Persian "observation" of the solar apogee in c. A.D. 450', *JNES* 24, 1965 :334-36.

—— 'The Greek influence on early Islamic mathematical astronomy', *JAOS* 93, 1973 :32-43.

—— 'Gregory Chioniades and Palaeologan astronomy', *Dumbarton Oaks Papers* 18, 1964 :135-60.

Especially significant for the important question of the transmission of Persian astronomy to the Byzantine west.

—— 'Astronomy and astrology in India and Iran', *Isis* 54, 1963 :229-46.

On BĪRŪNĪ, one of the most prolific Persian astronomers, who wrote most of his works in Arabic, there are several commemoration volumes, of uneven seriousness, that contain articles of general importance as well as particularly dealing with some aspect of BĪRŪNĪ's work. To name only a few:

IRAN: HIGH COUNCIL OF CULTURE AND ART, *Barrasīhā'ī dar bāra-yi Abū Raiḥān Bīrūnī bi-munāsabat-i hazāra-yi vilādat-i ū*, Tehran 1973.

—— *The commemoration volume of Bīrūnī International Congress in Teheran*, Tehran 1976.

These two volumes contain the papers in Persian, English and French read at the Congress.

SAID, Hakim Mohammed (ed), *Al-Bīrūnī commemoration volume*, Karachi 1979.

K͟HĀN, Aḥmad Saᶜīd, *Kitābs͟hināsī-yi Abū Raiḥān Bīrūnī*, tr. ᶜAbd al-ḥayy ḤABĪBĪ, Tehran 1973.

183 entries.

NAṢR, S H, *Kitābs͟hināsī-yi tauṣīfī-yi Abū Raiḥān Bīrūnī*, Tehran 1973.

194 items in Islamic and 354 in European languages.

S͟HĀBBĪ, ᶜAlī al-, *Zandagīnāma-yi Bīrūnī*, tr. Parviz AZ͟KĀ'Ī, Tehran 1973.

ṢAFĀ, Z͟abīḥallāh, *Ās͟ār u afkār-i Abū Raiḥān Bīrūnī*, Tehran 1973.

A valuable document illustrating the range of BĪRŪNĪ's interests is:

BĪRŪNĪ, Abū Raiḥān Muḥammad, *Risāla Abū Raiḥān fī kutub al-Rāzī*, (ed. and Persian tr.) Mahdī MUḤAQQIQ, Tehran 1973. French tr. P KRAUS, *Epître de Bêrûnî contenant le repertoire des ouvrages de Muhammad b Zakariya ar-Razi*, Paris 1936.

BOILOT, D J, 'L'oeuvre d'al-Bīrūnī, Essai bibliographique', *Melanges de l'Institut dominicain d'études orientales* 2, 1955 :161-256, 3, 1956 :391-96. Persian tr. Parvīz AZKĀ'Ī, *Karnāma-yi Bīrūnī*, Tehran 1973.

Lists 180 works by BĪRŪNĪ.

KENNEDY, E S, 'Biruni', *DSB*, *op.cit.*, 2.1.

On the work of al-KHWARIZMĪ:

SUTER, H, *Die astronomischen Tafeln des Muhammad b Mūsā al-Khwārizmī*, Copenhagen 1914.

NEUGEBAUER, O, *The astronomical tables of al-Khwārizmī*, Copenhagen 1962.

On the star-tables of ULUGH BEG:

BAILY, Francis, 'The catalogues of Ptolemy, Ulugh Beigh ...', *Memoirs of the Royal Astronomical Society*, vol.XIII, London 1843 :79-125.

KNOBEL, Edward Ball, *Ulugh Beg's catalogue of the stars*, Washington 1917.

SÉDILLOT, L A, *Prolégomènes des tables d'Oloug Beg*, Paris 1847, 1853.

Useful works on the Islamic nomenclature of the stars include:

EILERS, Wilhelm, *Sinn und Herkunft der Planetennamen*, Munich 1976.

IDELER, L, *Untersuchungen über den Ursprung und die Bedeutung der Sternnamen*, Berlin 1809.

KUNITSCH, Paul, *Arabische Sternnamen in Europa*, Wiesbaden 1959.

—— *Untersuchungen zur Sternnomenklatur der Araber*, Wiesbaden 1961.

Of more general nature studies-in-depth, are the following:

SAMSO, J, *Estudios sobre Abu Naṣr Manṣūr b ᶜAlī b ᶜIrāq*, Barcelona 1969.

A very comprehensive study of the extant works of BĪRŪNĪ's teacher and friend.

SAYILI, A, *The observatory in Islam*, Ankara 1960.

The most comprehensive study of the observatories and their activities especially those of Marāgha and Samarqand.

By way of introduction to the original research on planetary astronomy that was started at Marāgha, see

SABRA, A I, 'An eleventh-century refutation of Ptolemy's planetary theory', *Science and History: Studies in Honor of Edward Rosen*, Studia Copernicana XVI, The Polish Academy of Sciences Press, Wroclaw 1979 :117-31.

TOOMER, G, 'Ptolemaic astronomy in Islam', *Journal for the History of Astronomy* 8, 1977 :204-10.

The research itself, where the originality of the results reached, at Marāgha and thereafter, are related in modern terminology, is spread over several articles now collected in

The life and works of Ibn al-Shatir: an Arab astronomer of the fourteenth century, E S KENNEDY and I GHANEM (eds), Aleppo 1976.

A further up-dated bibliography is in

SALIBA, G, 'The first non-Ptolemaic astronomy at the Maraghah school', *Isis* 70, 1979 :571-76.

Some other studies dealing with the original astronomical texts are:

RUDLOFF, G, and Ad HOCHHEIM, 'Die Astronomie des Mahmud Ibn Muhammad Ibn Omar al-Ǧagmini', *ZDMG* 47, 1893 :213-75.

Contains the translation, into German, of the elementary astronomy of Jaghmīnī.

SAYILI, A, 'The introductory section of Ḥabashe's astronomical tables known as the Damascene *Zīj*', *Ankara Univertesi Dil ve Tarih-Coǧrafya Facultesi Dergisi* 13, 1955.

The works of Naṣīr al-dīn al-ṬŪSĪ are of extreme importance for the general development of Persian astronomy, for his *tazkira*, now edited as a Ph.D. dissertation at Harvard by Jamil RAJAB, became the standard text to be studied and commented upon for centuries after ṬŪSĪ's death. A comprehensive biblio-biography of ṬŪSĪ (in Persian) was published by:

RAŻAVĪ, Muḥammad Mudarris, *Aḥvāl va-āsār-i ... Naṣīr al-Dīn*, Tehran 1976.

5. *COSMOLOGY*

NASR, S H, *An introduction to Islamic cosmological doctrines*, Cambridge, Mass. 1964, rev.ed. London/Boulder 1978. Persian ed. *Naẓar-i mutafakkirān-i Islāmī dar bāra-yi ṭabīᶜat*, University of Tehran 890, Tehran 1963.

Mainly devoted to the works of Ikhwān al-Ṣafā', Bīrūnī, and Ibn Sīnā, but also contains several remarks of general nature and a good bibliography to introduce the student to the subject.

In addition, consult:

BURCKHARDT, Titus, 'Nature de la perspective cosmologique', *Études Traditionelles* 49, 1948 :216-19.

—— *Clé spirituelle de l'astrologie musulmane d'apres Mohyiddin ibn ᶜArabi*, Paris 1950; Milan 1974. English tr. Bulent RAUF, *Mystical astrology according to Ibn ᶜArabi*, Aldsworth, Glos. 1977.

CORBIN, Henry, *L'imagination créatrice dans le soufisme d'Ibn Arabi*, *op. cit.*, VI 2.10.

6. *OCCULT SCIENCES*

The two general works dealing with the subject of alchemy, astrology and related topics are:

SEZGİN, F, *GAS*, *op.cit.*, vols IV and VII.

ULLMANN, M, *Die Natur- und Geheimwissenschaften im Islam*, *op.cit.*, II 1.1.

The standard astrological text that gives a detailed picture of the actual writings of mediaeval Islam on the subject is:

BĪRŪNĪ, Abū Raiḥān Muḥammad, *Kitāb al-tafhīm li-awā'il ṣināᶜat al-tanjīm*, Persian text, Jalāl HUMĀ'Ī (ed), Tehran 1939. Arabic text, ed. and tr. R R WRIGHT, *The book of instruction in the elements of the art of astrology*, London 1934.

A specimen of a nineteenth-century Persian astrological document is provided by:

ELWELL-SUTTON, L P (tr. and ann.), *The horoscope of Asadullāh Mīrzā*, Leiden 1977.

Contains an explanatory glossary of astrological terms, and a bibliography.

Alchemical texts in European languages are:

HOLMYARD, E J, *Book of knowledge acquired concerning the cultivation of gold*. Edition of the Arabic text with a translation into English, Paris 1923.

This work is devoted to the study of the alchemical writings of Abu'l-qāsim Muḥammad b Aḥmad al-ᶜIrāqī (13th century).

RĀZĪ, Muḥammad b Zakarīyā, al-, *K. al-asrār wa-sirr al-asrār*, M DANISH-PUZHŪH (ed), Tehran 1964. German tr. Julius RUSKA, 'Al-Rāzī's Buch Geheimnis der Geheimnisse', *Quellen und Studien zur Geschichte der Naturwissenschaften und der Medizin* 6, 1937, and *ibid*. 4, 1935 :153-239.

Most of the works of J RUSKA deal with Islamic alchemy and should be sought in the standard bibliographical references given above. Similarly, HOLMYARD has contributed extensively to translating these sources into English. HOLMYARD has also written a text dealing with the history of alchemy in general including a large section for Islamic alchemy; see

HOLMYARD, E J, *Alchemy*, Harmondsworth 1968.

For other esoteric sciences, consult

HAMDANI, H F al-, 'A compendium of Ismāᶜīlī esoterics', *Islamic Culture* 2, 1937 :210-20.

7. *MATHEMATICS*

There is no comprehensive survey of Islamic mathematics, in spite of the fact that there are several historians working in the field; their works are still scattered in articles in several journals, for instance, *JHAS*, *op.cit*. Moreover, articles by E S KENNEDY, R RASHED, A ANBOUBA, A S SAIDAN, A YUSKEVICH, should be sought in the standard bibliographies.

The following works are noted here for their particular relevance, and as starting points for researchers:

AABOE, A, 'Al-Kashi's iteration method for the determination of sin 1°', *Scripta Mathematica* 20, 1954 :24-27.

DILGAN, H, 'Demonstration du Ve postulat d'Euclid par Shams-ed-Din Samarkandi', *Revue d'Histoire des Sciences* 13(3), 1960.

HAMADANIZADEH, J, 'Interpolation schemes in *Dastur al-Munajjimin*', *Centaurus* 22, 1978 :44-52.

The same author filed a dissertation at Columbia University in 1976 entitled *Medieval Interpolation Theory*, in which there is a discussion of interpolation schemes in several Persian sources.

HERMELINK, H, 'The earliest reckoning books existing in Persian language', *Proceedings of the XIVth International Congress of History of Science*, 1974 (pub. 1975) 3 :291-94.

IRANI, R, *Discussion of difficulties of Euclid by Omar Khayyam*, Tehran 1936.

IUSKEVICH, A P, *Les mathématiques arabes (VIIIe-XVe siècles)*, French tr. M CAZENAVE and K JAOUICHE, pref. R TATON, Paris 1976.

An excellent survey of Islamic mathematics, much of it relevant to Persian mathematicians such as ṬŪSĪ, KĀSHĪ, etc. with an updated bibliography with a special section on Russian works on Islamic mathematics.

KĀSHĪ, Ghiyās al-dīn Jamshīd al-, *Miftāḥ al-ḥussāb fī l-ḥisāb*, Nadīr NĀBULSĪ (ed), Ministry of Higher Education, Damascus 1977.

For secondary literature on this and other works of KĀSHĪ, see 'Kashi' in *DSB* (*op.cit.*, 2.1).

KASIR, D S, *The algebra of Omar Khayyam*, New York 1931.

KHAYYĀM, ᶜUmar, *Rasā'il*. Facsimile text with Russian tr. and comm. by B A ROZENFELD and A P YUSHKEVICH, Moscow 1961.

LUCKEY, P, *Die Rechenkunst bei Ǧamšīd b Masᶜūd al-Kāšī*, Wiesbaden 1951.

MAZAHERI, A, *La civilisation des eaux cachées*, Institut d'Études et de Recherches Intertechniques et Interculturelles (IDERIC), Études Préliminaires 6, Université de Nice, Nice 1973.

A study of KARAJĪ's work on the same subject.

—— *Les origines persanes de l'arithmétique*, IDERIC, Études Préliminaires 8, Nice 1975.

A study of KŪSHIYĀR's arithmetic.

RASHED, R, 'Resolution des équations numeriques et algèbre: Sharaf al-Dīn al-Ṭūsī, Viete', *Archives for History of Exact Sciences* 12, 1974 :244-90.

—— and A JABBAR, *Omar Khayyam: l'oeuvre algebrique d'Al-Khayyam*, tr. and comm., Inst. for the History of Arabic Science, Aleppo 1981.

ROZENFELD, B A, and S H TAQI-ZADEH, 'Mathematical methods used in construction of astronomical instruments in the Arab countries, Iran and Central Asia', *Proc. XIVth Int. Cong. Hist. Sc.*, 1974 (pub. 1975) 3 :339-42.

SCHOY, C, 'Al-Bīrūnī's computation of the value of Π', *American Mathematical Monthly* 33, 1926 :323-25.

SCHRAMM, M, 'Steps towards the idea of a function: a comparison between eastern and western science of the Middle Ages', *History of Science* 4, 1965 :70-103.

WOEPCKE, F, *L'algèbre d'Omar Alkhayyami*, Paris 1851.

A useful biographical work is:

QURBĀNĪ, Abu'l-qāsim, *Riyāżīdānān-i Īrānī az Khwārizmī tā Ibn Sīnā*, Tehran 1971.

Biographies of about 25 Iranian mathematicians and astronomers from the 2nd/8th to the 4th/10th centuries, with bibliographies.

For the relationship between geometry and Islamic art, see:

EL-SAID, Issam, and Ayşe PARMAN, *Geometric concepts in Islamic art*, World of Islam Festival, London 1976.

CRITCHLOW, Keith, *Islamic patterns: an analytical and cosmological approach*, New York/London 1976.

8. *MEDICINE*

General bibliographical material is contained in:

HAMARNEH, S, *Bibliography on medicine and pharmacy in medieval Islam*, Stuttgart 1964.

SEZGİN, F, *GAS*, *op.cit.*, vol.III.

ULLMANN, M, *Die Medizin in Islam*, *op.cit.*, II 1.1, English tr. *Islamic medicine*, Islamic Surveys 12, Edinburgh 1978.

Other surveys include:

BROWNE, E G, *Arabian medicine*, Paris 1933, Persian tr. Mas^cūd RAJABNIYĀ, *Ṭibb-i islāmī*, Tehran 1958.

CHRISTENSEN, Arthur, *Om Laegekunst hos Perserne*, Medicinsk-Historiske Smaaskrifter ved Vilhelm Maar, Copenhagen 1917.

ELGOOD, Cyril L, *A medical history of Persia and the eastern Caliphate from the earliest times until the year A.D. 1932*, Cambridge 1951.

—— *Safavid surgery*, Analecta medico-historica 2, Oxford 1966.

—— *Safavid medical practice, or, the practice of medicine, surgery and gynaecology in Persia between 1500 and 1750 A.D.*, London 1970.

LECLERC, L, *Histoire de la Médécine Arabe*, 2 vols, Paris 1876.

NAFICY, Abbas, *La médicine en Perse des origines à nos jours. Ses fondements théoriques d'après l'encyclopédie medicale de Gorgani*. The *Zakhīra-yi Khwārazmshāhī*, the first medical encyclopaedia in the Persian language.

NAJMĀBĀDĪ, Maḥmūd, *Tārīkh-i ṭibb dar Īrān-i pas az Islām ... az ẓuhūr-i Islām tā daurān-i Mughūl*, Tehran 1974.

NASR, S H, 'Life sciences, alchemy and medicine', *CHI*, vol.IV :396-418.

SIGERIST, H, *A history of medicine*, ch.III: Medicine in Ancient Persia, Oxford 1961.

Translations of texts, although partial, are of special interest for the flavour they give of the actual writings of mediaeval physicians.

GRUNER, O C, *A treatise on the Canon of Medicine of Avicenna incorporating a translation of the first book*, London 1930.

KONNING, Pieter de, *Trois traités d'anatomie arabes par Muḥammad Ibn Zakariyā al-Rāzī, Alī Ibn Abbās et Alī Ibn Sīnā*, Leiden 1903.

RĀZĪ, Muḥammad b Zakarīyā al-, *A treatise on the small-pox and measles*, Baltimore 1939.

SPINK, M S, and G L LEWIS (ed. tr. and comm.), *Albucasis on surgery and instruments*, University of California, Berkeley/Los Angeles 1973.

Translates only the surgical section of the work of Abu'l-Qāsim Khalaf b ʿAbbās al-ZAHRĀWĪ (c.A.D. 1013), with the Arabic and the English on facing pages.

TABARĪ, ʿAlī b Rabbān al-, *Paradise of Wisdom : Firdaus al-Ḥikma*, M Z SIDDIQI (ed), Berlin 1928.

A translation of the table of contents was published by M MEYERHOF in *Isis* 16, 1924, pp.6-54.

On the status of the physician in mediaeval Islam, see

ROSENTHAL, F, 'The physician in medieval Muslim society', *Bulletin of the History of Medicine* 52, 1978 :475-91.

On the transmission of Islamic Medicine to the west, see:

SCHIPPERGES, H, *Arabische Medizin in lateinischen Mittelalter, Sitz. der Heidelberg. Akad. Wiss. Math. NaturWiss. Klasse*, Berlin 1976.

SIDDIQI, M Z, *Studies in Arabic and Persian medical literature*, Calcutta 1959.

Useful general work.

Pharmacological material is included in HAMARNEH's *Bibliography*, *op. cit.*, but the following deserve a special notice:

SCHMUKER, Werner, *Die pflanzlische und mineralische Materia Medica in Firdaus al-Hikmah*, Bonner Orientalistische Studien, Bd.18, Bonn 1969.

A detailed etymological and pharmacological study of the drugs in *Firdaus al-Ḥikmah*, with bibliography and extensive footnotes.

BĪRŪNĪ, Abū Raiḥān al-, *Kitāb al-ṣaidana fī'l-ṭibb*, H M SAID and S HAMARNEH (ed. and tr.), *Book on pharmacy and materia medica*, 2 vols, Karachi 1973.

For an example of *Aqrābādhīn*-type literature on pharmacology see:

SAMARQANDĪ, Ḥāmid b Muḥammad al-, *The medical formulary of al-Samarqandi*, M LEVEY and N AL-KHALIDI (facs. and tr.), University of Pennsylvania, Philadelphia 1967.

Two bibliographical works dealing with the two major physicians of mediaeval Islam, RĀZĪ and AVICENNA, should be mentioned here:

ANAWATI, G-C, *Essai de bibliographie Avicenniene*. Ligue Arabe, Direction Culturelle. Cairo 1950.

NAJMĀBĀDĪ, Maḥmūd, *Mu'allafāt wa muṣannafāt-i Abū Bakr Muḥammad b Zakarīyā Rāzī*. Intishārāt-i Dānishgah-i Tihrān 500, Tehran 1960.

Further guides to source material include:

FOHNAHN, A M, *Zur Quellenkunde der persischen Medizin* Leipzig 1910.

NAJMĀBĀDĪ, Maḥmūd, *Fihrist-i kitābhā-yi chāpī-yi fārsī-yi ṭibbī va-funūn-i vābasta bi-ṭibb*, Tehran 1963. vol.1: Titles of books.

RICHTER-BERNBURG, L, *Persian medical manuscripts at the University of California, Los Angeles*. A descriptive catalogue. Malibu 1978.

9. *OTHER TRADITIONAL SCIENCES AND TECHNOLOGY*

The history of Islamic technology has yet to be written, although there are several sources in print, and several articles, as those of WIEDEMANN, have been known for some time. General histories of technology usually have small sections on Islamic technology, and they should be sought there. Of special interest for Persian technology are the following entries:

ALLAN, James W, *Persian metal technology 700-1300 A.D.*, Oxford Oriental Monographs, London 1979.

FUKAI, S, *Persian glass*, E B CRAWFORD (tr.), B TAKAHASHI (photos), Tokyo 1977.

GLUCK, Jay, and Sumi HIRAMOTO (ed), *A survey of Persian handicrafts*, Tehran/Ashiya 1977. Persian tr. *Sairī dar ṣanāyi^{c}-i dastī-yi Īrān*, Tehran 1977.

The most detailed and comprehensive survey of the subject; deals with much material omitted or only glancingly treated by WULFF (see below).

WILLIAMS, A, *The metallurgy of Muslim armour*. Seminar on Early Islamic Science, Monograph 3, Manchester University 1978.

WULFF, Hans E, *The traditional crafts of Persia*, Cambridge, Mass. 1966. The first comprehensive essay on the traditional crafts, containing an extensive glossary of Persian technical terms, pp.331-85 (a dictionary by itself), an annotated bibliography, pp.315-29, and a useful general bibliography, pp.305-14.

Texts in translation include:

BANŪ MŪSĀ b Shākir, *Kitāb al-ḥiyal*, A Y ḤASAN (ed), Aleppo 1981. English tr. Donald HILL, *The book of ingenious devices by the Banū (sons of) Mūsā b Shākir*, Dordrecht/Boston 1979.

JAZARĪ, Ibn al-Razzāz al-, *Kitāb fī maᶜrifat al-ḥiyal al-handasīya*, A Y HASAN (ed), Aleppo 1979. English tr. Donald HILL, *The book of knowledge of ingenious mechanical devices*, Dordrecht/Boston 1974.

KHĀZINĪ, Abul-Fatḥ ᶜAbd al-raḥmān al-, (c.1115), *Kitāb mīzān al-ḥikma*, Hyderabad 1940/41. English tr. (part) N KHANIKOFF, 'Analysis and extracts of *Kitāb mīzān al-ḥikma*, 'Book of the Balance of Wisdom', an Arabic work on the water-balance, written by al-Khāzinī in the twelfth century', *JAOS* 6, 1859 :1-128.

WINTER, H J J, 'Muslim mechanics and mechanical appliances', *Endeavour* 15, 1956 :25-38.

GEOGRAPHY AND TOPOGRAPHY

1. *GEOGRAPHY AND TOPOGRAPHY*

The bibliography for the geography of Iran is at once too complex and too
under-developed a subject to admit of succinct summary. Increasingly in
the 1960s and 1970s (though less certainly so now) fieldwork in Iran provided the raw material for research in many branches of physical and human
geography which transcend political boundaries. At the same time political
geography, or the national study of geography in Iran, has developed less
fast. Accordingly this chapter cannot attempt to provide the geomorpholo-
gist, the climatologist, or the demographer, with the depth of bibliographical information which he can obtain by using supranational bibliographical
guides to his own particular subject. Nor can it offer the researcher in
Iran, of whatever discipline, as immediately useful an introduction to the
geography of his country as he can obtain from local collections of reference material or through daily proximity to current research. This chapter
is designed instead as an auxiliary, for physical geography and geology
and for topography, for those away from Iran working in other fields of
Iranian studies.

1.1 *Works dealing with Iran*

Modern studies by Iranian geographers began during Riẓā S̲h̲āh's reign in
the army and at the Higher Teacher Training College and the University of
Tehran. In the period 1941-1979 much work was done in the provincial universities as well as Tehran University and by various governmental bodies,
notably the Survey and Mapping Organization (*Sāzmān-i Naqs̲h̲abardārī*), the
Meteorological Department (*Idāra-yi Havāshināsī*), the National Statistics
Centre (*Markaz-i Āmar-i Īrān*), the Agriculture Ministry's Soil Science Institute (*Mu'assasa-yi K̲h̲ākshināsī*), the Plan and Budget Organization's
Geological Survey (*Naqs̲h̲abardārī-yi Zamīnshināsī*) and study groups for Irrigation (*Ābyārī*) and Regional Development (*Ābādānī-yi Manṭiqa'ī*, i.e. of
remote and backward regions), and certain provincial establishments, among

which the Khūzistān Water and Power Authority (*Sāzmān-i Āb va Barq-i Khūzistān*) deserves special mention. These bodies published or made available important reports, maps, surveys, measurements, etc.

The main centres of academic research and teaching were the Tehran University Geographical Institute (*Mu'assasa-yi Jughrāfiyā*, a research institute), and the Geography Departments of the Universities of Tabrīz (Āzarbadāgān), Mashhad (Firdausī), Shīrāz (Pahlavī), Iṣfahān, and the National (Millī) University of Tehran. A Society of Iranian Geographers, founded in 1973, held six conferences and issued one number of its Iranian Geographers' Journal (*Majalla-yi Jughrāfiyādānān-i Īrān*) in 1976.

The rate at which research is published on a wide range of highly specialized subjects which bear on the geography of Iran militates against the production of a single international bibliography of the geography of Iran. As its title suggests, the following work is concerned solely with contributions in the Russian language within a limited range of years.

PETROV, M P, *Bibliografiya geografii Irana: Ukazatel' literatury na russkom yazyke, 1720-1954*, Ashkhabad 1955.

BURGESS, R L, *et al.*, *A preliminary bibliography of the natural history of Iran*, Tehran 1966- (in progress),

shows movements towards that goal, as does

GANJĪ, Muḥammad Ḥasan, and Javād ṢAFĪNIZHĀD, *Fihrist-i maqālāt-i jughrāfiyā'ī*, Tehran 1962,

which however is confined to articles in the Iranian press. Good articles with wholly or partly geographical contents appeared in the journals of the aforementioned universities and in the periodicals *Barrasīhā-yi tārīkhī* (published by the Army General Staff) and *Talāsh*, for instance, a study of the town and district of Sarakhs in its geographical, historical, ethnic and socio-economic aspects.

SAᶜĪDĪ, ᶜAbbas, 'Sarakhs', *Majalla-yi Dānishkada-yi Adabiyyat-i Dānishgāh-i Firdausī*, (see XIV 2.4.2).

The bibliography in

FISHER, W B (ed), *The land of Iran*, *CHI*, vol.I :741-64,

though its cut-off date is the mid-1960s, is the most straightforward introductory bibliography, at least until the publication of the 'systematic bibliography' promised 'at much greater length' as the eighth volume of the series.

General introductions to the geography of Iran, written in Persian, are:

RAZMĀRĀ, Ḥusain ᶜAlī, *Farhang-i jughrāfiyā-yi Īrān*, Sitād-i Ārtish, 10 vols, Tehran 1949-53.

This work, though deficient and now out of date in some respects, remains indispensable. The entries are names of towns and districts, mainly *dihīstāns* (groups of villages). The data comprise location, boundaries, climate, altitude, mountains, passes, rivers, water supplies, population, mother-tongue, religion, agriculture and stockbreeding, roads, bridges, railways, ports, and governmental buildings and services including schools. Ancient and mediaeval monuments are mentioned, but little or no historical information is given. The division into volumes is based on the ten provinces (*ustāns*) existing in 1949-53, when Kāshān was joined to Māzandarān, Zanjān to Gīlān, Āstārā to East Āzarbāyjān, and Yazd to Iṣfahān. Natural features such as mountains must be looked up under the district in which they are located. No coordinates of latitude and longitude are given.

For part of Iran, RAZMĀRĀ's work is now supplemented by

ADAMEC, Ludwig W, *Historical Gazetteer of Iran, Vol.I, Tehran and North West Iran*, Graz (Austria) 1976.

This valuable work in English covers the territory north and west of Kirmānshāh, Iṣfahān, Yazd, Dāmghān, and Gurgān. Mountains, etc. are listed in the entries, and coordinates are given. The population figures are those of the second (1966) census. Much of the historical information is about 19th century developments.

SĀZMĀN-I BARNĀMA, MARKAZ-I ĀMĀR-I ĪRĀN, *Farhang-i ābādīhā-yi Īrān*. Introduction and gazetteer by Luṭfallāh MUFAKHKHAM-PĀYĀN, and Havā ĀQĀYĀN, 27 vols, Tehran 1968, 2nd ed. 1971.

A dictionary of Iranian villages compiled from the 1966 census by the National Statistics Centre of the Plan Organization. The volumes (each with maps) are on the basis of the provinces. The data, presented in statistical tables, comprise population, area, buildings, water supply, land utilization, type of farming, livestock, businesses, social institutions, and roads of each village or group of villages.

KAIHĀN, Mas^{c}ūd, *Jughrāfiyā-yi mufaṣṣal-i Īrān*, 3 vols, Tehran 1931, 1932, 1933. Detailed geography of Iran: I Physical; II Historical; III Economic.

The author taught geography at the Higher Teacher Training College. After half a century, this work remains valuable.

FISHER, *The land of Iran* (*op.cit.*) has become the standard non-Persian introduction to the geography of Iran, superseding the same author's more extensive work

FISHER, W B, *The Middle East: a physical, social and regional geography*, London 1950.

Other works of variable value include

AHRENS, Peter Georg, *Die Entwicklung der Stadt Teheran: eine städtebauliche Untersuchung ihrer zukunftigen Gestaltung*. Deutsche Orient-Inst. Opladen 1966.

A study, with detailed maps, of the growth of Tehran during the present century.

BÉMONT, Fredy, *Les villes de l'Iran*. vols 1-2, Des cités d'autrefois à l'urbanisme contemporain. vol.3, Atlas de la civilisation iranienne. Repertoire analytique et critique de 225 ouvrages relatifs à l'Iran. Paris 1969-77.

EAST, W G, and O H K SPATE, *et al.*, *The changing map of Asia*, London 1971 (5th ed).

EHLERS, E, *Iran, Bibliographischer Forschungsbericht*, *op.cit.*, II 2.2.

GALLAS, Klaus, *Iran: Kulturstätten Persiens zwischen Wüsten, Steppen und Bergen*, Cologne 1976.

PRESCOTT, J R V, *et al.*, *Map of mainland Asia by treaty*, Melbourne 1975.

—— *Frontiers of Asia and south-east Asia*, Melbourne 1977.

SMITH, H H, *et al.*, *Area handbook for Iran*, American University Foreign Area Studies, Washington 1971.

STAMP, L D, *Asia: a regional and economic geography*, London 1967 (12th ed.).

UNITED KINGDOM, NAVAL INTELLIGENCE DIVISION, *Persia*, *op.cit.*, II 1.

Those seeking an introduction to the geology of Iran are more fortunate:

STAHL, A F, *Persien*. Handbuch der regionalen Geologie, Band V, Heft 6, Heidelberg 1911.

FURON, R, 'Géologie du plateau Iranien (Perse-Afghanistan-Béloutchistan)', Muséum National d'Histoire Naturelle. Memoires 7, Paris 1941.

NATIONAL IRANIAN OIL CORPORATION, *Explanation to the geologic map of Iran (1:2,500,000)*, with stratigraphical tables, index map and bibliography, Tehran 1959.

COMMISSION DE STRATIGRAPHIE DU CONGRÈS GÉOLOGIQUE INTERNATIONAL, *Lexique stratigraphique internationale*, Centre National de la Recherche scientifique, vol.iii, pt.9: Afghanistan, Iran, Turkey and Cyprus, Paris 1956.

RUTTNER, A, and O THIELE, 'Das UN-Projekt "Geological Survey Institute Iran": Organisation und Arbeitsergebnisse 1962-1968', *Verhandlungen der Geologischen Bundesanstalt* 2, 1969 :143-58.

EHLERS, E, *Iran: Bibliographischer Forschungsbericht*, *op.cit.*, II 2.2.

ROSEN, N C, *Bibliography of the geology of Iran*, Special Publications of the Geological Survey of Iran, 2, 1969.

Other researchers have to be content with more limited subject bibliographies and general reference works, including:

PETERSEN, A D, *Bibliography on the climate of Iran*, US Weather Bureau, Washington 1957.

GANJI, M H, 'The climates of Iran', *Bulletin de la Société de Géographie d'Egypte* 28, 1955 :195-299.

CLAPP, F G, 'Geology of eastern Iran', *Bulletin of the Geological Society of America* 51, 1940 :1-101.

UNITED KINGDOM, ADMIRALTY, *Geology of Mesopotamia and its borderlands*, London 1921.

More specific geographical studies, in Persian, give a flavour of work in progress:

KUMISYŪN-I YŪNISKŪ-YI ĪRĀN, *Īrānshahr*, 2 vols, 1963, 1964.

A survey of Iranian culture by leading scholars published by the UNESCO Commission for Iran. Pages 1-172 of volume I form a valuable geographical introduction (physical, geological, climate, regional (including historical), population, ethnic groups).

ᶜADL, Aḥmad Ḥusain, *Āb-u-havā-ye Īrān*, Tehran 1960.

—— *Taqsīmāt-i iqlīmī-yi rustanī-hā-yi Īrān*, Tehran 1960.

S̱ĀBITĪ, Ḥabīballāh, *Bar-rasī dar aqālīm-i ḥayāti-yi Īrān*, University of Tehran Publications, no.1231, Tehran 1969.

VADĪᶜĪ, Kāẓim, *Muqaddama bar jughrāfiyā-yi insānī-yi Īrān*, University of Tehran Publications, no.1231, Tehran 1970, 2nd ed. 1974.

Includes studies of nomadic pastoralism and of particular tribes, sedentary agriculture, types of settlements and houses, population distribution, frontiers, administrative units and boundaries.

ḤARĪRIYĀN, Maḥmūd, *Jughrāfiyā-yi iqtiṣādī-yi Īrān*, vol.I, Manābiᶜ-i giyāhī. Publications of the Higher Teacher Training College, no.36, Tehran 1971.

A treatise on plant resources and agriculture forming volume I of a promised series on the Economic Geography of Iran.

SAᶜĀDAT, Asad, and Amīr Hūshang AMĪNĪ, *Jughrāfiyā-yi iqtiṣādī-yi Īrān*, Dānishkada-yi Irṭibātāt-i ᶜUmūmī, no.13, 1971, 2nd ed. 1976.

A survey of contemporary Iranian economic geography: agriculture and stock breeding, mines, petroleum, petrochemicals, factory industries, handicraft industries, communications, internal and external trade, with much useful information and statistics. The authors do not only echo official plans, but also discuss difficulties.

BADĪᶜĪ, Rabīᶜ, *Jughrāfiyā-yi iqtiṣādī-yi Īrān*, Tehran 1968.

MUJTAHIDĪ, Aḥmad, *Shahr-hā va masā'il-i ān*, Iṣfahān 1970.

General, but refers to Iranian cities.

IMĀM-SHŪSHTARĪ, Muḥammad ^{c}Alī, *Tārīkh-i-jughrāfiyā-yi-Khūzistān*, Tehran 1953.

MUJTAHIDZĀDA, Parvīz, *Jughrāfiyā-yi tārīkhī-yi Khalīj-i Fārs*, University of Tehran Publications, no.1497, Tehran 1976.

Largely concerned with proving the correctness of the name 'Gulf of Fārs', and the incorrectness of 'Arab Gulf', from the testimony of classical Arabic geographers and early European cartographers.

SHAFAQĪ, Sīrūs, *Jughrāfiyā-yi Iṣfahān*, Iṣfahān 1976.

Published by the University of Iṣfahān. Physical and historical geography and population structure of the city of Iṣfahān.

Two series of geographical publications from Iran merit particular comment.

MU'ASSASSA-YI JUGHRĀFIYĀ-YI DĀNISHGĀH-I TIHRĀN, *Guzārishāt*.

Examples from this series are:

11. MU^{c}TAMID, Aḥmad, *Masā'il-i zamīnshināsī-yi chāla-yi Lūt*. HEINZELIN, J, *Ṣanāyi^c-i sangī-yi rūd-i Fahrij*, Tehran 1974.
12. KĀRDAVĀNĪ, Parvīz, *Shahdād tā Dih Salm: khāk, āb, pūshish-i giyāhī va auẓā^c-i kishāvarzī*, Tehran 1975.

MU'ASSASA-YI TAḤQĪQĀT-I IJTIMĀ^{c}Ī VA ^{c}ULŪM-I INSĀNĪ-YI DĀNISHGĀH-I ĀZARBĀDAGĀN, *Intishārāt*.

Examples from this series are:

6. FARĪD, Yadallāh, *Jughrāfiyā-yi shahrī* I, Tabrīz 1969.
11. *Ibid*. II, Tabrīz 1971.
16. ĀSĀYISH, Ḥusain, *Jughrāfiyā-yi ṣan^{c}atī-yi Īrān: bakhshī az ṣanāyi^c-i sangīn va nīm-sangīn*, Tabrīz 1975.

Examines regional distribution of investment and employment, changes which occurred in the 3rd and 4th five-year plan periods (1962-67 and 1967-72), and prospects under the 5th plan; gives detailed descriptions and statistics of the sugar refining, textile, iron and steel, machine-making, tractor, aluminium, and petro-chemical industries, and discusses problems of profitability and productivity.

1.2 *Basic reference works*

General researchers will soon be driven, along with geographers and geologists, to the world-wide geographical bibliographical tools, of which the chiefest are:

Geo abstracts, University of East Anglia, quarterly in 7 series:

A - Landforms and the quaternary; B - Climatology and hydrology; C - Economic geography; D - Social and historical geography; E - Sedimentology; F - Regional and community planning; G - Remote sensing, photogrammetry and cartography.

First published in 1960 by London School of Economics Department of Geography as a single series of *Geomorphological abstracts* (later *Geographical abstracts*).

Bibliographie géographique internationale, Centre national de la Recherche scientifique, annual, Paris 1891-.

ROYAL GEOGRAPHICAL SOCIETY, *New geographical literature and maps*, semi-annual, new series, London 1951-80.

Records additions to the library and map room of the Royal Geographical Society.

AMERICAN GEOGRAPHICAL SOCIETY, *Research catalogue of the A.G.S.*, 15 vols and suppls, Boston 1962.

Volume 12 covers Iran and the surrounding region.

—— *Current geographical publications*, 10 issues a year, Milwaukee 1938-.

Records additions to the Research catalogue.

The monitoring of geographical journals, in part achieved by the bibliographical tools just mentioned, is shown to be important by the frequency of occurrence of relevant articles in, for example, *The geographical journal* and (earlier) *Petermanns geographische Mitteilungen*. Some bibliographical control over this field is exercised (notably from Chicago) by

HARRIS, C D, and J D FELLMAN, *International list of geographical serials*, 3rd ed., University of Chicago Department of Geography 1980.

HARRIS, C D, *Annotated world list of selected current geographical serials*, 4th ed., University of Chicago Department of Geography 1980.

KISH, G (ed), *Bibliography of international geographical congresses 1871-1976*, Boston 1979.

Iranian serials of note for geology include

Report of the Geological Survey of Iran, (1964-);

Bulletin of the Iranian Petroleum Institute, (1964-);

Publications of the National Iranian Oil Company Geological Laboratories, (1964-).

More general reference tools with bibliographical content include

HARRIS, C D, *Bibliography of geography, part 1: Introduction to general aids*, University of Chicago Department of Geography 1976.

The most comprehensive handy guide available.

LOCK, C B M, *Geography and cartography*, London 1976.

First published in 1968 as *Geography: A reference handbook*.

MACKAY, J W, *An introductory guide to sources of information for the literature of geology*, University College London, Department of Geology 1971.

WARD, D C, and M WHEELER, *Geologic reference sources*, Metuchen, N.J. 1972.

RIDGE, J D, *Annotated bibliographies of mineral deposits in Africa, Asia (exclusive of the USSR) and Australasia*, Oxford 1976.

A rare example of a worldwide specialist bibliography which has particular relevance to Iran is

PAYLORE, P (comp), *Desertification: A world bibliography*, University of Arizona, Office of Arid Lands Studies, Tucson 1976.

2. *MAPS*

Techniques of map storage, cataloguing and consultation are not yet so far advanced that map collections can be used easily without an interpreter or a written guide. For western collections of maps of Iran, which have been formed so far from an area of which few current maps are available, an introduction to older map series and to particular collections may be useful. In the case of Iran, where until recent years even large-scale topographical mapping has been produced mainly by cartographic agencies outside the country, this is particularly so.

2.1 *Current surveys and map production in Iran*

Until 1973, when the two organizations merged, maps were produced in Iran by the National Geographic Organisation and the National Cartographic Centre. The new joint authority took the name of the National Geographic Organisation. The functions and responsibilities of the two constituent bodies is apparent from the history of their separate development after the Second World War (when mapping of Iran was in the hands of the belligerant powers). The National Geographic Organisation was at first a geographic department within the Military General Staff (earlier called 'General Staff Geographical Department', or with the suffix 'Imperial Iranian Army') and was responsible for preparing geodetic data and producing small- and medium-scale maps of the country. The National Cartographic Centre was created in 1953 at the instance of a cartographic adviser from France assisting the Iran Oil Company, and its policies developed by a Netherlands adviser, Professor W Schermerhorn, who visited Iran in 1954. The Centre co-ordinated the cartographic activities of various government departments, and has done a great deal of large-scale project and topographical mapping including the 1:10,000 Lar Valley series and town plans.

In 1970 these two bodies were seen as forming a four-pronged assault, with the National Iranian Oil Company (and other oil companies) and with private survey companies, on the mapping of Iran. The merger of 1973 seems to have changed this, though the Geological Survey Institute has continued to produce its maps separately, deriving topographical information from the products of the other two official bodies. Detailed information on progress in map publication is available only up to 1973 from United Nations reports (listed below), but gives a clear picture of accelerating progress with publication of sheets in the 1:250,000 and 1:50,000 topographical series. Much of this publication is in Persian, and this factor (together with the slow spread of the maps into reference collections outside Iran) ensures that collections of older Second World War maps (in English) retain their usefulness.

The difficulties in obtaining official mapping for use outside Iran have promoted commercial map publishers in Iran into unusual prominence, of which the Ṣahāb Geographic and Drafting Institute, and (to a lesser extent) the firm of Gītā Shināsī, have taken advantage.

2.2 *Sources of information on current map production*

Official catalogues of maps published have only rarely been issued by the two government mapping bodies. The few that are known include an index of publications of the Geographical Section, General Staff, apparently issued with the 1950 report of the Army Geographical Department, duplicated typescript catalogues of the National Cartographic Centre for 1966 and 1971, and separate map and publications lists (in duplicated typescript) from the Geological Survey of Iran for 1977. Reports issued by the Geological Survey of Iran (e.g. for 1972-73) also contain lists of maps. Such catalogues are by no means regular in appearance, whereas the Ṣahāb Geographic and Drafting Institute has issued frequent dated catalogues at least for the late 1960s and much of the 1970s.

Instead, one has to rely on contributions from the Iran authorities to the triennial United Nations Regional Cartographic Conferences for Asia and the Far East (UNRCCAFE):

UNRCCAFE 1 (Mussoorie 1955), vol.2, New York 1957 :49.

A short report on the establishment of the National Cartographic Centre.

—— 2 (Tokyo 1958), 'Report on cartographic activities in Iran', vol.2, New York 1961 :45-47.

By the National Cartographic Centre, giving a brief history of cartography in Iran and describing the structure and activities of the Centre.

—— 5 (Canberra 1967), 'Cartographic activities in Iran', vol.2, New York 1968 :94.

A short progress report by the National Cartographic Centre.

—— 6 (Tehran 1970), 'Cartographic activities of Iran', vol.2, New York 1974 : 35-37 and 13 maps.

The first report to bring together the activities of the National Geographic Organisation, the National Cartographic Centre, and the Geological Survey Institute.

—— 7 (Tokyo 1973), 'Iranian national report', vol.2, New York 1976 :39-44 and 9 maps.

The latest available report.

The index maps of published topographical map coverage and of progress with air survey work in the reports of the sixth and seventh conferences are particularly valuable, in the absence of up-to-date official catalogues.

World-wide catalogues show smaller-scale map series which cover Iran:

DIRECTORATE OF MILITARY SURVEY, *Ministry of Defence map and air chart sales catalogue*, London 1968.

Loose-leaf, amended by the issue of new pages.

UNITED NATIONS, Department of Economic and Social Affairs, *International map of the world on the millionth scale: Report*, New York, irregular.

Published every three-five years with interim supplements, containing lists of available sheets and of survey offices.

A general bibliographical with a useful coverage of Iran is

WINCH, K L, *International maps and atlases in print*, 2nd ed. London 1976.

The section on Iran comprises mainly Ṣahāb publications. Large-scale map series are generally absent.

World-wide map publication is recorded regularly in

CENTRE NATIONAL DE RECHERCHE SCIENTIFIQUE, *Bibliographie cartographique internationale*, Paris, annual.

The sections on Asian countries are disproportionately small, and inevitable delays in publication limit its usefulness as a monitor of current mapping. Before the publication of *International maps and atlases*, map retailers' catalogues were a unique form of reference aid. Still important is

Geo Katalog International, Stuttgart: Geo Center Internationales Landkartenhaus.

Volume 1 is a world-wide reference work revised annually, and volume 2 a loose-leaf catalogue of official map series and indices.

General map library accessions lists have useful sections on Iran:

New geographical literature and maps, *op.cit*.

British Library catalogue of printed maps: Accessions, London, annual.

Contains additions to *The British Museum catalogue of printed maps ....*

BODLEIAN LIBRARY MAP SECTION, *Selected map and book accessions*, Oxford, monthly.

DIRECTORATE OF MILITARY SURVEY (MINISTRY OF DEFENCE), *Selected accessions list of the map library*, London, monthly.

AMERICAN GEOGRAPHICAL SOCIETY, *Current geographical publications*, *op.cit.*, Milwaukee, 10 issues a year.

Includes a small section on maps.

General bibliographies of geography are rarely sufficiently detailed for information on maps; of general use, however, is

HARRIS, C D, 'Maps and atlases', *Bibliography of geography, Part 1: Introduction to general aids*, *op.cit*. 1.2, chap.10.

The following provide world-wide surveys of map accessions lists, map retailers, geographical journals and national bibliographies, but the information on sources for Iranian material is disappointingly superficial.

NICHOLS, H, *Map librarianship*, London 1976 :27-80.

LARSGAARD, M, *Map librarianship: an introduction*, Littleton, Colorado 1978.

STEPHENSON, R W, 'Published sources of information about maps and atlases', *Special Libraries* lxi, 1970 :87-98 and 110-12. Repr. in R DRAZNIOWSKY (ed), *Map librarianship: Readings*, Metuchen 1975.

For further general sources of bibliographical information see

LOCK, C B Muriel, *Modern maps and atlases*, London 1969 :468-79.

For a valuable dictionary-style compendium of useful facts, see

—— *Geography and Cartography*, 3rd ed., London 1976.

For the Middle East and Arab World generally, see

MEDLOCK, H, 'Maps and atlases of the Arab World', GRIMWOOD-JONES, *op.cit.* :123-33.

HALE, G A, 'Maps and atlases of the Middle East', *MESA bull*. 3, 1969, no.3 :17-39.

There are errors of fact (p.19) about the topographical mapping of Iran.

2.3 *Development of published map series to c.1950*

This section is derived chiefly from

The War Record 1914-1920 (Records of the Survey of India 20, 1925) pp.1-90 (especially pp.51-90); E O WHEELER, *The Survey of India during war and early reconstruction 1939-46* (Dehra Dun 1955); A B CLOUGH, *Maps and Survey*

(The Second World War 1939-1945: Army) ([London] 1952) pp.165-95; UNITED STATES DEPARTMENT OF THE ARMY, *Foreign Maps* (Technical Manual 5-248) (October 1963) pp.66-72.

Such Iranian topographical surveys as existed before the First World War were the result of reconnaissance or other specific surveys, many of them for military purposes. The chief exception to this was the first reliable general map of Iran

Persia. Compiled principally from original authorities by Captain O B C ST JOHN, by order of H.M. Secretary of State for India. 1:1,013,760 (16 miles to 1 inch), London/Stanford [1876],

which formed the basis for later maps at the same scale compiled by the Intelligence Branch, War Office (1886) and the Survey of India (1897) as the standard reference map of the country.

The whole of Iran fell within the tract of Asia for which the Survey of India was responsible, in accordance with the recommendations of the Seventh International Geographical Congress of 1899, for producing maps at the scale of 1:1,000,000. This tract was bounded on the west by the meridian of 44°E, and on the north by the parallel of 40°N; it included (nominally) the Persian Gulf and much of Arabia, and covered the Indian subcontinent as well as much of Central Asia and South-East Asia. After the report of the Indian Survey Committee in 1905 the resulting scheme divided all Southern Asia for mapping purposes into squares of 4° latitude and 4° longitude, numbering the squares from 1 to 136 from the north-west corner (44°E, 40°N) in north-south strips, each square to be contained on a single map at the 1:1,000,000 scale in the *India and adjacent countries* series. This series provided the basis for the 'Indian numbering' of larger-scale topographical maps produced subsequently by the Survey of India. In addition the Survey of India produced 1:1,000,000 sheets in the *International map of the word* format, of 4° latitude and 6° longitude, which provide the basis for the 'international numbering' of larger-scale topographical sheets. For fuller details see

COOK, A S, 'Maps', *South Asia Bibliography*, J D PEARSON (ed), Hassocks 1979.

The Survey of India was active in Mesopotamia and Persia during the First World War, and produced, besides a 1:126,720 series of sheets for Mesopotamia, maps in the 'Indian numbering' series for parts of Iran. Russian mapping in or before the First World War overlapped with the Survey of India work in covering Iran north of 36°N and west of 47°E at 1:84,000 (the 2-verst scale), as well as a series of 20-verst maps

(1:840,000) covering the whole of Iran. The Survey of India, which had taken on the additional responsibility in war-time for large-scale mapping of the area between 40°E and 44°E (using 'international numbering' for its maps of that strip), retained responsibility for mapping Iran until 1929, when it withdrew to 48°E, leaving western Iran the responsibility of the UK War Office. That arrangement persisted until the Second World War, when, at the Cairo Survey Conference of April 1940, the Survey of India resumed responsibility for all mapping east of 40°E (i.e. taking over the whole of Iran again). With the increasing demands on Survey of India resources in Eastern Asia in 1942 and 1943, the Survey of India surrendered the task of mapping west of 54°E to Middle East Land Force in 1942, and withdrew to 60°E in 1943 (leaving the whole of Iran to the Middle East Land Force (MELF) and the Persia and Iraq Force (PAIFORCE)). Though late war-time and post-war American and British map series relied heavily on pre-war Survey of India work (and early war-time India Field Survey Company revisions), the Survey of India was not thereafter involved in the mapping of Iran.

During the First World War the German military authorities had produced mapping of western Iran at 1:400,000 from Russian material. In the Second World War the German army improved on this with a coverage of Iran at 1:200,000 based on inter-war Survey of India maps.

The complexity of using collections of topographical and other maps drawn from series produced by five non-Iranian survey authorities over a period of 40 years suggests that the following list of map series may be useful:

1:1,000,000 (approximately 16 miles to 1 inch)

SURVEY OF INDIA. India and adjacent countries series, c.1910-1930s. Each sheet covers 4° latitude x 4° longitude. Index maps in Survey of India catalogues. 'Indian numbering'.

—— International map of the world series, c.1920-1930s. Each sheet covers 4° latitude x 6° longitude. Index maps in Survey of India catalogues. 'International numbering'.

German Military Series. Based on Survey of India *India and adjacent countries* series.

MIDDLE EAST LAND FORCE/DIRECTORATE OF MILITARY SURVEY (UK) series GSGS 2555 and GSGS 4646, 1941 onwards. International map of the world format and numbering.

DIRECTORATE OF MILITARY SERVICE (UK)/ARMY MAP SERVE (US), World series 1301. International map of the world format and numbering. Indices in Ministry of Defence catalogues and International Map of the World reports.

DEFENCE MAPPING AGENCY AEROSPACE CENTER (US) Operational Navigation Chart (ONC) aeronautical chart series. Indices in Ministry of Defence catalogues.

1:840,000

Russian Military Series, 20 verst scale, 1920s.

1:500,000 (approximately 8 miles to 1 inch)

German Military Series. Based on Survey of India *India and adjacent countries* series.

SURVEY OF INDIA. Indian Field Survey Company mapping, series PID 9001 (K404), 1940s. Includes sheets of UK aeronautical charting, series GSGS 4072.

DIRECTORATE OF MILITARY SURVEY (UK)/ARMY MAP SERVICE (US). World series 1404. Indices in Ministry of Defence catalogues.

DEFENCE MAPPING AGENCY AEROSPACE CENTER (US). Tactical Pilotage Chart (TPC) Aeronautical chart series. Indices in Ministry of Defence catalogues.

1:400,000

German Military Series, 1918. Based on Russian mapping. Western Iran only.

1:253,440 (4 miles to 1 inch)

SURVEY OF INDIA, North-western Trans-frontier series, 1888-1908.

—— Quarter-inch, or 'Degree sheet', series, 1912-46. Covers east of 40°E and south of 40°N. Series number K501. Some sheets reprinted by Middle East Land Force and Army Map Service.

MIDDLE EAST LAND FORCES. Quarter-inch series IDR [etc.] 9002, MDR 503, GSGS 3919 and K501. Covers west of 54°E. Some sheets reprinted by Army Map Service, 1941-47. Indian sheet sizes with 'international numbering'.

DIRECTORATE OF MILITARY SURVEY (UK). Quarter-inch series GSGS 3919 and K501. Reprints of Survey of India and Middle East Land Forces sheets with revisions. 1941 onwards. Indian sheet sizes with 'international numbering'.

1:250,000 (approximately 4 miles to 1 inch)

EDWARD STANFORD, Iraq and Persia series, 1921. 'Indian numbering'.

ARMY MAP SERVICE (US). K501 series. Photographic enlargements of quater-inch series GSGS 3919. Indian sheet sizes with 'international numbering'.

—— K502 series. Covers north and north-west Iran. International sheet sizes.

1:200,000

German Military Series, 1942. Based on Survey of India quarter-inch series.

Russian Military Series, 1941-42. Based on Survey of India quarter-inch series, and used for compiling GSGS 3919 series. 5 verst scale.

1:126,720 (2 miles to 1 inch)

SURVEY OF INDIA, 1914-18. Mesopotamia series of special sheets.

—— Half-inch series, 1920-23. Parts of Iran only.

1:100,000

Russian Military Series, 1938-41. Repr. from 1:84,000 series. Covers north and north-west Iran.

MIDDLE EAST LAND FORCES, Iraq-Iran series IDR [etc.] 9003, GSGS 4644 and K601. From British and Russian sources. Part of Iran only. 1941 onwards.

1:84,000

Russian Military Series, 1913-41. Based on surveys 1896-1914 north of 36°N and west of 47°E. Used by Middle East Land Forces in compiling quarter-inch series. 2 verst scale.

1:50,000

SURVEY OF INDIA, Iraq-Iran series K701, 1941-46. South-west Iran only.

MIDDLE EAST LAND FORCES, Series MDR 685 and GSGS 8035, 1946-47. Revision of preceding series.

—— Iraq-Iran series IDR [etc.] 9044, GSGS 8036 and K751-2 and 754-5, 1942-43. Scattered areas of Iran only.

1:25,000

—— Iraq-Iran series IDR 9005, GSGS 8037, and K852 and 856-8, 1942-43. West central Iran only.

—— Lar Valley series MDR 681, GSGS 4630 and K854, 1946-49.

1:10,000

—— Lar Valley series MDR 683, GSGS 4634 and K853, 1947-49.

Though the General Staff Geographical Department (the forerunner of the National Geographic Organisation) had been reprinting the 1:10,000, 1:50,000 and 1:84,000 series in Persian language editions, the topographical coverage of maps of Iran in the early 1950s could be summarized as giving a full 1:253,440 coverage, supplemented by 1:200,000 north-west of the Caspian Sea (with 1:84,000 coverage in the western part of that area), by 1:100,000 maps in the north and west, by a block of 1:50,000 sheets north of the Persian Gulf, by a sparse coverage of 1:25,000 and 1:50,000 maps in the west, and by detailed mapping of Lar Valley at 1:10,000 and 1:25,000.

2.4 *Development of published map series after 1950*

The main cover of topographical maps of Iran was maintained after 1950 by the National Geographic Organisation, rather than by the National Cartographic Centre (which developed large-scale project mapping), although the latter body did produce a 1:10,000 survey of Lar Valley. The early efforts of the National Geographic Organisation were to produce Persian language versions of maps compiled by British and American (and Russian) authorities. Later the work was concentrated in covering Iran with maps at three scales: 1:1,000,000, 1:250,000 and 1:50,000. At the time of the latest United Nations report (1973) only the 1:1,000,000 coverage had been completed; for the two larger scales the progress was tabulated as follows:

1:250,000 Up to 1970; 58; 1970-3: 50; Total needed: 136.

1:50,000 Up to 1967: 115; 1967-70: 180; 1970-3: 936; Total needed: 2650.

The following series, all published by the NATIONAL GEOGRAPHIC ORGANISATION, can be added to the list in the preceding section:

1:1,000,000

Reprint of 1942 Survey of India *India and adjacent countries* sheets, in Persian, 1949-60. Complete in 20 sheets.

Series K351. Persian language version of World 1301 series.

1:253,440

Reprint of Survey of India 'Degree sheets' in Persian.

1:250,000

Series K551. Persian language. Part coverage only. Index map in UNRCCAFE 7 report.

1:100,000

Reprint of part of Middle East Land Forces series K601, in Persian.

New mapping [not confirmed].

1:84,000

Reprint of Russian 1:84,000 series in Persian.

1:50,000

Enlargement of 1:253,440 series, 1936-49. Isolated sheets only.

Series K753. Persian language. Index map in UNRCCAFE 7 report.

1:20,000

Small area near Tehran, 1949-.

1:10,000

Small area near Tehran, 1944-50.

The report of the 1973 United Nations conference [UNRCCAFE 7] includes index maps to show not only the published topographical map coverage and sheet lines, but also the progress with air photography, at 1:50,000 in 1955-57 and at 1:20,000 in 1965-72.

The Geological Survey Institute has produced independent series of maps since the early 1950s, publishing first a map at 1:500,000 based on topographical maps at the 1:250,000 and 1:253,440 scales, and then, in 1957-62, developing two series of geological maps at 1:200,000 and 1:250,000, deriving topographical information from an otherwise unknown series of aeronautical charts at 1:250,000 (UNRCCAFE 6, vol.2, p.37) and the new 1:50,000 series. Index maps of all three geological series are included in the 1973 United Nations report.

2.5 *General and thematic maps and atlases*

Though the National Geographic Organisation produces a general map of Iran:

NATIONAL GEOGRAPHIC ORGANISATION, [*Iran*], 4 sheets, K302, Persian, 1:2,000,000,

the best general reference map is the Bartholomew map

JOHN BARTHOLOMEW & SON, *Iran*, 1:2,500,000, Bartholomew World Travel series, Edinburgh, revised frequently.

SAḤĀB Geographic and Drafting Institute issue a series of provincial maps at scales of 1:500,000 and 1:1,000,000 (see WINCH, *International maps and atlases*, p.274). Iran, like few other Asian countries, is susceptible to small-scale single-sheet mapping of an intelligible type, and SAḤĀB have developed this side of their work.

The reputation of the *Tübinger Atlas des Vorderen Orients* as a thematic atlas for Iran is high. The atlas, published in Wiesbaden from 1977 onwards, appears in irregular batches of loose map leaves forming annual folders. The atlas is in two parts, geography and history, and the geography part is in ten sections: relief and hydrology; geology; geomorphology; climate; hydrogeography; vegetation; natural regions; population; settlement; and economy and communications. The maps are based on four main scales: 1:8,000,000; 1:4,000,000; 1:2,000,000 and 1:1,000,000, giving rise to maps such as 'A X 15 - Iran Industry' and 'A x 16 - Arabian Persian Gulf Oil'.

Other atlases, published by SAḤĀB, include:

Atlas of Iran: White Revolution, Proceeds and Progresses, Tehran 1971.

Climatic Atlas of Iran, Tehran 1967,

as well as three historical atlases:

Atlas of Ancient and Historical Maps of Iran, Tehran 1971.

Aṭlas-i Tārīkhī-yi Īrān : Historical Atlas of Iran, Tehran 1971.

Atlas of Geographical Maps and Historical Documents of the Persian Gulf Tehran 1971.

ṢAFĀ, Ẕabīḥallāh, *Aṭlas-i farhangī-yi shahr-i Tihrān*, vol.I, Tehran 1976.

Also useful are three historical atlases of the Islamic world:

BRICE, William C (ed), *An historical atlas of Islam*, Amsterdam 1981.

HAZARD, H W, and H L COOKE, *Atlas of Islamic history*, Princeton Oriental Studies, 12, Princeton 1951.

ROOLVINK, R, *et al.*, *Historical atlas of the Muslim peoples*, Amsterdam 1957.

2.6 *Reference map collections*

For United Kingdom collections, see

BURKETT, J, *Special library and information services in the United Kingdom*, 2nd ed., London 1965 :291-96.

For overseas collections, see

RISTOW, W W, *World directory of map collections*, International Federation of Library Associations, München 1976.

The maps described so far are chiefly the topographical series produced by government authorities, the bulk of survey office work. Almost all library collections consist of such maps, although the completeness of coverage varies widely among libraries. In the United Kingdom three institutions are known to hold good collections of maps of Iran (chiefly the war-time and post-war British and American map production): the British Library (Map Library), the Royal Geographical Society Map Room, and the India Office Library and Records Map Room. Outside London the University Library in Cambridge and the Bodleian Library in Oxford hold good collections, but these institutions (as also those in London) embrace Iran in the general strength of coverage in their map collections. No specialist academic collections of maps are known to exist.

Collections of maps outside the United Kingdom can be consulted only on the basis of their general strengths. No information is available about map collections in Iran, nor (with one exception) in neighbouring countries.

ABDUL WAHEED KHAN, *Catalogue of maps in the Centre for Arab Gulf Studies*, vol.1, University of Basrah Centre for Arab Gulf Studies, Basra 1978.

Maps in official records, etc.

Maps abound in official records, but often to fulfil highly specific and ephemeral purposes. Collections of such maps exist, for Iran, in the Public Record Office and in the India Office Records, where they accompany official files and confidential prints. See the section 'Maps in official records, etc.' in

COOK, Andrew S, 'Maps' (*South Asian Bibliography*);

and particularly the section on maps of Iran in the India Office Political Department map collection (IOR: W/LPS/B) in the India Office Library and

Records, London.

2.7 *Place-finding gazetteers and indices*

Place-finding gazetteers are an essential aid to the proper use of topographical maps: without gazetteers such maps are like books without indices. Iran has been particularly well-served from the point of view of gazetteers, not all of them of the 'place-finding' type. For two official collections of gazetteers, see the section on Iran in the India Office Military Department Library (IOR: L/MIL/17/15) and in the India Office Political and Secret Department Library (IOR: L/P&S/20/C), which include a variety of older official gazetteers, including

LORIMER, J G, *Gazetteer of the Persian Gulf*, 6 vols, Calcutta 1908.

Early examples include

SURVEY OF INDIA, *Index to names appearing on the Southern* [*Northern*] *Persia sheet of the Southern Asia Series. Scale 1/2,000,000 or 1.014 inches to 32 miles*, Calcutta 1913 [1914].

GEOGRAPHICAL SECTION, GENERAL STAFF, *Index to names common to War Office and Indian Maps on the Turco-Persian Frontier (GSGS no.2841)*, HMSO, London 1917.

ARMY HEADQUARTERS INDIA (General Staff Branch), *Index of place names on Degree Sheets*, [Simla 1916] with first series of additions [1917].

PERMANENT COMMITTEE ON GEOGRAPHICAL NAMES FOR BRITISH OFFICIAL USE, *First* [*Second*] *list of names in Persia (South)* [*(North)*], London 1928 [1929], amended by addenda and corrigenda in *PCGN Circular* 19, 1947.

—— [*Provisional*] *List of Names (New Series): Persia*, London 1955.

GENERALSTAB DES HEERES, *Alphabetisches Namenverzeichnis der Kartenwerke Vorderasiens Iran (Westteil)* [*(Ostteil)*], Berlin 1942.

Gazetteer to the German 1:200,000 map series reprinted from Survey of India 1:253,440 maps.

SURVEY DIRECTORATE, GENERAL HEADQUARTERS, MIDDLE EAST [PAIFORCE], *Eastern* [*Western*] *Iran: Index Gazetteer showing place names on Quarter-inch series maps of Iran East* [*West*] *of 54°E*, Cairo 1945, [Baghdad 1944].

The current standard gazetteer for Iran is that published in the United States:

UNITED STATES BOARD ON GEOGRAPHIC NAMES, *NIS Gazetteer: Iran* [also issued as *Official Standard Names Gazetteer: Iran*], Washington 1956,

which supersedes

UNITED STATES BOARD ON GEOGRAPHIC NAMES, *Preliminary NIS Gazetteer: Iran*, Washington 1949.

A more modern development, though by no means yet complete for Iran, is

ADAMEC, L W (ed), *Historical gazetteer of Iran, op.cit.* 1.1.

Only the first volume (Tehran and Northwestern Iran) has appeared; the planned volumes are: Meshed and Northeastern Iran; Shiraz and Southwestern Iran (in two parts); and Bandar Abbas and Southeastern Iran. Each part is divided into four sections: a geographical and historical dictionary; a glossary of geographical etc. terms; a map section; and an index. It is the map section which excites curiosity, for the author has taken topographical maps from a wide variety of series (those so far identified in volume 1 are the 1:253,440 Survey of India, MELF and AMS maps, the 1:250,000 AMS maps, an otherwise unknown American map series probably at 1:250,000 with aeronautical information, and the 1:200,000 German pirate series from the Survey of India 1:253,440 maps). This motley collection he has reduced to a standard 1:300,000 scale to provide a workable (though internally inconsistent) atlas section to his gazetteer.

Supplementary world-wide gazetteers include

The Times index-gazetteer of the world, London 1965.

The Columbia-Lippincott Gazetteer of the World, New York 1952.

UNION POSTALE UNIVERSELLE, *Nomenclature international des bureaux de poste*, 3 vols, Berne 1968.

2.8 *Marine charts*

In a study of maps of Iran, attention deserves to be drawn to collections of navigation charts, both historical and current, on the coastline of Iran. Collections of charts by early marine surveyors for the East India Company (for example Alexander DALRYMPLE and James HORSBURGH) can be supplemented by early volumes of sailing directions for historical study. See the various editions of

HORSBURGH, J, *The Indian directory* [previously *Directions for sailing to and from the East Indies*], London 1809-64.

Modern Admiralty charts and pilots provide some topographical coverage of Iran's coastline. For charts see

HYDROGRAPHER OF THE NAVY, *Catalogue of Admiralty charts and other hydrographic publications*, Taunton, annual.

For an example of a pilot, see

HYDROGRAPHER OF THE NAVY, *Persian Gulf pilot*, various editions, Taunton, various dates.

3. *MUSLIM GEOGRAPHERS AND TRAVELLERS*

3.1 *General sources*

For a general survey of Islamic geographical literature and its principles, consult:

KRACHKOVSKII, I YU, *Arabskaya geograficheskaya literatura*, pub. as vol.4 of the author's collected works, *Izbrannye sochineniya*, Moscow 1958. Arabic tr. Ṣalāḥ al-dīn ᶜUthmān HĀSHIM, *Tārīkh al-adab al-jughrāfī al-ᶜarabī*, 2 vols, Cairo 1963-65.

KRAMERS, J H, 'Djughrāfiyā', *EI.1*, suppl.

AHMAD, S Maqbul, 'Djughrāfiyā', *EI.2*.

MIQUEL, A, *La géographie humaine du monde musulman jusqu'au milieu du XIe siècle*, 3 vols, Paris 1967-80.

SCHOLTEN, A, *Länderbeschreibung und Länderkunde im islamischen Kulturraum des 10. Jahrhunderts*, Paderborn 1976.

Biobibliographical information on Arab geographers can be found in the relevant sections of:

BROCKELMANN, C, *Geschichte der arabischen Litteratur*, *op.cit.*

Biobibliographical information on Persian geographers can be traced in:

STOREY, C A, *PL*, *op.cit.*

Consult especially in volume I, section N(p) on 'Travellers, pilgrims and tourists' (pp.1138-62), and in volume II, part 1, section D on 'Geography' (pp.117-92, no index).

WILBER, Donald N, 'Recent contributions to the historical geography of Iran', *Archaeologica orientalia in memoriam Ernst Herzfeld*, New York 1952 :267-78.

PETROV, Mikhail P, *Bibliografiya po geografii Irana; ukazatel' literatury na russkom yazyke 1720-1954*, Ashkhabad 1955.

Index to literature in the Russian language 1720-1954. Annotated references on the geography of Iran. Very useful for the earlier literature but not very comprehensive.

The most valuable secondary source on Muslim geography with regard to Iran is

LE STRANGE, G, *The lands of the Eastern Caliphate: Mesopotamia, Persia and Central Asia from the Moslem Conquest to the time of Timur*, Cambridge 1905, repr. 1966. Persian tr. Maḥmūd ᶜIRFĀN, *Jughrāfiyā-yi tārīkhī-yi sar-zamīnhā-yi khilāfat-i sharqī*, Tehran 1959.

The first chapter surveys the oriental sources for Iranian geography and topography, and is a valuable if outdated introduction. Chapters 11 to 30 deal with the actual geographical information on Iran and its interpretation, with many references to the original texts to substantiate each argument. The most important work in its field. An additional source containing sixteen maps is

SPRENGER, A, *Die Post- und Reiserouten des Orients*, Leipzig 1864, repr.
    Amsterdam.

3.2 *Individual texts and translations*

The most important geographical texts in Arabic and Persian dealing with Iran are listed below. The order is approximately that of the date of death of the author. Geographical information can also be extracted from other categories of Muslim literature, in particular:

(a) General historical texts, e.g. *Futūḥ al-buldān* by al-BALĀDHURĪ (see IX 3.5 below); *al-Kāmil fī 'l-tārīkh* by ᶜIzz al-dīn IBN AL-ATHĪR (published in fifteen volumes in Leiden in 1857-76 and thirteen volumes in Beirut in 1965-66); *Akhbār al-rusul wa'l-mulūk* by AL-ṬABARĪ (published in fifteen volumes in Leiden in 1879-1901 and ten volumes in Cairo in 1960-69), and *Ẓafarnāma* by Sharaf al-dīn ᶜAlī YAZDĪ (published in two volumes in Cairo in 1885-88 and in facsimile in Tashkent in 1972).

(b) Histories of individual towns, e.g. the anonymous *Fażā'il-i Balkh* (published in Tehran in 1971).

(c) Encyclopaedic works of general culture, e.g. *Murūj al-dhahab* by al-MASᶜŪDĪ (published in Paris 1861-77 in nine volumes, revised edition in seven volumes Beirut 1966-79, and in four volumes in Cairo in 1948), *Ṣubḥ al-aᶜshā fī ṣināᶜat al-inshā'* by al-QALQASHANDĪ (published in fifteen volumes in Cairo in 1964-72), and *Nihāyat al-arab fi funūn al-adab* by al-NUWAIRĪ (twenty-one volumes so far published in Cairo from 1923-). In general, however, the works mentioned below should prove sufficient for most enquiries.

3.2.1 *9th century AD*

KHWĀRIZMĪ, Muḥammad ibn Mūsā al-, *Das Kitāb ṣūrat al-arḍ*; herausgegeben
    ... von Hans v MŽIK. Bibliothek arabischer Historiker und Geographen,
    3, Leipzig 1926, repr. Baghdad.

3.2.2 *10th century AD*

ṢUHRĀB (Ibn Sarābiyūn/Ibn Serapion), *Das Kitāb ᶜaǧa'ib al-aḳālīm as-sabᶜa*;
    herausgegeben ... von Hans v MŽIK. Bibliothek arabischer Historiker
    und Geographen, 5, Leipzig 1930, repr. Baghdad.

Both these works are closely related and deal with mathematical rather than descriptive geography. The calculation of latitude and longitude was also an interest of the great Persian polymath, al-BĪRŪNĪ, examples of whose geographical methods can be seen in the extracts collected and edited by A Zaki Velidi TOGAN

BĪRŪNĪ, Muḥammad ibn Aḥmad Abū al-Raiḥān al-, *Biruni's picture of the world : Ṣifat al-ma^{c}mūra ^{c}alā al-Bīrūnī*, Memoirs of the Archaeological Survey of India, 52, Delhi 1937, repr. 1972.

IBN KHURDĀDHBIH, ^{c}Ubaid Allāh ibn ^{c}Abd Allāh (Ibn Khurradādhbih), *Kitâb al-masâlik wa'l-mamâlik* (Liber viarum et regnorum), auctore Ibn Khordâdhbeh et excerpta e Kitâb al-Kharâdj, auctore Kodâma ibn Dja^{c}far; quae cum versione Gallica edidit, indicibus et glossario instruxit M J de GOEJE. Bibliotheca geographorum arabicorum, 6, Leiden 1889, repr. Baghdad, without the French translation.

Only part of QUDĀMA ibn Ja^{c}far's *Kitāb al-kharāj* has been preserved; the extracts edited here are from sections five and six. *al-Masālik* was earlier translated as: 'Le livre des routes et des provinces; publié, traduit et annoté par C Barbier de MEYNARD', *JA*, série 6, no.5, 1865.

IBN RUSTA, Aḥmad ibn ^{c}Umar, *Kitâb al-A^{c}lâk an-nafisa*, VII, auctore ... Ibn Rosteh, et Kitâb al-boldân, auctore ... al-Jakûbî; edit. secunda, edidit M J de GOEJE, Bibliotheca geographorum arabicorum, 7, Leiden 1892, repr. Baghdad.

The geographical section of *al-A^{c}lāq al-nafīsa* (volume 7) is the only surviving part and was translated as

Les atours précieux; traduction de Gaston WIET, Cairo 1955.

YA^{c}QŪBĪ, Aḥmad ibn Abī Ya^{c}qūb al-, *Kitāb al-buldān*. French tr. Gaston WIET, *Les pays*, Textes et traductions d'auteurs orientaux, 1, Cairo 1937.

al-YA^{c}QŪBĪ is also the author of a historical text - *Ta'rīkh al-Ya^{c}qūbī* (published in Leiden in two volumes in 1883, and in three volumes in Najaf in 1939 and 1964) - which contains valuable geographical information. The four works mentioned above, by IBN KHURDĀDHBIH, QUDĀMA ibn Ja^{c}far, IBN RUSTA and AL-YA^{c}QŪBĪ are all road books, illustrating postal routes and imperial itineraries in the ^{c}Abbāsid Empire.

IBN AL-FAQĪH, Aḥmad ibn Muḥammad, al-Hamadhānī, [*Mukhtaṣar kitāb al-buldān*]. *Compendium libri Kitâb al-boldân*, quod edidit, indicibus et glossario instruxit M J de GOEJE, Bibliotheca geographorum arabicorum, 5, Leiden 1885, repr. Baghdad.

Only the abridgement of the original has come down to us; it was translated as

Abrégé du livre des pays, traduit de l'arabe par H MASSÉ, Damascus 1973.
al-Mukhtaṣar can be seen as a move away from the road book formula towards the inclusion of descriptive geography in *adab* literature, since it contains a great deal of cultural and general information.

IṢṬAKHRĪ, Ibrāhīm ibn Muḥammad al-, [*al-Masālik wa'l-mamālik*]. *Viae regnorum: descriptio ditionis moslemicae*, edidit M J de GOEJE, Bibliotheca geographorum arabicorum, 1, Leiden 1870.

A more recent edition, with a useful introduction is

al-Masālik wa'l-mamālik, ed. by Muḥammad Jābir ᶜAbd al-āl al-ḤĪNĪ, Cairo 1961.

An abridged edition of *al-Masālik* known as *Kitāb al-aqālīm* was published in facsimile as

Liber climatum ..., curavit J H MOELLER, Gotha 1839, repr. Baghdad.

The text thus published was translated as

Das Buch der Länder, aus dem arabischen übersetzt von A D MORDTMANN, Schriften der Akademie von Hamburg, 1, band 2, Abtheilung, Hamburg 1845.

An earlier, though partial translation, is

Il Segistan, ovvero il corso del fiume Hindmund, tr. from *Kitāb al-aqālīm* by Antonio MODINI, Milan 1842.

IBN ḤAUQAL, Muḥammad, Abū 'l-Qāsim, [al-Masālik wa-al-mamālik], *Viae et regna: description ditionis moslemicae*, edidit M J de GOEJE, Bibliotheca geographorum arabicorum, 1, Leiden 1873.

Also published under the Arabic title of *Ṣūrat al-arḍ* in two volumes (the projected third volume containing preface, indices and notes was never issued) as

Opus geographicum ..., edidit, collato textu 1, editionis aliisque fontibus adhibitis J H KRAMERS, 2 vols, Leiden 1938-39.

A translation was published under the auspices of UNESCO as

Configuration de la terre (Kitāb Ṣūrat al-arḍ), introduction et traduction avec index par J H KRAMERS et G WIET, 2 vols, Paris 1964.

AL-IṢṬAKHRĪ and IBN ḤAUQAL are the first systematic geographers in Arabic. On the relationship between their works, their joint source, al-BALKHĪ, and their Persian derivatives, see the books mentioned above (3.1) and the article by V MINORSKY, 'A false Jayhānī', *BSOAS* 13, 1949-50.

ABŪ DULAF, Misᶜar ibn al-Muhalhil, *Vtoraya zapiska*, ed., tr. and comm. by P G BULGAKOV and A B KHALIDOV, Moscow 1960.

Republished in Cairo with an Arabic introduction as

al-Risāla al-thāniyya, Cairo 1970.

An earlier edition and translation is

Travels in Iran (c.A.D.950), Arabic text with an English tr. and comm. by V MINORSKY, Cairo 1955.

ABU DULAF's first journey is generally held to be a fabrication, but his second, to North and West Iran and Armenia, is authentic and interesting.

Ḥudūd al-ʿĀlam, an anonymous work written around 980 and ed. in facs. as *Ḥudud al-ʿalem*, V BARTOL'D (ed), Leningrad 1930.

Later editions are

Ḥudūd al-ʿālam, Jalāl al-dīn TIHRĀNĪ (ed), Tehran 1933.

Ḥudūd al-ʿālam min al-mashriq ilā al-maghrib, Manūchihr SUTŪDA (ed), Tehran 1962.

A good translation with excellent annotations was published as

Ḥudūd al-ʿālam : the regions of the world: a Persian geography ..., tr. and explained by V MINORSKY, *GMS*, NS.11, London 1937, 2nd ed. C E BOSWORTH (ed), 1970.

Addenda to the annotations were published by MINORSKY in *BSOAS* 17/1, 1955, pp.250-70.

MASʿŪDĪ, ʿAlī ibn al-Ḥusain al-, *Kitâb al-tanbîh wa'l-ischrâf*, edidit M J de GOEJE, Bibliotheca geographorum arabicorum, 8, Leiden 1894, repr. Beirut.

Although of more interest to the historian than the geographer, the early chapters contain some topographical information. A translation was published as

Le livre de l'avertissement et de la revision, traduction par B CARRA DE VAUX, Paris 1896.

MUQADDASĪ, Muḥammad ibn Aḥmad al-, (*Aḥsan al-taqāsīm fi maʿrifat al-aqālīm*), *Descriptio imperii moslemici*, edidit M J de GOEJE, Bibliotheca geographorum arabicorum, 3, Leiden 1877, repr. Baghdad.

Various partial translations have been made, the fullest, including the description of Iran, being

Aḥsanu-t-taqāsīm fi maʿrifat-l-aqālīm, tr. from the Arabic and ed. by G S A RANKING and R F AZOO, vol.1, fascicles 1-4 (all published), Bibliotheca Indica 889, 952, 1001, 1258, Calcutta 1897-1910. 4 parts. (Scheduled for reprinting by Biblio Verlag.)

AL-MUQADDASĪ is considered by both LE STRANGE and SCHOLTEN to be the greatest of the Arab geographers.

MUNAJJIM, Isḥāq ibn Ḥusain al-, (*Ākām al-marjān fi dhikr al-madā'in al-mashhūra fī kull makān*) 'Il compendio geografico arabo di Isḥāq ibn al-Ḥusayn', ed. and tr. with an intro. by Angela CODAZZI, *Rendiconti d. R. Accad. Naz. dei Lincei, Cl. di Scienze Morali*, serie 6, col.5, 1929, repr. Baghdad without the Italian translation.

A brief descriptive study of the major cities known to the Muslims.

3.2.3 *11th century AD*

NĀṢIR KHUSRAU, (*Safarnāma*), *Sefer Nameh: relation du voyage de Nassiri Khosrau* ..., publié, traduit et annoté ... par C SCHEFER, Paris 1881, repr. Amsterdam. Another ed. Berlin 1923, repr. Tehran. For translations of extracts see STOREY, p.1140.

An interesting account of the author's journeyings through Iran, the Levant and Egypt in the eleventh century.

BAKRĪ, ᶜAbdallāh ibn ᶜAbd al-ᶜazīz, Abū ᶜUbaid al-, *Kitāb muᶜjam mā istaᶜjama*: das geographische Wörterbuch; nach den Handschriften ... herausgegeben von Ferdinand WÜSTENFELD, four parts in two volumes, Gottingen 1876-77.

A later edition using additional manuscripts is

Muᶜjam mā istaᶜjama min asmā' al-bilād wa-al-mawāḍiᶜ, Muṣṭafā al-SAQQĀ (ed), 4 vols in 2, Cairo 1945-51.

A list of places, mainly in the Arabian Peninsula, mentioned in early Arabic literature.

3.2.4 *12th century AD*

IBN AL-BALKHĪ, *The Fársnáma*, G LE STRANGE and R A NICHOLSON (eds), *GMS*, NS.1, London 1921.

The Fārsnāma was translated as

Description of the province of Fars in Persia at the beginning of the fourteenth century A.D., tr. ... by G LE STRANGE, Royal Asiatic Society monographs, 14, London 1912.

The translation was also published separately in the *JRAS* for 1912, where LE STRANGE correctly placed the author in the twelfth century. Apart from the description of Fārs, much of the text is an account of pre-Islamic Persian dynasties.

ZUHRĪ, Muḥammad ibn Abī Bakr al-, (*Kitāb al-jaᶜrafiyya*), 'Kitāb al-Djaᶜrafiyya: mappemonde du calife al-Ma'mūn reproduite par Fazārī (IIIe/IXe s.), rééditée et commentée par Zuhri (VIe/XIIe s.); texte arabe avec introduction en français ... par Mohammad HADJ-SADOK', *BEI* 21, 1968.

One of the earliest Muslim cosmographies, containing much general information.

IDRĪSĪ, Muḥammad ibn Muḥammad al-, *Opus geographicum, sive Liber ad eorum delectationem qui terras peragrare studeant*, consilio et auctoritate E CERULLI, *et al.*, Leiden 1970- in progress.

The eighth fascicle appeared in 1979, completing the edition of the text of *Nuzhat al-mushtāq fi ikhtirāq al-āfāq*. An introduction, translation, commentary, glossary and indices are promised.

A complete translation already exists

Géographie d'Edrisi, traduit de l'arabe en français ... par P Amédée JAUBERT, 2 vols, Paris 1836-40.

The most famous of all Arab geographical works, written by the court geographer of Roger II of Sicily. The work is arranged by climes, i.e. zones of latitude.

GHARNĀṬĪ, Muḥammad ibn ^{c}Abd al-raḥīm, Abū Ḥāmid al-, 'Le Tuḥfat al-albāb', Gabriel FERRAND (ed), *JA* 207, 1925.

Also known as al-Māzinī, the author travelled from Granada to Baghdad, and from the latter made expeditions to Iran and southern Russia.

3.2.5 *13th century AD*

YĀQŪT ibn ^{c}Abdallāh, al-Ḥamawī, (*Mu^{c}jam al-buldān*), *Geographisches Wörterbuch* ..., herausgegeben von Ferdinand WÜSTENFELD, 6 vols, Leipzig 1866-73.

A subject index to the above, the most important Arabic geographical dictionary, was published by Oskar RESCHER as

Sachindex zu Wüstenfelds Ausgabe von Jâqûts Mu^{c}ǧam al-buldân nebst einem alphabetsichen Verzeichnis der darin angeführten Werke, Stuttgart 1928.

The recent (1955-57) Beirut edition in five volumes is based on Wüstenfeld's text.

An abridgement of *Mu^{c}jam al-buldān*, including additional information was made by ^{c}Abd al-mun^{c}im ibn ^{c}Abd al-ḥaqq al-BAGHDĀDĪ probably in the fourteenth century, and published as

Lexicon geographicum cui titulus est: Marāṣid al-iṭṭilā^{c} ^{c}alā asmā' al-amkina wa-al-biqā^{c} ..., edidit J G J JUYNBOLL (et J J B GAAL), 6 vols, Leiden 1854-64.

A new edition is

Marāṣid al-iṭṭilā^{c} ^{c}alā asmā' al-amkina wa-al-biqā^{c}, ^{c}Alī Muḥammad al-BAJĀWĪ (ed), 3 vols, Cairo 1954-55, repr. Beirut.

In addition to his indispensable Mu^{c}jam al-buldān, YĀQŪT also produced a dictionary of topographical homonyms.

—— (*Kitāb al-mushtarik waḍ^can wa'l-muftariq saq^can*). *Jacut's Moschtarik. das ist: Lexicon geographischer Homonyme* ..., herausgegeben von Ferdinand WÜSTENFELD, Göttingen 1846, repr. Baghdad.

QAZVĪNĪ, Zakarīyā ibn Muḥammad al-, *Kosmographie*, herausgegeben von Ferdinand WÜSTENFELD, 2 vols, Göttingen 1848-49.

The second volume contains *Āthār al-bilād wa-akhbār al-^cibād* and is the source of much geographical information. The first volume contains *^cAjā'ib al-makhlūqāt wa-gharā'ib al-maujūdāt*, and is much more cosmographical in approach. The recent (1960-) Beirut editions of *Āthār al-bilād* follow WÜSTENFELD's edition and have good indices.

3.2.6 *14th century AD*

DIMASHQĪ, Muḥammad ibn ^cAlī al-, (*Nukhbat al-dahr fī ^cajā'ib al-barr wa-al-baḥr*), *Cosmographie*, texte arabe publié ... par A F MEHREN, St Petersburg 1866, repr. Leipzig, and later Baghdad. French tr. *Manuel de la cosmographie du Moyen Age*, tr. A F MEHREN, Copenhagen 1874, repr. Amsterdam.

An uncritical but comprehensive cosmographical work.

ABU 'L-FIDĀ', Ismā^cīl ibn ^cAlī, (*Taqwīm al-buldān*), *Géographie*, texte arabe publié ... par M REINAUD et MacGuckin de SLANE, Paris 1840, repr. Baghdad. French tr. (preceded by an important general study of Muslim geography), M REINAUD and S GUYARD, *Géographie*, 2 vols in 3, Paris 1848-83.

A systematic geography, enriched by the author's own observations during his travels in Syria, Egypt, Arabia, but not, unfortunately, Iran.

MUSTAUFĪ, Ḥamdallāh, *The geographical part of the Nuzhat-al-Qulūb* ..., ed. and tr. G LE STRANGE, *GMS* 23, 2 vols, Leiden/London 1915-19. cf also G LE STRANGE, *Mesopotamia and Persia under the Mongols in the fourteenth century A.D.*, Asiatic Society Monographs, 5, London 1903.

An important survey of Iran under the Īl-Khāns; MUSTAUFĪ wrote an equally distinguished history - *Tārīkh-i guzīda* (edited and translated in two volumes, London 1910-13) - which yields valuable geographical notices.

IBN BAṬṬŪṬA, Muḥammad ibn ^cAbdallāh, *Voyages*, texte arabe accompagné d'une traduction par C DEFRÉMERY et B R SANGUINETTI, 4 vols, Paris 1853-56.

The first, and major, edition of *Tuḥfat al-nuẓẓār fī gharā'ib al-amṣār wa-^cajā'ib al-asfār*. An incomplete English translation, including, however, Ibn BAṬṬŪṬA's description of Iran, was published as

The travels, A.D.1325-1354, tr. with revisions and notes ... by H A R GIBB, Hakluyt Society, 2nd series, nos. 110, 117, 141, 3 vols, London 1958-

71. Vols 1 and 2 repr. together by P KRAUS.

One of the world's greatest globetrotters, Ibn BAṬṬŪṬA spent thirty years away from his home in Morocco, visiting East and West Africa, Spain, the entire Muslim world, India, South-East Asia and the Far East.

AL-ḤIMYARĪ, Muḥammad ibn ᶜAbd al-Munᶜim, *al-Rauḍ al-miᶜṭār fi khabar al-aqṭār*, Iḥsān ᶜABBĀS (ed), Beirut 1975.

A well indexed and important geographical dictionary.

3.2.7 *15th century AD*

ḤĀFIẒ ABRŪ, ᶜAbdallāh ibn Luṭfallāh, *Jughrāfiyā-yi Ḥāfiẓ Abrū*, qismat-i rubᶜ-i Khurāsān va Harāt, Māyil HARAVĪ (ed), Tehran 1971.

Other parts of ḤĀFIẒ ABRŪ's geography exist in manuscript, as does the geographical section of his *Kitāb-i tārīkh*.

3.2.8 *17th century AD*

IṢFAHĀNĪ, Ṣādiq, *The geographical works of Sádik Isfaháni*, tr. by JC from original Persian manuscript in the collection of Sir William Ouseley, Oriental Translation Fund, London 1832.

3.2.9 *Persian travellers in modern times* (in alphabetical order)

AFSHĀR, Īraj, *Yādgārhā-yi Yazd*, Tehran 1970.

Exhaustive survey of archaeological and other monuments in the Yazd area. A second volume, which seems not to have appeared, was to cover the city of Yazd itself.

FARMĀN-FARMĀ, Firūz Mīrzā, *Safarnāma-yi Kirmān va Baluchistān*, Manṣūra NIẒĀM-MĀFĪ (ed), Tehran 1963.

A journey through the south of Iran undertaken in 1880.

FASĀ'Ī SHĪRĀZĪ, Ḥasan, *Fārsnāma-yi Nāṣirī*, Tehran 1895-96.

Volume II, which has not so far been translated, contains a great deal of geographical and local information regarding the south of Iran.

HIDĀYAT, Riżā Qulī Khān, (*Sifāratnāma-yi Khwārazm*), *Relation de l'ambassade au Kharezm de Riza Qouly Khan*, publié , traduite et annoté par C SCHEFER, 2 vols, Paris 1876-79.

JAMĀLZĀDA, Sayyid Muḥammad ᶜAlī, *Ganj-i shāyigān*, Berlin 1917.

Detailed economic survey of Iran.

MARĀGHĪ, Muḥammad Ḥasan Khān Ṣanīᶜ al-daula, Iᶜtimād al-salṭana, *Maṭlaᶜ al-shams*, 3 vols, Tehran 1884-86.

—— *Mir'āt al-buldān-i Nāṣirī*, 4 vols, Tehran 1876-80.

Alphabetical dictionary of Persian towns and villages, extending only to the letter *jīm*.

—— *Al-tadvīn fī aḥvāl jibāl Sharvīn*, Tehran 1893-94.

Description of part of the area of the Alburz mountains.

MUẒAFFAR AL-DĪN SHĀH QĀJĀR, *Safarnāma-yi Shāh-i Īrān*, Allahabad 1915.

Account of the Shah's visit to Europe in 1900.

NAJAF QULĪ MĪRZĀ, *Journal of a residence in England, and of a journey from and to Syria, of their Royal Highnesses Reeza Koolee Meerza, Najaf Koolee Meerza, and Taymoor Meerza ...*, tr. by Assaad Y KAYAT (Asᶜad Yaᶜqūb KHAYYĀṬ), 2 vols, London 1839.

Diary of one of the princes who travelled to England in 1835-36.

NĀṢIR AL-DĪN SHĀH QĀJĀR, *Rūznāma*, Tehran 1869.

Diary of the Shah's first visit to Khurāsān in 1867.

—— *Safarnāma*, Tehran 1889.

Second visit to Khurāsān.

—— *Rūznāma-yi safar-i humāyūnī bi-Māzandarān*, Tehran 1877. Russian tr. *Puteshestviye Shakha Nasr-ed-Dina po Mazanderana*, tr. by E KORIANDER, St Petersburg 1887.

—— *Rūznāma-yi safar az Ṭihrān ilā Karbalā*, Tehran 1870.

Diary of visit to Karbalā in 1870.

—— *Rūznāma-yi safar-i Farangistān*, Tehran 1874 etc. English tr. J W REDHOUSE, *The diary of H.M. The Shah of Persia during his tour through Europe in A.D.1873*, London 1874.

The Shah's first visit to Europe.

—— *Rūznāma*, Tehran 1879. English tr. A HOUTUM-SCHINDLER and Baron L de NORMAN, *A diary kept by His Majesty the Shah of Persia, during his journey to Europe in 1878*, London 1879.

—— *Rūznāma-yi safar-i sivvum-i Farangistān*, Bombay 1891.

The third journey, undertaken in 1889.

PAHLAVĪ, Riżā Shāh, *Safarnāma-yi Khūzistān*, Tehran 1976.

PĪRZĀDA, Muḥammad ᶜAlī, *Safarnāma-yi Ḥājī Pīrzāda*, Ḥāfiẓ FARMĀNFARMĀYĀN (ed), 2 vols, Tehran 1963-65.

The first part of volume I and the last part of volume II describe journeys from Tehran to Bushire in 1886 and from Bushire to Isfahan in 1889. The remainder of the book covers the intervening journey through India, Egypt and Europe to Paris and London, and back to Istanbul and thence via Egypt, Damascus and Baghdad to Baṣra and Shīrāz.

RIŻĀ QULĪ MĪRZĀ QĀJĀR, *Safarnāma-yi Riżā Qulī Mīrzā nava-yi Fatḥ ᶜAlī Shāh*, Aṣghar Farmānfarmā'ī QĀJĀR (ed), Tehran 1967.

Riżā Qulī Mīrzā accompanied a mission to Europe in 1836.

SHĪRĀZĪ, Mīrzā Ṣāliḥ, *Safarnāma*, Ismāᶜīl RĀ'ĪN (ed), Tehran 1968.

Accompanied the first party of Iranian students to Britain in 1813.

SUTŪDA, Manūchihr, *Az Āstārā tā Astārābād*, 2 vols, Tehran 1970, 1972. Journeys in the Alburz mountains.

4. *EUROPEAN TRAVEL ACCOUNTS 13th-20th CENTURIES*

There is a long tradition of European travellers who both visited Iran and left accounts of their experiences; George CURZON indeed conveniently lists most of them in the preface to volume I of his *Persia and the Persian Question*, London 1892, pp.16-18, from which it can be seen that the earliest yet recorded European visitor was Friar William de Rubruquis 1253. Mediaeval accounts, however, of which perhaps justifiably the most famous is the narrative of Marco Polo of his travels of 1271-94, are sporadic due to the limited nature of the contact between Europe and Iran and the practical difficulties of access. Accounts multiplied during the late 16th and 17th centuries as the Ṣafavids encouraged the presence of European diplomats, merchants and craftsmen, but naturally dwindled as the chaotic and unstable political situation of 18th century Iran made travel hazardous. With the establishment of peace by the victory of the Qājārs at the end of the 18th century the way lay open for the renewal of contact, and consequently diplomatic missions from England and France presented their credentials to the Iranian court. From these beginnings the 19th century witnessed an ever increasing flow of diplomats, merchants, soldiers, technicians, missionaries - whose activities were matched by their literary efforts both in official reports and in less formal memoirs. Such accounts naturally reflect the varied points of view and opportunities for observation of their writers; the best of them are extremely valuable records of historical events, economic and social conditions, Iranian life, customs and art. As they are no numerous the method adopted here is to present an annotated and necessarily selective list based on general criteria of interest of subject matter, standard of accuracy and detail, and clarity of presentation.

The most complete survey of European travellers to Iran, with bibliographies, is to be found in

GABRIEL, Alfons, *Die Erforschung Persiens*, Vienna 1952.

For supplementary reading a useful handlist of the main European travellers with brief biographies may be found in

STEVENS, Roger, *The Land of the Great Sophy*, London 1962, 2nd ed. 1971, 3rd ed. 1979 :309-12.

Accounts of how the British came to travel in Iran are contained in

SEARIGHT, Sarah, *The British in the Middle East*, London 1979.

WRIGHT, Denis, *The English among the Persians*, London 1977.

There is no totally satisfactory bibliography of travellers and their works but

BEVIS, Richard (comp and ed), *Bibliotheca Cisorientalia - an annotated checklist of early English travel books on the Near and Middle East*, Boston 1973,

may be consulted for further titles.

4.1 *13th-16th centuries - in chronological order*

POLO, Marco, *The travels of Marco Polo*, tr. and intr. by Ronald LATHAM, Folio Society, London 1958.

Accessible and well-edited version of Marco POLO's journeys of 1271-94.

ODERICUS, Matthuissi (Friar Oderic), *Itinerarum fratris Odorice ... de mirabilibus Orientalium Tartarorum : The journey of Friar Odericus concerning strange things which he saw among the Tartars of the East*, Richard HAKLUYT, The Principal navigations, vol.2, London 1598.

Friar ODERIC's journey took place c.1325.

GONZALES DE CLAVIJO, Ruy, *Embajada al Gran Tamorlan*, Seville 1582. *Narrative of the Embassy of R G de C to the court of Timour at Samarcand 1403-06*, tr. for the first time with notes, a preface and an introductory life of Timour Beg by C R MARKHAM, Hakluyt Society, London 1859; G LE STRANGE, *Embassy to Tamerlane 1403-1406*, Broadway Travellers, London 1928.

BARBARO, Josafa, and Ambrogio CONTARINI, 'Travels to Tana and Persia', *A narrative of Italian travels in Persia in the fifteenth and sixteenth centuries*, tr. and ed. C GREY, Hakluyt Society, XLIX, London 1873.

BARBARO and CONTARINI travelled to the court of Uzun Ḥasan in 1474-75.

JENKINSON, Anthony, *Early voyages and travels to Russia and Persia by A Jenkinson and other Englishmen*, E D MORGAN and C H COOTE (eds), 2 vols, Hakluyt Society, London 1886.

JENKINSON and his colleagues travelled to Persia on behalf of the British Muscovy Trading Company 1562-80.

ALESSANDRI, Vincentio d', *Narrative of Vincentio d'Alessandri, Ambassador to the King of Persia for the ... Republic of Venice*.

Included in Josafa BARBARO and Ambrogio CONTARINI, *op.cit*.

ALESSANDRI was in Persia in 1571.

LINSCHOTEN, Jan Huygen von, *The voyage of J H van Linschoten to the East Indies*, from the old English translation of 1598, 2 vols, Hakluyt Society, London 1885.

LINSCHOTEN's travels lasted from 1583 to 1589.

4.2 *17th century*[1]

CHARDIN, Sir John, *Voyages en Perse et autres lieux de l'Orient*, 10 vols, Amsterdam/Paris 1711. Abr. English tr. Sir Percy SYKES, *Travels in Persia*, London 1927.

A classic account of European experience in 17th century Persia. CHARDIN, a Huguenot jeweller, was in Persia 1666, 1669, 1673-77, and made the most of his opportunities to observe and document both the country and its customs.

DAULIER DESLANDES, André, *Les Beautez de la Perse ou la description de ce qu'il y a de plus curieux dans ce royaume*, Paris 1673. English tr. Sir Arnold WILSON, *The Beauties of Persia*, London 1926.

The author was in Persia in 1665.

DU MANS, Le Père Raphaël, *Estat de la Perse en 1660*, Paris 1890.

Contemporary account of Persia by the head of the Capuchin Mission to Isfahan.

FIGUEROA, García de Silva, *L'Ambassade du D Garcias de Silva Figueroa*, Paris 1667.

The embassy was in Persia from 1614 to 1619.

FRYER, John, *A new account of East India and Persia in eight letters, being nine years travels begun 1672 and finished 1681*, London 1698, and later Hakluyt Society 1909-16.

HERBERT, Sir Thomas, *A relation of some years travaile, begun Anno 1626 into Afrique and the greater Asia, especially the territories of the Persian Monarchie, and some parts of the oriental Indies ... of their religion, language, habit ... and other matters concerning them.* Together with the proceedings and death of the three late ambassadors, Sir D(odmore) C(otton), Sir R(obert) S(hirley) and the Persian Nogdi-Beg .... by T H(erbert) Esquier, London 1634, rev. and enl. by the author three times in 1638, 1665, and 1677. Abr. and ed. Sir William FOSTER, *Travels in Persia*, Broadway Travellers Series, London 1928.

HERBERT accompanied the ill-fated mission of Sir Dodmore Cotton of 1626-28. His account is a lively and well-observed record of Persian life and customs.

KAEMPFER, Engelbert, *Amoenitatum exoticarum politico-physico-medicarum fasciculi 5, quibus continentur variae relationes observationes et descriptiones rerum Persicarum et ulterioris Asiae.* Lemgoviae 1712. English tr. *Journey into Persia and other oriental countries*, London

---

[1] The lists that follow are each in alphabetical order of author's names.

1736.

KAEMPFER was in Persia 1684-88.

MANDELSLO, Jean-Albert de, English tr. John DAVIES, *The voyages and travels of J Albert de Mandelslo ... into the East Indies from 1638-1640*, London 1662. French tr. Adam WICQUEFORT, *Voyages célébres et remarquables faits de Perse aux Indes Orientales* par Gentilhomme des Ambassadeurs du Duc de Holstein en Muscovie et Perse, Amsterdam 1727.

The journeys took place 1638-40.

OLEARIUS, Adam, *Relation du voyage en Moscovie, Tartarie, et Perse*, Paris 1639. *The voyages and travels of the Ambassadors sent by Frederick Duke of Holstein to the Grand Duke of Muscovy and the King of Persia*. Begun in the year 1633 and finished in 1639. Containing a compleat history of Muscovy, Tartary, Persia and other adjacent countries. Tr. by J DAVIES, London 1662, 2 parts.

Also German and Dutch editions.

SANSON, Père, *Voyage ou relation de l'état present du Royaume de Perse. Avec une dissertation curieuse sur les moeurs, religion et gouvernement de cette état*, Paris 1695.

The account refers to a visit made in 1683.

STRUYS, John, *The voyages and travels of John Struys through Italy, Greece, Muscovy, Tartary, Media, Persia, East-India, Japan and other countries in Europe, Africa and Asia*. Tr. from the Dutch by John MORRISON, London 1684.

STRUYS was in Persia 1671-72.

TAVERNIER, Jean-Baptiste, *Recueil de plusieurs relations et traitez ... de J B Tavernier divisé en cinq parties ... II Relation de ce qui c'est passé dans la negociation des deputez qui ont esté en Perse et aux Indes ... pour l'establissement du commerce*, Paris 1679. English tr. J PHILLIPS and E EVERARD, 2 vols, London 1684.

TAVERNIER stayed in the East from 1629 to 1675.

TEIXEIRA, Pedro, *The travels of Pedro Teixeira with his 'Kings of Hormuz' and extracts from his 'Kings of Persia'*, tr. and ann. by W F SINCLAIR, London 1902.

TEIXEIRA was in Persia in 1604.

THÉVENOT, Jean de, *Relation d'un voyage fait au Levant*, 2 vols, Paris 1665-74. English tr. *The travels of Monsieur Thévenot into the Levant*, I Turkey; II Persia; III The East Indies, London 1687.

THÉVENOT made this journey 1664-67.

VALLE, Pietro della, *Viaggi di P della V divisi in tre parti cioè la*

Turchia, la Persia, e l'India, Rome 1650.

The journal of one of the best known Italian travellers to Persia 1616-23.

4.3 *18th century*

BELL, John, of Antermony, *Travels from St Petersburg in Russia to diverse parts of Asia*, 2 vols, Glasgow 1763.

This work includes an account of a journey to Iṣfahān 1715-18 in the suite of Artemy Petrovich Valaisky, Russian Ambassador to S͟hāh Ḥusain.

BRUIN, Cornelis de, *Voyages par la Moscovie en Perse et aux Indes Orientales*, Amsterdam 1718, tr. into English 1737.

The author was in Persia 1703-04.

CAMPBELL, Donald, *A journey overland to India, partly by a route never gone before by any European*, London 1796.

CAPPER, J, *Observations on the passage to India*, London 1785.

FORSTER, George, *A journey from Bengal to England, through the northern part of India, Kashmire, Afghanistan and Persia and into Russia by the Caspian Sea*, 2 vols, London 1798.

FORSTER travelled in Persia 1783-84.

FRANCKLIN, William, *Observations made on a tour from Bengal to Persia in the years 1786-87*, Calcutta 1788, London 1790.

HANWAY, Jonas, *An historical account of the British trade over the Caspian Sea, with the author's journal of travels from England through Russia into Persia, and back through Russia, Germany and Holland*. To which are added the revolutions of Persia during the present century with the particular history of the great usurper Nadir Kouli. 4 vols, London, 1st ed. 1753, 2nd rev.ed. 1754.

HANWAY was in Persia 1743-48 and his account is one of the most important contemporary European sources for the reign of Nadir Shah.

KRUSINSKI, J T, *Histoire de la dernière revolution de Perse*, The Hague 1728. English tr. *The history of the revolution of Persia*, London 1728, Dublin 1729.

KRUSINSKI was in Persia 1705-25 and was therefore able to give an eye-witness account of the collapse of the Ṣafavid dynasty.

OLIVIER, Guillaume Antoine, *Voyage dans l'Empire Othoman, l'Égypte et la Perse*, 3 vols, Paris 1801-07.

OLIVIER was in Persia 1796. His account gives a useful survey of late 18th century affairs.

PITTON DE TOURNEFORT, Joseph, *Voyage du Levant ... contenant l'histoire ancienne et moderne de plusieurs isles de l'Archipel de Constantin-*

ople, des côtes de la Mer Noire, de l'Arménie, de la Georgie, des frontières de Perse et de l'Asie mineure, etc., Paris 1717, 2 tom. Tr. into English 1757.

PITTON DE TOURNEFORT was in Persia 1701.

PLAISTED, Bartholomew, *A journey from Calcutta in Bengal, by sea, to Busserah; from thence across the Great Desert to Aleppo and from thence to Marseilles and through France to England in the year 1750*, London 1758.

4.4 *19th century*

BELL, Gertrude, *Safar Nameh. Persian pictures. A book of travel*, London 1894, repr. 1928 with intr. by E Denison ROSS.

Sketches of Persia in 1892.

BENJAMIN, Samuel G W, *Persia and the Persians*, London 1887.

Detailed account containing much information on contemporary arts and crafts in the 1880s.

BINNING, Robert B M, *A journal of two years travel in Persia, Ceylon, etc.*, 2 vols, London 1857.

Written in the form of a travel diary containing detailed observations on life and customs in 1850.

BISHOP, Isabella Bird, *Journeys in Persia and Kurdistan*, 2 vols, London 1891.

Excellent account full of accurately and objectively reported information on tribal and village life, urban life, customs and costume, in 1890-91.

BODE, C A de, *Travels in Luristan and Arabistan*, 2 vols, London 1845.

Journey in 1841 by a member of the Russian Legation in Tehran.

BRADLEY-BIRT, F B, *Through Persia from the Gulf to the Caspian*, London 1909.

Contains careful descriptions of the buildings and monuments seen en route. Especially useful for descriptions of contemporary Tehran and Iṣfahān.

BROWNE, Edward Granville, *A year amongst the Persians*, Cambridge 1893, repr. 1927.

A classic work describing contemporary Persian life as experienced by BROWNE and including famous personalities whom he met in 1887-88.

BUCKINGHAM, James S, *Travels in Assyria, Media and Persia etc.*, 2 vols, London 1829, 2nd ed. London 1830.

Includes detailed descriptions of major monuments. The journey was made in 1815.

COLLINS, Edward T, *In the kingdom of the Shah*, London 1896.

COLLINS was a doctor who visited the Ẓill-i Sulṭān, who wished to consult him about an eye disease. His book contains detailed observations on upper-class Persian life.

CURZON, George N, *Persia and the Persian question*, 2 vols, London 1892.

Exhaustively detailed compendium on all aspects of Persia based on information collected during a six months visit in 1889 and supplemented by copious reading. An indispensable source.

DROUVILLE, Gaspard, *Voyage en Perse pendant les années 1812 et 1813*, 2 vols, St Petersburg 1819, 2nd ed. Paris 1825.

DROUVILLE served as an officer in the Czar's service. His account is valuable as one of the earliest descriptions after the re-establishment of contacts between Europe and Iran.

DUPRÉ, André, *Voyage en Perse, fait dans les années 1807, 1808 et 1809*, Paris 1819.

EASTWICK, Edward B, *Journal of a diplomate's three years' residence in Persia*, 2 vols, London 1865.

Useful account for descriptions of contemporary Persian architecture. The three years covered the period 1860-63.

FERRIER, J P, *Voyages en Perse, dans l'Afghanistan, le Béloutchistan, et le Turkestan*, 2 vols, Paris 1860. *Caravan journeys and wanderings in Persia, Afghanistan, Turkestan and Beloochistan with historical notices of the countries lying between Russia and India*, London 1856.

Account valuable for descriptions of places visited in 1844-46 which were not on the usual route of visitors to Iran.

FEUVRIER, Joannès, *Trois ans à la cour de Perse 1889-1892*, Paris 1899, 2nd ed. Paris 1906.

FEUVRIER was personal physician to Nāṣir al-dīn Shāh. His account therefore contains detailed information about the personalities of the Persian court and its life and customs. He also gives an accurate contemporary plan and description of the Gulistān Palace in Tehran.

FLANDIN, Eugène, and Pascal COSTE, *Voyages en Perse*, 2 vols, Paris 1851.

Detailed account by two architects who planned and recorded the major monuments of Ṣafavid Iṣfahān in 1840-41.

FOWLER, George, *Three years in Persia*, London 1841-42.

FRASER, James Baillie, *Narrative of a journey to Khorassan ... in 1821 and 1822 including some account of the countries to the north east of Persia*, London 1825.

This work and the three following works by the same author are important because he explored areas well off the beaten track at the time, noting the monuments he saw and the manners and customs of village and tribal groups. His second journey was in 1834-35.

—— *Travels and adventures in the Persian provinces on the southern banks of the Caspian Sea*, with an appendix containing short notices on the geology and commerce of Persia, London 1826.

—— *A winter's journey from Constantinople to Teheran with travels through various parts of Persia*, 2 vols, London 1838.

—— *Travels in Koordistan, Mesopotamia, etc. including an account of parts of those countries hitherto unvisited by Europeans*, 2 vols, London 1840.

GOLDSMID, Sir Frederick John, *Telegraph and travel*, London 1874.

Account of the construction of the first telegraph line in Persia in the 1860s including descriptions of people and places encountered.

—— *Eastern Persia: an account of the journey of the Persian Boundary Commission 1870-72*, 2 vols, London 1876.

Account includes valuable local observations of life and customs in the areas visited.

HOLMES, William R, *Sketches on the shores of the Caspian, descriptive and pictorial*, London 1845.

Includes descriptions and plans of local architecture.

HOMMAIRE DE HELL, Xavier, *Les steppes de la mer caspienne*, Paris 1843. English tr. *Travels in the steppes of the Caspian Sea, the Crimea, the Caucasus, etc.*, London 1847.

—— *Voyage en Turquie et en Perse ... pendant les années 1846, 1847 et 1848*, 3 vols, Paris 1854-56.

Well-illustrated account.

JAUBERT, Pierre Amedée, *Voyage en Arménie et en Perse fait dans les années 1805 et 1806*, Paris 1821.

Good descriptions of contemporary Tehran.

KEPPEL, George, *Personal narrative of a journey from India to England*, London 1827.

The journey was made in 1824.

KINNEIR, J Macdonald, *A geographical memoir of the Persian empire*, London 1813. French tr. G DROUVILLE, 2 vols, St Petersburg 1827.

—— *Journey through Asia Minor and Koordistan*, London 1818.

LAYARD, A H, *Early adventures in Persia, Susiana and Babylonia including a residence among the Bakhtiyari and other wild tribes before the discovery of Nineveh*, 2 vols, London 1887.

Lived among the Bakhtiyārī tribes for two years (1840-42). Gives an account of contemporary Persian events from their point of view and describes their way of life.

LYCKLAMA A NIJEHOLT, T M Chevalier, *Voyage en Russie, au Caucase et en Perse*, 4 vols, Paris/Amsterdam 1872-75.

Account of two journeys in Persia in 1866 and 1867.

MACKENZIE, Charles Francis, *Safarnāma-yi shamāl*, tr. into Persian by Manṣūra IṬṬIḤĀDIYA (Niẓām-Māfī), Tehran 1980.

MACKENZIE was appointed in 1857 as the first British consul in Basht.

MALCOLM, Sir John, *Sketches of Persia*, 2 vols, London 1815.

Memoirs of the ambassador's third journey to Persia in 1810.

MORIER, James J, *A journey through Persia, Armenia and Asia Minor to Constantinople in the years 1808 and 1809 in which is included some account of the proceedings of His Majesty's Mission under Sir Harford Jones, Bart., to the Court of the King of Persia*, London 1812.

—— *A second journey through Persia, Armenia and Asia Minor to Constantinople between the years 1812 and 1816: with a journal of the voyage by the Brazils and Bombay to the Persian Gulph; together with an account of the proceedings of His Majesty's Embassy under Sir Gore Ousely, Bart.*, London 1818.

In these two works MORIER accurately reports all that he observed during his travels, and was the first traveller to publish an account of the Sāsānian ruins and rock reliefs at Bīshāpūr and to identify the tomb of Cyrus at Pasargadae.

NAPIER, Malcolm, *Five years in a Persian town*, London 1905.

Account of Yazd and its life by a missionary.

ORSOLLE, Ernest, *La Caucase et la Perse*, Paris 1885.

Excellent topographical descriptions including a detailed one of contemporary Tehran.

OUSELEY, Sir William, *Travels in various countries of the East more particularly Persia*, 3 vols, London 1819-23.

Accompanied his brother Sir Gore OUSELEY to Persia in 1811. Explored Fārs province extensively, recording archaeological sites at Dārāb, Fasā and Sarvistān. His book contains a notable survey of Persian antiquities including detailed notes on Persepolis and Pasargadae; he was also one of the first Europeans to research into Persian miniature painting.

PORTER, Sir Robert Ker, *Travels in Georgia, Persia, Armenia, Ancient Babylonia ... during the years 1817, 1818, 1819 and 1820*, 2 vols, London 1821-22.

Made more detailed and accurate descriptions and drawings than any of his contemporaries of Persian antiquities. First European to study Sāsānian reliefs at Tāq-i Bustān and to sketch reliefs at Bīsitūn. Also the first to visit Takht-i Sulaimān.

POWELL, T S, *Personal narrative of a journey through part of Persia in 1833-34*, London 1835.

PRICE, William, *Journal of the British Embassy to Persia*, London 1825.
Account written in diary form of the towns and monuments he encountered in 1811.

RICH, Claudius J, *Narrative of a residence in Koordistan, and on the site of ancient Nineveh; with journal of a voyage down the Tigris to Baghdad and an account of a visit to Shirauz and Persepolis*, 2 vols, London 1836.
RICH's account is valuable for his observations on Pasargadae and its role in Achaemenid history. He was also interested in Persian manuscripts, coins and seals. His journey took place in 1820.

ROCHEHUART, Comte Julien de, *Souvenirs d'une voyage en Perse*, Paris 1867.
Valuable and detailed accounts of contemporary Persian arts and crafts such as ceramic, metal and lacquer production.

ROSEN, Friedrich, *Oriental memories of a German diplomatist*, New York n.d. (1930?)
The author was in Persia in 1887, 1891-98, and 1898-99.

SHEIL, Lady, *Glimpses of life and manners in Persia*, London 1856.
Wife of the British Minister to the Persian court she was in a position to visit the family of Nāṣir al-dīn Shāh and has left a valuable account of their social life and costumes.

STACK, Edward, *Six months in Persia*, 2 vols, London 1882.
Written in the form of a daily travel diary (1881) containing useful descriptions of monuments.

SYKES, Ella, *Through Persia on a sidesaddle*, London 1898, 2nd ed. London 1901.

—— *Persia and its people*, London 1910.
In these two books she gives a detailed account of the various national groups in Persia together with details of manners and costume, as observed in 1894.

SYKES, Major Percy Molesworth, *Ten thousand miles in Persia or eight years in Iran*, London 1902.
Opened the British Consulate in Kerman in 1894 followed by consulates in Nuṣratābād, Turbat-i Ḥaidarī and Bīrjand. Work contains excellent descriptions of archaeological sites and monuments.

TANCOIGNE, J M, *Lettres sur la Perse et la Turquie d'Asie*, Paris 1819.

TEXIER, Charles, *Descriptions de l'Arménie, la Perse et la Mésopotamie publié sous les auspices des Ministères de l'Interieur et de l'Instruction publique*, 3 vols, Paris 1842-52.

Contains excellent drawings and plans of the major Persian monuments, made in 1838.

WARING, E Scott, *A tour to Sheeraz, by the route of Kazroon and Feerozabad; with various remarks on the manners, customs, laws, language and literature of the Persians. To which is added a history of Persia, from the death of Kureem Khan to the subversion of the Zand Dynasty*, London 1807.

Valuable account of Shīrāz and its products in 1802.

WILLS, C J, *In the land of the Lion and Sun or Modern Persia being experiences of life in Persia from 1866 to 1881*, London 1883, 2nd ed. 1891.

WILLS was a medical doctor with the Persian Telegraph Department working in Tehran, Hamadān, Işfahān and Shīrāz. He liked Persia and made the most of his professional contacts to leave excellent descriptions of social life, industry, and some of the best descriptions of Persian costume.

4.5 *20th century*

With the improvement in travel facilities during the twentieth century, travel accounts of Iran became at the same time more numerous and either more specialised or more trivial. A comprehensive bibliography of books and articles published up to the outbreak of the Second World War is given in GABRIEL, *op.cit*. The following selection also includes a few items not listed there, as well as some post-war accounts.

BLUNT, Wilfrid, *A Persian Spring*, London 1957.

A tour of Iran and Afghanistan in 1956.

BYRON, Robert, *The road to Oxiana*, London 1934, repr. 1981.

A journey through Iran undertaken in the 'thirties.

D'ALLEMAGNE, Henri R, *Du Khorassan au pays des Bakhtiaris*, 4 vols, Paris 1911.

A journey made in 1907. Extremely useful for information on contemporary arts and crafts. Copiously illustrated.

EMANUEL, W V, *The Wild Asses. A Journey through Persia*, London 1939.

Visit by an international student party in 1936.

GABRIEL, Alfons, *Durch Persiens Wüste*, Stuttgart 1935.

—— *Aus der Einsamkeiten Irans*, Stuttgart 1939.

GABRIEL visited Iran, mainly Balūchistān, in 1928, 1933 and 1937.

HALE, F, *From Persian Uplands*, London 1920.

Letters from a bank manager, 1913 to 1919.

HAY, H W, and Sidney, *By Order of the Shah*, London 1937.

Light-hearted and not always accurate account of travel in Iran in the 'thirties.

HUBBARD, G E, *From the Gulf to Ararat*, Edinburgh/London 1916.

Personal account of the International Boundary Commission of 1914.

JACKSON, A V Williams, *Persia, past and present*, a book of travel and research, New York 1906.

A journey of primarily archaeological interest undertaken during the first half of 1903.

MORTON, Rosalie Slaughter, *A Doctor's Holiday in Iran*, New York/London 1940.

Includes information on the position of women in Iran in the mid 'thirties.

NIEDERMAYER, O von, *Im Weltkrieg vor Indiens Toren*, Hamburg 1936.

Wartime expedition through Persia in 1915.

PAYNE, Robert, *Journey to Persia*, London 1951.

A journey undertaken in the spring of 1949 by the Asia Institute of New York.

RODKIN, Angela, *Unveiled Iran*, London n.d.

A journey through Iran in 1937.

ROSEN, Countess Maud von, *Persian Pilgrimage*, London 1937.

Somewhat idiosyncratic account but valuable for descriptions of Persian social life and customs during a period of transition.

SEVERIN, Timothy, *Tracking Marco Polo*, London 1964.

A journey through north Iran in 1961.

SITWELL, Sacheverell, *Arabesque and honeycomb*, London 1957.

The author visited Tehran, Mas͟hhad, Iṣfāhan and S͟hīrāz in 1956.

SMITH, Anthony, *Blind White Fish in Persia*, London 1953.

Valuable for the description of the *qanāt* system, as well as for glimpses of village life.

STARK, Freya, *The Valleys of the Assassins*, London 1934.

—— *Beyond Euphrates*, London 1951.

Accounts of the author's travels in Iran from 1929 to 1932.

STARMÜHLNER, Ferdinand, *Salzseen und Steppen*, Vienna 1956.

Journeys across Iran and Afghanistan in 1949-50.

STEIN, Sir Aurel, *Old Routes of Western Iran*, London 1940.

Narrative of an archaeological expedition in 1935-36.

STROMBERG, Kyra, *Der grosse Dürst*, Hamburg 1954.

Journey through Iran in 1951.

STUART, Donald, *The struggle for Persia*, London 1902.

A journey to Tehran in 1901.

SURATGAR, Olive, *I Sing in the Wilderness*, London 1951.

Experiences of an Englishwoman married to an Iranian university lecturer in 1936.

SYKES, P M, 'A fifth journey in Persia', *GJ* xxviii, 1906.

—— 'A sixth journey in Persia', *GJ* xxxvii, 1911 :1-19, 149-65.

—— 'A seventh journey in Persia', *GJ* xlv, 1915 :357-71.

Covers the author's journeys from 1902 to 1913.

WILSON, Sir Arnold, *S.W. Persia: A political officer's diary, 1907-1914*, London 1941.

Includes an eyewitness account of the discovery of oil at Masjid-i-Sulaimān in 1908.

5. *GUIDES AND PHOTOGRAPHIC RECORDS*

5.1 *Guide books*

The following guide-books have been selected, from a large number published both in Iran and elsewhere, for their compactness, accuracy and comprehensiveness. It must be borne in mind that, even when tourism in Iran is resumed, much of the information about hotels, restaurants, shops, and so on, will be out-of-date. Nevertheless, until revised editions have been compiled, those listed below will be found useful.

BOULANGER, Robert, *Hachette World Guides, The Middle East - Lebanon, Syria, Jordan, Iraq, Iran*, English tr. J S HARDMAN, Paris 1966. Section - Iran :767-1046.

Thorough and detailed guide which includes information accurate at the date of publication. Although certain facts have inevitably been superseded this is still the basic work of reference. It contains succinct introductory sections on Iran's geography, history, economic life, transport system and a select bibliography. These are followed by chapters devoted either to the most important cities or to certain routes. Within each type of chapter the information is admirably classified for ease of reference - practical information, list of main places of interest, then a careful account of each quarter, building, museum, etc. Select list of Persian phrases and words included.

—— *Les Guides Bleus - Iran, Afghanistan*, Paris 1974. Section on Iran :17-275.

Essentially an updated version of 'The Middle East ...' above though in less detail. Improvements, however, include detailed route maps and places classified in alphabetical order for quick reference. Select list of Persian words and phrases included.

FODOR, Eugene, *Fodor's Guide to Iran*, London 1977.

The most recent of those listed, living up to the standards of the series of which it forms a part.

HUREAU, Jean, *Iran today*, Paris 1975. Also published in French and German.

Beautifully illustrated guide-book.

MATHESON, Sylvia A, *Persia: an archaeological guide*, London 1972, 2nd ed. 1976. German tr. 1980.

The most detailed yet compact guide at present available which concentrates on archaeological sites and monuments from prehistory to the end of the Saljuq period (early 13th century) grouped by province. Especially valuable for the descriptive survey plus site plans of current archaeological work, which always needs constant revision as the additions to the second edition show. Text supplemented by chronological charts, bibliography and glossary.

MESHKATI, Nosratollah (MISHKĀTĪ, Nuṣratallāh), *Fihrist-i bināhā-yi tarikhī va amākin-i bāstānī-yi Īrān*, Tehran 1971. English tr. *A list of the historical sites and ancient monuments of Iran*, Tehran 1974.

Illustrated gazetteer of all monuments and sites registered by the National Organization for the Protection of the Historical Monuments of Iran grouped according to region. Includes monuments, especially for the Islamic period, not featured in the other guidebooks and provides translations of main inscriptions. Supplementary index classified according to function of monument.

SAMI, Ali, *Shiraz*, Shiraz, 2nd ed. 1971. English tr. Rev R N SHARP.

A discursive personalized account written by a Shīrāzī historian. Worth consulting as an addition to the more formally organized guide books especially for information on the monuments and gardens of local rather than international reputation.

STEVENS, Roger, *The land of the Great Sophy*, *op.cit.* 4.

Excellently written and enthusiastic account combining clear introductory sections on history, religion and art with nine chapters on monuments and sites grouped according to region. Second and third editions especially valuable for descriptions of otherwise little-known monuments and clear plans of all cities including the less frequently visited Qazvīn, Yazd, Kirmān. Excellent historical appendix of travellers to Iran and bibliography.

TAGG, Roger, *Travels with a Peykan*, Tehran 1975.

Practical account of author's travel experiences grouped into 35 tours beginning with short excursions from Tehran by car and extending into three-four day expeditions. Covers a geographical area radiating from Tehran to Ardabīl, Basṭām, Gunbad-i Qābūs in the north, to Hamadān in the west and to Naṭanz and Kāshān in the south. Includes descriptions and street plans of less frequently visited towns such as Simnān. Full of useful facts about driving conditions, travelling time, hotel stops and clear route directions. Basic Persian words and phrases included.

WAGRET, P (ed), *Nagel's encyclopedia guide*, Iran/Geneva 1972.

Extensive introduction to Iran's history, geography, economy, culture and art followed by chapters giving lively and detailed descriptions of major cities and regions. City plans do not, however, match the standard of the text.

5.2 *Volumes of photographs*

Guide-books may be of little practical use at present, when tourism in Iran has come to a standstill. In the absence of personal visits, photographs can help to convey something of the atmosphere of the land, its buildings and its inhabitants. The following list covers published works whose interest lies wholly or mainly in the photographs accompanying the text.

BALL, Warwick, and Antony HUTT, *Persian landscape: a photographic essay*, London 1978.

BENY, Roloff, *Persia, bridge of turquoise*, with essay and notes by Seyyed Hossein NASR and Mitchell CRITES, New York 1975.

—— and Mitchell CRITES, *Iran: elements of destiny*, New York 1978.

A pictorial rendering of life and art in Iran in the 20th century.

COSTA, A, *Persia*, with notes by Laurence LOCKHART, London 1957.

GHIRSHMANN, Roman, Vladimir MINORSKY, and Ramesh SANGHVI, *Persia: the immortal kingdom*, photographs by William MACQUITTY, London 1971.

GRAEFE, Axel von, *Iran: das neue Persien*, Berlin/Zurich 1937.

HOLTZER, Ernst, *Īrān dar yak-ṣad u sīzdah sāl pīsh*, ed. and tr. Muḥammad ᶜĀSIMĪ, part 1, Iṣfahān, Tehran 1976.

Photographs taken by a German telegraphist between 1864 and 1884. Text in German and Persian.

LOCKHART, Laurence, *Famous cities of Iran*, Brentford 1939, rev. and expanded, *Persian cities*, London 1960.

MORATH, Inge, *From Persia to Iran*, with notes by Edouard SABLIER, New York

1960.

WOOD, Roger, *Persia*, intr. by James MORRIS, notes by Denis WRIGHT, London 1969.

IX

HISTORY

1. *GENERAL*

1.1 *Introductory works*

Many introductory works on Iran contain an outline history of the country. Most of these are too sketchy and inaccurate to be of much use, but the following are worth mentioning (see also II 1.2).

BAUSANI, Alessandro, *I Persiani*, Florence 1962. English tr. J B DONNE, *The Persians*, London 1971.

BOYLE, J A (ed), *Persia: History and Heritage*, London 1978.

GHIRSHMANN, Roman, Vladimir MINORSKY, and Ramesh SANGHVI, *Persia: the immortal kingdom*, *op.cit*. VIII 5.2.

MINORSKY, Vladimir, 'Storia dell'Iran islamico', *Civiltà dell'oriente*, vol.I, Rome 1956 :459-513.

ROSS, E Denison, *The Persians*, Oxford 1931.

1.2 *General histories*

No really satisfactory general history of Iran exists, though the gap will be well filled when the *Cambridge History* is complete.

Cambridge History of Iran, vol.I, The land of Iran, W B FISHER (ed), Cambridge 1968; vol.IV, The period from the Arab invasion to the Saljuqs, R N FRYE (ed), Cambridge 1975; vol.V, The Saljuq and Mongol periods, J A BOYLE (ed), Cambridge 1968.

In the meantime we are dependent on

SYKES, Percy M, *A history of Persia*, 2 vols, London 1915, repr. and updated 1921, 1930. Persian tr. Sayyid Muḥammad Taqī FAKHR-DĀʿĪ Gīlānī, *Tārīkh-i Īrān*, Tehran 1944, 1951.

Old-fashioned in its method, it nevertheless offers a comprehensive account of Persian history from the earliest times to the present day.

A great deal of history is also available in

BROWNE, Edward G, *A literary history of Persia*, 4 vols. Originally published separately, 1902, 1906, 1920, 1924. Repr. as a set, Cambridge 1928, and subsequent reprints. Persian tr. ᶜAlī Pashā ṢĀLIḤ, *Tārīkh-i adabī-yi Īrān*, Tehran 1954.

In Persian the best known modern histories are

FURŪGHĪ Zukā' al-mulk, Muḥammad Ḥusain Khān, *Tārīkh-i Īrān*, Tehran 1905.

PARVĪZ, ᶜAbbās, *Tārīkh-i du hazār u panṣad-sāla-yi Īrān*, 3 vols, Tehran 1964.

RĀZĪ, ᶜAbdallāh, *Tārīkh-i mufaṣṣal-i Īrān*, Tehran 1938? repr. 1956.

A useful reference work is

PĀZĀRGĀD, Bahā' al-dīn, *Krunūlūzhī-yi tārīkhī-yi Īrān*, Tehran 1966.

Chronological outline of Iranian history, 2850 BC to 1963 AD.

In Russian the following works are useful.

GAFUROV, B G, *et al*, *Istoriya Tadzhikskogo naroda*, vol.I, Moscow 1963; vol.II (in two parts) 1964.

The first two volumes cover the general history of Khurāsān and Central Asia, volume III being concerned only with modern Tajikistan.

—— *Tadzhiki*, Moscow 1972.

General history of the Iranian areas of Central Asia from the earliest times to the first half of the 18th century.

PIGULEVSKAYA, N V, *et al.*, *Istoriya Irana s drevneishikh vremen do kontsa 18 veka*, Leningrad 1958. French tr. *L'histoire de l'Iran depuis les anciens temps jusqu'à la fin du XVIIIe siècle*. Persian tr. Karīm KISHĀVARZ, 2 vols, Tehran 1967.

The history of Iran is also covered in the general histories of the Islamic world, including

BROCKELMANN, Carl, *Geschichte der islamischen Völker und Staaten*, Munich/Berlin 1939. English tr. (rev.), Joel CARMICHAEL and Moshe PERLMANN, *History of the Islamic peoples*, London 1949, repr. 1979.

HODGSON, Marshall G S, *The Venture of Islam*, 1. The classical age of Islam; 2. The expansion of Islam in the middle periods; 3. The gunpowder empires and modern times. 3 vols, Chicago/London 1974.

HOLT, P M, Ann K S LAMBTON, and Bernard LEWIS (eds), *Cambridge History of Islam*, 2 vols, Cambridge 1970, repr. (paperback, 4 vols) 1977.

MUIR, William, *The Caliphate, its rise, decline and fall*, Edinburgh 1883 and reprs. New and rev.ed. 1915 and reprs.

SPULER, Bertold, *Geschichte der islamischen Länder*, 3 vols, Leiden 1952-59. English tr. F R C BAGLEY, *The Muslim world. A historical survey*, 4 vols, Leiden 1960-81.

General histories of neighbouring areas include

LONGRIGG, Stephen H, *Four centuries of modern Iraq*, Oxford 1925.

SYKES, Percy M, *A history of Afghanistan*, 2 vols, London 1940.

WILSON, Arnold T, *The Persian Gulf*, Oxford 1928.

The following reference works will be found useful.

AITCHISON, C U, *A collection of treaties, engagements and sanads relating to India and neighbouring countries*, Calcutta 1909, (4th rev.ed.)

Volume xii contains the treaties relating to Persia, the Arab principalities in the Persian Gulf, and Oman.

BOSWORTH, Clifford E, *The Islamic dynasties*, Edinburgh 1967, repr. 1980. Russian tr. P A GRYAZNAVICH, *Musulmanskiye dinastii*, Moscow 1971. Persian tr. Farīdūn BADRA'Ī, *Silsilahā-yi islāmī*, Tehran 1970.

This largely, but not entirely, supersedes

LANE-POOLE, Stanley, *The Mohammadan dynasties*, London 1893, repr. Beirut 1966. Russian tr. V BART'OLD, *Musul'manskiye dinastii*, St Petersburg 1899. Turkish tr. H EDHEM, *Duval-i islamiyya*, Istanbul 1927.

For those who require greater detail, the essential work is

ZAMBAUR, Eduard von, *Manuel de généalogie et de chronologie pour l'histoire de l'Islam*, Hanover 1927, repr. Bad Pyrmont 1955. Arabic tr. Aḥmad Maḥmud ḤASAN, *et al.*, *Mu*ᶜ*jam al-ansāb wa'l-usarāt al-ḥākima fī'l-ta'rīkh al-islāmī*, Cairo 1951, repr. Baghdad 1971.

GUILLON, A, *Essai bibliographique sur les dynasties musulmanes de l'Iran*, Madrid 1957.

Comprehensive list of dynasties with references to the relevant primary sources.

HUREWITZ, J C, *Diplomacy in the Near and Middle East: a documentary record*, 2 vols, Princeton/London 1956.

JUSTI, Ferdinand, *Iranisches Namenbuch*, Marburg 1895.

Pages 390-479 contain a series of genealogical tables of pre-Islamic and Islamic Iranian dynasties.

SAUVAGET, Jean, *Introduction à l'histoire de l'orient musulman. Éléments de bibliographie*, Paris 1943, rev. by Claude CAHEN, Paris 1961. English tr. *Introduction to the history of the Muslim east. A bibliographical guide*, Berkeley 1965.

1.3 *Classical histories in Persian and Arabic*

A comprehensive list of historical works in Persian will be found in

STOREY, C A, *Persian literature*, *op.cit.*, vol.I 'General history', :61-158, 1229-51; 'History of Persia', :237-366, 1268-1300.

Among the more important are

ṬABARĪ, Abū Jaᶜfar Muḥammad b Jarīr, *Kitāb akhbār al-rusul wa'l-mulūk*,

M J de GOEJE (ed), *Annales auctore Abu Djafar Muhammad b Djarīr al-Tabarī*, 15 vols, Leiden 1879-1901. 13 vols, Beirut 1965-66. German tr. (part), Th NOELDEKE, *Geschichte der Perser und Araber zur Zeit der Sasaniden*, Leiden 1879, repr. 1973. Persian tr. Abu'l-qāsim PĀYANDA, *Tārīkh-i Ṭabarī*, 12 vols, Tehran 1973-75. Persian abr. Abū ᶜAlī Muḥammad b Muḥammad al-BALᶜAMĪ, *Tarjama-yi tārīkh-i Ṭabarī* (c.352/964), Lucknow 1874, Cawnpore 1896, 1916. French tr. L DUBEUX and H ZOTENBERG, *Chronique de Abou-Djafar-Mohammed Tabari*, 4 vols, Paris 1867-74. English tr. (part), Elma MARIN, *The reign of al-Muᶜtaṣim (833-842)*, New Haven, Conn. 1951.

BĪRŪNĪ, Abū Raiḥān Muḥammad b Aḥmad, *Al-āthār al-bāqiya ᶜan al-qurūn al-khāliya*, C E SACHAU (ed), Leipzig 1877, repr. Leipzig 1923, Baghdad 1963. Persian tr. A DĀNĀSIRISHT, Tehran 1942, repr. 1973. English tr. C E SACHAU, *The chronology of ancient nations*, London 1879, repr. 1967. Russian tr. M A SALIE, vol.I, Tashkent 1957. Turkish tr. Ṣāliḥ ZAKĪ, Istanbul 1911.

Portions have been translated into other languages. The original work was composed c.400/1000.

GARDĪZĪ, Abū Saᶜīd ᶜAbd al-ḥayy, *Zain al-Akhbār*, Muhammad NAZIM (ed), E G Browne Memorial Series, 1, Berlin 1928. Muḥammad QAZVĪNĪ (ed), Tehran 1937. ᶜAbd al-ḥayy ḤABIBI (ed), Bunyād-i Farhang-i Īrān 27, Tehran 1968.

Written c.440/1050.

JŪZJĀNĪ, Abū ᶜUmar ᶜUsmān, Minhāj-i Sirāj, *Ṭabaqāt-i Nāṣirī*, W N LEES, Khādim ḤUSAIN, ᶜABD AL-ḤAYY (eds) (part only), Calcutta 1863-64. English tr. H G RAVERTY (starting with the Ṭāhirids), Bibliotheca Indica, 2 vols, Calcutta 1873-81, repr. New Delhi 1970, Lahore 1977.

Compiled in 657-8/1259-60.

RASHĪD AL-DĪN, Fażlallāh, *Jāmiᶜ al-tavārīkh*, vol.I, part 1, A A ROMASKEVICH (ed) *et al.*, Moscow 1965; vol.II, part 1, A A ALI-ZADE (ed), Moscow 1980; vol.III, A A ALI-ZADE (ed), with Russian tr. by A K ARENDS, Baku 1957. English tr. J A BOYLE, *The Successors of Genghis Khan*, New York 1971. See also HĀFIẒ-I ABRŪ below.

Originally written, in Arabic and Persian recensions, between 700/1300 and 710/1310. Translations of other parts are listed in STOREY, *op.cit.*

MUSTAUFĪ, Qazvīnī Ḥamdallāh, *Tārīkh-i guzīda* ... reproduced in facsimile ... with an introduction by E G BROWNE, *GMS*, vol.xiv, 1, Leiden/London 1910. ᶜAbd al-Ḥusain NAVĀ'Ī (ed), Tehran 1960. English tr. (abr.) Edward G BROWNE, *GMS*, vol.xiv, 2, Leiden/London 1913.

Written in 730/1330.

ḤĀFIẒ-I ABRŪ, S̲h̲ihāb al-dīn ᶜAbdallāh, *Zail-i Jāmiᶜ al-tavārīk̲h̲*, ed. and
    French tr. K̲h̲ān-bābā BAYĀNĪ, Paris 1936 (trans.), Tehran 1939 (text).
Covers the period from 706/1306 to 795/1392.

MĪR K̲H̲WĀND, Muḥammad b K̲h̲āvandshāh, *Raużat al-ṣafā*, Bombay 1848 etc. Teh-
    ran, 2 vols, 1853-56 (see also HIDĀYAT below 6.3.1), Lucknow 1874.

MĪR K̲H̲WĀND died in 903/1498, but his work was continued by other hands, in
the case of the Tehran edition to 1856. Numerous extracts have been published and translated (see STOREY I, :98-100).

K̲H̲WĀNDAMĪR, G̲h̲iyās̲ al-dīn, *Ḥabīb al-siyar fī ak̲h̲bār afrād al-bashar*, Teh-
    ran 1855, Bombay 1857. Jalāl al-dīn HUMĀ'Ī (ed), 4 vols, Tehran n.d.
    (1954?).

A general history to 930/1524.

Reference should also be made to III 1. and 4.

2. PRE-ISLAMIC IRAN

2.1 Archaeology

2.1.1 Bibliographies

There are two bibliographies dealing solely with the archaeology of Iran.

BALZER, Wolfgang and Leo TRÜMPELMANN, *Der deutschsprachige Beitrag zur*
    archäologischen und kunstgeschichtlichen Erforschung Irans: eine
    Bibliographie. Veröffentlichungen des Arbeitskreises Archäologie, 1,
    Band 1 (bis 1945), Türkenfeld 1977.

BERGHE, Louis van den, *Bibliographie analytique de l'archéologie de l'Iran*
    ancien. Avec la collaboration de B de WULF et E HAERINCK, Leiden 1979.
    Suppl.1, 1978-80, Leiden 1981.

The following works contain important sections on Iranian archaeology.

ABOLHAMD, Abdolhamid and Nasser PAKDAMAN, *Bibliographie française ...*, *op.*
    cit. II 2.2, vol.2, 'L'art, l'architecture et l'archeologie', :155-
    224.

AZMOUDEH (ĀZMŪDA), Aryan, *Kitābshināsī-yi hunar-i Īrān-i qabl az Islām*,
    Tehran 1977.

572 items in Persian.

—— *A bibliography of pre-Islamic Persian art*, Tehran 1977.

2872 items in European languages.

CRESWELL, Keppel A C, *A bibliography of the architecture, arts, and crafts*
    of Islam to 1st January 1960, Cairo 1961, cols 269-312. *Supplement*
    January 1960 to January 1972, Cairo 1973, cols 47-82, repr. 1978.

EHLERS, E, *Iran: ein bibliographischer Forschungsbericht*, *op.cit*. II 2.2,
    section 'Archaeological-historical literature', :137-67.

KARĪMĪ, Khusrau, *Kitābnāma-yi farhang va hunar-i Īrān dar daurān-i panjāh sāla-yi shāhanshāhi-yi Pahlavī*, Tehran 1976. Chapter 1, 'Architecture and archaeology'.

NAWĀBĪ, Yaḥyā Māhyār, *A bibliography of Iran, op.cit.* II 2.2, vol.3 :1-112.

PEARSON, J D, *A bibliography of pre-Islamic Persia, op.cit.* II 2.2, section D, :231-69.

PORADA, Edith, 'Bibliography for the art of ancient Iran', *Journal of the Ancient Near Eastern Society of Columbia University*, vol.9, 1977 :67-94.

Includes archaeological reports, particularly the works which have appeared since 1963.

RICKS, Thomas, T GOUTTIERE, D EGAN, *Persian studies, op.cit.* II 2.2, section VI, archaeology, :77-86.

2.1.2 *General surveys*

GHIRSHMAN, Roman, *Perse: Proto-iraniens. Mèdes. Achéménides*, Paris 1963.

—— *Parthes et Sassanides*, Paris ? . English tr. *Persian art: the Parthian and Sasanian dynasties*, London/New York 1962.

HERRMANN, Georgina, *The Iranian revival*, Oxford 1977.

HUOT, Jean-Louis, *Iran I. Des origines aux Achéménides*. Archaeologia Mundi. English tr. H S B HARRISON, *Persia I. From the origins to the Achaemenids*, Geneva/Paris/Munich 1970.

LUKONIN, Vladimir G, *Iran II. Des Séleucides aux Sassanides*. English tr. James HOGARTH, *Persia II. From the Seleucids to the Sassanids*, Geneva/Paris/Munich 1967.

— *Le plateau iranien et l'Asie centrale*. Des origines à la conquête islamique. Leurs relations à la lumière des documents archèologiques, Paris 1977.

SARRE, Friedrich, *Die Kunst des alten Persien*, Berlin 1923.

SCHIPPMANN, Klaus, *Die iranischen Feuerheiligtümer*, Berlin 1971.

Comprehensive bibliography on fire temple sites.

STEIN, Aurel, *Old Routes of Western Iran, op.cit.* VIII 4.5.

WATSON, P J, *Archaeological ethnography in western Iran*, Tucson 1979.

An archaeological survey by province for the period down to the Sasanians is

BERGHE, Louis van den, *Archéologie de l'Iran ancien*, Leiden 1959.

The National Organization for the Preservation of Iran's Ancient Monuments commissioned Nuṣrat Allāh MISHKĀTĪ to compile a list of archaeological sites.

Fihrist-i bināhā-yi tārīkhī va amākin-i bāstānī-yi Īrān, op.cit. VIII 5.1.

The period from the known beginnings to the end of the Saljūq rule is covered in

MATHESON, Sylvia A, *Persia: an archaeological guide*, *op.cit.* VIII 5.1.

Useful guides to later monuments are those published by Hachette and Nagel.

2.1.3 *Conference Proceedings*

Two international conferences are convened irregularly to discuss Iranian art and archaeology. The proceedings of both are published.

International Congress of Iranian Art and Archaeology (7th, München 1976), Berlin 1979. (*Archäologische Mitteilungen aus Iran:* Ergänzungsband 6.)

Symposium of Archaeological Research in Iran (2nd, Tehran 1973), Tehran 1974.

2.1.4 *Excavations*

The results of the excavations of successive expeditions have been continually published by various institutions such as the American Institute of Iranian Studies, the British Institute of Persian Studies, Deutsches Archäologisches Institut, Abteilung Teheran, Mission Archéologique en Iran, the Oriental Institute of the University of Chicago, the University of Pennsylvania, etc. The history of the archaeological excavations in Iran is given in

MA^cSŪMĪ, Ghulām Rizā, *Bāstānshināsī-yi Īrān*, Tehran 1976.

An annual survey of the excavations is contained in *Iran*, the journal of the British Institute of Persian Studies. Other journals devoted to Iranian antiquities are *Archäologische Mitteilungen aus Iran* (Berlin) and *Iranica antiqua* (Leiden).

Reports on individual sites are numerous; especially worthy of mention are

CONTENAU, G, and R GHIRSHMANN, *Fouilles de Tépé-Giyan, près de Nehavend 1931-32*, Musée du Louvre, Série Archéologique, Tom.III, Paris 1935.

GHIRSHMANN, R, *Fouilles de Sialk près de Kashan, 1933, 1934, 1937*, Musée du Louvre, Série Archéologique, Tom.IV, V, 2 vols, Paris 1938, 1939.

GODARD, André, *Le trésor de Ziwiyé (Kurdistan)*, Haarlem 1950.

STRONACH, David, *Pasargadae. A report on the excavations conducted by the British Institute of Persian Studies from 1961 to 1963*, Oxford 1978.

The records of the French Scientific Mission in Persia, begun by Jacques de MORGAN in 1894, are still of interest.

MORGAN, J de, *Mission scientifique en Perse*, I-II Études géographiques;

III Études géologiques; IV Recherches archéologiques; V Études linguistiques, 5 vols in 7, Paris 1894-1904.

—— *Mémoires de la Mission Archéologique en Iran*, 30 vols in 13, Paris 1900-47.

Cahiers de la Délégation Archéologique Francaise en Iran, Paris 1971-. Eleven fascicules published up to 1980.

The corpus of the inscriptions is in the process of being published by an international committee.

Corpus inscriptionum iranicarum, London 1955-. The supplement series has been published since 1972.

2.1.5 *Miscellaneous*

The standard is *SPA* (see XII 1. for details). Volume XV of the Japan reprint contains a bibliography of pre-Islamic art to 1938.

A guide to museums with Iranian collections is

NIZHAND, Saᶜīd, and ᶜAlī Aṣghar PARVĪNĪ, *Mūzahā-yi jahān va āsār-i hunarī-yi Īrān*, Shiraz 1971.

A wide-ranging periodical published before the Second World War is

Athār-é Īrān, Annales du Service Archéologique de l'Iran, Paris, I 1,2, 1936; II 1,2, 1937; III 1, 1938; IV 1949 (all published).

More recent publications are

PORADA, Edith, *The art of ancient Iran: pre-Islamic cultures*, with the collaboration of R H DYSON, rev.ed. New York 1969. German tr. 1962.

—— *Iran ancien*, Paris 1963. English tr. *Ancient Iran*, London 1965.

Current publications on Iranian archaeology down to the Sassanians have been compiled annually since 1974 by Peter CALMEYER in *Archäologische Mitteilungen aus Iran*, Neue Folge, section 'Archäologische Bibliographie'.

2.2 *Epigraphy*

A general introduction to Islamic epigraphy is J SOURDEL-THOMINE's contribution to the article 'Kitābāt' in the second edition of the *Encyclopaedia of Islam*. Persian epigraphy is discussed by A D H BIVAR in the same article under the heading 'Iran and Transoxiana', pp.228-31. As for pre-Islamic Iranian epigraphy, reference is made to *Études d'epigraphie, de numismatique et d'histoire de l'Iran ancien* by Ph GIGNOUX *et al*., Paris 1979, Travaux de l'Institut d'Études Iraniennes de l'Université de la Sorbonne Nouvelle, 9.

2.2.1 *Bibliographies*

ABOLHAMD, Abdolhamid, and Nasser PAKDAMAN, *Bibliographie française*, *op.cit.*

II 2.2.

The chapter on epigraphy is on pp.275-289 of the second volume.

CRESWELL, K A C, *A bibliography, op.cit.* 2.1.1.

The chapter on epigraphy, 'Specimens on stone', is on cols 675-714 of the original volume, cols 215-222 of the supplement.

DANI, Ahmad Hasan, *Bibliography of the Muslim inscriptions of Bengal (down to A.D. 1538)*, Dacca 1957, Suppl. *JAS Pakistan* 2, 1957.

MILES, George C, 'Epigraphy', *AI* 8, 1941 :105-08.

A full list of the Arabic inscriptions of Iran.

ḤIKMAT, ᶜAlī Aṣghar, *Naqsh-i pārsī bar aḥjār-i Hind*, Calcutta 1957.

Persian inscriptions in India.

PEARSON, J D, *Index islamicus (op.cit.) passim.*

WIET, Gaston, *L'exposition persane de 1931*, Cairo 1933.

2.2.2 *General works*

CAMERON, George G, *Persepolis treasury tablets*, Chicago 1948.

Apart from discussion of the language (Elamitic) of these documents, the introduction surveys the economic, social and religious aspects of the Achaemenid court.

COMBE, Étienne, *et al.*, *Répertoire chronologique de l'épigraphie arabe*, vols 1-9, Cairo 1931-37.

Short texts with bibliography of the inscriptions arranged chronologically; the earlier volumes are now seriously out of date.

FLURY, S, 'Le décor épigraphique des monuments de Ghazna', *Syria* 6, 1925 :61-90.

GROHMANN, Adolf, *Arabische Paläographie*, Teil 1-2, Öster. Akad. der Wiss., phil-hist. Kl.: Denkschriften; 94, Abhandlung 1-2, Wien 1967-71.

An elaborate treatment in the tradition of formal scholarship, but not very convenient to use. Many Persian inscriptions on hard materials are discussed and illustrated, with copious footnotes. The bibliography will presumably come in the following volume.

MILES, George C, 'Inscriptions on the minarets of Saveh, Iran', *Studies in Islamic art and architecture in honour of Professor K A C CRESWELL*, Cairo 1965 :163-78.

VOLOV, L, 'Plaited Kufic on Samanid epigraphic pottery', *AO* 6, 1966 :107-33.

2.3 *Palaeography and diplomatics*

ARBERRY, Arthur J, *Specimens of Arabic and Persian palaeography*, London 1939.

BAYĀNĪ, Mahdī, *Kitābshināsī-yi kitābhā-yi khaṭṭī*, Ḥusain Maḥbūbī ARDAKĀNĪ (ed), Tehran 1974.

FEKETE, Lajos, *Einführung in die persische Paläographie: 101 persische Dokumente*, G HAZAI (ed), Budapest 1977.

FRAGNER, Bert G, *Repertorium*, *op.cit.* III 4.1.

GROHMANN, Adolf, *Arabische Paläographie*, *op.cit.* 2.2.2.

An exhaustive treatise that contains numerous references to Persian palaeography.

MIRZA, H K, *Ancient Iranian systems of writing*, Bombay 1979, (Journal of the K R Cama Oriental Institute, no.47).

REYCHMAN, Jan, and Ananiasz ZAJACZKOWSKI, *Handbook of Ottoman-Turkish diplomatics*. Rev. and expanded tr. by A S EHRENKREUTZ, T HALASI-KUN (ed), The Hague 1968. Section II Persian palaeography :104-34.

Specimens of Persian manuscript, for the use of candidates for the Degree of Honour and High Proficiency Examination in Persian, Calcutta 1902.

Graded specimens of letters and documents in *shikasta* script from the late 19th century.

See also PEARSON, *Index Islamicus* (*op.cit.*), AFSHĀR, *Index Iranicus* (*op. cit.*).

2.4 *Numismatics*

A most useful introduction to the literature of Islamic numismatics is provided by

BATES, M L, 'Islamic numismatics', *MESA bull.* 12i, 1979 :1-16; 12ii, 1978; 13i, 1979 :3-21; 13ii, 1979 :1-9.

Intended as a 'guide for the historian, as an introduction to the literature and some of the problems of Islamic numismatics'. Part 4 contains 'Specialized studies in Islamic numismatics', which brings the story down to modern times.

For the period from the Arab invasion to the Saljuqs:

MILES, G C, 'Numismatics', *CHI*, IV :364-77.

An authoritative article, which includes much information on Iran *inter alia*, is

BIVAR, A D H, 'Muslim numismatics', *AIB* :208-20.

2.5 *Pre-Islamic history*

2.5.1 *General and introductory works*

FRYE, Richard N, *The heritage of Persia*, London 1962.

Concerned especially with the Iranian contribution to Near Eastern civilization, with stress on religious and cultural aspects. There is a useful chapter on the merging of Iranian and Arab societies after the Arab conquest, and a valuable bibliographical essay.

GHIRSHMANN, Roman, *L'Iran des origines à l'Islam*, Paris 1951. English tr. *Iran: from the earliest times to the Islamic conquest*, Harmondsworth 1954.

HINZ, W, 'Persia', *CAH*, I 23, 1963; II 7, 1964.

HUART, Clément, *La Perse antique et la civilisation iranienne*. L'évolution de l'humanité XXIV. Paris 1925, rev.ed. with L J DELAPORTE, *L'Iran antique - Elam et Perse - et la civilisation iranienne*, Paris 1943, rev.ed. 1952. English tr. M R DOBIE, *Ancient Persia and Iranian civilisation*, London/New York 1927.

LABAT, R, 'Elam', *CAH*, II 29, 1963. 'Elam and West Persia', *CAH*, II 32, 1964.

2.5.2 *Pre-Achaemenid history*

CAMERON, George G, *History of early Iran*, Chicago 1936, repr. Westport, Conn. 1968. French tr. *Histoire de l'Iran antique*, Paris 1937.

A history of Elam, based largely on archaeological sources. Still the standard work on the history of pre-Achaemenid Iran.

FRANKFORT, Henri, *The birth of civilisation in the Near East*, London 1951.

Primarily concerned with Mesopotamia and Egypt, there are references to Elam and south-west Iran.

GHIRSHMANN, Roman, *L'Iran et la migration des Indo-Aryens et des Iraniens*, Leiden 1977.

HERZFELD, Ernst, *Archaeological history of Iran*, London 1935. Persian tr. Tehran 1975.

Three lectures covering the period from the earliest times to the Sassanids, based on archaeological sources.

—— *Iran in the ancient East*, London/New York 1941.

For the history of the Medes two Russian works are available.

DYAKONOV, I M, *Istoriya Midii*, Moscow 1956.

ALIEV, I, *Istoriya Midii*, Baku 1960.

Two older works should also be mentioned, though allowance must be made for their deficiencies.

RAWLINSON, G, *The five great monarchies of the ancient eastern world*, Chaldaea, Assyria, Babylon, Media and Persia, 4 vols, London/New York 1862-67.

Media, the Third Monarchy, is dealt with in the first half of volume III, while Persia, the Fifth Monarchy, occupies the whole of volume IV.

PRASEK, J V, *Geschichte der Meder und Perser bis zur makedonischen Eroberung*, 2 vols, Gotha 1906, 1910.

The gap will be closed with the forthcoming publication of the second volume of the *Cambridge History of Iran*, edited by I GERSHEVITCH. The Median and Achaemenid periods.

2.5.3 *The Achaemenids*

OLMSTEAD, A T, *History of the Persian empire*, Chicago 1948.

Political, cultural and religious history.

ROGERS, Robert W, *A history of ancient Persia, from its earliest beginnings to the death of Alexander the Great*, New York/London 1929.

Based primarily on Greek sources.

EHTECHAM, M, *L'Iran sous les Achéménides*, Fribourg 1946.

Discussion of the organization of the empire and the provinces.

Mention may also be made of RAWLINSON, *op.cit.*, PRASEK, *op.cit.*, and of the forthcoming volume of the *CHI*, GERSHEVITCH (ed), *op.cit.*

2.5.4 *Alexander the Great, the Seleucids and the Parthians*

The only general history of the period is

GUTSCHMID, Alfred von, *Geschichte Irans von Alexander der Grossen bis zum Untergang der Arsaciden*, Tübingen 1888.

On the role of Alexander the Great in the history of western Asia:

ALTHEIM, Franz, *Alexander und Asien. Geschichte eines geistigen Erbes*, Tübingen 1953. French tr. *Alexandre et l'Asie. Histoire d'un legs spirituel*, Paris 1954.

—— *Zarathustra und Alexander.* Ein ost-westliche Begegnung, Frankfurt am Main 1960.

TARN, William W, *Alexander the Great*, 2 vols, Cambridge 1948, repr. 1950-51.

On the Seleucids the best sources are

BEVAN, E, *The house of Seleucus*, London 1902.

BIKERMAN, E, *Institutions des Séleucides*, Paris 1938.

BOUCHÉ-LECLERQ, A, *Histoire des Séleucides*, Paris 1914.

On the wider question of the spread of Hellenism in the east the following, though generally written from the European point of view, will be found useful.

ALTHEIM, Franz, *Weltgeschichte Asiens im griechischen Zeitalter*, 2 vols, Halle 1947-48.

—— *Geschichte Mittelasiens im Altertum*, Berlin 1970.

—— *Geschichte der Hunnen*, 5 vols, Berlin 1959-62.

Volumes 2-4, Die Hephthaliten in Iran, Kampf der Religionen, Die europäische Hunnen, are particularly relevant.

DROUSEN, J G, *Geschichte des Hellenismus*, 2 vols, Basle 1952.

JOUGUET, P, *L'impérialisme macédonienne et l'hellénisation de l'orient*, l'évolution de l'humanité XV, Paris 1926.

MEYER, Eduard, *Geschichte des Altertums*, 5 vols, Stuttgart/Darmstadt 1909-58.

Of particular relevance are volume III, 1937, Der Ausgang der altorientalischen Geschichte und der Aufstieg des Abendlandes bis zu dem Perserkriegen; volume IV, 1939, 1956; volume V, 1958, Das Perserreich und die Griechen.

RANOVICH, A B, *Ellenizm i ego istoricheskaya rol'*, Moscow 1950.

ROSTOVTZEFF, M I, *The social and economic history of the Hellenistic world*, vols I-III, Oxford 1941.

TARN, William W, *The Greeks in Bactria and India*, Cambridge 1938, rev.ed. 1951, 1966.

—— and G T GRIFFITH, *Hellenistic civilisation*, London 1927, rev.eds 1930, 1952, 1959.

For the history of the Parthian era the standard work is

DEBEVOISE, Neilson C, *A political history of Parthia*, Chicago 1938.

Also to be recommended:

COLLEDGE, Malcolm A R, *The Parthians*, London 1967.

Reference should also be made to GUTSCHMID, *op.cit.*, and to

RAWLINSON, G, *The sixth great oriental monarchy, Parthia*, New York 1873.

For the social history of the period, useful sources are

PIGULEVSKAYA, N, *Les villes de l'état iranien aux époques parthe et sassanide*, Paris 1963.

WIDENGREN, Geo, *Iranisch-semitisch Kulturbegegnung in der parthischen Zeit*, Cologne 1960.

Once again, mention must be made of the long awaited third volume of the *Cambridge History of Iran*.

YAR-SHATER, E (ed), *The Seleucid, Parthian and Sasanian periods*, (forthcoming).

2.5.5 *The Sasanids*

The standard work is

CHRISTENSEN, Arthur, *L'Iran sous les Sassanides*, 2nd ed. Copenhagen 1944.

Two older works are

NÖLDEKE, T, *Geschichte der Perser und Araber zur Zeit der Sasaniden*, *op. cit.* 1.3.

Largely a translation of the relevant portions of ṬABARĪ's history.

RAWLINSON, G, *The seventh great oriental monarchy. The Sasanians*, New York 1876.

Other useful works are

ALTHEIM, Franz, *Asien und Rom. Neue Urkunde aus sasanidischen Zeit*, Tübingen 1952.

—— *Die Araber in der alten Welt*, 3 vols, Berlin 1964-66.

—— and Ruth STIEHL, *Ein asiatischer Staat*. Feudalismus unter den Sasaniden und ihren Nachbarn, vol.I, Wiesbaden 1954.

CHRISTENSEN, Arthur, *Le règne du roi Kawadh I*, *op.cit.* VI 3.7.

LUKONIN, V, *Iran v epokhu pervikh Sassanidov*, Leningrad 1961.

And, of course, YAR-SHATER, *op.cit.*

2.5.6 *Social and cultural developments in pre-Islamic Iran*

While most of the works listed above refer to a greater or lesser degree to social and cultural history, the citations that follow are more specifically concerned with these aspects.

BALSARA, Pestanji Phirozshah, *Ancient Iran, its contribution to human progress*, Iran League Propaganda Publications no.18, Bombay 1936.

BRIANT, Pierre, *État et pasteurs au moyen orient ancien*, Cambridge 1981.

Especially concerned with the relationships of nomads and pastoralists with the Achaemenid Empire.

BUZURGZĀD, Ḥabīballāh, *Jas͟hnhā va aᶜyād-i millī va maẕhabī dar Īrān-i qabl az Islām*, Tehran 1971.

CHRISTENSEN, Arthur, *Les types du Premier Homme et du Premier Roi dans l'histoire légendaire des Iraniens*, part I, Stockholm 1918, part II, Leiden 1934.

—— *Les gestes des rois dans les traditions de l'Iran antique*, Paris 1936.

DHALLA, Maneckji Nusservanji, *Zoroastrian civilisation from the earliest times to the downfall of the last Zoroastrian empire*, New York 1922.

GEIGER, W, *Die ostiranische Kultur in Alterthum*. Erlangen 1882. English tr. Darab Peshotan SANJANA, *Civilisation of the eastern Iranians in ancient times*, London 1885, repr. SANJANA, *Collected works*, Bombay 1932 :81-333.

GODARD, André, *L'art de l'Iran*, Paris 1962. English tr. M HERON, *The art of Iran*, London 1965.

A useful survey of Iranian art, especially in the pre-Islamic period.

MAZAHERY, Aly Akbar, *La famille iranienne aux temps anté-islamiques*, Paris

1958.

PŪR-DĀVŪD, Ibrāhīm, *Farhang-i Īrān-i bāstān*, Tehran 1947.

On education in particular the following are useful.

BĪZHAN, Asadallāh, *Sair-i tamaddun va tarbiyat dar Īrān-i bāstān - daurahā-yi Avistā'ī va Mādī va Hakhāmanishī*, Tehran 1971.

—— *Chashmandāz-i tarbiyat dar Īrān-i pīsh az Islām*, Tehran 1972.

ḤIKMAT, ʿAlī Riżā, *Āmūzish u parvarish dar Īrān-i bāstān*, Tehran 1971.
A well-documented collection of essays on all aspects of education and training in the pre-Islamic period.

MODI, J J, *Education among the ancient Iranians*, Bombay 1905.

RAŻAVĪ, Masʿūd, *Tarbiyat-i Īrāniyān dar shāhanshāhī-yi Īrān-i pīsh az Islām*, Tehran 1971.

3. *ISLAMIC IRAN UP TO THE MONGOL PERIOD*

3.1 *Introduction*

The pre-Mongol history of Islamic Iran suffers - as do other periods of Iranian history, it must readily be admitted - from a lack of specialist, full-length books and monographs dealing with particular periods and dynasties on the one hand, and with specific regions of the Iranian world on the other. Hence much of this history has to be approached through general works on mediaeval Islamic history, through composite works on the general field of Iranian history (cultural, literary, religious, as well as straight political and dynastic history) such as the *Cambridge history of Iran*, and through articles in journals or collections of studies. Hence in what follows, certain articles will be noted where they are of especial importance or where books or monographs on the topic in question do not exist; but for detailed surveys of periodical literature and serials, recourse should of course be had to such standard reference works as the annual *Abstracta islamica*, published as supplements to *REI* from 1937, including books as well as articles, and J D PEARSON's *Index islamicus 1906-1955* and successive five-yearly supplements (*op.cit.*) section XXXI Persian history.

Secondly, it should be noted that, as elsewhere in this volume, it is impossible during this early period to confine oneself narrowly to the political boundaries of Iran as constituted roughly since the Qājār period. Culturally and politically, Iran has often been intimately linked with Semitic Mesopotamia and with the southern shores of the Persian Gulf and Oman, and dynasties whose main seat of power was in western Iran have at times also controlled much of Iraq (e.g. the Sāsānids, the Būyids, the

Qarā Qoyunlū and at times the Ṣafavids). In the northwest, the western coastlands of the Caspian Sea, as far north as Darband, have been historically linked with Iran until Russian expansionism there in the 18th and early 19th centuries. In the northeast, in ancient times very much *l'Iran extérieur*, a region of ethnically Iranian peoples, extended well into the steppes, that is, into Khwārazm and Transoxania, even though its present remnants comprise only a few pockets of Iranian speakers in Soviet Tājīkistān and in the upper Oxus-Pamirs region; the early Islamic history of the area, which under the caliphate came administratively within a vast and ill-defined governorship of Khurāsān and the East, was always closely-linked with that of the Iranian heartland proper. Likewise, the modern Iran-Afghanistan border is in many respects (e.g. topographically, linguistically and ethnically) an artificial one, not completely settled in the case of Sīstān till the opening years of the present century; here again, the mediaeval history of Iran has spilled over eastwards to cover some of what is now Afghanistan.

Finally, a section on translations of historical works bearing on Iran has been included, although translations of works dealing specifically with Iran are somewhat sparse. Translations of certain of the general chronicles for early Islamic history have been included (e.g. those by Balādhurī and Ṭabarī) where they contain a significant amount of material relevant to the history of Iran, but it should be borne in mind that translations exist of several other works in this genre containing a smaller proportion of material of Iranian interest (e.g. MASᶜŪDI's *Murūj al-dhahab*) and also of Arabic geographical works, such as YAᶜQŪBĪ's *Kitāb al-Buldān*, IBN RUSTA's *al-Aᶜlāq al-nafīsa* and IBN AL-FAQĪH's *Mukhtaṣar Kitāb al-Buldān*.

3.2 *General works on mediaeval Islamic history which contain sections relevant to the history of Iran during this period*

BROCKELMANN, C, *GAL*, *op.cit.* IX 1.2.
See sections on the Iranian world and the Turkish and Mongol incomers to it.
Encyclopaedia of Islam, 2nd ed. Leiden/London 1960-.

Certain general articles bear on our subject; see especially, art. 'Iran. v. History. (a) To the Turcoman invasions' (A K S LAMBTON); 'Kurds and Kurdistān. 2. History' (V MINORSKY and Th BOIS). There are articles on specific dynasties, e.g. 'Aḥmadilīs' (MINORSKY), 'Buwayhids' (Cl CAHEN), 'Ghaznawids' (B SPULER), 'Ghūrids' (C E BOSWORTH), 'Ildenizids' (BOSWORTH), 'Ilek-Khans' (BOSWORTH), 'Khwārazm-Shāhs' (BOSWORTH), 'Lur-i Buzurg', 'Lur-i Kūčik' (MINORSKY). Several articles on regions or provinces of Iran contain valuable historical information, e.g. 'Ādharbāydjān' (MINORSKY), 'Daylam' (MINORSKY), 'Fārs' (L LOCKHART), 'Khwārazm' (BOSWORTH), 'Khurāsān' (BOSWORTH), 'Kirmān' (LAMBTON), 'Ḳūhistān' (J H KRAMERS), 'Ḳūmis' (BOSWORTH), 'Luristān' (MINORSKY), as do the articles on individual towns; utilise now the *Index to Vols I-III*, Leiden/Paris 1979.

HOLT, LAMBTON, LEWIS (eds), *CHIs*, *op.cit.*, I *The central Islamic lands*.

See especially the chapters 'The Patriarchal and Umayyad caliphates' (L Veccia VAGLIERI), 'The ᶜAbbasid caliphate' (D SOURDEL), 'The disintegration of the caliphate in the East' (B SPULER).

MEZ, A, *Die Renaissance des Islâms*, Heidelberg 1932. English tr. S KHUDA-BUKHSH, *The renaissance of Islam*, Patna 1937.

Deals mainly with social, cultural and intellectual history, with considerable reference to the Iranian world.

RICHARDS, D S (ed), *Islamic civilisation 950-1150*, Papers on Islamic history, 3, Oxford 1973.

Contains several chapters concerning Iranian history, including also art, history and demography.

SAUNDERS, J J, *A history of medieval Islam*, London 1965.

Clearly-written, balanced account; good annotated bibliographies for further reading at the end of each chapter.

SPULER, B, *Geschichte*, *op.cit.* 1.2, vol.I, *The age of the caliphs*.

Succinct survey of trends and general features rather than a detailed narrative. Has good maps.

WELLHAUSEN, J, *Das arabische Reich und sein sturz*, Berlin 1902. English tr. M G WEIR, *The Arab kingdom and its fall*, Calcutta 1927.

A pioneer account of the Arab military supremacy during the Umayyad period, with emphasis on the disintegratory effect of the tribal conflicts, especially in Khurāsān, on the Arabs' unity.

3.3 *Works specifically concerned with Iran*

BARTHOLD, W, *Turkestan down to the Mongol invasion*, GMS, N.S. V, 3rd ed. with an additional chapter hitherto unpublished in English, tr. T MINORSKY and ed. C E BOSWORTH, London 1968.

A classic work by the 'Gibbon of Turkestan', with much of relevance for the history of eastern Iran.

BOSWORTH, C E, *Sīstān under the Arabs, from the Islamic conquest to the rise of the Ṣaffārids (30-250/651-864)*, ISMEO, Reports and memoirs XI, Rome 1968.

Surveys the history of this remote region of the far eastern fringes of the Islamic world, where Arab rule gradually gave way to that of local sectaries and ambitious military commanders.

—— *The Ghaznavids, their empire in Afghanistan and eastern Iran 994-1040*, Edinburgh 1963.

An analysis, rather than a connected narrative history, of the 'power state' of the most forceful empire known in eastern Islam till that date.

—— *The later Ghaznavids, splendour and decay: the dynasty in Afghanistan and northern India 1040-1186*, Edinburgh 1977.

Deals with the history, much more obscure than that of the preceding period, of the dynasty after it had been shorn of its western provinces by the Seljuqs.

—— *The mediaeval history of Iran, Afghanistan and Central Asia*, London 1977.

A collection of articles dealing with events from the first century of Islam till the Ghaznavid period.

—— (ed), *Iran and Islam, in memory of the late Vladimir Minorsky*, Edinburgh 1971.

Several articles in this book bear on the history of our period.

BROWNE, E G, *A literary history of Persia*, *op.cit*. I. *From the earliest times until Firdawsi*. II. *From Firdawsi to Sa*ᶜ*di*.

Still a standard reference book for Persian literature, with the literary information woven round a basis of attractively-written historical narrative and analysis.

BULLIET, R W, *The patricians of Nishapur, a study in medieval Islamic social history*, Harvard Middle Eastern Studies, 16, Cambridge, Mass. 1972.

Uses the biographical surveys of ulema, traditionists and littérateurs, especially ample for this town of eastern Iran, to build up a picture of the class of urban notables and to provide an analysis of their position within the fabric of urban societies in Khurāsān.

BUSSE, H, *Chalif und Grosskönig, die Buyiden im Iraq (945-1055)*, Beiruter Texte und Studien, 6, Beirut/Wiesbaden 1969.

Exhaustive and detailed study of this western branch of the Dailamī dynasty, whose history impinges to a considerable extent on that of southern and western Iran.

BOSWORTH, C E, 'Iran and the Arabs', *CHI*, III, *The Seleucid, Parthian and Sassanian periods*, E YARSHATER (ed), (forthcoming).

Deals with relations up to the age of the Prophet.

—— IV. *From the Arab invasions to the Saljuqs*, R N FRYE (ed).

Chapters 1-7 (various authors) deal with the Arab conquest of Iran, the establishment of caliphal control there, the disintegration of the caliphate and the rise of autonomous and then independent local dynasties.

—— V. *The Saljuq and Mongol periods*, J A BOYLE (ed).

Especially concerned with history are chapters 1, 'The political and dynastic history of the Iranian world (A.D. 1000-1217)' (C E BOSWORTH); 2, 'The internal structure of the Saljuq empire' (A K S LAMBTON); 5, 'The Ismā^cīlī state' (M G S HODGSON).

FRYE, R N, *The heritage of Persia*, *op.cit.* 2.5.1.

Chapter 7 deals with early Islamic Iran, at first culturally quiescent after the Arab invasions, then resurgent for the New Persian renaissance.

—— *The golden age of Persia: the Arabs in the East*, London 1975.

—— *Islamic Iran and Central Asia (7th-12th centuries)*, London 1979.

Thirty-six essays on various aspects of late Sasanid and early Islamic history.

GIBB, H A R, *The Arab conquests in Central Asia*, London 1923.

An account of the Arab raids into the Oxus valley and beyond, based primarily on the Arab chronicles.

HODGSON, M G S, *The order of the Assassins*, *op.cit.* VI 2.5.

The basic, detailed history of the sect plus its doctrines; good bibliographical appendix.

HORST, H, *Die Staatsverwaltung der Gross-selǧuqen und Ḫorazmšāhs 1038-1231, eine Untersuchung nach Urkundenformularen der Zeit*. Akad. der Wiss. und der Lit., Veroffentlichungen der Orientalischen Kommission, XVIII, Wiesbaden 1964.

Translations of contemporary documents, with a commentary on and survey of the administrative institutions under these two dynasties.

IQBĀL, ^cAbbās, *Vizārat dar ^cahd-i salāṭīn-i buzurg-i Saljūqī, az tārīkh-i tashkīl-i īn silsila tā marg-i Sulṭān Sanjar (432-552)*, Tehran University Publications, 520, Tehran 1959.

Purely compilatory in approach, but brings together useful material from both historical and literary sources on the viziers of the Saljuqs.

KAFESOǦLU, I, *Sultan Melikşah devrinde Büyük Selcuklu imparatorluǧu*, İstanbul Üniversitesi Edebiyat Fakültesi yayınlarından, 569.

The only monograph devoted to a specific Saljuq sultan.

—— *Harezmşahlar devleti tarihi (485-617/1092-1229)*, Türk Tarih Kurumu yayınlarından, VII, seri no.29, Ankara 1956.

Deals with the Turkish dynasty of Central Asia whose expansionist policies involved much of Iran proper and paved the way for the Mongol conquests.

KASRAVĪ, Sayyid Aḥmad, *Shahriyārān-i gum-nām. I, Dailamān. 2, Ravvādiyān.*

3, Shaddādiyān, Tehran 1930, repr. 1957.

A valuable work on the minor dynasties of the southwestern corner of the Caspian coastlands and of Azerbaijan by a noted scholar, described by MINORSKY as one who 'possessed the spirit of a true historian ... accurate in detail and clear in presentation'.

KLAUSNER, C L, *The Seljuk vezirate. A study of civil administration, 1055-1194*, Harvard Middle Eastern Monographs, 22, Cambridge, Mass. 1973.

Analyses the administrative structures and trends in government during this period.

KÖYMEN, M A, *Büyük Selçuklu imparatorluğu tarihi. II. Ikinci imparatorluk devri*, Ankara 1954.

Very detailed account of the Saljūq sultanate from the accession of Maḥmūd (1118) to the death of Sanjar (1157). Volumes I and III on the early and late Saljūq periods have never apparently appeared.

LAMBTON, A K S, *Landlord and peasant in Persia. A study of land tenure and land revenue administration*, London 1953, repr. 1969.

Essentially a history of landholding and an exposition of evolving types of tenure and irrigation, with important sections on the early period, including on such topics as the iqṭāᶜ's development and the increasing pastoralization brought about by Turkmen incomers from the Saljūq period onwards.

LEWIS, B, *The Assassins, a radical sect in Islam, op.cit.* VI 2.5.

Readable but scholarly presentation of the sect in both its Syrian and its Iranian manifestations; has a section of plates.

MARICQ, A, and G WIET, *Le minaret de Djam. La découverte de la capitale des sultans ghorides (XIIe-XIIIe siècles)*, Mémoires de la Délégation Archéologique en Afghanistan, XVI, Paris 1959.

Includes a useful historical commentary as background history of the Ghūrids.

MILES, G C, *The numismatic history of Rayy*, American Numismatic Soc., Numismatic Studies, 2, New York 1938.

An exemplary study demonstrating how the information from coins can be combined with that of the straightforward historical and literary sources to produce a meaningful narrative of political events for one of the chief towns of northern Iran (7th-14th centuries).

MINORSKY, V, *Studies on Caucasian history*, I, New light on the Shaddādids of Ganja; II, The Shaddādids of Ani; III, The prehistory of Saladin, London 1953.

Important studies on the history of Azerbaijan and Transcaucasia and their

Kurdish and Dailami dynasties in the pre-Mongol period.

—— *Iranica. Twenty articles : Bīst maqāla-yi Mīnūrskī*, Tehran University Publications, 775, Tehran 1964.

Contains several significant studies for our period, plus a valuable bibliography displaying this scholar's immense erudition and fecundity of production in the field of Iranian history.

—— *The Turks, Iran and the Caucasus in the Middle Ages*, London 1978.

NAFĪSĪ, Saʿīd, *Tārīkh-i khāndān-i Ṭāhirī*, I, Ṭāhir b Ḥusain, Tehran 1956.

The only volume ever published of a projected history of the Ṭāhirid line of governors in Khurāsān (821-73); purely traditional in its compilatory, uncritical approach.

NAẒIM, M, *The life and times of Sulṭān Maḥmūd of Ghazna*, Cambridge 1931.

Exhaustive and meticulous survey of the reign of the greatest of the Ghaznavids and his expansion into the Iranian and Indian worlds, if at times too laudatory and uncritical.

NÖLDEKE, Th, *Orientalische Skizzen*, Berlin 1892. English tr. J S BLACK, *Sketches from eastern history*, Edinburgh/London 1892.

Contains a still-useful pioneering study on the founder of the Ṣaffārid dynasty, Yaʿqūb b Laith, 'Yakub the Coppersmith and his dynasty'.

RABINO DI BORGOMALE, H L, 'Les dynasties du Māzandarān de l'an 50 avant l'hégire à l'an 1006 de l'hégire (572 a 1597-1598), d'après les chroniques locales', *JA* CCXXVIII, 1936 :397-474.

—— 'Les préfets du Califat au Ṭabaristān, de 18 à 328/639 à 939-40', *JA* CCXXXI, 1939 :237-74.

—— 'Les dynasties locales du Gîlân et du Daylam', *JA* CCXXXVII, 1949 :301-50.

Three of the most important of many studies on the local princes of the Caspian region by a former consul of H.B.M. at Rasht in Gīlān.

SADIGHI, G H, *Les mouvements religieux iraniens*, *op.cit.* VI 2.3.

Covers an important aspect of Iranian life during the first centuries of Islamisation, the continued recrudescence of Iranian national spirit and particularism in a religio-political form.

SANAULLAH, M F, *The decline of the Saljūqid empire*, Calcutta 1938.

Deals with the reigns of Malik-Shāh's sons, Maḥmūd, Berk-yaruq and Muḥammad, (1092-118).

SHABAN, M A, *The ʿAbbasid revolution*, Cambridge 1970.

Treats rather of the Arab tribes in Khurasan and their factional struggles as catalysts for the ensuing revolution.

SPULER, B, *Iran im frühislamischer Zeit, Politik, Kultur, Verwaltung und öffentliches Leben zwischen der Arabischen und der Seldschukischen Eroberung 633 bis 1055*, Akad. der Wiss. und der Lit., Veröffentlichungen der Orientalischen Kommission, II, Wiesbaden 1952.

Compilatory in approach, but a mine of information on all aspects of political, cultural and social history; especially full and accurate bibliography, valuable as a starting-point for further, detailed research.

3.4 *Works on the historical geography of Iran*

BARTHOLD, V V, *Istoriko-geograficheskii obzor Irana*, St Petersburg 1903, repr. in *Sochineniya* VII, Moscow 1971 :31-228. Persian tr. Tehran 1308/1930; an English tr. *Historical-geographical survey of Iran*, is in preparation by S SOUCEK, to be published by Princeton University Press.

LE STRANGE, G, *The lands of the eastern caliphate*, Cambridge 1905, repr. 1930, 1966.

Based essentially on the classical Arabic and Persian geographers of the period from the 9th to the 14th centuries; a standard, most useful work, with maps.

MARQUART, J, 'Ērānšahr nach der Geographie des Ps. Moses Xorenacᶜi', *Abh. der Göttingische Gesell. der Wiss.*, N.F. III/2, Berlin 1901.

Very erudite commentary on a brief Armenian geographical survey of Iran dating from the Sāsānid period, much of the commentary being relevant for the Islamic period.

MINORSKY, V (tr), *Ḥudūd al-ᶜālam*, *op.cit.* VIII 3.2.2.

Comprises a translation plus an extremely learned and far-ranging commentary by the translator. Another edition without translation, M SUTŪDA (ed), Tehran University no.727, Tehran 1961.

SCHWARZ, P, *Iran im Mittelalter nach den arabischen Geographen*, 9 parts, Leipzig/Zwickau/Berlin 1896-1935, repr. in one volume, Hildesheim 1969.

Very detailed descriptions, with verbatim translations from Arabic and other sources, wider in range than those used by LE STRANGE, but excludes K͟hurāsān and the eastern provinces.

3.5 *Persian and Arabic primary sources*

ABŪ DULAF Misᶜar b Muhalhil, *Travels in Iran (circa A.D. 950)*, text, English tr. and commentary by V MINORSKY, Cairo 1955.

Much information on physical geography, natural phenomena, historical geography, etc. of northeastern, northern and western Iran.

Tārīkh-i Sīstān, M BAHĀR (ed), Tehran 1935. English tr. Milton GOLD. ISMEO, Literary and historical texts from Iran, 2, Rome 1976. Russian tr. L P SMIRNOV, Moscow 1974.

One of the rich genre of local histories of Iranian towns and regions (goes up to the 11th century).

BAIHAQĪ, Abū 'l-faẓl, *Tārīkh-i Baihaqī* or *Tārīkh-i Masᶜūdī*, Saᶜīd NAFĪSĪ (ed), 3 vols, Tehran 1940, 1947, 1953. Russian tr. A K ARENDS, *Istoriya Masᶜuda 1030-1041*, 2nd ed. Moscow 1969.

The very detailed, almost day-to-day administrative diary of a Ghaznavid secretary, much of which deals with the clash of the Ghaznavids and the incoming Saljūq Turkmens.

AL-BALĀDHURĪ, Aḥmad B Yahyā, *Futūḥ al-buldān*, (*Liber expugnationis regionum*), M J de GOEJE (ed), Leiden 1870; 3 vols, Cairo 1956-57. English tr. P K HITTI and F C MURGOTTEN, *The origins of the Islamic state*, Columbia University Studies in History, Economics and Public Law, LXVIII, 2 vols, New York 1916, 1924. German tr. O RESCHER, Leipzig 1917, 1923.

Much of this deals with the overrunning of Iran by the Arabs and the early course of Islamisation.

IBN ISFANDIYAR, Muḥammad b Ḥasan, *Tārīkh-i Ṭabaristān*, ᶜAbbās IQBĀL (ed), 2 vols, Tehran n.d. (1941?). Abr. English tr. E G BROWNE, *History of Ṭabaristán*, GMS, II, Leiden/London 1905.

A local history of the Caspian coastlands.

JŪZJĀNĪ, Minhāj-i Sirāj, *Ṭabaqāt-i Nāṣirī*, *op.cit.* 1.3.

In effect, a special history of the Ghūrid dynasty and their expansion into Iran on the one side and India on the other; copious commentary by the translator, giving citations from parallel texts, but not always easily identifiable.

MISKAWAIH, Abū ᶜAlī Aḥmad, and continuators, *Tajārib al-umam*, etc. Facs. L CAETANI (ed), GMS, VII, 6 vols, Leiden 1909-17. 3 vols, n.p. 1914-16. English tr. accompanying the Arabic texts by D S MARGOLIOUTH and H F AMEDROZ, *The eclipse of the ᶜAbbasid caliphate*, 7 vols, Oxford 1920-21.

The prime source for the history of the Būyid amirates in northern, western and southern Iran, with much detail on administrative and social affairs in addition to political and military matters.

MUBĀRAKSHĀH, Fakhr-i Mudabbir, *Ādāb al-mulūk wa-kifāyat al-mamlūk*, English tr. (part), I M SHAFI, 'Fresh light on the Ghaznavids', *IC* XII, 1938 :189-234.

Anecdotes on the history of the Ghaznavids.

MÜNEJJIM-BĀSHĪ, *Jāmi*ᶜ *al-duwal*. Sections on eastern Caucasia tr. into English by V MINORSKY, *A history of Sharvān and Darband*, Cambridge 1958.
A late Ottoman Turkish universal history which preserves important early sources for this northwestern corner of the Iranian world; includes a copious commentary.

NARSHAKHĪ, Abū Bakr Muḥammad, Tārīkh-i Bukhārā. *Description topographique et historique de Boukhara*, Charles SCHEFER (ed), Paris 1892. Mudarris RAŻAVĪ (ed), Tehran 1939. English tr. R N FRYE, *The history of Bukhara*, Cambridge, Mass. 1954. Russian tr. N LYKOSHIN, Tashkent 1897.
On the early Islamic history of Central Asia and then that of the Sāmānid dynasty; copious notes and further references in the commentary.

NIẒĀM AL-MULK, Abū ᶜAlī Ḥasan, *Siyāsat-nāma*, Charles SCHEFER (ed), Paris 1891. ᶜAbbās IQBĀL (ed), Tehran 1941. Muḥammad QAZVĪNĪ and Murtażā Mudarris CHAHĀRDIHĪ (eds), Tehran 1955. French tr. Ch. SCHEFER, Paris 1893. German tr. K E SCHABINGER, Freiherr von Schowingen, Freiburg/Munich 1960. English tr. H DARKE, *The book of government or rules for kings*, London 1960, rev. 1976.

RĀVANDĪ, Abū Bakr Najm al-dīn Muḥammad b ᶜAlī, *Rāḥat al-ṣudūr va āyat al-surūr*, Muḥammad IQBĀL (ed), *GMS*, NS.ii, London 1921. French tr. (part), Charles SCHEFER, *Tableau du règne de Mouizz eddin Aboul Harith. Sultan Sindjar*, Paris 1886. C SCHEFER, Suppl. to *Siasset Nameh*, Paris 1897 :70-114.

ṬABARI, Muḥammad b Jaᶜfar al-, *Ta'rīkh al-rusul wa'l-mulūk*, *op.cit*. 1.3.
The English translation by Elma MARIN covers many important events in Iran, such as the rising of Bābak al-Khurramī and the fall of the Afshīn Ḥaidar.

4. *FROM THE MONGOL INVASION TO THE RISE OF THE SAFAVIDS*

4.1 *Introduction*

The incorporation of Iran into a great world empire in the 13th century has entailed certain consequences for the student of Iranian history during the Mongol period. Firstly, it has necessitated a familiarity with Mongol customary law and religious affiliations (including Nestorian Christianity and Buddhism as well as Shamanism); and hence works bearing on such aspects of Mongol culture have been included in this bibliography. Secondly, following the division of the empire after 1260 into a number of separate states Iran formed only the largest constituent part of the dominions of the Īl-Khāns, which simultaneously embraced the Caucasus region, Mesopotamia and Anatolia, as well as extending at times into Afghanistan. This applies also to Iran after its conquest in the late 14th century by Tīmūr, whose empire was smaller than that of the Mongols, but under whose dynasty strong cultural as well as political links were forged with Transoxania. Once again, therefore, our survey will not be confined within the boundaries of Iran as constituted at the present day. Under the Īl-Khāns, finally, Iran entered into a phase of sustained diplomatic and cultural relations with the outside world, and in particular with China and with Western Europe; both primary and secondary material pertaining to these important contacts is represented below, the latter in a special section (4.7).

Only the more indispensable items of periodical literature have been listed in this bibliography. As in the preceding section, for the majority of articles the reader is referred to the standard works such as the *Index Islamicus*, sections XXXI (Persian history) and XXXIVh (Central Asia: the Mongols), and the *Abstracta Islamica* supplements to *REI*; while D SINOR's *Introduction à l'étude de l'Eurasie centrale*, Wiesbaden 1963, pp.294ff, is a valuable guide to material on all aspects of Mongol history and culture.

4.2 *General works on Islamic history containing sections relevant to the history of Iran during this period*

BROCKELMANN, C, *Geschichte*, *op.cit*. IX 1.2.

Encyclopaedia of Islam, 2nd ed., *op.cit*.

See especially: 'Iran. v. History: (a) To the Turkoman invasions' (A K S LAMBTON); '(b) Turkomans to Present Day' (R M SAVORY). There are articles on specific dynasties: ''Aḳ Ḳoyunlu' (V MINORSKY); 'Čingizids' (B SPULER); 'Čūbānids' (SAVORY); 'Djalāyir, Djalāyirid' (J MASSON SMITH, Jr); 'Īlkhāns' (SPULER); 'Īndjū' (J A BOYLE); 'Ḳarā-Ḳoyunlu' (F SÜMER); 'Kart' (T W HAIG/SPULER). Valuable contributions are included also on individual rulers, e.g. 'Ghāzān' (W BARTHOLD/BOYLE), 'Hūlāgū' (BARTHOLD/BOYLE), and on specific regions and towns, e.g. 'Harāt' (R N FRYE).

HOLT, P M, A K S LAMBTON, and B LEWIS (eds), *The Cambridge History of Islam*, *op.cit*. I. *The central Islamic lands*.

See part II, chapter 1, 'The disintegration of the Caliphate in the East', (SPULER), especially pp.160-74.

SPULER, B, *The Muslim world, a historical survey*. II. *The Mongol period*, *op.cit*, 1.2.

A short but useful introduction to the entire period from the Mongol invasions down to 1500.

4.3 *General works on Iranian history*

BARTHOLD, W, *Turkestan down to the Mongol invasion*, *op.cit*. 3.3.

Chapter 4 is still the most detailed and critical survey of the first

Mongol invasion under Chingīz Khān in 1219-23, while chapter 5, 'Turkestan under Mongol domination (1227-1269)' is relevant for the history of the empire as a whole. The introductory study on 'Sources. II. The Mongol invasion' is similarly as yet unsurpassed.

BOYLE, J A (ed), *CHI*, V. *The Saljuq and Mongol periods.*

See chapters 4, 'Dynastic and political history of the Īl-Khāns', (BOYLE), 6, 'The socio-economic condition of Iran under the Īl-Khāns', (I P PETRUSHEVSKII), and 7, 'Religion under the Mongols', (A BAUSANI).

BROWNE, E G, *A literary history of Persia*, *op.cit.* II. *From Firdawsí to Sa^c dí*, and III. *A history of Persian literature under Tartar domination, 1265-1502.*

The historical background deals respectively with the era of the two great Mongol invasions and with that of the Īl-Khāns and their successors.

IQBĀL, ^c Abbās, *Tārīkh-i mufaṣṣal-i Īrān az istīlā-yi Mughūl tā i^c lān-i mashrūṭiyyat*, vol.I only published, Tehran 1933. 2nd ed. 1962.

The standard textbook in Persian for the Mongol period.

LAMBTON, A K S, *Landlord and peasant in Persia*, *op.cit.* 3.3.

See chapter 4, 'The Mongols and the break with tradition'.

MINORSKY, V, *The Turks, Iran and the Caucasus in the Middle Ages*, *op.cit.* 3.3.

A collection of sixteen articles, of which a few are concerned with the Mongol period but the majority with the 15th century.

4.4 *Works specifically concerned with the Mongols and with Mongol Iran*

The standard work on Iran under the Īl-Khāns is now

SPULER, B, *Die Mongolen in Iran: Politik, Verwaltung and Kultur der Ilchanzeit 1220-1350*, Iranische Forschungen I, Berlin 1939, 3rd rev.ed. 1968.

Includes analyses of administrative techniques, of military organization, and of relations with the various religious groups, and contains a fairly exhaustive bibliography.

For a more strictly narrative account, however, the older general works on Mongol history are still of some value.

D'OHSSON, Baron A C M, *Histoire des Mongols depuis Tchinguiz-Khan jusqu'à Timour Bey ou Tamerlan*, 4 vols, 2nd ed. Amsterdam/The Hague 1834-35. 3rd ed. Amsterdam 1852. (See vols III and IV.)

Utilises thoroughly the primary material in Arabic and Persian then available.

HOWORTH, Sir Henry H, *History of the Mongols from the ninth to the nine-*

teenth century, 3 vols in 4, London 1876-88, especially III, *The Mongols of Persia*.

The work of an ethnologist rather than a historian or linguist, relying greatly on secondary material and in this respect inferior to D'OHSSON. But it has the merit of including detailed chronological surveys of the local and successor dynasties.

BLOCHET, E, *Introduction à l'histoire des Mongols de Fadl Allah Rashid ed-Din*, GMS, XII, Leiden/London 1910.

Contains useful material on the political and diplomatic history of Īl-Khānid Iran gleaned partly from Chinese sources.

Modern works include

BOYLE, J A, *The Mongol World Empire 1206-1370*, Variorum reprs, London 1977.

A collection of articles pertaining to the history of the empire in general, some of which are of particular relevance to Iran.

PELLIOT, P, *Notes on Marco Polo*, 2 vols, Paris 1959-63.

Published posthumously as a glossary of proper names and terms, each with its own commentary: a good many of these pertain to Īl-Khānid Iran.

For a modern Persian study of the Īl-Khāns, see, in addition to IQBĀL's work mentioned previously,

MURTAŻAVĪ, M, *Taḥqīq dar bāra-yi daura-yi Īlkhānān-i Īrān*, Tabriz 1962.

Of the more recent works on Central Asian and Mongol history, see

GROUSSET, R, *L'Empire Mongol (1re phase)*. Eugène CAVAIGNAC, *Histoire du Monde*, VIII, 3, Paris 1941.

Takes the narrative down only as far as 1259, and consequently is of value only for the Mongol occupation prior to the Īl-Khāns.

—— *L'Empire des Steppes. Attila. Gengis Khan. Tamerlan*, Paris 1939, 4th ed. 1965. English tr. N WALFORD, *The Empire of the Steppes*, New Brunswick 1970.

Contains a succinct chronological survey of the entire Mongol period in Iran (chapter 5).

SAUNDERS, J J, *The history of the Mongol conquests*, London 1971.

A readable and very balanced account of the subjugation of Iran and its aftermath: see especially chapter 7.

The economic historiography of Iran, with the exception of the important chapter in LAMBTON's above-mentioned work, is dominated by the writings of

PETRUSHEVSKII, I P, *Zemledelie i agrarnye otnosheniya v Irane XIII-XIV vv*. Moscow 1960. Persian tr. K KISHĀVARZ, *Kishāvarzī va munāşabāt-i arżī dar Īrān*, 2 vols, Tehran 1965.

The author's views are more readily accessible, if in an abbreviated form, in his contribution to the *Cambridge History of Iran*, V. See also the regional study of

ALIZADE, A A, *Sotsial'no-ekonomicheskaya i politicheskaya istoriya Azerbaidzhana XIII-XIV vv.*, Baku 1954.

More specific are

JAHN, K, 'Paper currency in Iran. A contribution to the cultural and economic history of Iran in the Mongol period', *JAH* IV, 1970 :101-35.

MASSON SMITH, J, Jr, 'Mongol and nomadic taxation', *HJAS* XXX, 1970 :46-85.

The effects of the invasions upon Iran's long-term development have been the subject of some controversy: see now

LEWIS, B, 'The Mongols, the Turks and the Muslim polity', *Islam in history*, London 1973 :179-98.

On the subject of Mongol law, see

AYALON, D, 'The Great Yāsa of Chingiz Khān: a reexamination', *Studia Islamica* XXXIII, 1971 :97-140; XXXIV, 1971 :151-80; XXXVI, 1972 :113-58; XXXVIII, 1973 :107-56.

A criticism of the sources used by earlier authorities and of their conclusions.

4.5 *The local and successor dynasties*

Pending the appearance of the *Cambridge History of Iran*, VI. *The Timurid and Safavid periods*, there exists no individual work devoted to the century and a half between the extinction of the Īl-Khāns and the rise of the Ṣafavids. The following are monographs on individual dynasties which arose on the disintegration of the Īl-Khānid state:

BAYĀNĪ, Shīrīn, *Tārīkh-i āl-i Jalāyir*, Tehran 1966.

SUTŪDA, H Q, *Tārīkh-i āl-i Muẓaffar*, 2 vols, Tehran 1967-68.

GHANĪ, Qāsim, *Baḥs dar āsār va afkār va aḥvāl-i Ḥāfiẓ*, *op.cit.* VI 2.10, vol.I, *Tārīkh-i ʿaṣr-i Ḥāfiẓ*.

Concerned primarily with Fārs under Muẓaffarid rule.

MASSON SMITH, J, Jr, *The history of the Sarbadār dynasty 1336-1381 A.D. and its sources*, Paris 1970.

Now the standard work and including detailed analyses of both literary and numismatic sources.

For an alternative view, see

PETRUSHEVSKII, I P, 'Dvizhenie Serbedarov v Khorasane', *Uchenie Zapiski Instituta Vostokovedeniya* XIV, 1956 :91-162. Persian tr. K KISHĀVARZ, 'Nahżat-i Sarbadārān dar Khurāsān', *Farhang-i Īrān Zamīn* X, 1962 :124-224.

AUBIN, J, 'La fin de l'etat Sarbadar du Khorassan', *JA* CCLXII, 1974 :95-118.

—— 'Le khanat de Čaġatai et le Khorassan (1334-1380)', *Turcica*, VIII/2, 1976 :16-60.

Contains a great deal of useful material on the Kart rulers of Herat.

For the 15th century, the era of the Turcoman dynasties, two brief introductory surveys are available.

MINORSKY, V, 'La Perse au XVe siècle', *Orientalia Romana: essays and lectures*, I. Serie Orientale Roma, 17, Rome 1958 :99-117.

ROEMER, H R, 'Das türkmenische Intermezzo. Persische Geschichte zwischen Mongolen und Safawiden', *AMI*, n.F. IX, 1976 :263-97.

A further useful source is

HINZ, W, *Irans Aufstieg zum Nationalstaat im fünfzehnten Jahrhundert*, Berlin/Leipzig 1936.

Actually concerned with the rise of the Ṣafavids, it is of relevance also to the history of the two Turcoman dynasties.

SÜMER, F, *Kara Koyunlular (Başlangıçtan Cihan-Şah'a kadar)*, vol.I only published. Türk Tarih Kurumu Yayınlarından, VII, seri 49, Ankara 1967.

WOODS, J E, *The Aqquyunlu: clan, confederation, empire. A study in 15th/9th century Turko-Iranian politics*, Studies in Middle Eastern History, 3, Minneapolis/Chicago 1976.

The latter contains a valuable survey of the primary sources and a very full bibliography for the century as a whole. In addition, many of the articles of MINORSKY reprinted in *The Turks, Iran and the Caucasus*, *op.cit.*, illuminate particular aspects of the Turcoman period.

Besides the work of RABINO DI BORGOMALE on the Caspian territories mentioned above (3.3), there are a few other regional studies:

AUBIN, J, 'Les princes d'Ormuz du XIIIe au XVe siècle', *JA* CCXLI, 1953 :77-138;

FINSTER, B, 'Sistan zur Zeit timuridischer Herrschaft', *AMI*, n.F. IX, 1976 :207-15; and

IBRAGIMOV, D, *Feodal'nye gosudarstva na territorii Azerbaidzhana XV veka*, Baku 1962.

In part concerned with the Qarā- and Āq-Quyunlū, it treats also of the minor dynasty of the Shirvān-Shāhs.

4.6 *Tīmūr and the Tīmūrids*

There is as yet no single monograph on the Timurids, though the general histories, notably GROUSSET, *L'Empire des Steppes*, *op.cit.* 4.4, (chapter

7) provide an introductory summary. Tīmūr himself has been the subject of a number of studies, of which the only one in English is the semi-popular, but still useful, work of

HOOKHAM, H, *Tamburlaine the conqueror*, London 1962.

See also the more critical biography of

YAKUBOVSKII, A, 'Timur (opyt kratkoi kharakteristiki)', *Voprosy Istorii*, 8-9, 1946 :42-74.

The more famous of his successors have been covered to a certain extent in the following.

BARTHOLD, W, *Ulugbek i ego vremya*, Petrograd 1918, repr. in his *Sochinenie* II, part 2, Moscow 1964 :23-196. German tr. W HINZ, *Uluġ Beg und seine Zeit*, Leipzig 1935. English tr. V and T MINORSKY, *Four studies on the history of Central Asia*, 3 vols, Leiden 1956-62. II *Ulugh Beg*.

—— *Mir Ali-Šir i politicheskaya zhizn'*, Leningrad 1928, repr. in *Sochinenie*, II, part 2 :197-260. German tr. W HINZ, *Herat unter Husain Baiqara*, Leipzig 1938. English tr. V and T MINORSKY, in *Four Studies*, III *Mīr ᶜAlī-Shīr*, :1-72.

See further

SAVORY, R M, 'The struggle for supremacy in Persia after the death of Tīmūr', *Der Islam* XL, 1964 :35-65.

Sorts out numerous problems of chronology.

AUBIN, J, 'Deux sayyids de Bam au XVe siècle. Contribution à l'histoire de l'Iran Timouride', *Akad. Wiss. u. d. Lit. in Mainz. Abh. der geistes- und sozialwiss. Klasse*, 1956 :373-502.

Effectively a detailed study of Kirmān under Timurid rule during the first half of the century.

4.7 *Iran's contacts with the outside world during the 13th-15th centuries*

The standard work on relations with the Papacy is now

RICHARD, J, *La Papauté et les missions d'Orient au Moyen Age (XIIIe-XVe siècles)*, Collection de l'École Française de Rome, 33, Rome 1977.

See also

SORANZO, G, *Il Papato, l'Europa Cristiana e i Tartari*, Milan 1930.

Still of value for the more strictly diplomatic aspects.

A resumé of the most recent research is to be found in

BOYLE, J A, 'The Il-Khans of Persia and the Princes of Europe', *CAJ* XX, 1976 :25-40.

For the later period, see

PALOMBINI, B von, *Bündniswerben abendländischer Mächte um Persien 1453-*

1600, Freiburger Islamische Studien, I, Wiesbaden 1967.

For relations with China, see

JAHN, K, 'Wissenschaftliche Kontakte zwischen Iran und China in der Mongolenzeit', *Anzeiger der Österreichischen Akademie der Wissenschaften. Phil.-hist. Klass* CVI, 1969 :199-211.

4.8 *Works on the historical geography of Iran*

In addition to the works listed under this head in the pre-Mongol section, the following refer particularly to the Mongol period.

AUBIN, J, 'Réseau pastoral et réseau caravanier. Les grand'routes du Khurassan à l'èpoque mongole', *Le Monde Iranien et l'Islam* I, 1971 :105-30.

KRAWULSKY, D, *Iran-das Reich der Ilhane. Topographisch-historische Studie*, Wiesbaden 1978.

RABINO DI BORGOMALE, H L, 'Deux descriptions du Gilan du temps des Mongols', *JA* CCXXXVIII, 1950 :325-33.

See also 4.9.1 below, Ḥamdallāh MUSTAUFĪ.

4.9 *Primary sources*

It is a commonplace that for the Mongol period a far greater proportion of the primary source material is in Persian than for the preceding era. Nevertheless, non-Persian authorities continue to be virtually indispensable. Only those Arabic writers who devoted a more or less clearly defined section of their works to Iran are noticed below; and the reader should bear in mind that a great many details relevant to the history of the Īl-Khāns may be gleaned from the general chronicles of Mamlūk Egypt such as those of ABU'L-FIDĀ, al-MUFAḌḌAL, al-MAQRĪZĪ and IBN TAGHRĪBIRDĪ. In addition, it has seemed necessary to insert sources in other languages - Armenian, Syriac and Far Eastern - where these contain material of special relevance to the history of Iran.

There are two collections of translated extracts:

SPULER, B, *Geschichte der Mongolen, nach östlichen und europäischen Zeugnissen des 13. und 14. Jahrhunderts*, Zürich/Stuttgart 1968.

English tr. H and R DRUMMOND, *History of the Mongols*, London 1972.

Section III is devoted to material on the Īl-Khāns.

TIESENHAUSEN, Baron V G von, *Sbornik materialov otnosyashchikhsya k istorii Zolotoi Ordy*, 2 vols, I, St Petersburg 1884; II, A A ROMASKEVICH and S L VOLYN (eds), Moscow/Leningrad 1941.

The two volumes are composed respectively of Arabic and Persian sources. Strictly speaking, the extracts are concerned with the Mongols of Russia, but include details of relations with Iran.

Individual sources are listed below under four heads: (4.9.1) Chronicles and biographies; (4.9.2) Travellers' accounts; (4.9.3) Documents; and (4.9.4) Treatises and *Insha'*. Within each category they appear in chronological order.

4.9.1 *Chronicles and biographies*

NASAWĪ, Muḥammad b Aḥmad, *Sīrat al-sulṭān Jalāl al-dīn Mankubirtī*, ed. and tr. O HOUDAS, *Histoire du Sultan Djelal ed-Din Mankobirti, prince du Kharezm*, Publications de l'École des Langues Orientales Vivantes, IIIe série, 9 and 10, 2 vols, Paris 1891-95.

Volume II is the translation. An Arabic biography of one of the Mongols' principal enemies, incorporating a good deal of material on the first invasion of Iran.

HAENISCH, E (ed), *Die geheime Geschichte der Mongolen*, 2nd ed., Leipzig 1948.

The most accessible complete translation of the Mongol epic to date: its later chapters include details of the first invasion of Iran.

See also

—— 'Die letzten Feldzüge Cinggis Han's und sein Tod', *Asia Major*, IX, 1933 :503-51.

Translated extracts from Chinese and Mongolian sources on the conqueror's last years, including therefore his campaigns in Iran and Khwārizm.

JŪZJĀNĪ, *Ṭabaqāt-i Nāṣirī*, op.cit. 1.3.

Ṭabaqāt xvi and xxiii cover respectively the Khwārizm-Shāhs and the advent of the Mongols. For the defects of RAVERTY's commentary, see BARTHOLD, *Turkestan*, *op.cit.*, pp.60-61.

JUVAINĪ, Alā' al-dīn ᶜAṭā, *Tarīkh-i jahān-gushā*, M QAZVĪNĪ (ed), vols I and II, *GMS* xvi, 1/2, London/Leiden 1912, 1916; vol.III, facsimile, *RAS*, James G Forlong Fund, no.10, London 1931. English tr. J A BOYLE, *The history of the World-Conqueror*, 2 vols, Manchester 1958.

The work of a Persian bureaucrat in the service of the early Īl-Khāns, it embraces the Khwārizm-Shāhs and the Assassins, as well as the history of the Mongols down to 1256.

ṬŪSĪ, Naṣīr al-dīn, suppl. to JUVAINĪ's work. English tr. J A BOYLE, 'The death of the last ᶜAbbāsid Caliph: A contemporary Muslim account', *Journal of Semitic Studies*, VI, 1961 :145-61.

GANJAKEÇI, Kirakos, *Patmut^{c}yun Hayoç*. French tr. M F BROSSET, *Deux historiens arméniens, Kirakos de Gantzac, XIIIe siècle* .... vol.1 only, St Petersburg 1870.

An Armenian general chronicle, of considerable value for the Mongol occupation of the Caucasus and neighbouring regions down to c.1270.

DULAURIER, E, 'Les Mongols d'après les historiens arméniens', part 1 (Kirakos), *JA*, 5e série, XI, 1858 :192-155, 426-508; part 2 (Vardan Arawelçi), *JA*, 5e série, XVI, 1860 :273-322.

Translated extracts from the two early Armenian chroniclers.

BAR HEBRAEUS, *Chronicon Syriacum*, ed. and tr. E A Wallis BUDGE, *The Chronography of Gregory Abû l-Faraj ... commonly known as Bar Hebraeus*, 2 vols, Oxford/London 1932.

A universal history in Syriac, of which the later sections deal with the Īl-Khāns; an anonymous continuator brought the work down to 1297. Volume I is the translation.

BUDGE, E A Wallis (ed), *The Monks of Ḳûblâi Khân, Emperor of China*, London 1928.

MONTGOMERY, J A (ed), *The history of Yaballaha III, Nestorian patriarch, and of his vicar Bar Sauma*, New York 1927.

Translations (MONTGOMERY's is only a partial one) of the anonymous biography of the Nestorian prelate, including an account of the mission of his subordinate Rabbān Saumā from Iran to Europe in 1287.

IBN BĪBĪ, Naṣir al-dīn, *Saljūqnāma*, Turkish tr. Th. HOUTSMA (ed), *Histoire des Seldjoucides d'Asie Mineure d'après Ibn Bībī*. Recueil de textes relatifs à l'histoire des Seldjoucides, vol.III. Persian abr. *Mukhtaṣar-i Saljūqnāma*. *Ibid.* (ed), ... *d'après l'abrégé du Seldjouknāmeh d'Ibn Bībī*. Recueil ..., vol.IV, Leiden 1902. German tr. H W DUDA, *Die Seltschukengeschichte des Ibn Bibi*, Copenhagen 1959.

Essentially a history of the Saljūqids of Anatolia, it provides valuable insights into the Īl-Khāns' relations with a client state.

VAṢṢĀF, Shihāb al-dīn ^{c}Abdallāh, *Tajziyat al-amṣār va tazjiyat al-a^{c}ṣār*, ed. and German tr. J von HAMMER-PURGSTALL, *Geschichte Wassaf's*, vol.I only, Vienna 1856.

A detailed history of the Īl-Khāns down to c.1327, designed as a continuation of JUVAINĪ's work: this volume covers the period as far as 1284.

RASHĪD AL-DĪN, Fażlallāh, *Jāmi^{c} al-tavārīkh*, *op.cit.* 1.3.

A vast general history, compiled under the aegis of one of the Īl-Khāns' principal ministers: RASHĪD AL-DĪN was the subject of a special commemoration volume in 1970 (*CAJ* XIV) containing articles on various aspects of his epoch.

The section on the Īl-Khāns themselves was partially translated by E QUATREMÈRE, *Histoire des Mongols de la Perse*, volume I only, Paris 1836, reprinted Amsterdam 1968; and there now exists a complete Russian translation in *Dzhami-at-tavarikh*, III, Baku 1957, A A ALIZADE (ed) and A K ARENDS (tr). The earlier portions of the work, however, are of some importance for the history of Iran and of the Īl-Khāns: (the Turkish and Mongol tribes, and the history of the Mongols prior to Chingīz Khān) A A KHETAGUROV (tr), *Sbornik letopisei*, I, part 1, Moscow/Leningrad 1952; (the biography of Chingīz Khān) O I SMIRNOVA (tr), *Sbornik letopisei*, I, part 2, Moscow/Leningrad 1952; (the Great Khans from the death of Chingīz Khān to c.1303) J A BOYLE (tr), *The Successors of Genghis Khan*, London/New York 1971, and Yu P VERKHOVSKII (tr), *Sbornik letopisei*, II, Moscow/Leningrad 1960.

MUSTAUFĪ, Ḥamdallāh, *Tārīkh-i Guzīda*, *op.cit.*

A general history down to c.1330, containing a significant quantity of original material on the later Īl-Khāns: a full translation of this work is much to be desired. See also

—— *Nuzhat al-qulūb*, *op.cit.* VIII 3.2.6.

A vast cosmographical work, of which this section is of great value for the historical geography of Iran during the Mongol period.

GRIGOR of Akner, 'History of the Nation of the Archers (the Mongols) by Grigor of Akanc$^{c'}$, ed. and tr. R P BLAKE and R N FRYE, *HJAS* XII, 1949 :269-399. Repr. separately Cambridge, Mass. 1954.

A later Armenian authority (he died c.1335) on Mongol Iran, his work supplies a number of details even for the early period not found in Kirakos and Vardan.

AHARĪ, Abū Bakr al-Quṭbī al-, *Tārīkh-i Shaikh Uvais*, ed. and tr. J B VAN LOON, The Hague 1954.

A general history, dedicated to the second Jalāyirid ruler: the section edited covers the period from 1265-1359.

YAZDĪ, Ghiyās al-dīn ^{c}Alī, *Rūz-nāma-yi ghazavāt-i Hindūstān*, L A ZIMIN and W BARTHOLD (eds), Teksty po istorii Srednei Azii, no.1, Petrograd 1915. Russian tr. A A SEMENOV, *Dnevnik pokhoda Timura v Indiya*, Moscow 1958.

A diary of Tīmūr's Indian campaign in 1398, which is not without importance also for other aspects of Tīmūr's rule in South-West Asia.

SALMĀNĪ, Tāj al-dīn, *Shams al-ḥusn*. German tr. H R ROEMER, *Šams al-ḥusn, eine Chronik vom Tode Timurs bis zum Jahre 1409*, Akad. d. Wiss. u. d.

Lit. Veroff. d. orient. Kommission, VIII, Wiesbaden 1956.

A detailed chronicle of the first few years after Tīmūr's death.

YAZDĪ, Sharaf al-Dīn ᶜAlī, *Ẓafar-nāma*, Mawlawi M ILAHDAD (ed), 2 vols, Calcutta 1885-88; facsimile ed., Tashkent 1972. Abr. French tr. Pétis de la CROIX, *Histoire de Timur-Bec*, Paris 1722, Delft 1723. English tr. from the French, *The History of Timur Bec*, London 1723.

Regrettably the only translations of this valuable history of Tīmūr and his first successor Khalīl Sulṭān.

IBN ᶜARAB-SHĀH, Abu'l-ᶜabbās Aḥmad, *ᶜAjā'ib al maqdūr fī akhbār Tīmūr*. English tr. J H SANDERS, *Tamerlane or Timur, the Great Amir*, London 1936.

An Arabic biography of Timur which should be used with caution: the difficulties are compounded by a somewhat inadequate translation.

ḤĀFIẒ-I ABRŪ, ᶜAbdallāh, *Zail-i Jāmiᶜ al-tavārīkh*, *op.cit*. 1.3.

The continuation of the Iranian section of RASHĪD AL-DĪN's chronicle down to 1392-93: the translation is at times a poor rendering of a text which itself abounded in errors to be rectified in a later edition.

SCHMIDT-DUMONT, M (ed), *Türkmenische Herrscher des 15. Jahrhunderts in Persien und Mesopotamien nach dem Tariḫ al-Ġiyāṯī*. Islamkundliche Untersuchungen, 6, Freiburg i. Br. 1970.

Partial edition, with translation, of a general Arabic chronicle.

ISFIZĀRĪ, Muᶜīn al-dīn Muḥammad, *Raużat al-jannāt fī auṣāf madīna Harāt*. French tr. Barbier de MEYNARD, 'Extraits de la chronique persane de Herat', *JA*, 5e série, XVI, 1860 :461-520; XVII, 1861 :438-57, 473-522; XX, 1862 :268-319.

A local chronicle of Khurāsān down to 1470-71.

KHUNJĪ, Fażl-allāh b Rūzbihān al-, *Tārīkh-i ᶜĀlam-ārā-yi Amīnī*. Abr. English tr. V MINORSKY, *Persia in A.D. 1478-1490*, Royal Asiatic Soc. Mono. 16, London 1957.

A major source on the last rulers of the Āq-Qoyunlū dynasty.

4.9.2 *Travellers' accounts*

POLO, Marco, *Divisament dou Monde*, ed. and tr. A C MOULE and P PELLIOT, *The Description of the World*, 2 vols, London 1938.

To be used in conjunction with PELLIOT's *Notes on Marco Polo*, *op.cit*. 4.4.

IBN BAṬṬŪṬA, *Tuḥfat al-nuẓẓār*, *op.cit*. VIII 3.2.6.

The invaluable itinerary of a Moroccan pilgrim who visited Iran during the 1330s: volume II is especially relevant. Volume IV is being prepared by Professor C F BECKINGHAM.

ᶜUMARĪ, Abu'l-ᶜabbās Aḥmad, *Masālik al-abṣār fī mamālik al-amṣār*, ed. and tr. K LECH, *Das mongolische Weltreich*, Asiatische Forschungen, XXII, Wiesbaden 1968.

A detailed survey of the known world by an observer in Mamlūk Egypt, compiled chiefly from contemporary travellers' accounts and hence a most important source: LECH provides a very full commentary. Īl-Khānid Iran is dealt with in chapter 5.

IBN KHALDŪN, ᶜAbd al-raḥmān, *al-Taᶜrīf*. English tr. W J FISCHEL, *Ibn Khaldūn and Tamerlane, their historic meeting in Damascus, 1401 A.D. (803 A.H.): A study based on Arabic manuscripts of Ibn Khaldun's 'autobiography'*, Berkeley/Los Angeles 1952.

CLAVIJO, Ruy Gonzales de, *Embajada al Gran Tamorlan*, *op.cit.* VIII 4.1.

Narrative of a Castilian envoy to Tīmūr's court at Samarqand.

BARBARO, Josafa, and Ambrogio CONTARINI, 'Travels to Tana and Persia', *op. cit.* VIII 4.1.

The accounts of the two Italian visitors to Iran in the later 15th century, together with narratives of lesser importance dating from the 16th century.

4.9.3 *Documents*

MOSTAERT, A, and F W CLEAVES (eds), *Les lettres de 1289 et 1305 des ilkhans Argun et Öljeitü à Philippe le Bel*, Harvard-Yenching Institute, Scripta Mongolica Monograph Series, 1, Cambridge, Mass. 1962.

Now the standard edition, with translation and commentary, of the two letters.

TIEPOLO, M F (ed), *La Persia e la Repubblica di Venezia*, *op.cit.* III 4.1.4.

Contains the texts of the documents, together with a Persian translation.

4.9.4 *Treatises and Inshā'*

MINORSKY, V, and M MINOVI (eds), 'Naṣīr al-dīn Ṭūsī on finance', *Iranica. Twenty articles*, Tehran University Publications 775, Tehran 1964 :64-85.

Contains a translation of the discussion on finance drafted for one of the first two Īl-Khāns, together with a commentary.

RASHĪD AL-DĪN, *Mukātabāt*. Russian tr. A I FALINA, *Rashid ad-Din: Perepiska*. Pamyatniki Pis'mennosti Vostoka, XVII, Moscow 1971.

The correspondence of the great Īl-Khānid statesman. The authenticity of some of the letters has been questioned: see R LEVY, *JRAS*, 1946, pp.74-78.

ᶜALĀ-YI TABRĪZĪ, Falak, *Qānūn al-saᶜādat* and *Saᶜādat-nāma*, ed. and tr. M NABĪPŪR, *Die beiden persischen Leitfäden des Falak ᶜAlā-ye Tabrīzī*

über das staatliche Rechnungswesen im 14. Jahrhundert, Göttingen 1973.
The two major administrative manuals for the Mongol period.

HINZ, W (ed), 'Ein orientalisches Handelsunternehmen im XV. Jahrhundert', *Die Welt des Orients*, I, 1947-52 :313-40.
The translation of the anonymous economic treatise *Shams al-siyāq*.

DAVĀNĪ, Jalāl al-dīn Muḥammad, *ᶜArż-nāma*. English tr. V MINORSKY, 'A civil and military review in Fārs in 881/1476', *BSOAS* X, 1940-42 :141-78. Repr. in MINORSKY, *The Turks, Iran and the Caucasus*, *op.cit.*, no.15.

ROEMER, H R (ed), *Staatschreiben der Timuridenzeit: Das Šarafnāmä des ᶜAbdallāh Marwārīd*. Akad. d. Wiss. u. d. Literatur. Veröff. d. orient. Kommission, III, Wiesbaden 1952.
A collection, made during the Ṣafavid period, of documents largely dating from the era of the Tīmūrids.

4.10 *Ancillaries and hilfsmittel*

DOERFER, G, *Türkische und mongolische Elemente im neupersischen*. Akad. d. Wiss. u. d. Literatur. Veröff. d. orient. Komm, XVI, XIX, XX, XXI, 4 vols, Wiesbaden 1963-75.
An invaluable dictionary serving as a guide to the numerous Turkish and Mongol technical terms which begin to feature in Iranian historiography following the conquest.

5. *IRAN UNDER THE ṢAFAVIDS*

5.1 *Introduction*

Until very recent times, there has been a sad lack of interest in Iranian history on the part of Iranian and western scholars alike. The great 19th century works on Islamic history were written by men who were Arabists. Persian history, if dealt with at all, was treated as a somewhat baffling aberration, a curious and rather unimportant deviation from the mainstream of Islamic history. Even western scholars of the more recent past have been afflicted by the same syndrome. This is clearly demonstrated in the First Edition of the *Encyclopaedia of Islam* (Leiden 1913-38), in which articles on Iranian history are (with certain notable exceptions, such as those of Vladimir MINORSKY) often sketchy and inadequate; moreover, they contain errors of fact sometimes of a quite egregious kind. In addition, the coverage of Iranian history by the First Edition of the *Encyclopaedia of Islam* has major lacunae: for example, the article on Persian and Arabic historiography, published under the title *Ta'rīkh* in the *Supplement* to the First Edition (1938), completely ignores the existence of a rich Ṣafavid historiography. The neglect of their own history by Iranian scholars is less easy to explain. Doubtless an important factor has been the national predilection for the study of literature rather than history. It should be noted, too, that (again with some notable exceptions) much of the historical writing that does exist is narrative and descriptive rather than analytical in character, because of the dearth of Iranian historians trained in western methodology.

If there has been a neglect of Iranian history in general, the same is true *a fortiori* of Ṣafavid history. Prior to 1935, the history of Iran during the Ṣafavid period was almost *tabula rasa*. Even the basic chronology of the period had not been established with any degree of certainty. In 1936, Walther HINZ published his *Irans Aufstieg zum Nationalstaat im Fünfzehnten Jahrhundert*, and this was followed in 1943 by Vladimir MINORSKY's translation with commentary and notes of the *Tadhkirat al-Mulūk*, which is still the only manual of Ṣafavid administrative practice extant. These two works are landmarks in the study of Ṣafavid history by western scholars. Based on a careful study and analysis of the primary sources, above all the historical chronicles, they not only constituted a quantum progression in our knowledge of Ṣafavid history but suggested the lines of future research. Today, the historical framework of the Ṣafavid period is reasonably well established, and it is possible to obtain a fairly clear picture of Ṣafavid political and administrative institutions. Less progress has been made on economic and social studies of the Ṣafavid period, because, as Amin BANANI has pointed out, the historical chronicles, 'on material of value to economic and social historians ... are annoyingly vague and ambiguous', (*The social and economic structure of the Safavid empire in its heyday*, a paper submitted to the Harvard Colloquium on Tradition and Change in the Middle East, December 1967, p.14). Nevertheless, an encouraging start has been made in these areas too, by scholars such as Bert FRAGNER and R W FERRIER.

In view of the fact that it was the Ṣafavid rulers who laid the foundations of modern Iran, the almost total neglect of Ṣafavid history by Iranian scholars until a short time ago, is extraordinary. Sayyid Aḥmad KASRAVĪ published a series of penetrating studies on the origins of the Ṣafavids in the late 1920s, but nothing else of note appeared until the publication of Naṣrallāh FALSAFĪ's four-volume work *Zindigānī-yi Shāh ᶜAbbās-i Avval* (Tehran 1955-62), a work which in its way is as important as the pioneering works of western scholars on Ṣafavid history mentioned above.

The Ṣafavid period was notable for a remarkable flowering of the arts, and the literature on this aspect of Ṣafavid culture is voluminous. Under the Ṣafavids, there was a significant increase in diplomatic and commercial relations between Iran and western Europe, and the religious tolerance of Shāh ᶜAbbās the Great (1588-1629) encouraged Catholic religious Orders to establish convents at Iṣfahān and elsewhere. Again, the volume of literature on these aspects of the Ṣafavid period is considerable. Particularly valuable for the historian are the accounts left by European travellers of their visits to Ṣafavid Iran. The study of certain aspects of Ṣafavid cultural life, however, is still in its infancy. The neglect until recent times of Ṣafavid historiography has already been mentioned. Even more striking is the lack of any serious study of Ṣafavid literature as a whole. The scathing verdict on Ṣafavid poetry of E G BROWNE, extended by his Iranian contemporary Mīrzā Muḥammad Khān QAZVĪNĪ to a sweeping denunciation of the Ṣafavid period as a cultural desert, was accepted uncritically by subsequent scholars both in Iran and in the west. It was not until 1974, with the publication of Ehsan YAR-SHATER's seminal paper 'Ṣafavid literature: progress or decline', that any serious reconsideration of the received wisdom on this subject was made. The situation in regard to Ṣafavid philosophy is similar. According to most standard works on Islamic philosophy, IBN RUSHD, known to the west as AVERRÖES, who died in 1198 AD, was the 'last Muslim philosopher', and this mistaken view has been adopted by many modern Arab, Pakistani and Indian scholars. The resurrection of the important Ishrāqiyya or 'Illuminationist' school of Iranian philosophy, and the study of its further development at the hands of Ṣafavid philosophers, has been the work primarily of two scholars, one western, Henry CORBIN, and one Iranian, Seyyed Hossein NASR (Sayyid Ḥusain NAṢR).

The emphasis in the bibliography which follows will be on political and dynastic history, since cultural history (literature, religion and philosophy, science and technology, arts and crafts) will be covered by separate bibliographies, as will the general area of the social sciences. A few works of outstanding importance in these areas which are specifically relevant to the Ṣafavid period will, however, be listed for the convenience of the reader. A special section will be devoted to Ṣafavid travel literature, mentioned earlier as an important historical source for the period. Attention will be drawn to works which, though not confined to political history, nevertheless themselves contain useful bibliographies of the Ṣafavid period in general.

Articles in journals will not, as a general rule, be listed, since it is assumed that full use will be made of standard research tools such as J D

PEARSON's *Index Islamicus 1906-55*, Cambridge 1958, and subsequent supplements published at five-yearly intervals. On Ṣafavid matters, see particularly the articles by Jean AUBIN, Hafez F FARMAYAN, A K S LAMBTON, Laurence LOCKHART, V MINORSKY, J R PERRY, H R ROEMER, and R M SAVORY.

5.2 *Works of reference, festschrifts, and general works on Islamic and Iranian history which contain articles or chapters of importance for the history of the Ṣafavid period*

ARBERRY, A J, *et al*. (ed), *The Cambridge history of Iran*, Cambridge 1968-.
Only three volumes of this eight-volume project have appeared to date. Volume VI, publication of which has been expected for many years, is devoted to the Tīmūrid and Ṣafavid periods.

BOSWORTH, C E (ed), *Iran and Islam*, Edinburgh 1971.
Has several essays of relevance to the Ṣafavid period.

BRAUN, Hellmut, 'Iran under the Safavids and in the 18th century', SPULER, *The Muslim World*, Part III, *The last great Muslim empires*, *op.cit.* :181-218.
A sound introduction. Has useful bibliography.

BROWNE, E G, *A literary history of Persia*, *op.cit.*
Despite its title, this standard history of Persian literature contains much useful material of a historical and cultural nature. See especially volume IV for material on the Ṣafavids.

BUSSE, H, *Untersuchungen zum islamischen Kanzleiwesen*, Cairo 1959.
Of great use for determining the precise meaning of the technical vocabulary used in documents issued by Ṣafavid chancelleries.

Encyclopaedia of Islam, 2nd ed. *op.cit.*
See the general article 'Iran. v. history: (b) Turkomans to the present day', (R M SAVORY), vol.IV, pp.33-43; and the article 'Bārūd. v. The Ṣafawids' (R M SAVORY), vol.I, pp.1066-68, for a discussion of the use of firearms by the Ṣafavids.

See also the following articles on individual rulers, towns, institutions, etc., which contain information on the Safavids:

'ᶜAbbās I', R M SAVORY, vol.I :7-8.
'Ardabīl', R N FRYE, vol.I :625-26.
'Dārūgha', A K S LAMBTON, vol.II :162-63.
'Ghulām. ii. Persia', C E BOSWORTH, vol.II :1081-84.
'Īlāt', A K S LAMBTON, vol.III :1095-1110.
'Iṣfahān. (1) History', A K S LAMBTON; '(2) Monuments', J SOURDEL-THOMINE, vol.IV :97-107.

'Isma^cil I', R M SAVORY, vol.IV :186-87.

'Ḳizil-bāsh', R M SAVORY, vol.V :243-45.

In addition, the *Index* to volumes I-III, Leiden/Paris 1979, may now be used with advantage.

LAMBTON, A K S, *Landlord and peasant in Persia*, *op.cit.* 3.3.

Chapter V of this classic work on land tenure in Iran deals with the Ṣafavid period.

—— 'Persian biographical literature', Bernard LEWIS and P M HOLT (eds), *Historians of the Middle East*, Oxford 1962.

This paper contains some interesting remarks on Ṣafavid historiography.

MALCOLM, John, *The History of Persia from the most early period to the present time*, 2 vols, London 1815. Another ed., London 1829.

The greatest 19th century history of Iran. Offers shrewd insights not only into Ṣafavid history but also into the Iranian character.

MINORSKY, V, *A history of Sharvān and Darband*, Cambridge 1958.

Contains useful historical information on the Shīrvānshāhs, the arch-enemies of the early Ṣafavids, and valuable geographical data on the Caucasus regions subsequently incorporated into the Ṣafavid empire.

PIGULEVSKAYA, N V, *Istoriya Irana ...*, *op.cit.* 1.2.

Chapters 7-9 are on the Ṣafavids.

SAVORY, R M, 'Safavid Persia', *CHIs*, vol.I, part III/5 :394-429.

TOGAN, Z V, 'Sur l'origine des Safavides', *Mélanges Louis Massignon*, vol.III, Damascus 1957 :345-57.

Describes the (successful) attempt by the Ṣafavid family to obscure its own origins by falsifying the historical evidence, but appears unaware of earlier research by Sayyid Aḥmad KASRAVĪ on the same subject.

5.3 *Works specifically concerned with the Ṣafavid period*

BAYANI, K, *Les relations de l'Iran avec l'Europe occidentale à l'époque safavide*, Paris 1937.

An early work on the subject but still useful.

BELLAN, L-L, *Chah ^cAbbas* I, Paris 1932.

The only biography in a western language of the greatest of the Ṣafavid shahs. Based on the primary sources, but unfortunately lacks references to them.

BLUNT, WIlfrid and Wim SWAAN, *Isfahan: pearl of Persia*, London/Toronto 1966.

A visually beautiful record of the Ṣafavid capital.

FALSAFĪ, Naṣrallāh, *Zindigānī-yi Shāh ^cAbbās-i avval*, *op.cit.* 5.1.

A valuable work in Persian on the life and times of Shāh ᶜAbbās I.

GANDJEI, Tourkhan, *Il canzoniere di Šāh Ismāᶜīl Ḫaṭā'ī*, Naples 1959.

A critical edition of Shāh Ismāᶜīl's poems in Āzarī Turkish.

GAUBE, Heinze, and Eugen WIRTH, *Der Bazar von Isfahan*, Wiesbaden 1978.

An excellent, detailed study of the Royal Bazaar at Isfahan which is of great interest to the Ṣafavid historian.

GLASSEN, Erika, *Die frühen Safawiden nach Qazi Ahmad Qumi*. Islamkundliche Untersuchungen Band 5, Freiburg im Breisgau 1970.

A work of careful scholarship.

HINZ, W, *Irans Aufstieg zum Nationalstaat im fünfzehnten Jahrhundert*, Berlin/Leipzig 1936.

A pioneering and valuable work which gives a detailed account of the historical events which attended the rise of the Ṣafavid dynasty. Of particular interest is the account of the relations between the Ṣafavids and the Turcoman dynasties (Qarā Qoyūnlū and Āq Qoyūnlū).

—— 'Schah Ismaᶜil II. Ein Beitrag zur Geschichte der Safaviden', *Mitteilungen des Seminars für orientalische Sprachen an der K Friedrich-Wilhelms-Üniversität zu Berlin: Westasiatische Abteilung*, 36, 1933 :19-100.

The only detailed account of the reign of Shāh Ismāᶜīl II.

HORST, H, *Tīmūr und Hōjä ᶜAlī, Ein Beitrag zur Geschichte der Ṣafawiden*, Abh. d. Akad. d. Wiss. u. der Literatur in Mainz. Wiesbaden 1958.

Deals with the alleged meetings between Tīmūr and Khwāja ᶜAlī, the head of the Ṣafavid Order.

Iranian Studies, vol.VII, 1974.

This volume of the journal is a special issue devoted to the proceedings of the Iṣfahān colloquium held at Harvard University in January 1974. It contains many excellent papers on the Ṣafavid period written by specialists.

LOCKHART, Laurence, *The fall of the Ṣafavī dynasty and the Afghan occupation of Persia*, Cambridge 1958.

The standard work on the subject.

MAZZAOUI, M M, *The origins of the Ṣafawīs*, Wiesbaden 1972.

A doctoral thesis on the subject.

MINORSKY, Vladimir (ed. tr. and annot.), *Tadhkirat al-Mulūk*, *GMS*, NS XVI, London 1943.

A landmark in Ṣafavid studies. Invaluable not only because it is an English translation of the only extant manual of Ṣafavid administration, but for the translator's 'Prolegomena' on the social and economic background of the Ṣafavid state and on questions of state organization; for his extraordinarily erudite commentary on the text; and for the appendices on various aspects of Ṣafavid history.

QUIRING-ZOCHE, Rosemarie, *Isfahan im 15. und 16. Jahrhundert: ein Beitrag zur persischen Stadtgeschichte*, Freiburgh 1980.

RIAZUL ISLAM, *Indo-Persian relations*, Tehran 1970.

The only comprehensive account of relations between the Ṣafavids and the Mughal empire in India.

—— *A calendar of documents on Indo-Persian relations (1500-1750)*, vol.I, Iranian Culture Foundation and Institute of Central and West Asian Studies, Tehran/Karachi 1979.

ROEMER, H R, *Der Niedergang Irans nach dem Tode Ismāᶜīl's des Grausamen 1577-1581*, Würzburg/Aumühle 1939.

The history of the first few years of the weak Sulṭān Muḥammad Shāh.

ROSS, Sir E Denison, 'Early days of Shāh Ismāᶜīl', *JRAS*, 1896 :250-340.

Based on the relevant portion of British Library MS. Or.3248, the best manuscript source for the first part of the reign of the founder of the Ṣafavid dynasty.

—— *Sir Anthony Sherley and his Persian adventure*, Broadway Travellers Series, London 1933.

SARWAR, Ghulam, *The history of Shah Ismāᶜīl Ṣafawī*, Aligarh 1939.

A well-annotated narrative of the events of the reign of Shāh Ismāᶜīl I.

SAVORY, Roger, *Iran under the Safavids*, Cambridge 1980.

SOHRWEIDE, H, 'Der Sieg der Ṣafaviden in Persien und seine Rückwirkungen auf die Schiiten Anatoliens im 16. Jahrhundert', *Der Islam*, Band 41, 1965 :95-223 (Hamburg thesis).

A solid and reliable work.

SÜMER, Faruk, *Safevî devletinin kuruluşu ve gelişmesinde Anadolu Türklerinin rolü*, Ankara 1976.

Contains valuable information on the principal *qizilbāsh* tribes.

5.4 *Contemporary accounts by visitors to and residents in Ṣafavid Iran*

For details of the extremely rich European travel literature relating to the Ṣafavid period, see V MINORSKY, *Tadhkirat al-Mulūk*, pp.6-9. For details of the various editions of the travellers, see the work by John EMERSON, listed below (5.5).

The Huguenot jeweller Jean CHARDIN (*op.cit*. VIII 4.2) is without question the doyen of the European travellers who visited Iran during the Ṣafavid period and left an account of their visit. His extraordinarily accurate and perceptive descriptions of the Ṣafavid system of government both complement and corroborate the *Tadhkirat al-Mulūk*.

The following works in this category are of especial interest:

A Chronicle of the Carmelites in Persia, 2 vols, London 1939.

Should be used with caution, since the Carmelite fathers were naturally inclined to assess the Ṣafavid shahs primarily on the basis of their attitude toward Christians resident in Iran. In addition, the historical data is not always accurate. Nevertheless, this work affords interesting insights into the history of the period.

BOXER, C R (ed), *Commentaries of Ruy Freyre de Andrade*, Broadway Travellers Series, London 1930.

A valuable contemporary account of Portuguese activities in the Persian Gulf in the 17th century, including a description of the capture of Hurmuz by a combined Anglo-Persian force in 1622.

DU MANS, R, *Estat de la Perse en 1660*, *op.cit.* VIII 4.2.

HERBERT, Sir Thomas, *Travels in Persia*, *op.cit.* VIII 4.2.

LE STRANGE, G (tr. and ed), *Don Juan of Persia, A Shiᶜah Catholic*, Broadway Travellers Series, London 1926.

A translation of the *Relaciones*, itself a Castilian translation of a diary kept by a *qizilbāsh* officer who was one of four secretaries accompanying a Ṣafavid ambassador to Europe at the beginning of the 17th century.

BARBARO and CONTARINI, *Travels to Tana and Persia*, *op.cit.* VIII 4.1.

5.5 *Unpublished Ph.D. theses*

Valuable material on Ṣafavid history is contained in a number of unpublished theses. Among them are:

BRAUN, H, *Eine unerschlossene Darstellung des Lebens des ersten Safawidenschahs*, Göttingen 1946.

DICKSON, M B, *Shāh Ṭahmāsb and the Uzbegs*, Princeton 1958.

EMERSON, John, *Ex Occidente Lux. Some European sources on the economic structure of Persia between about 1630 and 1690*, Cambridge 1969.

The bibliography to this thesis contains a valuable summary of the editions of the works of the European travellers to Ṣafavid Iran.

SAVORY, R M, *The development of the early Ṣafawid State under Ismāᶜīl and Tahmāsp*, London 1958. (Some material subsequently published in journals.)

5.6 *Persian historical chronicles*

MUNSHĪ, Iskandar Beg, *Tārīkh-i ᶜĀlam-ārā-yi ᶜAbbāsī*, Tehran 1896. Another ed. Tehran 1955. English tr. Roger M SAVORY, *History of Shah ᶜAbbas the Great*, Persian Heritage Series, no.28, 2 vols, Boulder, Col. 1978.

QAZVĪNĪ, Muḥammad Ṭāhir Vaḥīd, *ᶜAbbās-nāma*, Ibrāhīm DIHGĀN (ed), Arāk 1950.

Contemporary, rather flowery biography of Shāh ᶜAbbās II.

QUMMĪ, Qāẓī Aḥmad, *Khulāṣat al-tavārīkh*, ed. and tr. H MÜLLER, *Die Chronik* ..., Wiesbaden 1964.

RŪMLŪ, Ḥasan, *Aḥsan al-tavārīkh*, ᶜAbd al-ḥusain NĀVĀ'Ī (ed), Tehran n.d. repr. 1979. English tr. C N SEDDON, *A chronicle of the early Ṣafawīs*, Gaekwad's Oriental Series no.69, Baroda 1934.

A much abridged and somewhat unreliable translation.

6. *MODERN HISTORY*

6.1 *From the fall of the Ṣafavids to the reign of Nādir Shāh*

The last years of the Ṣafavid dynasty and the subsequent occupation of Iran by the Afghans are fully covered in

LOCKHART, Laurence, *The fall of the Ṣafavi dynasty*, *op.cit.* 5.3.

Includes an extensive bibliography of works in Persian and various European languages.

For the reign of Nādir Shāh himself the best source is still the same author's work:

—— *Nadir Shah. A critical study based mainly upon contemporary sources*, London 1938.

Both of the above works contain a full list of contemporary sources, of which the most important are

CLAIRAC, Louis de la Mamye, *Histoire de Perse depuis le commencement de ce siècle*, Paris 1750.

FRASER, James, *The history of Nadir Shah*, London 1742.

HANWAY, Jonas, *An historical account of the British trade over the Caspian Sea*, *op.cit.* VIII 4.3.

The first three volumes include an account of HANWAY's own experiences in Persia, while the fourth volume is devoted to the life and reign of Nādir Shāh.

KĀẒIM, Muḥammad, *Nāma-yi ᶜālam-ārā-yi Nādirī*. Facsimile edition ed. by N D MIKLUKHO-MAKLAI, 3 vols, Moscow 1960-66.

KRUSINSKI, J T, *Histoire de la dernière revolution de Perse*, *op.cit.* VIII 4.3.

MARᶜASHĪ ṢAFAVĪ, Mirzā Muḥammad Khalīl, *Majmaᶜ al-tavārīkh dar tārīkh-i inqirāẓ-i Ṣafavīya va vaqāyiᶜ-i baᶜd*, ᶜAbbās IQBĀL (ed), Tehran 1949.

A useful secondary source on Nādir Shāh's foreign relations is

HEKMAT, Mohammad-Ali (ḤIKMAT, Muḥammad ᶜAlī), *Essai sur l'histoire des relations politiques irano-ottomanes de 1722 à 1747*, Paris 1937.

6.2 *The Zand period*

Source material on the Zand period is not very abundant, a useful bibliography being available in what is also the standard work:

PERRY, John R, *Karim Khan Zand. A history of Iran, 1747-1779*, Chicago/London 1979.

The principal contemporary sources are

ᶜALī RIẒĀ SHĪRĀZĪ b ᶜAbd al-karīm, *Das târîkh-i Zendîje*, Ernst BEER (ed), London 1888.

A florid account of events from the death of Karīm Khān to the accession of Āg̲h̲a Muḥammad Qājār.

GULISTĀNA, Abu'l-ḥasan, *Mujmal al-tavārīkh-i baᶜd-i Nādiriyya*, Mudarris RAẒAVĪ (ed), Tehran n.d. (1951).

From the death of Nādir S̲h̲āh to the reign of Karīm Khān.

ḤUSAINĪ al-Muns̲h̲ī, Maḥmūd b Ibrāhīm al-Jāmī al-, *Tārīkh-i Aḥmad-S̲h̲āhī*.

Facsimile edition ed. D SAIDMURADOV, 2 vols, Moscow 1974.

History of Afghanistan from the death of Nādir S̲h̲āh to the reign of Aḥmad S̲h̲āh Durrānī.

MARᶜAS̲h̲Ī ṢAFAVĪ, Mīrzā Muḥammad Khalīl, *op.cit.*

Continues up to 1207/1793.

MĪRZĀ MUḤAMMAD, *Rūznāma-yi Mīrzā Muḥammad Kalāntar-i Fārs*, ᶜAbbās IQBĀL (ed), Tehran 1946.

NĀMĪ IṢFAHĀNĪ, Muḥammad Ṣādiq Mūsavī, *Tārīkh-i gītī-gus̲h̲ā*, Saᶜīd NAFĪSĪ (ed), Tehran 1938.

The reign of Karīm Khān.

Important European sources are

FRANCKLIN, William, *Observations made on a tour, op.cit.* VIII 4.3.

The author spent eight months in Shiraz as guest of Jaᶜfar Khān.

WARING, E Scott, *A tour to Sheeraz, op.cit.* VIII 4.4.

Among useful secondary studies of the period the following may be mentioned.

FARĀMARZĪ, Ḥasan, *Karīm Khān Zand va k̲h̲ilīj-i Fārs*, Tehran 1967.

HIDĀYATI, Hādī, *Tārīkh-i Zandīya*, Tehran 1955.

The reign of Karīm Khān.

AMIN, A A, *British interests in the Persian Gulf, 1747-1780*, Leiden 1967.

6.3 *The early Qājār period to 1848*

6.3.1 *Contemporary sources*

ʿABD AL-RAZZĀQ Bēg Maftūn b Najaf Qulī Khān, *Ma'āsir-i sulṭāniyya*, Tabriz 1826. English tr. H J BRYDGES, *The dynasty of the Kajars*, London 1833.

The Persian edition continues to 1825, the English translation only to 1811. History of the reign of Fatḥ ʿAli Shāh.

FASĀ'Ī, Ḥasan, *Fārsnāma-yi Nāṣirī*, Tehran 1895, repr. 1965. English tr. (vol.I), Heribert BUSSE, *History of Persia under Qājār rule*, New York /London 1972.

History of the Qājār period from 1789 to 1882, with special reference to Fārs. The translation has a useful bibliography, and tables of prime ministers, provincial governors and viziers.

HIDĀYAT, Riżā Qulī Khān, *Raużat al-ṣafa-yi Naṣiri*, *op.cit.* VI 3.8.2.

Edition and continuation of MĪR KHWĀND's history (see above 1.3) up to the author's own time.

MALCOLM, John, *The history of Persia*, *op.cit.* 5.2.

The second volume starts in 1722, and is concerned mainly with the history of the rise of the Qājārs.

SIPIHR, Muḥammad Taqī, *Tārīkh-i Qājāriyya. Nāsikh al-tavārīkh*, vol.IX, Tehran 1856.

This volume contains the history of the Qājār dynasty up to the date of publication.

6.3.2 *Secondary sources*

The most useful general histories of this period are

MARKHAM, Clements R, *A general sketch of the history of Persia*, London 1870, 1874, repr. 1978.

WATSON, Robert Grant, *A history of Persia from the beginnings of the nineteenth century to the year 1858*, London 1866.

Also highly relevant are

FERRIER, J P, *History of the Afghans*, London 1858.

KAYE, John W, *History of the war in Afghanistan*, 2 vols, London 1851. 3 vols, London 1874 (3rd ed).

Two interesting biographies are

NAJMĪ, Nāṣir, *Īrān dar miyān-i ṭūfān*, Tehran n.d. (1957).

Mainly a biography of ʿAbbās Mīrzā.

PAKRAVAN, Emineh, *Agha Mohammad Ghadjar*, Essai biographique, Tehran 1953.

For a survey of Iran's foreign relations during this period and subsequently, see

RAMAZANI, Rouhollah K, *The foreign policy of Iran, 1500-1941*, Charlottesville, University of Virginia 1966.

Other works in the same field are

AFSCHAR, Mahmoud, *La politique européenne en Perse*, Berlin 1921.

ATKIN, Muriel, *Russia and Iran 1780-1828*, Minneapolis 1980.

BADDELEY, J F, *The Russian conquest of the Caucasus*, London 1908.

BĪNĀ, ᶜAlī Akbar, *Tārīkh-i siyāsī va dīplūmāsī-yi Īrān*, Tehran 1954.

Covers the period from 1721 to 1828, but with special emphasis on the Qājār reign.

INGRAM, Edward, *The beginning of the great game in Asia 1828-1834*, Oxford 1979.

MAḤMŪD, Maḥmūd, *Tārīkh-i ravābiṭ-i siyāsī-yi Īrān va Ingilīs dar qarn-i nūzdahum-i mīlādī*, 8 vols, Tehran 1949-54.

A massive compilation, to be used with care.

YAPP, M E, *Strategies of British India: Britain, Iran and Afghanistan 1798-1850*, Oxford 1980.

Social and economic studies are to be found in

ALGAR, Hamid, *Religion and state in Iran, 1785-1906*, Berkeley/Los Angeles 1969.

HAMBLY, Gavin, 'An introduction to the economic organization of early Qājār Iran', *Iran*, 2, 1964 :69-81.

Examines some of the significant factors in the economic structure of Iran during the period 1779-1813.

HERSHLAG, Z Y, *Introduction to the modern economic history of the Middle East*, 2nd rev.ed., Leiden 1980.

Deals with the area of the Ottoman Empire, its successor states, and Iran since 1800.

ISSAWI, Charles, *The economic history of Iran, 1800-1914*, London 1971.

NAFĪSĪ, Saᶜīd, *Tārīkh-i ijtimāᶜī va siyāsī-yi Īrān dar daura-yi muᶜāṣir*, vol.I, Tehran 1956.

Covers the period from the accession of the Qājārs to the end of the first war with Russia.

6.4 *The Qājār regime, 1848-1906*

6.4.1 *Contemporary sources*

Several of the Persian histories mentioned in the last section continue to be relevant for the early part of this period, including ᶜABD AL-RAZZĀQ, FASĀ'Ī, HIDĀYAT and SIPIHR. To these may be added

MARĀGHĪ, Muḥammad Ḥasan Iᶜtimād al-salṭana, *Al-ma'āsir va l-āsār*, Tehran 1889.

The first forty years of Nāsir al-dīn Shāh's reign.

KHWURMŪJĪ, Muḥammad Jaᶜfar, *Ḥaqāyiq al-akhbār-i Nāṣirī*, Tehran 1867, new ed. Ḥusain KHADĪV-JAM (ed), Tehran 1965.

Concerned mainly with the first nineteen years of Naṣir al-dīn Shāh's reign.

Personal memoirs start to be of value in the study of this period.

BAHRĀMĪ, ᶜAbdallāh, *Khāṭirāt az ākhir-i salṭanat-i Naṣir al-dīn Shāh tā avval-i kūditā*, Tehran n.d. (1965).

HIDĀYAT, Mahdī Qulī (Mukhbir al-salṭana), *Khāṭirāt va khatarāt*, Tehran 1950, 2nd ed. 1965.

MUSTAUFĪ, ᶜAbdallāh, *Sharh-i zandagānī-yi man, yā tārīkh-i ijtimāᶜī va idārī-yi daura-yi Qājār*, 3 vols in 4, Tehran 1945-47.

Volume I covers the Qājār period up to the death of Nāsir al-dīn Shāh; volume II runs from 1896 to 1918; volume III (2 parts) from 1918 to 1925.

6.4.2 *Secondary sources*

Many of the sources already cited continued to be relevant for the second half of the nineteenth century, including ALGAR, FERRIER, ISSAWI, KAYE, MAḤMUD, MARKHAM, NAFĪSĪ, RAMAZANI, and WATSON.

The most comprehensive work, though concerned more with late nineteenth century Iran, is

CURZON, George N, *Persia and the Persian question*, *op.cit*. VIII 4.4.

A massive survey of Iran towards the end of the Qājār period, based on personal observation as well as on documented sources. Allowance must be made for the author's imperial sentiments.

The standard modern work is

AVERY, Peter W, *Modern Iran*, London 1965.

Covers the history of Iran from the beginning of the nineteenth century to the 1960s.

Another valuable source, in spite of the eccentricities of its author, is

GOBINEAU, A de, *Trois ans en Asie de 1855 à 1858*, 2 vols, Paris 1859.

The same author's second book on Iran, while it is concerned more with religious matters, also contains important historical material.

—— *Les religions et les philosophies dans l'Asie centrale*, *op.cit*. VI 3.8.2.

The story of the foreign concessions granted by Nāsir al-dīn Shāh and his successors is told in

LITTEN, Wilhelm, *Persien von der 'pénétration pacifique' zum 'Protektorat'*, Berlin/Leipzig 1920.

TAIMŪRĪ, Ibrāhīm, *ᶜAṣr-i bīkhabarī, yā tārīkh-i imtiyāzāt dar Īrān*, Tehran 1953.

The same author describes the first successful opposition to the granting of concessions.

—— *Taḥrīm-i tanbākū: avvalīn muqāvamat-i manfī dar Īrān*, Tehran n.d. (1949).

Another important work on the same subject is

KEDDIE, Nikki R, *Religion and rebellion in Iran: the tobacco protest of 1891-1982*, London 1966.

A footnote to KAYE's history of the Afghan wars (*op.cit.*) is

OUTRAM, J, *Lieut.-General Sir James Outram's Persian campaign in 1857*, London 1860.

Biographies of key figures include

(Amīr-i Kabīr)

ĀDAMIYYAT, Farīdūn, *Amīr-i kabīr va Īrān*, 3 vols, Tehran 1944-45.

The standard account of the great mid-century reforming minister.

(Mīrzā Malkum Khān)

ALGAR, Hamid, *Mirzā Malkum Khān. A biographical study in Iranian modernism*, Berkeley/Los Angeles/London 1973.

A somewhat hostile account of the well-known reformer. A selection from his writings is contained in

Majmūʿa-yi āsār-i Mīrzā Malkum Khān, Muḥammad Muḥīṭ ṬABĀṬABĀ'Ī (ed), Tehran 1948.

(Jamāl al-dīn Afghānī or Asadābādī)

ASADĀBĀDĪ, Mīrzā Luṭfallāh Khān, *Sharḥ-i ḥāl va āsār-i ... Sayyid Jamāl al-dīn Asādābādi*, Tehran 1947.

ḤALABĪ, ʿAlī Aṣghar, *Zandagī va safarhā-yi Sayyid Jamāl al-dīn Asadābādī*, Tehran 1971.

KEDDIE, Nikki R, *An Islamic response to imperialism*, Berkeley/Los Angeles 1968.

—— *Sayyid Jamāl al-Dīn 'al-Afghānī'*, Berkeley/Los Angeles/London 1972.

MAHDAVĪ, Aṣghar, and Īraj AFSHĀR (ed), *Majmūʿa-yi asnād va madārik-i chāp na-shuda dar bāra-yi Sayyid Jamāl al-dīn mashhūr bi-Afghānī*, Tehran 1963.

For foreign relations, in addition to RAMAZANI, *op.cit.*, reference may be made to

GREAVES, R L, *Persia and the defence of India, 1884-1892*, London 1959.

KAZEMZADEH, Firuz, *Russia and Britain in Persia, 1864-1914*, London 1968.

Other works in the political, social and economic fields include

BAKHASH, Shaul, *Iran: monarchy, bureaucracy and reform under the Qajars, 1858-1896*, London/Oxford 1968.

LAMBTON, A K S, 'Persia: the breakdown of society', *CHI*, vol.I :430-46.

A valuable series of articles on various aspects of Qājār society is provided by

FLOOR, W M, 'The Lūṭīs - a social phenomenon in Qājār Persia', *Die Welt des Islams*, NS, vol.XIII, 1971 :103-20.

—— 'The market police in Qājār Persia', *Die Welt des Islams*, NS, vol. XIII, 1971 :212-29.

—— 'The office of kalāntar in Qājār Persia', *JESHO*, 14, 1971 :153-68.

—— 'The police in Qājār Persia', *ZDMG*, 123, 1973 :293-315.

—— 'The guilds in Iran - an overview from the earliest beginnings till 1972', *ZDMG*, 125, 1975 :99-116.

—— 'The merchants in Iran', *ZDMG*, 126, 1976 :101-35.

—— 'The customs in Qājār Iran', *ZDMG*, 126, 1976 :281-311.

—— 'Bankruptcy in Iran', *ZDMG*, 127, 1977 :61-76.

—— 'The bankers (*ṣarrāf*) in Qājār Iran', *ZDMG*, 129, 1979 :263-81.

6.5 *From the Constitutional Revolution to the aftermath of the 1914-1918 War*

A number of works already cited continue to be relevant: AFSCHAR, AVERY, ISSAWI, KAZEMZADEH, LITTEN, RAMAZANI.

Further works of a general character include

ḤUSĀM-I MUᶜIZZĪ, Najaf Qulī, *Tārīkh-i ravābiṭ-i siyāsī-yi Īrān bā dunyā*, 2 vols, Tehran 1946, 1947.

The first volume provides a general survey of Iran's foreign relations from the Achaemenids to the Ṣafavids, followed by a more detailed study of relations with Russia up to the 1917 revolution. Volume II is concerned with relations with Britain up to the constitutional period, together with an account of the Iranian Ministry of Foreign Affairs.

MUᶜTAMID, Maḥmūd Farhād, *Tārīkh-i ravābiṭ-i siyāsī-yi Īrān va ᶜUsmānī*, 2 vols, Tehran 1947, n.d.

Still the most important work on the Constitutional Revolution is

BROWNE, Edward G, *The Persian revolution, 1905-1909*, Cambridge 1910, which may be supplemented by

—— *The press and poetry of modern Persia*, *op.cit.* IV 1.

Although primarily an annotated catalogue of newspapers published during the constitutional period, together with a study of political poetry, it provides a considerable amount of information on the politics of the day.

In recent years a great many studies of the constitutional movement have been published in Iran and elsewhere, ranging from personal memoirs to analytical studies. Among these may be listed

ABRAHAMIAN, Ervand, 'The crowd in the Persian revolution', *IS* 2(4), Autumn 1969 :128-50.

ĀDAMIYYAT, Farīdūn, *Īdi'uluzhi-yī nihżat-i mashrūṭiyyat-i Īrān*, Tehran 1976.

—— *Afkār-i ijtimāᶜī va siyāsī va iqtiṣādī dar āsār-i muntashar na-shuda-yi daurān-i Qājār*, Tehran 1977.

Two studies of ideological trends in the constitutional movement.

BĀSTĀNĪ-PĀRĪZĪ, *Talāsh-i āzādī*, Tehran 1962, 3rd imp. 1976.

An account of the constitutional movement and its aftermath woven around the life of Mushīr al-daula (Ḥasan Pīrniyā) (1874-1935), statesman and historian.

BIHZĀD, Karīm Ṭāhirzāda, *Qiyām-i Āzarbāyjān dar inqilāb-i mashrūṭiyyat-i Īrān*, Tehran n.d. (1955?)

DĀVŪDĪ, Mahdī, *ᶜAin al-daula va rizhīm-i mashrūṭa*, Tehran 1963.

HAIRI, Abdul-Hadi, *Shiᶜism and constitutionalism in Iran*, Leiden 1977.

A study of the role played by the Persian residents of Iraq in Iranian politics.

HARAVĪ, Muḥammad Ḥasan Adīb, *Tārīkh-i paidāyish-i mashrūṭiyyat-i Īrān*, Tehran 1953.

ISKANDARĪ, ᶜAbbās, *Tārīkh-i mufaṣṣal-i mashrūṭiyyat-i Īrān*, 2 vols, Tehran n.d., 1943.

KASRAVĪ, Aḥmad, *Tārīkh-i mashrūṭiyyat-i Īrān. Tārīkh-i hijdah-sāla-yi Āzarbāyjān*, 1st ed. Tabriz 1935-41 (suppl. to *Paimān*), 6 parts; 2nd ed. (rev.), parts 1-2 (in 3 vols), Tehran 1940-43; parts 3-6, Tehran 1954.

KIRMĀNĪ, Nāẓim al-islām, *Tārīkh-i bīdārī-yi Īrāniyān*, 3 vols, Tehran 1910, repr. 1967-70.

Important contemporary history of the revolution.

MALIKZĀDA, Mahdī, *Tārīkh-i inqilāb-i mashrūtiyyat-i Īrān*, 7 vols, Tehran n.d. (1949-53?)

PAVLOVICH, M, V TIRIA, S IRANSKI, *Inqilāb-i mashrūṭiyyat-i Īrān*. M HŪSHYĀR (tr), Tehran 1951.

Study of the social and political aspects of the constitutional movement, continuing to 1925. First published in Moscow in 1925.

ṢAFĀ'Ī, Ibrāhīm, *Rahbarān-i mashrūṭa*, Tehran 1965.

Biographies of 24 leading figures in the constitutional movement.

Contemporary international developments affecting Iran are discussed in

CHURCHILL, Rogers Platt, *The Anglo-Russion convention of 1907*, Cedar

Rapids, Iowa 1939.

McLEAN, David, *Britain and her buffer-state: the collapse of the Persian empire, 1890-1914*, Roy.Hist.Soc. Stud. in Hist., ser.14, London 1979.

Post-constitution developments are described at first hand in

SHUSTER, W Morgan, *The strangling of Persia*, New York (1912) 1920.

The author was Treasurer-General of the Persian Government from 1911-1912.

McDANIEL, Robert A, *The Shuster mission and the Persian constitutional revolution*, Minneapolis 1974.

The impact of the Great War on Iran is described in PAVLOVICH, (*op.cit.*) and in

ĀDAMIYYAT, Muḥammad Ḥusain Ruknzāda, *Fārs va jang-i bain-al-milal*, Tehran 1933.

—— *Dalīrān-i Tangistān*, Tehran 1931, rev.ed. 1948.

A somewhat romanticised account of tribal operations in the south of Iran.

Other aspects of the same theatre are the subject of

MIROSHNIKOV, L I, *Iran in World War I*, Moscow 1963. Persian tr. ᶜA DUKHĀNIYYĀTĪ, *Īrān dar jang-i jahānī-yi avval*, Tehran 1965.

Lectures read at Harvard University in November 1962.

OLSON, W J, *Anglo-Iranian relations during World War I*, London 1981.

SIPIHR, Muvarrikh al-daula, *Īrān dar jang-i buzurg 1914-1918*, Tehran 1957.

SYKES, Christopher, *Wasmuss, the German Lawrence*, London 1936.

Events during the period between the Russian revolution and the coup d'état of February 1921 are covered in the following works, apart from those already mentioned:

ĀZARĪ, Sayyid ᶜAlī, *Qiyām-i Shaikh Muḥammad Khiyābānī*, Tehran 1950.

Khiyābānī was the leader of an anti-government rebellion in Āzarbāyjān between 1917 and 1920.

FATEMI, Nasrollah Saifpour, *Diplomatic history of Persia, 1917-1923*, New York 1952.

In spite of the title, the book ends effectively with the Irano-Soviet Treaty of February 1921.

KAPUR, Harish, *Soviet Russia and Asia 1917-1927*, Geneva 1966.

A study of Soviet policy towards Turkey, Iran and Afghanistan.

RAVASANI, Shapur, *Sowjetrepublik Gilan: die socialistische Bewegung im Iran seit Ende des 19. Jh. bis 1922*, Berlin 1973.

Apart from the general surveys mentioned above, much relevant information is to be found in the memoirs already cited: BAHRĀMĪ, HIDĀYAT (Khāṭirāt), MUSTAUFĪ, and in

DAULATĀBĀDĪ, Yaḥyā, *Tārīkh-i muᶜāṣir yā ḥayāt-i Yaḥyā*, 4 vols, Tehran n.d. (1949-57).

Various political, social and economic aspects of this period are dealt with in

BENAB, Y, 'Political organisations in Iran: a historical review', *RIPEH*, 3(1), 1979 :30-80.

BHARIER, Julian, *Economic development in Iran 1900-1970*, London 1971.

JAMĀLZĀDA, Sayyid Muḥammad ᶜAlī, *Ganj-i shāyigān*, *op.cit.* VIII 3.2.9.

A comprehensive economic survey of the country immediately before the Great War.

Legal and constitutional aspects of post-1906 Iran are discussed in

NAKHAI, M, *L'évolution politique de l'Iran*, Brussels 1938.

TAVALLALI, Djamchid, *Le parlement iranien*, Lausanne 1954.

Two Arabic works discuss the problem of the Arab population of south-west Iran.

ḤALŪ, ᶜAlī Niᶜma al-, *Al-Muḥammara: madīna wa imāra ᶜarabiyya*, Baghdad 1972.

NAJJĀR, Muṣṭafā Muḥammad al-, *Al-tarīkh al-siyāsī li-imārat ᶜArabistān al-ᶜarabiyya*, Cairo 1971.

Useful bibliographies, guide to manuscript and archival material, and text of some original documents.

6.6 *The coup d'état of 1921 and the reign of Riżā Shāh*

An important work linking the post-constitution developments to the rise of Riżā Khān is

BAHĀR, Muḥammad Taqī Malik al-shuᶜarā, *Tārīkh-i mukhtaṣar-i aḥzāb-i siyāsī: inqirāż-i Qājāriyya*, vol.I (all published), Tehran 1944.

Written by an active participant in the events of the time, this volume breaks off at the Conference of Lausanne in 1923.

The standard work on Riżā Shāh's life and reign is

WILBER, Donald N, *Riza Shah Pahlavi: the resurrection and reconstruction of Iran 1878-1944*, Hicksville 1975.

Particularly valuable is its exhaustive bibliography of works in Persian and European languages.

Further sources on the coup d'état and the accompanying international events, in addition to AVERY, BĀSTĀNĪ-PĀRĪZĪ, DAULATĀBĀDĪ, HIDĀYAT, MUSTAUFĪ (*op.cit.*), are

ARFA, Hassan, *Under five shahs*, London 1964.

BALFOUR, James Moncrieff, *Recent happenings in Persia*, Edinburgh/London 1922.

BUTLER, Rohan, and J P T BURY (ed), *Documents on British foreign policy 1919-1939*, 1st ser. vol.XIII, ch.3: 'Persia, Jan.6 - March 31, 1920', HMSO, London 1963.

IRONSIDE, Maj.-Gen. Sir Edward, *High road to command*, Lord IRONSIDE (ed), London 1972.

LESUEUR, Emile, *Les Anglais en Perse*, Paris 1922.

MAHRAD, Ahmad, *Iran auf dem Weg zur Diktatur - Militarisierung und Widerstand 1919-1925*, Hanover 1972, repr. 1976.

—— *Die deutsch-persischen Beziehungen von 1918-1933*, Bern/Frankfurt a/M, 1979.

MAKKĪ, Ḥusain, *Tārīkh-i bīst-sāla-yi Īrān*, vol.I, Kūditā-yi 1299; vol.II, Muqaddamāt-i taghyīr-i salṭanat; vol.III, Inqirāż-i Qājāriyya va tashkīl-i silsila-yi Pahlavī, Tehran 1945-46, repr. 1979.

TEMPERLEY, H W V, 'The liberation of Persia', *A history of the Peace Conference at Paris*, vol.VI, part 5 :206-17, London 1924.

ULLMAN, Richard H, *Anglo-Soviet relations 1917-1921*, vol.III, *The Anglo-Soviet accord*, Princeton 1972.

ZURRER, Werner, *Persien zwischen England und Russland 1918-1925*, Grossmachteinflüsse und nationalen Wiederaufsteig am Beispiel des Iran, Bern/Frankfurt/Las Vegas 1978.

Iran's early relations with the Soviet Union are also fully described in

LENCZOWSKI, George, *Russia and the west in Iran*, Ithaca, New York 1949.

Amongst other valuable material on the period, this work contains an account of the Jangalī movement of Mīrzā Kūchik Khān. Other sources for this movement are

FAKHRĀ'Ī, Ibrāhīm, *Sardar-i jangal: Mīrzā Kūchik Khān*, Tehran 1967.

MARTCHENKO, M, 'Kutchuk Khan', *RMM*, XL, 1920 :98-116.

Other dissident movements and the measures taken by Rizā Khān to suppress them are described in

ĀZARĪ, ᶜAlī, *Qiyām-i kulunil Muḥammad Taqī Khān Pisyān dar Khurāsān*, Tehran 1950.

BAHRĀMĪ, Dabir-i aᶜzam Farajallāh, *Yād-dāsht-hā-yi sirrī-yi Rizā Shāh*, Tehran n.d.

A record of the campaign against Shaikh Khazᶜal.

BAṢRĪ, ᶜAlī al-, *Mudhakkarāt Riḍā Shāh*, Baghdad 1950. Persian tr. Muḥammad Ḥusain IṢTAKHR, *Yāddāshthā-yi Rizā Shāh*, Tehran 1956; Shahrām KARĪMLŪ, *Yāddāshthā-yi Aᶜlāḥażrat-i Rizā Shāh-i Kabīr*, Tehran 1971.

Alleged memoirs of Rizā Khān during his period as Commander-in-Chief and Prime Minister.

JAHĀNBĀNĪ, Amānallāh, *ᶜAmaliyyāt-i qushūn dar Balūchistān*, Tehran 1928, repr. 1957.

YĀSAMĪ, Rashīd, *Safarnāma-yi Shāhanshāh bi-Khūzistān*, Tehran 1923.

Another aspect of Riżā Khān's early career is described in

MILLSPAUGH, Arthur C, *The American task in Persia*, New York 1925.

The author was Administrator-General of the Finances of Persia from 1921 to 1927.

General accounts and memoirs of Riżā Shāh and his reign, in addition to those in AVERY and HIDĀYAT, *op.cit.*, include

BANANI, Amin, *The modernization of Iran, 1921-1941*, Stanford 1961.

BLÜCHER, Wipert von, *Zeitenwende in Iran*, Biberach an der Riss 1949.

A diplomat's reminiscences.

ELWELL-SUTTON, L P, *Modern Iran*, London 1941, and reprs. Persian tr. ᶜAlī JAVĀHIR KALĀM, Tehran 1946; ᶜAbd al-ᶜaẓīm ṢABŪRĪ, Tehran 1956.

—— 'Reza Shah the Great: founder of the Pahlavi dynasty', *Iran under the Pahlavis*, George LENCZOWSKI (ed), Stanford 1978 :1-50.

ESSAD-BEY, *Reza Schah: Feidherr, Kaiser, Reformator*, Vienna 1936. English tr. Paul Maerken and Elsa BRANDEN, *Reza Shah*, London 1938.

A rather laudatory account.

KHWĀJA-NŪRĪ, Ibrāhīm, *Bāzīgarān-i ᶜaṣr-i ṭalā'ī*, 6 parts, Tehran 1943-44.

Biographies of eleven personalities of the Riżā Shāh era.

MAHRAD, Ahmad, *Iran unter der Herrschaft Reza Schahs*, Frankfurt/New York 1977.

MELZIG, Herbert, *Resa Schah: die Aufstieg Irans und die Grossmächte*, Stuttgart 1936.

MIHRKHWĀH, Niᶜmatallāh, *Kitāb-i Riżā Shāh*, Tehran 1946.

MUKHTĀRĪ, Ḥabīballāh, *Tārīkh-i bīdārī-yi Īrān*, Tehran 1947.

NŪRĪ ISFANDYĀRĪ, Fatḥallāh, *Rastākhīz-i Īrān*, Tehran 1956.

Mainly news items and articles translated from foreign sources.

PAHLAVĪ, Muḥammad Riżā Shāh, 'Riżā Shāh-i Kabīr', *Mardān-i khwud-sākhta*, Ibrāhīm KHWĀJA NŪRĪ (ed), Tehran 1956.

—— *Mission for my country*, London 1961. Persian ed. *Ma'mūriyyat barāyi vaṭanam*, Tehran.

POLACCO, Angelo, *L'Iran di Rezà Scià Pahlavi*, Venice 1937.

ṢADĪQ, ᶜĪsā, *Yādgār-i ᶜumr*, Tehran 1960, repr. 1961.

Memoirs of a one-time Minister of Education.

ṢĀDIQĪ-PŪR, ᶜAbd al-riżā (ed), *Yādgār-i guzashta: majmūᶜa-yi sukhanrānīhā-yi aᶜlāḥażrat-i faqīd Riżā Shāh-i Kabīr*, Tehran 1968.

SHEEAN, Vincent, *The new Persia*, New York 1927.

SIASSI, Ali Akbar, *La Perse au contact de l'occident*, Paris 1931.

UPTON, Joseph M, *The history of modern Iran: an interpretation*, Cambridge, Mass. 1960.

VIZĀRAT-I IṬṬILĀʿĀT, *ʿAṣr-i Pahlavī*, vol.I, Riżā Shāh-i Kabīr, Pahlavī-yi avval, Tehran 1967.

Of interest for its many contemporary photographs.

Foreign affairs are dealt with in RAMAZANI, *op.cit.*, and in

MAHRAD, Ahmad, *Die deutsch-persische Beziehungen von 1918-1933*, Bern/ Frankfurt a/M, 1979.

—— *Die Wirtschafts- und Handelsbeziehungen zwischen Iran und dem nationalsozialistischen Deutschen Reich*, Anzali 1979.

MAHRAD's books are particularly valuable for the reproduction of original documents, many of which are also contained in supplementary volumes.

MANSHŪR GARAKĀNĪ, M A, *Siyāsat-i daulat-i shūravī dar Īrān az 1296 tā 1306*, Tehran 1947.

MATINE-DAFTARY, Ahmad Khan, *La suppression des capitulations en Perse*, Paris 1930.

MESBAH ZADEH, Mostafa, *La politique de l'Iran dans le Société des Nations*, Paris 1906.

REZUN, Miron, *The Soviet Union and Iran: Soviet policy in Iran from the beginnings of the Pahlavi dynasty until the Soviet invasion in 1941*, Geneva 1981.

Economic questions are specifically dealt with in BHARIER, *op.cit.*, and

FATEH, Moustafa Khan, *The economic position of Persia*, London 1926.

FÜRSTENAU, G, *Das Verkehrswesen Irans*, Munich 1935.

JAZĀYIRĪ, Shams al-dīn, *Qavānīn-i māliyya va muḥāsabat-i ʿumūmī va muṭālaʿa-yi būdja az ibtidā-yi mashrūṭiyyat tā ḥāl*, Tehran 1956.

KAZEMI, Parviz, *Le commerce extérieur de la Perse*, Paris 1930.

MALEKPUR, Abdullah, *Die Wirtschaftsverfassung Irans*, Berlin 1935.

MIGLIORINI, Elio, *Strade e commercio dell'Iran*, Messina/Milan 1939.

SOHEILY, Hossein, *Essai sur l'industrialisation de l'Iran*, Montreux 1950.

YEGANEGI, E, *The recent financial and monetary history of Persia*, New York 1934.

A variety of educational and social questions are dealt with in

ʿALAVĪ, Buzurg, *Panjāh u si nafar*, Tehran 1943, and reprs.

A first-hand account by one of the defendants of the trial and imprisonment of the '53' accused of communism in 1937.

BĀMDĀD, Badr al-mulūk, *Zan-i īrānī az inqilāb-i mashrūṭiyyat tā inqilāb-i safīd*, 2 vols, Tehran 1968-69. English tr. F R C BAGLEY, *From darkness into light*, Hicksville, New York 1977.

SADĪQ, ʿĪsā, *Tārīkh-i mukhtaṣar-i taʿlīm u tarbiyat*, Tehran 1937, repr. 1938, 1940. Rev.ed. *Sair-i farhang dar Īrān va maghrib-zamīn*, Tehran 1953. New rev.ed. *Tārīkh-i farhang-i Īrān*, Tehran 1957, repr. 1959.

WOODSMALL, Ruth Frances, *Moslem women enter a new world*, London 1936.

6.7 *The Second World War and its aftermath*

The Allied occupation of Iran is discussed in LENCZOWSKI, *op.cit.*, and in CENTRAL OFFICE OF INFORMATION, *Paiforce*. The official story of the Persia and Iraq Command 1941-1946, London 1948.

FATEMI, Faramarz S, *The USSR in Iran*, New York 1980.

A study of Irano-Soviet relations between 1941 and 1947, with an epilogue on the Iranian revolution of 1978-79.

KHĀN MALIK Yazdī, Muḥammad, *Arzish-i masāʿī-yi Īrān dar jang-i 1939-1945*, Tehran 1945.

KŪHĪ KIRMĀNĪ, Ḥusain, *Az Shahrīvar 1320 tā fājiʿa-yi Āzarbāyjān*, 2 vols, Tehran n.d. (1947), 1950.

LĀRŪDĪ, Nūrallāh, *Asīrān*, Tehran 1953.

An account of the nationalists interned by the British between 1943 and 1945, including a full list of the internees.

MOTTER, T H Vail, *The Persian corridor and aid to Russia*, Office of the Chief of Military History, Washington 1952.

RAMAZANI, Rouhollah K, *Iran's foreign policy 1941-1973: a study of foreign policy in modernizing nations*, Charlottesville 1975.

SCHULTZE-HOLTHUS, Bernhardt, *Frührot in Iran*, Abenteuer im deutschen Geheimdienst, Esslingen 1952. English tr. Mervyn SAVILL, *Daybreak in Iran*. A story of the German Intelligence Service, London 1954.

SKRINE, Clarmont, *World war in Iran*, London 1962.

STEPPAT, Fritz, *Iran zwischen den Weltmächten 1941-1948*, Oberursel 1948.

Most of the above are also relevant to the internal affairs of Iran during the immediate post-war period. In addition, reference should be made to the following:

JAZANĪ, Bizhan, *Tārīkh-i sī-sāla-yi Īrān*, 2 vols, n.p., n.d.

A left-wing view of the period. JAZANĪ was one of a left-wing group arrested in the '60s, who subsequently died in prison.

KAI USTUVĀN, Ḥusain, *Siyāsat-i muvāzana-yi manfī dar majlis-i chahārdahum*, 2 vols, Tehran 1949, 1950.

MĀNĪ, Shukrallāh, *Tārīkhcha-yi nihżat-i kārgarī dar Īrān*, Tehran 1946.

MILLSPAUGH, Arthur C, *Americans in Persia*, Washington 1946.

Account of the author's second financial mission to Iran.

QĀSIMĪ, Aḥmad, *Ḥizb-i Tūda-yi Īrān chi mīkhwāhad va chi mīgūyad?* Tehran 1943.

An official statement of the aims of the Tūda Party.

Sair-i kumūnīzm dar Īrān az Shahrīvar 1320 tā Farvardīn 1336, Tehran 1957.
A semi-official exposé of communist activities in Iran.

ZABIH, Sepehr, *The communist movement in Iran*, Berkeley/Los Angeles 1966.

The crisis of 1945-46, the establishment of the autonomous government in Āzarbāyjān, and the ensuing national and international developments are described in several of the foregoing, including F S FATEMI, KŪHĪ KIRMĀNĪ, RAMAZANI, STEPPAT, and ZABIH, and also in

EAGLETON, William, *The Kurdish republic of 1946*, London/New York 1963.

HAMZAVI, A H, *Persia and the powers*, London n.d. (1946).
Contains an appendix of documents relating to the Security Council hearings of 1946.

HOUMAYOUNPOUR, Parviz, *L'affaire d'Azarbaïdjan*, Lausanne 1967.

ROOSEVELT, Archie, 'The Kurdish republic of Mahabad', *MEJ*, I, iii, 1947 :247-69.

ROYAL INSTITUTE OF INTERNATIONAL AFFAIRS, *Survey of international affairs.* The Middle East 1945-1950, part II(i) Persia :56-105, London 1954.

SECURITY COUNCIL, *Official records, first year, first series*, no.1, Jan - Feb 1946 :31-71, and annexes 2a, 2b; no.2, Apr - Jun 1946 :27-152, 201-14, 146-52, 287-305; and annexes 2a-2k, London/New York 1946.

VAN WAGENEN, Richard W, *The Iranian case, 1946*, United Nations Action series, New York 1952.

Although the Baḥrain case was not particularly prominent during the period under consideration, two works deal specifically with the problem:

ADAMIYAT, Fereydoun, *Bahrein Island, a legal and diplomatic study of the British-Iranian controversy*, New York 1955.

FAROUGHY, Abbas, *The Bahrein Islands 750-1951.* A contribution to the study of power politics, New York 1951.

6.8 *The Muṣaddiq period 1951-1953*

Since the premiership of Dr Muṣaddiq was dominated by the oil dispute, many of the works cited here deal with the dispute itself as well as with the internal politics of the period. Other works on the oil industry are listed in XIV 4.4.

Asnād-i naft, Tehran 1951.
An official compendium of documents relevant to the dispute.

ATYEO, Henry C, 'Political developments in Iran, 1951-1954', *MEA*, 5, Aug-Sep. 1954 :249-59.

BULLARD, Reader, 'Behind the oil dispute in Iran: a British view', *Foreign Affairs*, 31(3), 1953 :461-71.

CHISHOLM, A H, 'Anglo-Iranian answers Iran with facts', *The Oil Forum*, 6, (Special Insert i-xviii), April 1952.

Correspondence between His Majesty's Government in the United Kingdom and the Persian Government, and related documents concerning the oil industry in Persia, February 1951 to September 1951, HMSO, London 1951.

EDEN, Anthony, 'Oil, October 1951 - March 1955', *Full Circle*, London 1960 :189-223.

ELWELL-SUTTON, L P, *Persian oil: a study in power politics*, London 1955, repr. Westport, Conn. 1975. Russian tr. N PAISOV, *Iranskaya neft'*, Moscow 1956. Chinese tr. Baoyong ZHENG, *Yilang shiyou*, Beijing 1958.

FATEMI, N S, *Oil diplomacy, powder-keg in Iran*, New York 1954.

FĀTIḤ, Muṣṭafā, *Panjāh sāl-i naft dar Īrān*, Tehran 1956.

FORD, Alan W, *The Anglo-Iranian oil dispute of 1951-1952*. A study of the role of law in the relations of states. Berkeley/Los Angeles 1954.

GHOSH, Sunil Kanti, *The Anglo-Iranian oil dispute*, Calcutta 1960.

INTERNATIONAL COURT OF JUSTICE, *Anglo-Iranian Oil Co. case (United Kingdom v Iran)*. Pleadings, oral arguments, documents. Leiden 1952.

—— *ibid*. Judgement of July 22, 1952. ICJ Reports, Leiden 1952 :93-171.

INTERNATIONAL LABOUR OFFICE, *Labour conditions in the oil industry in Iran*, Geneva 1950.

ISKANDARĪ, ʿAbbās, *Naft va Baḥrain, yā ʿAbbās Iskandarī dar khidmat-i majlis-i pānzdahum*, Tehran 1952.

Although intended as personal propaganda for the author, the book contains a number of interesting documents and other information.

KEMP, Norman, *Abadan: a first-hand account of the Persian oil crisis*, London 1953.

LENCZOWSKI, George, 'Iran's deepening crisis', *CH*, 24, April 1953 :230-36.

LEVY, Walter J, 'Economic problems facing a settlement of the Iranian oil controversy', *MEJ*, 8(1), 1954 :91-95.

LISĀNĪ, Abu'l-fazl, *Ṭalā-yi siyāh yā balā-yi Īrān*, Tehran n.d. (1951).

LOCKHART, Laurence, 'Causes of the Anglo-Persian oil dispute', *RCAJ*, XL, ii, 1953 :134-50.

The AIOC view of the oil dispute.

MAKKĪ, Ḥusain, *Kitāb-i siyāh*, Tehran 1951.

Documents, correspondence, Majlis debates relating to the oil dispute.

NOORI, Hossein Shiekh-Hosseini, *A study of the nationalization of the oil industry in Iran*, Ed.D. thesis, Univ. of Northern Colorado, 1965.

O'CONNELL, D P, 'A critique of the Iranian oil litigation', *ICLQ*, 9, 1955 :267-93.

Persia-Consortium Agreement, Tehran n.d. (1954).

The English and Persian texts of the 1954 agreement between the Iranian Government and the Oil Consortium.

ROOSEVELT, Kermit, *Counter-coup: the struggle for the control of Iran*, New York 1979.

RŪḤĀNĪ, Fu'ād, *Tārīkh-i millī shudan-i ṣanᶜat-i naft-i Īrān*, Tehran 1973.

SHWADRAN, B, 'The Anglo-Iranian oil dispute, 1948-1952', *MEA*, 5, 1954 :193-231.

ZABIH, Sepehr, *The Mossadegh era: roots of the Iranian revolution*, Chicago 1981.

6.9 *The Pahlavī regime 1953-1978*

Books on the post-1953 development of the Pahlavī regime in Iran are numerous. In addition to those already cited (ARFA, AVERY, BHARIER, PAHLAVI, and RAMAZANI), the following deal with general historical and political aspects.

ABRAHAMIAN, Ervand, *Iran between two revolutions*, Princeton 1982.

AMIRSADEGHI, Hossein, and R W FERRIER (ed), *Twentieth century Iran*, London 1977.

BILL, James Alban, *The politics of Iran.* Groups, classes and modernization, Columbus, Ohio 1972.

BINDER, Leonard, *Iran: political development in a changing society*, Berkeley/Los Angeles 1962.

COTTAM, Richard, *Nationalism in Iran*, Pittsburgh 1964. 2nd ed. ... *updated through 1978*, Pittsburgh 1979.

Dast-āvardhā-yi inqilāb, Tehran 1976.

Text of and notes on the first seventeen points of the White Revolution.

FISCHER, Michael M J, *Iran: from religious dispute to revolution*, Cambridge, Mass./London 1980.

Though primarily concerned with the role of religion in Iranian society in modern times, the author has much of interest to say about contemporary politics.

JACQZ, Jane (ed), *Iran: past, present and future*, Aspen Institute for Humanistic Studies, New York 1976.

Though overtaken by events so far as the future is concerned, the book is a valuable survey of conditions in Iran in the mid-seventies.

KATOUZIAN, Homa, *The political economy of modern Iran. Despotism and pseudo-modernism 1926-1979*, London 1981.

An exhaustive, if somewhat one-sided, account of the Pahlavī regime.

KEDDIE, Nikki R, *Roots of revolution: an interpretive history of modern*

Iran, New Haven 1981.

KEDOURIE, Elie, and Sylvia G HAIM (ed), *Towards a modern Iran: studies in thought, politics and society*, London 1980.

Kitāb-i siyāh dar bāra-yi sāzmān-i afsarān-i Tūda, Tehran 1955.

A semi-official account of the Tūda network said to have been unearthed during the years following the events of August 1953.

LENCZOWSKI, George (ed), *Iran under the Pahlavis*, Stanford, California, 1978.

Chapters by twelve European and American scholars on various aspects of the Pahlavī regime. This is perhaps the most objective of the various books produced in celebration of the fiftieth anniversary of the accession of Riẓā Shāh.

MERIP Reports, nos 37, 40, 43, Washington, DC 1975.

PAHLAVI, Muḥammad Riẓā Shāh, *Mission for my country*, *op.cit.*

—— *Inqilāb-i safīd*, Tehran 1966. English tr. *The White Revolution*, Tehran 1966.

—— *Bi-sūyi tamaddun-i buzurg*, Tehran 1978.

The Shah's vision of Iran's future.

RUBIN, Barry, *Paved with good intentions*. The American experience and Iran, New York/Oxford 1980.

Account of the American involvement in Iran during the Pahlavī regime.

SAIKAL, Amin, *The rise and fall of the Shah*, Princeton Univ. Press/Sydney/Melbourne 1980.

YAR-SHATER, Ehsan (ed), *Iran faces the seventies*, New York 1971.

Contributions on many aspects of contemporary Iranian society ranging from land reform to music and literature.

ZONIS, Marvin, *The political élite of Iran*, Princeton 1971, repr. 1976.

Study of the role of personalities and social classes in the political and social structure of Pahlavi Iran.

Apart from numerous references in the works already cited, foreign affairs are particularly the subject of

CHUBIN, Shahram, and Sepehr ZABIH, *The foreign relations of Iran: a developing state in a zone of great power conflict*, Berkeley/Los Angeles 1975.

COTTRELL, Alvin J (ed), *The Persian Gulf states: a general survey*, Baltimore/London 1980.

KELLY, J B, *Britain and the Persian Gulf*, Oxford 1968.

MONROE, Elizabeth, *The changing balance of power in the Persian Gulf*, New York 1972.

RAMAZANI, Rouhollah K, *The Persian Gulf: Iran's role*, Charlottesville 1972.

—— *The Persian Gulf and the Straits of Hormuz*, Delaware 1979.

Reference must also, of course, be made to the same author's *Iran's foreign policy 1941-1973*, *op.cit.*

For economic, social and legal questions, see chapter XIV.

Chronologies of current events throughout the Middle East have been maintained since their first publication by

Oriente Moderno, monthly, Rome 1921-.

Middle East Journal, quarterly, Washington 1947-.

Other useful chronologies are

Keesings Contemporary Archives, Bristol 1931-.

The Middle East and North Africa, *op.cit.* II 1.

Middle East Annual Review, Saffron Walden 1974-.

The revolution of 1978-79 and its aftermath is the subject of chapter XV of the present work. Many publications by dissident writers appeared outside Iran during the preceding decades, and these are very fully listed in

BEHN, Wolfgang, *The Iranian opposition in exile*. An annotated bibliography of publications from 1341/1962 to 1357/1979 with selective locations, Wiesbaden 1979.

The following works, not all of which come within the scope of BEHN, are of interest for the dissident movements of the period.

ABRAHAMIAN, Ervand, 'The guerrilla movement in Iran, 1963-77', *MERIP Reports*, 86, Washington, DC 1980 :3-21.

ALAVI, Bozorg, *Kämpfendes Iran*, Berlin 1955.

—— *Das Land der Rosen und der Nachtigallen*. Kreuz und quer durch Iran, Berlin 1957.

KISHĀVARZ, Farīdūn, *Man muttaham mīkunam kumīta-yi markazī-yi ḥizb-i Tūda-yi Īrān*, Tehran 1978.

Critique of Tūda Party leadership by a former leader.

Kunfidirāsyūn-i dānishjūyān-i Īrānī, Tehran 1977.

Government-sponsored 'exposé' of Iranian student activities overseas.

NIRUMAND, Bahman, *Persien. Modell eines Entwicklungslande* oder *die Diktatur der freien Welt*, Reinbek bei Hamburg 1967. English tr. *Iran. The new imperialism in action*, New York 1969.

7. *LOCAL HISTORIES*

A number of local histories have already been cited because of their importance as records of contemporary events. A full list of the older local histories is contained in STOREY, *op.cit.*, volume I, pp.348-432. The following selection includes some of the more important, together with some supplementary titles and information.

Arāk

DIHGĀN, Ibrāhīm, and Abū Turāb HIDĀ'Ī, *Tārīkh-i Arāk*, 2 vols, Arāk 1950, 1960.

Bukhārā

NARSHAKHĪ, Abū Bakr Muḥammad b Jaʿfar, *The history of Bukhara*. Tr. from a Persian abridgement of the Arabic original, by R N FRYE. Medieval Academy of America, publ. no.61, Cambridge, Mass. 1954.

The Arabic original was written in 332/943, the Persian abridgement and continuation in 574/1178.

Caucasus

BUTKOV, P G, *Materialy dlya novoy istorii Kavkaza s 1722 po 1803 g.*, 3 vols, St Petersburg 1896.

Fārs

IBN AL-BALKHĪ, *Fārsnāma*, *op.cit.* VIII 3.2.4.

FASĀʿĪ, Ḥasan, *Fārsnāma-yi Nāṣirī*, *op.cit.* 6.3.1.

Iṣfahān

JĀBIRĪ ANṢĀRĪ, Shaikh, *Tārīkh-i Iṣfahān va Rayy*, vol.I, Iṣfahān 1943.

Volume II was intended to contain biographies of distinguished Iṣfahānīs, but seems never to have appeared.

Khurāsān

MARĀGHĪ, Muḥammad Ḥasan Khān, *Maṭlaʿ al-shams*, *op.cit.* VIII 3.2.9.

Khūy

ĀQĀSĪ, Mahdī, *Tārīkh-i Khūy*, Tabrīz 1971.

Khūzistān

KASRAVĪ, Ahmad, *Tārīkh-i pānsad-sāla-yi Khūzistān*, Tehran 1934, repr. 1954.

Kirmān

HIMMAT, Maḥmūd, *Tārīkh-i mufaṣṣal-i Kirmān*, Kirmān 1971.

Kurdistān

BIDLĪSĪ, Sharaf al-dīn, *Sharafnāma*, V VÉLIAMINOF-ZERNOF (ed), 2 vols, St Petersburg 1860-62. French tr. F B CHARMOY, *Chèref-Nâmeh ou fastes de la nation kourde de Chèref-ou'ddîne*, St Petersburg 1868-75.

Nīshāpūr

FRYE, R N (ed), *The histories of Nishapur*, Harvard Oriental Series, 45, Cambridge, Mass. 1955.

Facsimile of three Arabic manuscripts: al-Nīsābūrī al-KHALĪFA, (tr), *Kitāb aḥwāl Nīsābūr*; ʿAbd al-ghāfir b Ismāʿīl al-FĀRISĪ, *Kitāb al-siyāq li-ta'rīkh Nīsābūr*; Ibrāhīm b Muḥammad al-ṢARĪFĪNĪ, *Muntakhab min kitāb al-siyāq li-ta'rīkh Nīsābūr*.

Qazvīn

GULRĪZ, Sayyid Muḥammad ᶜAlī, *Mīnūdar yā bāb al-janna-i Qazvīn*, Tehran 1958.
Description and history of Qazvīn compiled from classical and modern sources.

Sīstān

Tārīkh-i Sīstān, Muḥammad Taqī BAHĀR (ed), *op.cit.* 3.5.
The main part was completed in the 5th/11th century, with an anonymous continuation to the end of the 7th/13th century.

Ṭabaristān

IBN ISFANDYĀR, Muḥammad b Ḥasan, *Tārīkh-i Ṭabaristān*, *op.cit.* 3.5.
Written in 613/1216, with an anonymous continuation to c.750/1350.

MARᶜASHĪ, Ẓahīr al-dīn, *Tārīkh-i Ṭabaristān va Rūyān va Māzandarān*, St Petersburg 1850; Tehran 1954.
Written towards the end of the 9th/15th century.

DORN, B (tr and ann.), *Muhammedanische Quellen zur Geschichte der südlichen Küstenlander des kaspischen Meeres*, St Petersburg 1850-58.

ḤAKĪMIYĀN, Abuᶜl-fatḥ, *ᶜAlaviyyān-i Ṭabaristān*, University of Tehran, no.1265, Tehran 1969.

8. *THE MARTIAL ARTS AND SPORTS*

8.1 *Introduction*

Iran has ancient traditions of organized warfare, for the Achaemenids, Parthians and Sasanids had successively built up powerful empires through their military machines. To the Parthians was due the emphasis, characteristic of all subsequent Iranian military systems up to the Turkish and Mongol invasions, on the mailed, heavily-armed cavalryman (*savār*); whilst connections between northern Iran and the adjacent Inner Asian steppe lands favoured the use of the bow, so that the 'Parthian shot', fired by a rider to his rear with deadly accuracy, was already known in Greco-Roman literature. Moreover, in Islamic times, the importance of the mounted archer (*fāris*) received an impetus as, from the 9th century onwards, Turkish and other steppe peoples, supreme exponents of the archer's skills, came to form a significant element of armies in Iran, the counterpart of the Daylamīs from north-west Iran, famed as infantrymen and as fighters with the spear and javelin. From the later 15th century onwards, in Āq Qoyunlū and early Ṣafavid times, the use of artillery and handguns became general, until in Shāh ᶜAbbās's reign (1588-1629), the army included a regular corps of musketeers (*tufangchiyān*). However, Iran in the 19th century lagged far behind, for instance, the Ottoman empire and Egypt in the adoption of western-type armies and weaponry, continuing to depend largely on tribal and local forces for defence. Even in the first decades of the 20th century, the only really effective military force was the Russian-directed Persian Cossack Brigade, and the creation of a really modern Persian army was the work of Riżā Shāh Pahlavī and his son Muḥammad Riżā.

8.2 *Bibliographical indications*

There is no full-scale, single work which provides a history of Iranian armies and warfare, and information has to be gleaned from articles or from sections in more general works. For the pre-Islamic period, see

MODI, J J, 'Archery in ancient Persia', *Journal of the Asiatic Society, Bombay*, XXV, 1917-21 :175-86,

and the sections on military organization in

CHRISTENSEN, A, *L'Iran sous les Sassanides*, *op.cit*. IX 2.5.5.

For the Islamic period, see various articles in the *Encyclopaedia of Islam*, 2nd ed., Leiden/London 1960-, either specifically on Iranian institutions or practices, such as 'Ispahbadh', (C E BOSWORTH), and 'Lashkar', (A K S LAMBTON), or also sections on Iran within wider articles, such as 'Bārūd. v', (R M SAVORY), 'Fīl. As beasts of war', 'Ghulām. ii', 'Ḥarb. v', 'Ḥiṣār. iii', 'Ispahsālār. i', and 'Iṣṭabl. iv', (all by BOSWORTH). There are sections on military organization in

SPULER, B, *Iran im fruhislamischer Zeit*, *op.cit*. 3.3.

—— *Die Mongolen in Iran*, *op.cit*. 4.4, :399-421.

A Persian classic on the military arts is now available.

FAKHR-I MUDABBIR, *Ādāb al-ḥarb wa 'l-shajāᶜa*, A S KHWĀNSĀRĪ (ed), Tehran 1967. Facsimile ed. A ZAJACZKOWSKI, *Le traité iranien de l'art militaire 'Ādāb al-Ḥarb wa-š-Šaǧāᶜa' du XIIIe siècle*. Zakl. Or. Pol. Akad. Nauk, prace orient., XXI, Warsaw 1969. Translation of certain anecdotes from it by I M SHAFI, 'Fresh light on the Ghaznavîds', *IC*, XII, 1938 :189-234. See also E McEWEN below.

Studies of the armies of three specific mediaeval Iranian dynasties, those of the Ṣaffārids, the Būyids and the Ghaznavids, are to be found in

BOSWORTH, C E, *The medieval history of Iran, Afghanistan and Central Asia*. Variorum reprs, London 1977, arts. III, XVII for the first two, and as 'Ghaznevid military organization', *Der Islam*, XXXVI, 1960 :37-77.

On the techniques of siege warfare and its machinery, see also the relevant sections in

HUURI, K, *Zur Geschichte des mittelalterlichen Geschützwesens aus orientalischen Quellen*, Societas Orientalis Fennica, Studia Orientalia, IX, 3, Helsinki 1941.

On the topic of archery, see

LATHAM, J D, 'The archers of the Middle East: the Turco-Iranian background', *Iran*, VIII, 1970 :97-103.

McEWEN, E, 'Persian archery texts: Chapter eleven of Fakhr-i Mudabbir's *Ādāb al-ḥarb* (early thirteenth century)', *IQ*, XVIII, 1974 :76-99.

For a general survey of the early modern period, see

YAPP, M E, 'The modernization of Middle Eastern armies in the nineteenth century: a comparative view', V J PARRY and M E YAPP (eds), *War, technology and society in the Middle East*, London 1975 :357-59.

For recent decades,

COTTRELL, A J, R J HANKS, and F T BRAY, 'Military affairs in the Persian Gulf', A J COTTRELL, *et al.* (eds), *The Persian Gulf states*, *op.cit.* 6.9, :151-59.

Descriptions of Persian arms and armour will be found in XII 5.5.

Hunting and field sports, which instilled the equestrian skills and the handling of weapons, and the game which was generally regarded as providing practice in miniature for actual battle tactics, i.e. chess, were important adjuncts of the military art. See for the game of polo, so frequently depicted in Persian miniature painting, the *EI*, 2nd ed., art. 'Čawgān', (H MASSÉ), and for falconry, 'Bayzara' (F VIRÉ); this last contains little specifically relating to Iran, but note, from its bibliography,

PHILLOTT, D C, *The Báz-Náma-yi Náṣiri, a Persian treatise on falconry*, London 1908.

Another relevant work is

NASAVĪ, Abu'l-Hasan ᶜAlī b Aḥmad, *Bāz-nāma*, ed. and intr. ᶜAlī GHARAVĪ, Publications of Markaz-i Mardum-shināsī-yi Iran, no.10, Tehran 1975.

For chess, see

EI, 1st ed., Leiden/London 1906-38, art. 'Shaṭrandj' (B CARRA DE VAUX).

MURRAY, H J R, *A history of chess*, Oxford 1911.

9. *SOCIAL AND INTELLECTUAL HISTORY*

9.1 *General*

There are comparatively few books dealing specifically with the social history of Iran, and reference must be made to works on the Islamic world as a whole.

GRUNEBAUM, G von, *Medieval Islam. A study in cultural orientation*, Chicago 1946.

KREMER, Alfred von, *Culturgeschichte des Orients unter den Chalifen*, 2 vols, Vienna 1875-77. English tr. (part), S KHUDA-BUKHSH, *The Orient under the Caliphs*, Calcutta 1920.

MEZ, Adam, *Die Renaissance des Islam*, *op.cit.* 3.2.

POLAK, J E, *Persien. Das Land und zeine Bewohner*, Leipzig 1865.

SCHWARZ, P, *Iran im Mittelalter*, *op.cit.* 3.4.

9.2 *Social Institutions*

BĀMDĀD, Badr al-mulūk, *Zan-i Īrānī ...*, *op.cit.* 6.6.

DENNETT, Daniel C, *Conversion and the poll tax in early Islam*, Cambridge, Mass./London 1950.

LEVY, Reuben, *An introduction to the sociology of Islam*, 2 vols, London 1931, 1933. Re-issued as *The social structure of Islam*, Cambridge 1957.

MAZAHERY, Aly Akbar, *La vie quotidienne des musulmans au moyen âge: Xe au XIIIe siècle*, Paris 1951.

MUŻĀRIʿĪ, ʿAdnān, *Tārīkh-i iqtiṣādī va ijtimāʿī-yi Īrān az āghāz tā Ṣafaviyya*, Tehran 1969.

PERROY, Edouard (ed), *Le moyen âge: l'expansion de l'orient et la naissance de la civilisation occidentale*, Paris 1955.

TRITTON, A S, *The Caliphs and their non-Muslim subjects*. A critical study of the Covenant of Umar, London 1930.

9.3 *Political and social theory*

Texts

Significant classical works on Islamic political and social theory, especially in the Iranian area, include

FĀRĀBĪ, Abū Naṣr al-, *Ārā' ahl al-madīnat al-fāḍila*, A N NĀDIR (ed), Beirut 1959. Persian tr. Sayyid J SAJJĀDĪ, *Andīsha-hā-yi ahl-i madīna-yi fāżila*, Tehran 1975.

—— *Fuṣūl al-Madanī: aphorisms of the statesman*, ed. and tr. D M DUNLOP, Cambridge 1961.

FAŻLALLĀH B RŪZBIHĀN Iṣfahānī, *Sulūk al-mulūk*. English tr. M ASLAM, *Muslim conduct of state*, Islamabad 1974.

GHAZZĀLĪ, Muḥammad, *Kīmiyā-yi saʿādat*, *op.cit.* VI 5.2.

—— *Naṣīḥat al-mulūk*, Jalāl HUMĀ'Ī (ed), Tehran 1936-38, rev.repr. 1972. English tr. F R C BAGLEY, *Ghazālī's Book of Counsel for kings*, London 1964.

KAI-KĀVŪS b Iskandar, *Qābūs-nāma*, R LEVY (ed), London 1951. English tr. R LEVY, *A mirror for princes*, London 1951. Russian tr. Y E BERTELS, Moscow 1953.

MĀWARDĪ, ʿAlī b Muhammad, *Kitāb al-Bughyat al-ʿulyā fī adab al-dunyā wa'l-dīn*, Būlāq 1922 (many other editions). German tr. O RESCHER, *Das kitâb „adab ed-dunjâ wa'ddîn"*, 3 vols, Stuttgart 1932-33.

MUSTAUFĪ, Yūsuf b ʿAlī, *Khirad-nāma*, A BURŪMAND (ed), Tehran 1968.

NIẒĀM AL-MULK, Abū ʿAlī Ḥasan b ʿAlī Khwāja, *Siyāsatnāma*, *op.cit.* 3.5.

NIẒĀMĪ ʿARŪẒĪ Samarqandī, Aḥmad b ʿUmar, *Chahār maqāla*, *op.cit.* VII 3.

SAMANDAR, Khwāja, Tirmidhī, *Dastūr al-mulūk*, ed. with Russian tr. M A SALAKHETDINOVA, Moscow 1971.

ṬŪSĪ, Naṣīr al-dīn, *Akhlāq-i Nāṣirī*, *op.cit.* VI 5.2.

Studies

BADIE, B, 'La philosophie politique de l'hellénisme musulman: l'oeuvre de Nasired-Din Tusi', *Revue française de science politique*, XXVII, 2, Paris 1977 :190-304.

DĀVARĪ, Riḍā, *Falsafa-yi madanī-yi Fārābī*, Tehran 1975.

GAUDEFROY-DEMOMBYNES, Maurice, *Les institutions musulmanes*. English tr. John P MACGREGOR, *Muslim institutions*, London 1950.

KREMER, Alfred von, *Geschichte der herrschenden Ideen des Islams*, Leipzig 1868.

LAMBTON, Ann K S, *Theory and practice in medieval Persian government*, London 1980.

Eleven reprinted studies, including 'Islamic political thought', 'Justice in the medieval Persian theory of kingship', and 'Islamic mirrors for princes'.

—— *State and government in medieval Islam*, Oxford 1981.

LAMMENS, H, *L'Islam: croyances et institutions*, Beirut 1926. English tr. E Denison ROSS, *Islam: beliefs and institutions*, London 1929.

LERNER, Ralph, and Muhsin MAHDI (ed), *Medieval political philosophy: a sourcebook*, Ithaca 1972.

MACDONALD, Duncan B, *Development of Muslim theology, jurisprudence and constitutional theory*, New York 1903.

RASĀ'Ī, Dāvūd, *Ḥukūmat-i islāmī va nazar-i Ibn-i Khaldūn*, Tehran 1969.

ROSENTHAL, E I J, *Political thought in medieval Islam: an introductory outline*, Cambridge 1958.

9.4 *History of education*

AḤMADĪPŪR, Ḥusain, *Taʿlīm u tarbiyat dar du qarn-i akhīr*, Tabrīz 1953.

ARDAKĀNĪ, Ḥusain Maḥbūbī, *Tārīkh-i taḥavvul-i dānishgāh-i Tihrān va mu'assasāt-i ʿālī-yi āmūzishī-yi Īrān dar daura-yi khujasta-yi Pahlavī*, Tehran 1971.

—— *Tārīkh-i mu'assasāt-i tamaddunī-yi jadīd dar Īrān*, 2 vols, Tehran 1975, 1978.

A well-documented survey of education in Iran, with chapters on the pre-Ṣafavid, Ṣafavid, Afshār and early Qājār periods; the foundation of the *Dār al-funūn* and other colleges, private and foreign schools, and so on.

DODGE, Bayard, *Muslim education in medieval times*, Washington 1962.

ḤIKMAT, ʿAlī Aṣghar, 'Farhang-i āmūzish va parvarish', *Irānshahr*. Kumīsyūn-i millī-yi Yūniskū (UNESCO), Tehran 1967 :1165-246.

A reliable survey of Iranian education from pre-Islamic times to the present day, with details of schools, colleges and universities, minority and foreign schools, women's education, etc.

JUNDĪSHĀPŪR UNIVERSITY, *Āmūzish dar Īrān az ʿahd-i bāstān tā imrūz*, Ahvāz 1971.

A concise history up to 1920, with a chronology of the main events from 1921 to 1970.

ṢADĪQ, ʿĪsā, *Modern Persia and her educational system*, New York 1931.

—— *Tārīkh-i mukhtasar-i taʿlīm u tarbiyat*, *op.cit.* 6.6.

ʿĪsā ṢADĪQ was the most influential educationalist in modern times, serving more than once as Minister of Education.

ṢAFĀ, Ẕabīḥallāh, *Tārīkh-i ʿulūm va adabiyyāt-i Īrānī*, Tehran 1968.

Concerned mainly with pre-Islamic and traditional Islamic schools.

—— 'Madrasa', *Īrānshahr. Kumīsyūn-i millī-yi Yūniskū (UNESCO)*, Tehran 1963 :714-44.

A discussion of Islamic maktabs and madrasas, with some comparisons with modern developments.

TALAS, Asad, *La madrasa nizamiyya et son histoire*, Paris 1939.

TRITTON, A S, *Materials on Muslim education in the middle ages*, London 1957.

ZAʿFARĀNLŪ, Qudratallāh Raushanī, *Amīr-i Kabīr va Dār al-funūn*, Tehran 1975.

See also XIV 2.5.

X

LANGUAGES

1. *GENERAL BIBLIOGRAPHICAL AND REFERENCE SOURCES ON IRANIAN LANGUAGES*

1.1 *Surveys*

At the beginning of this century the current state of Iranian studies was summed up in the monumental two-volume *Grundriss der iranischen Philologie* (Strassburg 1895-1904), edited by W GEIGER and E KUHN. Although in many respects outdated - in particular it inevitably gives no account of the numerous Iranian languages discovered during this century - it contains many articles which remain unsurpassed in comprehensiveness. The quantity of material which has appeared since then precludes mention here of more than a few general works. Preference has been given to recent publications and to those which are most accessible.

REICHELT, H, 'Iranisch', *Grundriss der indogermanischen Sprach- und Altertumskunde, II: die Erforschung der indogermanischen Sprachen*, Bd. 4, Hälfte 2, Berlin 1927 :1-84.

A detailed survey of research on the Iranian languages up to about 1925.

Handbuch der Orientalistik, *op.cit.*, Abt. 1: Bd. 4: Abs. 1: Linguistik, Abs. 2: Literatur, Lfg. 1.

Contains survey articles, rather variable in length and depth of coverage, on Iranian languages and literature. M DRESDEN's 'Survey of the history of Iranian studies' in Abschnitt 2, Lfg. 1, pp.168-90, gives a lucid account of the subject up to 1962. Other articles are mentioned under appropriate language headings below.

RYPKA, J, *History of Iranian literature*, Dordrecht 1968.

A revised version of *Dějiny perské a tadžické literatury*, Prague 1956, and German translation, *Iranische Literaturgeschichte*, Leipzig 1959. Persian translation, Tehran 1975.

Yazyki Asii i Afriki, II: Indoevropeiskie yazyki: iranskie yazyki, dardskie yazyki; dravidiiskie yazyki, Moscow 1968.

Grammatical sketches of the Iranian languages, pp.7-315.

MACKENZIE, D N, 'Iranian languages', T SEBEOK (ed), *Current trends in linguistics. Vol.5: linguistics in South Asia*, The Hague 1969 :450-77. This article contains an extensive analytical bibliography as do several in volume six of the same series which have been listed individually under language headings below.

Opyt istorico-tipologicheskogo issledovaniya iranskikh yazykov, 2 vols, Moscow 1975.

A typological analysis of Iranian languages.

ORANSKIJ, I M, *Les langues iraniennes*, tr. J BLAU, Paris 1977.

A translation, with additional bibliography, of *Iranskie yazyki*, Moscow 1963. It gives a brief historical account of most of the Iranian languages.

—— *Iranskie yazyki v istoricheskom osveshchenii*, Moscow 1979.

1.2 *Bibliographies*

HENNING, W B, *Bibliography of important studies on old Iranian subjects*, Tehran 1950.

Despite its title, this covers all Iranian languages other than Persian. It lists nothing published after 1946.

PEARSON, J D (ed), *A bibliography of pre-Islamic Persia*, *op.cit.* II 2.2.

The first attempt at a comprehensive bibliography. It lists, without annotation, most relevant monographs and periodical articles published up to about 1970.

ZWANZIGER, R, 'Bibliographie: Iran, 1977-1980', *Archiv für Orientsforschung*, 27, 1980 :492-507.

Bibliography of recent publications without annotation.

The following serials contain good sections on current publications of articles and monographs.

Bibliographie linguistique : linguistic bibliography, Utrecht 1937-.

Short annotations are included where necessary, and reference is made to reviews.

MLA international bibliography of books and articles on the modern languages and literatures, Modern Languages Association of America, New York 1922-.

Besides these works, bibliographical information is also given in I AFSHAR's *Index Iranicus*, Tehran 1961-, and J PEARSON's *Index Islamicus*, Cambridge and London 1958-77, and *Quarterly Index Islamicus*, 1977-, which are described in more detail in II 3. See also *Abstracta Iranica* in section 1.4 below.

1.3 *Encyclopaedieas and collections*

Encyclopaedias in general have been described earlier in chapter II, but it may be worth giving special mention to:

Dānishnāma-yi Īrān u Islam: encyclopaedia of Iran and Islam, I YĀRSHĀṬIR, Tehran 1976.

Contains much information on Iranian languages, consisting partly of articles translated from the *Encyclopaedia of Islam*, and partly of new articles. See also *Encyclopaedia Iranica*, *op.cit.* II 1.

Monumentum H S Nyberg, 4 vols, Acta Iranica, 4-7, Tehran/Liège 1975.

Volumes 1-3 are a Festschrift. Volume 4 contains reprints of NYBERG's articles on Iranian religion.

HENNING, W B, *Selected papers*, 2 vols, Acta Iranica, 14 and 15, Tehran/Liège 1977.

Includes reprints of most of his articles, and many reviews.

1.4 *Periodicals*

Only those journals which consistently contain a high proportion of relevant material have been included here.

Zeitschrift für Indologie und Iranistik, Leipzig 1922-36.

Münchener Studien zur Sprachwissenschaft, Munich 1952-.

Indo-Iranian Journal, Dordrecht 1957-.

Studia Iranica, Leiden 1972-.

A supplementary series *Abstracta Iranica*, 1978-, contains useful bibliographical information in the form of reviews and abstracts.

Studien zur Indologie und Iranistik, Reinbeck 1975-.

1.5 *Series*

Corpus inscriptionum Iranicarum, London (except for part 2, vol.3, portfolio 1, which was published in Moscow), 1955-.

This series publishes inscriptions and documents from Iran, regardless of language, and in Iranian languages from outside Iran, up to the early Ṣafavid period. It includes facsimile and text volumes.

Acta Iranica: encyclopédie permanente des études iraniennes ..., Leiden 1974-.

This series publishes monographs and collections of articles on Iranian subjects.

Pahlavi codices and Iranian researches, K M Jamasp ASA and M NAWABI (eds), Shiraz 1976.

Contains works on Pahlavi and Avestan including a reprint, nos.41-49, of nine volumes in the important series of facsimilies *Codices Avestici et Pahlavici Bibliothecae Universitatis Hafniensis ...*, A CHRISTENSEN (ed),

12 volumes, Copenhagen 1931-44.

Iranisches Personennamenbuch, M MAYRHOFER (ed), Vienna 1977-.
A major project intended to provide a dictionary of all the personal names in the Iranian languages. Volume 1, by the editor, deals with Old Iranian names.

2. *OLD IRANIAN LANGUAGES*

Unfortunately there is no written evidence of most of the languages of ancient Iran from which the numerous mediaeval and modern Iranian languages are derived. The only Old Iranian languages of which substantial records survive are Old Persian, which is known from inscriptions of the Achaemenian period (sixth to fourth centuries BC), and Avestan, the language of the Zoroastrian scriptures. The earliest of these, the 'Gathas' of Zarathushtra, are traditionally thought to have been composed in about the sixth century BC, and some scholars would assign them to a still earlier period, but the Avestan literature was probably not put into writing before the Sassanian period.

Two articles in the *HdO*, Abt.1, Bd.4, survey the Old Iranian languages and their literatures, namely K HOFFMANN's 'Altiranisch' in Abschnitt 1, pp.1-19, and I GERSHEVITCH's 'Old Iranian literature' in Abschnitt 2, Lfg. 1, pp.1-30. J DUCHESNE-GUILLEMIN, 'L'étude de l'iranien ancien au vingtième siècle' (published first in *Kratylos* 7, 1962, pp.1-44, and reprinted in the author's *Opera minora*, volume 1, Tehran 1974, pp.9-52), provides a bibliographical account of Old Iranian studies up to about 1961. This is continued up to 1968 in E BENVENISTE's article 'Old Iranian' in *Current trends in linguistics*, volume 6, pp.9-25. Information on more recent publications is to be found in the articles by KELLENS and MAYRHOFER cited below under the respective headings of Avestan and Old Persian.

The historical grammar of the Old Iranian languages was treated in great detail by C BARTHOLOMAE in his two chapters 'Vorgeschichte der iranischen Sprachen' and 'Awestasprache und Altpersisch' in the *Grundriss der iranischen Philologie*, Bd.2, Abt.1, pp.1-248. BARTHOLOMAE also compiled a comprehensive dictionary, *Altiranisches Wörterbuch* (Strassburg 1904), with a supplementary volume, *Zum altiranischen Wörterbuch* (Strassburg 1906). Though in some respects antiquated, these works have not been superseded. In particular, they remain the most detailed and authoritative dictionary and grammar of Avestan (for Old Persian more recent works are available).

The scanty remains of the ancient Scythian and Sarmatian languages have recently received comprehensive treatment in V I ABAEV's chapter 'Skifosarmatskie narechiya' in the volume *Osnovy iranskogo yazykoznaniya: Drevne-iranskie yazyki*, Moscow 1979, pp.272-364.

2.1 *Avestan*

KELLENS, J, 'L'avestique de 1962 à 1972', *Kratylos* 16, 1971 (pub. 1973) :1-30.

—— 'L'avestique de 1962 à 1972: addenda et corrigenda', *Kratylos* 18, 1973 (pub. 1975) :1-5.

These two articles continue the work of DUCHESNE-GUILLEMIN, *op.cit.*, but for Avestan only.

SCHLERATH, B, *Awesta-Wörterbuch. Vorarbeiten*, Bd.1: *Index locorum zur Sekundärliteratur des Awesta*; 2: *Konkordanz*, Wiesbaden 1968.

The dictionary itself has not yet appeared.

JACKSON, A V W, *An Avesta grammar in comparison with Sanskrit*, part I: *Phonology, inflection, word-formation, with an introduction on the Avesta*, Stuttgart 1892. (No more published.)

A less detailed grammar than BARTHOLOMAE's, *op.cit.*, but very convenient.

REICHELT, H, *Awestisches Elementarbuch*, Heidelberg 1909.

Particularly useful for its section on syntax (pp.218-387), a subject not covered elsewhere.

GELDNER, K F, *Avesta: the sacred books of the Parsis*, 3 vols, Stuttgart 1886-96.

The standard edition of the principal Avestan texts.

Works published since 1972 include the following.

KELLENS, J, *Les noms-racines de l'Avesta*, Wiesbaden 1974.

—— *Fravardīn Yašt (1-70): introduction, édition et glossaire*, Wiesbaden 1975.

INSLER, S, *The Gathas of Zarathustra*, *op.cit.* VI 3.2.

Edition with translation, commentary, and word-list.

MONNA, M C, *The Gathas of Zarathustra*, *op.cit.* VI 3.2.

Includes a complete glossary to the Gathas.

KUIPER, F B J, *On Zarathustra's language*. Mededelingen der Koninklijke Nederlandse Akademie van Wetenschappen, Afd. Letterkunde. Nieuwe Reeks. Deel 41, no.4, Amsterdam 1978.

2.2 *Old Persian*

MAYRHOFER, M, 'Das Altpersische seit 1964', *W B Henning memorial volume*, London 1970 :276-98.

—— 'Neuere Forschungen zum Altpersischen'. *Donum Indogermanicum: Festgabe für Anton Scherer*, Heidelberg 1971 :41-66.

Two articles containing analytic bibliography up to 1968 and 1970 respectively.

KENT, R G, *Old Persian: grammar, texts, lexicon*, 2nd rev.ed. New Haven 1953.

The standard collection of Old Persian inscriptions, with a grammar and complete glossary.

BRANDENSTEIN, W, and M MAYRHOFER, *Handbuch des Altpersischen*, Wiesbaden 1964.

Though less comprehensive than the preceding work, this handbook is more modern in approach.

MAYRHOFER, M, *Supplement zur Sammlung der altpersischen Inschriften*. Österreichische Akad. d. Wiss. Phil.-hist. Klasse. Sitzungsberichte. Bd. 338, Vienna 1978.

A supplementary collection of Old Persian inscriptions not included in KENT's edition.

Many publications since 1970 have been largely concerned with Old Persian as recorded in Elamite texts. Amongst these the following may be mentioned.

—— *Onomastica persepolitana: das altiranische Namengut der Persepolis-Täfelchen*. Österreichische Akad. der Wiss. Phil.-hist. Klasse. Sitzungsberichte, Bd.286, Vienna 1973.

HINZ, W, *Neue Wege im Altpersischen*, Wiesbaden 1973.

—— *Altiranisches Sprachgut der Nebenüberlieferungen*, Wiesbaden 1975.

GERSHEVITCH, I, 'The alloglottography of Old Persian', *Transactions of the Philological Society*, 1979 :114-90.

Another preoccupation has been the Old Persian cuneiform script and its origin, the most recent detailed discussions of which are the following.

LECOQ, P, 'Le problème de l'écriture cunéiforme vieux-perse', *Hommage universel* 3, Acta Iranica 3, Tehran/Liège 1974 :25-107.

HOFFMANN, K, 'Zur altpersischen Schrift', *idem*, *Aufsatze zur Indoiranistik*, Bd.2, Wiesbaden 1976 :620-45.

3. *MIDDLE IRANIAN LANGUAGES*

The term Middle Iranian is used to refer to the forms of Iranian languages spoken during the period from the disintegration of the Achaemenid empire up to early Islamic times. From a linguistic point of view, the attested Middle Iranian languages may be classified into two clearly defined groups: Western Middle Iranian, consisting of Middle Persian and Parthian, and Eastern Middle Iranian, namely Sogdian, Saka (Khotanese and Tumshuq Saka),

Bactrian, and Choresmian.

A brilliant and personal analysis of the common features and individual peculiarities of the Middle Iranian languages (other than Saka), with many incidental bibliographical references, is W B HENNING's 'Mitteliranisch' in *HdO*, Abt.1, Bd.4, Abschnitt 1, 1958, pp.20-130. For a survey of more recent work up to about the end of 1968, with detailed bibliography, see M J DRESDEN's article 'Middle Iranian' in *Current Trends in Linguistics*, volume 6, pp.26-63. The relevant part of D N MACKENZIE's article 'Iranian languages' in volume 5 of the same series, which covers the publications of a similar period, is also well worth consulting.

An important ancillary source for Middle Iranian linguistics is provided by the Armenian language. Although Armenian is a non-Iranian language (see 7.3 below), a large part of its vocabulary is borrowed from Iranian. The standard collection of material is in

HÜBSCHMANN, H, *Armenische Grammatik: I. Teil: Armenische Etymologie*, Leipzig 1897, repr. Hildesheim 1962 :9-280.

More recent major works are

BOLOGNESI, G, *Le fonti dialettali degli imprestiti iranici in armeno*, Milan 1960.

BENVENISTE, E, 'Eléments parthes en arménien', *REA* 1, 1964 :1-39.

The following language-by-language guide lists a few of the basic tools for the study of each language (dictionaries, grammars, chrestomathies), together with a selection of publications too recent to be included in the surveys by HENNING, DRESDEN, and MACKENZIE, or in the more specialized bibliographical works mentioned at the beginning of the appropriate sections below.

3.1 *Western Middle Iranian*

Since the Western Middle Iranian languages are closely connected with one another, both linguistically and historically, they are most conveniently treated together. Middle Persian (Pahlavi), the language of the province of Fars, was the official language of the Sasanian state. It is documented by a wide variety of sources: Sasanian and early Islamic inscriptions, Zoroastrian and (to a lesser extent) secular literature, Manichean texts (and one Christian text) from Central Asia, coins, seals, ostraca, papyri, etc. Parthian, the official language of the Arsacid empire, is known from secular documents (inscriptions, ostraca, etc.) of the Arsacid and Sasanian periods, and from Central Asian Manichean texts.

3.1.1 *General*

ROSSI, A V, *Linguistica mediopersiana 1966-1973: bibliografia analitica*, Supplemento 5 agli *AION* 35, Naples 1975.

A very detailed analytic bibliography, intended as a continuation of those of DRESDEN and MACKENZIE, *op.cit.*, but for Middle Persian only. Includes a section on work in progress (pp.75-78).

BRUNNER, C J, *A syntax of Western Middle Iranian*, Delmar, New York 1977.

3.1.2 *Inscriptional Middle Persian and Parthian*

GIGNOUX, P, *Glossaire des inscriptions pehlevies et parthes*, Corpus Inscriptionum Iranicarum, Suppl. Series, vol.1, London 1972.

BACK, M, *Die sassanidischen Staatsinschriften: Studien zur Orthographie und Phonologie des Mittelpersischen der Inschriften zusammen mit einem etymologischen Index des mittelpersischen Wortgutes und einem Textcorpus der behandelten Inschriften*. Acta Iranica 18, Tehran/Liège 1978.

HUMBACH, H, and P O SKJAERVØ, *The Sassanian inscription of Paikuli*, Wiesbaden 1978-.

DIAKONOFF, I M, and V A LIVSHITS, *Parthian economic documents from Nisa*, D N MACKENZIE (ed), Corpus Inscriptionum Iranicarum, London 1976-.

A comprehensive edition, of which three volumes of plates (out of a projected five) and one fascicle of the first Text-volume have so far appeared.

3.1.3 *Zoroastrian Pahlavi*

Two useful surveys of the Zoroastrian Pahlavi literature (including secular texts) may first be mentioned.

TAVADIA, J C, *Die mittelpersische Sprache und Literatur der Zarathustrier*, Leipzig 1956.

BOYCE, M, 'Middle Persian literature', *HdO*, Abt.1, Bd.4, Abschnitt 2, Lfg. 1 :31-66.

Sent to press in 1958, but with bibliographical additions up to 1967.

MACKENZIE, D N, *A concise Pahlavi dictionary*, London 1971.

A reliable basic vocabulary, containing about 4000 words in Pahlavi script, transliteration, and transcription, together with the equivalent forms in Manichean Middle Persian, New Persian, etc. An English-Pahlavi index is included.

BAHĀR, Mihrdād, *Vāzhanāma-yi guzīdahā-yi Zād-aspram*, Tehran 1972.

A Pahlavi-Persian glossary to the 'Selections of Zādspram'.

NYBERG, H S, *A manual of Pahlavi*, 2 vols, Wiesbaden 1964, 1974.

Includes selected texts, notes, etymological glossary, and grammatical sketch. A convenient introductory handbook, marred by many idiosyncracies.

SALEMANN, C, 'Mittelpersisch', *GIP*, Bd.1, Abt.1 :249-332. English tr. L BOGDANOV, *A Middle-Persian grammar*, Bombay 1930.

The only full-scale grammar of Pahlavi, antiquated but still useful.

PERIKHANYAN, A G, *Sasanidskii sudebnik: 'Kniga tysyachi sudebnykh reshenii' (Mātakdān ī hazār dātastān)*, Erevan 1973.

Edition and translation of an important legal text, with glossary.

ĒMĒTĀN, Āturpāt-i, *The wisdom of the sages*, *op.cit.* VI 3.2.

Text, translation, commentary and glossary.

KOTWAL, F M, and J W BOYD (eds), *Ērbadīstān ud Nirangistān: facsimile edition of the manuscript TD*, Harvard Iranian series 3, Cambridge, Mass. 1980.

MACUCH, M (ed), *Das sasanidische Rechtsbuch 'Mātakdān i hazār dātistān' Teil II*. Abhandlungen für die Kunde des Morgenlandes, Bd.45, 1, Wiesbaden 1981.

3.1.4 *Manichean Middle Persian and Parthian*

BOYCE, M, *A catalogue of the Iranian manuscripts*, *op.cit.* III 3.2.2.

Contains detailed bibliography of work on the Middle Persian, Parthian, and Sogdian texts in Manichean script.

—— 'The Manichaean literature in Middle Iranian', *HdO*, Abt.1, Bd.4, Abschnitt 1, Lfg.1 :67-76.

A general survey, with further bibliography up to 1967.

SUNDERMANN, W, 'Arbeiten an den iranischen Turfantexten seit 1970', *JA* 269, 1981 :37-45.

Includes bibliography of recent work on the Middle Persian, Parthian, and Sogdian texts.

Two further works by M BOYCE provide an excellent introduction to the language and content of the Manichean texts, while the most essential works on their grammar remain the studies of the Middle Persian and the Parthian verb by HENNING and GHILAIN respectively.

BOYCE, M, *A reader in Manichaean Middle Persian and Parthian: texts with notes*, Acta Iranica 9, Tehran/Liège 1975.

—— *A word-list of Manichaean Middle Persian and Parthian*, with a reverse index by R ZWANZIGER, Acta Iranica 9a, Tehran/Liège 1977.

Many of the texts included in BOYCE's *Reader* are translated in

ASMUSSEN, J P, *Manichaean literature: representative texts, chiefly from Middle Persian and Parthian writings*, Delmar, New York 1975.

HENNING, W B, 'Das Verbum des Mittelpersischen der Turfanfragmente', *ZII* 9, 1933 :158-253, repr. in HENNING's *Selected papers*, vol.1, *op.cit.* 1.3, :65-160.

GHILAIN, A, *Essai sur la langue parthe: son système verbal d'après les textes manichéens du Turkestan oriental*, Louvain 1939.

The following important text-editions, each including translation, commentary, glossary, and facsimiles, have appeared recently.

MACKENZIE, D N, 'Mani's *Šābuhragān* [I]-II', *BSOAS* 42, 1979 :500-34; 43, 1980 :288-310.

SUNDERMANN, W, *Mitteliranische manichäische Texte kirchengeschichtlichen Inhalts*, Berliner Turfantexte, 11, Berlin 1981.

Includes Sogdian texts also.

3.2 *Sogdian*

Sogdian, the mediaeval language of the area around Samarqand in present-day Soviet Tajikistan, is known both from an archive of secular documents found at Mt Mug in the Sogdian homeland and from the much more extensive material, including Buddhist, Manichean, and Christian manuscripts, discovered in Chinese Turkestan. Sogdian inscriptions, moreoever, have been found as far afield as Kirghizia, Mongolia, and Tibet.

Works mentioned in the preceding section on Manichean Middle Persian and Parthian as being relevant also to (Manichean) Sogdian should be consulted in addition to those listed here.

UTZ, D A, *A survey of Buddhist Sogdian studies*, Tokyo 1978.

Contains a good bibliography up to 1976.

HANSEN, O, 'Die buddhistische und christliche Literatur', *HdO*, Abt.1, Bd.4, Abschnitt 2, Lfg.1 :77-99.

A survey-article covering Khotanese as well as Sogdian. Particularly valuable for its information on unpublished Sogdian manuscripts.

GERSHEVITCH, I, *A grammar of Manichean Sogdian*, Oxford 1954.

Based primarily on Manichean material, but equally essential for the study of all varieties of Sogdian.

ISKHAKOV, M M, *Glagol v sogdiiskom yazyke (dokumenty s gory Mug)*, Tashkent 1977.

On the verbal forms in the documents from Mt Mug.

YOSHIDA, Y, 'On the Sogdian infinitives', *Journal of Asian and African studies* 18, Tokyo 1979 :181-95.

SIMS-WILLIAMS, N, 'The Sogdian sound-system and the origins of the Uyghur script', *JA* 269, 1981 :347-60.

RAGOZA, A N, *Sogdiiskie fragmenty tsentral'noaziatskogo sobraniya Instituta Vostokovedeniya*, Moscow 1980.

An edition (including facsimiles) of an important new collection of texts. To be read in conjunction with the following article.

SIMS-WILLIAMS, N, 'The Sogdian fragments of Leningrad', *BSOAS* 44, 1981 :231-40.

3.3 *Saka*

Two Middle Iranian Saka languages are known, both written in the Indian Brahmi script. An extensive Buddhist literature and many secular documents dating from the seventh to the tenth century AD survive in Khotanese, the language of the kingdom of Khotan, modern Ho-t'ien in the Sinkiang Uigur Autonomous Region of China. The closely-related dialect of Tumshuq is attested by less than twenty documents.

EMMERICK, R E, *A guide to the literature of Khotan*, Tokyo 1979.

Includes valuable advice on the study of Khotanese as well as information on manuscripts and editions of the texts themselves.

DRESDEN, M J, 'Khotanese (Saka) manuscripts: a provisional handlist', *Varia 1976*, Acta Iranica 12, Tehran-Liège 1977 :27-85.

A detailed list of the manuscripts with references to publications. Includes (pp.82-84) a bibliography of Tumshuq Saka.

BAILEY, H W, 'Languages of the Saka', *HdO*, Abt.1, Bd.4, Abschnitt 1 :131-54.

A survey of the principal linguistic features of the two dialects.

—— *Dictionary of Khotan Saka*, Cambridge 1979.

A largely etymological dictionary, excluding the substantial foreign (chiefly Indian) element in the Khotanese vocabulary.

KONOW, S, *Primer of Khotanese Saka: grammatical sketch, chrestomathy, vocabulary, bibliography*, Oslo 1949.

Still useful for aspects of Khotanese grammar not included in the next.

EMMERICK, R E, *Saka grammatical studies*, London 1968.

The first volume of a detailed, up-to-date grammar.

—— 'The vowel phonemes of Khotanese', *Festschrift for Oswald Szemerényi ...*, B BROGYANYI (ed), Current issues in Linguistic Theory, 11, Amsterdam 1979 :239-50.

3.4 *Bactrian*

The language of the Kushan kingdom of Bactria is known principally from a single well-preserved inscription in Greek script, of which three copies have been excavated at Surkh Kotal in the north of Afghanistan. Other sources include coins, seals, ostraca, and a few manuscript fragments.

DAVARY, G D, 'A list of the inscriptions of the pre-Islamic period from Afghanistan', *Studien zur Indologie und Iranistik*, 1, 1977 :11-22.

Covers the Bactrian inscriptions of Afghanistan, but not those of Pakistan or the USSR.

HUMBACH, H, *Baktrische Sprachdenkmaler*, 2 vols, Wiesbaden 1966, 1967.

A valuable collection of material, with excellent plates. Articles by HENNING, GERSHEVITCH, *et al*. (see DAVARY's list) provide an essential corrective to HUMBACH's often idiosyncratic interpretations.

More recently discovered Bactrian inscriptions have been published by V A LIVSHITS and others in the following collective works.

STAVISKII, B Y (ed), *Buddiiskie peshchery Kara-tepe v starom Termeze*, Moscow 1969.

—— *Buddiiskii kul'tovyi tsentr Kara-tepe ...*, Moscow 1972.

—— *Novye nakhodki na Kara-tepe ...*, Moscow 1975.

KRUGLIKOVA, I T, (ed), *Drevnyaya Baktriya*, vyp. [1]-2, Moscow 1976, 1979.

3.5 *Choresmian (Khwarezmian)*

The language of mediaeval Khwārizm is known from two types of source: coins, documents, and inscriptions of the second to eighth centuries AD, written in the indigenous Choresmian script, and much later materials in Arabic script (eleventh to fourteenth centuries). Most important amongst the latter are the Choresmian glosses in a manuscript of ZAMAKHSHARĪ's Arabic dictionary *Muqaddamat al-adab* (see 4.2.2).

An idea of the grammar and linguistic peculiarities of Choresmian can be obtained from the writings of W B HENNING (conveniently listed on p.38 of DRESDEN's article 'Middle Iranian', *op.cit.*) At the time of his death HENNING had completed only a small part of a projected Choresmian dictionary, published posthumously as

HENNING, W B, *A fragment of a Khwarezmian dictionary*, D N MACKENZIE (ed), London 1971.

BENZING, J, *Das chwaresmische Sprachmaterial einer Handschrift der 'Muqaddimat al-adab' von Zamaxšarī*, Bd.1: Text, Wiesbaden 1968.

A transliteration of the Choresmian glosses to ZAMAKHSHARĪ's dictionary, together with text and translation of the Arabic and Persian versions.

MACKENZIE, D N, 'The Khwarezmian glossary I-V', *BSOAS* 33, 1970 :540-59; 34, 1971 :74-90, 314-30, 521-37; 35, 1972 :56-73.

An extended review of BENZING's work.

—— 'Khwarezmian imperfect stems', *Mélanges linguistiques offerts à Émile*

Benveniste, Paris 1975 :389-95.

4. *NEW PERSIAN*

4.1 *General works and bibliographies*

4.1.1 *Bibliographies*

ABOLHAMD, Abdolhamid, and Nasser PAKDAMAN, (ABU'L-ḤAMD, ᶜAbd al-Ḥamīd, and Nāṣir PĀKDĀMAN), *Bibliographie française de civilization Iranienne op.cit.* II 2.2.

Modern Persian in volume II, pp.25-36.

KĀẒIMĪ, Aṣghar, *Fihrist-i kitābhā-yi ālmānī dar bāra-yi Īrān*, University of Tehran Publications 1303, Tehran 1970.

Dictionaries and grammars, pp.15-17.

ṢABĀ, Muḥsin, *Kitābhā-yi firānsa dar bāra-yi Īrān : Bibliographie française d'Iran*, University of Tehran Publications 1077, 3rd ed. Tehran 1966.

Dictionaries and grammars, pp.114-17.

MĀHYĀR NAVĀBĪ, Yaḥyā, *Kitābshināsī-yi Īrān : A Bibliography of Iran*, *op.cit.* II 2.2, vol.III, Persian language and literature.

LAZARD, G, 'Persian and Tajik', T SEBEOK (ed), *Current trends op.cit.* 1.1, vol.VI :64-135.

Contains extensive bibliography.

YARSHATER, Ehsan, 'Iran and Afghanistan', T SEBEOK (ed), *Current trends in linguistics*, vol.VI, The Hague 1970 :669-89.

4.1.2 *General works*

LEVY, R, *The Persian language*, London 1951.

Contains bibliography.

LENTZ, W, 'Das Neupersische', *HdO* 1, IV. 1, Leiden 1958 :179-221.

Bibliography on pp.218-21.

WINDFUHR, G L, *Persian grammar: history and state of its study*, The Hague 1979.

KHĀNLARĪ, P N, *Tārīkh-i zabān-i fārsī*, Iranian Culture Foundation Publications 24, 156, 214, 253, 272.

There is a very poor English translation of volume II published in India.

—— *A history of the Persian language*, tr. N H ANSARI, Delhi 1979.

—— *Zabān-shināsī va zabān-i fārsī*, Tehran 1964.

A collection of articles on various aspects of Iranian philology and linguistics and Persian grammar.

4.2 *Dictionaries*

4.2.1 *Modern dictionaries*

Monolingual

ADĪB-ṬŪSĪ, Muḥammad Amīn, *Farhang-i lug͟hāt-i adabī*, Faculté des Lettres de Tabriz: Institut d'Histoire et de Civilization Iraniennes Publications, 4, 6, 17, 3 vols, Tabriz 1967-72.

AURANG, Sargurd, *Farhang-i Aurang*, Tehran 1958.

DĀ^c^Ī AL-ISLĀM, Muḥammad ^c^Alī, *Farhang-i Niẓām*, 5 vols, Hyderbad 1929-38.

DIHK͟HUDĀ, ^c^Alī Akbar, *et al.*, *Lug͟hat-nāma*, Tehran 1948-81. 26,475 pages in about 260 fascicules.

Mammoth encyclopaedia incorporating material from many previous dictionaries and reference works.

MU^c^ĪN, Muḥammad, *Farhang-i fārsī (mutavassiṭ)*, 6 vols, Tehran 1963-73.

NAFĪSĪ, ^c^Ali Akbar (Nāẓim al-aṭibbā'), *Farhang-i Nafīsī*, 5 vols, Tehran 1938-56.

Bilingual

English

ARYANPŪR KĀS͟HĀNĪ, ^c^Abbās, *The new unabridged English-Persian Dictionary (Farhang-i kāmil-i ingilīsī-fārsī)*. With the collaboration of Jahāns͟hāh ṢĀLIḤ, vols 1-5, Tehran 1963-65.

BOYLE, J A, *A practical dictionary of the Persian language*, London 1949.

HAIM, S, *The larger English-Persian dictionary*, 2 vols, Tehran 1959-60, and reprints.

—— *New Persian-English dictionary*, 2 vols, Tehran 1934-36, and reprints.

—— *The shorter English-Persian dictionary*, Tehran 1956, and reprints.

—— *The one-volume English-Persian dictionary*, Tehran 1952.

—— *The one-volume Persian-English dictionary*, Tehran 1953, and reprints.

LAMBTON, A K S, *Persian vocabulary*, Cambridge 1954, and reprints.

MUNTAẒIM, Mīr ^c^Alī Aṣg͟har, *The new English-Persian dictionary*, Tehran 1967.

Two differing editions, large (26 cm) and small (18 cm) with the same title.

STEINGASS, F, *A comprehensive Persian-English dictionary*, London 1892, and reprints.

French

NAFĪSĪ, Sa^c^īd, *Dictionnaire Française-Persan*, 2 vols, Tehran 1930-31, and reprints.

G͟HAFFĀRĪ, Jalāl al-dīn, *Farhang-i Ghaffārī*, Persian-French, 8 vols, Tehran 1956-58.

German

JUNKER, Heinrich F J, and Bozorg ALAVI, *Persisch-Deutsches Wörterbuch*,

Leipzig 1965.

EILERS, Wilhelm, *Deutsch-persisches Wörterbuch*, Wiesbaden 1959-.

Russian

MILLER, B V, *Persidsko-Russkii slovar'*, Moscow 1960.

RUBINCHIK, Yu A, *Persidsko-russkii slovar' : Farhang-i pārsī bi-rūsī*, Moscow 1970.

Latin

VULLERS, I A, *Lexicon persico-latinum etymologicum*, 2 vols, Bonn 1855-64.

4.2.2 *Classical dictionaries*

For full descriptions of many of the dictionaries named below see

RIEU, C, *A catalogue of the Persian manuscripts in the British Museum*, *op. cit.* III 3.2.2, vol.II :491-510.

NAQAVĪ, Shahryār, *Farhang-nivīsī-yi fārsī dar Hind va Pākistān*. Tehran 1962.

Monolingual

ASADĪ ṬŪSĪ, Abū Manṣūr ᶜAlī b Aḥmad, *Lughat-i Furs*, Paul HORN (ed), Berlin 1897; ᶜAbbās IQBĀL (ed), Tehran 1940.

5th/11th century.

FAKHRĪ IṢFAHĀNĪ, Shams al-dīn Muḥammad (Shams-i Fakhrī), *Miᶜyār-i Jamālī*, part four, C SALEMANN (ed), Casani 1887; Ṣādiq KIYĀ (ed), University of Tehran Publications 486, Tehran 1958.

8th/14th century.

IBRĀHĪM, Badr al-dīn, *Farhang-i zafānguyā va jahānpūyā*, S I BAEVSKII (ed), Moscow 1974.

Facsimile and edited text of a 9th/15th century dictionary.

INJŪ, Mīr Jamāl al-dīn Ḥusain, *Farhang-i Jahāngīrī*, Lucknow 1876; R ᶜAFĪFĪ (ed), 3 vols, Mashhad 1972-76.

Compiled c.1600.

JĀRŪTĪ, Abu'l-ᶜalā' ᶜAbd al-mu'min, (Ṣafī Kaḥḥāl), *Majmūᶜa al-Furs*, ᶜAzīzallāh JUVAINĪ (ed), Iranian Culture Foundations Publications 259, Tehran 1977.

Compiled on similar lines to *Lughat-i Furs* of ASADĪ, 8th/14th century.

See also NAKHJIVĀNĪ below.

NAKHJIVĀNĪ, Muḥammad b Hindūshāh, *Ṣiḥāḥ al-Furs*, ᶜAbd al-ᶜalī ṬĀᶜATĪ (ed), BTNK Persian Texts Series 12, Tehran 1963.

Compiled in 8th/14th century, on similar lines to ASADĪ's *Lughat-i Furs*.

PĀDSHĀH, Muḥammad ('Shād'), *Farhang-i Ānandrāj*, Muḥammad DABĪR-SIYĀQĪ (ed), 7 vols, Tehran 1956.

Compiled in India c.1888 and first printed in Calcutta.

—— *Farhang-i mutarādifāt va iṣṭilāḥāt*, Tehran 1967.

First printed in Calcutta in 1874 and recently issued as a companion volume to *Farhang-i Ānandrāj*.

TABRĪZĪ, Muḥammad Ḥusain b Khalaf, ('Burhān'), *Burhān-i qāṭi*c, Muḥammad MUcĪN (ed), 5 vols, Tehran 1963.

Comprehensive dictionary compiled c.1062/1651.

TATTAVĪ, cAbd al-rashīd, *Farhang-i Rashīdī*, 2 vols, Calcutta 1875, repr. Tehran 1958.

Bilingual

DIHLAVĪ, Qāḍī Khān Badr Muḥammad, (Dhārwāl), *Dastūr al-ikhwān*, 2 vols, Sacīd Najafī ASADALLĀHĪ (ed), Iranian Culture Foundation Publications 96, 104, Tehran 1970-72.

9th/15th century Arabic-Persian dictionary; volume II consists of an index of the Persian words.

KURDĪ NĪSHĀPŪRĪ, Adīb Yacqūb, *Kitāb al-balgha*, Mujtabā MĪNUVĪ and Fīrūz ḤARĪRCHĪ (eds), Iranian Culture Foundation publications 244, Tehran 1976.

Composed in 438 AH, this is the oldest Arabic-Persian dictionary.

MAIDĀNĪ, Abu'l-faḍl Aḥmad b Muḥammad, *al-Sāmī fi'l-asāmī*, vol.I, facsimile of MS dated 601 AH, Iranian Culture Foundation Publications 15, Tehran 1966; vol.II, Index of Persian words and phrases by Muḥammad DABĪR-SIYĀQĪ, Iranian Culture Foundation Publications 199, Tehran 1973.

5th-6th/11th-12th century Arabic-Persian dictionary.

ṬIFLĪSĪ, Abu'l-faḍl Ḥubaish b Ibrāhīm, *Qānūn-i adab*, Ghulām Riẓā ṬĀHIR (ed), 3 vols, Iranian Culture Foundation Publications 108, 115, 127, Tehran 1971-72.

6th/12th century Arabic-Persian dictionary arranged in order of final letters of Arabic words.

ZAMAKHSHARĪ, Maḥmūd b cUmar, *Muqaddamat al-adab (Pīshrau-i adab)*, Muḥammad Kāẓim IMĀM (ed), vol.I, Nouns. In two separate parts - text and index; vol.II, Verbs. Text and index together. University of Tehran Publications 848, 962, Tehran 1963.

The author lived 467/1075 to 538/1144.

ZAUZANĪ, Abū cAbdallāh Ḥusain b Aḥmad, *Kitab al-maṣādir*, Taqī BĪNISH (ed), 2 vols, Mashhad 1961-66.

5th/11th century dictionary of Arabic verbs explained in Persian.

4.2.3 *Specialized dictionaries*

Technical and scientific

ABU'L-ḤAMD, ᶜAbd al-ḥamīd (ed), *Farhang-i iṣṭilāḥāt-i ḥuqūqī. Dictionaire juridique*, Iranian Culture Foundation Publications 178, 257, 2 vols, Tehran 1977.

Persian-French.

ĀSHŪRĪ, Dāryūsh, *Vāzhagān-i falsafa va ᶜulūm-i ijtimāᶜī*, vol.I, English-Persian, Tehran 1976.

A second French-English volume was promised; it is uncertain whether it ever appeared.

COMMISARIAT À L'ÉNERGIE ATOMIQUE FRANÇAIS, *Farhang-i vāzhahā-yi atumī, fārsī-ingilīsī-farānsa*. Lexique nucléaire, tr. Samad FARRUKHĪ, Masᶜūd KISRĀ'Ī, and Nāṣir RŪḤĀNĪ-ZĀDA, Tehran 1978.

Farhang-i iṣṭilāḥāt-i ḥisābdārī, Iranian Culture Foundation Publications 86, Tehran 1969.

Financial terms; Persian-English with English-Persian index.

GĪV, Āqāsī, *Farhang-i daryā'ī-yi ingilīsī-fārsī*, Tehran 1978.

GOEDECKE, W, *Farhang-i nuvīn-i iliktrūnīk, irtibāṭāt, barq*, English-Persian dictionary of electronics, communications and electricity. Tr. Shukrī HARĀTĪ, Tehran 1980.

GŪNĪLĪ, Abu'l-ḥasan, *Farhang-i iṣṭilāḥāt-i kishāvarzī*, University of Tehran Publications 1203, Tehran 1968.

English-Persian dictionary of agriculture.

ḤABĪBĪ, Bahrām, *Farhang-i ālmānī-fārsī (Deutsch-Persisch Fachwörterbuch)*, Wiesbaden 1964.

German-Persian vocabulary for the natural sciences, medicine and agriculture.

JAMES, Glenn, and R C JAMES, *Farhang-i riyāżiyyāt*. Mathematics dictionary, English-Persian, tr. Afshīn ĀZĀDMANISH, Tehran 1976.

KAIHĀNĪ, ᶜAlī, *Farhang-i muṣavvar-i ᶜulūm-i ṭabīᶜī*, Tehran 1980.

KHWĀNSĀRĪ, Muḥammad, *Farhang-i iṣṭilāḥāt-i mantiqī*, Iranian Culture Foundation Publications 252, Tehran 1977.

KISHĀVARZ, Bahman, *Farhang-i ḥuqūqī-yi ingilīsī bi-fārsī*, Tehran 1977.

KOR OGLY, Kh G, *Persidsko-russkii i russko-persidskii obshcheekonomicheskii i vneshnetorgovyi slovar'*, Moscow 1957.

MAIMANDĪ-NIZHĀD, Muḥammad Javād, *Farhang-i asāmī-yi ᶜilmī-yi giyāhān*. Tehran University Publications 1110, Tehran 1967.

POUR-MOGHADDAM, Reza Agha (Rižā Āghā PŪR-MUQADDAM), *Illustrated scientific and technical dictionary of chemistry*, English-Persian/Persian-English, Tehran 1977.

RAHJŪ, Ḥusain, *Vāzha-nāma-yi ijtimāᶜī-siyāsī-yi islāmī*, n.p. 1979.

SĀBITĪ, Ḥabīballāh, *Dirakhtān va dirakhtcha-hā-yi Īrān : Trees and shrubs of Iran*, University of Tehran Publications 1037, Tehran 1966.

SCHLIMMER, L, *Terminologie médico-pharmaceutique et anthropologique française-persane*, University of Tehran Publications 330, Tehran 1956.

SHĀHRYĀRĪ, Parvīz (ed), *Farhang-i iṣṭilāḥāt-i ᶜilmī : A dictionary of scientific terms, covering mathematics, astronomy, physics, chemistry, geology, zoology and botany*, Iranian Culture Foundation Publications 100, Tehran 1970.

Persian-French and English with indices English-Persian and French-Persian.

ṬABĀṬABĀ'Ī, Muḥammad, *Farhang-i iṣṭilāḥāt-i pizishkī : A dictionary of medical terms*, Iranian Culture Foundation Publications 132, 133, 2 vols, Tehran 1973.

Volume I, Persian-French and English; volume II, English-Persian and French-Persian.

TAVĀNĀ, Jalāl al-dīn, *Farhang-i iṣṭilāḥāt-i naft*, Iranian Culture Foundation Publications 3, 2 vols, Tehran 1966-68.

English and Russian-Persian.

—— *Technical dictionary of oil industry terms, English-French-German-Persian*, 2 vols, Tehran 1966-68.

ZĀHIDĪ, Ismāᶜīl, *Vāzha-nāma-yi giyāhī : Botanical dictionary*, University of Tehran Publications 509, Tehran 1959.

Text arranged in order of scientific (Latin) names; separate indices of English, French, German, Arabic and Persian names.

Etymological dictionaries

HORN, Paul, *Grundriss der neupersischen Etymologie*, Strassburg 1893.

A pioneering work that, for all its shortcomings, has not been superseded. It should be used in conjunction with H HÜBSCHMANN's extended review, *Persische Studien*, Strassburg 1895.

RĀZĪ, Hāshim, *Farhang-i iṣṭilāḥāt-i khārijī dar zabān-i fārsī*, Tehran 1960.

SHĪR, Addī, *Kitāb al-alfāz al-fārisīya al-muᶜarraba*, Beirut 1908, repr. Tehran 1965.

Dictionaries of idioms, slang, etc.

AMĪNĪ, Amīr-Qulī, *Farhang-i ᶜavāmm*, 2nd enl.ed., 3 vols, Isfahan 1971, 1974.

ARDASHĪRJĪ, Shāpūr, ('Reporter'), *Farhang-i iṣṭilāḥāt-i fārsī bi inglīsī*, University of Tehran Publications 1337, Tehran 1975.

JAMĀLZĀDA, Sayyid Muḥammad ᶜAlī, *Farhang-i lughāt-i ᶜāmmiyāna*, Muḥammad Jaᶜfar MAḤJŪB (ed), Publications of Farhang-i Īrān-zamīn 7, Tehran 1962.

RAHMATĪ, Yūsuf, *Farhang-i ^{c}ammiyāna*, Tehran 1951.

Glossaries to specific works

AMĪRĪ, Minūchihr, *Farhang-i dārū-hā va vāzha-hā-yi dushvār yā taḥqīq dar bāra-yi Kitāb al-abniya fī ḥaqāyiq al-adwiya* of Abū Manṣūr ^{c}Alī HARAVĪ, Iranian Culture Foundation Publications 171, Tehran 1974.

GAUHARĪN, Ṣādiq, *Farhang-i lughāt va ta^{c}bīrāt-i Masnavī*, University of Tehran Publications 479, 545, 608, 744, 744/5, 6, 7; 7 vols, Tehran 1958-75.

MUḤAQQIQ, Mahdī, *Taḥlīl-i ash^{c}ār-i Nāṣir-i Khusrau*, University of Tehran Publications 987, Tehran 1965.

OSMANOV, M N O, *Chastotnyi slovar' Unsuri*, Moscow 1970.

Computerized concordance of the *Dīvān* of ^{c}UNSURĪ.

UTAS, Bo, *A Persian Sufi poem: vocabulary and terminology*, London/Malmö 1978.

Concordance, frequency word-list, statistical survey, Arabic loanwords, and Ṣūfī-religious terminology as used in the *Ṭarīq al-taḥqīq*, Bo UTAS (ed), Lund 1973.

WOLFF, F, *Glossar zu Firdosis Schahname*, Berlin 1935.

SHAFAQ, Riżāzāda, *Farḥang-i Shāhnāma*, Tehran 1941.

Many editions of texts are provided with glossaries, e.g.

RŪMĪ, Jalāl al-dīn, *Kullīyāt-i Shams*, Badī^{c} al-zamān FURŪZĀNFAR (ed), vol. VII, University of Tehran Publications 743, Tehran 1966 :179-468.

4.3 *Grammars*

4.3.1 *Literary/classical*

ALAVI, Bozorg, and Manfred LORENZ, *Lehrbuch der persischen Sprache*, Munich 1967.

AMIN-MADANI, Sadegh, and Dorothea LUTZ, *Persische Grammatik*, Heidelberg 1972.

ARENDS, A K, *Kratkii sintaksis sovremennogo persidskogo literaturnogo yazyka*, Moscow/Leningrad 1941.

ATEŞ, Ahmed, and Abdülvehhâb TARZĪ, *Farsça grameri*, Istanbul 1954.

BOYLE, J A, *Grammar of Modern Persian*, Wiesbaden 1966.

D'ERME, G M, *Grammatica del neopersiano*, Istituto universitario orientale, Seminario di studi asiatici, serio minor 9, Naples 1979.

ELWELL-SUTTON, L P, *Elementary Persian grammar*, Cambridge 1963, repr. with key 1972.

HUMĀYŪN-FARRUKH, ^{c}Abd al-raḥīm, *Dastūr-i jāmi^{c}-i zabān-i fārsī*, Tehran 1960.

KHĀNLARĪ, P N, *Dastūr-i zabān-i fārsī*, Tehran 1972, and reprints.

LAMBTON, A K S, *Persian grammar*, including key, Cambridge 1953, and reprints.

LAZARD, G, *Grammaire du persan contemporain*, Paris 1957.

—— *La langue des plus anciens monuments de la prose persan*, Paris 1963.

MUᶜĪN, Muḥammad, *Ṭarḥ-i dastūr-i zabān-i fārsī*, rev.ed. Tehran 1961-63; 1, Mufrid va jam', 1961; 2, Ism-i maṣdar, ḥāṣil-i maṣdar, 1962; 3-4, Iẓāfa, 1962; 5, Ism-i jins va maᶜrifa, nakira, 1963.

OVCHINNIKOVA, I K, and A K MAMEDZADE, *Uchebnik persidskogo yazyka*, Moscow 1966.

PHILLOTT, D C, *Higher Persian grammar*, Calcutta 1919.

Though out-of-date in arrangement and approach, it contains a wealth of detail not available elsewhere, particularly with reference to the differences between Iranian and Afghan Persian.

ROSSI, Ettore, *Grammatica di persiano moderno*, Rome 1947.

ST CLAIR-TISDALL, W, *Modern Persian conversation-grammar*, with key, 3rd ed., London/Heidelberg 1923.

4.3.2 *Phrase-books, teach-yourself, etc.*

ELWELL-SUTTON, L P, *Colloquial Persian*, London 1941, and reprints.

HINZ, Walther, *Persisch. Praktischer Sprachführer*, Berlin 1963.

Fourth revised edition of *Persisch I. Leitfaden der Umgangssprache*, Berlin 1955.

MONTEIL, V, *Le persan contemporain. Textes et vocabulaires*, Paris 1955.

SHAKI, Mansour, *Moderni perska frazeologie a konverzace : Modern Persian phrase-book : Iṣṭilāḥāt-i fārsī*, Prague 1963.

In Czech, English and Persian, including a gramophone record of Persian speech sounds.

SHĪRĀZĪ, Mu'ayyid, *Today's Persian for foreign students*. Book 1 (Easy Persian), Pahlavī University, Shīrāz 1972; Book 2 (Pleasant Persian), Pahlavī University, Shīrāz 1978.

SOBHANI (ṢUBḤĀNĪ), Farhād, *Persisches Lehr-und Lesebuch für die Umgangssprache*, Berlin 1962.

Two records are available to accompany this grammar.

ṢUTŪDA, Minūchihr, *Persian for English-speaking people*, Faculty of Letters, University of Tehran; University of Tehran Publications 1025, 2 vols, Tehran 1961, 1965.

WINDFUHR, G, and H TEHRANISA, *Modern Persian: elementary level*, Ann Arbor, Mich. 1979.

WINDFUHR, G, *et al.*, *Modern Persian: intermediate level*, vol.I, Ann Arbor, Mich. 1980.

—— *Modern Persian: intermediate level*, vol.II, draft, Ann Arbor, Mich. 1979.

Final edition expected Winter 1981.

4.3.3 *Readers*

ARBERRY, A J, *Modern Persian reader*, Cambridge 1944.

DRESDEN, M J, *et al.*, *A reader in modern Persian*, American Council of Learned Societies: Program on Oriental Languages, A.6, New York 1958.

GELPKE, Rudolph, *Modern Persian texts*, Selection, introduction and glossary, Wiesbaden 1962.

HAIDARI, A A, *Modern Persian reader*, London 1975.

JAZAYERI, M A, and H H PAPER, *Modern Persian reader*, I, Elementary, with M FARZAN; II, Intermediate, with M FARZAN; III, Advanced, with P W AVERY and M FARZAN, Ann Arbor, Mich. 1962.

KAMSHAD, H, *A modern Persian prose reader*, Cambridge 1968.

4.4 *Miscellaneous*

AHSAN, Shakoor, *Modern trends in the Persian language*, Islamabad 1976.

GAPRINDASHVILI, Sh G, and Dzh Sh GIUNASHVILI, *Fonetika Persidskogo yazyka*, Tbilisi 1964.

ĪZADPARAST, Nūrallāh, *Dastūr-i zabān-i Sa^{c}dī*, Tehran 1980.

A study of the grammar, syntax and vocabulary of the language used by Sa^{c}dī.

KAPRANOV, V A, *'Lughati Furs' Asadi i ego mesto v istorii tadzhikskoi (farsi) leksikografii*, Dushanbe 1964.

PEISIKOV, L S, *Leksikologiya sovremennogo persidskogo yazyka*, Moscow 1975.

TOWHIDI (TAUḤĪDĪ), Jalil, *Studies in the phonetics and phonology of modern Persian*, Hamburg 1974.

SAMAREH, Yadollah, *The arrangement of segmental phonemes in Farsi*, Tehran 1977.

5. *AFGHAN-PERSIAN, TĀJĪK, JUDAEO-PERSIAN*

LAZARD, Gilbert, 'Persian and Tajik', SEBEOK, *op.cit.*, *Current trends*, vol.VI :64-96.

Contains (pp.77-96) a very full bibliography of recent works on Persian, Tājīk, Afghan (Darī) Persian, Judaeo-Persian, etc., up to March 1968.

LENTZ, Wolfgang, 'Das Neupersische', *HdO* I, IV. 1 :179-221.

The bibliography (pp.218-221) is less exhaustive than LAZARD's, but contains some useful references.

The following list supplements these bibliographies with a number of more recent works, and also includes some of the more important works listed in them.

5.1 *Afghan Persian*

5.1.1 *Dictionaries*

AFGHĀNĪ-NAVĪS, ʿAbdullāh, *Afghān Qāmūs - Fārsī bi-Pashtū*, 3 vols, Kābul 1957-58.

—— *Lughāt-i ʿāmmiyāna-yi fārsī-yi Afghānistān*, Kābul 1961.

BADAKHSHĪ, Shāh ʿAbdullāh, *Da Afghānistān da dzīno zh bo au lahjo qāmūs*, Kābul 1960.

Multilingual vocabulary in Pashto, Persian, Shughnī, Sanglēchī, Vākhī, Ishkāshmī and Munjī.

KISELEVA, L N, and V I MIKOLAICHIK, *Dari-Russkii Slovar'*, Moscow 1978. 21,000 words.

5.1.2 *Grammars*

FARHÂDI, Abd-ul-Ghafûr, *Le Persan parlé en Afghanistan. Grammaire du Kâboli*, Paris 1955.

DOROFEEVA, L N, *Yazyk Farsi-Kabuli*, Moscow 1960.

BĪTĀB, Malik al-shuʿarā, *Dastūr-i zabān-i fārsī*, Kābul 1961.

ENTEZĀR, E, and D J BURNS, *Farsi reference manual: basic course*, mimeographed, Putney, Vt. 1964.

ḤAMĪDĪ, A, *Dastūr-i zabān-i darī*, Kābul 1968.

NAGHAT-SAʿĪDĪ, Muhammad Nasīm, *Dastūr-i zabān-i muʿāsir-i darī*, Kābul 1969.

5.1.3 *Miscellaneous*

PAKHALINA, T N, 'On the system of vowel phonemes in Kabuli-Persian'. Paper prepared for the XXVI International Congress of Orientalists, Delhi 1964, Moscow 1963.

NAGHAT-SAʿĪDĪ, Muḥammad Nasīm, 'Sākht va anvāʿ-i kalima-yi murakkab dar zabān-i darī', *Majalla-yi Adab* 1/2, Kābul 1968.

ZAGREBEL'NYI, V N, 'Nekotorye sotsiologicheskiye aspekty proniknoveniya anglitsizmov v dari', *Leksikologiya i grammatiki vostochnikh yazykov*, Moscow 1975 :3-13.

URALOV, Kh U, 'Nekotorye modeli teknicheskikh terminov-sushchestvitel'nikh yazyka dari', *ibid.* :14-23.

5.2 *Tājīk*

5.2.1 *Dictionaries*

RAKHIMI, M V, and L V USPENSKAYA, *Tadzhiksko-russkii slovar'*, Moscow 1951.

40,000 words.

ARZUMANOV, D, and Kh K KARIMOV, *Russko-tadzhikskii slovar'*, Moscow 1957.

14,000 words.

SHUKUROV, M Sh, *et al.*, *Farhangi zaboni tojiki*, 2 vols, Moscow 1969.

Tājīk-Tājīk dictionary. 45,000 words.

AINI, Sadriddin, *Lughati nim tafsilii tojiki baroi zaboni adabii tojik. Kulliyot*, vol.XII, Dushanbe 1976.

11,400 words. Tājīk-Tājīk dictionary of literary words, originally compiled in 1938 by one of Tājīkistān's leading writers and scholars.

All the above are in the Cyrillic script with a check-list in Arabic script.

FOZILOV, M, *Farhangi iborahoi rekhtai zaboni hozirai tojik*, 2 vols, Moscow 1963.

About 6,500 idiomatic and proverbial phrases in Cyrillic script.

5.2.2 *Grammars, etc.*

NIYOZMUHAMMADOV, B, Sh NIYOZI, and L BUZURGZODA, *Grammatikai zaboni tojiki.* Qismi I. Fonetika va morfologiya baroi maktabhoi haftsola va miyona. Qismi II. Sintaksis. Stalinabad 1955, and subsequent revisions.

ARZUMANOV, S, and O DZHALOLOV, *Zaboni tojiki: Uchebnik tadzhikskogo yazyka dlya vysshikh uchebnykh zavedenii*, Dushanbe 1969.

SOKOLOVA, V S, *Fonetika tadzhikshogo yazyka*, Moscow/Leningrad 1949.

JURAYEV, Ghaffor, *Lahjahoi arabhoi tojikzabon*, Dushanbe 1975.

MURVATOV, Jamolkhon, *Shevahoi Tojikoni atrofi Andijon*, Dushanbe 1974.

LORENZ, Manfred, 'Postpositionen im Tāǧikischen', *Mitt. d. Inst. f. Orientforschung* XIII/3, Berlin 1967 :382-93.

—— 'Zur Herausbildung der modernen tâǧikischen Literatursprache', *Wiss. Zeitschr. d. Humboldt-Univ. Ges.-Sprachw.*, R. XXI/2, Berlin 1972 :257-62.

—— 'Eine besondere Funktion des Aorists von *budan* im Tâǧikischen', *Zeitschr. f. Phonetik. Sprachwiss. u. Kommunikationsforschung.*, Band 32, Heft 5, Berlin 1979 :571-75.

5.3 *Judaeo-Persian*

A number of articles on Judaeo-Persian are cited in LAZARD, *op.cit.*, by ASMUSSEN, PAPER, MACKENZIE and LAZARD himself. Attention may be drawn to one earlier work.

ABRAHAMIAN, Roubène, *Dialectes des Israélites de Hamadan et d'Ispahan (et dialecte de Baba Tahir)*, Paris 1936.

The following have appeared recently.

YAR-SHATER, Eḥsan (YĀR-SHĀṬIR, Iḥsān), 'The Jewish communities of Persia and their dialects', *Memorial Jean de Menasce*, Louvain 1974 :453-66.

—— 'The hybrid language of the Jewish community of Persia', *JAOS* 97/1, January-March 1977 :1-7.

PAPER, Herbert (ed), *A Judaeo-Persian Pentateuch*, Leiden 1972.

The text of the oldest Judaeo-Persian Pentateuch translation, BM, Or.5446.

ASMUSSEN, J P, *Studies in Judeo-Persian literature*, Leiden 1973.

6. *MODERN IRANIAN LANGUAGES*

Numerous languages belonging to the Iranian family are spoken over an area extending from Pakistan and Soviet Central Asia to Iraq and the Caucasus. This section is concerned with all these languages with the exception of Persian and Tājīkī (see 4. and 5. above).

A convenient starting-point is the masterly survey by G MORGENSTIERNE, 'Neu-iranische Sprachen' in *HdO*, Abt.1, Bd.4: Iranistik, Abschnitt 1: Linguistik, Leiden 1958, pp.155-78. Within a very few pages MORGENSTIERNE provides an incisive characterization and classification of the modern Iranian languages, together with a selective bibliography containing about 100 titles.

More recent work up to about 1966 and 1968 respectively is reviewed in two overlapping articles in the series *Current trends in linguistics*, T A SEBEOK (ed).

MACKENZIE, D N, 'Iranian languages', *Current trends ...*, vol.5, The Hague 1969 :450-77.

Covers Old and Middle Iranian, Persian and Tājīkī, as well as the other modern Iranian languages. Bibliography of books and articles, preceded by a concise critical analysis.

REDARD, G, 'Other Iranian languages', *Current trends ...*, *op.cit.*, vol.6 :97-135.

Covers all the modern Iranian languages except Persian and Tājīkī, Pashto and Kurdish; also includes the Dardic languages, which are non-Iranian. Bibliography of books and articles, with detailed critical comments on many of the works listed.

The most extensive work of this kind is

ORANSKIJ, I M, *Die neuiranischen Sprachen der Sowjetunion*, tr. W WINTER,

2 vols, The Hague 1975.

History of studies, with comprehensive bibliography from pre-revolutionary times to 1969, on the Iranian languages spoken in the Soviet Union (Persian-Tājīkī, Ossetic, Yaghnobi, Pamir languages, Balūchī, Tātī, Tālishī, Kurdish).

The selective bibliography which follows consists principally of items published during the last ten years or so, and thus not included in the surveys listed above, together with a small number of particularly useful or basic works, regardless of their date of publication. The order of the individual languages in this bibliography is based on the arrangement of MORGENSTIERNE's 'Übersicht über die neuiranischen Sprachen und Mundarten' (*op.cit.*, pp.167-76), beginning with Ossetic in the Caucasus, at the extreme north-west corner of the Iranian linguistic area, and continuing clockwise via Soviet Central Asia, Afghanistan and Pakistan, to Iran, the Caspian and Kurdistan.

6.1 *General works*

The principal works which deal with the modern Iranian languages as a whole have already been mentioned above. Amongst more recent publications one may refer to

SMIRNOVA, I A, *Formy chisla imeni v iranskikh yazykakh: znachenie i funktsionirovanie*, Leningrad 1974.

A comparative study of numerals in certain modern Iranian languages.

MORGENSTIERNE, G, *Irano-Dardica*, Wiesbaden 1973.

A collection of essays including many on the modern Iranian languages. Indexed.

6.2 *Ossetic*

Ossetic is spoken by some half million people in the Caucasus, chiefly in the South Ossetic Autonomous Region (part of the Georgian SSR) and the North Ossetic Autonomous SSR. There are two main dialects, Iron, which forms the basis of the standard literary language, and the more archaic Digor or Digoron. Ossetic has had a continuous written tradition since the end of the eighteenth century.

ISAEV, M I, *Ocherki po istorii izucheniya osetinskogo yazyka*, Ordzhonikidze 1974.

On the history of Ossetic studies.

MILLER, V F, and A A FREIMAN, *Osetinsko-russko-nemetskii slovar'*, 3 vols, The Hague 1972.

A reprint of the standard Ossetic dictionary (covering both dialects), originally published in Leningrad 1927-34.

BIGULAEV, B B, *et al.*, *Osetinsko-russkii slovar'*, 3rd enl.ed., Ordzhonikidze 1970.

About 28,000 entries, as compared with 20,000 in the first edition (Moscow 1952) and 27,000 in the second (Ordzhonikidze 1962). Iron only. Especially valuable for current usage.

ABAEV, V I, *Istoriko-etimologicheskii slovar' osetinskogo yazyka*, 3 vols, Moscow 1958-79.

Includes, in addition to the etymological analysis, many citations showing how the words are used.

BIELMEIER, R, *Historische Untersuchung zum Erb- und Lehnwortschatzanteil im ossetischen Grundwortschatz*, Frankfurt am Main 1977.

A re-examination of the theory of MARR, ABAEV, and others, that a 'Caucasian substrate' has contributed significantly to the formation of the basic vocabulary of Ossetic.

ABAEV, V I, *A grammatical sketch of Ossetic*, tr. S P HILL, Bloomington 1964.

A reliable and readily accessible grammar of Iron. Originally published in Russian, in several versions, both as a supplement to various dictionaries (1950 onwards) and separately (Ordzhonikidze 1959).

ISAEV, M I, *Digorskii dialekt osetinskogo yazyka: fonetika, morfologiya*, Moscow 1966.

A Digoron grammar with texts and translations.

TEKHOV, F D, *Vyrazhenie modal'nosti v osetinskom yazyke*, Tiflis 1970.

On the expression of modality in Ossetic.

ABAEV, V I, W BELARDI, and N MINISSI, 'Profilo grammaticale dell' osseto letterario moderno', *AION-L* 6, 1965 :49-68.

Includes (pp.55-56) two useful comparative tables showing some of the many alphabets (Cyrillic, Roman, Georgian) and transcriptions which have been employed for Ossetic.

DUMÉZIL, G, *Légendes sur les nartes: suivies de cinq notes mythologiques*, Paris 1930.

On the Nart saga, the Ossetic traditional literature.

6.3 *Yaghnobi*

Yaghnobi is spoken by about 2000 people in the Tajik SSR. It possesses a unique place in Iranian historical linguistics as the only surviving language closely related to mediaeval Sogdian.

ANDREEV, M S, and E M PESHCHEREVA, *Yagnobskie teksty: s prilozheniem yagnobsko-russkogo slovarya*, Moscow 1957.

A large collection of Yaghnobi texts, with Russian translations and a glossary including etymological information.

KHROMOV, A L, *Yagnobskii yazyk*, Moscow 1972.

A short grammar, with a few texts and a supplement to the glossary of *Yagnobskie teksty*.

6.4 *Pamir languages*

In the Pamir mountains and the surrounding area (including parts of the USSR, Afghanistan, Pakistan, Kashmir and Chinese Sinkiang) numerous Iranian languages are spoken. The list of titles which follows keeps, as far as possible, to the order in which the languages are listed here: the Shughnī group (Shughnī, Khufī, Roshanī, Bartangī, Oroshorī, Sarīkolī), Yāzghulāmī, Wakhī, Ishkashmī and Sanglēchī, Munjī and Yidgha.

PAKHALINA, T N, 'Sravnitel'nyi obzor pamirskikh yazykov', *Strany i narody vostoka*, vyp. 16, *Pamir*, A N ZELINSKII (ed), Moscow 1975 :222-50.

A comparative survey of the Pamir languages.

PAYNE, J R, 'The decay of ergativity in Pamir languages', *Lingua* 51, 1980 :147-86.

EDELMAN, D I, 'History of the consonant systems of the North-Pamir languages', *Indo-Iranian Journal* 22, 1980 :287-310.

MORGENSTIERNE, G, *Etymological vocabulary of the Shughni group*, Wiesbaden 1974.

Covers both the Shughnī group proper and Yāzghulāmī, as does the article by EDELMAN.

KARAMSHOEV, D, *Kategoriya roda v pamirskikh yazykakh (shugnano-rushanskaya gruppa)*, Dushanbe 1978.

On the category of gender in the Shughnī group.

ZARUBIN, I I, *Shugnanskie teksty i slovar'*, Moscow 1960.

NAWATA, T, *Shughni*, Asian and African grammatical manuals, 17, Tokyo 1979.

A brief outline grammar in English.

SOKOLOVA, V S, *Rushanskie i khufskie teksty i slovar'*, Moscow 1959.

—— *Bartangskie teksty i slovar'*, Moscow 1960.

KARAMKHUDOEV, N, *Bartangskii yazyk: fonetika i morfologiya*, Dushanbe 1973.

ZARUBIN, I I, 'Oroshorskie teksty i slovar'', *Pamirskaya ekspeditsiya 1928 g.: trudy ekspeditsii*, vyp. 6, *Lingvistika*, Leningrad 1930.

KURBANOV, Kh, *Roshorvskii yazyk*, Dushanbe 1976.

Oroshori grammar with some texts.

PAKHALINA, T N, *Sarykol'skii yazyk: issledovanie i materialy*, Moscow 1966.

Sarikoli texts and grammar.

—— *Sarykol'sko-russkii slovar'*, Moscow 1971.

EDEL'MAN, D I, *Yazgulyamskii yazyk*, Moscow 1966.

Yazg̲h̲ulami̅ texts and grammar.

—— *Yazgulyamsko-russkii slovar'*, Moscow 1971.

PAKHALINA, T N, *Vakhanskii yazyk*, Moscow 1975.

Wak̲h̲i̅ grammar, texts and glossary.

GRYUNBERG, A L, and I M STEBLIN-KAMENSKII, *Yazyki vostochnogo gindukusha: vakhanskii yazyk: teksty, slovar', grammaticheskii ocherk*, Moscow 1976.

The most comprehensive work on Wak̲h̲i̅.

KIEFFER, C M, 'Einführung in die Wakhi-Sprache und Glossar', *Grosser Pamir: Österreichisches Forschungsunternehmen 1975 in den Wakhan-Pamir/ Afghanistan*, R SENARCLENS DE GRANCY and R KOSTKA (eds), Graz 1978 :345-74.

MORGENSTIERNE, G, *Indo-Iranian frontier languages*. Vol.2, *Iranian Pamir languages (Yidgha-Munji, Sanglechi-Ishkashmi and Wakhi)*, Oslo 1938, 2nd ed. 1973.

Historical grammar, texts and glossary for each of the languages named in the title, together with an English-Iranian index to the words cited in this and other publications by the same author.

PAKHALINA, T N, *Ishkashimskii yazyk: ocherk fonetiki i grammatiki, teksty i slovar'*, Moscow 1959.

GRYUNBERG, A L, *Yazyki vostochnogo gindukusha: mundzhanskii yazyk: teksty, slovar', grammaticheskii ocherk*, Leningrad 1972.

SOKOLOVA, V S, *Geneticheskie otnosheniya mundzhanskogo yazyka i shugnano- yazgulyamskoi yazykovoi gruppy*, Leningrad 1973.

On the relationship between Munji̅ and the S̲h̲ughni̅ group.

6.5 *Pashto*

Pashto is spoken by some 20 million people, chiefly in Afghanistan, where it has the status of a national language, and in north-west Pakistan. The principal dialect division is between the south-west ('Pashto') and the north-east ('Pakhto') dialects. Pashto possesses a written literature dating back to the sixteenth century.

Paṣto Quarterly, Kabul 1977-.

Contains articles of varying quality on Pashto language, literature, folklore, etc.

ASLANOV, M G, *Afgansko-russkii slovar' (pushtu)*, Moscow 1966.

About 50,000 entries.

LEBEDEV, K A, L S YATSEVICH, and Z M KALININA, *Russko-afganskii slovar' (pushtu)*, Moscow 1973.

About 32,000 entries.

PAX̌TO ṬOLENA, *Pax̌to qāmūs*, 2 vols, Kabul 1951-54.

Pashto-Persian dictionary.

—— *English-Pushtu dictionary*, Kabul 1975.

RAVERTY, H G, *A dictionary of the Puk'hto, Pus'hto, or language of the Afghāns*, London 1860, 2nd ed. 1867.

Pashto-English dictionary, still not superseded.

MORGENSTIERNE, G, *An etymological vocabulary of Pashto*, Oslo 1927.

SHAFEEV, D A, *A short grammatical outline of Pashto*, tr. H PAPER, Bloomington 1964.

A convenient basic grammar of standard Afghan Pashto, originally published in Russian in 1955.

LORENZ, M, *Lehrbuch des Pashto (Afghanisch)*, Leipzig 1979.

A graded introductory course based on the current literary language.

ELFENBEIN, J H, 'Laṇḍa, zor Wėla! Waṇecī', *Archiv orientální* 35, 1967 :563-606.

A detailed account (in English) of the aberrant Wanetsi dialect spoken in Baluchistan.

ZYĀR, M A, *Die Nominalkomposita des Paschto*, Bern 1974.

BEČKA, J, *A study in Pashto stress*, Prague 1969.

A purely descriptive analysis. On the Pashto accent from a historical point of view the two following articles may be consulted.

DYBO, V A, 'Afganskoe udarenie i ego znachenie dlya indoevropeiskoi i balto-slavyanskoi aktsentologii, I: imennaya aktsentuatsiya', *Balto-slavyanskie issledovaniya*, Moscow 1974 :67-105.

MORGENSTIERNE, G, 'Traces of Indo-European accentuation in Pashto?', *Norsk tidsskrift for sprogvidenskap* 27, 1973 :61-65.

TEGEY, H, *The grammar of clitics: evidence from Pashto (Afghani) and other languages*, Kābul 1978.

KALININA, Z M, *Ocherki po leksikologii sovremennogo literaturnogo pushtu*, Moscow 1972.

On the vocabulary of modern literary Pashto.

PANJAB UNIVERSITY, *Tārīkh-i adabīyāt-i Musulmānān-i Pākistān u Hind*, vol. 13, Lahore 1971 :1-183.

History of Pashto literature, in Urdu.

ṢĀBIR, A, *Jadīd Pashto adab*, Peshawar 1974.

An extensive account in Urdu of Pashto literature, with short biographies of some authors.

HEWADMAL, Z, *Farhang-i zabān u adabīyāt-i Pax̌to*, Kābul 1977-.

Volume I is a biographical dictionary, in Persian, of Pashto writers.

BĪNAWĀ, ᶜA, *Osanai līkwāl*, 3 vols, Kabul 1961-67.

A biographical anthology, in Pashto, of 19th and 20th century writers of Pashto.

6.6 *Parāchī and Ormurī*

Parāchī, with a few thousand speakers in villages north of Kābul, and the two dialects (Logar, south of Kabul, and Kaniguram in Pakistani Wazīristān) of the now almost extinct Ormurī are the only surviving languages of the South-East Iranian group. The fundamental work on both these languages is

MORGENSTIERNE, G, *Indo-Iranian frontier languages*. Vol.I: *Parachi and Ormuri*, Oslo 1929, 2nd ed. 1973.

Includes texts and translations, historical grammar and glossaries.

KIEFFER, C M, 'Études Parāči, I-', *Studia Iranica* 6-, 1977-.

A series of articles comprising Parāchī texts, ethnographical and linguistic studies. Includes additions to MORGENSTIERNE's glossary.

—— 'The approaching end of the relict South-East Iranian languages *Ōrmuṛi* and *Parāči* in Afghanistan', *Linguistics* 191, 1977 :71-100.

—— 'Le multilinguisme des Ormuṛs de Baraki-Barak (Afghanistan): note sur des contacts de dialectes: ōrmuṛi, paṣ̌tō et persan kāboli', *Studia Iranica* 1, 1972 :115-26.

6.7 *Balūchī*

Balūchī is spoken over a wide area of south-east Iran and southern Afghanistan and Pakistan. There is also a small colony of Balūchī speakers in the region around Marv in the Turkmen SSR. The total number of Baluches was estimated in 1959 at something between 1½ and 2½ million. Written literature in Balūchī hardly existed before the present century, but there is a flourishing oral tradition.

ELFENBEIN, J H, *The Baluchi language: a dialectology with texts*, London 1966.

—— *A vocabulary of Marw Baluchi*, Naples 1963.

A glossary, with etymological notes and an English-Balūchī index, to the Russian publications on the Balūchī spoken in the Turkmen SSR.

BARKER, M A, and A K MENGAL, *A course in Baluchi*, 2 vols, Montreal 1969.

A graded introductory course based on the Rakhshānī dialect.

DAMES, M L, *Popular poetry of the Baloches*, 2 vols, London 1907.

Still the largest and most important collection of Balūchī traditional literature, with translations and notes.

PANJAB UNIVERSITY, *Tārīkh-i adabīyāt-i Musulmānān-i Pākistān u Hind*, *op. cit.* 6.5, vol.14 :344-406.

History of Balūchī literature, in Urdu.

QĀDIRĪ, K Al-, and ^{c}A BRĀHŪ'Ī, *Balochī, Brāhū'ī: ma^{c} ta^{c}āruf-i muṣannifīn*, Karachi 1973.

In Urdu. A bibliography of Balūchī (and Brāhū'ī) books printed in Pakistan from 1947 to 1972, including biographical details of the authors.

6.8 *Dialects of South and Central Iran*

It would unduly imbalance the present survey even to list the names of the innumerable languages and dialects of Iran. One must be content simply to mention a few of the more substantial of recent monographs and articles dealing with some of these languages. The list which follows, under the two headings of 'Dialects of South and Central Iran' and 'Dialects of North Iran and the Caspian', is arranged in approximately geographical order, starting from the Persian Gulf (where one dialect, Kumzarī, is spoken beyond the borders of Iran, on the Masandam peninsula (Oman) and ending at the Caspian (where Tātī and Tālishī are spoken on the far side of the Soviet frontier).

SKJAERVØ, P O, 'Notes on the dialects of Minab and Hormoz', *NTS* 29, 1975 :113-28.

KAMIOKA, K, and M YAMADA, *Lārestāni studies*. I: *Lāri basic vocabulary*, Tokyo 1979.

MAHAMEDI, H, 'On the verbal system in three Iranian dialects of Fārs', *Studia Iranica* 8, 1979 :277-97.

LECOQ, P, *Le dialecte de Sivand*, Wiesbaden 1979.

LAM^{c}A, M, *Farhang-i ^{c}āmmiyāna-yi ^{c}ashāyir-i Būyir-Aḥmadī va Kūhgīlūya*, Tehran 1970.

EILERS, W, *Westiranische Mundarten aus der Sammlung Wilhelm Eilers*, Bd.1: *die Mundart von Chunsar*. Bd.2: *die Mundart von Gaz*, Wiesbaden 1976-79.

LECOQ, P, 'Le dialecte d'Abyāne', *Studia Iranica* 3, 1974 :51-63.

—— 'Le dialecte d'Abu Zeyd Ābād', *Monumentum H S Nyberg* II, Acta Iranica 5 :15-38.

MACKINNON, C, 'The dialect of Giō', *Studia Iranica* 6, 1977 :211-47.

6.9 *Dialects of North Iran and the Caspian*

AZAMI, C A, and G L WINDFUHR, *A dictionary of Sangesari: with a grammatical outline*, Tehran 1972.

YAR-SHATER, E, *A grammar of Southern Tati dialects*, The Hague 1969.

MOKRI, M, *La grande assemblée des fidèles de vérité au tribunal sur le mont Zagros en Iran (Dawra-y dīwāna-gawra): livre secret et inédit en gourani ancien: texte critique, traduction, introduction et commentaires avec des notes linguistiques et glossaire*, Paris 1977.

KERIMOVA, A A, A K MAMEDZADE, and V S RASTORGUEVA, *Gilyansko-russkii slovar'*, Moscow 1980.

Includes a Russian-Gīlānī index.

RASTORGUEVA, V S, *et al.*, *Gilyanskii yazyk*, Moscow 1971.

PIREIKO, L A, *Talyshsko-russkii slovar'*, Moscow 1976.

A pocket dictionary with about 6,600 entries. Includes a Russian-Tālishī index and a grammatical sketch.

LAZARD, G, 'Le dialecte tâleši de Mâsule (Gilân)', *Studia Iranica* 7, 1978 :251-68.

—— 'Textes en tâleši de Mâsule', *Studia Iranica* 8, 1979 :33-66.

—— 'Glossaire Mâsulei', *Studia Iranica* 8, 1979 :269-75.

6.10 *Kurdish*

The extensive territory occupied by Kurdish in the heart of Asia Minor crosses the frontiers of five states: Iran, Iraq, Syria, Turkey and the USSR. The total number of Kurdish speakers in Kurdistan has been estimated, very approximately, at 12 million, and small groups are found also in other parts of Iran and the USSR. The numerous Kurdish dialects may conveniently be divided into a northern and a southern group, often called Kurmanjī and Sōrānī respectively, the principal representative of the latter being the dialect of Sulaimanīya, which has official status in Iraq.

MACKENZIE, D N, *Kurdish dialect studies*, 2 vols, London 1961-62.

The fundamental work on the grammar and dialectology of the Kurdish dialects of Iraq. Volume 1 contains texts and translations.

WAHBY, T, and C J EDMONDS, *A Kurdish-English dictionary*, Oxford 1966, 2nd ed. 1970.

Based on a normative form of the official Sulaimānī dialect.

McCARUS, E N, *A Kurdish-English dictionary: dialect of Sulaimania, Iraq*, Ann Arbor 1967.

BEDIR KHAN, D, and R LESCOT, *Grammaire kurde (dialecte kurmandji)*, Paris 1970.

BLAU, J, *Le kurde de ᶜAmādiya et de Djabal Sindjār: analyse linguistique, textes folkloriques, glossaires*, Paris 1975.

—— *Manuel de kurde (dialecte Sorani)*. Grammaire, textes de lecture, vocabulaire kurde-francais et francais-kurde. Institut d'études iraniennes de l'Université de la Sorbonne nouvelle. Documents et ouvrages de référence, 2, Paris 1980.

BAKAEV, Ch Kh, *Yazyk kurdov SSSR: sravitel'naya kharakteristika govorov*, Moscow 1973.

KURDOEV, K K, *Grammatika kurdskogo yazyka: na materiale dialektov kurmandzhi i sorani*, Moscow 1978.

JASTROW, O, 'Zur Phonologie des Kurdischen in der Türkei', *Studien zur Indologie und Iranistik* 3, 1977 :84-106.

Includes texts and translations.

TSABOLOV, R L, *Ocherk istoricheskoi fonetiki kurdskogo yazyka*, Moscow 1976.

—— *Ocherk istoricheskoi morfologii kurdskogo yazyka*, Moscow 1978.

7. *NON-IRANIAN LANGUAGES OF IRAN*

7.1 *Arabic*

Comparatively little has been written on the Arabic dialects of Iran, but they are similar to those of Iraq and in particular to those of the Southern Mesopotamian region.

Basic works for the study of these dialects are:

MEISSNER, B, 'Neuarabische Geschichten aus dem Iraq', *Beiträge zur Assyriologie und semitischen Sprachwissenschaft*, 5i, 1903 :i-lviii, 1-148.

WEISSBACH, F H, *Beiträge zur Kunde des Irak-Arabischen*, Leipzig 1930.

These have been updated by

DENZ, A, 'Die Verbalsyntax des neuarabischen Dialektes von Kwayriš (Irak) mit einer einleitenden allgemeinen Tempus- und Aspektlehre', *Abhand. für die Kunde des Morgenlandes*, 40i, 1971.

Other important works are:

VAN WAGONER, M Y, *Spoken Iraqi Arabic*, vol.1 (with records), New York 1949; Key to exercises, New York 1960; vol.2, Washington, DC 1958.

McCARTHY, R J, and F RAFFOULI, *Spoken Arabic of Baghdad*, 2 vols, Beirut 1964-65.

BLANC, Haim, 'Iraqi Arabic studies', H SOBELMAN (ed), *Arabic dialect studies: a selected bibliography*, Washington, DC 1962 :48-57.

Recent works include:

ERWIN, W M, *A short reference grammar of Iraqi Arabic*, Washington, DC 1963.

MALAIKA, Nisar, *Grundzüge der Grammatik des arabischen Dialektes von Bagdad*, Wiesbaden 1963.

BLANC, H, *Communal dialects in Baghdad*, Cambridge, Mass. 1964.

EDZARD, D O, 'Zum Vokabular der Maᶜdān-Araber in südlichen Iraq', G WIESSNER (ed), *Festschrift für Wilhelm Eilers: ein Dokument der internationalen Forschung zum 27 September 1966*, Wiesbaden 1967 :305-17.

HOSPERS, J H (ed), *A basic bibliography for the study of the Semitic languages*, vol.2, Leiden 1974.

Iraqi Arabic: pp.97-99.

INGHAM, B, 'Urban and rural Arabic in Khūzistān', *BSOAS* 36, 1973 :533-53.

—— 'Regional and social factors in the dialect geography of Southern Iraq and Khūzistān', *BSOAS* 39, 1976 :62-82.

—— 'Languages of the Persian Gulf', A J COTTRELL (ed), *The Persian Gulf states*, *op.cit*. IX 6.9, :314-33.

—— *North East Arabian dialects*, London 1981.

7.2 *Aramaic*

Modern Eastern Aramaic, also called Syriac and Assyrian, is spoken by Christians and Jews in the North Eastern part of Iraq, in Turkey and in Iran in the areas around Lake Urūmīya (Riżā'īya) with small communities in most of the large towns.

A recent study of the grammar which includes a most useful bibliographical introduction to the subject is

TSERETELI, K, *Grammatik der modernen assyrischen Sprache (Neuostaramäisch)*, Leipzig 1978. English tr. *The modern Assyrian language*, Mocow 1978.

Both works are revised editions of *Sovremennyi assiriiskii yazyk*, Moscow 1964.

For a survey of modern literature see

MACUCH, R, *Geschichte der spät- und neusyrischen Literatur*, Berlin 1976.

Basic reference works are:

NÖLDEKE, T, *Grammatik der neusyrischen Sprache am Urmia-See und in Kurdistan*, Leipzig 1868.

MACLEAN, A J, *A dictionary of the dialects of vernacular Syriac as spoken by the Eastern Syrians of Kurdistan, North-West Persia, and the plain of Mosul; with illustrations from the dialects of the Jews of Zakhu and Azerbaijan, and of the Western Syrians of Tur ᶜAbdin and Maᶜlula*, Oxford 1901.

ORAHAM, A J, *Oraham's dictionary of the stabilized and enriched Assyrian language and English*, Chicago 1943.

Includes many words omitted by MACLEAN.

More recent publications are:

GARBELL, I, *The Jewish Neo-Aramaic dialect of Persian Azerbaijan: linguistic analysis and folkloristic texts*, The Hague 1965.

HETZRON, R, 'The morphology of the verb in modern Syriac (Christian colloquial of Urmi)', *JAOS* 89, 1969 :112-27.

7.3 *Armenian*

Apart from school text-books published by the Armenian community in Iran, there are few specific studies of Armenian as used in Iran. It belongs, however, to the Eastern dialect as also spoken in the Armenian Republic of the Soviet Union, and of this dialect there are numerous studies, mainly in Russian. The following may be noted, though it must be borne in mind that the modern Soviet orthography differs in certain respects from that still used in Iran.

A comprehensive bibliography of both the eastern and the western dialects appears in

CONNOLLY, M J, 'Synchronic Armenian', *Current Trends in Linguistics*, vol. VI :160-75.

See also

GODEL, Robert, 'Diachronic Armenian', *ibid.*, :139-59.

Č'UGASYAN, B L, *Hay-Iranakan grakan arnč'ut'yunner*, Erevan 1963.

NAJARIAN, H, *Turk-Iranakan haraberut'yunnere XVI darum u XVII dari arajin kesin ev Hayastanė*, Erevan 1961.

The essential trends and issues of Armenian linguistics are discussed in

GREPPIN, John A C, 'An overview of Armenian linguistics', *Journal of Armenian Studies* I, Autumn 1975 :54-64,

and in the journal

Annual of Armenian Linguistics, 1980-.

A valuable list of publications on Armenian linguistics is to be found in

SCHMITT, R, 'Die Erforschung des Klassisch-Armenischen seit Meillet (1936)', *Kratylos* 17, 1972 :1-68.

The first International Conference on Armenian Linguistics was held in Philadelphia in 1979.

GREPPIN, J A C, *Proceedings*, Delmar 1980.

The standard works on Armenian language are

HÜBSCHMANN, H, *Armenische Grammatik*, *op.cit.* X 3.

MEILLET, A, *Études de linguistique ...*, *op.cit.* X 3.

AČARYAN, H, *Liakatar k'erakanut'yun hayoc' lezvi*, Erevan 1952-71.

BOLOGNESI, G, *Le fonti dialettali ...*, *op.cit.* X 3.

BENVENISTE, E, 'Elements parthes ...', *op.cit.* X 3.

7.3.1 *Grammars*

Among recent grammars three works deserve attention.

ABEGHIAN, A, *Neuarmenische Grammatik*, Berlin 1936.

THOMSON, R W, *An introduction to classical Armenian*, New York 1975.

BARDAKJIAN, K B, and R W THOMSON, *A textbook on modern western Armenian*, New York 1977.

Grammars with special relevance to eastern Armenian include

DIRR, A, *Praktisches Lehrbuch der ostarmenischen Sprache*, Vienna 1912.

FAIRBANKS, G, and E STEVICK, *Spoken East Armenian*, New York 1958.

FINCK, F N, *Lehrbuch der neuostarmenischen Litteratursprache*, Marburg 1902.

GHARIBYAN, A, *Kratkii kurs armyanskogo yazyka*, Erevan 1965. English tr. M J CONNOLLY.

MINASSIAN, Martyros, *Grammaire d'arménien oriental*, Delmar 1981.

MOVSESSIAN, P L, *Armenische Grammatik*, Vienna 1959.

SEVAK, G, *Žamanakakic' hayoc' lezvi daṡent'ac'*, Erevan 1967.

7.3.2 *Dictionaries*

ABRAHAMYAN, Ṙ, *Pahlaverén-Parsakerén-Hayerén-Ṙuserén-Anglerén baṙaran*, Erevan 1965.

Polyglott dictionary of Pahlavi, Persian, Armenian, Russian and English.

AGHAYAN, E B, *Ardi hayeréni bac'atrakan baṙaran*, 2 vols, Erevan 1976.

ČAGMAGČYAN, Y Y, *Ėndarjak baṙaran angleréné-hayeren*, Beirut 1979.

KHNDRUNI, Tigran, and Martiros GUŠAGČEAN, *Hayeréné-anglerén ardi baṙaran*, Beirut 1970.

KOUYOUMDJIAN, Mesrop G, *A comprehensive dictionary of Armenian-English*, Cairo 1961, repr. 1972.

—— *A comprehensive dictionary of English-Armenian*, Cairo 1961.

TER PALATYANC', G, *Baṙaran parskerén*, Constantinople 1826.

Zamankakic' hayoc' lezvi bac'atrakan baṙaran, 4 vols, Erevan 1972-80.

An explanatory dictionary of modern eastern Armenian.

7.3.3 *Studies*

ADJARIAN, H, *Classification des dialectes arméniens*, Paris 1909.

ALLEN, W S, 'Notes on the phonetics of an Eastern Armenian speaker', Trans. Phil.Soc., London 1950 :180-206.

The narrator was a resident of Ābādān originating from New Julfa, Iṣfahān.

ASATRYAN, M E, *Žamanakakic' hayoc' lezvi jevabanut'yan narc'er*, Erevan 1970.

Questions on the morphology of modern Armenian.

GRIGORYAN, A, *Hay barbaragitut'yun dasėnt'ac'*, Erevan 1957.

Text-book of Armenian dialectology.

KHACHATRIAN, Robert, '"Zhulfimskoi yazyk"', uponimaemyi V.N. Tatishchevym.' *Lrabar hasarakakan gitut'yunneri/Vestnik obshchestvennykh nauk*. Haykakan SSR Gitut'yunneri Akademiya/Akademiya Nauk Armyanskoi SSR, part 10, Erevan 1976 :68-70.

Concerning the Armenian dialect of Julfa.

Two works on the Armenian dialect of Chahārmaḥal are

ANDREASEAN, V, *C'armahal gawaṙė*, New Julfa 1977.

EDGAREAN, A, *Irani č'armahal gawaṙė*, Tehran 1963.

7.4 *Turkish*

DOERFER, G, 'Irano-altaistica: Turkish and Mongolian languages in Persia and Afghanistan', *Current trends in linguistics*, vol.VI, 1970 :217-34.

A thorough survey of the Turkish dialects of Iran which were known to the author at the time of publication. The extensive bibliography lists Iranian works as well as those in Western languages.

Since 1970 much new material has been published including several articles by DOERFER and others, details of which may be found in *Linguistic bibliography* and *Index Islamicus Quarterly*, *op.cit*. Amongst the most substantial works of recent years are

7.4.1 *Āzarī*

AMIRPUR-AHRANDJANI, M, *Der aserbeidschanische Dialekt von Schahpur: Phonologie und Morphologie*, Islamkundliche Untersuchungen, 11, Freiburg 1971.

DOERFER, G, 'Zum Vokabular eines aserbaidschanischen Dialektes in Zentralpersien', *Voprosy tyurkologii: K shestidesyatiletiyu akademika AN Azerb. SSR M Sh Shiralieva*, Baku 1971 :33-62.

BRANDS, H W, *Aserbaidschanische Chrestomathie: Texte des 20. Jahrhunderts*. Frankfürter türkologische Arbeitsmittel, Bd.1, Wiesbaden 1977.

ISHRĀQĪ, ᶜAbbās, *Mīkhwāham Turkī-yi Āzarbāyjānī yād bigīram*, Tabriz 1978.

HANEDA, K, and A GANJELU, *Tabrizi vocabulary on Azeri-Turkish dialect in Iran*, Studia culturae islamicae, 13, Tokyo 1979.

Z, M T, *Müᶜāşır Azarbayjān dilinin şarfı-naḥvı*, Tehran c.1980.

7.4.2 *Other dialects*

DOERFER, G, *Khalaj materials*. Indiana Univ. Publications. Uralic and Altaic series, 115, The Hague 1971.

BOZKURT, M F, *Untersuchungen zum Boǰnurd-Dialekt des Chorasantürkischen.* Dissertation zur Erlangung des Doktorgrades der Phil. Fak. der Georg-August-Universität Göttingen, Göttingen 1975.

FÁZSY, S, *Das Bodschnurdi, ein türkischer Dialekt in Chorasan, Ostpersien.* Thesis, Zurich Univ. Phil. Fak. 1, 1977, Zurich 1977.

DOERFER, G, 'Das Chorasantürkische', *Türk dili araştırmaları yilliği*, Belletin 1977 :127-204.

—— and S TEZCAN, *Wörterbuch des Chaladsch (Dialekt von Xarrab)*, Budapest 1980.

XI

LITERATURE

1. *GENERAL INTRODUCTION*

Until the 1950s the definition of Persian literature held by most Iranists was considerably different from what it is now a generation later. In the past, Persian literature was considered to designate almost anything written, and this idea is reflected in the older histories of this literature, both Persian and western. The gradual change of focus in the definition of Persian literature which has come about since World War II is characterized on the one hand by a narrowing of the range of forms and genres considered to be literature, and on the other hand by an expansion of this new scope to include oral as well as written genres. Today Persian literature is generally understood to include poetry, belletristic prose, a few 'classic' discursive works, and oral narratives of various genres. This change in the notion of Persian literature has been brought about, in part, by evolving academic concerns such as the idea that Persian literature should be studied in the context of the disciplinary study of literature, and by the development of new academic fields such as the formal study of folklore. These changing concerns are reflected in this section of the *Guide*, both in the categories of works listed, and in the works themselves.

The prevailing definition of Persian literature has influenced the bibliographical organization of it. The first major efforts in this direction were the catalogues of Persian manuscripts held in the large European libraries. The contents of these catalogues were classified under a set of headings which included topics as well as literary forms, and 'literature' was not separately designated *per se*. In the 1930s bibliographies in Persian on individual writers or literary forms began to be compiled, but it was not until the 1950s that bibliographies of literature in its more restricted sense started to appear in increasing numbers in Iran and in the west.

From even this very brief account it should be apparent why the bibliographical coverage of Persian literature is uneven. Bibliographies of a more general nature are likely to be available in English or another western language, while many of the specialized bibliographies are in Persian. The following entries are not meant to be a guide to Persian literature, but rather a guide to bibliographical sources for, and representative studies and translations of, Persian literature.

1.1 *Bibliographies and general works*

Among the general bibliographies, there are specific sections on literature in its more restricted sense of belles lettres in: *Index Islamicus*; *Bibliografiya Irana*; *Bibliografiya Afganistana*; *Index Iranicus*; *Rahnumā-yi Kitāb*; *Āyanda*; *Kitābshināsī-yi Millī*; and *Kitābhā-yi Dah Sāla*. Older material can be found in *Orientalische Bibliographie*. C A STOREY, *Persian literature*, and its Russian translation and revision by Yu E BREGEL are general classified bibliographies dealing with literature in its widest sense of 'written texts'.

MLA International Bibliography (annual).

A selective source for books and articles on Persian literature in Persian and other languages. Beginning in 1967, items of Persian interest were listed in the general Near- and Middle-East subsection of the larger section on Oriental and African literatures. Since 1968 there has been a special section for Iran in the Near- and Middle-East subsection.

WILBER, Donald N, 'Iran: Bibliographical Spectrum', *Review of National literatures*, 2:1, 1971 :161-81.

A bibliographical essay covering works in Persian and western languages on Persian literature, translations, and anthologies.

FOUCHÉCOUR, C -H de, 'Les Iranica dans la deuxième édition de l'Encyclopédie de l'Islam', *Studia Iranica* 1, 1972 :313-33; 2, 1973 :115-18; 8, 1979 :305-15.

A classified list, which includes a separate section on literature, through volume IV of *EI.2*.

GULBUN, Muḥammad, *Bibliography of language and writing*, Tehran 1977.

HANAWAY, William L, Jr, 'Persian literature', L BINDER (ed), *The study of the Middle East*, New York 1976 :453-78.

A general survey of the study of Persian literature in Iran and the west, with a selective bibliography of 149 items including literary history and criticism, and editions of texts.

Abstracta Iranica, 1978-.

Issued as supplements to *Studia Iranica*. Abstracts of selected articles published since 1 January 1977 / 1 Farvardīn 1356. Articles in any language are abstracted and classified under various headings, including literature.

2. *HANDBOOKS OF LITERATURE*

KHĀNLARĪ, Zahrā, *Farhang-i adabiyāt-i fārsī-yi darī*, Tehran 1969.
A general handbook of Persian literature, with information on authors, books, literary characters, historical personages important in literature, and the technical terminology of rhetoric, prosody, and astronomy.

3. *HISTORIES OF LITERATURE*

3.1 *General*

BROWNE, Edward Granville, *A literary history of Persia*, *op.cit.* IX 1.2.
Presents Persian literary history chronologically and linked to the major ruling dynasties. While this standard, basic reference work on Persian literature is out of date in a few respects, age has not significantly sapped its vitality.
ARBERRY, A J, *Classical Persian literature*, London 1958.
Written for students and the general reader, this work traces the history of Persian literature in its broad sense from the beginning of the 3rd/9th to the end of the 9th/15th century.
MORRISON, G, Julian BALDICK, and Shafīʿī KADKANĪ, *History of Persian Literature*, *op.cit.* II 1.1.
Includes chapters on Persian literature from the earliest times to the time of Jāmī, mediaeval Ṣūfī literature in Persian prose, Persian Ṣūfī poetry up to the 9th/15th century, and Persian literature from the time of Jāmī to the present day.
RYPKA, Jan, *History of Iranian literature*, *op.cit.* X 1.1.
A composite work, which includes very extensive bibliographies for each chapter. The topics covered are: Avesta, Ancient Persian Inscriptions, Middle Persian literature; History of Persian literature up to the beginning of the 20th century; Persian literature of the 20th century; Persian learned literature from its beginnings up to the end of the 18th century (this chapter is by Felix TAUER. See also his 'Two additional chapters to my outline of the Persian learned literature', *Archiv Orientální* 39, 1971, pp.268-83); Tajik literature from the 16th century to the present; Iranian folk-literature; Persian literature in India; An outline of Judeo-Persian literature. Despite the title, there are no discussions or bibliographies of literature in modern Iranian languages other than Persian and Tajik.
PAGLIARO, Antonio, and Alessandro BAUSANI, *Storia della letteratura*

persiana, Milan 1960.

Covers pre-Islamic Iranian literature, as well as Persian literature of the Islamic period. The major focus is on Persian poetry, and the valuable features of the work are its discussion of poetry by genre rather than chronologically, and its attempt to be analytical and critical rather than descriptive.

ETHÉ, Hermann, 'Neupersische Litteratur', W GEIGER and E KUHN (eds), *Grundriss der iranischen Philologie*, 2 vols, Strassburg, 1895-1905, II :212-368.

A scholarly account, still valuable, of the principal poets and prose writers. This work was translated into Persian and published in Tehran 1958.

HORN, Paul, *Geschichte der persischen Litteratur*, Leipzig 1901.

Deals mainly with poetry, by genre, with a short chapter on the history of Persian prose. A more 'popular' account than that of ETHÉ.

BERTEL'S, Y E, *Ocherk istorii persidskoi literatury*, Leningrad 1928.

A succinct but learned work.

NAFĪSĪ, Saᶜīd, *Tārīkh-i naẓm va nas̱r dar Īrān va dar zabān-i fārsī*, 2 vols, Tehran 1965.

A list of poets and prose writers, arranged chronologically by century (with an alphabetical index), from the 2nd/8th to the 10th/16th century. Includes some biographical information, and lists of works.

SHAFAQ, Ṣādiq Riẓāzāda, *Tārīkh-i adabiyāt-i Īrān*, Shīrāz 1942, repr. 1962. Revised and expanded 1973.

Covers the pre-Islamic literature of Iran, and the literature of the Islamic period through the early 20th century. The arrangement is chronological, by dynasty, and there are special chapters on literature in India and Azerbaijan.

Literaturnye imena arabskikh i persidskikh avtorov. Part II: Imena persidskikh avtorov. Book 1: Persidsko-tadzhikskiye avtory (VII-XV vv), Moscow 1979.

A useful check-list of Persian writers with brief details and alternative forms of their names. In Russian and Persian.

ṢAFĀ, Ẕabīḥallāh, *Tārīkh-i adabiyāt dar Īrān*, Tehran 1959-77.

Four volumes (in five) have been published. A chronological presentation of the political, social, religious, scientific, and literary history of Iran from the Arabic conquest to the beginning of the 10th/16th century. Much little-known material and many examples of poetry and prose are given.

3.2 *Regional*

3.2.1 *Indo-Pakistan Subcontinent*

SCHIMMEL, Annemarie, *Islamic literatures of India*, Wiesbaden 1973.

A bibliographical essay which includes many references to Persian works, along with works in Arabic and Turkish.

GHANI, Muhammad ᶜAbdu'l, *Pre-Mughal Persian in Hindūstān*, Allahabad 1941.

—— *A history of Persian language and literature at the Mughal court*, 3 vols, Allahabad 1929-30.

Descriptive, anecdotal accounts, with abundant examples in Persian and in translation.

MAREK, Jan, 'Persian literature in India', Jan RYPKA, *History*, *op.cit.*, :711-34.

The most useful general source for material on Persian literature in the Subcontinent.

RAHMAN, M L, *Persian literature in India during the time of Jahangir and Shah Jahan*, Baroda 1970.

SADARANGANI, H I, *Persian poets of Sind*, Karachi 1956.

Discusses approximately eighty Persian-writing poets in Sind, from the 13th to the 20th century.

DEVARE, T N, *A short history of Persian literature at the Bahmani, the Adilshahi and the Qutbshahi courts - Deccan*, Poona 1961.

Surveys the rise and development of Persian language and literature in the Deccan from the establishment of the Bahmani sultanate to the fall of the kingdom of Golconda.

TIKKU, G L, *Persian poetry in Kashmir, 1339-1846*, Berkeley 1971.

Includes an extensive bibliography.

KOKAN, Muhammad Yousuf, *Arabic and Persian in Carnatic, 1710-1960*, Madras 1974.

Includes many examples in Persian and Arabic.

3.2.2 *Tajikistan*

BEČKA, Jiří, 'Tajik literature from the 16th century to the present', Jan RYPKA, *History*, *op.cit.*, :483-605.

Includes an extensive bibliography.

BRAGINSKII, I S, *Ocherki iz istorii tadzhikskoi literatury*, Stalinabad 1956.

3.2.3 *Asia Minor*

KHUSRAUSHĀHĪ, Riżā, *Shiᶜr va adab-i fārsī dar āsyā-yi ṣaghīr*, Tehran 1971.

Includes a bibliography of Persian literature written in Asia Minor to the 16th century.

3.3 *Period*

3.3.1 *9th-11th century AD*

LAZARD, Gilbert, 'The rise of the New Persian language', *CHI*, IV :595-632.

3.3.2 *12th-13th century AD*

RYPKA, Jan, 'Poets and prose writers of the late Saljuq and Mongol periods', *CHI*, V :550-625.

The bibliography includes translations of Persian works.

3.3.3 *15th century AD*

YĀR-SHĀṬIR, Iḥsān, *Shi^{c}r-i fārsī dar ^{c}ahd-i Shāhrukh*, Tehran 1955.

3.3.4 *18th-20th century AD*

ĀRYANPŪR, Yaḥyā, *Az Ṣabā tā Nīmā*, 2 vols, Tehran 1971.

Covers the period from the beginning of the Qājār period to the early 1920s.

3.3.5 *20th century AD*

KUBÍČKOVÁ, Věra, 'Persian literature of the 20th century', Jan RYPKA, *History*, *op.cit.*, :353-418.

ALAVI, Bozorg, *Geschichte und Entwicklung der modernen persischen Literatur*, Berlin 1964.

YAR SHATER, Ehsan, 'The modern literary idiom', *Iran Faces the Seventies*, *op.cit.* IX 6.9, :284-320.

A survey of 20th century poetry, prose fiction, and drama.

JAZAYERY, Mohammad Ali, 'Recent Persian literature: observations on themes and tendencies', *Review of national literatures*, 2:1, 1971 :11-28.

Relates 20th century literature to the Iranian social order.

3.4 *Shorter surveys*

LEVY, Reuben, *An introduction to Persian literature*, New York 1969.

A useful, short history of poetry and discursive prose, focusing on major writers and 'classic' works, with some discussion of the formal characteristics of Persian verse.

BRUIJN, J T P de, 'Literature', *EI.2*, s.v. Iran.

A general survey of poetry and belletristic prose from the early Islamic period to the beginning of the 20th century. Includes a substantial bibliography.

ISTIʿLĀMĪ, Muhammad, *Bar-rasī-yi adabiyāt-i imrūz*, 3rd ed., Tehran 1976.
Contains nine chapters which survey the history and present state of poetry, prose fiction, drama, scholarly writing, and literature written for children and young adults.

KIYĀ NŪSH, Mahmūd, *Bar-rasī-yi shiʿr va nasr-i fārsī-i muʿāṣir*, Tehran 1972.
Eleven articles, all previously published, about major contemporary writers and some of their works.

3.5 *Poetry*

LAZARD, Gilbert, *Les premiers poètres persans*, 2 vols, Tehran/Paris 1964.
Biographical data, texts, and translations of the works of twenty-two poets of the 9th and 10th centuries.

ELWELL-SUTTON, L P, 'The "Rubāʿī" in early Persian literature', *CHI*, IV :633-57.
Discusses writers of quatrains up to and including ʿUmar Khayyām (d.525/1131).

BRAGINSKII, I S, *12 Miniatyur ot Rudaki do Dzhami*, Moscow 1976.
Essays on poets and poetry.

—— *Iz istorii Tadzhikskoi narodnoi poezii*, Moscow 1956.
Covers poetry from pre-Islamic times through the 18th century, with a very extensive bibliography.

YĀR SHĀTIR, Iḥsan, *Shiʿr-i fārsī dar ʿahd-i Shāhrukh*, *op.cit.* 3.3.3.
Deals with poets who flourished in the first half of the 15th century.

SHIBLĪ NUʿMĀNĪ, *Shiʿr al-ʿajam*, tr. from the Urdu by Muḥammad Taqī Fakhr-i Dāʿī GĪLĀNĪ, 5 vols, Tehran 1935-60.
A history of Persian poetry from the 3rd/9th to the 11th/17th century, with particular emphasis on Saʿdī, Ḥāfiẓ, and the major poets writing in the Indian style. No general index.

ḤIKMAT, ʿAlī Aṣghar, 'Shiʿr-i fārsī dar ʿaṣr-i muʿāṣir', *Nakhustīn kungra-yi navīsandagān-i Īrān*, Tehran 1947 :11-40.

MACHALSKI, Franciszek, *La littérature de l'Iran contemporain*, 3 vols, Wroclaw 1965-80.
Despite the title, it deals only with poetry, and covers the period 1880-1976. Many examples in Persian and in translation in volumes I and II, and in translation only in volume III.

ISHAQUE, M, *Modern Persian poetry*, Calcutta 1943.

'A general survey with a critical estimate of the position of modern Persian poetry', pp.xi-xii. Includes selections in Persian.

RAHMAN, Munibur, *Post-Revolution Persian verse*, Aligarh 1955.

A critical account, including selections in Persian with English translations.

KLYASHTORINA, V B, *'Novaya Poeziya' v Irane*, Moscow 1975.

Discussion and analysis of Persian poetry from the 1950s to the 1970s.

MĪR SĀDIQĪ, Maimanat, *Kitābshināsī-yi shiᶜr-i nau dar Īrān*, Tehran 1976.

Lists 497 items by 152 poets, published between 1922 and 1971, with an index by title. It is important to see also the following entry.

MAḤĀMIDĪ, Ḥamīd, [Review of MĪR ṢĀDIQĪ's bibliography], *Edebiyāt* 3, 1978 :107-17.

Adds 172 new titles, and carries the bibliography through 1977.

OUSELEY, G, *Biographical notices of Persian poets, with critical and explanatory remarks*, London 1846.

3.5.1 *Epic poetry*

NÖLDEKE, Theodor, *Das iranische Nationalepos*, 2nd ed., Berlin 1920. English tr. L BOGDANOV, Bombay 1930.

The fundamental study of the origins and development of the Iranian epic, and of FIRDAUSI's *Shāhnāma*.

HANAWAY, William L, Jr, 'The Iranian epics', Felix J OINAS (ed), *Heroic epic and saga*, Bloomington, Indiana 1978 :453-78.

A survey focusing on *Shāhnāma* and the epic tradition, the post-*Shāhnāma* epics, and the development of the popular romances.

MOLÉ, M, 'L'épopée iranienne après Firdōsī', *La Nouvelle Clio*, 5, 1953 :377-93.

Especially useful because of its detailed listing of manuscripts.

ṢAFĀ, Ẕabīḥullāh, *Ḥamāsa-sarā'ī dar Īrān*, 2nd ed., Tehran 1954.

An extensive survey and discussion of Persian epic poetry in its broadest sense, focusing on extended narrative poetry from the national, the historical, and the religious traditions.

3.6 *Prose*

LAZARD, Gilbert, *La Langue des plus anciens monuments de la prose persane*, *op.cit.* X 4.3.1.

Discusses over seventy prose texts written between the 10th and the 12th centuries.

ELWELL-SUTTON, L P, 'Ḳiṣṣa in Persian literature', *EI.2*, s.v. Ḳiṣṣa.

A survey, with bibliography, of genres of fiction in classical and modern Persian.

KAMSHAD, Hasan, *Modern Persian prose literature*, Cambridge 1966.

A history of 20th century prose writing, with the emphasis on the works of Ṣādiq HIDĀYAT. Accompanying this is his *A modern Persian prose reader*, Cambridge 1968, containing selections in Persian, with glossary, from many of the writers discussed in his earlier work.

KOMISSAROV, D S, *Ocherky sovremennoi persidskoi prozy*, Moscow 1960.

Deals with 20th century prose from the 1920s to the 1950s.

GELPKE, Rudolf, *Die iranische Prosaliteratur im 20. Jahrhundert*, 1. Teil, Wiesbaden 1962.

No more published. Discusses the literary and socio-political background of 20th century prose writing. Useful bibliography.

DORRI, Dzhakhangir Kh, *Persidskaya satiricheskaya proza*, Moscow 1977.

Concentrates on the 19th and 20th centuries.

IBRĀHĪMĪ ḤARĪRĪ, Fāris, *Maqāma-nivīsī dar adabiyāt-i fārsī*, Tehran 1967.

The history of Persian *maqāma* writing through the 19th century, and its Arabic antecedents.

KHĀNLARĪ, Parvīz Nātil, 'Nasr-i fārsī dar daura-yi akhīr', *Nakhustīn kungra-yi navīsandagān-i Īrān*, Tehran 1947 :128-74.

3.7 *Tazkiras*

Tazkiras provide biographical information about individuals, and in the case of poets, selections from their works. STOREY, *op.cit.*, concerns only poets, while the following two works cite *tazkiras* which include scholars and Ṣūfīs as well as poets. Frequently the scholars and Ṣūfīs were also poets.

STOREY, C A, *Persian literature*, I:2, :781-923.

Cites more than 150 *tazkiras* of poets, and provides extensive annotations, including notes on manuscripts and printed editions.

GULCHĪN MAᶜĀNĪ, Ahmad, *Tārīkh-i tazkirahā-yi fārsī*, 2 vols, Tehran 1969-71.

Lists 529 *tazkīras*, with extensive annotations and quotations.

NAQAVĪ, ᶜAlī Riẓā, *Tazkira-nivīsī dar hind va pākistān*, Tehran 1964.

Cites 92 Persian *tazkiras* written in India and Pakistan from the 11th to the 20th century. Full annotations and many quotations.

KHAYYĀMPŪR, ᶜAbd al-rasūl, *Farhang-i sukhanvarān*, Tabriz 1961.

An index to 150 *tazkiras*.

4. *BIBLIOGRAPHIES AND STUDIES OF MAJOR AUTHORS*

To the extent possible, the works listed in this section have been selected for their bibliographical usefulness.

Ṣadr al-Dīn Ainī

BRAGINSKII, I S, *Hayot va ējodiyoti Sadriddīn Aynī*, Dushanbe 1968.

—— *Sadriddin Aini: Zhizn' i tvorchestvo*, 2nd ed., Moscow 1978.

Amīr Khusrau of Delhi

MIRZA, Mohammad Wahid, *The life and works of Amir Khusrau*, Delhi 1935, repr. 1974.

Amir Khusrau: critical studies, Islamabad 1975.

BAKOEV, Muhammadvafo, *Hayot va ējodiyoti Khusravi Dehlavi*, Dushanbe 1975.

Asadī Ṭūsi

MINORSKY, Vladimir, 'Vīs u Rāmīn: a Parthian romance', *Iranica*, *op.cit.*, :151-99.

Farīd al-dīn ^{c}Aṭṭār

RITTER, Helmut, *Das Meer der Seele*, *op.cit.* VI 2.4.

FURŪZĀNFAR, Badī^{c} al-Zamān, *Sharḥ-i aḥvāl va naqd va taḥlīl-i āsār-i ^{c}Aṭṭār*, Tehran 1960-61.

Muḥammad Taqī Bahār

NĪKŪHIMMAT, A, *Zindagānī va āsār-i Bahār*, 2 vols, Kirmān 1955.

Concentrates on BAHĀR's poetry about, inspired by, or concerning others. Little bibliography, but useful for setting BAHĀR among his contemporaries.

^{c}IRFĀNĪ, ^{c}Abd al-Ḥamīd, *Sharḥ-i aḥvāl va āsār-i Malik al-Shu^{c}arā Muḥammad Taqī Bahār*, Tehran 1956.

LORAINE, M B, 'A memoir on the life and poetical works of Maliku'l-Shu^{c}arā' Bahār', *IJMES* 3, 1972 :140-68.

Farrukhī Sīstānī

YŪSUFĪ, Ghulām Ḥusain, *Farrukhī Sīstānī*, Mashhad 1962.

Firdausī (see also the entries under *Epic poetry*)

AFSHĀR, Īraj, *Kitābshināsī-yi Firdausī*, 2nd ed., Tehran 1976.

Ḥāfiẓ

BROMS, Henri, *Towards a Hafiz bibliography*, Helsinki 1969.

HILLMANN, Michael C, *Unity in the Ghazals of Hafez*, Minneapolis 1976.

REHDER, Robert M, 'Persian poets and modern critics', *Edebiyāt* 2, 1977 :91-117.

Hidāyat, Ṣādiq

KOMISSAROV, D S, and A ROZENFEL'D, *Sadek Khedayat: biobibliograficheskii ukazatel'*, Moscow 1958.

FLOWER, Richard L G, *Sadeq-e Hedayät, 1903-1951: Eine literarische Analyse*, Berlin 1977.

Includes a list of HIDĀYAT's works, with a summary and discussion of each.

KRÜGER, Eberhard, *Zum Verhältnis von Autor und Werk bei dem modern-persischen Erzähler Sādeq Hedāyat*, Freiburg 1977.

GULBUN, Muḥammad, *Kitābshināsī-yi Ṣādiq Hidāyat*, Tehran 1977.

HILLMANN, Michael C (ed), *Hedāyat's 'The Blind Owl' forty years after*, Austin, Tex. 1978.

Iqbāl, Muḥammad

WAHEED, K A, *A bibliography of Iqbal*, Karachi 1965.

SCHIMMEL, Annemarie, *Gabriel's wing*, Leiden 1963.

Jalāl al-dīn Rūmī

ÖNDER, Mehmet, *et al.*, *Mevlāna Bibliografyası*, 2 vols, Ankara 1973.

SCHIMMEL, Annemarie, *The triumphal sun: a study of the works of Jalāloddin Rumi*, London 1978.

Jamālzāda, Muḥammad ᶜAlī

DORRI, Dzhakhangir Kh, *Dzhamal'-zade*, Moscow 1972.

Jāmī, ᶜAbd al-raḥmān

AFSAḤZOD, Aᶜlokhon, *Ruzgor va osori Abdurraḥmani Jomi*, Dushanbe 1980.

Khāqānī

REINERT, Benedikt, *Hāqānī als Dichter*, Berlin 1972.

Manūchihrī

CLINTON, Jerome W, *The Divan of Manūchihrī Dāmghānī: a critical study*, Minneapolis 1972.

Neshāt + Mejmar. Mulloahmadov, Mirzo. Nishot va Mijmar. Dushanbe, 1983.

Qā'ānī

KUBÍČKOVA, Věra, *Qāānī: poète persan du XIXe siècle*, Prague 1954.

Rūdakī

TAL'MAN, Rina O, *Rudaki*, Dushanbe 1965.

MIRZOYEV, ᶜAbdulghani, *Abū ᶜAbdallāh Rūdakī*, Stalinabad 1958.

—— *Rudaki: Zhizn' i tvorchestovo*, Moscow 1968.

NAFĪSĪ, Saᶜīd, *Muḥīṭ-i zindagānī va aḥvāl va ashᶜār-i Rūdakī*, Tehran 1963.

Saᶜdī

MASSÉ, Henri, *Essai sur le poète Saadi, suivi d'une bibliographie*, Paris 1919.

DASHTĪ, ᶜAlī, *Qalamrau-i Saᶜdī*, Tehran 1960.

^{c}Umar Khayyām

POTTER, Ambrose George, *A bibliography of the Rubáiyát of Omar Khayyám*, London 1929.

Fitzgerald's Rubáiyát: centennial edition ... with a check-list of the Rubáiyát collection in the Colby College library, Waterville, Maine 1959.

DASHTĪ, ^{c}Alī, *In search of Omar Khayyam*, tr. L P ELWELL-SUTTON, London 1971.

A translation of his *Damī bā Khayyām*, 2nd ed., Tehran 1969.

HUMĀ^{c}Ī, Jalāl al-dīn, *Khayyāmī-nāma*, Tehran 1967.

YAGĀNĪ, *Nādira-yi ayyām Ḥakīm ^{c}Umar-i Khayyām*, Tehran 1963.

^{c}Unṣurī

OSMANOV, M -N, *Chastotnyi slovar' Unsuri*, *op.cit.* X 4.2.3.

A frequency-count of words, and a concordance to the poetry of ^{c}Unṣurī.

Vāṣifī

BOLDYREV, A N, *Zainaddin Vasifi*, Stalinabad 1957.

A detailed study of Vāṣifī (16th century), the author of *Badāyi^{c} al-Vaqāyi^{c}*.

5. *ANTHOLOGIES*

5.1 *General*

ḤIKMAT, ^{c}Alī Aṣghar (comp), *Pārsī-yi naghz*, Tehran 1951.

Eighteen selections of poetry and prose written in 'pure' (i.e. unarabicized) Persian, with extensive notes.

MAHMŪDĪ Bakhtiyārī, ^{c}Alī Qulī, *Ganj-i gauhar*, Tehran 1970.

Selections of poetry and prose from Bal^{c}amī to Ḥāfiẓ.

SAJJĀDĪ, Żiyā al-dīn, *Durr-i darī*, Tehran 1977.

Selections from classical and modern poetry and prose, including translations into Persian, accompanied by a discussion of Persian literary style and a sketch of Persian grammar.

KHIBRAZĀDA, ^{c}Alī Aṣghar, *Guzīda'ī az adab-i fārsī*, 2 vols, Tehran 1970, 1973.

Prose and poetry, both classical and modern, arranged under subject headings.

5.2 *Poetry*

5.2.1 *General*

ṢAFĀ, Zabīḥallāh, *Ganj-i sukhan*, 3 vols, Tehran 1960-61.

Selected poems arranged under authors from Rūdakī to Bahār.

5.2.2 *Early*

MUṢAFFĀ, Maẓāhir, *Pāsdārān-i sukhan*, vol.I, Tehran 1956.
Selections from poets from Rūdakī to Shahīd, with biographical notes and extensive commentaries.

MIRZOYEV, Abdulgani, *Ash'ori hamasroni Rūdakī*, Stalinabad 1958.
Includes an extensive glossary.

DABĪR-SIYĀQĪ, Muḥammad, *Pīshāhangān-i shiʿr-i pārsī*, Tehran 1972.
Poetry from the earliest times to the early 11th century, with explanatory notes and a glossary.

ḤAMĪDĪ, Mahdī, *Bihisht-i sukhan*, 2 vols, Tehran 1958-59.
Selections from thirty-eight poets from the earliest times to the 13th century.

NAFĪSĪ, Saʿīd, 1963, *op.cit.* 4.
Contains brief notes and quotations from all known poets prior to and contemporary with Rūdakī.

See also LAZARD, *op.cit.* 3.5.

5.2.3 *Modern*

ISHAQUE, M, *Sukhanvarān-i Īrān dar ʿaṣr-i ḥāzir*, 2 vols, Delhi 1933-37.
Selections from eighty-four poets, with biographical information.

BURQAʿĪ, Sayyid Muḥammad Bāqir, *Sukhanvarān-i nāmī-yi muʿāṣir*, Tehran 1950.
Selections from eighty-six poets who lived after 1921.

HAMĪDĪ, Mahdī, *Daryā-yi gauhar*, vol.III, Tehran 1956.
Selections from sixty-five poets of the 19th and 20th centuries.

KĀR, Firīdūn, *Shāhkārhā-yi shiʿr-i muʿāṣir-i Īrān*, Tehran 1958.
Selections from thirty-five poets of the twentieth century.

RAḤMĀN, Munīb al-, *Bar-guzīda-yi shiʿr-i fārsī-yi muʿāṣir*, 2 vols, Aligarh 1958-63.
Volume I contains selections from thirty-nine poets who write in the classical style. Volume II has selections from thirty-two poets writing in modern verse forms.

FARRUKHZĀD, Furūgh, *Az Nīmā tā baʿd*, Tehran 1968.
Selections from thirteen contemporary poets.

KHABĪR, Hurmuz, *Shiʿr-i muʿāṣir-i Īrān*, Tehran 1969.
Selections from twenty-six contemporary poets, with biographical data.

ḤUQŪQĪ, Muḥammad, *Shiʿr-i nau az āghāz tā imrūz (1301-1350)*, Tehran 1972.
Selections from twenty-five poets, with biographical and bibliographical information.

5.2.4 *Poetry by women*

ISHAQ, M, *Four eminent poetesses of Iran, with a brief survey of Iranian and Indian poetesses of Neo-Persian*, Calcutta 1950.

Includes selections in Persian with some English translations.

KISHĀVARZ, Ṣadr, *Zanānī ki bi fārsī shiᶜr gufta-and: Az Rābiᶜa tā Parvīn*, Tehran 1955.

Selections from 106 women poets.

MUSHĪR SALĪMĪ, ᶜAlī Akbar, *Zanān-i sukhanvar*, 3 vols, Tehran 1956-58.

Lists over 250 women poets, with samples of their poetry.

— Poetry by Europeans. Saksena, R.B. European + Indo-European Poets of Urdu + Persian. Lucknow, 1941.

5.2.5 *Poetry by Jews*

NETZER, Amnon, *Muntakhab-i ashᶜār-i fārsī az āsār-i Yahūdīyān-i Īrān*, Tehran 1973.

Extensive selections from ten poets, with a glossary.

5.3 *Prose*

5.3.1 *General*

ṢAFĀ, Zabīḥallāh, *Nasr-i fārsī az āghāz tā ᶜahd-i Niẓām al-Mulk-i Ṭūsī*, Tehran 1968.

The first half of the book is a history of Persian prose, and the second half contains twenty-four short samples from writers from the early 10th to the late 11th century.

JAVĀDĪ, Ḥasan Ṣadr Ḥāj Sayyid, *Ganjīna-yi nasr-i pārsī*, Tehran 1961.

Selections from sixteen writers from the 10th to the 20th century.

KISHĀVARZ, Karīm, *Hazār sāl-i nasr-i pārsī*, 5 vols, Tehran 1966.

Short selections of prose from the 10th to the 20th century with a glossary for each section.

KHAṬĪB RAHBAR, Khalīl, *Guzīna-yi nasr-i fārsī*, Tehran 1969.

One hundred selections, from the 10th to the 20th century, including some translations into Persian, with explanatory notes.

5.3.2 *Modern*

NAFĪSĪ, Saᶜīd, *Shāhkārhā-yi nasr-i fārsī-yi muᶜāṣir*, 2 vols, Tehran 1951-53.

Selections from eight 20th century prose writers.

KĀR, Firīdūn, *Panj shuᶜla-yi jāvīd*, Tehran 1954.

Short stories by five 20th century authors.

ḤAMĪDĪ, Mahdī, *Daryā-yi gauhar*, vol.I, Tehran 1964.

Short stories by eighteen 20th century authors.

6. *LITERARY STUDY AND CRITICISM*

6.1 *Theory and criticism*

BRAGINSKY, I S, 'Periodization in Persian literature', *Central Asian Review* 12, 1964 :132-39.

A translation of an article in Russian published in 1963. BRAGINSKY's periodization scheme, while not ideal, is the most useful one suggested so far.

SCOTT, Charles C, *Persian and Arabic riddles: a language-centred approach to genre definition*, Bloomington, Indiana 1965.

WINDFUHR, Gernot, 'A linguist's criticism of Persian literature', Richard N FRYE (ed), *Neue Methodologie in der Iranistik*, Wiesbaden 1974 :331-52.

Suggests how current linguistic theories and methods can be used in the analysis and criticism of poetry.

MUᶜĀẒID, Mīhandukht, *Kitābshināsī-yi naqd-i kitāb*, Tehran 1976.

An index to reviews of 1062 books.

ZARRĪNKŪB, ᶜAbd al-Ḥusain, *Naqd-i adabī*, 2nd ed., 2 vols, Tehran 1975.

A history of literary criticism in the western and the Perso-Arab traditions, from Aristotle to the present day.

NIẒĀMĪ ᶜARŪẒI, Aḥmad ibn ᶜUmar, *Chahār maqāla*, *op.cit.* VII 3.

In the chapter on poets, the author discusses the nature of poetry and the craft of being a poet.

RĀZĪ, Shams al-dīn Muḥammad ibn Qais al-, *al-Muᶜjam fī maᶜāyīr ashᶜār al-ᶜajam*, Mudarris RAẒAVĪ (ed), Tehran 1959.

Important for the author's observations on the nature and qualities of poetry.

BARĀHINĪ, Riẓā, *Ṭilā dar mis*, Tehran 1968.

Presents a theory of poetry, and essays on a number of poets.

NŪRĪ ᶜALĀ'Ī, Ismāᶜīl, *Ṣuvar va asbāb dar shiᶜr-i imrūz*, Tehran 1969.

SHAFĪᶜĪ KADKANĪ, Muḥammad Riẓā, *Mūsīqī-yi shiᶜr*, Tehran 1979.

A discussion of the aesthetic function of rhyme in mediaeval and modern poetry. Written in 1963.

—— *Ṣuvar-i khiyāl dar shiᶜr-i fārsī*, Tehran 1971.

A lengthy theoretical discussion of poetic imagery, based on Persian, Arabic, and western sources, followed by an examination of the imagery used by eighteen poets through the 5th/11th century.

6.2 *Stylistics*

BAUSANI, Alessandro, 'Contributo a una definizione dello "Stile indiano" della poesia persiana', *Annali dell'Istituto universitario orientale di Napoli*, NS 7, 1958 :167-78.

An attempt to define the special characteristics of Indian style poetry, and how it differs from earlier and later poetry.

FOUCHÉCOUR, C -H, de, *La description de la nature dans la poésie lyrique persane du XIe siècle*, Paris 1969.

An exhaustive listing, with some discussion, of references to nature in the major poets of the 11th century.

HEINZ, Wilhelm, *Der indische Stil in der persischen Literatur*, Wiesbaden 1973.

An examination of the vocabulary and rhetorical structure of poetry written between the 15th and the 18th centuries.

OSMANOV, M N, *Stil' persidsko-tadzhikskoi poezii IX-X v.v.*, Moscow 1974.

A concordance, in Russian and Persian, of similes, metaphors, metonyms, and antitheses in the poetry of the 9th and 10th centuries.

RĀMĪ, Sharaf al-dīn, *Anīs al-^{c}ushshāq*, ^{c}Abbās IQBĀL (ed), Tehran 1946.

A classified list of words used as images in classical Persian poetry for parts of the body. Translated into French by C HUART, Paris 1875.

BAHĀR, Muḥammad Taqī, *Sabk-shināsī*, 2nd ed., 3 vols, Tehran 1958, repr. 1976.

A fundamental survey of the changes in prose style from the 10th through the 19th century.

MU^{c}ĪN, Muḥammad, *Mazdayasnā va adab-i pārsī*, Tehran 1959.

MAḤJŪB, Muḥammad Ja^{c}far, *Sabk-i khurāsānī dar shi^{c}r-i fārsī*, Tehran 1966.

An exhaustive discussion of Persian poetic style from the early Islamic period to the end of the 5th/11th century.

PĀDISHĀH, Muḥammad, *Farhang-i mutarādifāt va iṣṭilāḥāt*, Tehran 1967.

A topical dictionary of figurative language, with examples from Persian poetry. Compiled in the late 19th century.

RAHMAN, Mojibur, *Allusions and references in Persian poetry*, Calcutta 1974.

Four hundred and fifty-nine entries based on allusions to Islamic religious works, Persian history and literature, Perso-Arabic astronomical and scientific terms, and important historical and geographical names and terms, including some from India.

DARYĀGASHT, Muḥammad Rasūl (ed), *Ṣā'ib va sabk-i hindī*, Tehran 1976.

Twenty papers read at a conference on *Ṣā'ib* (1601-77) and Indian-style poetry.

6.3 *Prosody and rhetoric*

Western-language manuals of prosody and rhetoric have generally been based on or translated from earlier Persian and Arabic works. Since the traditional formulation of the principles of Persian prosody did not vary over the centuries, only a small but representative sample of these manuals is provided here. The number of rhetorical devices recognized by the prosodists, however, increased considerably between the 11th and the 19th centuries. The works listed below give a fair sample of these. For a discussion of many of these devices, see E G BROWNE, *A literary history of Persia*, *op.cit.*, II, pp.46-78.

GARCIN DE TASSY, Joseph, *Rhétorique et prosodie des langues de l'orient musulman*, 2nd ed., Paris 1873, repr. Amsterdam 1970.

The second edition is a fuller treatment of the subject than is the first edition of 1843.

BLOCHMANN, H, *The prosody of the Persians*, Calcutta 1872, repr. Amsterdam 1970.

RÜCKERT, Friedrich, *Grammatik, Poetik und Rhetorik der Perser*, W PERTSCH (ed), Gotha 1874, repr. Wiesbaden 1976.

RĀDŪYĀNĪ, Muḥammad ibn ᶜUmar al-, *Tarjumān al-balāgha*, Ahmed ATEŞ (ed), Istanbul 1949.

The earliest surviving manual of prosody in Persian, written in the late 10th or early 11th century. This edition includes a facsimile of the manuscript.

VAṬVĀṬ, Rashīd al-dīn, *Ḥadāyiq al-siḥr fī daqāyiq al-shiᶜr*, ᶜAbbās IQBĀL (ed), Tehran n.d. (1930), repr. in VAṬVĀṬ's *Divān*, Saᶜīd NAFĪSĪ (ed), Tehran 1960 :621-707.

Written in the second third of the 12th century.

RĀZĪ, Shams al-dīn Muḥammad ibn Qais al-, *al-Muᶜjam ...*, *op.cit.* 6.1.

Completed shortly after 630/1232-33. The most important of the mediaeval books of prosody.

KĀSHIFĪ, Kamāl al-dīn Ḥusain Vāᶜiẓ, *Badāyiᶜ al-afkār fī ṣanāyiᶜ al-ashᶜār*, Raḥim MUSILMĀNQULUF (ed), Moscow 1977.

This edition consists of a facsimile of the manuscript, critical apparatus, and introductions in Persian and Russian.

THIESEN, F, *A manual of classical Persian prosody*, Leiden 1980.

6.3.1 *Poetic metre*

While the manuals of prosody treat the subject in the traditional manner, the two works listed below are reformulations of the basis of Persian metre.

ELWELL-SUTTON, L P, *The Persian metres*, Cambridge 1976.

An entirely new analysis of the Persian metrical system.

KHĀNLARĪ, Parvīz Nātil, *Vazn-i shiʿr-i fārsī*, Tehran 1966.

A modest advance beyond the boundaries of the traditional system.

Thiesen, Finn. A Manual of Classical Persian Prosody. Wiesbaden, 1982.

6.4 *Comparative studies*

Interest in the comparative study of Persian and other literatures has been stronger in the west than in Iran. In the past these studies tended to cluster around three foci: Firdausī-Arnold; Khayyām-Fitzgerald; and Ḥāfiẓ-Goethe, but recently new areas have been explored.

BEARD, Michael, 'Character and psychology in Hedayat's *Buf-e Kur*', *Edebiyāt* 1, 1976 :207-18.

EKHTIAR, Mansur, *Emerson & Persia*, Tehran 1976.

HONARMANDI, Hassan, *André Gide et la littérature persane: recherches sur les sources persanes de l'oeuvre de Gide*, Paris 1973.

JAVADI, Hasan, 'Matthew Arnold's "Sohrab and Rustum" and its Persian Original', *Review of National Literatures*, 2:1, 1971 :61-73.

ibid., Persian Literary Influence on English Literature. Calcutta, 1983.

JOHNSON, Janette S, '"The Blind Owl", Nerval, Kafka, Poe and the Surrealists: affinities', Michael C HILLMANN (ed), *Hedāyat's 'The Blind Owl' forty years after*, Austin, Texas 1978 :125-41.

MOHANDESSI, Manoutcher, 'Hedāyat and Rilke', *Comparative literature* 23, 1971 :209-16.

RANNIT, Aleksis, 'Iran in Russian poetry', *Slavic and East European Journal* 17, 1973 :265-72.

Discusses works published in the period 1824-1970.

Remy, Arthur. The Influence of Persia and India on the Poetry of India. N.Y., 1901.

ROSE, Ernst, 'Persian mysticism in Goethe's "West-Östlicher Divan"', *Review of National Literatures*, 2:1, 1971 :92-111.

SAFFARI, Kokab, *Les légendes et contes persans dans la littérature anglaise des XVIIIe et XIXe siècles jusqu'en 1859*, Paris 1972.

SCHIMMEL, Annemarie, 'The emergence of the German Ghazal', Muhammad Umar MEMON (ed), *Studies in the Urdu Ġazal and prose fiction*, Madison, Wisconsin 1979 :168-74.

SCHMIDT, Richard, *Das Kathākāutukam des Çrīvara verglichen mit Dschāmī's Jusuf und Zuleikha, nebst Textproben*, Kiel 1893.

YOHANNAN, John D, *Persian poetry in England and America: a 200-year history*, Delmar, New York 1977.

Bibliography of translations of Persian poetry into English. See also under 9. below.

AMĪRĪ, Manūchihr, *Māthyu Ārnuld: Suhrāb va Rustam*, Shiraz 1975.

7. *FOLKLORE AND POPULAR LITERATURE*

Many examples of popular literature can be found in the works on the languages and dialects spoken in Iran. The regional and local ethnographies in Persian, such as *Farhang-i mardum-i Sarvistān* (Tehran 1969) by Sādiq HUMĀYŪNĪ, and *ᶜAqāyid va rusūm-i ᶜāmma-yi mardum-i Khurāsān* (Tehran 1970) by Ibrāhīm SHUKŪRZĀDA, are another source. Special note should be taken of the publications of the Markaz-i Pizhūhish-hā-yi Mardumshināsī va Farhang-i ᶜĀmma, especially its journal *Mardumshināsī va Farhang-i ᶜĀmma-yi Īrān*. In addition, many articles on folklore and popular literature can be found in the journal *Hunar va Mardum*.

7.1 *General*

HIDĀYAT, Ṣādiq, *Nivishta-hā-yi parākanda*, Tehran 1955.

Includes many articles on Persian folklore and popular beliefs.

CEJPEK, Jiří, 'Iranian folk-literature', Jan RYPKA, *History*, *op.cit.*, :607-709.

The chapter is accompanied by an extensive but unclassified bibliography which includes much material bearing on the folklore and popular literature of the Persians and Tajiks as well as various other Iranian peoples such as Kurds and Ossetes.

BOULVIN, Adrienne, *Contes populaires persans du Khorassan*, 2 vols, Paris 1975.

Seventy folktales in French translation, a thematic analysis, and a selective, classified bibliography.

HUMĀYŪNĪ, Ṣādiq, *Yāzdah maqāla dar zamīna-yi farhang-i ᶜāmma*, Shīrāz 1977.

Bibliogrofiyai Fol'klorshinosii Tojik (1872-1968), 2 vols, Dushanbe 1979.

A comprehensive, classified list of works in Tajik and Russian.

AMONOV, Rajab, *et al.*, *Kulliyoti Fol'klori Tojik/Svod Tadzhikskogo Folklora*. Vol.I, Masalho va afsonaho dar borai haivonot/Basni i skazki o zhivotnykh, Moscow 1981.

In Russian and Tajik. The first volume of a series based on texts in the archives of the Rudaki Academy of the Tajik SSR. With introduction, tables, maps, and more than 100 texts of animal stories selected from some 2,000 in the archives.

RANELAGH, E L, *The past we share. The Near Eastern ancestry of western folk literature*, London 1979.

7.2 *Collections of tales*

CHRISTENSEN, Arthur, *Contes persanes en langue populaire*, Copenhagen 1918.

—— *Persiske Aeventyr*, Copenhagen 1924. German tr. *Märchen aus Iran*, Jena

1939; *Persische Märchen*, Dusseldorf/Köln 1958. English tr. (part), *Persian folktales*, London 1971.

ROMASKEVICH, A A, *Persidskiye narodnye skazki*, Moscow 1934.

ṢUBḤĪ MUHTADĪ, Fażlallāh, *Afsānahā*, 2 vols, Tehran 1944-46.

—— *Afsānahā-yi kuhan*, 2 vols, Tehran 1947-49.

—— *Dizh-i hūsh-rubā*, Tehran 1951.

—— *Dīvān-i Balkh*, Tehran 1952.

KŪHĪ KIRMĀNĪ, Ḥusain, *Pānzdah afsāna az afsānahā-yi rūstā'ī-yi Īrān*, Tehran 1954.

New edition of a collection of fourteen tales first published in 1936. French translation in volume II of

MASSÉ, Henri, *Croyances et coutumes persanes, suivies de contes et chansons populaires*, 2 vols, Paris 1938. English tr. *Persian beliefs and customs*, New Haven 1954.

AMĪNĪ, Amīr Qulī, *Dāstānhā-yi amsāl*, 3rd ed., Isfahan 1973.

The stories associated with Persian proverbs.

ANJAVĪ SHĪRĀZĪ, Sayyid Abu'l-qāsim, *Qiṣṣahā-yi Īrānī*, 3 vols, Tehran 1974-76.

—— *Mardum va Shāhnāma*, Tehran 1975.

Popular versions of tales from the *Shāhnāma*.

—— *Mardum va Firdausī*, Tehran 1976.

Popular beliefs about Firdausī, and popular versions of tales from the *Shāhnāma*.

LORIMER, D L R, and E O, *Persian tales, written down for the first time in the original Kermānī and Bakhtiārī*, London 1919.

In spite of the title, only the English translation is given.

AMONOV, R, and K ULUGZODA, *Afsonahoi khalkii Tojiki*, Stalinabad 1957.

About 250 stories in Tajik Persian. Regrettably the compilers and their colleagues have edited the texts into literary form (Taḥrīr va taṣḥīḥ-i adabī).

DAMES, M Longworth, *Popular poetry of the Baloches*, *op.cit.* X 6.7.

Volume I includes a discussion of Balūchī poetry, and translations of sixty-four poems and short prose pieces; volume II contains the original texts in transcription, accompanied by grammatical notes and glossary.

Further titles dealing with popular beliefs, customs and practices will be found in XIV 2.2.4.

7.3 *Wit and humour*

LESZCZYŃSKI, Georg L, *'Hikayat': Persische Schnurren*. Berlin 1918.

Sixty-four jokes translated from Persian.

KUKA, Mehrjibhai N, *Wit, humour and fancy of Persia*, Bombay 1923.

First published in 1894 under the title, *The wit and humour of the Persians*. Some examples in Persian.

MASANI, R P, *Court poets of Iran and India: an anthology of wit and verse*, Bombay 1938.

Examples in Persian with English translation.

ĀZ̲AR YAZDĪ, Mahdī, *Labk̲hand*, Tehran 1954.

Over 1000 jokes and anecdotes in Persian.

RAMAŻĀNĪ, Muḥammad, *Mullā Naṣr al-dīn*, Tehran 1954.

Includes almost 600 stories.

MADANĪ, Ḥusain, *Z̲hukir*, Tehran n.d. (196 ?)

Jokes and anecdotes about women.

PIZIS̲H̲KZĀD, Īraj, *Āsmūn va Rīsmūn*, Tehran 1963.

Humorous sketches and skits.

7.4 *Proverbs and aphorisms*

7.4.1 *In Persian*

ZHUKOVSKII, V A, *Obraztsy persidskago narodnago tvorchestva*, St Petersburg 1902.

Examples in Persian with Russian translation.

PHILLOTT, D C, 'Common saws and proverbs collected, chiefly from dervishes, in Southern Persia', *Memoirs of the Asiatic society of Bengal*, 1, 1906 :302-37.

Three hundred and fifty-eight Persian proverbs with English translation or equivalent.

DIHK̲H̲UDĀ, ʿAlī Akbar, *Ams̲āl va ḥikam*, 4 vols, Tehran 1931.

About 20,000 proverbs, mainly from literary sources, with explanations.

BONELLI, Luigi, *Detti proverbiali persiani*, Rome 1941.

RAḤMATĪ, Yūsuf, *Farhang-i ʿāmmiyāna*, *op.cit.* X 4.2.3.

HABALARŪDĪ, Muḥammad ʿAlī, *Majmaʿ al-ams̲āl*. Ṣadiq KIYĀ (ed), Tehran 1965.

Over 2000 proverbs, collected in Hyderabad (Deccan) in 1049/1639.

—— *Jāmiʿ al-tams̲īl*, Tehran 1953.

A collection of proverbs and stories collected in 1054/1644.

ELWELL-SUTTON, L P, *Persian proverbs*, London 1954.

English translations of Persian proverbs, with notes on their origin and use.

ḤAIM, Sulaimān, *Żarbalmas̲alhā-yi fārsī va inglīsī*, Tehran 1956.

FOZILOV, M, *Pandu hikmatho*, Stalinabad 1961.

—— *Aforizmy*, Dushanbe 1963.

—— *Pandu hikmat*, Dushanbe 1963.

—— *Zarbulmasalu maqolho dar tamsil*, Dushanbe 1975.

—— *Farhangi zarbulmasal*, Dushanbe 1975.

BIHRANGĪ, Ṣamad, and Bihrūz DIHQĀNĪ, *Matalhā va chīstānhā*, Tabriz 1966.

SUHAILĪ, Mahdī, *Żarbalmasalhā-yi maʿrūf-i Īrān*, Tehran 1970.

Proverbs, with explanations and occasions for use.

BURQAʿĪ, Yaḥyā, *Kāvishī dar amsāl va ḥikam-i fārsī*, Tehran 1972.

Proverbs, with the stories that gave rise to them.

SHUʿAʿĪ, Ḥamīd, *Amsāl-i shiʿr-i fārsī*, Tehran 1972.

One thousand and sixty-seven lines of poetry that have become proverbial, with references to their sources, and to parallel expressions.

AMĪNĪ, Amīr Qulī, *Dāstānhā-yi amsāl*, *op.cit.* 7.2.

ANJAVĪ SHĪRĀZĪ, Sayyid Abū al-qāsim, *Tamsīl va masal*, Tehran 1973.

The stories associated with Persian proverbs.

KOROGLY, Kh G, *Persidskiye poslovitsy, pogovorki i krylatye slova*, 2nd ed., Moscow 1973.

Proverbs, aphorisms, and verses in Persian with Russian translation.

PARTAU-YI ĀMULĪ, Mahdī, *Amsāl va ḥikam*, Tehran 1974.

Sixty-five proverbs with stories of their origin and explanations of their use.

JAMSHĪDĪPŪR, Yūsuf, *Farhang-i amsāl-i fārsī*, Tehran 1968.

Persian proverbs with brief explanations.

ḤALABĪ, ʿAlī Aṣghar, *Adab-i fārsī*, Tehran 1979.

'Familiar quotations' and the stories behind them.

7.4.2 *In dialects and other languages*

MUJTAHIDĪ, ʿAlī Aṣghar, *Amsāl va ḥikam dar lahja-yi maḥallī-yi Āzarbāyjān*, Tabriz 1955.

ARZHANGĪ, Hūshang, *Taʿbīrāt va iṣṭilāḥāt va amsāl-i mushtarak-i fārsī va Āzarbāyjānī*, Tabriz 1958.

DĀVARĪ, Bahrām, *Żarbalmasalhā-yi Bakhtiyārī*, Tehran 1964.

PĀYANDA, Maḥmūd, *Masalhā va iṣṭilaḥāt-i Gīl va Dailam*, Tehran 1973.

8. *LITERATURE FOR CHILDREN AND YOUNG ADULTS*

Serious efforts toward writing, translating, and publishing books for young people began in Iran in the middle 1960s. Since then considerable progress has been made. The bibliographies listed below cite translations as well as works originally in Persian.

ĀZARPŪR, Āzar, *Kitābshināsī-yi kitābhā-yi munāsib barāyi kūdakān*, Tehran 1973.

BANĪ ĀDAM, Ḥusain, *Kitābshināsī-yi nivishtahā-yi fārsī barāyi kūdakān va naujavānān*, Tehran 1968.

Eight hundred items, divided by three age-groups, and classified within each group.

ĪMĀN, Lailī, *Guzarī dar adabiyāt-i kūdakān*, Tehran 1973.

KIYĀ NŪSH, Maḥmūd, *Shiʿr-i kūdak dar Īrān*, Tehran 1973.

Deals with poetry written in Persian and other languages for children.

ḤAQĪQĪ, Maḥmūd, *Kitābshināsī-yi tauṣīfī-i kitābhā-yi munāsib barāyi naujavānān*, Tehran 1974.

9. *TRANSLATIONS*

Bibliographical coverage of translations from Persian is uneven in general, but better for translations published since the early 1950s than for previous periods. The major difficulty is locating translations of less than book length. *Index Islamicus* is the best current source for translated books and articles.

Index Translationum, Quarterly, Paris 1932-40. Annual, Paris 1948-.

Lists translated books only. Arranged by country, and then by general Dewey Decimal System categories: section 8 covers Literature. The country is a general indication of the language *into* which a book has been translated. Under Iran, therefore, will be found works translated into Persian. There is a general author index to each volume. For translations into English, see also the following entry.

Cumulative index to English translations, 1948-1968, 2 vols, Boston 1973.

An index to volumes 1-21 of the *Index Translationum*, New Series. It lists books only, and is arranged alphabetically by author, or by title if no author is given.

WINDFUHR, Gernot L, and John R WORKMAN, 'Literature in translation - Iranian into English', *MESA bull.*, 7:1, February 1973 :9-41.

Lists 334 items, most of which are books, plays, short stories, and poems, but the coverage of 20th century poetry is highly selective. Also included are selective lists of translations of popular literature, and of works translated from Pashtu, Judeo-Persian, Baluchi, and Kurdish. Some brief annotations. Some entries are not for translations, but rather for discussions of literature.

YOHANNAN, John D, *Persian poetry in England and America*, *op.cit.* 6.4.

Includes the most extensive bibliography available of translations of

Persian poetry into English. Does not include translations of 20th century poetry. No annotations.

HILLMANN, Michael C, *Twentieth century Persian literature in translation: a bibliography*, Washington, DC 1976.

Includes only translations into English. Some annotations. If used in conjunction with WINDFUHR and WORKMAN, *op.cit.*, reasonably good coverage will result, particularly with respect to 20th century poetry.

LITTLEFIELD, David W, *The Islamic Near East and North Africa*, *op.cit.* II 2.3.

The section on Persian literature (nos 325-359) is carefully selected, with extensive annotations. There are indices by author, title, and subject.

BIRNBAUM, Eleazar, *Books on Asia from the Near East to the Far East*, Toronto 1971.

A guide for the general reader. Pages 60-61 and 73-79 list forty-four Persian literary works translated into English or French, with annotations. This selection overlaps only partially with LITTLEFIELD, *op.cit.*

SENNY, Jacqueline, *Contributions à l'appréciation des valeurs culturelles de l'Orient: traductions françaises de littératures orientales*, Brussels 1958.

Pages 97-118 list 215 translations from Persian to French, published from the 17th to the 20th centuries. There are indices of authors, translators, and titles. No annotations.

BESTERMAN, T, *A world bibliography of oriental bibliographies*, *op.cit.*, II 2.4.

The bibliographies of Persian writers cited by BESTERMAN are all listed above in 4.

FISCHEL, Walter J, 'The Bible in Persian translation', *Harvard Theological Review* 45, 1952 :3-45.

Extensive bibliography in the footnotes.

9.1 *Representative translations*

The following is a selective list of translations into French, German, Italian, and Russian. This list is not intended to be comprehensive. For translations into English, see the bibliographies listed at the beginning of this section.

9.1.1 *French*

ASADĪ ṬŪSĪ *Le livre de Gerchāsp*, 2 vols, Paris 1926, 1951.

Volume I translated by C HUART; volume II by H MASSÉ.

ᶜAṬṬĀR, Farīd al-dīn, *Le livre divin*, tr. F RŪḤĀNĪ, Paris 1961.

GURGĀNĪ, Fakhr al-dīn, *Le roman de Wīs et Rāmīn*, tr. H MASSÉ, Paris 1959.

FARĀMARZ ibn Khudādād, *Samak-e ayyār*, vol.I, tr. Frédérique RAZAVI, Paris 1972.

FIRDAUSĪ, *Le livre des rois*, tr. J MOHL, Paris 1838-78.

HIDĀYAT, Ṣādiq, *La chouette aveugle*, tr. Roger LESCOT, Paris 1953.

RŪMĪ, Jalāl al-dīn, *Odes mystiques*, tr. E de VITRAY-MEYEROVITCH, Paris 1973.

—— *Le livre du dedans*, tr. E de VITRAY-MEYEROVITCH, Paris 1975.

JAMĀLZĀDA, Muḥammad ᶜAlī, *Choix de nouvelles*, tr. S CORBIN and H LOTFI, Paris 1959.

NIẒĀM AL-MULK, *Siyāsat-nāmè*, tr. C SCHEFER, Paris 1893.

NIẒĀMĪ, *Le roman de Chosroès et Chīrīn*, tr. H MASSÉ, Paris 1970.

NIẒĀMĪ ᶜARŪẒĪ, *Les quatre discours*, tr. I de GASTINES, Paris 1968.

ẒAHĪRĪ, Samarqandī, *Le livre des sept vizirs*, tr. D BOGDANOVIĆ, Paris 1975.

9.1.2 *German*

FIRDAUSĪ, *Das Buch der Könige*, tr. U von WITZLEBEN, Düsseldorf 1961.

ḤĀFIẒ, *Gedichte aus dem Diwan*, tr. R D KEIL, Düsseldorf 1962.

RŪMĪ, Jalāl al-dīn, *Licht und Reigen*, tr. C BÜRGEL, Bern 1974.

MUḤAMMAD ᶜALI, Naqīb al-mamālik, *Liebe und Abenteuer des Amir Arsalan*, tr. R GELPKE, Zürich 1965.

NIẒĀM AL-MULK, *Siyāsatnāma*, tr. K E SCHABINGER, Freiburg/Munich 1960.

NIẒĀMĪ, *Lejla und Medshnun*, tr. R GELPKE, Zürich 1963.

—— *Die sieben Geschichten der sieben Prinzessinnen*, tr. R GELPKE, Zürich 1959.

Persische Märchen, tr. A CHRISTENSEN, Düsseldorf 1958.

Persische Meistererzähler der Gegenwart, tr. R GELPKE, Zürich 1961.

SAᶜDĪ, *Hundertundeine Geschichte aus dem Rosengarten*, tr. R GELPKE, Zürich 1967.

9.1.3 *Italian*

FIRDAUSĪ, *Il libro dei Re*, tr. Francesco GABRIELI, Turin 1969.

NIẒĀMĪ, *Le sette principesse*, tr. A BAUSANI, Bari 1967.

ᶜUMAR KHAYYĀM, *Quartine*, tr. A BAUSANI, n.p. 1956.

9.1.4 *Russian*

CHŪBAK, Ṣādiq, *Izbrannoe*, tr. D KOMISSAROV and Z OSMANOVA, Moscow 1972.

GURGĀNĪ, Fakhr al-dīn, *Vis i Ramin*, tr. S LIPKIN, Moscow 1963.

FIRDAUSĪ, Shāhnāma, tr. C BANŪ-LĀHŪTĪ, *et al.*, Moscow 1957-69.

ḤĀFIẒ, *Sto semnadtsat' gazelei*, tr. G PLISETSKOV, Moscow 1981.

HIDĀYAT, Ṣādiq, *Izbrannye Proizvedeniya*, tr. A Z ROZENFEL'D, *et al.*, Moscow 1957.

RŪMĪ, Jalāl al-dīn, *Pritchi*, tr. V DERZHAVIN, Moscow 1963.

KAMĀL KHUJANDĪ, *Lirika*, tr. A ADALIS, *et al.* Moscow 1976.

NIZĀMĪ, *Pyat Poém*, tr. K LIPSKEROV, *et al.*, Moscow 1968.

RŪDAKĪ, *Lirika*, tr. V LEVIK and S LIPKIN, Moscow 1969.

SA^c^DĪ, *Gulistan*, tr. R ALIEV and A STAROSTIN, Moscow 1957.

—— *Bustan*, tr. V DERZHAVIN and A STAROSTIN, Moscow 1962.

10. *LITERARY JOURNALS*

The following journals are entirely or primarily devoted to literary subjects. Those published in Iran are all in Persian, and published in Tehran unless otherwise stated; those for which no closing date is given were still publishing in 1979, but their present state is uncertain.

10.1 *Published in Iran*

Ārash, 1340/1961 - 1346/1967, 1359/1981-

Armaghān, 1298/1919-

Āyanda, vols. 1-3, 1304/1925 - 1307/1928; vol.4, 1338/1959 - 1339/1960; vol.5, 1358/1979-

Dānish, 1327/1948 - 1334/1955.

Mihr, 1312/1933 - 1319/1940.

Payām-i Nau, 1323/1944 - 1333/1954.

Payām-i Navīn, 1337/1958-

Rahnumā-yi Kitāb, 1337/1958 - 1358/1979.

Majalla/Nashrīya-yi Dānishkada-yi Adabīyāt-i Dānishgāh-i

Tabrīz (*Āzarbādigān*) 1327/1948-

Tihrān, 1332/1953-

Iṣfahān, 1343/1964-

Mashhad (*Firdausī*) 1344/1965-

Sukhan, 1322/1943-

Yādgār, 1323/1944-

Ta^c^līm va Tarbiyat (later *Āmūzish va Parvarish*), 1304/1925 - 1326/1947.

Yaghmā, 1327/1948 - 1358/1979.

10.2 *Published elsewhere*

Edebiyāt, Philadelphia 1976-

Publishes articles in English on Middle Eastern literatures, and always has at least one on Persian.

Iranian Studies, New Haven, Conn. (later Chestnut Hill, Mass.) 1967-.

Articles in English on literary and historical subjects.

Kāva (*Kaveh*), Munich 1963-

In Persian and German.

XII

ARTS AND CRAFTS [1]

1. *INTRODUCTION*

In the field of art and architecture, perhaps even more than in the field of history, it is crucial to bear in mind the notion of a Greater Iran spreading far beyond the present political boundaries of the country. The pottery of early ᶜAbbāsid Mesopotamia and the Tīmūrid architecture of Central Asia are more central to an understanding of the Iranian tradition than any contemporary work in these media from Iran proper. Throughout the period covered in this survey the art of Afghanistan was firmly within the orbit of Iran. Strong though intermittent Iranian influence characterises the art of Anatolia and Soviet Āẕarbāyjān between the 13th and 15th centuries.

Besides this impact of Iranian modes on neighbouring lands by a process of natural extension one must also take account of the radiating influence of Iranian art throughout the Islamic world. For sheer output pre-modern Iran has no rivals among other Islamic countries. Moreover at certain times, such as the high and late mediaeval period, and in certain media, such as painting, Iran possessed the most vigorous and advanced artistic tradition in the Islamic world. Not surprisingly, it exercised a radiating influence which made itself felt from Egypt to Bengal. Only North Africa, itself under the spell of Muslim Spain, remained immune. It follows from these remarks that much valuable work on Iranian art is contained in general histories of Islamic art.

Islamic art history is a comparatively recent feature of Iranian studies, and the development of the discipline has been spasmodic. Much valuable information was amassed by, or more frequently lies buried in, the account of the early European travellers to the country. Such material mostly concerns architecture. Among the 19th century travellers were some - like TEXIER, LAURENS, and COSTE - whose prime aim was, it seems, to record the monuments

[1] For a survey of works on pre-Islamic art and architecture see IX 2.1.

as scientifically as possible. The turn of the century saw the advent of such professional art historians as SARRE, HERZFELD and DIEZ, all of whom undertook arduous pioneering fieldwork and published scores of monuments hitherto unknown to European scholarship. In many respects their works are still not superseded. The same cannot be said of the contemporary work on the minor arts, which featured lavishly illustrated folios whose texts were often astonishingly inaccurate and skimpy.

The 1930s inaugurated a decisive change for the better. In the minor arts the principal event was the great exhibition of Iranian art held in London in 1931. Most of the finest known illustrated Iranian manuscripts were on show, and other fields were almost equally well represented. The catalogue of the miniatures exhibited - *Persian miniature painting* (see Laurence BINYON, J V S WILKINSON, and Basil GRAY) - is still the standard handbook on the subject. Even interest in architecture experienced a fillip as a result of the photographs and reconstructions in the exhibition. Similar though lesser exhibitions in France, the USA and the Soviet Union followed. These exhibitions confronted specialists in the minor arts with a huge quantity of hitherto unfamiliar material which generated much creative scholarship. In Iran itself a national Archaeological Service was set up and its director, André Godard, founded the journal *Āthār-é Īrān* to publish the numerous monuments recorded as part of the Service's work. Meanwhile the American Arthur Upham POPE, to whose enthusiasm international interest in Iranian architecture was largely due, himself founded the American Institute for Iranian Art and Archaeology, which also published a journal recording the indefatigable activity of its members. This effort culminated in

POPE, Arthur Upham, and Phyllis ACKERMAN (eds), *A survey of Persian art from prehistoric times to the present*, 6 vols, London/New York 1938-39. Repr. 17 vols, Ashiya, Japan 1977.

Equally indispensable is the basic bibliography

CRESWELL, K A C, *A bibliography*, *op.cit.* IX 2.1.1.

Also useful is

MĀFĪ, ᶜAbbās, *Kitābshināsī-yi hunar*, Tehran 1976.

In Iran itself the pace of research activity and fieldwork slackened markedly for the next twenty years, but the 1960s saw the establishment in Tehran of British, German and French Institutes catering principally for archaeological and architectural interests. The parallel activity of Iranian government organizations has meant that the country's monuments are now in the main known and adequately recorded though not many have been published thoroughly. The principal excavations of Islamic material since 1930 have been at Rayy, Nīshāpūr, Sīrāf and Iṣfahān. More recently, in the 1970s, Iranian scholars have excavated more and more Islamic sites and have produced detailed gazetteers of the country; their contribution to the field has become increasingly significant.

In the minor arts, notably painting, ceramics and metalwork, the volume of significant scholarship since 1940 has been greater than in architecture. More specialists have concerned themselves with these fields and much of the material, lodged in western museums and frequently exhibited, is easily accessible. Museum curators have been the crucial factor in this development. Much more precise dating and assessment of styles and provenance are now possible and a comparatively new field - Islamic iconography - is being mapped out. For information on the techniques of the minor crafts, reference should be made to the works by Jay and Sumi GLUCK and Hans E WULFF, *op.cit.* VII 9.

Until the last fifty years most published work on Iranian art could fairly be described as amateur. Even since that time, the discipline has too often tried to run before it could walk. There have been too many surveys and too few monographs. Some areas and objects have suffered from overpublication at a low level of competence, so that a given range of illustrations becomes hackneyed and belies the variety of Iranian art. However, the continued vitality of public interest makes it inevitable that works of both *haute* and *basse vulgarisation* will continue to dominate among books on Iranian art. Yet there are still no serious, up-to-date, full-length books dealing with the history of Persian ceramics or Persian metalwork as a whole. Very few of the major museums have published serious catalogues of their holdings in the Iranian minor arts, although numerous fine catalogues of private collections have appeared. There is an urgent need for selective annotated bibliographies of the major fields. Unpublished theses will increasingly form a key component of such bibliographies. Perhaps the major desideratum, however, is much more work relying primarily on written sources - poetry, history (especially local chronicles), archives and inscriptions. The gap in this area reflects the extreme rarity of scholars of Iranian art who have a firm control of Near Eastern languages. The meaning of hundreds of miniature paintings is obscured because their accompanying texts have not been identified; most of the inscriptions on Saljūq and Īlkhānid pottery remain unpublished; lists of craftsmen are still very incomplete. Native scholars are obviously best fitted for such tasks, and the most efficient way of accomplishing them could well be to make them co-operative ventures. A 'Documentary survey of Persian art' was in fact inaugurated by POPE in the 1930s but never completed. Finally, attention might be drawn to the need for translations of key Russian works, especially on architecture, archaeology, epigraphy and ceramics. This body of material, of crucial importance in the pre-Saljūq and Tīmūrid periods, is rendered difficult of access both because few Islamic art historians know Russian and because the relevant journals and reports are very hard to find in western libraries.

Two useful periodicals are

Hunar va mardum, Ministry of Culture and Art, monthly, Tehran 1963-79.

Naqsh va nigār, Department of Fine Arts, six-monthly, Tehran 1955-58.

2. *PAINTING AND THE ART OF THE BOOK*

ADLE, Chahriyar, 'Recherche sur le module et le tracé correcteur dans la miniature orientale', *Le monde iranien et l'Islam* III, 1975 :81-104.

A valuable analysis of the compositional principles underlying mature Persian painting.

AFSHĀR, Īraj (ed), *Ṣaḥḥāfī-yi sunnatī*, Tehran 1978.

AGA-OGLU, Mehmet, *Persian bookbindings of the fifteenth century*, Ann Arbor 1935.

Handy monograph on a neglected subject.

ARBERRY, A J, E BLOCHET, M MINOVI, J V S WILKINSON, and B W ROBINSON, *The Chester Beatty Library. A catalogue of the Persian manuscripts and miniatures*, Dublin 1959-62.

Basic account of one of the finest collections of Persian miniatures. Unfortunately the catalogue entries are often somewhat thin and the illustrations, though fine, are too few in number.

ARNOLD, T W, *Painting in Islam*, Oxford 1928, repr. New York 1965.

Still the only book on the subject which utilizes to the full a wide range of literary sources and thus places book painting firmly within its religious and social context.

—— *The Old and New Testaments in Muslim religious art*, Oxford 1932.

The wealth of evidence presented here decisively repudiates the notion that Islamic societies operated a ban on religious painting.

ATASOY, Nurhan, 'Four Istanbul albums and some fragments from fourteenth century Shah-namehs', *AO* VIII, 1970 :19-48.

This material permits a tentative reconstruction of the metropolitan style of the later 14th century.

BARRETT, Douglas, *Persian painting of the fourteenth century*, London 1952.

A sure and readable guide to the period.

BEHZAD, H Taherzadeh, 'The preparation of the miniaturist's materials', *SPA* :1921-27.

Useful technical summary.

BINYON, Laurence, J V S WILKINSON, and Basil GRAY, *Persian miniature painting*, Oxford 1933.

Though originally intended as an exhibition catalogue, this has remained the standard handbook ever since it was published; a classic.

BRIAN, Doris, 'A reconstruction of the miniature cycle in the Demotte Shah Namah', *AI* VI, 1939 :97-112.

The indispensable foundation for all later studies of this key manuscript.

DUDA, Dorothea, 'Die Malerei unter den Djalairiden. I. Unter Shaykh Hasan Buzurg', *Der Islam* 48, 1972 :28-76.

—— 'Die Malerei in Tabriz unter Sultan Uwais und Husain', *Der Islam* 49, 1972 :153-220.

The most detailed monographic account of Jalā'irid painting so far published.

ETTINGHAUSEN, Richard, 'Bihzad', *Encyclopaedia of Islam*, 2nd ed., I :1211-14.

An excellent and full account of the most famous Persian painter; the *oeuvre* attributed to him is cautiously restricted.

—— 'Manuscript illumination', *SPA* :1937-74.

Still the best account of the subject.

—— 'Persian ascension miniatures of the fourteenth century', *Accademia Nazionale dei Lincei, Convegno 'Volta'*, Atti XII, 1957 :360-83.

A pioneering attempt to place the earliest *Miᶜrāj Nāma* illustrations in their religious and stylistic context.

—— 'On some Mongol miniatures', *Kunst des Orients* III, 1959 :44-65.

Presents among other new material the earliest paintings to be associated with Īlkhānid Iran. Largely devoted to material in the Topkapı Saray.

FALK, S J, *Qajar paintings. Persian oil paintings of the 18th and 19th centuries*, London 1972.

The only monographic study of this material.

GOLOMBEK, Lisa B, 'Toward a classification of Islamic painting', R ETTINGHAUSEN (ed), *Islamic art in the Metropolitan Museum of Art*, New York 1972 :23-34.

A challenging and original attempt to show that the greatest Persian painting is much more than 'mere' illustration and can express a subtle understanding of the nuances of the text, and occasionally even satire.

GRABAR, Oleg, 'Notes on the iconography of the "Demotte" Shah-Namah', R H PINDER-WILSON (ed), *Paintings from Islamic lands*, Oxford 1969 :32-47.

Isolates the major themes of these illustrations, chief among which are scenes involving death and legitimacy.

GRAY, Basil, *Persian painting*, Geneva 1961.

A comprehensive, reliable text and numerous magnificent colour plates make this the best popular handbook currently available.

—— *The illustrations of the World History of Rashid al-Din*, London 1978.

Reproduces, with brief commentary, all the illustrations in the manuscript formerly belonging to the Royal Asiatic Society.

—— 'Chinese influence in Persian painting: 14th and 15th centuries', W WATSON (ed), *The westward influence of the Chinese arts from the 14th to the 18th century*, London 1973 :11-19.

Shows how the seminal influence exerted by Chinese painting on 14th century Persian work had declined to mere chinoiserie by the 15th century.

—— (ed), *The arts of the book in Central Asia. 14th-16th centuries*, Paris/ London 1979.

A digest of recent research on Persian painting from 1300-1600, with contributions from leading specialists and valuable material on calligraphy, illumination and book-binding. Indispensable and of excellent quality throughout.

GRUBE, Ernst J, *Muslim miniature paintings from the XIIth to XIXth century from collections in the United States and Canada*, Venice 1962.

—— *Islamic paintings in the collection of H P Kraus*, New York 1972.

—— *Miniature Islamiche nella collezione del Topkapi Sarayi Istanbul*, Padua 1975.

All three books follow the catalogue format and are distinguished by a combination of detailed, exhaustive description and analysis and a full bibliography which lists ample comparative material for each item or group of items. Excellent general bibliographies in each case.

—— 'Persian painting in the fourteenth century. A research report', *The memorial volume of the VIth International Congress of Iranian Art and Archaeology, Oxford, September 11th-16th 1972*, Tehran 1976 :113-29.

—— 'The *Kalilah wa Dimnah* of the Istanbul University Library and the problem of early Jalairid painting', *Akten des VII. Internationalen Kongresses für Iranische Kunst und Archäologie. München 7-10 September 1976*, Berlin 1979 :491-507.

A useful conspectus of a still neglected period in metropolitan painting: the years between 1350 and 1396. Both articles are concerned almost exclusively with material in Istanbul.

GRATZL, Emil, 'Book covers', *SPA* :1975-94.

Useful general survey, though inadequately illustrated.

GUEST, G D, *Shiraz painting of the sixteenth century*, Washington 1949.

An unaccountably neglected monograph with many original observations; includes an early attempt to identify a compositional module in Persian painting.

HARAVĪ, Māyil, *Lughāt va iṣṭilāḥāt-i fannī-yi kitābsāzī*, Tehran 1975.

Includes terms in bookbinding, illumination and painting.

HILLENBRAND, Robert, *Imperial images in Persian painting*, Edinburgh 1977.

Traces by means of selected examples some of the major themes of Persian painting; most of the 80-odd illustrations are hitherto unpublished.

IPŞIROǦLU, M S, *Painting and culture of the Mongols*, tr. E D PHILLIPS, London 1967.

Attempts to associate major groups of 14th and 15th century paintings with Mongol rather than Persian culture; many excellent colour plates, especially of paintings attributed to Muḥammad Siyāh Qalam.

—— *Saray Alben. Diezsche Klebebände aus den Berliner Sammlungen*, Wiesbaden 1964.

Full catalogue raisonnée of the little-known collections of Īlkhānid painting in Tübingen and Berlin.

IVANOV, A A, 'The life of Muhammad Zaman: a reconsideration', *Iran* XVII, 1979 :65-70.

Disposes of several vulgar errors about Muḥammad Zamān.

KAZI AKHMED, (QAŻĪ AḤMAD), *Traktat o kalligrafakh i khudozhnikakh*, tr. and ann. B N ZAKHODER, Moscow/Leningrad 1947. English tr. V MINORSKY, *Calligraphers and painters*. A treatise by Qāḍī Aḥmad, son of Mīr Munshī (c.1015/1606), Washington 1959.

This translation is especially useful for the light it sheds on the nature of connoisseurship and on the status of the artist in Ṣafavid Iran.

KIRKETERP-MØLLER, Hertha, *Det Islamiske Bogmaleri*, Copenhagen 1974.

KLIMBURG-SALTER, Deborah, 'A Sufi theme in Persian painting: the Diwan of Sultan Ahmad Ğalā'ir in the Freer Gallery of Art, Washington DC', *Kunst des Orients* 11, 1976-77 :43-84.

Monographic treatment of a crucial Jalā'irid manuscript.

KÜHNEL, Ernst, 'Die Baysonghur-Handschrift der Islamischen Kunstabteilung', *Jahrbuch der preuszischen Kunstsammlungen* LII, 1931 :133-52.

Full publication of one of the earliest examples of the early Tīmūrid school of Shīrāz.

—— 'Painting and the art of the book', *SPA* :1829-97.

A detailed but somewhat pedestrian account.

LAWRIE, A P, 'Materials in Persian miniatures', *Technical Studies in the Field of the Fine Arts* III, 1934 :146-56.

Of fundamental importance to the subject.

MARTIN, F R, *The miniature painting and painters of Persia, India and Turkey*, London 1912.

For a long time this was the major textbook, largely because of its unrivalled array of plates. These are still useful but the text is best ignored.

MELIKIAN-CHIRVANI, A S, *Le roman de Varqe et Golšāh*, Paris 1970.

Monographic treatment (including a complete translation of the text) of perhaps the earliest cycle of Persian paintings to survive. All are illustrated and the analogies with other media are explored *in extenso*.

RICE, D Talbot, *The illustrations to the 'World History' of Rashid al-Din*, B GRAY (ed), Edinburgh 1976.

Brief introductory chapters preface short commentaries on the pictures themselves, and attributions are suggested. All the pictures are illustrated in black and white and in colour microfiche.

ROBINSON, B W, *A descriptive catalogue of the Persian paintings in the Bodleian Library*, Oxford 1958.

Detailed catalogue of a major collection; especially useful for the comprehensive lists of 'manuscripts for comparison' and for the detailed indices.

—— *Persian miniature paintings from collections in the British Isles*, London 1967.

Essentially an illustrated account, arranged chronologically, of the development of metropolitan and provincial schools, with terse descriptive notes on the individual items.

—— *Persian paintings in the India Office Library*, London 1976.

Largely Ṣafavid material; lavishly illustrated, with useful subject index.

—— 'Two manuscripts of the "Shahnama" in the Royal Library, Windsor Castle. I: Holmes 150 (A/5) and II: Holmes 151 (A/6)', *Burlington Magazine* CX, 1968 :73-78, 133-38.

Very detailed publication of two high-quality Ṣafavid manuscripts; part II deals with a manuscript of 1648 which displays marked originality. Excellent close-ups.

—— 'The court painters of Fath ᶜAlī Shāh', *Eretz Israel* 7, L A Mayer Memorial Volume, 1963 :94-105.

A detailed and profusely illustrated study which breaks much new ground.

—— *et al.*, *Islamic painting and the arts of the book*, London 1976.

Catalogue of a private collection rich in court painting of the Tīmūrid, Turcoman and early Ṣafavid periods. Lavishly illustrated in colour.

ROGERS, J M, *Myth and ceremony in Islamic painting*, London 1978.

A catalogue largely confined to material in the British Museum and the British Library. No illustrations, but many of the entries are engagingly written and exhibit curious learning.

SARRE, F, *Islamische Bucheinbände*, Berlin 1923.

The scope of the book allows the Persian contribution to be assessed vis-à-vis other Islamic traditions of book-binding. Excellent plates.

—— and E MITTWOCH, *Zeichnungen von Riza Abbasi*, Munich 1914.

Still the only detailed treatment of a corpus of Persian drawings; the epigraphic material is exhaustively published.

SCHROEDER, Eric, *Persian miniatures in the Fogg Museum of Art*, Cambridge, Mass. 1942.

Easily the best-written book on Persian painting yet to appear; original, provocative, erudite. A classic.

—— 'Ahmad Musa and Shams al-Din: a review of fourteenth-century painting', *AI* VI, 1939 :113-42.

A magisterial assessment of the Demotte *Shāhnāma*; still the best work published on that manuscript. Even the errors in the interpretation are entertaining.

SCHULZ, P W, *Die persisch-islamische Miniaturmalerei*, Leipzig 1914.

Far ahead of its time in its accuracy and sensitivity to style; perhaps the only major work on the subject published before 1933 which can still be read with profit.

SIMPSON, M S, *The illustration of an epic: the earliest* Shahnama *manuscripts*, New York/London 1979.

On the basis of an extremely detailed study of all the 'small' *Shāhnāmas* not attributed to Shīrāz, a group of three of them is attributed to Baghdad around 1300. The development of the *Shāhnāma* as a vehicle for illustration is also examined. A pioneering work.

SIMS, Eleanor G, 'Late Safavid painting: the Chehel Sutun, the Armenian houses, the oil paintings', *Akten des VII. Internationalen Kongresses für Iranische Kunst und Archäologie. München 7-10 September 1976*, Berlin 1979 :408-18.

Traces the links between mural, easel and book painting in the late Ṣafavid period and notes the debt which this painting owes to Europe and to Mughal

India; the discussion focuses on the paintings in the Chihil Sutūn.

—— 'Five seventeenth-century Persian oil paintings', *Persian and Mughal Art*, London 1976 :223-48.

A highly original study which shows that the determined eclecticism of the later Ṣafavid court could even produce oil paintings of European type.

SOUCEK, Priscilla P, 'Niẓāmī on painters and painting', R ETTINGHAUSEN (ed), *Islamic Art in the Metropolitan Museum of Art*, New York 1972 :9-21.

An attempt to define a mediaeval philosophy of representation by following up hints in the text of Niẓāmī.

STCHOUKINE, I, *La peinture Iranienne sous les derniers ᶜAbbâsides et les Îl-Khâns*, Bruges 1936.

—— *Les peintures des manuscrits Tîmûrides*, Paris 1954.

—— *Les peintures des manuscrits Safavis de 1502 à 1587*, Paris 1959.

—— *Les peintures des manuscrits de Shah Abbas Ier à la fin des Safavis*, Paris 1964.

These four volumes represent the work of a life-time devoted to Islamic, and particularly Persian, painting. Each volume presents the major manuscripts of the period in question, complete with short descriptions of the major paintings and a critical bibliography. The monochrome plates are well chosen and of excellent quality. STCHOUKINE had a sound critical judgement, an acute sense of style and an unrivalled familiarity with the paintings themselves. His volumes are therefore the cornerstone of future work.

STRIKA, Vincenzo, 'Note introduttive a un estetica islamica: la miniatura persiana', *Rendiconti della Accademia dei Lincei* 28, 1973 :699-727.

Challenging attempt to define the underlying ideas which have shaped traditional Persian painting.

SWIETOCHOWSKI, K L, 'The development of traditions of book illustration in pre-Safavid Iran', *Iranian Studies* 7(1/2), 1974 :49-71.

—— 'Some aspects of the Persian miniature painter in relation to his texts', Peter J CHELKOWSKI (ed), *Studies in art and literature of the Near East in honor of Richard Ettinghausen*, Salt Lake City/New York 1974 :111-31.

Both these studies examine the painter's response to the text before him and his efforts to vary inherited formulae.

—— 'The historical background and illustrative character of the Metropolitan Museum's *Mantiq al-Tayr* of 1483', R ETTINGHAUSEN (ed), *Islamic art in the Metropolitan Museum of Art*, New York 1972 :39-72.

Sets the manuscript in the context of contemporary Harātī work; includes some penetrating comments on Bihzād and his probable role in the royal atelier.

TITLEY, N M, *Miniatures from Persian manuscripts. A catalogue and subject index of paintings from Persia, India and Turkey in the British Library and the British Museum*, London 1978.

An invaluable working tool which at last renders accessible over 11,000 Islamic paintings in the British Library and British Museum. Each painting is described, a brief bibliography is given for each manuscript or detached leaf, and the subject index is some 150 pages long.

WELCH, Anthony, *Shah ᶜAbbas and the arts of Isfahan*, New York 1973.

Places later Ṣafavid painting firmly within the context of 17th century Persian society and polity, and emphasises the links between painting and other media.

—— *Artists for the Shah*, New Haven 1976.

Assesses the role of Siyāvush, Ṣādiqī Beg and Riẓā in the formation of later Ṣafavid painting and explores the interplay of personalities between painters and patrons.

—— 'Painting and patronage under Shah ᶜAbbas I', *Iranian Studies* VII(3/4), 1974 :458-507.

Analyses the work of six painters of the period and shows why the patronage of Shah ᶜAbbas was less important to the development of painting than that of some of his predecessors.

WELCH, S Cary, *Royal Persian manuscripts*, London 1976.

Lavishly illustrated survey of the finest productions of the reign of Shāh Ṭahmāsp.

—— *Wonders of the age*, New York 1979.

Catalogue of an exhibition devoted mainly to the Houghton Shāhnāma and, to a lesser extent, to the British Library Niẓāmī of 1539-43.

—— and M B DICKSON, *The Houghton Shahnama*, Cambridge, Mass. 1981.

The definitive publication of the Houghton Shāhnāma executed at Tabrīz in the 1520s and 1530s.

WELLESZ, Emmy, 'Eine Handschrift aus der Blütezeit frühtimuridischer Kunst', *Wiener Beiträge zur Kunst und Kulturgeschichte Asiens* X, 1936 :3-24.

Well-documented account of an exquisite manuscript from the atelier of Baisunghur.

3. *ARCHITECTURE*

ADLE, C, and A S MELIKIAN-CHIRVANI, 'Les monuments du XIe siècle du

Dâmqân', *Studia Iranica* 1, 1972 :229-97.

An intensive investigation of a well-defined group of monuments whose complex epigraphy had largely balked earlier scholars. Penetrating analysis of the funerary cult in mediaeval Iran.

ANJUMAN-I ĀS̲ĀR-I MILLĪ.

Among the long series of monographs published by this body are a number of architectural gazetteers of individual cities or provinces with descriptions of their monuments and inscriptions. Examples include

MUṢṬAFAVĪ, M T, *Iqlīm-i Pārs*, Tehran 1964. English tr. N SHARP, Chippenham 1978.

KARĪMĀN, H, *Rayy-i bāstān*, Tehran 1966.

AFS̲H̲ĀR, Īraj, *Yādgārhā-yi Yazd*, *op.cit.* VIII 3.2.9.

SUTŪDA, Manuc̲h̲ihr, *Az Āstārā ta Astārābād*, *op.cit.* VIII 3.2.9.

KĀRANG, ᶜA ᶜA, *Ās̲ār-i bāstānī-yi Āz̲arbāyjān*, Tehran n.d.

NARĀQĪ, Ḥ, *Ās̲ār-i tārīk̲h̲ī-yi s̲h̲ahristānhā-yi Kās̲h̲ān va Naṭanz*, Tehran n.d.

VARJĀVAND, Parvīz, *Sar-zamīn-i Qazvīn*, Tehran 1970.

BAKHTIAR, A A, 'The Royal Bazaar of Isfahan', *Iranian Studies* 7(3/4), 1974 :320-47.

Concise architectural and socio-historical summary based on profound knowledge of the complex.

BRANDENBURG, Dietrich, *Samarkand. Studien zur islamischen Baukunst in Uzbekistan (Zentralasien)*, Berlin 1972.

Useful compendium based largely on Russian sources.

BRETANITSKY, L S, *Zodchestvo Azerbaidzhana, XII-XV vv, i ego mesto v arkhitekture Perednego Vostoka*, Moscow 1966.

Profusely illustrated survey concentrating on the monuments of Soviet rather than Iranian Āz̲arbāyjān.

COHN-WIENER, Ernst, *Turan. Islamische Baukunst in Mittelasien*, Berlin 1930.

Magnificent album of photographs, some of vital historical interest because they have since collapsed or been restored. Brief notes on each monument.

DIEZ, Ernst, *Churasanische Baudenkmäler*, Berlin 1918.

The first and still the best attempt to characterize the monuments of this key province. Valuable epigraphical appendix by Max van BERCHEM.

—— *Persien. Islamische Baukunst in Churâsân*, Darmstadt 1923.

An undeservedly neglected book packed with original and stimulating ideas generated by DIEZ's journeys in northern, central and eastern Iran. Particularly illuminating are the separate discussions of building types, materials, and spatial organization.

ETTINGHAUSEN, R, 'The "Beveled Style" in the post-Samarra period', G C MILES (ed), *Archaeologica Orientalia in Memoriam Ernst Herzfeld*, Locust Valley 1952 :72-83.

Places mediaeval Iranian stucco in its wider historical and geographical context, and documents the formative influence of Samarran work on later periods.

—— 'Some comments on medieval Iranian art', *Artibus Asiae* XXXI(4), 1969 :276-300.

Includes a novel and provocative analysis of the origins and uses of the 4-Īvān plan.

FLURY, Samuel, 'La Mosquée de Nayin', *Syria* XI, 1930 :43-58.

An epigraphical analysis of the type pioneered by FLURY, using alphabetical tables; complements the earlier architectural and epigraphic study of this mosque in *Syria* II, 1921, pp.230-34, 305-16.

GALDIERI, Eugenio, *Iṣfahān: Masǧid-i Ǧumᶜa*, Rome 1972-73.

The definitive album of plates though the commentary only partially supersedes that of GODARD (q.v.).

—— 'Quelques précisions sur le Gunbad-é Nizam al-Mulk d'Isfahan', *Revue des Études Islamiques* XLIII, 1975 :96-122.

This meticulous study forces a complete revision of earlier theories about the southern side of the mosque.

GODARD, André, *The art of Iran*, *op.cit.* IX 2.5.6.

The fruit of more than thirty years' work in Iran; presents in succinct and telling form a host of provocative insights and generalizations.

—— 'Les anciennes mosquées de l'Īrān', *AeI* I(2), 1936 :187-210, and *Arts Asiatiques* 3, 1956 :48-63, 83-88.

A classic if flawed analysis of how the Iranian mosque developed.

—— 'Iṣfahān', *AeI* II(1), 1937.

Still the best brief guide available; gives texts and translations of many inscriptions and provides a check-list of monuments. To be consulted in conjunction with HUNARFAR's comprehensive work.

—— 'Khorāsān', *AeI* IV(2), 1949 :7-150.

The only rival to DIEZ's work; it treats monuments he did not know, notably Ribāṭ-i Sharaf.

—— 'Voûtes iraniennes', *AeI* IV(2), 1949.

The sole serious comprehensive study of mediaeval Iranian vaulting.

—— 'Historique du Masdjid-é Djumᶜa d'Iṣfahān', *AeI* I(2), 1936 :213-82.

Outdated in the earlier sections, but it remains a useful *aide-mémoire*.

GOLOMBEK, L B, *The Timurid Shrine at Gazur Gah*, Toronto 1969.

Monographic study of a key Tīmūrid monument; especially valuable for the functional analysis of Gāzur Gāh.

—— 'The cult of saints and shrine architecture in the fourteenth century', D K KOUYMJIAN (ed), *Near Eastern Numismatics, Iconography, Epigraphy and History. Studies in Honor of George C Miles*, Beirut 1974 :419-30.

Useful introduction to the problems presented by shrine complexes.

GRABAR, Oleg, 'The visual arts', *CHI* IV :331-51; V :629-41.

These contributions highlight the problems which mediaeval Iranian architecture continues to pose, and they propose some tentative solutions. They are not just summaries; they tackle the subject afresh in a most invigorating manner.

HARB, Ulrich, *Ilkhanidische Stalaktitengewölbe: Beiträge zu Entwurf und Bautechnik*, Berlin 1978.

Lucid geometrical analyses result in the identification of various categories of *muqarnas* vaults.

HILL, Derek, and Oleg GRABAR, *Islamic architecture and its decoration*, London 1967.

Comprehensive and invaluable assemblage of photographs, with brief captions and a pioneering introductory essay.

HILLENBRAND, Robert, 'Saljūq monuments in Iran. I. The Masjid-i Jāmi^c, Qurva', *Oriental Art*, N.S. XVIII, 1972 :1-14; 'II. The "Pīr" Mausoleum at Tākistān', *Iran* X, 1972 :45-55; 'III. The domed Masǧid-i Ǧāmi^c of Suǧās', *Kunst des Orients* X, 1975 :49-79; 'IV. The mosques of Nūshābād', *Oriental Art*, N.S. XXII, 1976 :265-77.

Detailed presentations of unfamiliar Saljūq buildings.

HUNARFAR, Luṭfallāh, *Ganjīna-yi āsār-i tārīkhī-yi Iṣfahān*, Iṣfahān 1971.

A superb compendium of information; indispensable.

HUTT, A M, and L W HARROW, *Islamic architecture. Iran 1*, London 1977.

—— *Islamic Architecture. Iran 2*, London 1978.

Attractively produced picture books showing many unfamiliar details. Brief introductions and captions.

MASSON, M E, and G A PUGACHENKOVA, 'Shakhri Syabz pri Timure i Ulug Beke - I', tr. J M ROGERS, *Iran* XVI, 1979 :103-26.

Detailed study of one of the finest Tīmūrid monuments extant, the Āqsarāi. To be read in conjunction with NEMTSEVA (q.v.).

MILES, G C, 'The inscriptions of the Masjid-i Jāmi^c at Ashtarjān', *Iran* XII, 1974 :89-98.

A model of how to do such work.

MORTON, A H, 'The Ardabil shrine in the reign of Shah Tahmasp I', *Iran* XII, 1974 :31-64, and *Iran* XIII, 1975 :39-58.

Utilises much contemporary literary material to show how much change the shrine has undergone over the centuries and what role it played in the life of the city.

MOYNIHAN, Elizabeth B, *Paradise as a garden in Persia and Mughal India*, London 1979.

More on India than on Persia, but a useful *coup d'oeil* of Ṣafavid gardens especially.

NEMTSEVA, N B, 'Istoki kompozitsii i etapy formirovaniya ansamblya Shakhi-Zinda', tr. with additions, J M ROGERS and ᶜA YĀSĪN, 'The origins and architectural development of the Shāh-i Zinde', *Iran* XV, 1977 :51-73.

Invaluable survey of the organic growth of this complex.

O'KANE, Bernard, 'The Madrasa al-Ghiyās̱iyya at Khargird', *Iran* XIV, 1976 :79-92.

The definitive account of the finest Iranian madrasa.

POPE, Arthur U, *Persian architecture*, London 1965.

Handy one-volume illustrated account of Persian architecture. The photographs are magnificent though the text is indifferent and full of careless errors.

—— and Phyllis ACKERMAN (eds), *SPA*, *op.cit.* 1.

Despite its uneven quality which is partly due to the large number of contributors, this is the foundation for all serious work on Persian architecture. The sections on pre-Saljūq and Saljūq architecture by Eric SCHROEDER deserve special praise. The illustrative material is sumptuous and of first-rate quality.

PUGACHENKOVA, G A, *Puti razvitiya arkhitektury Yuzhnogo Turkmenistana pory rabovladeniya i feodalizma*, Moscow 1958.

The most usable general survey of pre-Tīmūrid, largely Islamic, architecture in Central Asia. Invaluable for its assembly of plans and photographs.

—— 'Les monuments peu connus de l'architecture médiévale de l'Afghanistan', *Afghanistan* XXI(1), 1968 :17-52.

Important for its drawings of the Balk̲h̲ mosque and for its account of unfamiliar Tīmūrid monuments.

RAINER, R, *Anonymes Bauen in Iran*, Graz 1977.

Lavishly produced survey of vernacular architecture.

REMPEL, L I, *Arkhitekturni ornament Uzbekistana*, Tashkent 1961.

Unsurpassed in its detailed coverage of the principles and types of Islamic architectural ornament; the book is relevant for Islamic architecture in general.

ROSINTAL, J, *Pendentifs, trompes et stalactites dans l'architecture orientale*, Paris 1928.

—— *Le réseau*, Paris 1937.

Though superseded in some respects, these are still especially valuable guides to Persian vaulting, largely through the use of lucid diagrams. The illustrative material is in fact largely Persian.

SARRE, Friedrich, *Denkmäler Persischer Baukunst*, Berlin 1901-10.

Its value lies principally in its photographs, probably the finest ever published of Persian buildings. The monographic treatment of Ardabīl is especially useful (to be read in conjunction with WEAVER, q.v.).

SAUVAGET, J, 'Observations sur quelques mosquées seldjoukides', *Annales de l'Institut d'Etudes Orientales*, Faculté des Lettres de l'Université d'Alger, IV, 1938 :81-120.

Blistering attack on GODARD's theory about the origins of the Iranian mosque; but this article is itself seriously flawed. A useful corrective to slipshod method.

SEHERR-THOSS, Sonia P, and Hans S, *Design and color in Islamic architecture*, Washington 1968.

The finest collection of colour plates of Iranian architecture yet assembled. Lengthy captions.

SIROUX, Maxime, *Caravansérails de l'Iran*, Cairo 1949.

The only comprehensive monograph on the subject; to be supplemented by material in the articles of W KLEISS in *Archaeologische Mitteilungen aus Iran*, NF, II, 1968, ff.

—— *Anciennes voies et monuments routiers de la région d'Ispahân*, Cairo 1971.

Especially useful for its accounts of little-known mosques in this area.

SMITH, Myron B, 'Material for a corpus of early Iranian Islamic architecture - I. Masdjid-i Djum^{c}a, Demāwend', *Ars Islamica* II, 1935 :153-73; 'II. Manār and masdjid, Barsīān (Iṣfahān)', *ibid.* IV, 1937 :1-40; 'III. Two dated Seljuk monuments at Sīn (Isfahan)', *ibid.* VI(1), 1939 :1-10.

These articles are models of how such monographic investigations of Iranian buildings should be executed. They share with the iceberg the characteristic that most of their substance is not obviously apparent. Some of the information that SMITH had collected but never published on brickwork techniques and on vaulting is to appear in a posthumous book currently under preparation by Princeton University Press.

—— 'The Manārs of Iṣfahān', *AeI* 1(2), 1936 :313-58.
Excellent meaty handlist, well illustrated and provided with the salient facts.

SOURDEL-THOMINE, Janine, 'Deux minarets d'époque seldjoukide en Afghanistan', *Syria* XXX, 1953 :108-36.
Presents hitherto unread or mis-read inscriptions as well as a convenient check-list of Saljūq minarets.

—— 'Inscriptions seldjoukides et salles à coupoles de Qazwin en Iran', *REI* XLII, 1974 :3-43.
Corrects earlier readings of these inscriptions and places the buildings firmly within their social and historical context.

STRONACH, D B, and T Cuyler YOUNG, Jr, 'Three octagonal Seljuq Tomb Towers from Iran', *Iran* IV, 1966 :1-20.
Thorough publication of important newly-discovered monuments in western Iran.

ṬABĀṬABĀ'Ī, Mudarris, *Turbat-i pākān*, 2 vols, Qumm n.d.
The best account of the monuments of the city.

USEINOV, M, L S BRETANITSKY, and A SALAMZADE, *Istoriya arkhitekturi Azerbaidzhana*, Moscow 1963.
Convenient and lavishly illustrated general survey.

WEAVER, M E, *The conservation of the Shrine of Sheikh Safi at Ardebil: second preliminary study*, UNESCO, Paris 1971.
Continues and greatly expands the brief account given in the same author's *Preliminary study on the conservation problems of five Iranian monuments*, UNESCO, Paris 1970; focuses on the structural history of the buildings. To be read in conjunction with MORTON, q.v.

WILBER, Donald N, 'The development of mosaic faïence in Islamic architecture in Iran', *Ars Islamica* VI, 1939 :16-47.
Meticulously researched and documented study; its conclusions have weathered extremely well.

—— with Margaret S WILBER, *Persian gardens and garden pavilions*, Tokyo 1962.
The only serious account of the subject, produced not only by architectural historians but by passionate gardeners. A book that is worthy of its subject.

—— *The architecture of Islamic Iran. The Il Khānid period*, Princeton 1955.
A pioneering work. General chapters on history and architecture, themselves carefully judged summaries, are followed by a detailed catalogue of some 100 monuments. This is perhaps the single most useful book on mediaeval

Persian architecture.

WULFF, Hans E, *The traditional crafts of Persia*, *op.cit.* VII 9.

Detailed account of the varied techniques involved in architecture and kindred fields. Lavishly illustrated with photographs and explanatory drawings. Indispensable.

ZANDER, Giuseppe, *Travaux de restauration de monuments historiques en Iran*, Rome 1968.

This book summarizes much fairly recent restoration work on Ṣafavid buildings in Iṣfahān and the surrounding area.

4. *CERAMICS*

4.1 *General*

No general handbook devoted entirely to Persian pottery exists. Nevertheless, Persian wares take pride of place in most general histories of Islamic pottery.

ALLAN, J W, *Medieval Middle Eastern pottery*, Oxford 1971.

Concise, reliable, informative; includes a useful technical glossary. This is one of the best brief introductions to the subject currently available. The wares illustrated are all in the Ashmolean Museum, Oxford.

ATIL, Esin, *Ceramics from the world of Islam*, Washington 1973.

Over a hundred pieces, all in the Freer Gallery of Art, are illustrated and each is given a lengthy catalogue entry. Many have side as well as frontal views, and inscriptions are often transcribed and translated in full.

FEHÉRVÁRI, Géza, *Islamic pottery. A comprehensive study based on the Barlow Collection*, London 1973.

Very fully illustrated. Useful summary of current knowledge.

GRUBE, Ernst J, *Islamic pottery of the eighth to the fifteenth century in the Keir Collection*, London 1976.

Extremely full and detailed catalogue of the best contemporary private collection. Includes long lists of comparable pieces. The classified bibliography, which features 20 sub-sections, is the most useful working tool on the subject yet published.

HOBSON, R L, *A guide to the Islamic pottery of the Near East*, London 1932.

Summarizes the major historical and stylistic developments; all the objects illustrated are in the British Museum.

LANE, Arthur, *Early Islamic pottery*, London 1947.

—— *Later Islamic pottery. Persia, Syria, Turkey, Egypt*, revised by R H PINDER-WILSON, London 1972.

The unchallenged classics in the field.

—— *A guide to the collection of tiles*, London 1960.

Though its scope is confined to the collection of the Victoria and Albert Museum, this work is the only reliable handbook on Islamic, principally Persian, tilework.

POPE, Arthur U, 'The ceramic art in Islamic times. A. The history', *SPA* :1446-1666,

The longest single treatment of the subject yet published, with useful line drawings.

WALLIS, Henry, *The Godman Collection. Persian ceramic art in the collection of Mr F Du Cane Godman*, London 1891-94.

Catalogues the finest private collection of Persian wares ever formed. Since much of the collection is still not accessible to the public, the documentary value of the plates outweighs the disadvantages of the rather dated text.

WILKINSON, C K, *Iranian ceramics*, New York 1963.

Exhibition catalogue with brief notes on each object. The plates are well chosen to highlight the principal schools and contrast Islamic pottery with earlier ceramic styles in Iran.

4.2 *Early Islamic*

LANE, Arthur, 'The early sgraffito ware of the Near East', *TOCS*, 1937-38 :33-54.

Sets Iranian ware in this technique in the context of similar Byzantine and Syrian production.

MAYSURADZHE, Z, *Keramika Afrasiyaba*, Tiflis 1958.

Important for its treatment of the neglected unglazed wares though it also deals with the epigraphic pottery.

PÉZARD, Maurice, *La céramique ancienne de l'Islam et ses origines*, Paris 1920.

With its exhaustive text and 153 well-chosen plates, this is still a basic handbook.

ROSEN-AYALON, Miriam, *The unglazed Islamic pottery of Susa*, Paris 1977.

The fullest account of early Islamic unglazed ware in Iran; perhaps more detailed than its subject warrants.

SAYKO, E V, *Glazuri keramiki Srednei Azii VII-XIIvv*, Dushanbe 1963.

Sets the epigraphic ware firmly in the context of earlier and later local production.

SCERRATO, U, 'Islamic glazed tiles with moulded decoration from Ghazni', *EW* XIII, 1962 :263-87.

Detailed publication of a rare series of monochrome glazed, square tiles with figural designs.

TASHKHODZHAYEV, S S, *Khudozhestvennaya polivnaya keramika Samarkanda IX-nachala XIII v*, Tashkent 1964.

Summarizes a doctoral thesis on the glazed ware of Samarqand.

VOLOV, L, 'Plaited Kufic on Samanid epigraphic pottery', *op.cit.* IX 2.2.2.

Seminal analysis of the decorative function of inscriptions on pottery. Also contains a convenient handlist of the proverbs used on this ware.

WILKINSON, C K, *Nishapur. Pottery of the early Islamic period*, New York 1973.

The definitive account of the ceramics found in the Nīshāpūr excavations. Examines the links with similar pottery from Samarqand.

ZICK-NISSEN, Johanna, '"Ghabri-Ware" und "Nischapur-Keramik"', *Keramos* 64, 1974 :35-46.

Discusses the themes shared by two distinct traditions of mediaeval 'folk' pottery. The assembly of so many examples of Gabrī/Garrūs ware is especially useful.

4.3 *Saljūq*

It is often impossible to date a given object of this period within fifty years even if there is general agreement that it was produced, say, between 576/1180 and 670/1270. The Mongol invasion of 614/1217 marks only a political divide and typically 'Saljūq' wares were certainly produced after this date. The presence of an entry in this section, therefore, should not be taken to mean that its content is not also relevant to the Īl-Khānid period.

BAHRAMI, Mehdi, *Gurgan Faiences*, Cairo 1949.

A fundamental work establishing the existence of a previously unknown school of Saljūq pottery. It gives the fullest account yet published of the verse inscriptions on Saljūq pottery.

—— 'Le problème des ateliers d'étoiles de faience lustrée', *Revue des Arts Asiatiques* X, 1936 :180-91.

Exploits the epigraphic evidence of the tiles themselves.

—— 'Contribution à l'étude de la céramique musulmane de l'Īrān', *AeI* III(2), 1938 :109-29.

Useful discussion of kilns and unglazed wares.

ETTINGHAUSEN, Richard, 'Evidence for the identification of Kashan pottery', I, III, 1936 :44-75.

To be read in conjunection with WATSON's article, q.v.

—— and G D GUEST, 'The iconography of a Kashan lustre plate', *AO* IV, 1961

:25-64.

A model analysis of the complex layers of meaning, especially Ṣūfī symbolism, contained within an apparently neutral narrative subject.

LANE, Arthur, 'Sung wares and the Seljuq pottery of Persia', *TOCS* XXII, 1946-47 :9-30.

A reminder of the perennial strength of Chinese influence on Persian pottery. Saljūq soft-paste wares imitating porcelain are examined.

WATSON, Oliver, 'Persian lustre-painted pottery. The Rayy and Kashan styles', *TOCS* XL, 1973-75 :1-20.

Finally disposes of the theory that a separate Rayy style existed.

WILLIAMSON, A G, 'Regional diversities in medieval Persian pottery in the light of recent investigations', *Sixth International Congress of Iranian Art and Archaeology. Summaries of Papers*, Oxford 1972 :97.

Shows that only the finest pottery was traded throughout Iran; other types were often locally imitated.

4.4 *Īl-Khānid*

BAHRAMI, Mehdi, *Recherches sur les carreaux de revêtement lustré dans la céramique persane du XIIIe au XIVe siècle (Etoiles et croix)*, Paris 1937.

Proves *inter alia* that much of the repertoire of lustre tiles was equally valid for secular and religious buildings.

NAUMANN, R, 'Eine keramische Werkstatt des 13. Jahrhunderts auf dem Takht-i-Suleiman', *Beiträge zur Kunstgeschichte Asiens. In Memoriam Ernst Diez*, O ASLANAPA (ed), Istanbul 1963 :301-07.

—— and E NAUMANN, 'Ein Kösk des Abaqa Chan auf dem Tacht-i Sulaimān', *Forschungen zur Kunst Asiens. In memoriam Kurt Erdmann*, O ASLANAPA and R NAUMANN (eds), Istanbul 1969 :35-65.

These two articles establish the importance of Takht-i Sulaimān as a short-lived centre of ceramic production, notable especially for its *lājvardīna* tiles with Far Eastern animal motifs.

REITLINGER, Gerald, 'Sultanabad. Classification and chronology', *TOCS* XX, 1944-45 :25-34.

Still the most thorough treatment of these wares yet published.

4.5 *Post-Mongol*

CENTLIVRES-DEMONT, Micheline, *Une communauté de potiers en Iran. Le centre de Meybod (Yazd)*, Wiesbaden 1971.

Excellent study of a contemporary community of potters with a detailed analysis of their products. It also shows that they work in a tradition which may be traced back to the Ṣafavid period.

GRAY, Basil, 'Blue-and-white vessels in Persian miniatures of the 14th and 15th centuries', *TOCS* XXIV, 1948-49 :23-30.

Uses dated or datable paintings of court scenes to construct a chronology and typology of the early Persian blue-and-white wares.

GRUBE, Ernst J, 'Notes on the decorative arts of the Timurid Period', *Gururājamañjarika. Studi in onore di Giuseppe Tucci*, Naples 1974 :233-79.

The only serious attempt so far to define a Tīmūrid style which imposes itself across the boundaries of medium and technique. In so doing he gives Tīmūrid pottery a context it previously lacked. Lavishly illustrated. Reprinted (without illustrations or notes) in *Afghanistan* XXIV(2-3), 1971, pp.60-75.

LANE, Arthur, 'The so-called "Kubachi" wares of Persia', *BM* LXV, 1939 :156-62.

Attempts to localise and date the products of the major school of figure-decorated pottery in post-Tīmūrid Iran.

LUSCHEY-SCHMEISSER, Ingeborg, 'The pictorial tile cycle of Hašt Behešt in Isfahan and its iconographic tradition', *ISMEO*, Rome 1978.

Detailed study of the tile decoration of a Ṣafavid palace.

REITLINGER, Gerald, 'The interim period in Persian pottery: an essay in chronological revision', *AI* V, 1938 :155-78.

Classifies 14th and 15th century wares, principally 'Varamin' ware, blue-and-white 'Miletus' and 'Kubachi'.

SCARCE, Jennifer M, 'Ali Mohammad Isfahani, tilemaker of Tehran', *Oriental Art*, NS 22(3), 1976 :278-88.

Traces the biography and career of a 19th century tilemaker with a comprehensive list of his works.

—— 'Function and decoration in Qajar tilework', *Islam in the Balkans and Persian art and culture of the 18th and 19th centuries*, Royal Scottish Museum, Edinburgh 1979 :75-86.

Traces the evolution of styles and techniques of 19th century tilework using dated monuments.

—— 'The tile decoration of the Gulestan Palace at Tehran - an introductory survey', *Proceedings of VIIth Congress*, :635-41.

Documents the revival of Sasanian themes and the infiltration of European influence in Qājār tilework.

WATSON, Oliver, 'Persian lustre ware from the 14th to the 19th centuries',

Le Monde Iranien et l'Islam III, 1975 :63-80.

Suggests a revised dating for many pieces previously thought to be mediaeval and demonstrates the continuity of lustre manufacture in Iran.

WULFF, Hans E, *The traditional crafts of Persia*, *op.cit.*, part 3, 'Building crafts and ceramic crafts', :133-64.

Detailed account of ceramic production concentrating on contemporary methods and wares.

4.6 *Dated wares*

ETTINGHAUSEN, Richard, 'Dated Faience', *SPA* :1667-96.

The most convenient catalogue yet published.

4.7 *Technique*

ALLAN, J W, 'Abū'l-Qāsim's treatise on ceramics', *Iran* XI, 1973 :111-20.

Translation of basic text giving mediaeval recipes; includes detailed commentary.

HOBSON, R L, 'The ceramic art in Islamic times: techniques', *SPA* :1697-1702.

A convenient summary.

RITTER, H, J RUSKA, F SARRE, and R WINDERLICH, *Orientalische Steinbücher und persische Fayencetechnik*, Istanbul 1935.

Edition and German translation, with commentary on the art-historical, chemical and mineralogical aspects of the text, of Abū'l-Qāsim's treatise.

RÖDER, Kurt, 'Zur Technik der persischen Fayence im 13. und 14. Jahrhundert', *ZDMG* LXXXIX, 1935 :225-42.

Attempts to equate the information in Abū'l-Qāsim's treatise with the evidence of the pottery of that period.

SCHULTZE-FRENTZEL, U, and H SALGE, 'Glazes and decorating colours of Persian Islamic ceramics examined by X-radiography, and transparent Seljuq glazes examined by electron-probe microanalysis', *Kunst des Orients* X(1/2), 1975 :80-90.

Describes some of the newly developed scientific techniques which have helped in deciding the authenticity of certain wares.

5. *METALWORK*

5.1 *General*

ALLAN, J W, *Persian metal technology*, *op.cit.* VII 9.

Contains much information on ores, metallurgy and techniques; based on extensive reading of primary sources. The only handy guide to this subject.

BARRETT, Douglas, *Islamic metalwork in the British Museum*, London 1949.

Very concise survey; excellently illustrated.

FEHÉRVÁRI, Geza, *Islamic metalwork of the eighth to the eighteenth century in the Keir Collection*, London 1976.

Publishes numerous hitherto unknown inscriptions and an extraordinarily wide range of objects. Some two-thirds of the 171 pieces in the collection are Iranian. All the objects are illustrated.

MAYER, L A, *Islamic metalworkers and their works*, Geneva 1959.

Still a unique compilation, with most useful bibliographies for each entry.

MELIKIAN-CHIRVANI, A S, *Le bronze iranien*, Paris 1973.

Presents some 56 pieces, almost entirely unpublished, drawn largely from the Musée des Arts Decoratifs, Paris. Excellent photographs, including many details, with useful introductions establishing the major schools. An indispensable handbook.

—— 'Les calligraphes et l'art du bronze', *Iran* (pub. by the *Institut National des Langues et Civilisations Orientales*), Paris 1972 :138-49.

—— 'Iranian metalwork and the written word', *Apollo* CIII, 1976 :286-91.

—— 'Les thèmes ésotériques et les thèmes mystiques dans l'art du bronze iranien', S H NASR (ed), *Mélanges offerts à Henry Corbin*, Tehran 1977 :376-406.

All three studies emphasize with full documentation the religious significance of many metalwork inscriptions.

SARRE, F, *Erzeugnisse Islamischer Kunst. Teil I. Metall*, Berlin 1906.

Reliable for its descriptions and treatment of epigraphy though not always for provenance.

SCERRATO, U, *Metalli Islamichi*, Milan 1966.

Illustrated entirely in colour; many of the pieces are in Italian collections and not widely known.

5.2 *Early Islamic*

DIAKONOV, M M, 'Bronzovaya plastinka pervikh vekov Khidzhry', *Trudy Otdela Vostoka* (Gosudarstvenniy Ermitazh) IV, 1947 :155-79.

DIMAND, M S, 'A review of "Sasanian and Islamic metalwork" in *A Survey of Persian Art*', *AI* VIII, 1941 :192-214.

See below, s.v. HARARI (5.3) and ORBELI (5.2).

HARPER, Prudence O, 'An eighth century silver plate from Iran with a mythological scene', *IAMMA* :153-68.

Uses a specific object to illustrate the problems of the 'transitional' metalwork identified variously as 'late Sasanian' or 'early Islamic'.

MARSHAK, B I, 'Bronzovoy kuvshin iz Samarkanda', *Srednei Aziya i Iran*, Leningrad 1972 :61-90.

—— *Sogdiskoe serebro*, Moscow 1971.

These two studies present much unfamiliar material in bronze and silver from the immediately pre-Islamic and early Islamic periods in Central Asia.

MELIKIAN-CHIRVANI, A S, 'The white bronzes of early Islamic Iran', *Metropolitan Museum of Art Journal* 9, 1974 :123-56.

Largely Khurāsānian material, which is now definitively located for the first time.

ORBELI, J A, 'Sasanian and early Islamic metalwork', *SPA* :716-70.

The first attempt to construct a serious chronology, typology and provenance for metalwork of this period. As such it has inevitable defects, many of them chronicled by DIMAND *op.cit.*

ROSEN-AYALON, Miriam, 'Four Iranian bracelets seen in the light of early Islamic art', *IAMMA* :169-86.

Very little Iranian mediaeval jewellery or gold metalwork survives. This article discusses some representative pieces and adduces a wealth of analogous material.

SAUVAGET, Jean, 'Remarques sur les monuments omeyyades. II: Argenteries "sassanides"', *JA* CCXXXII, 1940-41 :19-37.

Seeks by rigorous definition of appropriate criteria to prove that much 'Sasanian' metalwork is in fact early Islamic. Most of these arguments are now generally accepted.

5.3 *Saljūq*

AGA-OGLU, Mehmet, 'The use of architectural forms in Saljuq metalwork', *AQ* VI, 1943 :92-98.

Recent literary research has established the symbolic connotations of domical forms in metalwork, a theme only hesitantly advanced here.

ALLAN, J W, 'Silver: the key to bronze in early Islamic Iran', *KdO* XI(1/2), 1977 :5-21.

Discusses the effects of the 11th century 'silver famine' on Saljūq patronage and taste.

—— *Nishapur. Metalwork of the early Islamic period*, New York 1982.

Catalogues the material found in the excavations sponsored by the Metropolitan Museum of Art, New York. The range of types is much wider than in any other books on Iranian metalwork.

BAER, Eva, 'An Islamic inkwell in the Metropolitan Museum of Art', *IAMMA* :199-211.

—— 'A brass vessel from the tomb of Sayyid Baṭṭāl Ghāzī. Notes on the interpretation of thirteenth-century Islamic imagery', *Artibus Asiae* XXXIX(3-4), 1977 :299-335.

These two articles range far wider than the single object on which each ostensibly focuses; they offer a useful introduction to the varied iconography of mediaeval Iranian metalwork.

DIMAND, M S, 'Saljuk bronzes from Khurasan', *BMMA*, NS 4, 1945 :87-92.

A useful introduction to the material treated in much greater depth by MELIKIAN-CHIRVANI.

DIAKONOV, M M, 'Bronzoviy vodoley 1206g.', *Mémoires ... IIIe Congrès* :45-52.

Describes perhaps the outstanding aquamanile of mediaeval Iran.

ETTINGHAUSEN, Richard, 'The Bobrinski "Kettle": patron and style of an Islamic bronze', *GBA* XXIV, 1943 :193-208.

Perhaps the first sustained attempt to fix a piece of Iranian metalwork in its historical, social and iconographic context.

GIUZALIAN, L T, 'The bronze qalamdan (pen-case) 542/1148 from the Hermitage Collection (1936-1965)', *AO* VII, 1968 :95-119.

Contains much information on the technique of manufacture and the precise status of the maker (a merchant). The latter discussion embraces also pieces dated 578/1182 and 604/1206.

HARARI, R, 'Metalwork after the early Islamic period', *SPA* :2466-529.

Like ORBELI's contribution *op.cit.*, a pioneering study, now badly dated in places but still useful as the most detailed general survey currently available.

MARCHAL, Henri, 'L'art du bronze islamique d'Afghanistan', *La Revue du Louvre et des Musées de France* XXIV(1), 1974 :7-18.

A useful general survey; for more detailed studies see below, s.v. SCERRATO.

MELIKIAN-CHIRVANI, A S, 'The westward progress of Khurasanian culture under the Seljuks', *AIA* :110-25.

Argues for the eastern Iranian origin of much so-called 'Anatolian' metalwork.

—— 'Les bronzes du Khorâssân', *SI* 3, 1974 :29-50; 4, 1975 :51-71, 187-205; 5, 1976 :203-12; 6, 1977 :185-210; 8, 1979 :7-32.

These detailed studies have established beyond question what was earlier only suspected - that eastern Iran was the principal centre of mediaeval metalwork in Iran. The distinctive traits of that school - in material, technique, decorative themes, iconography, symbolism, and epigraphy - are painstakingly identified, and a host of hitherto unknown craftsmen's and patrons' names have been deciphered. A remarkable, single-handed achievement.

SCERRATO, Umberto, 'Ogetti metallici di età islamica in Afghanistan', *Annali dell'Istituto Universitario Orientale di Napoli*, NS IX, 1960 :95-130; XIV, 1964 :673-714; XXI, 1971 :455-66; XXII, 1972 :287-310.

Consists largely of material from Ghaznī, a good deal of it excavated. These articles bring central Afghanistan into sharper focus as an offshoot of the school of Khurāsān, though still firmly within its orbit.

5.4 *Mongol*

ATIL, E, 'Two Il-ḫanid candlesticks at the University of Michigan', *KdO* 8, 1972 :3-33.

Relates these objects to a school in Āzarbāyjān which drew inspiration for its iconography from manuscript paintings. Especially useful for its information on the Labours of the Months.

BAER, E, 'The Nisan Tasi: a study in Persian-Mongol metalware', *KdO* 9, 1973-74 :1-46.

Detailed study of a most unusual covered brass basin made for the Īlkhānid sultan Abū Saᶜīd, probably in Āzarbāyjān; the piece is especially notable for its animated friezes.

GIUZALIAN, L T, 'Tri indzhuidskikh bronzovykh sosuda. K voprosu o lokalizatsii yugo-zapadnoi gruppy srednevekovoi khudozhestvennoi bronzy Irana', *Trudy dvadtsat'pyatogo Mezhdunarodnogo Kongressa Vostokovedov. Moskva 9-16 Avgusta 1960*, II, Moscow 1963 :174-78.

Establishes the existence of an important provincial school at Shīrāz on the basis of signatures on three Īnjūyid brasses.

MELIKIAN-CHIRVANI, A S, 'Bassins iraniens du XIVe siècle au Musée des Beaux-Arts', *BMML* IV, 1969 :189-206.

—— 'Bronzes et cuivres iraniens du Louvre, I. L'école du Fars au XIVe siècle', *JA* CCLVII, 1969 :19-36.

Uses above all the evidence of titulature to define the characteristics of this local school in south-western Iran.

5.5 *Post-Mongol*

BAER, Eva, 'Traditionalism or archaism? Reflections on a 19th century bronze bucket', *Islam in the Balkans and Persian art and culture of the 18th and 19th centuries*, Royal Scottish Museum, Edinburgh 1979 :87-94.

Traces the survival of motifs from 12th century metalwork in the 19th century.

MELIKIAN-CHIRVANI, A S, 'Un plumier d'époque timouride au Musée des Beaux-Arts', *BMML* IV, 1969 :265-69.

Tīmūrid metalwork is surprisingly rare. This article is a useful introduction to a little-known period.

—— 'Safavid metalwork: a study in continuity', *IS* 7(iii-iv), 1974 :543-85.

The only monographic treatment of Ṣafavid metalwork yet to be published; particular emphasis is laid on distinctively Ṣafavid forms and on inscriptions.

SCERRATO, Umberto, 'Coppia di candelabri di Iṣfahān di epoca Qāǧār', *Muzeo Nationale d'Arte Orientale* 3, Arte Orientale in Italia II, Rome 1971 :27-48.

A detailed discussion including a valuable analysis of iconography.

5.6 *Arms and armour*

BOUDOT-LAMOTTE, A, *Contribution à l'étude del'archerie musulmane*, Damascus 1968.

ELGOOD, Robert (ed), *Islamic arms and armour*, London 1979.

Includes

ELWELL-SUTTON, Laurence P, 'Persian armour inscriptions' :5-19.

FLINDT, Torben W, 'Some nineteenth-century arms from Bukhara' :20-29.

GORELIK, Mikhail V, 'Oriental armour of the Near and Middle East from the eighth to fifteenth centuries as shown in works of art' :30-63.

IVANOV, Anatoliy, 'A group of Iranian daggers of the period from the fifteenth century to the beginning of the seventeenth, with Persian inscriptions' :64-77.

LATHAM, J Derek, and William F PATERSON, 'Archery in the lands of Eastern Islam' :78-87.

MELIKIAN-CHIRVANI, Assadullah Souren, 'Bucklers, covers or cymbals? A twelfth-century riddle from Eastern Iran' :98-111.

—— 'The tabarzins of Loṭfᶜalī' :116-35; cf 'Appendix' :240-41.

MILLER, Yuri A, 'Iranian swords of the seventeenth century with Russian inscriptions in the collection of the State Hermitage Museum' :136-48.

NICOLLE, David C, 'An introduction to arms and warfare in classical Islam' :163-86.

ŻYGULSKI, Jr, Zdzislaw, 'Islamic weapons in Polish collections and their provenance' :214-38.

GERMAN, Michael C, *A guide to Oriental daggers and swords*, London 1967.

Very lavishly illustrated survey.

GRANCSAY, Stephen V, 'The New Galleries of Oriental arms and armor', *Bulletin of the Metropolitan Museum of Art*, NS XVI, 1958 :241-56.

HUURI, Kalervo, *Zur Geschichte des mittelalterlichen Geschützwesens aus orientalischen Quellen*, *op.cit.* IX 8.1.

See especially pp.94-192.

JACOB, Alain, *Armes blanches de l'islam*, Paris 1975.

Fine range of colour plates.

KALUS, Ludvik, 'Boucliers circulaires de l'orient musulman (évolution et utilisation)', *Gladius* XII, 1974 :59-133.

KOHZAD, Ahmad ᶜAlī, 'Uniformes et armes des gardes des sultans de Ghazna', *Afghanistan* VI, 1951 :48-53.

LAKING, Guy Francis, *The Wallace Collection. Catalogue: Oriental Arms and Armour*, London 1914.

LATHAM, J Derek, 'The archers of the Middle East: the Turco-Iranian background', *Iran* VIII, 1970 :97-103.

LAUFER, Berthold, *Chinese clay figures. Part I. Prolegomena on the history of defensive armor*, Field Museum of Natural History, Publication 177, Anthropological Series XIII, no.2, Chicago 1914.

MAYER, Leo Ary, *Islamic armourers and their works*, Geneva 1962.

McEWEN, E, 'Persian archery texts:' *op.cit.* IX 8.2.

MELIKIAN-CHIRVANI, A S, 'Four pieces of Islamic metalwork: some notes on a previously unknown school', *AARP* 10, 1976 :24-30.

NICOLLE, David C, *Early medieval Islamic arms and armour*, Madrid 1976.

Contains much Persian material drawn from visual and literary sources; especially valuable for its 151 explanatory drawings.

POTIER, Otmar Baron, 'Waffengeschichtliches aus dem Wiener Jagdteppich', *Zeitschrift für historische Waffen- und Kostümkunde* IX, 1921 :4-10.

ROBINSON, H Russell, *Oriental Armour*, London 1967.

SCHÖBEL, Johannes, *Türkenschatz*, Leipzig 1974.

Despite the title, much Persian material.

STÖCKLEIN, Hans, 'Arms and armour', *SPA* III :2555-85.

STONE, George C, *A glossary of the construction, decoration and use of arms and armor in all countries and in all times, together with some closely related subjects*, Portland, Maine 1934.

Especially useful for its 875 illustrations.

TUSHINGHAM, A D, 'Persian enamels', Muhammad Y KIANI and Akbar TAJVIDI (eds), *The Memorial Volume of the Vth International Congress of Iranian Art & Archaeology. Tehran-Isfahan-Shiraz 11th-18th April 1968*, II, Tehran 1972 :211-22.

VIANELLO, G, *Armi e armature orientali*, Milan 1966.

ZAKI, ᶜAbd al-Raḥmān, 'Islamic swords in Middle Ages', *Bulletin de l'Institut d'Égypte* XXXVI, 1955 :365-79.

Discusses *inter alia* the evolution of the curved form, based on evidence from Persian miniatures.

ZELLER, Rudolf, and Ernst ROHRER, *Orientalische Sammlung Henri Moser-Charlottenfels. Beschreibender Katalog der Waffensammlung*, Bern 1955.

6. *CALLIGRAPHY*

The Islamic calligraphic arts developed throughout the Islamic world as an extension of painting, book-making, architecture, and many other arts, and, even more than in the case of the other arts, it is difficult to draw a line between what is strictly Iranian and what is more generally Islamic. The following bibliography therefore includes a number of works that are not directly connected with Iran, but which help to illuminate Iranian techniques in the field of calligraphy. In this chapter, too, we are concerned primarily with calligraphy as an art; for works concerned with the reading and decipherment of manuscripts, documents and letters, see IX 2.3.

6.1 *General works and bibliographies*

AZIZA, Mohamed, *La calligraphie arabe*, Tunis 1973.

In spite of the title, the book surveys the whole field of Islamic calligraphy, with numerous specimens.

KHATIBI, Abdelkebir, and Mohammed SIJELMASI, *The Splendour of Islamic Calligraphy*, New York 1975.

KÜHNEL, Ernst, *Islamische Schriftkunst*, Berlin 1942, repr. Graz 1972.

LINGS, Martin, *The Quranic art of calligraphy and illumination*, World of Islam Festival Series, London 1976.

SCHIMMEL, Annemarie, *Islamic Calligraphy*, Iconography of Religions, Section XXII, Islam: fasc.1, Leiden 1970.

ṬĪBĪ, Muḥammad ibn Ḥasan al-, *Jāmiᶜ maḥāsin kitābat al-kitāb*, Ṣalāḥ al-dīn al-MUNAJJID (ed), Beirut 1962.

Facsimile edition of a 10th/16th century study of the method of Ibn al-Bawwāb (4th/10th century).

WELCH, A, *Calligraphy in the arts of the Muslim world*, Austin, Texas 1979.

ZAKARIYA, Mohamed U, *The calligraphy of Islam: reflections on the state of the art*, Georgetown University 1979.

A brief study of Islamic calligraphy, with comparative specimens of forty different calligraphic styles, ancient and modern.

6.2 *History and biography*

BAYĀNĪ, Mahdi, *Aḥvāl va āsār-i khwushnavīsān*, 3 vols, Tehran 1966-69.

—— *Aḥvāl va āsār-i Mīr ʿImād*, Anjuman-i Dūstdārān-i Kitāb, Tehran 1951.

Lecture delivered at the opening of an exhibition of Mīr ʿImād's work.

HUART, Clément, *Les calligraphes et les miniaturistes de l'orient musulman*, Paris 1908, repr. Osnabrück 1972.

HUMĀYŪNFARRUKH, Rukn al-dīn, *Sahm-i Īrāniyān dar paidāyish va āfarīnish-i khaṭṭ dar jahān*, Tehran 1971.

ĪRĀNĪ, Ḥājī Mīrzā ʿAbd al-muḥammad Khān, *Kitāb-i paidāyish-i khaṭṭ va khaṭṭāṭān*, Cairo 1926-27.

KAZI-AKHMED (Qāżī Aḥmad), *op.cit.* 2.

6.3 *Specimens of fine calligraphy*

BAYĀNĪ, Mahdī, *Fihrist-i namūna-yi khuṭūṭ-i khwush-i Kitābkhāna-yi Shāhanshāhī-yi Īrān*, *op.cit.* III 3.2.1.

Specimens of fine calligraphy from the Imperial Library of Iran with descriptions.

Chand rubāʿī az Khayyām bi-khaṭṭ-i Mīr, Anjuman-i Dūstdārān-i Kitāb, Tehran 1952.

FAŻĀ'ILĪ, Ḥabīballāh, *Aṭlas-i Khaṭṭ*, Iṣfahān 1971.

A history of calligraphy with lavish specimens. The book itself is calligraphed in *nastaʿlīq*.

GHULAM, Yousif, *Introduction to the art of Arabic calligraphy*, Shīraz 1970.

The book has been very carelessly produced, with pages out of order, illustrations misplaced, etc. But it is useful for the specimens and transcriptions of varieties of Kufic script.

HASAN, Khan Sahib Maulvi Zafar, *Specimens of calligraphy in the Delhi Museum of Archaeology*, Memoirs of the Archaeological Survey of India, no.29, Calcutta 1926.

KHAṬṬĀṬ, Hāshim Muḥammad al-, *Qawāʿid al-khaṭṭ al-ʿarabī*, Baghdad 1961.

Rules for the writing of the main calligraphic styles.

Namūna'ī chand az khuṭūṭ-i khwushnavīsān, Anjuman-i Dūstdārān-i Kitāb, Tehran n.d.

Namāyishgāh-i khaṭṭ, Iranian Calligraphers' Assoc., London 1976.

Catalogue of an exhibition.

Obraztsy kalligrafii Irana i Srednei Azii XV-XIV vv, Moscow 1963.

Forty-five specimens from the Saltykov-Shchedrin Library in Leningrad.

ZAIN AL-DĪN, Nājī, *Muṣawwar al-khaṭṭ al-ʿarabī*, Baghdad 1968.

—— *Badā'iʿ al-khaṭṭ al-ʿarabī*, Baghdad 1972.

Two lavishly illustrated atlases of Islamic calligraphy.

7. *CARPETS, TEXTILES AND COSTUME*

Introductory remarks

At a cursory glance the literature available on these subjects seems extensive, but a more critical examination reveals that comparatively little of it can be recommended with confidence. Carpets well illustrate the nature of the problem. The carpets of Persia, and indeed of all the Islamic lands, are not only of cultural importance; they are also extremely popular and desirable collectors' pieces. Consequently a large proportion of the literature published caters to the interest of the collector and the commercial market. While some of this literature - particularly the detailed sale catalogues - is useful, much consists of glossy illustrated books which have little to offer as far as their texts are concerned. The serious student, therefore, is best directed towards the classic works of the pioneer, mainly German, scholars - LESSING, VON BODE, ERDMANN, KÜHNEL, MARTIN, RIEGL and SARRE - which still form the basis of the subject. The works in English chosen here include the more reliable studies of classical carpets and relatively new works on tribal rugs which employ the methods of ethnographical fieldwork. Persian textiles have received less concentrated attention than carpets but here too some of the same problems arise, if in a less acute form. Recommended works fall between pioneer studies which are still the standard reference material and more specialist technical reports. The iconography of this material remains an unaccountably neglected field. Finally, the subject of costume has received almost no serious attention and the rich source material provided by miniature paintings, literature, surviving examples of garments and direct field observation still remains for the most part untapped.

7.1 *General*

AGA-OGLU, Mehmet, *Safavid rugs and textiles*, New York 1941.

The only monographic treatment of the Ṣafavid material in these fields.

SPUHLER, Friedrich, *Islamic carpets and textiles in the Keir Collection*, London 1978.

Thorough account of one of the best private collections of this material. See especially pp.80-118 on Persian carpets.

7.2 *Textiles*

ANAVIAN, Rahim and George, *Royal Persian and Kashmir brocades*, Kyoto 1975.

Sumptuously produced volume with excellent illustrations.

BUNT, Cyril G E, *Persian fabrics*, Leigh-on-Sea 1963.

Illustrates a wide range of principally Ṣafavid textiles.

FALKE, Otto von, *Kunstgeschichte der Seidenweberei*, Berlin 1913. Abbr. English version, *Decorative silks*, New York 1922.

Parts of sections VI-VIII cover the Iranian world, always in the wider context of the western and Far Eastern traditions; the text is still largely relevant and the range of illustrations unsurpassed. The English edition retains most the the plates.

GEIJER, Agnes, *Oriental textiles in Sweden*, Copenhagen 1951.

Discussion of Persian textiles and costumes including those presented to Queen Christina in 1644.

HAYWARD GALLERY, *The arts of Islam*, London 1976.

Textiles: pp.65-118; includes a selection of fine quality Persian textiles, all described in detail and illustrated.

HOFENK DE GRAAF, Judith, Mechtild LEMBERG, Gabriel VIAL, various articles, *Bulletin de Liaison du Centre International d'Étude des Textiles Anciens*, nos.37, 1973 I; 38, 1973 II; 39-40, 1974 I-II; 43-44, 1976 I-II.

Group of studies concerning the authenticity of Būyid silks.

KÜHNEL, Ernst, '"Stoffe" in *A Survey of Persian Art*, Rezension', *AI* VII, 1940 :109-20.

Especially useful for Ṣafavid textiles.

LOMBARD, Maurice, *Études d'economie médiévale III. Les textiles dans le monde mussulman du VIIe au XIIe siècle*, Paris 1978.

Excellent study of mediaeval textile production and commerce.

MARTIN, Fredrik R, *Die Persischen Prachtstoffe im Schlosse Rosenborg in Kopenhagen*, Leipzig 1901.

Study of a group of Persian velvets presented to the Duke of Holstein by the Persian embassy of 1639.

MURDOCH SMITH, Robert, *Persian art*, London 1876, 3rd ed. 1895.

Textile fabrics: pp.45-51; needlework, embroidery and block printing: pp. 51-58. Still the standard text on the subject.

POPE, Arthur Upham, *et al.*, *Woven treasures of Persian art*, Los Angeles 1959.

Well-illustrated catalogue of an exhibition of 153 items of which about one-third are pre-Ṣafavid.

REATH, Nancy A, and Eleanor B SACHS, *Persian textiles and their technique from the sixth to the eighteenth centuries, including a system for general textile classification*, New Haven 1937.

A handy conspectus of the field.

SERJEANT, Robert B, *Islamic textiles*, Beirut 1972.

An invaluable and uniquely detailed compilation of the literary evidence bearing on the production of mediaeval Islamic textiles. Previously published in article form in *Ars Islamica* IX-XVI, 1942-48, without the index.

SHEPHERD, Dorothy G, 'Technical aspects of the Buyid silks', *SPA* :3090-99.

Discussion of a controversial group of early Persian textiles.

—— 'The authenticity of the Rayy silks', *Bulletin de Liaison du Centre International d'Etude des Textiles Anciens* 39-40, 1974.

Summarizes much of the information previously published in her articles in the *Bulletin of the Cleveland Museum of Art*; this is the most complete defence of the authenticity of these silks so far published.

—— and Walter B HENNING, 'Zandanījī identified?', Richard ETTINGHAUSEN (ed), *Aus der Welt der islamischen Kunst*, Festschrift für Ernst Kühnel zum 75 Geburtstag am 26.10.1957, Berlin 1959 :15-40.

A classic piece of detective work identifying a Central Asian silk type hitherto known only from texts.

WIET, Gaston, *Soieries persanes*, Cairo 1947.

Detailed publication of a group of apparently Būyid textiles from Rayy, with full historical and epigraphical notes.

7.3 *Carpets*

BEATTIE, May H, *Carpets of Central Persia*, London 1976.

Despite the catalogue format, this is a model monographic treatment of a specific group of carpets; it contains much valuable technical information.

SYLVESTER, David, and Joseph McMULLAN, *Islamic carpets from the collection of Joseph V McMullan*, Hayward Gallery, London 1972.

Exhibition catalogue with excellent entries on the history and development of carpet studies and the making of carpets.

BODE, Wilhelm von, and Ernst KÜHNEL, *Vorderasiatische Knüpfteppiche aus älterer Zeit*, Brunswick 1955, 4th ed. English tr. Charles G ELLIS, *Antique rugs from the Near East*, London 1970.

Still the unchallenged classic in the field; particularly useful for its analysis of rugs depicted in European paintings.

DIMAND, Maurice S, and Jean MAILEY, *Oriental rugs in the Metropolitan Museum of Art*, New York 1973.

The definitive catalogue of one of the world's great collections. Chapter 5, pp.27-116: catalogue entries and discussion of Persian carpets.

EDWARDS, A C, *The Persian carpet: a survey of the carpet-weaving industry of Persia*, London 1953.

The fruit of a lifetime's experience in the carpet industry, much of it spent in Iran itself. Many of the observations on technique are relevant for antique carpets. Arranged according to geographical areas, with useful notes on common designs and their variants.

ERDMANN, Kurt, *Der orientalische Knüpfteppich: Versuch einer Darstellung seiner Geschichte*, Tübingen 1955. English tr. Charles G ELLIS, *Oriental carpets - an account of their history*, London 1962.

Of central importance for the study of the antique carpet.

—— *Siebenhundert Jahre Orientteppiche. Zu seiner Geschichte und Erforschung*, Herford 1955. English tr. Hanna ERDMANN (ed), May H BEATTIE and H HERZOG, *Seven hundred years of oriental carpets*, London 1970.

Collects some forty-two of ERDMANN's articles on carpets; valuable for material on the history of carpet studies, on the major public collections, on dated carpets, on Turkish carpets and on carpets depicted in western and oriental paintings.

—— '"The art of carpet making" in *A Survey of Persian Art*', *AI* VII, 1940 121-91.

Absolutely indispensable to the use of POPE's text in the *Survey*.

ETTINGHAUSEN, Richard, 'Ḳālī', *EI*, *Suppl*., 1938 :106-11.

The most convenient short history of oriental rugs available.

—— 'New light on early animal carpets', Richard ETTINGHAUSEN (ed), *Aus der Welt der islamischen Kunst*, *op.cit*. 7.2, :93-116.

Collates evidence from paintings with a Konya carpet of c.1450-1550, and shows the relationship of this material to Mamlūk embroideries.

—— 'The Boston Hunting Carpet in historical perspective', *Boston Museum Bulletin* LXIX, 1971 :70-81.

Traces the history of the iconography of this genre.

——, Maurice S DIMAND, and Louise W MACKIE, *Prayer rugs*, Washington 1974.

The first major publication on this subject; sections on history, iconography and major areas of production are supplemented by an exhaustive catalogue.

GROTE-HASENBALG, Werner, *Der Orientteppich: seine Geschichte und seine Kultur*, Berlin 1922.

Still a useful general work covering the whole range of antique and modern rugs.

KENDRICK, Albert F, and Creassey E C TATTERSALL, *Hand-woven carpets. Oriental and European*, London 1922, repr. Dover 1973.

Persian carpets are given a separate chapter; excellent chapters on technique (including materials, colours and shapes) and on design.

LESSING, Julius, *Altorientalischer Teppichmuster nach Bildern und Originalen des XV und XVI Jahrhunderts*, Berlin 1877. English tr. London 1879.

The earliest attempt to classify carpet designs.

—— *Orientalische Teppiche*, Berlin 1891.

A continuation of his work of 1877.

McMULLAN, Joseph, *Islamic carpets*, New York 1965.

Section on Persian rugs: pp.47-156.

MARTIN, Fredrik R, *A history of Oriental carpets before 1800*, Vienna 1908.

A pioneer study and historical survey.

POPE, Arthur U, 'The art of carpet making. History', *SPA* III :2257-430.

This was the first really detailed account of antique Persian rugs which drew on extensive practical field experience of modern rugs in Iran itself. Despite the many faults necessarily attendant on such a pioneering effort, and the many over-confident attributions, this is still a text basic to an understanding of the subject.

RIEGL, Alois, *Altorientalische Teppiche*, Leipzig 1891.

The first attempt to produce an overall historical survey.

RUDENKO, Sergei I, *Kultura naseleniya gornogo Altaya v skifskoe vremya*, Moscow/Leningrad 1953. English tr. M W THOMPSON, *Frozen tombs of Siberia. The Pazyryk burials of Iron Age horsemen*, London 1970.

The most easily accessible discussion of the earliest surviving carpet.

SARRE, Friedrich, and Hermann TRENKWALD, *Old Oriental carpets*, tr. A F KENDRICK, Vienna/Leipzig 1926 and 1929.

Still a largely reliable guide, magnificently illustrated. The original German texts on which this translation was based are *Orientalische Teppiche*, 1892, and *Altorientalische Teppiche*, 1908. The colour plates have been separately published in paperback form by Dover Editions, New York 1979.

STEAD, Rexford, *The Ardabil carpets*, Los Angeles 1974.

Discussion of the second Ardabīl carpet now in the Los Angeles County Museum. The first, one of the most famous Persian carpets of the Ṣafavid period, is in the Victoria and Albert Museum, London.

7.4 *Tribal rugs*

ALLGROVE, Joan, *et al.*, *The Qashqa'i of Iran*, Whitworth Art Gallery, Manchester 1976.

Exhibition catalogue which sets Qas͟hqā'i rugs, costume and textiles firmly in the context of the tribal environment. It illustrates the keen interest which tribal material is currently evoking. Similar but less detailed work has been done on Turcoman textiles and rugs.

BLACK, David, and Clive LOVELESS (eds), *Rugs of the wandering Baluch*, London 1976.

Catalogue of an exhibition devoted to a specific group of tribal rugs.

—— *Woven gardens. Nomad and village rugs of the Fars province of southern Persia*, London 1979.

Discussion of designs, techniques, dyes and types of rug based on a group of exhibited pieces.

—— *The undiscovered kilim*, London 1978.

One of the few serious books devoted to this subject.

DIMAND, Maurice S, *Peasant and nomad rugs of Asia*, New York 1961.

Indispensable general guide.

FRANCHIS, Amadeo de, and Jenny HOUSEGO, *Tribal animal covers from Iran*, Rug Society, Tehran 1975.

Thirty-two pieces are described with the aim of presenting tribal weaving to a wider public.

—— and John WERTIME, *Lor and Bakhtiyari flatweaves*, Rug Society, Tehran 1976.

Pioneer study devoted to identifying and describing two distinctive groups of tribal weaving.

HOUSEGO, Jenny, *Tribal rugs. An introduction to the weaving of the tribes of Iran*, London 1978.

Clearly presented general account of the main groups of tribal weaving. The plentiful illustrations include rugs, textiles and also studies of the peoples who wove and used them.

MACKIE, Louise, and John THOMPSON (eds), *Turkmen tribal carpets and traditions*, The Textile Museum, Washington 1980.

Detailed and up-to-date study with valuable chapters on the historical and social background based on an exhibition of ninety-five carpets.

PETSOPOULOS, Yanni, *Kilims: the art of tapestry weaving in Anatolia, the Caucasus and Persia*, London 1979.

The first comprehensive account yet published on the subject.

7.5 *Techniques*

ACKERMAN, Phyllis, 'Persian weaving techniques. A History', *SPA* III :2175-220.

Still the most detailed account available.

—— 'Textiles of the Islamic periods. A. History', *SPA* III :1995-2162.

A very full history laying much stress on technique and iconography.

ALVAND, Aḥmad, *Sanᶜat-i nassājī dar Īrān*, Tehran n.d.

COLLINGWOOD, Peter, *The techniques of rug weaving*, London 1968.

Comprehensive and thorough treatment of the subject by a first-class craftsman.

EMERY, Irene, *The primary structure of fabrics, an illustrated classification*, The Textile Museum, Washington 1966. Rev.ed. 1980.

Standard treatment of the subject.

JACOBY, Heinrich, 'Materials used in the making of carpets', *SPA* III :2456-65.

POPE, Arthur U, 'The technique of Persian carpet weaving', *SPA* III :2431-36.

TATTERSALL, Creassey E C, *Notes on carpet knotting and weaving*, Victoria and Albert Museum, London 1927, 2nd ed. 1969.

Useful though incomplete summary of technical information.

WULFF, Hans E, *The traditional crafts of Persia*, *op.cit.* VII 9, :172-239.

Detailed accounts with local vocabulary of crafts of spinning, dyeing, weaving, embroidery and block printing.

7.6 *Costume*

ALLGROVE, Joan, *The Qashqa'i of Iran*, *op.cit.* 7.4.

Includes detailed account of costume.

ANDREWS, Peter and Mügül, *et al.*, *The Turcoman of Iran*, Abbot Hall Art Gallery, Kendal 1971.

Study of costume and jewellery set within their material environment.

—— *Türkmen needlework. Dressmaking and embroidery among the Türkmen of Iran*, Central Asian Research Centre, London 1976.

Excellent well-researched study.

DOZY, Reinhart P A, *Dictionnaire détaillé des noms des vêtements chez les Arabes*, Amsterdam 1845.

This work has not yet been surpassed as the most accurate and comprehensive treatment of the subject.

FALK, S J, *Qajar paintings*, *op.cit.* XII 2.

Persian paintings of this type and period are excellent sources for costume detail. This volume has copious and excellent colour illustrations.

FIROUZ, Iran Ala, *Silver ornaments of the Turkoman*, Tehran 1978.

Detailed study based on original fieldwork of the types, function and techniques of women's jewellery of the Yomut, Tekke and Göklen Türkmen. Lavishly illustrated.

GOETZ, Hermann, 'The history of Persian costume', *SPA* III :2227-56.

Attempts to provide a comprehensive historical synthesis.

SCARCE, Jennifer M, 'The development of women's veils in Persia and Afghanistan', *Costume, the Journal of the Costume Society*, no.9, London 1975 :4-14.

Historical and typological analysis of veiling traditions.

—— 'A Persian brassiere', *AARP* no.7 :15-21.

Detailed study of Persian female underwear.

—— *Middle Eastern costume from the tribes and cities of Iran and Turkey*, Royal Scottish Museum, Edinburgh 1981.

A short meaty text incorporating much local vocabulary is set off by early photographs and engravings and by excellent colour photographs of life-size models.

TILKE, Max, *Oriental costumes, their designs and colours*, London 1922.

Useful general survey.

—— *Costume patterns and designs*, New York 1956.

A survey of costume patterns and designs of all periods and nations from antiquity to modern times. Useful outline of basic principles of costume cut and construction.

ŻIYĀPŪR, Jalīl, *Pūshāk-i bāstānī-yi Īrāniyān*, Tehran 1964.

Persian costume from the earliest times up to the Sāsānian period.

—— *Pūshāk-i īlhā*, Tehran 1967.

Tribal costumes.

See also VIII 4. The following travel accounts have detailed descriptions of costume:

15th century

GONZALES DE CLAVIJO, Ruy.

17th century

CHARDIN, Sir John.

19th-20th centuries

BINNING, Robert B M; BISHOP, Isabella Bird; D'ALLEMAGNE, Henri R; FRASER, James Baillie; LAYARD, Austen H; PORTER, Sir Robert Ker; RICH, Claudius; ROSEN, Countess Maud von; SHEIL, Lady; SYKES, Ella; and WILLS, Charles J.

XIII

PERFORMING ARTS

1. *MUSIC*

The kind of Persian music best known to connoisseurs of Persian culture is the set of twelve modal suites (*dastgâh*), which derive ultimately from the Persian-Arab music of the mediaeval period. Often described as the art, or 'classical', music of Iran, this refined and meditative music is of interest to only a minority of Iranians. Religious, regional and popular musics play a more significant role in modern Iranian society.

1.1 *Introductory works*

CARON, N, and D SAFVATE (D SAFVAT), *Iran. Les Traditions Musicales*, Paris 1966.

As yet, perhaps the best general work on the subject. Besides the art music system, deals with other kinds of music, with music history, and the role of traditional music in modern Iran.

FARHAT, H, *The Traditional Art Music of Iran*, Tehran 1973.

This brief work outlines the principal characteristics of the art music system.

ZONIS, E, *Classical Persian music: an introduction*, Cambridge, Mass. 1973.

Covers much the same ground as N CARON and D SAFVATE, *op.cit.*, 1966, but less wide-ranging.

These three works include descriptions and illustrations of Persian musical instruments.

1.2 *Bibliographies*

A comprehensive bibliography of Persian music has yet to be published. M T MASSOUDIEH, (M T MAS^{c}ŪDĪYA), 'Die Musikforschung in Iran. Eine bibliographische Übersicht', *Acta Musicologica*, 1976, pp.12-20, is one important bibliographical essay. A second part, reviewing the most recent literature, is to be published by M T MASSOUDIEH, in *Acta Musicologica* in the near future.

An extensive bibliography of Persian music is given by E ZONIS, *op.cit.* 1.1. Critical comments on this bibliography are included in a review by G TSUGE, *Asian Music*, 1974, volume 2, pp.51-60. (B NETTL gave the book a more favourable review in *Ethnomusicology*, 1974, pp.323-24.)

Another useful bibliographical source for the mediaeval period is O WRIGHT, *The modal system of Arab and Persian music A.D. 1250-1300*, Oxford 1978.

J JENKINS, and P R OLSEN, *Music and musical instruments in the world of Islam*, London 1976, give an extensive bibliography for Islamic music which includes many works on Persian music.

ERDMANN, Kurt, 'Bibliography on history, theory and character of Persian music', POPE, *SPA*, *op.cit.* XII 1, vol.XVI, cols 617-40.

MASHĀYIKHĪ, Vīdā, *Kitābshināsī-yi mūsīqī*, Tehran 1976.

1.3 *History of Persian music*

It is sometimes suggested that there is a relationship between contemporary Persian music and the music of ancient Greece (see, for example, E ZONIS, *op.cit.* 1.1, pp.29-30). Such assertions must, for several reasons, be treated with extreme caution; nevertheless, it is clear that Greek and Persian musical systems shared certain elements in ancient times.

A summary of Persian music history is given by H G FARMER, 'An outline history of music and musical theory', in *SPA* III, pp.2783-804. A more condensed statement of FARMER's views is given in the entry for 'Persian Music' in *Grove's dictionary of music and musicians*, 5th edition, London 1954. P ACKERMAN, 'The character of Persian music', in POPE, *SPA*, *op.cit.* XII 1, volume III, pp.2805-17, discusses the role of music in Persian society from ancient to modern times.

Information about music in the Parthian and Sassanian periods is given in the following articles:

BOYCE, M, 'The Parthian *Gōsān* and Iranian minstrel tradition', *JRAS*, 1/2, 1957 :10-45.

BROWNE, E G, 'Bārbad and Rūdagī, the minstrels of the houses of Sāsān and Sāmān', *JRAS*, 1899 :54-69.

CHRISTENSEN, A, 'La vie musicale dans la civilisation des Sassanides', *Bulletin de l'Association Français des Amis de l'Orient* 20/21, 1936.

D'ERLANGER, Rodolphe, *La musique arabe*, 6 vols, Paris 1930-59.

Contains the French translation of al-FĀRĀBĪ's *Kitāb al-mūsīqī al-kabīr*, AVICENNA's *Kitāb al-shifā* (section on music), and two treatises by Ṣafī al-dīn URMAVĪ.

The exact nature of the reciprocal influences between Arab and Persian musics in the Islamic period is still a matter for debate. It is clear that by the 13th century AD a system of musical modes had developed that was common to both Arab and Persian cultures. This 'Systematist School' is considered in detail by O WRIGHT, *op.cit.*, 1978.

The modern period is covered best by Persian authors.

KHĀLIQĪ, R, *Sarguzasht-i mūsīqī-yi Īrān*, vol.I, Tehran 1954; vol.II, Tehran 1955.

Volume I describes the lives and contributions of Persian musicians in the second half of the 19th century, with brief introductory chapters on the history of music prior to the 19th century. Volume II deals with the life and works of the musician VAZĪRĪ.

—— *Mūsīqī-yi Īrān*, Tehran 1963.

Describes more recent developments in the 20th century.

MASSOUDIEH, M T, (MAS^cŪDĪYA, M T), 'Tradition und Wandel in der persischen Musik des 19. Jahrhunderts', R GÜNTHER (ed), *Musikkulturen Asiens, Afrikas und Ozeaniens im 19. Jahrhunderts*, Regensburg 1973 :73-94.

Discusses various genres of Persian music found in the 19th century.

1.4 *Dastgāh system of art music*

The art music system consists of twelve modal suites (*dastgāh*). Each *dastgāh* consists of a number of separate modes (*gūsha*, pl. *gūsha-hā*), only some of which are utilized in a single performance of the *dastgāh*. Transitions from one mode to another in the course of the performance of a *dastgāh* involve various kinds of modulation. Each mode consists of a set of intervals with certain tonal functions and constitutes a 'melody model' upon which improvisation is based. The twelve *dastgāh-hā* and their constituent *gūsha-hā* collectively constitute the *radīf*, the repertory of Persian art music. The *radīf* has been described and transcribed in western staff notation in a number of publications.

FARHAT, H, *The Dastgāh concept in Persian music*, Ph.D. diss., Los Angeles 1965.

Detailed analysis of the modes of the *radīf* and their essential melodic characteristics; types of modulation; transcriptions of performances in each mode.

GERSON-KIWI, E, *The Persian doctrine of Dastga-composition*, Tel-Aviv 1963.

Discussion of the *dastgāh* principle, with analysis of two *dastgāh-hā*, *Shūr* and *Abū-^cAtā*.

HIDĀYAT, Mahdī Qolī, *Majma^c al advār*, Tehran 1938.

Description of the *radīf* according to the 19th century traditions, with musical notations to illustrate a number of pieces.

KHĀLIQĪ, R, *Naẓarī bi mūsīqī*, Tehran 1937.

Exposition of the theory of Persian music propounded by VAZĪRĪ (see below) with fragmentary notations of selected *gūsha-hā*.

KHATSCHI, K (KHAṬCHĪ, K), *Der Dastgâh; Studien zur neuen persischen Musik*, Regensburg 1962.

Contains a brief analytical study of the twelve *dastgāh-hā*.

MA'AROUFI, M, and M BARKECHLI, (MAᶜRŪFĪ, M and M BARKISHLĪ) *Radīf-i mūsīqī-yi Īrān* (also titled *La musique traditionelle de l'Iran*), Tehran 1963.

This important work contains a full transcription of the *radīf* as played and notated by MAᶜRŪFĪ on the *tār* (long necked double chested lute), with explanatory text in Persian and French by BARKISHLĪ. This version of the *radīf* is in the tradition established by Mīrzā ᶜABDALLĀH.

MASSOUDIEH, M T (MASᶜŪDĪYA, M T), *Le Radif vocal par Ostād Mahmud Karimi*, Tehran 1977.

Transcriptions of the *radīf* according to the singer Maḥmūd Karīmī.

VAZĪRĪ, A N, *Mūsīqī-yi naẓarī*, Tehran 1934.

An expanded exposé of the theories of Persian music that first appeared in his *Dastūr-i Tār* (see section 1.9 below), with musical notations for analytical purposes.

1.5 *Technical aspects of performance*

Besides the works cited in section 1.4 above various matters pertaining to the performance of art music are discussed in greater detail in the following.

KHĀLIQĪ, R, 'Mudūlāsiyūn dar mūsīqī-yi Īrānī', *Majalla-yi mūsīqī*, Tehran 1961.

Discusses the important principle of modulation from one mode to another.

MASSOUDIEH, M T (MASᶜŪDĪA, M T), *Āwāz-e-Šūr, zur Melodiebildung in der persischen Kunstmusik*, Regensburg 1968.

Detailed analysis of *Dastgāh-yi Shūr*.

NETTL, B, 'Notes on Persian classical music of today. The performance of the Hesār section as part (Gusheh) of Dastgāh Chahārgāh', *Orbis Musicae* 1972 :175-92.

Considers the musical function of one *gūsha* in the context of the *dastgāh* as a whole.

—— 'Aspects of form in the instrumental performance of the Persian Âvâz',

Ethnomusicology, 1974 :405-14.

Examination of the *dastgāh* as a highly sophisticated musical form analogous in some ways to the sonata allegro.

—— and B FOLTIN, *Daramad of Chahargah: a study in the performance practice of Persian music*, Detroit 1972.

Comparative analysis of forty-three performances of a single mode in an attempt to isolate certain principles of improvisation in Persian music.

TSUGE, G, 'Rhythmic aspects of the *Âvâz* in Persian music', *Ethnomusicology*, 1970 :205-27.

Argues that the rhythmic organization of the unmetred *āvāz* style of singing is based on the poetic metres of the *ᶜarūẓ* system.

ZONIS, E, *op.cit.* 1.1.

Chapters four and five deal with improvisation, rhythm and form.

1.6 *Religious and ceremonial musics*

Religious music in Iran includes various types of *qarā'at* (reading, recitation or singing of the Holy *Qur'ān*) and other forms of religious singing. Most characteristic of Persian culture are those associated with *Muḥarram*, the month of mourning: (1) *Nauḥa*, chants sung by groups of men walking in processions while beating their chests, commonly performed during the first ten days of *Muḥarram*; (2) *Rauża*, addresses, partially sung, by *mullās*, dealing with the martyrdom of the Saints; (3) *Taᶜzīya*, dramatic re-enactment of the martyrdom of the Saints, when the protagonists sing and the antagonists speak - see 3 below. Ṣūfī ritual also uses types of music. Ceremonial music consists of the singing with *dumbak* (large goblet drum) accompaniment for the *Zūr-khāna*; another type of ceremonial music now virtually abandoned was played by the large ensemble known as *Naqqāra-khāna*.

Rather little has been written about religious and ceremonial musics. N CARON and D SAFVATE, *op.cit.* 1.1, chapter 15, give some information. Several relevant entries are given in

Encyclopédie des musiques sacrées, vol.I, J PORTE (ed), Paris 1968:

BOUBAKEUR, S H, 'Psalmodie coranique' :338-403.

While not concerned specifically with Persian practice gives an important exposition of the principles of Qur'ānic recitation.

CARON, N, 'La musique shiite en Iran' :430-40.

Various types of religious music, especially those involved in *Taᶜzīya*.

MAUGUIN, B, 'L'appel à la prière dans l'Islam' :404-08.

Not specifically concerned with Persian practice.

MOKRI, M (MUKRI, M), 'La musique sacrée des Kurdes "Fidèles de vérité", en Iran' :442-53.

Use of music and musical instruments by *Ahl-i Ḥaqq* sect.

Persian art music also has its spiritual aspect, a matter discussed in these two papers:

DURING, J, 'Éléments spirituels dans la musique traditionelle iranienne contemporaire', *Sophia Perennis*, 1975 :129-54.

NASR, S H, 'The influence of Sufism on traditional Persian music', *Studies in comparative religion*, 1972 :225-34.

1.7 *Regional and popular musics*

Only a few of the many varieties of regional music, many of them associated with ethnic minorities, have been covered by researchers, while popular music has received very little attention.

BLUM, S, 'Persian folksong in Meshed (Iran), 1969', *Yearbook of the International Folk Music Council*, 1974 :86-114.

—— 'The concept of the *ᶜĀsheq* in Northern Khorasan', *Asian Music* IV/1, 1972 :27-47.

KUCKERTZ, J, and M T MASSOUDIEH (M T MASᶜŪDĪYA), *Musik in Būšehr, Süd-Iran*, Wilhelming 1976.

LOEB, L D, 'The Jewish musician and the music of Fars', *Asian Music* IV/1, 1972 :3-14.

MASSOUDIEH, M T (M T MASᶜŪDĪYA), 'Hochzeitslieder aus Balūčestān', *Jahrbuch für musikalische Volks und Völkerkunde*, Berlin 1973.

MUBA<u>SHSH</u>IRI, L, *Āhanghā-yi maḥallī*, Tehran 1959.

Notations of regional songs from several parts of Iran.

NETTL, B, 'Persian popular music in 1969', *Ethnomusicology*, 1972 :218-39.

AMĀNALLĀHĪ, Sikandar, *Pi<u>zh</u>ūhi<u>sh</u>ī dar bāra-yi navāzandagān-i sunnatī-yi Īrān*, Shiraz 1977.

1.8 *Musical change in the 20th century*

Several studies have been made of recent processes of musical change.

BLUM, S, 'Changing roles of performers in Meshed and Bojnurd, Iran', B NETTL (ed), *Eight Urban Music Cultures*, Urbana 1978.

NETTL, B, 'Attitudes toward Persian music in Tehran, 1969', *Musical Quarterly*, 1970 :183-97.

—— 'Persian classical music in Tehran: the process of change', B NETTL (ed), *Eight Urban Music Cultures*, *op.cit.*

Puts forward the contentious thesis that contemporary Persian art music might well be considered part of the western musical system.

ZONIS, E, 'Classical Persian music today', E YAR-SHATER (ed), *Iran Faces the Seventies*, *op.cit.* IX 6.9.

BEEMAN, William O, 'You can take music out of the country, but .... The dynamics of change in Iranian musical tradition', *Asian Music* VII/2, 1976.

1.9 *Twentieth century compositions and teaching manuals*

There have been a number of important Iranian musicians in the 20th century. Perhaps the most influential was A N VAZĪRĪ. His book *Dastūr-i tār*, Berlin 1922, is particularly significant because it was the first work to deal with theoretical aspects of Iranian music to be published after an hiatus of several centuries. The theory of the octave divided into 24 quarter-tones advanced by its author is not generally accepted today. Other works by VAZĪRĪ are:

Dastūri-i jadīd-i tār, Kitāb-i avval, Tehran 1936.

Dastūr-i vīyulun, Tehran 1933.

A second important Iranian musician is A H ṢABĀ, whose teaching manuals for various instruments include a number of pieces of significance composed within the framework of the *dastgāh* system. His works are cited by E ZONIS, *op.cit.* 1.1, p.226. Two other musicians of note listed by E ZONIS are A JĀHID and L PĀYĀN.

1.10 *Discography of Persian music*

Of the many long-play recordings of Persian art music published in the west the following are of particular value: they contain performances by some of Iran's finest traditional musicians and they have been reviewed by leading experts whose comments provide the listener with important additional information for understanding and appreciating the music.

A musical anthology of the Orient: Iran I and II

Two 12" 33 rpm discs. Barenreiter-Musicaphon. UNESCO Collection. BM 30 L 2004 and 2005.

Reviewed by Hormoz FARHAT, *Ethnomusicology*, 1962, pp.239-41.

Classical music of Iran - Dastgāh systems

Two 12" 33 rpm discs. Ethnic Folkways FW 8831/8832. Ella ZONIS (ed).

Reviewed by Gen'ichi TSUGE, *Ethnomusicology*, 1971, pp.152-54.

Musique persane

One 12" 33 rpm disc. Stereo. OCORA OCR 57. Recorded by Mohammad JAHANFARD. Notes by Hormoz FARHAT (in English and French).

Reviewed by Manoochehr SADEGHI, *Ethnomusicology*, 1973, pp.354-56.

2. *SECULAR THEATRE*

2.1 *Introduction*

In pre-Islamic Iran (from prehistoric times up to 640 AD) indigenous rituals, ceremonies (rejoicing or mourning), dances and festivals were performed. Some of these remain up to the present time. In ancient Iran (from Alexander to the Sasanians) Greek plays were also performed at the courts of the princes. Persian poets have often mentioned shadow plays (mainly *Fānūs-i khiyāl*) and puppet theatre (*Luᶜbatbāzī* or *Khaima-yi shabbāzī*). Jesters and buffoons are at the roots of traditional comedy and this type of improvised theatre played a less important part than the religious drama. From the second half of the 19th century, under western influence, authors like M F A ĀKHUNDZĀDA and MĪRZĀ ĀQĀ Tabrīzī, wrote plays. Theatre gradually developed from 1918 to reach a considerable level between 1960-80.

Lists of books and articles on performing arts and media can be found in general bibliographies (see II 2.1).

The main specialized bibliographies are

TAᶜĀVUNĪ, Sh, *Kitābshināsī-yi ti'ātr va sīnimā*, Tehran 1976.

ḤAMZALŪ, B, *Kitābshināsī-yi mauẓūᶜī-yi risānīhā-yi hamigānī*, Tehran 1979.

DASTMĀLCHI, Mahīn, *Kitābshināsī-yi risānī-hā-yi gurūhī*, Tehran 1977.

KUTUBĪ, M, *Fihrist-i maṭālib dar bāra-yi maṭbūᶜāt, rādyū, sīnimā va tilivīzyūn dar Īrān*, Mimeo'd, Tehran 1968.

KARĪMĪ, Khusrau, *Kitābnāma-yi farhang va hunar-i Īrān*, *op.cit.* IX 2.1.1.
A list of Iranian films and plays (120 items) on pp.69-94.

—— *Fihrist-i maqālāt-i sīnimā'ī*, vol.II (1350-1353), Tehran 1977.

2.2 *General works on secular theatre*

CHODZKO, A, *Le Théatre Persan, choix de téazies ou drames*, Paris 1878.
Mainly on *Taᶜziya* with a general introduction on Persian theatre.

BERTELS, E, *Persidskii Teatr*, Rossiiskii Institut Istorii Iskustv, IV, Leningrad 1924.

KRYMSKII, Agatangel, *Perskiy Teatr. Kiev*, 1925. English tr. Volodimir PECHENUK, *The Persian theatre: its origin and development*, Tehran 1977 (not published).
This work is basically important for *Taᶜziya* but chapters on comedies, puppet theatre and European type drama are included.

JANNATĪ ᶜAṬĀ'Ī, A, *Bunyād-i nimāyish dar Īrān*, Tehran 1955.
Contains a helpful list of printed plays in Persian.

REZVANI, M, *Le théatre et la danse en Iran*, Paris 1962.
Full of valuable information but without a scholarly concept.

BAIẒĀ'Ī, B, *Namāyish dar Īrān*, Tehran 1965.

The best on the subject. A new enlarged and corrected edition is in preparation.

YAR-SHATER, E, 'Development of Persian drama', P J CHELKOWSKI (ed), *Iran: continuity and variety*, New York 1971.

GAFFARY, F, 'Secular theatre in Iran', *McGraw-Hill Encyclopedia of World Drama*. (In the press.)

A concise article on all aspects of Iranian non-religious theatre.

—— 'The theatrical movement of the Iranians', *Bibliographical anthology on theatrical movement*, New Orleans 1982.

ARYANPŪR, Yaḥyā, 'Namāyishnāma-navīsī', *Az Ṣabā tā Nīmā*, vol.II, Tehran 1971 :288-315. 5th impr. 1978.

CHELKOWSI, Peter J, 'Popular entertainment, media and social change in 20th century Iran', *CHI*, vol.VII (forthcoming).

2.3 *Ancient rituals and festivals*

General and interesting chapters in M REZVANI, *op.cit.*, and especially in B BAIẒĀ'Ī, *op.cit.*

For masks in the Mithra cults:

TUSCAN, R A, *Mithra et le mithriacisme*, Paris 1981.

VERMASEREN, M, *Mithra*, Paris/Bruxelles 1960. English tr., London 1963.

For the ceremonies in Transoxiana:

YAR-SHATER, E, 'Taᶜziyeh and pre-Islamic mourning rites in Iran', P J CHELKOWSKI (ed), *Taᶜziyeh: ritual and drama in Iran*, New York 1979.

For Piandjikent (USSR) wall paintings:

BUSSAGLI, M, *Painting of Central Asia*, Geneva 1963.

TALBOT-RICE, T, *Ancient arts of Central Asia*, London 1965.

For the iconography of human disguise:

ETTINGHAUSEN, R, 'The dance with Zoomorphic masks and other forms of entertainment seen in Islamic art', *Arabic and Islamic studies in honour of H A R Gibb*, Leiden 1965.

2.4 *Shadow and puppet theatre*

Useful chapters in A KRYMSKII, *op.cit.*, M REZVANI, *op.cit.*, and especially B BAIẒĀ'Ī, *op.cit.*, and a good résumé in M AND, *Karagöz*, Istanbul 1979.

JACOB, Geo, *Geschichte des Schattentheaters in Morgen- und Abendland*, Hanover 1925.

2.5 *Traditional comedy*

Chapters in M REZVANI, *op.cit.*, and particularly B BAIẒĀ'Ī, *op.cit.*, and

F GAFFARY, *op.cit.* Also a general introduction and the text of a play in M B MU'MINĪ, *Tiyātr-i Karīm Shīra'ī*, Tehran 1978.

For the meaning of popular performance:

BEEMAN, W O, 'A full arena', M BONINE and N KEDDIE (eds), *Modern Iran: the dialectics of continuity and change*, Albany 1981 :361-81.

—— 'Why do they laugh? An approach to humor in traditional Iranian theatre', *Journal of American Folklore*, 1982.

2.6 *Western style theatre*

E BERTELS, *op.cit.*, A KRYMSKII, *op.cit.*, M REZVANI, *op.cit.*, and E G BROWNE, *Literary History of Persia*, *op.cit.* vol.IV, contain general references.

JANNATĪ ^{c}ATĀ'Ī, *op.cit.*, has a list of printed plays written or translated into Persian.

In 1956 two Soviet Āzarbāijānī scholars proved in an article that the comedies attributed to Mīrzā MALKAM Khān were in fact written by MĪRZĀ ĀQĀ Tabrīzī:

MUḤAMMADZĀDA, H, and A IBRĀHĪMOV, 'Mīrzā Malkam Khānā ^{c}āyed ḥisāb aidīlan pīeslarīn aṣīl mu'allifī hāqīqindā', *Āzarbāyjān S.S.R. ^{c}ilmlar Akadimiası, Niẓami ādinā adabiyāt va dīl institūsūnūn āsār ları*, vol.9, 1956.

The best texts of ĀKHUNDZĀDA's plays are those of his Persian translator, M J QARĀJADĀGHĪ, *Tamsīlāt*, Tehran 1970.

The best editions of MĪRZĀ ĀQĀ Tabrīzī's plays are those of:

ṢADĪQ, H, *Namāyishnāmahā-yi Mīrzā Āqā Tabrīzī*, Tehran 1975.

MU'MINĪ, M B, *Chahār tiyātr-i Mīrzā Āqā Tabrīzī*, Tehran 1977.

The best book on the life and thought of ĀKHUNDZĀDA is

ĀDAMIYYAT, F, *Ākhundzāda*, Tehran 1970.

The following are the principal translations of M F A ĀKHUNDZĀDA's plays into western languages:

BARBIER DE MEYNARD, C A, 'L'Alchimiste', *JA*, vol.128, Janvier 1886 :1-67.

—— 'L'Ours et le Voleur', *Recueil de textes et de traductions publiés par l'École des Langues Orientales*, Paris 1889.

BAZIN, L, *Comédies de M.F.A. Akhundov*, Paris 1962.

BOUVAT, L, 'L'avare', *JA*, vol.164, 1904 :259-331 and 365-456.

—— *Monsieur Jourdan*, Paris 1906.

BRICTEUX, A, *L'avare*, Liège, Paris 1934.

CHODZKO, A, 'L'aventure du Vizir du Khān de Lenkoran', *Bulletin de l'Athénée Oriental*, vol.3, 1883 :81ff.

CILLIÈRE, A, *Deux Comédies Turques*, ('Vazir de Lenkoran' et 'Les Procureurs'), Paris 1888.

HAGGARD, W H D, and G LE STRANGE, *The Wazir of Lankuran*, London 1882.

LE STRANGE, G, 'The Alchemist', *JRAS*, NS XVIII, part 1, January 1886.

LESZCYNSKI, G L, *Der Alchimist*, Berlin 1920.

LOEBEL, D, and C Fr WITTMAN, *Der Vezier von Lenkoran*, Leipzig n.d.

ORSOLLE, E I, 'La comédie Persane' (Les plaideurs), *Revue Britannique*, Janvier 1887 :5-40.

ROGERS, A, *Three Persian plays*, ('The pleaders of the court', 'The bear that knocked down the robber', and 'Monsieur Jourdan'), London 1890.

SEATON, E A, *The complete translation of the Wukalā-i-murāfaᶜa*, Heiderabad 1911.

WAHRMUND, Ad, *Neupersische Schauspiele*, Wien 1889.

The principal translations of MĪRZĀ ĀQĀ Tabrīzī's plays are in French:

BRICTEUX, A, *Les comedies de Malkom Khan*, Liège/Paris 1933.

NICOLAS, A L M, 'Voyage d'Echref Khan à Téhéran', *RMM*, vol.3, no.9, Aug-Sept. 1907 :10-37.

M BAKTĀSH, wrote a documented series of articles on the theatre of 1850-1890 in the quarterly *Faṣlnāma*, nos.1-5, Tehran 1977-78.

F GAFFARY, *op.cit.*, has the most up-to-date information on contemporary theatre.

Programmes and photographs of the Shīrāz Arts Festival are listed in *Festival of arts: the first ten years*, Tehran 1976.

Nigāhī bi sī va panj sāl-i ti'ātr-i mubāriz, Jāmiᶜa-yi hunarī-yi ANĀHĪTĀ (ed), Tehran 1979.

Including a biography of the actor and stage director, ᶜA Ḥ Nūshīn.

A recent journal on theatre is

Ṣaḥn-i muᶜāṣir, Esfand 1359, Farvardīn 1360, Tehran 1981.

3. *TAᶜZIYA*

3.1 *General works and bibliographies*

The most comprehensive study of *taᶜziya* is to be found in

CHELKOWSKI, Peter (ed), *Taᶜziyeh: ritual and drama in Iran*, New York 1979.

This contains a very full 'bibliographical spectrum' on which the following notes are largely based.

General studies include

AYOUB, Mahmoud, *Redemptive suffering in Islām. A study of the devotional aspects of 'Āshūrā' in Twelver Shiᶜism*, The Hague 1978.

BAIẒĀ'Ī, Bahrām, *Namāyish dar Īrān*, *op.cit.* 2.2.

BAUSANI, Alessandro, 'Il dramma di Karbala e la sofferenzâ redentrice', *Persia Religiosa*, Milan 1959.

BERTELS, E, *Persidskii Teatr*, *op.cit.* 2.2.

CEJPEK, Jiří, 'Iranian folk literature', *op.cit.* XI 7.1.

CERULLI, Enrico, 'Le theatre persan et ses origines', *La Nouvelle Clio* VII-IX, Brussels 1955-57.

GRUNEBAUM, G E von, *Muhammadan festivals*, London 1958.

HUMĀYŪNĪ, Ṣādiq, *Taᶜziya va taᶜziya-khwānī*, Tehran 1975.

KRYMSKI, Agatangel, *op.cit.* 2.2.

MAMNOUN, Parviz, *Taᶜzija. Schiitisch-persisches Passionsspiel*, Vienna 1967.

MASSÉ, Henri, *Croyances et coutumes ...*, *op.cit.* XI 7.2.

MONCHI-ZADEH, Davoud (MUNSHĪZĀDA, Dā'ūd), *Taᶜziya, das persische Passionsspiel*, Stockholm 1967.

MÜLLER, Hildegard, *Studien zum persischen Passionsspiel*, Freiburg 1966.

ROSSI, Ettore, and Alessandro BOMBACI, *Elenco di drammi religiosi persiani*, Rome 1961.

Catalogue of CERULLI's collection of 1055 *taᶜziya* manuscripts deposited in the Vatican Library.

REZVANI, M, *op.cit.* 2.2.

VIROLLEAUD, Charles, *Le theatre persan, ou le drame de Kerbela*, Paris 1950.

YAR-SHATER, Ehsan, 'Development of Persian drama, in the context of cultural confrontation in Iran', Peter CHELKOWSKI (ed), *Iran. Continuity and Variety*, New York 1970-71.

3.2 *History of the study*

Taᶜziya-khwānī (*shabīh-khwānī*, or more generally *taᶜziya*) is a Shīᶜa ritual drama that came into existence in the middle of the 18th century as the result of long mourning rituals commemorating the death of Ḥusain, the third Shīᶜa Imām, on the plain of Karbalā in Muḥarram 61/680.

The origin of these rituals cannot be traced. Comparisons have been made with the mourning for Siyāvush in pre-Islamic Iran and Tammuz in Mesopotamia, and there are references to them from the period of the Būyid dynasty (320-454/932-1062). What is certain is that the first year of Ṣafavid rule, 907/1501, coincided with the writing of a book that gave birth to a new type of Muḥarram observance, the *rauża-khwānī*.

KĀSHIFĪ, Ḥusain Vāᶜiẓ, *Raużat al-shuhadā*. The most recent edition was published in Tehran in 1962.

Two and a half centuries later it served as the warp through which the lyrics and the texts of the *taᶜziya* dramas were woven. The first description of dramatic performances in this connection is given by FRANCKLIN, William, *Observations made on a tour*, *op.cit.* VIII 3.2. Thereafter many European travellers witnessed and described such performances (see VIII 4.4).

The middle of the 19th century saw the beginning of scholarly research into the *Ta^{c}ziya*.

CHODZKO, Alexandre, *Djungui Chéhâdat*, Paris 1855.

—— *Théâtre persan*, *op.cit.* 3.2.

Translation of five out of CHODZKO's collection of thirty-three plays, the manuscripts of which are in the Bibliothéque Nationale. For further texts and translations see below, 3.3.

BEREZIN, Ilya, *Puteshestiviye po severnoi Persi*, Kazan 1852.

Includes a detailed account of what goes on in a *takiya* (arena) before the performance begins, as well as a commentary on the language, text, staging and acting of *ta^{c}ziya*.

GOBINEAU, Auguste Comte de, *Les religions et les philosophies dans l'Asie Centrale*, *op.cit.* VI 3.8.2.

Somewhat exaggerated and not always precise, but had a great impact on scholars and literati in Europe. Contains a translation of the play 'The Marriage of Qāsim'.

LASSY, Ivan J, *The Muharram mysteries among the Azerbaijan Turks of Caucasia*, Helsingfors 1916.

CALMARD, Jean, 'Le mécénat des représentations de Ta^{c}ziyè', *Le monde iranien et l'Islam*, Paris 1976-77.

3.3 *Texts and translations*

Only a few of CHODZKO's collection of thirty-three plays have been published, either in text or translation. Apart from those published by CHODZKO himself, these include

VIROLLEAUD, Charles, *La passion de l'Imam Hossein*, Paris 1929.

Number 24 of CHODZKO's collection. Text and translation.

GENERET, Abbé R H de, *Le martyre d'Ali Akbar. Drame persan*, Liège/Paris 1946.

Translation of CHODZKO's no.18.

NĀMDĀR, Zahrā Iqbāl, *Jung-i Shahādat*, Tehran 1976.

The text of six plays from CHODZKO's collection.

Other texts include

PELLY, Sir Lewis, *The miracle plays of Hasan and Husain*, 2 vols, London 1879, repr. Farnborough 1970.

English translation of thirty-seven plays. Unfortunately the Persian texts have not been preserved.

LITTEN, Wilhelm, *Das Drama in Persien*, Berlin/Leipzig 1929.

Facsimile text of fifteen plays.

DUDA, Herbert, 'Das persische Passionsspiel', *Zeitschrift für Missionskunde und Religionswissenschaft*, vol.49, 1934.

Number 1 of LITTEN's collection.

MASSIGNON, Louis, 'Le Majlis de Mansûr-e Hallâj, de Shams-e Tabrizi et du mollâ de Roum', *REI*, 1955.

Translation of a text from the CERULLI collection.

BAUSANI, Alessandro, 'Drammi populari inediti persiani sulla leggenda di Salomone e della Regine di Saba', *Atti del Convegno Internazionale di Studi Etiopici*, Rome 1960 :167-209.

Selections from the CERULLI collection.

FOROUGH, Mehdi, *A comparative study of Abraham's sacrifice in Persian passion plays and western mystery plays*, Tehran n.d.

HUMĀYŪNĪ, Ṣādiq, *op.cit.* 3.1.

Contains the text of four plays.

—— *Farhang-i mardum-i Sarvistān*, Tehran 1970.

Contains the text of two plays.

HUNARĪ, Murtaẓā, *Ta^{c}ziya dar Khur*, Tehran 1975.

BAIẒĀ'Ī, Bahrām, 'Gūsha-yi shast bastan-e dīv', *Ārish*, no.1, Tehran 1961.

An example of a 'comic' *ta^{c}ziya*.

MÜLLER, Hildegard, *op.cit.* 3.1.

Text and translation of a play, *Adam and Eve*, from the CERULLI collection.

ṢAYYĀD, Parvīz, *Ta^{c}ziya-yi Ḥurr*, Tehran 1972.

GHAFFĀRĪ, Farrukh, and Māyil BAKTĀSH, *Ti'ātr-i Īrānī*, Tehran 1971-72.

A number of *ta^{c}ziya* texts have appeared in popular 'chap-book' form.

4. *DANCE*

The ancient classical dances performed at court or for wealthy people have died out. M REZVANI, *op.cit.*, has research on the subject and has gathered information on Iranian classical and folk dances (with bibliography).

For a historical outline of pre-Islamic dances:

ZUKĀ, Y, 'Raqṣ dar Īrān', *Majalla-yi Mūsīqī*, vol.3, no.79 and following, Tehran 1963.

Also

—— 'Tārīkh-i raqṣ dar Īrān', *Hunar va Mardum*, nos.191/192, 193, 1978-79.

KHĀLĪQĪ, R, *Sarguzasht-i mūsīqī-yi Īrān*, *op.cit.* 1.3.

5. *FILM*

5.1 *Iranian*

The first movie camera was introduced into Persia by the Shah Muẓaffar al-dīn in 1900, and his chief photographer, Mīrzā Ibrāhīm Khān, was the first Iranian cameraman. At the beginning of the century release and exhibition of foreign films started with Mīrzā Ibrāhīm Ṣaḥḥāfbāshī. In the early twenties the first newsreels were shot by Khānbābā Khān Muᶜtaẓidī and the first silent feature films were produced in the early thirties ('Ḥājī Āqā' by Uhāniān). ᶜAbd al-ḥusain Sipantā directed Persian talkies in India (1932-35). National production started on a regular basis in 1947 with Ismāᶜīl Kūshān. From 1958 the first tentative quality cinema began and reached an international level in 1969.

For the pre-history of cinema:

GHAFFĀRĪ, F, 'Jām-i Jam, fānūs-i khiyāl va khaima-yi shab-bāzī', *Fīlm va zandagī*, no.5.

NAFICY, H, 'Film in Iran: a brief critical history', *Quartery Review of Film Studies* 4, 1979.

For a biography of the pioneer Ṣaḥḥāfbāshī by F GAFFARY, see *Safarnāma-yi Ibrāhīm Ṣaḥḥāfbāshī*, M MUSHĪRĪ (ed), Tehran 1979.

General literature:

GAFFARY, F, *Le cinéma en Iran*, Tehran 1973.

The best résumé but must be up-dated and enlarged.

SHUᶜĀᶜĪ, H, *Farhang-i sīnimā'ī-yi Īrān*, Tehran 1975.

UMĪD, J, 'Farhang-i fīlmhā-yi sīnimā-yi Īrān', *Sīnimā*, no.33, 1356; no.34, 1357; no.35, 1357; no.36, 1357, Tehran 1977-78.

A useful dictionary of Iranian films.

Guzārish-i faᶜāliyathā-yi farhangī dar Īrān. Vizārat-i Farhang va Hunar. 1347, 1348, 1349, 1350, 1351, 1352, 1353, 1354, 1355, 1356, Tehran 1968-77.

Contains annual reports and data on film activities.

TEHRANIAN, M, *Socio-economic and communications indicators in development planning: a case study of Iran*, UNESCO, Paris 1980.

Includes data and analysis on traditional media, theatre, press, printing and publishing, film, broadcasting, advertising, telecommunications, libraries and documentation centres, tapes and records, informatics.

Also to be noted:

NAFICY, Hamid, 'Cinema as a political instrument', M BONINE and N KEDDIE (eds), *op.cit.* 2.5, :341-60.

—— 'Nonfiction fiction: documentaries on Iran', *Iranian Studies* XII, nos.3-4, Summer-Autumn 1979 :217-38.

—— 'Iranian feature films: a brief critical history', *Quarterly Review of Film Studies* V, no.1, Fall, 1979.

5.2 *Non-Iranian*

For films on Asia made in the United States see

CYR, Helen W, *A filmography of the Third World*. An annotated list of 16mm films, Metuchen, NJ 1976.

Films on Iran are listed in the section on Southwest Asia on pp.41-51; Afghanistan follows on pp.51-53.

More complete lists can be found in

MOUTSATSOS, Barbara, and Christine EICKELMAN, 'Directory of films on the Middle East', *MESA bull*. 5(1), 1971 :39-55; 6(1), 1971 :44-50; 9(2), 1975 :45-57.

Brief details of content, with film rental and sales agencies.

For British films on the Middle East reference should be made to

British National Film Catalogue, quarterly, with annual cumulations, 1963-. Classified list of all films made in the United Kingdom, with title and subject indices and full details of distributors.

An account of the making of an individual film is to be found in

COOPER, Merian C, *Grass*, New York 1925.

Description of the classic documentary on the Bakhtiyārī migration, made in 1924 by COOPER with Ernest B SCHOEDSACK and Marguerite HARRISON.

Nearly fifty years later another film, in sound and colour, was made of this migration by Anthony HOWARTH and David KOFF, described in a mimeographed brochure:

BROOKS, David H M, *People of the wind*, Durham 1981.

6. *RADIO AND TELEVISION*

The first radio station was inaugurated in Tehran in April 1940. In October 1958 the commercial company of 'Tilivīziyūn-i Īrān' started the first TV stations in Tehran and Ābādān. In October 1966 the state-owned National Iranian Television (Tilivīziyūn-i Millī-yi Īrān) began to work in Tehran and later radio services were added to it. In 1978 three channels (two in Persian and one in English) worked with two million sets watched by some eleven million spectators constituting a third of the entire population.

TEHRANIAN, M, *op.cit*. 5.1.

The best on the subject.

KUTUBĪ, M, *Tilivīziyūn dar Tihrān*, Tehran 1969.

—— *Importance et portée de la télévision en Iran*, mimeo., Tehran 1970.

—— 'Bāztāb-i piyāmhā-yi khānivāda, madrasa va tilivīziyūn dar nazd-i kūdakān', *Nāma-yi ᶜulūm-i ijtimāᶜī*, no.2, Spring, Tehran 1976 :71-203.

MAJLISĪ, H, 'Rādyū va tilivīziyūn dar Īrān', *Īrānshahr* II, Tehran 1964 :1520-29.

MOWLANA, H, 'Technology versus tradition: communication in the Iranian revolution', *Journal of Communication* 29(3), Summer 1979.

TEHRANIAN, M, F HAKIMZADEH, and M L VIDALE, *Communication policy for national development*, London 1977.

Includes articles by A BANANI, 'Communications policy for Iran', and M TEHRANIAN, 'The future of broadcasting in Iran'.

7. *ZŪRKHĀNA*

The traditional Iranian gymnasium, *Zūrkhāna* (the house of strength), is probably of pre-Islamic origin. The exercises are performed in a large round pit (*gaud*), the floor of which is kissed on entrance by the athletes; indulging in movement with heavy maces (*mīl*), metal arches with chains (*kabbāda*) and massive wooden shields (*sang*), and wrestling (by seizing the rival's belt), they train themselves in martial arts. A man (*murshid*) directs the exercises with the rhythms of a drum made of pottery (*żarb*) and a bell accompanied with his chantings in praise of religion and epic heroes of the Shāh Nāma. The athletes, from the beginners (*naucha*) to the masters (*pahlavān*), wear short embroidered leather tights and are expected to abide by ethic rules aiming at altruism and noble causes (*javānmardī*).

The best book on the subject is

PARTAU BAIŻĀ'Ī, H, *Tārīkh-i varzish-i bastānī-yi Īrān*, Tehran 1958.

Also

KAZEMEYNI, K K, *The Zour Khaneh, traditional Persian gymnasium*, (in collaboration with Professor C N BARNARD for the English edition, and Teresa BATTESTI for the French one), Tehran 1970.

INṢĀFPŪR, Gh, *Tārīkh va farhang-i zūrkhāna*, Tehran 1976.

BAHĀR, Mihrdād, 'Varzish-i bāstānī-yi Īrān va rīshahā-yi tārīkhī-yi ān', *Chīstā*, no.2, Mihr 1360, Tehran 1981.

XIV

SOCIAL SCIENCES

1. *INTRODUCTION*

1.1 *Iran and the social sciences*

Although the term 'social sciences' (*ᶜulūm-i-ijtimāᶜī*) has gained ground in Iran only during the past quarter century, scholars within the country and abroad have been looking at its society, government, and economy for centuries. In recent years, many of Iran's practitioners in political science, sociology, and economics have been foreign-trained. University curricula and research activities have tended to reflect the prevailing influences, largely from Europe (especially France) prior to the 1939-45 War and, thereafter, from the United States - up to the fall of the Pahlavi dynasty in 1979. Internal realities have also influenced the direction of emphasis in Iranian social science. Much work in political science and economics has avoided 'controversy' in the face of reaction to commentary seen as critical of government, though sociology and related disciplines have, until 1979 at least, been seen as generally less contentious, as has human geography.

A succinct 1974 review of developments, problems and achievements is given in 'The state of the social sciences in Iran' by Hamid ENAYAT, *MESA Bulletin* 8(3), 1974, pp.1-12. Further detail on practicalities and on trends and emphases appears in Rouhollah K RAMAZANI's 'Research facilities in Iran', *MESA Bulletin* 3(3), 1969, pp.53-61. Both writers discuss the growth of teaching and research centres and of libraries with a focus on the social sciences, particularly since the opening, in 1958, of Tehran University's Institute for Social Studies and Research. Typical of the strengthened support services to emerge in recent years was the Iranian Documentation Centre (IRANDOC) which, after 1970, offered reference services, publishing, and other facilities. IRANDOC has produced a bulletin of social science abstracts (from 1970) and an index (*fihrist*) to articles in Iranian journals (from 1971).

The later years of the 1970s saw an accelerated proliferation of research and graduate study centres in Iran, taking advantage of the boom induced by the quadrupling of oil prices. Among these were the Institute of Rural Studies, the Centre of Cultural Studies, the Royal Philosophical Society, the Humanities Research Centre, the Riẓā Shāh Kabīr University, and the Iran Communication and Development Institute. Such bodies contributed to social sciences by the translation of foreign books, graduate teaching, and original research. Overall, of course, the last years of the decade were dominated by the intellectual trends leading to the Islamic Revolution. There was an unprecedented upsurge of interest - stimulated by some relaxation of censorship in this area - in the social and ideological history of Shī'ī Islam, while elsewhere, some of those more concerned with political matters of the moment added to the burgeoning output of 'underground' material.

Since the 1979 Islamic Revolution, social science in Iran has been abruptly redirected. The sponsorship or encouragement of research and study on topics related to economic growth, industrialization, the White Revolution, etc., has been replaced by official concern for redefinition of priorities and targets in terms of religion. Ex-patriate university and college staffs have left the country and a number of teaching departments - and, on occasion, some universities - have been closed. Many Iranian teachers and researchers have been subjected to purges. Others planning sabbatical or study leave, in Iran or abroad, have been called upon to show the relevance of their plans to the aims of the Revolution. Foreign social scientists visiting Iran report uncertainty in matters of permission, co-operation, and sources of data. Predictably, the publication of some statistical and other periodic material has been interrupted or modified. Chapter XV of this *Guide* examines the implications of the changes for Iranian studies in general.

Meanwhile, chapter XIV has four parts. The first goes on to list a number of general works on Iran as a supplement to the coverage of reference works in earlier chapters and as a forerunner to the other three parts of this chapter - on People, Government, and the Economy. A principal criterion in the selection of titles here, as elsewhere in this volume, has been their accessibility. Many of the theses listed in this chapter are accessible through University Microfilms International in Ann Arbor, Michigan or London. The format of presentation varies, partly in response to the nature of the available material and the topics covered. Most of the titles listed are in English, though numbers of Persian language items are indicated for some subjects. An attempt has been made to include at least a sample of titles in French, German, and other languages.

Needless to say, the definition of 'social science' in this chapter is nothing if not flexible. The overlap with several of the earlier chapters is as obvious as it is necessary. In general, the social sciences are seen as emphasizing the period since about 1953 - though many items are listed which go back in time or which are believed to provide useful context and background to the understanding and analysis of contemporary Iranian society.

1.2 *General works*

Only those general works primarily concerned with the social sciences are included in the chapter. However, other references on the social sciences may be found in chapter II (Bibliographies and Reference Works). Meanwhile, basic statistical sources, and the institutions which produce them and other material, are indicated in chapter V (Official Publications) - and elsewhere in this present chapter. No apology is made for the inclusion of titles under more than one heading where this is thought likely to be helpful.

ABBOTT, John, *The Iranians: how they live and work*, Newton Abbott 1977.

A brief introduction to the country and its peoples, their history, traditions and present way of life. Comprehensive, but necessarily somewhat superficial. Bibliography.

UNITED KINGDOM - NAVAL INTELLIGENCE DIVISION, *Persia*, *op.cit.* II 1.

Describes topography and coastal features, natural resources, history, peoples, administration and government, public health, agriculture and industry, economy, towns, and communications. Statistical appendices. Maps.

AFSHAR, Iraj, 'Basic information on collecting Persian materials for the development of Iranian and Islamic studies', *MESA bull.* 10(1), 1976 :11-19.

Indicates important research institutes and centres, publishers, collections, bibliographies, and catalogues.

AMERICAN UNIVERSITY FOREIGN AREA STUDIES DIVISION, *Area Handbook for Iran*, (by Harvey H SMITH, *et al.*), US Government Printing Office, Washington DC 1971 (a revision of *US Army Handbook for Iran*, Washington 1963).

A thorough survey of modern Iran, with sections on government, politics, religion, economy, population, education, health, judicial system, administration, services, armed forces, together with an historical introduction. Bibliography.

AMIRSADEGHI, H, and R W FERRIER (eds), *Twentieth-century Iran*, *op.cit.*

IX 6.9.

American, British and Iranian specialists provide an introduction to the history of Iran in the 20th century and examine the development of the Iranian oil industry, the economy, foreign policy, and the country's strategic role.

ARASTEH, A Reza, *Man and society in Iran*, Leiden 1970 (repr. of 1964 ed.).

Written with J ARASTEH, this sociological perspective on Iranian peoples and society (including values, family life, social character) and their antecedents also attempts to predict trends.

ARFA, General Hassan, *Under five Shahs*, London 1964.

Memoirs of General ARFA, spanning the years 1895-1963. The author played a part in many major events.

ARMAJANI, Yahya, *Iran*, Englewood Cliffs, Jew Jersey 1972.

An interpretive essay on the antecedents of contemporary Iranian society.

AVERY, Peter, *Modern Iran*, London 1965.

Comprehensive study of Iran from the beginning of the 19th century to the reign of Muḥammad Riẓā S͟hāh Pahlavī. Bibliography.

BÉMONT, Fredy, *L'Iran devant le progrès*, Paris 1964.

Examines developments in agriculture, industry, transport and communications, the social services and foreign trade.

BONINE, Michael E, and Nikki R KEDDIE (eds), *Modern Iran*, *op.cit*. XIII 2.5.

Twenty essays on history, religion, anthropology, geography, sociology, economics, linguistics, government, etc: discusses western influence and the creation of a dual economy *and* a dual society. See also abridged paperback version.

COTTRELL, Alvin J, *et al*. (ed), *The Persian Gulf states*, *op.cit*. IX 6.9.

This large reference volume brings together material on the region's history, both tribal and international, and on its geography, culture, religion, law, sociology, arts, military affairs and economics.

EHLERS, Eckart, *Iran: Grundzuge einer geographischen Ländeskunde*, Darmstadt 1980.

A very comprehensive social and physical geography, with sections on sources, history, physical environment, resources, modernization, natural regions, and a bibliography.

—— *Iran: a bibliographic research survey*, *op.cit*. II 2.2.

ELWELL-SUTTON, L P, *A guide to Iranian area study*, *op.cit*. II 2.2.

Brief introductory essays with references on aspects of Iranian culture, history, economic, social and administrative structure: detailed chronology and bibliographies.

FISHER, W B (ed), *The land of Iran*, *CHI*, vol.1.
Despite its title, this comprehensive collection includes eleven chapters on 'The Land', three on 'The People', seven on 'Economic Life', and a conclusion on 'The Personality of Iran' by the editor.

GEHRKE, Ulrich and Harald MEHNER (eds), *Iran: Natur-Bevölkerung - Geschichte - Kultur - Staat - Wirtschaft*, Tübingen 1976, 2nd ed.
Describes natural resources, population and society, culture and traditions, political organization, economy and development. Appendices with statistical tables.

GRAHAM, Robert, *Iran: the illusion of power*, London 1980, 2nd ed.
Forthright analysis of Iran's economic and political system from oil wealth (especially after 1973) to revolt against the Shah.

HALLIDAY, Fred, *Iran: dictatorship and development*, Harmondsworth 1979, 2nd ed.
Economic, social and political developments in Iran in the 20th century and particularly since the early 1960s. Maps, bibliography.

Iran Almanac and Book of Facts, Echo of Iran, annual, Tehran 1961.
A handbook of information on economic and social developments.

Iranian Studies - journal of the society for Iranian studies, quarterly, Chestnut Hill, Mass. 1967.
Articles of social science interest and detailed book reviews.

JACOBS, Norman, *The sociology of development. Iran as an Asian case study*, New York 1966.
A detailed analysis of the problems inherent in implementing development programmes, how they are affected by the structure of political authority and the society upon which they are imposed. Bibliography.

JACQZ, Jane E (ed), *Iran: past, present and future*, *op.cit.* IX 6.9.
Studies of land reform, rural modernization, agricultural development, migration, the economics of oil, human resources, and income distribution.

KEDOURIE, Elie, and Sylvia HAIM (eds), *Towards a modern Iran*, *op.cit.* IX 6.9.

The Middle East and North Africa (until 1964-65 *The Middle East*), annual, Europa Publications, London 1948.
The section on Iran briefly describes the country's physical and social geography, its history and recent political developments, and the economy. It also includes a statistical summary and basic information on the government, diplomatic representation, judicial system, press, radio and television, banking, trade and industry, transport, tourism and education.

Middle East Journal, quarterly, Middle East Institute, Washington, DC 1947-.

Articles on social science subjects, chronology of events, texts of documents, lists and reviews of recent publications (books and periodical articles). Perhaps a first point of reference for the social scientist studying contemporary Iran.

RĀVANDĪ, Murtaẓā, *Tārīkh-i ijtimāᶜī-yi Īrān*, 3 vols, Tehran 1977.

Social history of Iran from earliest times: the nature and structure of Iranian society.

SAHEBJAM, Freidoune, *L'Iran des Pahlavis*, Paris 1966.

With a preface by MUḤAMMAD RIẒĀ SHAH, this survey stresses the 1939-45 War period and subsequent developments, especially those involving oil, reform, and planning.

SCHWEIZER, Günther (ed), *Interdisziplinäre Iran-Forschung. Beiträge aus Kulturgeographie, Ethnologie, Soziologie und neuerer Geschichte*, Wiesbaden 1979.

Fourteen contributions by various authors, seven in German, four in English and three in French (with summaries of all papers in English, French, German and Persian).

UPTON, Joseph M, *The history of modern Iran: an interpretation*, Cambridge, Mass. 1960.

Section on Pahlavī period.

VREELAND, Herbert H (ed), *Iran*, Human Relations Area Files, New Haven 1957.

A comprehensive survey of the land, people, society, government, political and cultural life, economy, education and health.

WILBER, Donald N, *Iran, past and present*, Princeton 1976, 8th ed.

General survey of Iran's physical features, history and culture. Chapters on the Pahlavi period describe the government, the people and their way of life, the development of resources and services. Appendices on the Iranian calendar, weights and measures; bibliography.

YAR-SHATER, Ehsan (ed), *Iran faces the seventies*, *op.cit.* IX 6.9.

Papers from a 1960 conference (Columbia University), including land reform and cooperatives, the economy, capital formation, politics, social change, religion, education, emigration, etc.

2. *PEOPLE*

2.1 *Demography*

Iran's first national census in 1956 showed a population of nearly nineteen million in a land of 1.65 million square kilometres. By 1980 there were twice as many people, with a high birth rate (about 44 per thousand per year) and a relatively low mortality rate (less than 20 per thousand).

Current expectations look to another doubling of the country's population by the very early years of the next century. Some 44 per cent of the present population is under 15 years of age (23 per cent in the United Kingdom), with only 4 per cent over 64 (14 per cent in the UK). The urban population accounts for 47 per cent of the total with Tehran, the capital and outstanding metropolitan area, taking a growing share. Much of the increase represented migration from Iran's 45,000 villages to towns and cities.

General characteristics of Iran's population are portrayed in census and other demographic data published since 1956 by the Iranian Statistical Centre and other branches of Government in Tehran and the provinces. *A bibliography on the population and manpower in Iran*, by Jamshid MOMENI, Pahlavi University Press, Shiraz 1975, is partially annotated and includes references to census data, other official publications, newspapers, and academic journals. The same writer edited *The population of Iran: a selection of readings*, East-West Center, Honolulu, and Pahlavi University, Shiraz 1977 - a collection of previously published articles on Iran's demography, population, manpower, urbanization, etc. and on problems of forecasting and projection. Comment and analysis of population trends is also available in articles and books such as:

AMANI, Mehdi, 'Vue d'ensemble sur la situation demographique de l'Iran', *Rev. géog Lyon* 48(2), 1973 :141-63.

BEHNAM, J, 'Population', *The land of Iran*, *CHI*, vol.I :468-85.

BÉMONT, Fredy, *Les villes de l'Iran*, *op.cit.* VIII 1.1, :65-88.

CLARK, Brian D, 'Iran: changing population patterns', J I CLARKE and W B FISHER (eds), *Populations of the Middle East and North Africa*, London 1971 :68-96.

FIROOZI, Ferydoon, 'Iranian census 1956 and 1966: a comparative analysis', *MEJ* 14(2), 1968 :220-28.

GOBLOT, H, 'La structure de la population de l'Iran', *L'Éthnographie*, NS 57, 1963 :33-54.

LIEBERMAN, Samuel S, 'Prospects for development and population growth in Iran', *Population and development review* 5(2), 1979 :293-317.

Focus on demographic trends, particularly population growth, as a factor in development.

PAKDAMAN, Nasser, 'Étude critique du recensement général de l'Iran', *Tiers-monde* 6(21), 1965 :231-46.

Most of the above titles deal in part with the patterns of contemporary population relocation in Iran. More specialized studies on this include:

HEMMASI, Mohammad, *Migration in Iran: a quantitative approach*, Shiraz 1974.

HILL, Robert N, *Interprovincial migration and its effect on settlement patterns in Iran for the intercensal period 1956-1966*, Ph.D. thesis, Princeton University 1973.

HOURCADE, Bernard, 'Migrations de travail et de loisir dans l'Elbourz de Téhéran', *Rev. géog Lyon* 53(3), 1978 :229-40.

MAUROY, Hubert de, 'Mouvements de population dans la communauté assyro-chaldéenne en Iran', *Rev. géog Lyon* 43(3), 1968 :333-56.

SHADMAN-VALAVI, Mohammad, *An analysis of the determinants of migration in Iran*, Ph.D. thesis, North-Western University 1974.

TABIDIAN-KHORASGANI, Mohamad-Reza, *The relationship between rural-urban population redistribution and distribution of non-labor resources and income in rural areas in Iran (1966-1976)*, Ph.D. thesis, Pennsylvania State University 1979.

TAVAKKOL, Abdolamir, *Determinants of migration into urban areas of Iran*, Ph.D. thesis, Kansas State University 1979.

During the 1960s and 1970s considerable sums were spent by the Tehran authorities on population problems. In 1967, a Population and Family Planning Division was set up in the Ministry of Health to co-ordinate measures to reduce the rate of population growth - though at an annual 3 per cent in 1980 (compared with a world figure of about 1.7) this remains among the highest in South-West Asia and the Middle East. Iranian family planning services have been increasingly integrated within the health delivery system while changes, after 1973, in the law on abortion and sterilization, removed some of the restrictions in those areas. A sample of titles since 1967:

AGHAJANIAN, Akbar, *Community characteristics, socioeconomic status, and fertility in rural communities of Iran*, Ph.D. thesis, Duke University 1978.

ᶜAJAMĪ, Ismāʼīl, 'Differential fertility in peasant communities: a study of six Iranian villages', *Population Studies* 30(3), 1976 :453-63.

Based on a 1974 survey of six villages 50-80 km north of Shiraz.

MINISTRY OF HEALTH, Iran, *A checklist of Iranian population and family planning documents 1945-1972*, Family Planning Division, Tehran 1972.

See other Ministry of Health material.

MOHSENI, M, and M MOTABAR, 'Fécondité et planning familial parmi les nomades', *Sociologia Ruralis* 16(3), 1976 :197-207.

On the Qashqāʼī.

MOORE, Richard, Khalil ASAYESH, and Joel MONTAGUE, 'Population and family planning in Iran', *MEJ* 28(4), 1974 :396-408.

PADIDAR-NIA, Hossein, *Population dynamics in Iran: new estimates of mortality and fertility*', Dr. P.H. thesis, University of Texas HSC at Houston School of Public Health 1977.

PĀYDĀRFAR, ^{c}Alī A, *et al.*, *The population and family planning program in Iran: an inventory of manpower, facilities, and services*, University of North Carolina (Carolina Population Center), Chapel Hill 1972.

PLAN ORGANIZATION, DEPARTMENT OF HEALTH AND SOCIAL WELFARE, *Plan of action of population and family planning program for the years 1346-1351 (1967-1972)*, Tehran 1967.

See other Plan Organization material.

The links between population, education, and manpower attracted an increasing number of writers during the 1970s. Among these outside the Iranian Government service itself have been:

AMMADI, Mohammad Reza, *Trends and projection of population, education, and manpower planning in Iran*, Ph.D. thesis, University of Missouri 1975.

BALDWIN, George B, 'The Iranian brain drain', YAR-SHATER (ed), *Iran faces the seventies*, *op.cit.* IX 6.9.

BARTSCH, William H, 'The industrial labour force of Iran: problems of recruitment, training and productivity', *MEJ* 25(1), 1971 :15-30.

See author's Ph.D. thesis, *Labour supply and employment creation in the urban areas of Iran, 1956-1966*, School of Oriental and African Studies, University of London 1970.

BEHKISH, Mohammad M, *Economics of investing in human capital: the case of Iran*, Ph.D. thesis, Indiana University 1977.

ELKAN, Walter, 'Employment, education, training, and skilled labour in Iran', *MEJ* 32(2), 1977 :175-87.

HIRSCH, Étienne, *et al.*, *Employment and income policies for Iran*, International Labour Office, Geneva 1973.

Report and recommendations of ILO mission (1971-72).

JOHNSON, Gail Cook, *High-level manpower in Iran: from hidden conflict to crisis*, New York 1980.

LIAGHAT, Gholam A, 'Changes in a new middle class through the analysis of census data. The case of Iran between 1956-1966', *MEJ* 34(3), 1980 :343-49.

2.2 *Social groups*

The first part of this section has considered quantitative aspects of the population of contemporary Iran. The following passages review qualitative aspects of Iran's people - their divisions into groups and communities on the basis of social, ethnic, religious, linguistic, economic, tribal or other ties and classifications.

2.2.1 *Communities and groups*

Between 1960 and 1978 there was an unprecedented proliferation of ethnographic field studies in Iran but many of the best works remain in the form of unpublished theses, not all accessible in xerox or microfilm form. Thus, despite a considerable expansion in the information available on culture and society, general works on Iran still frequently rely on outdated and inaccurate images of tribal society, the role of women in rural communities, etc. One recent survey of Iranian society, based on many sources, is Michael FISCHER's 'Persian society: transformation and strain', in *Twentieth Century Iran*, AMIRSADEGHI and FERRIER (ed), 1977, *op.cit.* IX 6.9. A more general survey is provided by Jamshīd BIHNĀM and Shāhpūr RĀSIKH in their introduction to the sociology of Iran, *Ṭarḥ-i muqaddamātī-yi jāmiᶜa-shināsī-yi Īrān*, volume 1, Tehran 1960. The proliferation of field studies was such that the coverage of different geographical areas and categories of society was unsystematic, so that a few areas have been worked over by several different scholars while large gaps in information remain. In particular, it seems that Fredrik BARTH's pioneer study, *Nomads of south Persia: the Basseri tribe of the Khamseh Confederacy*, London 1961, together - perhaps - with a lingering fascination with the exotic, led European and North American researchers, at least initially, to concentrate on pastoral nomadic tribes rather than on peasant or urban society. BARTH's work has inspired many studies of nomadic and tribal groups. Nevertheless its limitations should now be recognized. First, the brevity of his fieldwork and the rigorous framework he uses to explain Basseri social forms expose the book to the criticism that it gives little information apart from that required in the development of the argument. Secondly, in the absence of other published studies, various aspects of Basseri pastoral economy and social organization have been, misleadingly, taken as typical of pastoral nomadic society in Iran.

Far more detail on material culture (though less on social organization) can be found in C FEILBERG's earlier study of the Papi Lurs, *Les Papis*, National Museum, Copenhagen 1952. Lur tribesmen, both nomadic and settled, have more recently been studied by

BLACK-MICHAUD, J, 'An ethnographic and ecological survey of Luristan, western Persia: modernization in a nomadic pastoral society', *MES* 10(2),

1974 :210-28.

AMANOLAHI-BAHARBAND, Sekandar, *The Baharvand, former pastoralists of Iran*, Ph.D. thesis, Rice University, Texas 1975.

The two major tribal groups of southwestern Iran, the Bakhtiyārī and the Qashqā'ī, have each been studied by several scholars. The Bakhtiyārī are the subject of

BAKHTIYĀRĪ, A, *Tārīkh-i Bakhtiyārī*, Tehran 1966.

BAKHTIYĀRĪ, Ḥ Pizhmān, 'Bakhtiyārī dar guzashta-yi dūr', *Vaḥīd* iii/2,3,4, 1966.

DIGARD, J-P, 'Histoires et anthropologies des sociétés nomades: le cas d'une tribu de l'Iran', *Annales: Économies. Societies. Civilisations* 28(6), 1973 :1423-35.

—— *Techniques des nomades Baxtyâri d'Iran*, Cambridge 1981.

EHMANN, Dieter, *Baḫtiyaren - persiche Bergnomaden im Wandel des Zeit*, Wiesbaden 1975.

GARTHWAITE, Gene R, 'Khans and kings: the dialectics of power in Bakhtiyari history', BONINE and KEDDIE (eds), *Modern Iran*, *op.cit*. XIII 2.5, :159-72.

—— 'The Bakhtiyari Ilkhani: an illusion of unity', *IJMES* 8(2), 1977 :145-60.

The Qashqā'ī have been the subjects of a major study by Pierre OBERLING, *The Qashqa'i nomads of Fars*, The Hague 1974: see also his 1960 Ph.D. thesis, Columbia University, New York, on *The Turkic peoples of southern Iran*. Results of several ethnographic studies beginning to appear include:

BECK, Lois, 'Economic transformation among Qashqa'i nomads, 1962-1978', BONINE and KEDDIE (eds), *Modern Iran*, *op.cit*. XIII 2.5, :99-121.

—— 'Herd owners and hired shepherds: the Qashqa'i of Iran', *Ethnology* 19(3), 1980 :327-51.

MARSDEN, David J, 'The Qashqai nomadic pastoralists of Fars Province', *The Qashqai of Iran*, Whitworth Art Gallery, World of Islam Festival, Manchester 1976 :9-18.

SALZER, Richard E, *Social organization of a nomadic pastoral nobility in southern Iran: the Kashkuli Kuchek tribe of the Qashqai*, Ph.D. thesis, University of California, Berkeley 1974.

SHAFII, F, M MOHSENI, and M MOTABAR, 'Formal education in a tribal society, Iran', *Sociologia Ruralis* 17(1/2), 1977 :151-57.

Among groups to the north, the Kurds look back to the short-lived Mahābād Republic of 1945-46 and across the border to the Kurds in the oil rich northern part of Iraq. Some sources are:

MUKRĪ, Muḥammad Kaivānpūr (M MOKRI), *ᶜAshayir-i Kurd*, 2nd ed, part 1, Tehran 1954.

—— 'Le mariage chez les Kurdes', *L'Éthnographie*, Paris 1962 :42-68.

NIKITINE, Basil, *Les Kurdes: étude sociologique et historique*, Imprimerie Nat., Paris 1950, repr. 1975.

QĀSIMLŪ, ᶜAbd al-Raḥmān (A R GHASSEMLOU), *Kurdestan and the Kurds*, Prague/ London 1965.

YĀSAMĪ, Ghulām Riżā Rashid, *Kurd va paivastagī-yi nizhādī va tārīkhi-yi ū*, Tehran n.d. (c.1941).

RUDOLPH, W, 'Gründzuge sozialer Organization bei den westiranischen Kurden', *Sociologus* 17(1), 1967 :19-39.

ZAKĪ BEG, Muḥammad Amīn, *Khulāṣa tārīkh al-Kurd wa Kurdistān*, tr. Muhammad ᶜAli ᶜAWNI, from Kurdish to Arabic, 2 vols, Cairo 1939-48. (Vol.1 repr. in Baghdad 1961.)

Religious and ethnographic works are included among some 300 Kurdish titles listed in *Kitēbkhānay kurdī* by Mustafā NARĪMĀN, Kirkuk 1960. Zh. S MUSAELYAN, in *Bibliografiya po kurdoveniyu*, Moscow 1963, lists over 2,700 monographs and periodical articles, more than half of which represent Russian-language material. The comprehensive *ISK's Kurdish bibliography*, edited by Silvio VAN ROOY and Kees TAMBOER, International Kurdistan Society, Amsterdam 1968, 2 volumes, is classified but under broad subject headings. *The Kurds in Iran: a selected and annotated bibliography* by Wolfgang BEHN, London 1977, fills the gap between 1966 and 1975 for monographs. A complementary work is Elizabeth E LYTLE's *Bibliography of the Kurds, Kurdistan, and the Kurdish question*, Monticello, Ill., 1977, Exchange bibliography; 1301, citing predominantly articles from serials not included in J D PEARSON's *Index Islamicus*. Whereas half the titles in *The Kurds in Iran* are in non-western languages, LYTLE's work covers almost exclusively western-language material.

The main source on the Shāhsivan of nearby Āzarbāyjān is Richard TAPPER's *Pasture and politics: economics, conflict and ritual among Shahsevan Nomads of northwestern Iran*, London 1979, following his 1972 thesis, at the University of London, which gives a comprehensive analysis of Shāhsivan culture at the time of TAPPER's field work in 1965-66. A major contribution of *Pasture and politics* is clarification of what TAPPER calls 'the primary nomadic community'. Another work is

SCHWEIZER, Günther, 'Nordost-Azerbaidschan und Shah Sevan Nomaden: Strukturwandel einer nordwestiranischen Landschaft und ihrer Bevölkerung', G Z BEIHEFT (ed), *Erdkundliches Wissen* 26, Wiesbaden 1970 :81-148.

For northeastern Iran, W G IRONS provides a major source, *The Yomut Turkmen of Iran: a study of social organization among a Central Asian Turkic-speaking population*, University of Michigan, Ann Arbor 1975, with a special focus on kinship and tribal political relations. The Balūch of southeastern Iran have been studied by anthropologists B SPOONER, who has written *inter alia* 'Politics, kinship and ecology in southeast Persia', *Ethnology* 8(2), 1969, pp.139-52, and P SALZMAN, who produced 'The proto-state in Iranian Baluchistan', R COHEN and E SERVICE (eds), *The origins of the state*, Philadelphia 1978, and other articles following his 1972 University of Chicago thesis on *Adaptation and change among the Yarahmadzai Baluch*. The Afshār of Kirmān have recently been admirably described by the cultural geographer Georg STÖBER in *Die Afshar Nomadismus im Raum Kerman* (Zentraliran), Marburg/Lahn: Marburger Geog. Schriften; Hft 76, 1978, which contains useful maps and documentation.

Further titles on aspects of nomadic and tribal society in Iran are

BAHMAN BEGI, Muḥammad, 'Manners and customs of the tribes of Fars', Vincent MONTEIL, *Les Tribus du Fars et la sédentarisation des Nomades*, Paris 1966.

This chapter is a translation of *ᶜUrf va ᶜādāt dar ᶜashāyir-i Fārs*, Tehran 1945-46.

BARTH, Fredrik, 'The land use pattern of migratory tribes of South Persia', *Norsk Geografisk Tidsskrift* XVII, 1959-61 :1-11.

—— 'Nomadism in the mountain and plateau areas of south-west Asia', *Arid Zone Research* xviii, Paris 1962.

—— 'Capital, investment and the social structure of pastoral nomad groups in south Persia', R FIRTH and B S YAMEY (eds), *Capital saving and credit in peasant societies*, London 1964 :69-81.

BĀVAR, Maḥmūd, *Kūhgīlūya va īlāt-i ān*, Tehran 1945.

FAZEL, G Reza, *Economic organization and change among the Boyer Ahmad*, Ph. D. thesis, University of California, Berkeley 1971.

—— 'The encapsulation of nomadic societies in Iran', C NELSON (ed), *The desert and the sown: nomads in the wider society*, Inst. of Int. Studies, Research Series no.21, Univ. of California, Berkeley 1973 :129-42.

HOURCADE, Bernard, 'Les nomades du Lâr face aux problèmes de l'expansion de Téhéran', *Rev. géog. Est.* 17(1/2), 1977 :37-51.

IRONS, William G, and N DYSON-HUDSON (eds), *Perspectives on nomadism*, Symposium on Nomadic Societies, New Orlean 1969, Leiden 1972.

See contributions on Balūch (SALZMAN and SPOONER) and Turkmen (IRONS).

LAMBTON, Ann K S, 'Īlāt', *Encyclopaedia of Islam* III, 1971 :1095-110.
Historical review of tribal groups of Iran.
MONTEIL, Vincent, *Les tribus du Fars et la sédentarisation des nomades*, Paris 1966.
SCHAFGHI, S, 'Nomaden im heutigen Iran', *Zeitschrift für Ausländische Landwirtschaft* 13(4), 1974 :345-59.
SINGER, A F W, *A study of the impact of social and cultural change upon the ethnic identity in eastern Iran*, D.Phil. thesis, Oxford University 1976.
STAUFFER, Thomas R, 'The economics of nomadism in Iran', *MEJ* 19(3), 1965 :284-302.
SUNDERLAND, Eric, 'Pastoralism, nomadism and the social anthropology of Iran', *CHI* I :611-83.

2.2.2 *Religion*

Contemporary studies of the place of religion in Iranian society include Michael M J FISCHER's *Iran: from religious dispute to revolution*, *op.cit.* IX 6.9; P SALZMAN's 'Islam and authority in tribal Iran', *The Moslem World* 65, 1975, pp.186-95, and B SPOONER's 'Religion and society today: an anthropological perspective', E YAR-SHATER (ed), *Iran faces the seventies*, *op.cit*. Religion *per se* is a major topic within chapter VI of this *Guide*. Some writings on religious communities in Iran are

BOYCE, M, *A Persian stronghold of Zoroastrianism*, Oxford 1977.
DĀMGHĀNĪ, Muḥammad Taqī, *Aḥvāl-i shakhṣiya-yi Zardushtiyān-i Īrān*, Tehran 1955.
ENGLISH, Paul W, 'Die Auswirkung neuzeitlicher Strömungen auf eine alte persische Minderheit', *Bustan*, Hft 4, 1966 :18-22.
Especially on Zoroastrianism.
FISCHER, M, *Zoroastrian Iran between myth and praxis*, *op.cit.* VI 1.2.
FRANZ, E, *Minderheiten in Iran: Dokumentation zur Ethnographie und Politik*, Hamburg 1981.
GABRIEL, Alfons, *Religionsgeographie von Persien*, *op.cit.* VI 1.2.
GOLDSTEIN, J, *Interwoven identities: religious communities in Yazd, Iran*, Ph.D. thesis, Princeton University 1978.
See especially on Muslims.
KIELSTRA, Nico, *Two essays on Iranian society*, Papers on European and Mediterranean Societies 5, Univ. of Amsterdam, Amsterdam 1976.
The first essay is on popular religious belief in a south Persian village.
LOEB, Laurence D, *Outcast: Jewish life in southern Iran*, *op.cit.* VI 3.9.

MAGNARELLA, Paul J, 'A note on aspects of social life among the Jewish Kurds of Sanandaj', *Jewish Journal of Sociology* 11(1), 1969 :51-58.

MAUROY, Hubert de, *Les Assyro-Chaldéens dans l'Iran d'aujourd'hui*, *op.cit.* VI 3.10.

—— 'Les minorités non-musulmanes dans la population iranienne', *Rev. géog. Lyon* 48(2), 1973 :165-206.

MODARRESSI, T, 'The Zar cult in south Iran', Raymond PRINCE (ed), *Trance and possession states*, Montreal 1968.

SA[c]ĪDĪ, Ghulām Ḥusain, *Ahl-i havā*, University of Tehran Press, Inst. for Social Research, Tehran 1966-67.

Zar cults along the Gulf.

SCHWARTZ, Richard M, *The structure of Christian-Muslim relations in contemporary Iran*, *op.cit.* VI 3.10.

SPECTOR, Earl Daniel, *A history of the Persian Jews*, *op.cit.* VI 3.9.

THAISS, G, 'Religious symbolism and social change: the drama of Husain', N KEDDIE (ed), *Scholars, saints and sufis*, *op.cit.* VI 2.10.

Based on 1973 thesis (same title) at Washington University, St Louis.

—— 'The bazaar as a case study of religion and social change', YAR-SHATER (ed), *Iran faces the seventies*, *op.cit.* IX 6.9, :189-216.

2.2.3 *Language*

Iran's languages *per se* are the subject of chapter X of this *Guide*. For their part, social scientists have long been concerned with language as a basis for differentiation between groups, as is evident from many of the titles on tribes and minority groups listed above. There are, however, few studies with a primary focus on the sociology or politics of the linguistic pattern in Iran, where over one-third of the population do not have the official Persian as a first language. One article, 'What is (Iranian) national character? A sociolinguistic approach', by William BEEMAN, *Iranian Studies* 9(1), 1976, pp.22-48, examines the role of the communication system in 'national' consciousness. The same writer has written 'The hows and whys of Persian style: a pragmatic approach', Ralph W FASOLD and Roger W SHUY (eds), *Studies in language variation*, Georgetown University Press, Washington, DC 1977, pp.269-82. Among other work on aspects of the social science of language are, Michael C HILLMAN 'Language and social distinctions in Iran', M BONINE and N R KEDDIE (eds), *Modern Iran*, *op.cit.* XIII 2.5, and *A sociolinguistic analysis of modern Persian*, a 1978 Ph.D. thesis at the University of Kansas, by Yahya MODARESSI-TEHRANI.

2.2.4 *Folklore*

Material on aspects of the folklore of Iran is indicated at a number of points in this *Guide*, most notably in the coverage of folk and popular literature in chapter XI. MASSÉ's work listed there provides a bibliographic point of departure on aspects of folklore which are not primarily verbal or literary (Henry MASSÉ, *Croyances et coutumes persanes*, *op.cit.* XI 7.2). *Hunar va Mardum*, a periodical produced by the Ministry of Culture in Tehran up to 1979, covers a wide range of folklore topics - children's games, names of implements, ceremonies, etc.

Particular parts of Iran are subjects for studies of folklore: for example

HUMĀYŪNĪ, Ṣādiq, *Gushahā'ī az ādāb u rusūm-i mardum-i Shīrāz*, Tehran 1974.

—— *Farhang-i mardum-i Sarvistān*, *op.cit.* XI 7.

KATĪRĀ'Ī, Maḥmūd, *Az khisht tā khisht*, Tehran 1970.

Popular customs in Tehran.

LAMAʿA, Manūchihr, *Farhang-i ʿāmmiyāna-yi ʿashāyir-i Būyir Aḥmadī va Kūhgīlūya*, *op.cit.* X 6.8.

SHUKŪRZĀDA, Ibrāhīm, *ʿAqāyid u rusūm-i ʿāmma-yi mardum-i Khurāsān*, *op.cit.* XI 7.

The Persian New Year, Naurūz, is the special concern of monographs such as

SAYYID, Fu'ād ʿAbd-al-muʿṭī, al-, *Al-Nūrūz wa atharuhu fī'l-adab al-ʿarabī*, Beirut 1972.

Naurūz and its influence on the Arabs.

AZKĀ'Ī, Parvīz, *Naurūz - tārīkhcha va marjaʿ-shināsī*, Markaz-i mardumshin-āsī, Tehran 1974.

HUNARĪ, Murtaẓā, *Ā'īn-hā-yi Naurūzī*, Markaz-i mardumshināsī, Tehran 1974.

Games have been the subject of several studies:

ANJAVĪ-SHĪRĀZĪ, Sayyid Abu'l-qāsim, *Bāzīhā-yi namāyishī*, Tehran 1973.

Dramatic games, many played only by women.

BAHĀR, Muḥammad Taqī Malik al-shuʿarā, 'Bāzīhā-yi Īrānī', *Taʿlīm u tarbiyat* 12, 13, Tehran 1934.

JAHĀNSHĀH, Ḥusain, *Qāb-bāzī dar Īrān*, Tehran 1971.

Other titles on aspects of Iranian folklore include

ANJAVĪ-SHĪRĀZĪ, Sayyid Abu'l-qāsim, *Jashnhā va ādāb va muʿtaqidāt-i zamistān*, 2 vols, Tehran 1973-75.

DONALDSON, Bess Allen, *The wild rue. A study of Mohammedan magic and folklore in Iran*, London 1938.

An accessible account by a missionary's wife: useful, with caution.

HIDĀYAT, Ṣādiq, *Nairangistān*, Tehran 1963.

MUSÉUM NATIONAL D'HISTOIRE NATURELLE (MUSÉE DE L'HOMME), *Objets et mondes* 11, fasc.2, Paris 1971.

Special issue on Iran, with articles on aspects of folk culture, including costume, hair-styles, date-palm cultivation, coffee-house paintings, etc.

—— *Iran: hommes du vent, gens de terre*, Paris 1971.

Illustrated catalogue of exhibition in Paris, May-October 1971: valuable for photographs of artifacts on view, plus text.

ŻIYĀPŪR, Jalīl, *Pūshāk-i īlhā*, Tehran 1967.

Tribal costumes.

2.2.5 *Women*

However otherwise differentiated, the women of Iran are increasingly the subjects of studies by social scientists. *Women in the Muslim World*, L BECK and Nikki R KEDDIE (eds), Harvard University Press, Cambridge, Mass., 1978, contains case studies on the Būyir Aḥmad (FRIEDL), Marāgha (GOOD), Iṣfahān (GULICKS), Qashqā'ī (BECK), and Shāhsivan (N TAPPER) and other contributions on Iranian women.

Other titles are

ARASTEH, A Reza, 'The struggle for equality in Iran', *MEJ* 18(2), 1964 :189-205.

BĀMDĀD, Badr al-mulūk, *Zan-i Irani* ..., *op.cit.* IX 6.6.

FAZEL, G Reza, 'Social and political status of women among pastoral nomads: the Boyr Ahmad of southwest Iran', *Anthropological Quarterly* 50(2), 1977 :77-89.

ṢADR, Ḥasan, *Ḥuqūq-ī zanān dar Islām va Urupā*, Tehran 1963.

TAPPER, Nancy, 'Matrons and mistresses: women and boundaries in two Middle Eastern tribal societies', *Archives Européennes de Sociologie* 21, 1980 :59-78.

On the Shāhsivan.

WRIGHT, S, 'Prattle and politics: the position of women in Doshman Ziari', *Journal of the Anthropological Society of Oxford* 9(2), 1978 :98-112.

Having reviewed Iranian society in terms of the social science coverage of groups differentiated by ethnic origin, tribe, minority, religion, language, sex, etc., this chapter now looks at rural (2.3) and urban (2.4) Iran. Such distinctions clearly represent the bibliographer's convenience rather than any real disjunction between tribe, group, village, and city. Evidently, people may belong to a number of groups and categories. Equally, there are fundamental links between town and country, while rural culture is reproduced as well as transformed by migrants to the towns and cities. No tribal group, village community, or city can be understood except in the contexts of the State, of Islam, and of regional, national, and international economic, social, and political structures.

2.3 *Villages and rural change*

The non-tribal peasant villagers of Iran until recently formed the major element in the population. Yet no significant monograph has been published in English though, in the last two decades, Iranian social scientists have produced studies, both in published and thesis form, on a limited variety of village communities. Ann LAMBTON's *Landlord and peasant in Persia*, London 1969, *op.cit.* IX 3.3, is basic reading on traditional land tenure and agriculture, while in *The Persian land reform, 1962-1966*, she provides essential background to a topic which has dominated both official and academic interest in rural Iran in recent years. Some of the material now available is

ʿAJAMĪ, Ismāʾīl, 'Social classes, family demographic characteristics and mobility in three Iranian villages', *Sociologia Ruralis* 9(1), 1969 :62-72.

With special reference to land reform.

—— *Shishdāngī*, Shiraz 1969.

A case study of the effects of land reform on a village.

—— and M MUHĀJIR-YAZDĀNĪ, *Bīhābād*, Univ. of Tehran Press, Tehran 1967-68.

ALBERTS, Robert C, *Social structure and culture change in an Iranian village*, Ph.D. thesis, Univ. of Wisconsin, Madison 1963.

Comprehensive account of a village near Tehran.

ĀL-I AḤMAD, Jalāl, *Aurāzān*, Tehran 1954, repr. 1970.

—— *Tāt-nishīn-hā-yi bulūk-i zahrā*, Tehran 1958, 3rd ed. 1974.

BERTHAUD, Edmond, 'La vie rurale dans quelques villages chrétiens de l'Azerbaidjan occidental', *Rev. géog. Lyon* 43(3), 1968 :291-331.

CONNELL, John, 'Economic change in an Iranian village', *MEJ* 28(3), 1974 :309-14.

CRAIG, Daniel, 'The impact of land reform on an Iranian village', *MEJ* 32(2), 1978 :141-54.

EHLERS, Eckart, and Javad SAFI-NEZHAD, 'Formen kollektiver Landwirtschaft in Iran: Boneh', *Beiträge zur Kulturgeographie des islamischen Orients*, Marburger Geog. Schriften, Marburg 1979.

See other titles by Eckart EHLERS, 4.2.

FISHĀRAKĪ, Parīdukht, *Dāristān, ākharīn ābādī-yi ḥāshiya-yi Lūt*, Geog. Inst.

Univ. of Tehran, Tehran 1970.

Dāristān, a village on the margin of the Lūt.

GŪDARZĪ-NIZHĀD, Shāhpūr, *Rustā-hā-yi Asadābād: jughrāfiyā-yi insānī va iqtiṣādī*, Geog. Inst., Univ. of Tehran, Tehran 1975.

On villages in the Asadābād district of Hamadān province.

HANESSIAN, John Jr, 'Yosouf-Abad, an Iranian village', *AUFS: Reports Service, Southwest Asia Series* 12 (6 parts), 1963.

HAYDEN, L J, 'Living standards in rural Iran. A case study', *MEJ* 3(2), 1949 :140-50.

HOLMES, J E, *A study of social organization in certain villages in west Khurasan, Iran: with special reference to kinship and agricultural activities*, Ph.D. thesis, Univ. of Durham 1975.

HOOGLUND, E, 'The khushnishin population of Iran', *I.Stud.* 6(4), 1973 :229-45.

Refers to landless agricultural workers.

IRANIAN STATISTICAL CENTRE (Markaz-i Āmār-i Īrān), *Village Gazetteer* (Farhang-i ābādīhā-yi Īrān/kishvar), 27 vols, Tehran 1968, *et seq.*

Compiled, by the Plan Organization, from the 1966 Census. Data, by village (with location maps), on population, area, buildings, water, land use, farming, institutions, communications, etc.

KEDDIE, Nikki R, 'Stratification, social control, and capitalism in Iranian villages', R ANTOUN and I HARIK (eds), *Rural politics and social change in the Middle East*, Indian Univ. Press, Bloomington, Indiana 1972 :364-402.

With special reference to land reform.

KHUSRAVĪ, Khusrau, *Jāmiʿa-shināsī-yi rūstāʿī-yi Īrān*, Univ. of Tehran, Tehran 1972-73.

Attempts to construct a theory of Iranian rural society.

—— (KHOSROVI, Khosrow), 'Les paysans sans terre en Iran: les Khochnechin', *Sociologia Ruralis* 23(3/4), 1973 :289-93.

KIELSTRA, Nico, *Two Essays on Iranian Society*, *op.cit.* 2.2.2.

Second essay is on the impact of agrarian reform on village social structure.

MARSDEN, David J, *The social organization of selected villages in the Marvdasht Plain, Fars province, southern Iran*, Ph.D. thesis, Univ. of Durham 1981.

MILLER, W Green, 'Hosseinabad: a Persian village', *MEJ* 18(4), 1964 :483-98.

With special reference to land reform.

MIR-HOSSEINI, Ziba, *Changing aspects of economy - family structures in*

Katardasht, a district in northern Iran, up to 1978, Ph.D. thesis, Univ. of Cambridge 1980.

Study of four villages - government policy implications, migration, society, etc.

ŌNO, Morio, 'On socio-economic structure of Iranian villages - with special reference to *deh*', *The Developing Economies* 5(3), Inst. of Asian Economic Affairs, Tokyo Sept. 1967 :446-62.

Landlord (mālik) and peasant (raᶜīyat) relationships.

POUR HEKMAT, Abol Fazl, *La société rurale, les collectivités et les conseils locaux en Kurdistan et Azerbaidjan (Iran)*, D.Univ. thesis (sociology), Univ. of Paris-Sorbonne 1973.

ṢAFĪ-NIZHĀD, Javād, *Munugrāfī-yi dih-i Ṭālibābād*, Tehran 1966.

Important study of a village near Tehran.

—— *Buna*, Univ. of Tehran Press, Tehran 1972.

On a traditional form of agricultural co-operation: in Persian.

SAᶜĪDĪ, Ghulām Ḥusain, *Īlkhchī*, Tehran Univ. Press, Tehran 1964.

Account of an Ahl-i Ḥaqq village in Āzarbāyjān.

SALMANZADEH, Cyrus, *Agricultural change and rural society in southern Iran*, Middle East and North African Studies Press, Cambridge 1980.

SPOONER, Brian, 'Continuity and change in rural Iran', P CHELKOWSKI (ed), *Iran: continuity and variety*, New York Univ. Center for Near Eastern Studies and the Center for International Studies, New York 1971 :1-19.

VADĪᶜĪ, Kāẓim, *Muqaddama bar jughrāfiyā-yi insānī-yi Īrān*, *op.cit.* VIII 1.1.

Studies of pastoralism, tribes, agriculture, settlement, population, human geography.

VOSSOUGHI, Mansour, *Les changements sociaux dans les villages iraniens à la suite de la reforme agraire'*, Univ. of Paris V, thesis, 3ème cycle (sociology), 1974.

2.4 *Urban and regional development*

Michael E BONINE provides one point of entry to academic work on urban Iran. His *Urbanization and city structure in contemporary Iran and Afghanistan: a selected annotated bibliography*, Monticello, Illinois 1975 (Exchange Bibliography no.875) lists over 100 items in English and other western languages, while his article on 'The morphogenesis of Iranian cities', *Annals of the Association of American Geographers* 69(2), 1979, pp.208, 244, indicates a number of sources. A Persian introduction to the study of Iranian cities is *Muqaddama bar ravish-i taḥqīq-i shahr-hā-yi Īrān* by Yadallāh FARĪD, Social and Human Sciences Research Institute, Publication 7, University of Āz̲ārbādagān, Tabriz 1970. Another comprehensive study is *Les Villes de l'Iran. Des cités d'autrefois à l'urbanisme contemporain* by Fredy BÉMONT, *op.cit.* VIII 1. This examines environmental, demographic, and historical factors in the development of Iranian urbanization and looks in detail at Tehran, Mas̲h̲had, and Ābādān and, more briefly, at some twenty other towns. Other titles on general and comparative aspects of urban Iran include:

ADIBI, Hossein, *An analysis of the social, economic, and physical aspects of urbanization in Iran*, Ph.D. thesis, United States International Univ. 1972.

UNITED KINGDOM - NAVAL INTELLIGENCE DIVISION, *Persia*, *op.cit.* II 1.

Chapter 13, 'Ports and Inland Towns'.

AMERICAN UNIVERSITY FOREIGN AREA STUDIES DIVISION, *Area handbook for Iran*, *op.cit.* 1.2.

Chapter 6, 'Social Structure'.

ANSCHÜTZ, Helga, 'Persische Stadttypen: eine vergleichende Betrachtung der Städte Teheran-Isfahan-Abadan-Chorramschahr und Buschir in Iran', *Geographische Rundschau* 19(3), 1967 :105-10.

Contrasts between the traditional city, such as Iṣfahān, and new cities, such as Ābādān.

BHARIER, Julian A, 'The growth of towns and villages in Iran, 1900-1966', *MES* 8(1), 1972 :51-61.

CLARK, Brian D, and Vincent F COSTELLO, 'The urban system and social patterns in Iranian cities', *Transactions of the Institute of British Geographers* 59, 1973 :99-128.

Three cities (Ārān/Bīdgul, Kās̲h̲ān, and Kirmāns̲h̲ah) are compared in terms of factors influencing contemporary social patterns.

EHLERS, Eckart, 'Rentenkapitalismus und Stadtentwicklung im islamischen Orient. Beispiel: Iran', *Erdkunde* 32(2), 1978 :124-42.

ENGLISH, Paul Ward, 'Selections from *City and Village in Iran*', L E SWEET (ed), *Peoples and Cultures of the Middle East*, vol.2: *Life in cities, towns and countryside*, New York 1970 :308-43.

GAUBE, Heinz, *Iranian cities*, New York Univ. Press, New York 1979.

From 1977 lectures, based on broad array of sources, including chapters on theoretical/historical considerations and on Iṣfahān and Bam.

GAUGLITZ, K-G, 'Eigentümlichkeiten des Wegesystems in iranischen Städten: die Entstehung von Gassen und Sackgassen', *Orient* 10, Hamburg 1969 :162-69.

KOPP, Horst, 'Städte im östlichen iranischen Kaspitiefland: ein Beitrag zur

Kenntnis der jüngeren Entwicklung orientalischer Mittel- und Kleinstädte', *Mitteilungen der Fränkischen Geographischen Gesellschaft* (Erlangen) 20, 1973 :33-197.

KORTUM, Gerhard, 'Hafenprobleme Irans im nördlichen persischen Golf', *Geographische Rundschau* 23(9), 1971 :354-62.

LAPIDUS, Ira M, 'The traditional Muslim cities: structures and change', L Carl BROWN (ed), *From medina to metropolis*, Princeton 1973 :51-69.

Puts the Iranian city in its traditional Middle Eastern and Islamic context.

LOCKHART, Laurence, *Persian cities*, London 1960.

Short glimpses at twenty-three major Iranian cities: focus is historical rather than structural/functional.

PLANHOL, Xavier de, 'Geography of settlement', *CHI* I :409-67.

SCHARLAU, Kurt, 'Moderne Umgestaltungen im Grundriss iranischer Städte', *Erdkunde* 15(3), 1961 :180-91.

The modernization of Iranian cities after 1926.

SCHWEIZER, Günther, 'Bevölkerungsentwicklung und Verstädterung in Iran', *Geographische Rundschau* 23(9), 1971 :343-53.

Urban population changes, especially 1956-66.

WIRTH, Eugen, 'Strukturwandlungen und Entwicklungstendenzen der orientalischen Stadt', *Erdkunde* 22(2), 1968 :101-28.

Structural changes in Middle Eastern cities, with examples from Iran: maps of Iranian cities and bazaars.

2.4.1 *Tehran*

With its outstanding primacy in the urban hierarchy of Iran, the capital, Tehran, has attracted most interest from social scientists and planners. A selection of the available material is

AHRENS, Peter G, *Die Entwicklung der Stadt Tehran*, *op.cit.* VIII 1.1.

Physical environment demography, city structure: maps, photographs.

BAHRAMBEYGUI, H, *Tehran: an urban analysis*, Tehran 1977.

Based on 1972 M.A. thesis at the University of Durham.

BÉMONT, Fredy, *Les villes de l'Iran*, *op.cit.* VIII 1.1, :89-145.

CHASTELAND, Jean-Claude, and Mehdi AMANI, *Projections de la population de Téhéran, 1956-1991*, Inst. for Social Studies and Research, Univ. of Tehran, Tehran 1966.

DAGRADI, Piero, 'Due capitali nella steppa: Ankara e Tehran', *Revista Geografica Italiana* 70(3), 1963 :271-306.

The two developed after being made capitals: Tehran in 1787 - though modernization there came only after 1925.

FIROOZI, Ferydoon, 'Tehran - a demographic and economic analysis', *MES* 10(1), 1974 :60-76.

HOURCADE, Bernard, 'Téhéran: évolution récente d'une métropole', *Méditerranée* 2ème ser. 16(1), Aix-en-Provence 1974 :25-41.

Employment structures and spatial patterns of commercial and other activities.

KAZEMI, Farhad, *Poverty and revolution in Iran: the migrant poor, urban marginality and politics*, New York Univ. Press, New York/London 1980.

Based on field work in Tehran in 1974-75 and 1977, this study has a special focus on squatters and factory workers and on the frustrations which left them ready for revolution.

KHAVIDI, Rahim, *Low-income public housing and neighbourhood planning and development in the city of Tehran, Iran*, Ph.D. thesis, Univ. of Wisconsin, Milwaukee 1978.

PLANHOL, Xavier de, 'Geography of settlement', *op.cit.* 2.4 :445-61.

—— 'De la ville islamique à la métropole iranienne: quelques aspects du développement contemporain de Téhéran', *Mémoires et Documents, Centre National de la Recherche Scientifique* 9(4), 1964 :59-77.

SEGER, Martin, 'Zum Dualismus der Struktur orientalischer Städte: das Beispiel Teheran', *Mitteilungen der Österreichischen Geographischen Gesellschaft* 121(2), Vienna 1979 :129-59.

—— *Teheran: eine stadtgeographische Studie*, Vienna 1978.

THAISS, Gustav, 'The Bazaar as a case study of religious and social change', E YAR-SHATER (ed), *Iran faces the seventies*, *op.cit.*, :189-216.

UNIVERSITY OF TEHRAN, *Atlas de Téhéran: équipements et loisir à Teheran*, Inst. for Social Studies and Research, Tehran Univ., Tehran 1969.

Maps of the distribution of major public services, plus tables and text.

VIEILLE, Paul, *Marché des terrains et societé urbaine: recherche sur la ville de Téhéran*, Paris 1970.

Based on a 1961 study of land use and values.

—— and K MOHSENI, 'Ecologie culturelle d'une ville islamique: Téhéran', *Rev. géog. Est.* 9(3/4), 1969 :315-59.

Spatial patterns of selected luxury services.

2.4.2 *Other Iranian cities*

Representative titles on Iranian cities other than Tehran (listed alphabetically by city) are

ĀBĀDĀN

BÉMONT, Fredy, *Les villes de l'Iran*, *op.cit.*, :269-82.

PLANHOL, Xavier de, 'Abadan: tissu urbain, attitudes et valeurs', *Rev. géog. Est.* 9(3/4), 1969 :361-78.

—— 'Abadan: morphologie et fonction du tissu urbain', *Rev. géog. Est.* 4(4), 1964 :337-85.

Includes cadastral surveys, house plans, and demographic data.

BAM

GAUBE, Heinz, *Iranian cities*, *op.cit.*, chap.4, 'Bam - a provincial center'.

EHLERS, Eckart, 'Die Stadt Bam und ihr Oasen-Umland/Zentraliran: ein Beitrag zu Theorie und Praxis der Beziehungen ländlicher Raume zu ihrem kleinstädtischen Zentrum im Orient', *Erdkunde* 29(1), 1975 :38-52.

BANDAR ᶜABBĀS

SCHWEIZER, Günther, *Bandar ᶜAbbas und Hormoz: Schicksal und Zukunft einer iranischen Hafenstadt am persischen Golf*, Tübinger Atlas des Vorderen Orients, Wiesbaden 1972.

HAMADĀN

GHAFFARZADEH, H, *Hamadan. An evaluation of the urban planning process*, Ph.D. thesis, Univ. of Aberdeen, Aberdeen 1979.

IṢFAHĀN

BAKHTIAR, Ali, 'The Royal Bazaar of Isfahan', R HOLOD (ed), *Studies on Isfahan*, part 1 (see below).

Includes maps and photographs.

BLUNT, Wilfred, *Isfahan, pearl of Persia*, *op.cit.* IX 5.3.

GAUBE, Heinz, *Iranian cities*, *op.cit.*, chap.3, 'Isfahan - the capital'.

—— and Eugen WIRTH, *Der Bazaar von Isfahan*, *op.cit.* IX 5.3.

GULICK, John, 'Private life and public face: cultural continuities in the domestic architecture of Isfahan', R HOLOD (ed), *Studies on Isfahan*, part 2 (see below).

Continuity between older and newer parts of the city.

HOLOD, Renata (ed), *Studies on Isfahan: proceedings of the Isfahan Colloquium*, 2 parts, Soc. of Iranian Studies, *I.stud.* 7(1/4), Boston 1974.

Stresses arts, architecture and history.

S̲H̲AFAQĪ, Sīrūs, *Jug̲h̲rāfīyā-yi Iṣfahān*, Univ. of Iṣfahān, Iṣfahān 1974.

Physical setting, historical background and population.

KARAJ

BAHRAMBEYGUI, H, *A geographical analysis of Karaj: a satellite city in the urban region of Tehran*, Ph.D. thesis, Univ. of Durham 1978.

COSTELLO, Vincent F, *Kashan. A city and region of Iran*, Centre for Middle Eastern and Islamic Studies, Univ. of Durham, London/New York 1976.

Argues for a distinctly Persian - rather than Middle Eastern - city. Tests models of dichotomy and continuity. Based on 1971 Ph.D. thesis (University of Durham) *Settlement relations in the city and region of Kashan, Iran.*

—— 'The industrial structure of a traditional Iranian city', *TESG* 64(2), 1973 :108-20.

Modern and traditional spatial patterns: textiles as a major example.

KIRMĀN

BECKETT, P H T, and E D GORDON, 'Land use and settlement round Kerman in southern Iran', *GJ* 132(4), 1966 :476-90.

ENGLISH, Paul Ward, *City and village in Iran: settlement and economy in the Kerman Basin*, Univ. of Wisconsin Press, Madison 1966.

Based on 1961-62 field work: argues that urban dominance explains the functional regional integration centred on the city. Also analyzes the towns of Jūpār and Māhān.

—— 'Culture change and the structure of a Persian city', *The Texas Quarterly* 9(2), 1966 :158-72, repr. in *Traditionalism and modernism in the Muslim Middle East*, Carl LEIDEN (ed), Univ. of Texas Press, Austin 1968.

Zoroastrians as example of social change.

SPOONER, Brian, and Philip C SALZMAN, 'Kirman and the Middle East: Paul Ward English's *City and village in Iran: settlement and economy in the Kerman Basin*', *Iran: Journal of the British Institute of Persian Studies* 7, 1969 :107-13.

Review and criticism.

KIRMĀNSHĀH

CLARKE, John I, and Brian D CLARK, *Kermanshah: an Iranian provincial city*, Dept. of Geog. and Centre for Middle Eastern and Islamic Studies, Univ. of Durham, Durham 1969.

Analysis of commercial and industrial patterns: maps and aerial photographs.

MALĀYIR

MOMENI, Mostafa, *Malayer und sein Umland: Entwicklung, Struktur und Funtionen einer Kleinstadt in Iran*, Marburger Geog. Schriften, Marburg/Lahn 1976.

MARĀGHA

GOOD, Mary Jo, *Changing patterns of hierarchy and inequality in provincial Iran: a case study of an Azarbaijani town*, Ph.D. thesis, Harvard Univ. 1976.

MASHHAD

BÉMONT, Fredy, *Les villes de l'Iran*, *op.cit.*, :147-78.

DARWENT, David, *Urban growth in relation to socio-economic development and westernization: a case study of the city of Mashhad, Iran*, Ph.D. thesis, Univ. of Durham, Durham 1966.

PAGNINI ALBERTI, Maria P, *Strutture commerciali di una città di pellegrinaggio: Mashhad (Iran nord-orientale)*, Inst. of Geog., Univ. of Trieste, Udine 1971.

Retail patterns analyzed on the basis of a computer programme. Map of all retail outlets; illustrations and aerial photographs.

QAZVĪN

ROTBLAT, Howard J, 'Social organization and development in an Iranian provincial bazaar', *Economic Development and Cultural Change* 23(2), 1975 :292-305.

—— 'Structural impediments to change in the Qazvin bazaar', *I.stud.* 5(4), 1972 :130-48.

Social anthropological emphasis.

QUM

BAZIN, Marcel, 'Qom, ville de pèlerinage et centre régional', *Rev. géog. Est.* 13(1/2), 1973 :77-136.

Based on 1968-70 field work: looks at the 'pilgrimage quarter', commercial activities and Qum's regional influence.

RASHT

EHLERS, Eckart, 'Die Städte des südkaspischen Küstentieflands', *Erde* 102(1), Berlin 1971 :6-33.

SARAKHS

SAʿĪDĪ, ʿAbbās, 'Taḥavvul-i jamʿīyat-paẕīrī dar Sarakhs', *Majalla-yi Dānishkada-yi Adabīyāt va ʿUlūm-i Insānī-yi Mashhad*, (later *MDAUI - Dānishgāh-i Firdausī*) 39, 1974 :432-59; 40, 1974 :565-94.

Implications of population growth for Sarakhs.

—— 'Sarakhs-i dīrūz va imrūz', *Majalla-yi Dānishkada-yi Adabīyāt va ʿUlūm-i Insānī-yi Mashhad*, (later *MDAUI - Dānishgāh-i Firdausī*) 31, 1972 :710-33; 32, 1972 :1001-015; 33, 1973 :140-58; 34, 1973 :387-410; 36, 1973 :732-77.

SIMNĀN

CONNELL, John (ed), *Semnan: Persian city and region*, Univ. of London, London 1969.

Five papers on Department of Geography, University College, expedition.

SHĪRĀZ

CLARKE, John I, *The Iranian city of Shiraz*, Dept. of Geog., Univ. of Durham, Durham 1963.

Especially commercial development: maps and aerial photographs.

LOEB, Laurence D, *Outcast: Jewish life in southern Iran*, *op.cit.* 2.2.2.

PAYDARFAR, Ali A, 'Differential life-styles between migrants and non-migrants: a case study of the city of Shiraz, Iran', *Demography* 11(3), 1974 :509-20.

Factor analysis of 34 variables identified from 1061 interviews.

ṬABAS

EHLERS, Eckart, 'City and hinterland in Iran: the example of Tabas/Khorassan', *TESG* 66(5), 1977 :282-96.

TABRĪZ

SCHWEIZER, Günther, 'Tabriz (Nord-West Iran) und der Tabrizer Bazar', *Erdkunde* 26(1), 1972 :32-46.

Urban evolution and structure: analysis of the commercial patterns of the bazaar (with map).

YAZD

BONINE, Michael E, *Yazd and its hinterland: a central place system of dominance in the central Iranian plateau*, Ph.D. thesis, Univ. of Texas, Austin 1975.

Physical and historical factors affecting patterns of settlement and commerce.

BOYCE, Mary, 'The Zoroastrian houses of Yazd', C E BOSWORTH (ed), *Iran and Islam: in memory of the late Vladimir Minorsky*, Edinburgh Univ. Press, Edinburgh 1971 :125-47.

FISCHER, Michael M J, *Zoroastrian Iran: between myth and praxis*, *op.cit.* VI 1.2.

Religious groups: includes a description of Yazd.

GOLDSTEIN, J, *Interwoven identities: religious communities in Yazd, Iran*, *op.cit.* 2.2.2.

2.4.3 *Planning*

Many of the above have some concern with planned change in Iranian cities and urban regions. Writings which have a primary focus on such planning include

CLARK, Brian D, 'Urban planning in Iran', John I CLARKE and H BOWEN-JONES (eds), *Change and development in the Middle East: Essays in honour of*

W B Fisher, London/New York 1981 :280-88.

COSTELLO, Vincent F, 'Tehran', M PACIONE (ed), *Problems and planning in Third World cities*, London 1981 :156-86.

Past and present planning problems.

DÜLEC, Bahri, *et al.*, *Bazar Teheran*, Hochschule der Künste, Fachbereich Architektur (Probleme der internationalen Stadtentwicklung), Berlin 1979.

Extremely critical analysis of urban planning.

MOZAYENI, Manootchehr, 'City planning in Iran: evolution and problems', *Ekistics* 38(228), 1974 :264-67.

Reviews legislation affecting the restructuring of Iranian municipalities since 1925 and considers the impact on urban areas of national development plans.

ROBERTS, M Hugh P, 'Iran: Shahestan Pahlavi, a new city centre for Tehran', *An urban profile of the Middle East*, London 1979 :161-79.

The departments of government most directly concerned with urban problems and planning prior to the 1979 Revolution were the Plan Organization and the Ministry of Housing and Local Government Development, while official information was made available by the Demographic and Social Statistics Department and other sections of the Statistical Centre. Typical of such official material was the collection of town plans for five selected provinces produced by the Plan and Budget Organization in 1975. The same office (Sāzmān-i Barnāma, Daftar-i ṭarḥhā va guzārishhā) had previously published *Urban development in Iran*, by Hidāyat NAKHJAVĀNĪ and Jamshīd DĀRĀ'Ī, edited by Maḥmūd INĀYAT, and translated by Roger COOPER, 1967.

Many such reports involved foreign specialist advisers. One such was the 1969 *Tarḥ-i jamᶜī-yi Tihrān* (Tehran Master Plan) edited by ᶜAbd al-ᶜAzīz FARMĀNFARMĀYĀN and Victor GRUEN for the Plan Organization. In 1973, the Societé Française d'Études et de Réalisation de Transports Urbains was commissioned for a 'Tehran Transportation Plan'. Overall, however, most such involvement came from US personnel and it is to American government and development agencies that one must turn for material - much of it restricted or produced in very limited quantities.

The First and Second National Economic Development Plans (1947-1961), like their successors, stressed industrialization and sector-oriented planning priorities, with no overall urban development programme. In the Third Plan (1962-66), however, plans were prepared for selected cities and, in 1965, a Higher Council for City Planning was set up. Between 1966 and 1972, the Fourth Plan included a scheme to build a new centre for Tehran:

it also saw the 1968 Urban Renovation and Development Act which gave greater powers to municipalities. The Fifth Plan (1972-78), the last before the Islamic Revolution, continued the trend towards more comprehensive city planning taking account of social and economic factors as well as of physical planning concerns. In 1975, a Centre for National Spatial Planning was established and a 'Strategy Plan' produced, in the following year, to integrate urban development into broader regional and national planning efforts. This reflected concerted efforts to get away from the over-centralized type of urban decision-making within which initiatives in Iranian cities and towns had generally been *ad hoc* and remedial.

Many of the items on aspects of the Iranian economy in 4.1 below deal with planning. Three from that section are

BALDWIN, George B, *Planning and development in Iran*, Baltimore 1967.

DAFTARY, Farhad, 'Development planning in Iran: a historical survey', 1973.

NAINI, A, 'Entwicklungsplanung in Iran', 1975.

2.4.4 *Regions*

During the last years of the monarchy it was clear that concern with imbalances and inequalities between Iranian regions were growing. Much of this interest was focused on inter-regional and rural-urban migration - most notably to Tehran. A number of government and other agencies were involved, including the Plan and Budget Organization which produced, for example, (and generally in Persian) 'Social and economic development plans' for Coastal Province, 3 volumes, 1975; Chahārmahal and Bakhtiyārī Province, 2 volumes, 1976; and Yazd Province, 2 volumes and Annexe, 1976.

Despite its 1945 date, *Persia* in the Geographical Handbook Series, *op. cit.* II 1, remains a valuable introduction to the regional variety within Iran. It deals with aspects of both the human and physical patterns in the country and gives a 'Regional Description of the Land' (pp.34-118). A selection of more recent titles on regions and regional development in Iran is

ANSCHÜTZ, Helga, 'Die Verkehrswege des Iran und ihre Bedeutung für die Erschliessung des Landes', *Geographische Rundschau* 19(6), 1967 :221-25.

LOEFFLER, Reinhold, 'Recent economic changes in Boir Ahmad: regional growth with development', *I.stud.* 9(4), 1976 :226-87.

NARAGHI, E, 'Regional studies in Iran', *Multidisciplinary aspects of regional development*, Organization for Economic Cooperation and Development (OECD), Paris 1969.

RICHARDSON, M W, 'Regional planning in Iran', *Growth and Change* 3. 1975 :16-19.

WRIGHT, George E, Jr, *Regional inequality in the economic development of Iran, 1962-1970*, 2 vols, Ph.D. thesis, Univ. of Michigan 1977.

Further sources, maps as well as written material, are indicated in chapter VII of this *Guide*, while further titles on national planning and general aspects of regional change are to be found in 4.1 and 4.2 below.

2.4.5 *Social services*

MOHSENI, Manouchehr, 'Patients and their resort to health care. Attitudes towards the use of medical and sanitary services in Iran', *International Social Science Journal* XXIX(3), 1977 :473-82.

PRIGMORE, Charles S, *Social work in Iran since the White Revolution*, University of Alabama 1976.

2.5 *Education*

Since 1935, many institutions of education in Iran have published reports, yearbooks, etc. Nearly fifty of these are listed in

BANĪ ĀDAM, Ḥusain, *Kitābshināsī-i mauẓūᶜī-i Īrān*, *op.cit.* II 2.1, :225-30.

In 1972, Ānūsh Huvsipiyān ĀZĀDIYĀN listed publications from the Ministry of Education in *Ṣūrat-i nashriyyāt-i vizārat-i āmūzish va parvarish*, Tehran. See chapter V of this *Guide* for further details of sources on education. Among non-official descriptions of the development of education in Iran during the Pahlavī period, the following deserve note.

BANANI, Amin, *The modernization of Iran, 1921-1941*, *op.cit.* IX 5.1.

Contains an account of educational developments in the context of Riżā Shāh's reforms.

GEHRKE, Ulrich, and Harald MEHNER, *Iran: Natur - Bevölkerung ...*, *op.cit.* II 1.

Chapter on education (pp.283-317) covers the types and levels of schools, universities, Literacy Corps, etc.

ḤIKMAT, ᶜAlī Aṣghar, 'Farhang-i āmūzish va parvarish', *Īrānshahr*, National UNESCO Commission in Iran, Tehran 1967 :1165-246.

Survey of the education system in Iran.

KIMIACHI, Bigan, *History and development of broadcasting in Iran*, Ph.D. thesis, Bowling Green State Univ., Ohio 1978.

SHIᶜĀRĪNIZHĀD, ᶜAlī Akbar, *Farhang-i iṣṭilāḥāt-i tarbiyatī, jāmiᶜa-shināsī, ravānpizishkī, ravānkāvī, falsafī*, Tabriz 1965.

Dictionary of educational and related terms.

ṬŪSĪ, Muḥammad ᶜAlī, *Sāzmān-i idārī-yi kishvar va qavānīn-i farhangī*, Tehran 1966.

Organization and laws of education.

On the broader issues of the philosophy and priorities of the Iranian system of education the works of cĪsā ṢADĪQ (a founder and later Chancellor of the University of Tehran and six times Minister of Education) were influential over several decades:

ṢADĪQ, cĪsā Khān, *Ravish-i nuvīn dar tacLīm va tarbiyat*, Tehran 1935: later revised as *Ravish-i nuvīn dar āmūzish va parvarish*, Tehran 1956 (the 17th edition was published in 1968).

—— *Chihil guftar*, Tehran 1973.

Articles and lectures on history and problems of Iranian education: see especially 'The philosophy of regionalization of education in Iran'.

—— *Yādgār-i cumr*, 4 vols, Tehran 1959-77.

Memoirs.

Other work on a variety of educational questions includes:

AMĪR-HŪSHMAND, Fatḥallāh, *Falsafa-yi āmūzish va parvarish*, 2nd ed., Tehran Univ. Pub. no.333, repr. Sāzmān-i Tarbiyat-i Mucallim va Taḥqiqāt-i Tarbiyati, Tehran 1964.

Philosophy of education.

ĀRĀSTA, A Riżā, *Majmūca-yi maqālāt va sukhanrānīhā-yi tarbiyatī va falsafī*, Tehran 1969.

Critical studies of educational goals (from 1955), including a study of Tehran University.

—— *Education and social awakening in Iran, 1850-1868*, Leiden, 2nd rev.ed. 1971.

BĀMDĀD, Badr al-Mulūk, *Taclīm va tarbiyat-i dimūkrāsī dar Īrān*, Tehran 1950.

Education for democracy in Iran.

HAKIM, Maryam, *Education and modernization in Iran: planning and impact of educational policy*, Ph.D. thesis, State Univ. of New York, Binghamton 1980.

HENDERSHOTT, Clarence, *Politics, polemics, and pedagogues*, New York 1975.

Account of the Point Four/USAID educational advisers, 1951-1967. Discusses *inter alia* problems of agricultural and technical education and of Tehran and Shīrāz (Pahlavī) Universities. Compares US and Iranian education systems.

HOSSEINI-FOULADI, Fereydoon, *A study of educational policy formulation in Iran, 1962-1977: establishment of Education Corps and Educational Revolution Decree*, Ed.D. thesis, The Catholic Univ. of America 1979.

HŪSHYĀR, Muḥammad Bāqir, *Uṣūl-i āmūzish va parvarish*, Tehran Univ. Pub. no.398, Tehran 1956, 2nd ed.

This book on the purpose and practice of education echoes the work of German educators, Kirchensteiner and Heinz: it strongly influenced Iranian educational circles.

JUNDĪ-SHĀPŪR UNIVERSITY, *Āmūzish der Īrān*, *op.cit.* IX 9.4.

KANĪ, ᶜAlī, *Sāzmān-i farhangī-yi Īrān*, Tehran Univ. Pub. no.229, Tehran 1954, repr. as Pub. no.453, 1960.

The structure of Iranian education: a critical source book.

KARROUBY, Sorour, *The new educational system in Iran: a general survey of problems and suggestions for improvements*, Ph.D. thesis, Univ. of Illinois, Urbana-Champaign 1977.

SALIMIAN, Jafar, *A survey of selected policies and the practice of public educational administration in Iran*, Ed.D. thesis, Univ. of Akron, Ohio 1980.

SHARIFZADEH, Mansour, *The development and management of human resources in Iran*, Ph.D. thesis, North Texas State Univ. 1979.

Aspects of higher education in Iran have been discussed *inter alia* by

AFẒAL, Manuchihr, Farīdūn BĀZARGĀN, *et al.*, *Rāhnamā-yi āmūzish-i ᶜālī dar Īrān*, Tehran 1969.

Guide to higher education.

AGHAZADEH, Ahmad, *Higher education and investment in human capital: the case of Iran*, Ph.D. thesis, Florida State Univ. 1977.

ARDAKĀNĪ, Ḥusain Maḥbūbī, *Tārīkh-i taḥavvul-i dānishgāh-i Tihrān* ..., *op. cit.* IX 9.4.

BRAMMER, Lawrence M, 'Problems of Iranian university students, *MEJ* 18(4), 1964 :443-50.

COPELAND, W A, *American influence on the development of higher education in Iran*, Ph.D. thesis, Univ. of Pennsylvania 1973.

Gives account of the Presbyterian mission schools (chapter 2) and of university cooperative projects in the period 1951-1967.

DOERR, Arthur, 'An assessment of educational development: the case of the Pahlavi University, Iran', *MEJ* 22(3), 1968 :317-23.

Describes the largely unsuccessful attempt to reorganize Pahlavī University (Shīrāz) with help from the University of Pennsylvania.

EICHER, Carl K (ed), *An analysis of US-Iranian cooperation in Higher Education*, American Council on Education, Overseas Liaison Committee, Washington, DC 1976.

FARJADI, Gholamali, *Economics of study abroad: the case of Iranian students in the US*, Ph.D. thesis, New York Univ. 1980.

KUTUBĪ, Murtażā, *Masā'ilī chand dar bārā-yi āmūzish-i ᶜālī va dānishgāhhā dar Īrān*, Tehran 1969.

A sociological study of university problems.

—— *Tārīkh-i mu'assasāt-i tamaddun-i jadīd dar Īrān*, *op.cit.* IX 9.4.

NASSEFAT, M, and J MADANI-WELLS, 'Iranian students abroad', *I.rev.int.rel.* 7, 1976 :19-48.

SHAHLAPOUR, Parvin, *Development of higher education and high level manpower needs in Iran*, Ph.D. thesis, Univ. of Missouri-Columbia 1978.

TABAN, Hossein Hozi, *Higher education and its development in Iran*, Ed.D. thesis, Univ. of Northern Colorado 1979.

ZONIS, Marvin, 'Higher education and social change: problems and prospects', E YAR-SHATER (ed), *Iran faces the seventies*, *op.cit.* IX 6.9.

Other works on the history of education in Iran are listed in chapter IX 6.4.

A well-known study which identifies problems in primary education is Ṣamad BIHRANGĪ's *Kand u kāv dar masāyil-i tarbiyatī-yi Āẕarbāyjān*, Tehran 1964; reprinted Arlington, Virginia 1977. The village experience of this Tabrīzī school teacher greatly adds to this book: he discusses the use of Persian in Āẕari-Turkish speaking villages, the unintelligibility of school-books, teacher motivation, the bureaucracy, and the inadequacy of school inspection. Other representative titles on primary and secondary schooling, literacy, teachers, and the educational requirements of different social groups are

AGHILIPOUR, A, *Lutte contre l'analphabétisme dans le monde, et l'armée du savoir en Iran*, D. de l'Univ. thesis, Univ. of Paris V, 1973.

ALAGHBAND, Ali, *The public school teacher in Iran: social origin, status, and career orientation*, Ph.D. thesis, Southern Illinois Univ. 1973.

ARASTEH, A Reza (ĀRĀSTA, ᶜA Riżā), *Faces of Persian youth: a sociological study*, Leiden 1970.

BĀMDĀD, Badr al-mulūk, *Taᶜlīm va tarbiyat-i dukhtarān dar Īrān*, Tehrān 1950. Education for girls.

HANNA, Barbara, *Der Kampf gegen das Analphabetentum in Iran*, Deutschen Orient-Inst., Opladen 1966.

LYKO, Dieter, *Gründung, Wachstum, und Leben der evangelischen christlichen Kirchen in Iran*, *op.cit.* VI 3.10.

Contains material on the American Presbyterian and English Episcopal mission schools and the German-English schools for the blind.

MINISTRY OF EDUCATION, *Majmūᶜa-yi tarḥhā-yi āmūzish va parvarish-i kishvar*, Tehran 1967.

Plans for school education, with suggested syllabuses and teacher training courses: see also *Education Statistics* prepared by the Ministry's Bureau of Statistics 1970, 1972, etc.

NAVABPOUR, Mehdi, *The role of the Iranian secondary school principal as perceived by principals, teachers, and school supervisors*, Ph.D. thesis, George Peabody College for Teachers, Tennessee 1977.

ṢĀḤIB AL-ZAMĀNĪ, Nāṣir al-dīn, *Javānī-yi pur-ranj: pizhūhish dar bāra-yi masā'il-i javānān*, Tehran 1967.

Penetrating study of youth problems by one-time Director of the Mental Health Department of the Health Ministry: includes sections on the inadequacy of study and specialization, employment and military service, Iranian students abroad, etc.

SHAFII, F, M MOHSENI, and M MOTABAR, 'Formal education in a tribal society, Iran', *op.cit.* 2.2.1.

On the tent schools of the Qashqā'ī tribe.

SOHRAB, Rouhanguise, *Problèmes des élèves du cycle secondaire à Téhéran*, thesis (3ème cycle), Univ. of Paris V, 1974.

STREET, Brian, 'The mullah, the Shahnameh and the madrasseh', *Asian Affairs* LXII(3), October 1976.

Reactions of villagers to state schools.

WATERFIELD, Robin E, *Christians in Persia*, *op.cit.* VI 3.10.

Contains material on mission schools.

Increasing interest was being shown in vocational and technical education as part of broader concerns for manpower needs and the development of human resources. Some typical titles are

BARTSCH, William H, 'The industrial labor force of Iran: problems of recruitment, training and productivity', *op.cit.* 2.1.

ELKAN, Walter, 'Employment, education, training and skilled labor in Iran', *op.cit.* 2.1.

KHAVARPOUR, F A, *The problem of manpower planning for rural to urban migrants in Esfahan Province, Iran: the need for an educational development policy*, Ph.D. thesis, Univ. of Michigan 1980.

LOTFIPOUR, Khosrow, *A study of vocational education in Iran (Tehran)*, Ph.D. thesis, Iowa State Univ. 1977.

NASSEHY TABRIZI, Guitty, *Technical education in Iran: attitudes of students and employers*, Ph.D. thesis, Univ. of Illinois, Urbana-Champaign 1979.

NOORI, Mohammad Hassan, *Education and training to meet manpower needs for the energy industries in Iran*, Ph.D. thesis, Univ. of Missouri-Columbia 1978.

3. *GOVERNMENT*

3.1 *International relations*

These notes on Iran's contemporary international relations (3.1), internal politics and administration (3.2), and law (3.3) should be read in conjunction with both the review of material on recent history (chapter IX 6) and the assessment of the impact of the 1979 Islamic Revolution (chapter XV). Clearly much that has been written recently about Iran's international links has become redundant except in the context of the study of the Pahlavī dynasty as a phase which has ended. Much more assumes a new importance as scholars and others look back over past decades to identify developments which have culminated in the events since late 1978 to produce a revolution in both the internal order and the international posture of Iran.

The Middle East Journal, published by the Middle East Institute in Washington, DC, provides an accessible 'Chronology' of major events involving Iran. Appearing in each of the four annual issues, this provides names, dates and other useful details and indicates sources of information. The same journal also maintains a section of new books on political and related topics and a bibliography of articles published in over 250 periodicals, including the *Bank Markazi Iran Bulletin*, Tehran, *Iranian Studies*, Los Angeles, the *Journal of Social Sciences and Humanities*, Shīrāz, the *Revue iranienne de relations internationales*, Tehran, and *Sophia Perennis*, Tehran.

A number of general works, which contain description basic to this section have been named elsewhere. The *Area Handbook for Iran*, Foreign Area Studies Division, American University, Washington, DC 1971, is one of these. Another is the earlier *Persia*, produced in London by the United Kingdom Admiralty in 1945. Europa Publications' *The Middle East and North Africa* is another comprehensive reference work, as is the *Iran Almanac and Book of Facts*, produced by the Echo of Iran up to 1978. Analytical, rather than descriptive, surveys are also listed in 1.2 above. Particularly useful among these, as general introductions to Iran's government and politics, at least prior to the Revolution, are *Twentieth-Century Iran*, AMIRSADEGHI, 1977, *Iran: dictatorship and development*, HALLIDAY, 1979, *Iran under the Pahlavis*, LENCZOWSKI, 1978, and *Iran, past and present*, WILBER, 1963.

3.1.1 *USA*

Iran's relations with the major powers have been studied in a number of works on the later Pahlavī period. A sample of the available titles with a special focus on Iranian links with the United States, prior to the 1979 Revolution, is

ALEXANDER, Yonah, and Allan NANES (eds), *The United States and Iran: a documentary history*, University Publications of America, Frederick, Maryland 1981.

Reports, papers, correspondence, documents (including some previously unprinted).

ARCILESI, Salvatore A, *Development of United States foreign policy in Iran, 1949-1960*, Ph.D. thesis, Univ. of Virginia 1965.

BOZEMAN, A, 'Iran: US foreign policy and the tradition of Persian statecraft', *Orbis* 23(2), 1979 :387-402.

IRANI, G, 'American diplomacy in Iran: a review of the literature', *I.rev. int.rel.* 4, 1975 :169-72.

RAMAZANI, Rouhollah K, 'Iran and the United States: an experiment in enduring friendship', *MEJ* 30(3), 1976 :322-34.

RUBIN, Barry, *Paved with good intentions*, *op.cit.* IX 6.9.

SADEGHI, K, 'American-Iranian relations', *I.rev.int.rel.* 9, 1977 :45-67.

UNITED STATES SENATE, *Sale of ANWACS to Iran*, Hearings, Subcommittee on Foreign Assistance, 18 July - 19 Sept. 1977, Washington, DC 1977.

3.1.2 *USSR*

On relations between Iran and the Soviet Union in recent years, reference can be made to

FATEMI, Faramarz S, *The USSR in Iran*, *op.cit.* IX 6.7.

Special focus on 1941-47.

GHOREICHI, Ahmad, *Soviet foreign policy in Iran, 1917-1960*, Ph.D. thesis, Univ. of Colorado 1965.

KAIHĀN, Mahdī, *Dah-sāl-i kumak-i iqtiṣādi va fannī-i Ittiḥād-i Shūravī ba-Īrān, 1344-1354*, Stockholm 1976.

A Tūda publication on Soviet economic and technical aid to Iran between 1966 and 1976.

PARVIN, Manoucher, 'Political economy of Soviet-Iranian trade: an overview of theory and practice', *MEJ* 31(2), 1977 :31-43.

WASSERBERG, Arlyn B, *Politics of Soviet interference: Soviet foreign policy towards Iran*, Ph.D. thesis, City Univ. of New York 1979.

3.1.3 *Other foreign policy*

Further titles covering a variety of aspects of Iranian foreign policy are

BURRELL, R, 'Iranian foreign policy: strategic location, economic ambition, and dynastic determination', *Journal of International Affairs* 29(2), 1975 :129-38.

CHUBIN, Shahram, 'Iran's foreign policy 1960-1976: an overview', AMIRSADEGHI and FERRIER (eds), *Twentieth-Century Iran*, *op.cit.*, :197-222.

COTTRELL, Alwin J, *Iran: diplomacy in a regional and global context*,

Washington, DC 1975.

ELAHI, Cyrus, *Society and foreign policy in Iran*, Ph.D. thesis, The American Univ., Washington, DC 1970.

HEKMAT, Hormoz, *Iran's response to Soviet-American rivalry, 1951-1962: a comparative study*, Ph.D. thesis, Columbia Univ., New York 1974.

KUNIHOLM, Bruce R, *The origins of the Cold War in the Near East: great power conflict and diplomacy in Iran, Turkey, and Greece*, Princeton Univ. Press, Princeton, NJ 1980.

Suggests that traditional power relationships in the 'Northern Tier' contributed significantly to the Cold War.

LAMBTON, Ann K S, 'The impact of the West on Persia', *International Affairs* 33(1), 1957 :12-25.

MARTIN, Laurence, 'The future strategic role of Iran', AMIRSADEGHI and FERRIER (eds), *Twentieth-Century Iran*, 1977 :223-52.

A pre-1979 Revolution view.

MOZAFARI, M, 'Les nouvelles dimensions de la politique étrangère de l'Iran', *Politique Étrangère* 40(2), 1975 :141-60.

RAMAZANI, Rouhollah K, *Iran's Foreign Policy, 1941-1973*, *op.cit.* IX 6.7.

ZABIH, Sepehr, 'Iran's international posture: de facto nonalignment with a pro-Western alliance', *MEJ* 24(3), 1970 :302-18.

From the perspective of Tehran, the country's foreign relations were, from 1967, systematically surveyed in the annual publications *Ravābiṭ-i khārijī-yi Īrān* and *Akhbār va asnād* from the Ministry of Foreign Affairs. This Ministry issued a collection of bilateral treaties in two volumes, *Majmūʿa-i muʿāhadāt-i dū jāniba-yi muʿtabar ... tā sāl-i 1349(1970-71)*. The Information and Press Department of the same Ministry published occasional surveys of Iran's foreign policy in western languages.

3.1.4 *Middle East policy*

Iran is the largest Gulf state and has conducted a vigorous foreign policy in the area, particularly since the British withdrawal in 1971. A comprehensive review of 'Persian Gulf Studies' is provided by Emile A NAKHLEH, *MESA bull.* 11(2), 1977, pp.31-43. Another contemporary source is Alvin J COTTRELL (ed), *The Persian Gulf states*, *op.cit.* IX 6.9. Mohammad-Reza DJALILI considers the common problems and prospects of Iran and its neighbours in *La Golfe Persique: problèmes et perspectives*, Paris 1978: the fourth part of his book looks at foreign powers and the Gulf.

Iran has long been linked with states and issues in the wider Middle Eastern region. Much of the relevant historical material is covered in chapter IX and elsewhere in this *Guide*. A selection of titles on the contemporary regional involvements of Iran (up to 1979) follows.

ALAOLMOLKI, Nozar, *Emergence of regional hegemonical power: Iran as a case study in the Persian Gulf*, Ph.D. thesis, Miami Univ., Ohio 1977.

AMIN, Sayed Hassan, *International and legal problems of the Gulf*, Wisbech 1981.

AMIRIE, Abbas (ed), *The Persian Gulf and Indian Ocean in international politics*, Inst. of Int. Political and Economic Studies, Tehran 1976.

Proceedings of a 1975 conference in Tehran: descriptive essays rather than critical analysis of Pahlavī Iran.

AMIRSADEGHI, Hossein (ed), *The security of the Persian Gulf*, London 1981.

BAHRAMPOUR, Firouz, *Iran: emergence of a Middle Eastern power*, New York 1970.

BANUAZIZI, Ali, 'Iran: the making of a regional power', A L UDOVITCH (ed), *The Middle East: oil, conflict, and hope*, Lexington, Mass. 1976.

CHUBIN, Shahram, and M FARD-SAIDI, *Recent trends in Middle East politics and Iran's foreign policy options*, Inst. for Int. Political and Economic Studies, Tehran 1975.

—— and Sepehr ZABIH, *The foreign relations of Iran*, *op.cit.* IX 6.9.

COOLEY, John K, 'Iran, the Palestinians, and the Gulf', *Foreign Affairs* 57(5), 1979 :1017-034

EHRENBURG, E, and W MALLMAN, *Rüstung und Wirtschaft am Golf. Iran und seine Nachbarn (1965-1978)*, Deutsches Orient-Inst., Hamburg 1978.

GIL BENUMEYA, R, 'El Imperio del Iran, corazón del Oriente', *Revista de Politica Internacional* 117, Madrid 1971 :123-30.

HALE, William, and Julian BHARIER, 'CENTO, RCD, and the northern tier: a political and economic appraisal', *MES* 8(2), 1972 :217-26.

KELLY, J B, 'The Persian claim to Bahrain', *International Affairs* 33(2), 1957 :12-25.

From India Office and other documentary sources.

LONG, David E, *The Persian Gulf: an introduction to its peoples, politics, and economics*, Boulder, Colorado 1976.

MacDONALD, Charles G, 'Iran's strategic interests and the law of the sea', *MEJ* 34(3), 1980 :302-22.

MAHDAVĪ, ^{c}Abd al-Riżā Hūshang, *Tārīkh-i ravābiṭ-i khārijī-yi Īrān*, Tehran 1970.

MELAMID, Alexander, 'The Shatt al-Arab boundary dispute', *MEJ* 22(3), 1968 :351-57.

MINISTRY OF FOREIGN AFFAIRS, *Ravābiṭ-i daulat-i shāhanshāhī-yi Īrān bā duval-i ḥauza-yi mas'ūliyyat-i idāra-yi avval-i siyāsī*, Tehran 1976.

Relations with Iraq, Saudi Arabia, Kuwait, and Yemen.

PATRICK, Robert Bayard, *Iran's emergence as a Middle Eastern power*, Ph.D. thesis, Univ. of Utah 1973.

RAMAZANI, Rouhollah K, *The Persian Gulf and the Straits of Hormuz*, *op.cit.* IX 6.9.

—— 'Iran and the Arab-Israeli conflict', *MEJ* 32(4), 1978 :413-28.

—— 'Iran's search for regional cooperation', *MEJ* 30(2), 1976 :173-86.

—— 'Emerging patterns of regional relations in Iranian foreign policy', *Orbis* 18(4), 1975 :1043-069.

—— *The Persian Gulf: Iran's role*, *op.cit.* IX 6.9.

—— *The northern tier: Afghanistan, Iran, and Turkey*, Princeton, NJ 1966.

REPPA, Robert Bruce, Sr, *Israel and Iran: bilateral relationships and effect on the Indian Ocean Basin*, New York 1974.

SHAOUL, Eshach Emran, *Cultural values and foreign policy decision-making in Iran: the case of Iran's recognition of Israel*, Ph.D. thesis, George Washington Univ. 1971.

SINGH, K, 'The security of the Persian Gulf', *I.rev.int.rel.* 9, 1977 :5-26.

TOWLIAT, Mohsen, *Iran as a regional power in the Persian Gulf*, Ph.D. thesis, Claremont Graduate School 1978.

WEINBAUM, M G, 'Iran and Israel: the discreet entente', *Orbis* 18(4), 1975 :1070-087.

WYMAR, Benno, *Regional cooperation for development: Iran, Pakistan, and Turkey*, Ph.D. thesis, Univ. of Nebraska, Lincoln 1973.

ZABIH, Sepehr, 'Iran's policy toward the Persian Gulf', *IJMES* 7(3), 1976 :345-58.

—— and Shahram CHUBIN, *Iran's foreign relations: a developing state in a zone of great power conflict*, Univ. of California Press, Berkeley 1974.

3.2 *Internal politics and administration*

The introductory comments and many of the titles in 3.1 above bear directly on the internal politics and administration of Iran. Other relevant material is to be found, in this chapter, in 2.2 (Social groups) and 3.3 (Law), while much of relevance to the historical dimension of the contemporary structure and function of Iranian government appears in chapter IX. Included in an article, 'Observations on sources for the study of nineteenth- and twentieth-century Iranian history', are comments by Hafez F FARMAYAN on the constraints and limitations characteristic of academic writing on history and politics in Pahlavī Iran - except for some upsurge of activity in the

1940s and 1950s (*IJMES* 5(1), 1974, pp.32-49).

Hamid ENAYAT reviews the background of political science in pp.3-5 of his 1974 article on 'The state of the social sciences in Iran' (*op.cit.* 1.1). He points to the links with legal studies - and with French political science - up to the mid-1960s when the American unit system was introduced at the University of Tehran and a second university was established in Tabrīz. Up to 1979 many teachers of political science were trained in the United States or Europe: many showed the rejection of Islam's Islamic tradition in favour of western priorities which were, in their turn, to be the objects of counter-rejection in 1979. To this has been added the internal political climate of Iran which has generally discouraged free debate and question.

Despite the constraints, however, it was possible for Aqdas MALIK and Hamid ENAYAT (ᶜINĀYAT) to list some 900 Persian-language titles in their annotated political science bibliography, *Kitāb-shināsī-yi tawṣīfī-yi ᶜulūm-i siyāsī dar Īrān*, University of Tehran Publication no.1448, Tehran 1975. Meanwhile, a primary source for domestic politics have been the parliamentary debates (first record in 1906 in *Majlis*). Debates of the National Assembly have been published separately as *Muẕākarāt*, while the official gazette, *Rūz-nāma-yi rasmī-yi kishvar-i shāhanshāhī-yi Īrān*, has been produced by the Ministry of Justice since 1945. The political science output on Iran reflects the realities and changes within the system itself. Many works have appeared with a primary focus on the central position of the Pahlavī monarchy, but without rigorous critical analysis. Just as logically there was, during the later 1970s, an upsurge of interest in studies on the social and ideological history of Shīᶜī Islam. This found expression, for example, in the publication of over two hundred essays and lectures by ᶜAlī SHARĪᶜATĪ, founder of radical sociology in revolutionary Iran: see his eight-volume *Majmūᶜa-i āsār* (Solon, Ohio/Aachen 1977-1979).

In the later 1960s and 1970s opposition groups with various complexions and locations produced a range of material important to the student of the 1979 Revolution. Reflecting the cultural contrasts among Iran's Persian and minority groups have been studies of the concept of nationalism and of the conflict between groups within Iran and between them and Tehran. (Some of this material is listed in 2.2 above.) Meanwhile administration and local government *per se* have attracted less attention than might have been expected except, as seen, from the perspective of law.

3.2.1 *Government*

Some general works covering the politics and government of Iran in the

Pahlavī period are

ARABADZHYAN, A Z (ed), *et al.*, *Iran: ocherki noveyshey istorii*, Soviet Academy of Sciences, Moscow 1976.

Essays on Iran's recent history: see especially re 1953-61, pp.262-318, and re 1960s and 1970s, pp.319-468.

BANANI, Amin, *The modernization of Iran*, *op.cit.* IX 5.1.

Legislative and statutory reforms (army, health, education, etc.) under Reza Shah: based primarily on Persian sources. Bibliography.

BAUSANI, Alessandro, *The Persians*, *op.cit.* IX 1.1.

BILL, James A, *The politics of Iran*, *op.cit.* IX 6.9.

Thoughtful study of Iranian society and of the political aspirations and disaffections of classes and groups.

BINDER, Leonard, *Iran: political development in a changing society*, *op. cit.* IX 6.9.

Important study of the political and social structure of Iran in the 1950s.

COTTAM, Richard W, *Nationalism in Iran*, *op.cit.* IX 6.9.

The revised 1979 edition has an additional chapter on the 1978 events leading up to the Revolution. Studies relationships between Iranian nationalism and imperialism and Islam.

FISCHER, Michael M J, *Iran: from religious dispute to revolution*, *op.cit.* IX 6.9.

Based on pre-Revolution field work, this looks at Iranian society on the verge of metamorphosis.

GRAHAM, Robert, *Iran: the illusion of power*, *op.cit.* 1.2.

HALLIDAY, Fred, *Iran: dictatorship and development*, *op.cit.* 1.2.

KASTER, Heinrich L, *Iran heute*, Vienna 1974.

Broad survey of religious and student opposition, Tudeh, National Front, terrorism, etc.

LAMBTON, Ann K S, 'The impact of the West on Persia', *op.cit.* 3.1.3.

Government and the rise of nationalism: the historical background.

LENCOWSKI, George (ed), *Iran under the Pahlavis*, *op.cit.* 6.9.

Chapters by twelve writers, with bibliographies. Does not identify the first stirrings of the revolution to come.

MARLOWE, John, *Iran: a short political guide*, New York 1963.

A very effective, albeit brief, general guide to Iran's recent political history.

MILANYAN, M D, *Gosudarstvenniy stroy sovremennogo Irana*, Soviet Academy of Sciences, Moscow 1973.

The government structure of contemporary Iran: role of the Shah, parliament, constitution, legislature, judiciary, etc.

PAHLAVI, Muḥammad Reza (Shah), *The White Revolution*, *op.cit.* IX 6.9.

3.2.2 *Political parties*

Titles on the parliament of Iran and the country's political parties during the reign of Muḥammad Riẓā S̲h̲āh include

ABRAHAMIAN, Ervand V, 'Communism and communalism in Iran: The *Tudah* and the *Firqah-i Dimukrat*', *IJMES* 1(4), 1970 :291-316.

See author's 1969 Ph.D. thesis, *Social bases of Iranian politics: the Tudeh party, 1941-53*, Columbia University, New York.

ASHRAFI, Mehdi, *Development and transformation of political parties in Iran (1941-1975)*, Ph.D. thesis, Claremont Graduate School, California 1977.

BINDER, Leonard, 'The cabinet of Iran: a case study in institutional adaptation', *MEJ* 16(1), 1962 :29-47.

D'ERME, G, 'I partiti politici in Persia dal 1941 al 1944', *Oriente Moderno* 50(3), 1971 :213-35.

ELWELL-SUTTON, Laurence P, 'Political parties in Iran: 1941-1948', *MEJ* 3(1), 1949 :45-62.

MILLER, William G, 'Political organization in Iran: from *dowreh* to political party', *MEJ* 23(2), 1969 :159-67, and 23(3), 1969 :343-50.

MOHAMMADI-NEJAD, Hassan, 'The Iranian parliamentary elections of 1975', *IJMES* 8(1), 1977 :103-16.

RAZI, G Hossein, 'Genesis of party in Iran: a case study of the interaction between the political system and political parties', *I.stud.* 3(2), 1970 :58-90.

Sair-i kumūnīzm dar Īrān az S̲h̲ahrivār 1320 ta 1336, Tehran 1957.

S̲H̲AJĪᶜĪ, Zuhra, *Namāyandigān-i Majlis-i S̲h̲aurā-yi Millī dar bīst u yak daura-yi qānūnguzārī*, Tehran 1965.

The representatives of the National Consultative Assembly during twenty-one legislative periods.

ṢIDDĪQ, Javād, *Milliyyat va inqilāb dar Īrān*, New York 1973.

WEINBAUM, Marvin G, 'Iran finds a party system: the institutionalization of Iran Novin', *MEJ* 27(4), 1973 :439-55.

ZABIH, Sepehr, *The Communist movement in Iran*, *op.cit.* IX 6.7.

Authoritative: based on 1963 Ph.D. thesis at the University of California, Berkeley.

ZONIS, Marvin, *The political elite of Iran*, *op.cit.* IX 6.9.

Solidly based on psycho-sociological research, including interviews: the management of the elite by the Shah.

3.2.3 *Religion*

Among the growing literature on recent and contemporary implications of religion in the Iranian political scene are

AKHAVI, Shahrough, *Religion and politics in contemporary Iran: clergy-state relations in the Pahlavi period*, State Univ. of New York Press, Albany 1980.

Penetrating review of the fluctuating relations between the Islamic clergy, the ulama, and the government of Iran since 1925.

BAYAT-PHILIPP, Mangol, 'Shi'ism in contemporary Iranian politics: the case of Ali Shari^{c}ati', KEDOURIE and HAIM (eds), *Towards a modern Iran*, *op. cit.* 1.2, :155-68.

BINDER, Leonard, 'The proofs of Islam: religion and politics in Iran', George MAKDISI (ed), *Arabic and Islamic studies in honor of H A R Gibb*, Harvard Univ. Press, Cambridge, Mass. 1965 :118-40.

DOROSHENKO, Ye A, *Shiitskoye dukhovyenstovo v sovryemyennom Irane*, Soviet Acad. of Sciences, Moscow 1975.

The Shiite clergy in contemporary Iran: role in political structure and conflict with the monarch; substantial bibliography, including Persian-language sources.

FISCHER, Michael M J, *Iran: from religious dispute to revolution*, op.cit. IX 6.9.

FLOOR, Willem M, 'The revolutionary character of the Iranian ulama: wishful thinking or reality?' *IJMES* 12(4), 1980 :501-24.

GAROUSSIAN (Riazi-Davoudi), Vida, *The* ulema *and secularization in contemporary Iran*, Ph.D. thesis, Southern Illinois Univ. 1974.

KEDDIE, Nikki R, 'The roots of the Ulama's power in modern Iran', Nikki R KEDDIE (ed), *Scholars, saints, and sufis*, op.cit. VI 2.10.

—— *Iran: religion, politics and society, collected essays*, London 1980.

Six of the eight essays have been previously published.

—— 'Iran: change in Islam: Islam and change', *IJMES* 11(4), 1980 :527-42.

KHUMAINĪ, Āyatullāh Sayyid Rūḥullāh.

See chapter XV of this *Guide*.

LAMBTON, Ann K S, 'Islamic society in Persia', (inaugural lecture delivered March 9, 1954), L E SWEET (ed), *Peoples and cultures of the Middle East*, vol.1, *Depth and diversity*, New York 1970 :74-101.

RICHARD, Yann, *Le Shi'isme en Iran*, op.cit. VI 2.4.

3.2.4 *Nationalism*

The nature of Iranian nationalism, and the relationships between various groups and the centre, are subjects of

DIGARD, Jean-Pierre, 'Les nomades et l'état central en Iran: quelques enseignements d'un long passé d'"hostilité réglementée"', *Peuples Mediterranéens* 7, 1979 :37-53.

EAGLETON, William, Jr, *The Kurdish Republic of 1946*, *op.cit.* IX 6.7.

ELWELL-SUTTON, Laurence P, 'Nationalism and neutralism in Iran', *MEJ* 12(1), 1958 :20-32.

RAMAZANI, Rouhollah K, 'The autonomous republic of Azarbaijan and the Kurdish People's Republic: their rise and fall', Thomas T HAMMOND and Robert FARRELL (eds), *The anatomy of Communist takeovers*, Yale Univ. Press, New Haven/London 1975 :448-74.

ROOSEVELT, Archie, 'The Kurdish Republic of Mahabad', *op.cit.* IX 6.7.

SALZMAN, Philip C, 'National integration of the tribes of modern Iran, *MEJ* 25(3), 1971 :325-36.

SAVORY, Roger M, 'Modern Persia', *Cambridge History of Islam*, vol.1, Cambridge Univ. Press 1970 :595-626.

VAHDAT, M, *The Soviet Union and the movement to establish autonomy in Iranian Azarbaijan*, Ph.D. thesis, Indiana Univ. 1958.

3.2.5 *Monarchy*

Further titles on the monarchy and on the structure of power and administration in Iran up to 1979 include

ARGHEYD, Kamal, *The role of value systems in the process of social change: the Shah-People Revolution of Iran*, DBA thesis, Harvard Univ. 1978.

BAYNE, E A, *Persian kingship in transition: conversations with a monarch whose office is traditional and whose goal is modernization*, AUFS, New York 1968.

BESHARAT, Ali Reza, 'The role of local government in social development: Iran', *Ekistics* 28(169), 1969 :435-39.

BILL, James A, 'Modernization and reform from above: the case of Iran', *Journal of Politics* 32(2), Feb. 1970 :3-18.

—— 'The plasticity of informal politics: the case of Iran', *MEJ* 22(2), 1973 :131-51.

GABLE, Richard W, 'Culture and administration in Iran', *MEJ* 13(4), 1959 :407-21.

GREAVES, Rose, '1942-1976: the reign of Muhammad Riza Shah', AMIRSADEGHI and FERRIER (eds), *Twentieth-century Iran*, *op.cit.*, :53-91.

KARANJIA, Rustom Khurshedji, *Mind of a monarch: biography of the Shah*, London 1977.

KATOUZIAN, Homa, *The political economy of modern Iran*, *op.cit.* IX 6.9.

Less on Iran's economy than on its political development, from an anti-Pahlavī perspective.

KAZEMI, Farhad, 'The military and politics in Iran: the uneasy symbiosis', KEDOURIE and HAIM (eds), *Towards a modern Iran*, *op.cit.* IX 6.9, :217-40.

KEDDIE, Nikki R, 'Class structure and political power in Iran since 1796', *I.stud.* 11, 1978 :305-80.

Developments since 1941 covered from p.318.

—— 'The Iranian power structure and social change 1800-1969: an overview', *IJMES* 2(1), 1971 :3-20.

KNAPP, Wilfrid, '1921-1941: the period of Riza Shah', AMIRSADEGHI and FERRIER (eds), *Twentieth-century Iran*, *op.cit.*, :23-51.

KUKLAN, Hooshang, 'Civil service reform in Iran: myth and reality', *International Review of Administrative Sciences* 43(4), Brussels 1977 :345-51.

MAHDAVY, Hossein, 'The coming crisis in Iran', *Foreign Affairs* 44(1), 1965 :134-46.

MAHRAD, Ahmad, *Iran unter der Herrschaft Reza Schahs*, Frankfurt/New York 1977.

Critical treatment of Riżā Shāh: extensive use of German sources.

MOZAFARI, M, 'Transformations sociales et problèmes politiques en Iran', *Politique Étrangère* 43(5), 1978 :557-78.

NAHAVANDI, Hushang, 'La politique d'independence de l'Iran', *I.rev.int.rel.* 7, 1976 :5-18.

RAMAZANI, Rouhollah K, 'Iran's "White Revolution": a study in political development', *IJMES* 5(2), April 1974 :124-39.

REZUN, Miron, 'Reza Shah's court minister: Teymourtash', *IJMES* 12(2), 1980 :119-37.

Until 1932 ᶜAbd al-Ḥusain Khān Taimūrtāsh was second in power only to Riżā Shāh.

SAVORY, Roger M, 'The principles of homeostasis considered in relation to political events in Iran in the 1960s', *IJMES* 3(3), 1972 :282-302.

THORPE, James A, *The mission of Arthur C Millspaugh to Iran, 1943-1945*, Ph.D. thesis, Univ. of Wisconsin-Madison 1973.

UNITED STATES, HOUSE OF REPRESENTATIVES, *Human Rights in Iran*, (Hearing, Subcommittee on International Organizations, Committee on International Relations), Government Printing Office, Washington, DC 26 Oct. 1977.

VIEILLE, Paul, *La féodalité et l'état en Iran*, Paris 1975.

—— and A H BANI-SADR (eds), *Pétrole et violence: terreur blanche et résistance en Iran*, Paris 1974.

WARNE, William E, *Mission for peace: Point-Four in Iran*, Indianapolis/New York 1956.

ZONIS, Marvin, 'The political élite of Iran: a second stratum', Frank TACHAU (ed), *Political élites and political development in the Middle East*, Cambridge, Mass. 1975 :192-216.

In the later years of the reign of Muḥammad Riżā Shāh, there was a substantial increase in the volume of protest material, most of it published outside Iran and some of it difficult to obtain. The best introduction to this material, for the period up to the 1979 Revolution, is Wolfgang BEHN's *The Iranian opposition in exile*, *op.cit.* IX 6.9. The same writer has also compiled a comprehensive article on 'The revolution of the pen: Iranian underground publications 1963-1978', in *Middle East studies and libraries: a felicitation volume for Professor J D Pearson*, B C BLOOMFIELD (ed), London 1980, pp.13-22.

3.3 *Law*[1]

3.3.1 *Constitutional law*

The Constitution of Iran, prior to 1979, consisted of (a) the Fundamental Law (Qānūn-i asāsī) of 30 December 1906, (b) the Supplementary Fundamental Law of 7 October 1907, and (c) amendments of 12 December 1925, 8 May 1949, and 7 September 1967. English translations of (a) and (b) are to be found in Edward G BROWNE, *The Persian Revolution*, *op.cit.* IX 6.5, and of (a), (b), and (c) in the *Iran Almanac 1968*. See also Ann K S LAMBTON's article *Dustūr* (Iran) in the *Encyclopaedia of Islam* (2nd edition); Helen M DAVIS, *Constitutions, electoral laws, treaties of states in the Near and Middle East*, Durham (North Carolina) 1947; and A A AL MARAYATI, *Middle Eastern constitutions and electoral laws*, New York 1961. For comparison of the modern laws of Iran with those of other Moslem countries, a useful work is Herbert J LIEBESNY, *The law of the Near and Middle East: readings, cases, and materials*, Albany, New York 1975. See also Sir Norman ANDERSON, *Islamic Law in the Modern World*, New York 1959.

Further titles on the roots of law in Iran are

AGHABABIAN, Raphaël, *Législation iranienne actuelle*, vol.I, ... interessant les étrangers et les iraniens à l'étranger, Tehran 1939; vol.II, Lois constitutionelles, code civil iranien, statuts particuliers, Paris 1951.

[1] For material on Islamic law see VI 6.

MANṢŪR, ᶜAlī (Manṣūr al-mamālik), *Tārīkh-i qānūn va ḥukūmat*, Univ. of Tehran, Tehran 1960.

History of statute law and government administration.

ṢĀLIH, ᶜAlī Pāshā, *Quvva-yi muqannina va quvva-yi qaẓā'īya (naẓarī bi tārīkh-i ḥuqūq-i Īrān va sāzmānhā tā shahrīvar 1341)*, Tehran 1964.

Legislative and judicial power: sources of Iranian law: see also short version in *Īrānshahr*, volume 2, UNESCO, Tehran 1964, pp.986-1013.

ṢĀNIᶜĪ, Parvīz, *Ḥuqūq va ijtimāᶜ dar rābiṭa-yi ḥuqūq bā ᶜavāmil-i ijtimāᶜī*, Tehran 1968.

On law and society.

Further general works on Iranian law, together with selected compendium and glossary material, are

ABU'L-ḤAMD, ᶜAbdul-Ḥamīd, *et al.*, *Farhang-i iṣṭilāḥāt-i ḥuqūqī, Fārsī-Farānsa*, vol.I, (alif-ṣād), Iranian Culture Foundation, Scientific and Technical Glossaries, 7, Tehran 1974.

Legal terms in Persian and French (to letter ṣād).

ᶜALAVĪ, Riẓā, *Kullīyāt-i ḥuqūq*, Higher Accountancy Inst., Tehran 1969.

Compendium of Iranian law.

GEHRKE, Ulrich, 'Rechtswesen', Ulrich GEHRKE and Harald MEHNER (eds), *Iran: Natur, Bevölkerung ...*, *op.cit.* II 1, :238-58.

Description of the legal system.

ḤAIDARIĀN, Maḥmūd, *Mabādī-yi ᶜilm-i ḥuqūq*, College of Literature and Foreign Languges, pub.8, Tehran 1973.

Fundamentals of jurisprudence.

JAᶜFARĪ LANGARŪDĪ, Muḥammad Jaᶜfar, *Dānishnāma-yi ḥuqūqī*, Univ. of Tehran, Tehran 1964-66, repr. Tehran 1973.

Legal encyclopaedia: statutes, regulations, evidence, registration, the courts, etc.

—— *Tirmīnūlūzhī-yi ḥuqūq*, Tehran 1967.

Legal terminology.

The laws passed by the Iranian parliament since 1906 have been published as *Majmūᶜa-yi qavānīn-ī mauẓūᶜa va muṣavvabāt* and, since 1961, as *Majmūᶜa-i qavānīn ... daura-i qānūn-guzārī-i Majlis-i Shūrā-yi Millī*. An index for 1906-1971 was published in 1972. See also the *National Union Catalog* (Library of Congress) which lists (under 'Iran') laws, statutes, etc. and (by municipality) ordinances and local laws. Entries on Iranian law can be found in *Index to Foreign Legal Periodicals*, which has a geographical index.

Further titles on Iranian constitutional law include

BŪSHIHRĪ, Jaᶜfar, *Ḥuqūq-i asāsī, ḥuqūq-i taṭbīqī-yi asāsī*, 2 vols, Tehran

Univ. pub.1161 (1 & 2), Tehran 1973.

Iranian and comparative constitutional law.

ᶜIRĀQĪ, Aḥmad, *Ḥuqūq-i asāsī-yi Īrān*, Tehran 1953.

Iranian constitutional law.

KAMĀNGAR, Aḥmad (ed), *Qānūn-i asāsī va qavānin-i jazā'ī ba tamām-i iṣlāḥāt tā sāl-i 1336*, Tehran 1958, repr. 1967.

The law of the constitution and penal laws, with amendments to 1957.

LOCKHART, L, 'The constitutional laws of Persia: an outline of their origin and development', *MEJ* 13(4), 1959 :372-88.

RAḤĪMĪ, Muṣṭafā, *Qānūn-ī asāsī-yi Īrān va uṣūl-i dimūkrāsi*, Tehran 1968.

Iranian constitution and government.

3.3.2 *Civil law*

The development of civil - including family - law during the later Pahlavī period is covered by

ᶜĀMILI, Bāqir, *Huqūq-i khānvāda*, College for Girls, Tehran 1971.

Family law.

ᶜAMĪD, Mūsā, *Hiba va vaṣiyāt dar ḥuqūq-i madanī-yi Īrān*, ᶜAbbās FARBUD (ed), Farbud pub.17, Tehran 1963.

Bequest and testamentary disposition.

HINCHCLIFFE, Doreen, 'The Iranian Family Protection Act', *ICLQ* 17(2), 1968 :516-21.

IMĀMĪ, Sayyīd Ḥasan, *Ḥuqūq-i madanī*, 8 vols, Tehran Univ. pub.213, 251, 439, 550, 639, 886, Tehran 1954-1963; vols. 1 & 2 repr. 1961.

The most comprehensive treatise on civil law.

Iran Almanac and Book of Facts.

A translation of the Family Protection Law of 1967 appeared in the 1968 *Iran Almanac*. Other English translations and summaries of various laws appear in annual editions between 1962 and 1976.

KĀTŪZIYĀN, Amīr Nāṣir, *Kulliyāt-i ḥuqūq-i madanī*, 2 vols, Univ. of Tehran pub.1182(1) and 1182(2), Tehran 1970.

Compendium of civil law.

—— *Taḥavvulat-i ḥuqūq-i khuṣuṣī*, Univ. of Tehran pub.1274, Tehran 1970.

Changes in private law.

—— *Vaṣīyat dar ḥuqūq-i madanī-yi Īrān*, Tehran 1960.

Testamentary disposition.

KISHĀVARZ ṢADR, Muhammad ᶜAlī (ed), *Āyīn va ravish-i dādrasī-yi madanī*, Tehran 1965.

Rules and methods of civil procedure.

NAQAVI, Sayyid ᶜAlī Riẓā, *Family Laws of Iran*, Islamic Research Inst., Islamabad 1971.

Includes text and translation of 1967 Family Protection Law.

ṢĀBĪ, Mūsā, *The Civil Code of Iran*, Tehran 1973.

ṢADR, Ḥasan, *Ḥuqūq-ī zanān dar Islām va Urūpā*, *op.cit.* 2.2.5.

Women's rights in Islam and in Europe.

SHĀYAGĀN, ᶜAlī, *Ḥuqūq-i madanī-i Īrān*, vol.I, Tehran 1965, 3rd ed.

3.3.3 *Criminal law*

Some Persian-language titles on the country's criminal law are

ᶜALAVĪ, Maḥmūd Riẓā, *Jurmshināsī*, Tehran 1970.

Criminology.

ᶜALĪ ĀBĀDĪ, ᶜAbd al-ḥusain, *Ḥuqūq-i jinā'ī*, Univ. of Tehran pub.271, 1955; 490, 1958, Tehran.

Criminal law.

KISHĀVARZ ṢADR, Muḥammad ᶜAlī (ed), *Āyīn va ravīya-yi dādrasī-yi kaifarī, bā qavānīn-i Dīvān-i Kaifar*, Tehran 1969.

Procedures and appeals.

MUᶜTAMID, Muḥammad ᶜAlī, *Ḥuqūq-i jazā'ī-yi ᶜumūmī*, Univ. of Tehran pub. 1367(1), Tehran 1972.

PĀD, Ibrāhīm, *Ḥuqūq-i kaifarī-yi ikhtiṣāṣī*, Tehran 1968.

Penal law applicable to the armed forces, civil service, judiciary, etc.

ṢADĀRAT, ᶜAlī, *Huqūq-i jazā va jurmshināsī*, Tehran 1961.

Penal law and criminology.

ṢĀNIᶜĪ, Parvīz, *Huqūq-i jazā'ī-yi ᶜumūmī*, National Univ. of Tehran, Tehran 1972.

General penal law.

3.3.4 *Commercial law*

Commercial law is the subject of *Ḥuqūq-i bāzargānī* by ᶜAbd al-ḥamīd AᶜẒAMI ZANGANA and edited by Suhrāb AMĪNĪYĀN, third edition, Tehran 1968, and of *The Commercial Code of Iran: Treatise I, Joint Stock Companies*, translated and edited by Mūsā ṢĀBĪ, second edition, 1976. Copyright is the subject of Muḥammad MUSHĪRIYĀN's *Ḥaqq-i mu'allif va ḥuqūq-i taṭbīqī*, Tehran 1960.

Three titles on aspects of labour law are

BAHRAMY, Ahmad Ali, *La législation internationale du travail et son influence sur le droit iranien: aspects internationaux du problème économique et social*, Geneva 1963.

The law of labour, social security, etc.

MIHR, Farhang, *Ḥuqūq-i kār*, Higher Accountancy Inst., Tehran 1974.

JAZĀYIRĪ, Shams al-dīn, *Ḥuqūq-i kār va bīmahā-yi ijtimāʿī*, Univ. of Tehran pub.1016, Tehran 1965.

Labour and social insurance laws.

3.3.5 *Administration*

Titles on administrative law include

ABŪ'L-ḤAMD, ʿAbd al-ḥamīd, *Ḥuqūq-i idārī: istikhdām-i kishvarī va mas'ūlīyat-i madanī-yi daulat*, Univ. of Tehran pub.1258, 2 vols, Tehran 1972.

State liability in civil service employment.

SANJĀBĪ, Karīm, *Ḥuqūq-i idārī-i Īrān*, Tehran 1963.

SHĪDFAR, Zain ul-ʿābidīn, *Ḥuqūq-i ʿumūmī va idārī*, Univ. of Tehran pub.443, Tehran 1957.

Administrative law concerning minerals, public works and services, planning and the Plan Organization, and the Council of State.

ṬABĀṬABĀ'Ī MU'TAMINĪ, Manūchihr, *Ḥuqūq-i idārī*, 2 vols, Univ. of Tehran pub.992(1) and 992(1), Tehran 1970.

ZANDĪ, Hūshang (ed), *Majmūʿa-yi qavānīn va muqarrarāt-i shahrdārīhā va khadamāt-i shahrī*, Tehran 1969.

Laws and regulations relating to municipalities.

The 1963 work on international labour law by Ahmad Ali BAHRAMY has been mentioned. A more general survey of the application of foreign laws and regulations within Iran, *Iʿmāl va ijrā-yi qavānīn va aḥkām-i bīgāna dar Īrān*, by Shams al-dīn ʿĀLAMĪ was published in Tehran in 1967. Public international law is the subject of *Ḥuqūq-i bain-al-milalī-yi ʿumūmī* by Manūchihr GANJĪ, Tehran 1969, while Muḥammad NAṢĪRĪ deals with private international law in *Ḥuqūq-i bain-al-milalī-yi khuṣūṣī*, Tehran 1959. With both international and domestic relevance is Ḥasan SUTŪDA ṬIHRĀNĪ's 1965 review of maritime and aviation law, *Ḥuqūq-i daryā'ī va havā'ī*, University of Tehran Publication 976, Tehran. Another study of the law of relations between states is *Ḥuqūq-i bain al-milalī-yi ʿumūmī* by Muḥammad ṢAFDARĪ and revised by Aḥmad Hūshang SHARĪFĪ, 2 volumes, University of Tehran Publication 694, Tehran 1961 (volume 1), and 997, 1962 (volume 2), reprinted 1967. Among topics concerning Iran covered is sovereignty over sea zones and air space.

3.3.6 *Rights*

After 1963 there was increasing interest in human rights and the enforcement of official policy in Iran. A 1957 law authorized the trial of cases of terrorism, espionage, and subversion under martial law, without the previously necessary declaration of a state of emergency, and instituted the National Security and Intelligence Organization (*Sāzmān-i amnīyat va iṭṭilāʿāt-i kishvar*: SAVAK). Subsequent legislation placed further offences such as sabotage, hijacking, and also drug-smuggling under martial law. SAVAK and the military courts were criticized in the west because it arrested authors and intellectuals and because accused persons were obliged to have officially chosen military officers as defence counsel. See William J BUTLER and Georges LEVASSEUR, *Human rights and the legal system in Iran*, (two reports), Geneva 1976, published by the International Commission of Jurists, for an excellent outline of both the civil and the military penal law (see list of theses in French on matters of Iranian penal law in LEVASSEUR's report). On human rights and international support for them, see also *Ḥuqūq-i bashar va ḥimāyat-i bain al-milalī-yi ān*, Tehran 1969, by Aḥmad MATĪN DAFTARĪ. For a full coverage of political and legal developments since the Revolution of February 1979, and the departure from Tehran of Muḥammad Riẓā Shāh Pahlavī, see chapter XV.

4. *ECONOMY*

4.1 *The national economy*

The Iranian economy is only moderately covered in the available literature. Constraints facing the production of comprehensive works include shortages of reliable data and limited time series of statistics, often making trend-identification difficult. Persian-language material is particularly limited in scope, quantity and authenticity. Statistics on politically contentious subjects are frequently unreliable if not absent. Language may be a difficulty for the non-Iranian researcher. Though many official figures on general release have, in recent decades, carried English or French translations, the position since 1979 remains unclear - though evidently some sources are continuing to publish, at least in all-Persian format.

For an introduction to the contemporary Iranian economy, BHARIER, 1971, offers a systematic analysis of developments through the twentieth century to 1970, including an assessment of national accounts and of the development of individual sectors. A general work, the Admiralty Handbook *Iran*, 1945 (*op.cit.* II 1), looks at the years prior to the 1939-45 War, and gives detail on the regional as well as national economies.

While official publications (see also chapter V above) of the Iranian government and agencies must be treated with care since they contain statistics and views often with an optimistic bias, some are important sources for the study of the economy. In particular, the *Annual Report and Balance Sheet* of the Central Bank of Iran (Bānk-i Markazī-yi Īrān), which has appeared each March since 1962, includes data on financial and economic indicators, budgets, and price indices. The Bank's *Bulletin*, (English-language edition from 1962, bi-monthly to 1973 and quarterly thereafter: also concurrent Persian edition), augments material from this source, as does its *Investor's Guide to Iran* and *National Income of Iran* which have appeared from time to time. A subject index of economic articles, 1961-1966 (*Fihrist mauẓūʿī-yi maqālāt-i iqtiṣādī, 1340-1344*), listing over 1800 entries in Iranian periodicals, was produced by the Bank's library in 1967 and was followed by similar publications extending the coverage to 1976.

The Industrial and Mining Development Bank of Iran has issued an eighteen year series of annual reports (to March 1978) giving general reviews of the economy as well as data on industrial concerns in which the Bank had interests. Annual statistical yearbooks on trade are available, while census materials for the years 1956, 1966 and 1976 have also been published. Periodic census of agriculture and industry, often on a sample basis, has been undertaken and published either through the ministries or the Iranian Statistical Centre which in 1977, to name just three examples, issued the results of 1973 censuses of rural and urban household expenditure and a set of 'Statistics of Mines for the Whole Country for 1976'. Government banks, such as the Industrial Credit Bank and the Agricultural Development Bank, publish annual reports and statistical materials. The Plan (and Budget) Organization's output of published material runs from 1948 and is the major source of official statements on the successive budgets and development plans. Many have appeared through the Statistical Centre: see its 1978 'Selected List of Persian Publications' (in Persian) and other bibliographies. See also the *Sālnāma* and its English-language version, the *Statistical Yearbook*. Other regular items prior to the 1979 Revolution were development plans and their supplementary materials in both Persian and English. A bibliography of the Statistical Centre is *Fihrist-i nashrīyāt-i Markaz-i Āmār-i Īrān tā pāyān-i sāl-i 1353*, Tehran 1974. A bibliography of Plan Organization publications received at the Iranian Documentation Centre in Tehran, entitled *Fihrist-i nashrīyāt-i Sāzmān-i Barnāma*, Tehran 1972, was compiled by Ānūsh Huvsipiyān ĀZĀDIYĀN. He also produced a bibliography of the Ministry of Economics, *Fihrist-i nashrīyāt-i Vizārat-i Iqtiṣād*, Tehran 1973. Two hundred publications from this ministry are listed in

Kitābshināsī-yi mauẓūʿī-yi Īrān, Ḥusain BANĪ ĀDAM (ed), *op.cit.* II 2.1, pp.182-96.

A few significant periodical publications are concerned with the Iranian economy. Among those worth attention on a selective basis are *Taḥqiqāt-i Iqtiṣādī* published, mainly in west European languages, by the University of Tehran, the *Iranian Economic Review* from the same source and (since 1958) *Iran, A Quarterly Economic Review* from the Economist Intelligence Unit in London. Excellent summaries of economic conditions and trends in Iran are often included in reviews such as the annual *The Middle East and North Africa*, Europa Publications, and *Middle East Annual Review*, World of Information, Saffron Walden. Barclays Bank and Lloyds Bank are among commercial institutions publishing brief but up-to-date surveys of the Iranian economy and market trends.

As yet there are few Persian language materials on the Iranian economy, except agriculture. *Tehran Economist*, mainly in Persian with occasional English language summaries, is a monthly containing current items.

The period 1921-1941 is covered by many works listed in this *Guide*. Particularly useful as introductions to economic conditions and changes are

UK NAVAL INTELLIGENCE DIVISION, *Persia*, 1945, *op.cit.* 1.2.
A complete survey of Iran, with reviews of each sector of the economy.

BANANI, Amin, *The modernization of Iran*, *op.cit.* IX 6.6.
A description of the attempt by Riẓā Shāh to develop the human and physical resources of Iran, though in eulogistic terms.

MILLSPAUGH, A C, *Americans in Persia*, *op.cit.* IX 6.7.
MILLSPAUGH's view of Iran and its problems when he revisited the country at the invitation of the United States government. See also his *The American task in Persia*, *op.cit.* IX 6.6, in which he outlined the country's financial problems and the means for their solution.

A selection of titles on the economy, finance, and planning of Iran under Muḥammad Riẓā Shāh, 1941-1979, arranged alphabetically, is

AFSHAR, Kamran, *A monetary estimate of Iran's GNP, 1900-1975*, Ph.D. thesis, Florida State Univ. 1977.

AMIRSADEGHI, H, and R W FERRIER, *Twentieth century Iran*, *op.cit.* IX 6.9.
Especially chapters 4 and 5.

AMUZEGAR, Jahangir, *Iran: an economic profile*, Middle East Institute, Washington 1977.

—— and M Ali FEKRAT, *Iran: economic development under dualistic conditions*, Univ. of Chicago Press, Chicago 1971.

An examination of the counter position of national and petroleum sectors of the economy and its retarding effects on development.

ASKARI, Hossein, and Majin SHOHREH, 'Recent economic growth in Iran', *MES* 12(3), 1976 :105-23.

BADĪʿĪ, Rabīʿ, *Jughrāfiyā-yi iqtiṣādī-yi Īrān*, *op.cit.* VIII 1.1.

BALDWIN, George B, *Planning and development in Iran*, *op.cit.* 2.4.3.

An account of Iran's first attempt at economic planning, based on the author's participation in the planning process from 1958-1961.

BÉMONT, Fredy, *L'Iran devant le progrès*, *op.cit.* 1.2.

Essays on Iran's economic situation with some statistical data not available elsewhere.

BARTSCH, Wm H, and Julian BHARIER, *The economy of Iran*, *op.cit.* II 2.2.

BHARIER, Julian, *Economic development in Iran 1900-1970*, *op.cit.* IX 6.5.

A wide-ranging review of the development of the Iranian economy from the late Qājārs to the end of the 1970s, with special reference to changing economic structure.

BRICAULT, Giselle C, *Major companies of Iran*, 1978-79 ed., London 1978.

DAFTARY, Farhad, 'Development planning Iran: a historical survey', *I.stud.* 7, 1973 :176-228.

Succinct outline of national plans from the 1950s. See also author's 1971 Ph.D. thesis, University of California, Berkeley, on *Economic development and planning in Iran, 1955-1967.*

ELKAN, Walter, 'Employment, education, training and skilled labor in Iran', *op.cit.* 2.1.

Assessment of problems facing Iran during the period of rapid economic growth after 1970.

FIROOZI, Ferydoon, 'Income distribution and taxation laws of Iran', *IJMES* 9(2), 1978 :73-87.

Review of the evolution of the tax system and some of its implications.

—— 'The Iranian budgets: 1964-1970', *IJMES* 5(3), 1974 :328-43.

FISHER, W B, *The land of Iran*, *CHI*, vol.I.

GRAHAM, Robert, *Iran: the illusion of power*, *op.cit.* 1.2.

HALLIDAY, Fred, *Iran: dictatorship and development*, *op.cit.* 1.2.

HAMMEED, Kamal A, and Margaret N BENNETT, 'Iran's future economy', *MEJ* 29(4), 1975 :418-32.

INTERNATIONAL BANK FOR RECONSTRUCTION AND DEVELOPMENT, *Economic situation and prospects of Iran*, Washington, DC 1958.

A short survey as prelude to financing by IBRD.

Iran Almanac and Book of Facts, *op.cit.* 1.2.

JABBARI, Ahmad, *Distribution of income and expenditures in Iran*, Ph.D. thesis, Washington Univ. 1978.

JACOBS, Norman, *The sociology of development*, *op.cit.* 1.2.

Conflict between development strategies and traditional institutions and between rational economic action and non-economic considerations.

JENAB, Parviz, *The role of the Third Plan in economic development, Iran: a case study, 1963-1967*, Ph.D. thesis, Indiana Univ. 1977.

KATOUZIAN, Homa, *The political economy of modern Iran*, *op.cit.* IX 6.9.

LANGER, F, *Iran: oil money and the ambitions of a nation*, Hudson Inst., Paris 1975.

Short examination of changes in the Iranian economy after the oil boom of the early 1970s.

LENCZOWSKI, George (ed), *Iran under the Pahlavis*, *op.cit.* IX 6.9.

See chapters on economic planning and oil policy.

LIEBERMAN, Samuel S, 'Prospects for development and population growth in Iran', *op.cit.* 2.1.

LOONEY, Robert E, *The economic development of Iran, 1959-1981*, New York 1973.

McLACHLAN, Keith S, 'The Iranian economy, 1960-76', AMIRSADEGHI and FERRIER (eds), *Twentieth-century Iran*, *op.cit.* IX 6.9.

A review of changes resulting from the Shah's modernization programme.

MADANI, Ahmad S, *An econometric model of development for an oil-based economy: the case of Iran*, Ph.D. thesis, Univ. of Colorado 1976.

MAHAMEDI, A, *Iran's involvement in the World Bank*, Ph.D. thesis, Univ. of Pennsylvania 1980.

MOGHTADER, Hushang, 'The impact of increased oil revenue on Iran's economic development, 1973-76', KEDOURIE and HAIM (eds), *Towards a modern Iran*, *op.cit.* IX 6.9, :241-62.

MOLAVI, M A, 'Les blocages du développement en Iran', *Tiers-Monde* 8(30), 1967 :349-70.

Review of plan aims and constraints.

MÜLLER, Wilhelm, *Die wirtschaftlichen Entwicklungsprobleme Irans*, Geographischen Inst. der Hochschule für Welthandel, Vienna 1971.

NAINI, A, 'Entwicklungsplanung in Iran', *Orient* 16(4), 1975 :105-30.

NOORBAKHSH, Mohsen, *Dynamic consideration of trade agreements. Case study: Iran*, Ph.D. thesis, Univ. of California, Davis 1979.

OLSEN, P Bjorn, and P N RASMUSSEN, 'An attempt at planning in a traditional state: Iran', Everett E HAGEN (ed), *Planning economic development*, Homewood, Illinois 1963 :223-51.

OVERSEAS CONSULTANTS INC., *Report on the Seven-Year Development Plan*, 5 vols, New York 1949.

Discussion of the first plan, by its US consultants.

PESARAN, M H, 'Income distribution and its major determinants in Iran', JACQZ (ed), *Iran: past, present and future*, *op.cit.* IX 6.9, :267-86.

PLAN ORGANIZATION, *Iran's Fifth Development Plan, 1973-1978, Revised - A Summary*, Tehran 1975.

—— *Fourth National Development Plan, 1968-1972*, Tehran 1968.

Official proposals, with sectoral analysis and financial allocations.

—— *Outline of the Third Plan, 1341-1346*, Tehran 1963.

Aims and strategies for 1962-68.

—— *Review of the Second Seven Year Plan Program of Iran*, Tehran 1960.

Mid-stage official view of the second plan (1334/1955 to 1341/1962).

RAFII, Farshad, *Joint ventures and transfer of technology to Iran: the impact of foreign control*, DBA thesis, Harvard Univ., Mass. 1978.

RASADI, A, (Aḥmad ᶜAlī RAṢADĪ), *Innostranni kapital v Irane posle vtoroy mirovoy voyni (1945-1967 gg.)*, Inst. of World Economy and Int. Relations, Moscow 1973.

Foreign capital in Iran, 1945-67; especially US aid.

RĀVANDĪ, Murtaẓā, *Tārikh-i ijtimāᶜī-yi Īrān*, 3 vols, *op.cit.* 1.2.

RAVASANI, Schapour, *Iran. Entwicklung der Gesellschaft, der Wirtschaft und des Staates*, Stuttgart 1978.

National economic development.

SAᶜĀDAT, A, and A H AMĪNĪ, *Jughrāfiyā-yi iqtiṣādi-yi Īrān*, *op.cit.* VIII 1.1.

Economic geography of Iran: discussion of official plans and development constraints.

SHAFA, Hossein Soleymanian, *An analysis of the impact of investment incentives on the rental cost of capital: the case of Iran*, Ph.D. thesis, Univ. of Texas, Dallas 1978.

SHAHIDI, Hushang, *Economic growth and the distribution of income in Iran*, Ph.D. thesis, Colorado State Univ. 1977.

SHAHROODI, Muhammad Reza, *The Iranian budgetary system and patterns of government expenditure, 1960-1976*, Ph.D. thesis, Syracuse Univ., New York 1978.

SHARIPOV, U Z, *Byudzhet i byudzhetnaya sistema Irana*, Soviet Academy of Sciences, Moscow 1976.

The budgetary system of Iran, especially in the 1950s and 1960s: bibliography.

TIKHONOV, N S, *Zapadnogermanskii kapital v Irana*, Azarbaijan Academy of

Sciences, Baku 1972.

West German aid after 1945 - and ideological penetration.

YAR-SHATER, Ehsan, *Iran faces the seventies*, *op.cit.* IX 6.9.

See especially, chapters 1, 2, and 3.

VAEZ-ZADEH, Muhammad Reza, *Optimal economic growth with exhaustible resources and absorptive capacity constraint: the case of Iran*, Ph.D. thesis, Johns Hopkins Univ., Maryland 1977.

VAN NIEUWENHUIJZE, C A O, 'Iranian development in a sociological perspective', *Der Islam* 45(1/2), 1969 :64-80.

Social phenomena and the probability of development: in the context of Norman JACOBS' *The sociology of development*, *op.cit.* 1.2.

4.2 *Agriculture*

Agricultural and related matters in Iran have attracted large numbers of written contributions from western and Iranian scholars. A definitive introduction to the evolution of the country's agrarian structure is provided by Ann K S LAMBTON, *Landlord and peasant in Persia*, *op.cit.* IX 3.3, who was also responsible for the equally significant *The Persian land reform 1962-1966*, London 1969. This later publication is among the most comprehensive analyses of the implementation and effects of the land reform programme of the 1960s.

Agriculture features prominently in many of the works listed in 4.1 above. Further titles providing an overview of developments in the sector are

ARESVIK, Oddvar, *The agricultural development of Iran*, New York 1976.

Takes an optimistic view of the potential.

BEAUMONT, Peter, 'Water resource development in Iran', *GJ* 140(3), 1974 :418-31.

BEHESCHTI, M, 'Iran', *World atlas of agriculture*, vol.2, Asia and Oceania, Istituto Geografico de Agostini, Novara 1973 :253-66.

Environment, land use, crops, animal husbandry, agricultural economy: survey.

BOWEN-JONES, Howard, 'Agriculture', *CHI*, vol.I, :565-98.

CAREY, Jane P C, and Andrew G CAREY, 'Iranian agriculture and its development: 1952-1973', *IJMES* 7(3), 1976 :359-82.

FAO, *Agriculture sector planning: a report of the joint Iran/FAO workshop in Tehran, May, 1975*, Food and Agriculture Organization, Rome 1976.

FRIEVALDS, John, 'Farm corporations in Iran: an alternative to traditional agriculture', *MEJ* 26(2), 1972 :185-93.

GHADIRI, B, 'The experience of rural co-operatives and co-operative unions in Iran', *Taḥqiqāt-i iqtiṣādi*, 10(29/30), 1973 :80-105.

GITTINGER, J Price, *Planning for agricultural development - the Iranian experience*, Nat. Planning Assoc., Washington, DC 1965.

Developments in the early 1960s.

KARAMI, Ezatollah, *An appraisal of the extension service in Iran as perceived by extension specialists and extension agents*, Ph.D. thesis, Ohio State Univ. 1979.

KAZEMIAN, Gholam Hossein, *The impact of US technical aid on the rural development of Iran*, New York 1968.

MADJID, Muhammad Gholi, *Policies concerning sugar production in Iran*, Ph.D. thesis, Cornell Univ., New York 1978.

MASSARRAT, M, 'Asiatische Produktionsweise (Iran)', H ASCHE (ed), *Studien über die dritte Welt*, Geographische Hochschulmanuskripte, no.4, Göttingen 1977 :3-125.

Organization of Iranian agriculture.

MOJTAHED, Ahmad, *Economic development of the livestock in Iran*, Ph.D. thesis, Iowa State Univ. 1977.

PLANHOL, Xavier de, 'Le déboisement de l'Iran', *Annales de Géographie* 78(430), 1969 :625-35.

REZAZADEH, Farhad, *Agricultural development in Iran: evaluation of state planning and policies in relation to agriculture*, Ph.D. thesis, Iowa State Univ. 1979.

WEINBAUM, M G, 'Agricultural policy and development politics in Iran', *MEJ* 31(4), 1977 :434-50.

4.2.1 *Land reform*

Since Iran's General Land Reform Law of 1959, the redistribution of large estate land and its economic and social consequences have commanded the attention of many writers, including Ann LAMBTON (see above). The initial Law was followed by others, in 1960 and 1962, while a Ministry of Land Reform and Rural Co-operatives was established in 1968. By 1970, the Central Organization of Rural Co-operatives had a constitution. Further legislation followed the setting-up, in the same year, of the Ministry of Co-operation and Rural Affairs - which was itself incorporated into the Ministry of Agriculture and Natural Resources in 1976. Such official agencies have produced statistics and literature, though not all totally objective.

Partisanship is certainly evident in much of the writing on land reform. D R DENMAN's *The King's vista: a land reform which has changed the face of*

Persia, Berkhamsted 1973, examines the Iranian programme in some detail and with more sympathy for the Pahlavī regime than is found elsewhere. Other titles on land reform include

BERGMANN, Herbert, *The impacts of large-scale farms on development in Iran: a case study of certain aspects of the Iranian agrarian reform*, Verlag der SSIP-Schriften, Saarbrücken 1975.

CRAIG, Daniel, 'The impact of land reform', *op.cit.* 2.3.

DRESKORNFELD, Friedrich, *Agrarstrukturwandel und Agrarreform in Iran*, Saarbrücken 1976.

GHARATCHEDAGHI, Cyrus, *Landverteilung in Waramin. Ein Auftakt zur Agrarreform im Iran*, Schriften des Deutschen Orient-Inst., Opladen 1967.

Distribution of land in Varamin.

HOOGLUND, Eric James, *The effects of the land reform program on rural Iran, 1962-72*, Ph.D. thesis, Johns Hopkins Univ. 1975.

KATOUZIAN, M A, 'Land reform in Iran, a case study in the political economy of social engineering', *Journal of Peasant Studies* 1(2), 1974 :220-39.

KEDDIE, Nikki R, 'The Iranian village before and after land reform', *JCH* 3(3), 1968 :69-91.

KHOSROVI, Khosrow, 'Les paysans sans terre en Iran: les Khochnechin', *op. cit.* 2.3.

MALEK, Hossein, 'Après la réforme agraire iranienne', *Annales de Géographie* 75(409), 1966 :268-713.

Land reform offers limited solutions and new problems.

McLACHLAN, Keith S, 'Land reform in Iran', *CHI*, vol.I, :684-713.

MIRZADEH, A, *Land reform and rural economy in Iran: selected bibliography*, Iranian Documentation Center (IRANDOC), Tehran 1973.

MOGHADAM, Reza, 'Land reform and rural development in Iran', *Land Economics* 48(2), 1972 :160-68.

PLANCK, Ulrich, 'Die Reintegrationsphase der iranischen Agrarreform', *Erdkunde* 29(1), 1975 :1-9.

Three titles (*op.cit.* 2.2.1) deal with economic aspects of pastoralism:

BARTH, Fredrik, 'The land use pattern of migratory tribes of south Persia'.

BLACK-MICHAUD, Jacob, 'An ethnographic and ecological survey of Luristan'.

STAUFFER, Thomas R, 'The economics of nomadism in Iran'.

4.2.2 *Regions*

Agricultural and rural characteristics of selected regions and provinces of Iran are fairly plentiful. A selection of titles is

ATAI, M, 'Economic report on agriculture in the Iṣfahān and Yazd areas', *Taḥqiqāt-i iqtiṣādī* 3(9/10), 1965 :69-152.

BAGLEY, Frank R C, 'A bright future after oil: dams and agro-industry in Khuzistan', *MEJ* 30(1), 1976 :25-35.

BEAUMONT, Peter, 'Qanats on the Varamin Plain', *Transactions, Institute of British Geographers* 45, 1968 :169-79.

Study of the traditional qanāt irrigation system in an area south-east of Tehran.

BECKETT, P H T, and E D GORDON, 'Land use and settlement around Kerman in southern Iran', *op.cit.* 2.4.2.

Includes coloured maps of land use and settlement.

DJAVAN, Djafar, *Structures agraires et économie rurale dans la plaine de Tabriz*, thesis (3ème cycle), Univ. of Caen 1973.

EHLERS, Eckart, *Iran: Grundzuge einer geographischen Ländeskunde*, *op.cit.* II 2.2.

—— *Traditionelle und moderne Formen der Landwirtschaft in Iran: Siedlung, Wirtschaft und Agrarsozialstruktur im nördlichen Khuzistan seit dem Ende des 19 Jahrhunderts*, Marburger Geographische Schriften, Marburg 1975.

—— 'Agrarsociale Wandlungen in kaspischen Tiefland Nordpersiens', *Verhandlungen des Deutschen Geographentages* 38, Wiesbaden 1971 (1972) :289-311.

—— 'Nordpersiche Agrarlandschaften: Landnutzung und Sozialstruktur in Ghilan und Mazanderan', *Geographische Rundschau* 23(9), 1971 :329-42.

Environment and land use.

FLOWER, D J, 'Water use in north-west Iran', *CHI*, vol.I, :599-610.

GHAZI, I, *The Dez multi-purpose dam scheme, Khuzestan: a socio-economic analysis*, Ph.D. thesis, Univ. of Durham 1977.

GOODELL, G, 'Agricultural production in a traditional village of northern Khuzistan', *Marburger Geographische Schriften* 64, 1975 :245-89.

GŪDARZĪ-NIZHĀD, Shāhpūr, *Kangāvar, jughrāfiyā-yi insānī va iqtiṣādī*, Geog. Inst., Univ. of Tehran, Tehran 1973.

Human and economic geography of Kangāvar district in Kirmānshāh province.

HARTL, Martin, *Das Najafabadtal: Geographische Untersuchung einer Kanatlandschaft im Zagrosgebirge (Iran)*, Geog. Inst., Univ. of Regensburg 1979.

Water supply, agriculture and settlement in an area north-east of Iṣfahān.

HOURCADE, Bernard, 'Le processus de la déprise rurale dans l'Elbourz de Téhéran (Iran)', *Revue de Géographie Alpine* 64(3), Grenoble 1976 :365-88.

A traditional system of tree cultivation and cattle breeding is now surrounded by an urban-dominated economy: land reform and nationalization of ranges have accelerated change.

KHAYAMI, Seyd Mortaza, *An appraisal of the efficiency of resource utilization in the Ghazvin Agricultural Development Project in Iran*, Ph.D. thesis, Pennsylvania State Univ. 1978.

KORTUM, Gerhard, *Die Marvdasht-Ebene in Fars*, Geog. Inst., Univ. of Kiel, Kiel 1976.

—— 'Ländliche Siedlungen im Umland von Shiraz', Reinhard STEWIG and Horst-Günter WAGNER (eds), *Kulturgeographische Untersuchungen im islamischen Orient*, Geog. Inst., Univ. of Kiel, Kiel 1973 :177-212.

Land use and rural settlement in the hinterland of Shīrāz.

NAJAFI, Yadolah, *Adoption of agricultural innovations and the use of information services and media in a selected rural community in Iran*, Ph.D. thesis, Univ. of Maryland 1978.

POUR-FICKOUI, Ali, and Marcel BAZIN, *Élevage et vie pastorale dans le Guilân (Iran septentrional)*, Dept. of Geog., Univ. of Paris-Sorbonne, Paris 1978.

RAHEMI, Nejar Azar, *La vie rurale et l'évolution de l'agriculture dans la région de Varamine (Iran)*, thesis (3ème cycle), Univ. of Paris 1974.

SAHAMI, C, *L'économie rurale et la vie paysanne dans la province sud-caspienne de l'Iran: le Guilân*, Inst. of Geog., Univ. of Clermont-Ferrand 1965.

SALMANZADEH, Cyrus, *Agricultural change and rural society in southern Iran*, *op.cit.* 2.3.

SCHOWKATFARD, F D, and M FARDI, 'Sozialökonomische Auswirkungen der landwirtschaftlichen Aktiengesellschaft in Iran: Fallstudie eines Dorfes der Provinz Fars', *Zeitschrift für ausländische Landwirtschaft* 11(2), 1972 :120-37.

VIEILLE, Paul, 'La société rurale et le développement agricole du Khouzistan', *Année Sociologique*, 3rd ser., 1965 :85-112.

YAZDANI, L, *Utilisation des eaux souterraines dans le Khorasan méridional*, thesis (3ème cycle), Univ. of Paris 1977.

ZAHEDANI, Abdolhossain, *Iran: evaluation of agricultural development strategy, 1962-1972*, Ph.D. thesis, Univ. of California, Davis 1974.

A linear programming approach.

The Institute for Economic Research of the University of Tehran has been responsible for studies of the rural economy which have appeared in *Taḥqīqāt-i iqtiṣādī*. These have included lengthy articles on Khūzistān (three, 1965), Āzarbāyjān (five, 1968), Khurāsān and the Central Ustān (six,

1969), Hamadān and Kirmānshāhān (seven, 1970), Sīstān and Balūchistān (seven, 1970), etc.

The Ministry of Agriculture has produced both topic- and place-related material, though much of it is difficult to obtain. Statistics *per se* are more easily accessible: a variety of publications and reports have appeared since the *First National Census of Agriculture* was prepared by the Department of Public Statistics in Tehran in 1960. See also the *Results of Agricultural Census, 1972* (1974), and the *Preliminary Results of Census of Rural Agriculture 1977* (1978), produced - also in Persian - by the Statistical Centre in Tehran. The relevant sections of documents from the Plan Organization (see 4.1 above) are generally stronger on strategy and intention than on evaluation and analysis. Annual reports of the Agricultural Bank of Iran, Tehran, constitute another source.

An important example of the work of international organizations on Iranian agriculture is the series of 1970-71 reports by the Food and Agriculture Organization of the United Nations. Under the general title, *Iran: integrated planning of irrigated agriculture in the Varamin and Garmsar Plains*, FAO (UNDP IRA 12N1-12N9), there were nine reports on agriculture, resources, planning, management, etc. - several with relevance to Iranian agriculture outside the specific project areas. The Pahlavī government also maintained close links with individual foreign countries and national development agencies. The most important of these has been the United States' Agency for International Development (AID) and its predecessors.

4.3 *Industry*

4.3.1 *Modern*

Industry (other than petroleum-related, see 4.4 below) is less well covered for Iran than is agriculture, though BANANI, *op.cit.* IX 5.1, gives a view of the industrial programme under Riẓā Shāh. BALDWIN, *op.cit.* 2.4.3, looks at the more recent period, as does Richard E BENEDICK in *Industrial finance in Iran*, Graduate School of Business Administration, Harvard University, Boston 1964, where he examines the origins and expansion of industrial finance after 1945. Industrial development since 1970 is treated by GRAHAM, *op.cit.* 1.2, and HALLIDAY, *op.cit.* 1.2. Again, attention is drawn to the reports and other publications from government ministries in Tehran. See, for example, the *Annual Industrial Survey* (Ministry of Economy), *Foreign Trade Statistics of Iran* (Ministry of Finance), and *Report on the Industrial Census of Iran* (Ministry of Interior). Banks constitute another source: an example is the *Annual Report* series of the Industrial and Mining

Development Bank of Iran, giving details of the Bank's funding activities (with locations). Other titles on the modern industrial sector in Iran include

ĀSĀYISH, Ḥusain, *Jughrāfiyā-yi ṣanᶜatī-yi Īrān: bakhsh-ī az ṣanāyiᶜ-i sangīn va nīm-sangīn*, Social and Human Research Inst., Univ. of Āzarbāyjān, Tabrīz 1975.

Geography of industrial investment, employment, regional distribution, plans, productivity, etc.

BAGHSHOMALI, Hamid, *Optimal economic planning with a structural break: a study of the impact of the steel industry on the Iranian economy*, Ph.D. thesis, Univ. of California, Los Angeles 1973.

A multi-sectored, multi-period linear programming model is used to analyse the inter-industry effects of Iran's first integrated steel mill.

CAREY, Jane Perry Clark, and Andrew G CAREY, 'Industrial growth and development planning in Iran', *MEJ* 29(1), 1975 :1-15.

DEUTSCHES ORIENT INSTITUT, *Probleme des Transportsektors in den Ländern des arabischen Ostens und Iran*, Hamburg 1976.

FAHIM-NADER, Mahnaz, *Import-substitution industrialization in Iran*, Ph.D. thesis, Univ. of Maryland 1978.

HARRISON, J V, 'Minerals', *CHI*, vol.I, :489-516.

HOEPPNER, R R, 'Probleme des iranischen Verkehr und Transport-systems und seiner projektierten Entwicklung', *Orient* 17(3), Hamburg 1976 :77-105.

KASHANI, Kamran, *Promotion of manufactured exports from Iran: a study on the effectiveness of public policy*, DBA thesis, Harvard Univ. 1974.

KORBY, Wilfried, *Probleme der industriallen Entwicklung und Konzentration in Iran*, Tübinger Atlas des Vorderen Orients, Wiesbaden 1977.

KORTUM, Gerhard, 'Hafenprobleme Irans im nordlichen persischen Golf', *op. cit.* 2.4.

McLACHLAN, Keith S, 'Planning industrialization', *Iran Report*, Focus Research Ltd., London 1975.

MADJTUBI, Mahmoud, *Les ouvriers urbains dans les industries textiles d'Hispahan*, thesis (3ème cycle), Univ. of Paris X, 1971.

MELAMID, Alexander, 'Industrial activities', *CHI*, vol.I, :517-51.

—— 'Communications, transport, retail trade and services', *CHI*, vol.I, :552-64.

NAJMABADI, Farrokh, 'Strategies of industrial development in Iran', JACQZ (ed), *Iran: past, present and future*, *op.cit.* 1.2, :105-21.

The then Minister of Industry on government strategies for rapid industrialization for the 1970s.

RAJI, Seyed Mohammad, *The evolution and modernization of industrial relations system in Iran*, Ph.D. thesis, Graduate School of Business Admin., New York University 1972.

SADIGH, Piruz, *Impact of government policies on the structure and growth of Iranian industry*, Ph.D. thesis, School of Oriental and African Studies, University of London 1975.

SHAHROUDI, Mohammed, *Participative management and the industrial development of Iran*, Ph.D. thesis, United States International Univ. 1975.

SPILLANE, James J, *The housing production process in Iran*, Ph.D. thesis, Graduate School of Business Admin., New York Univ. 1972.

TABRIZICHE, Sirousse, *Spatial economics of manufacture in Iran*, Ph.D. thesis, Columbia Univ., New York 1970.

4.3.2 *Traditional*

Some writers and, increasingly, official agencies have devoted attention to the traditional industrial sector of Iran as in other developing countries. A selection of such titles is

BEAZLEY, Elizabeth, and Michael HARVERSON, *Living with the desert. Working buildings of the Iranian plateau*, London 1982.

CENTLIVRES-DEMONT, M, *Une communauté de potiers en Iran*, *op.cit.* XII 4.5.

COSTELLO, Vincent F, 'The industrial structure of a traditional Iranian city', *op.cit.* 2.4.2.

DHAMIJA, Jasleen, *Living tradition of Iran's crafts*, New Delhi 1979.

Socio-economic organization of guilds: links between crafts and daily life.

DILLON, R, *Carpet capitalism and craft involution in Kirman, Iran*, Ph.D. thesis, Columbia Univ., New York 1976.

Bazaar economy, with anthropological emphasis.

EDWARDS, A C, *The Persian carpet*, *op.cit.* XII 7.3.

FLOOR, W M, 'The guilds of Iran - an overview from the earliest beginnings to 1972', *op.cit.* IX 6.4.2.

Guilds in Iranian bazaar life.

MAHALLATI-CHIRAZI, Salaheddine, *L'industrie artisanale de la céramique et du tapis en Iran*, thesis (3ème cycle), Univ. of Tours 1973.

MOHADJER FARROKH, Parviz, *Culture traditionelle et travail industriel: les problèmes d'adaptation des ouvriers dans quelques usines de Teheran*, thesis (3ème cycle), Univ. of Paris V, 1974.

ROTBLAT, Howard J, 'Social organization and development in an Iranian provincial bazaar', *op.cit.* 2.4.2.

See also Ph.D. thesis, *Stability and change in an Iranian provincial bazaar (example of Qazvin)*, University of Chicago 1972.

SCHWEIZER, Gunther, 'Tabriz (Nordwest-Iran) und der Tabrizer Bazar', *op. cit.* 2.4.

WULFF, Hans E, *The traditional crafts of Persia*, *op.cit.* VII 9.

A major source, especially on urban trades and crafts: wide-ranging survey, well illustrated, with explanatory technical vocabulary.

4.4 *Oil*

Development of the Iranian oil industry: international and domestic aspects, Praeger, New York 1976, by Fereidun FESHARAKI, is one of a number of valuable general surveys. Others are Ronald W FERRIER's 'The development of the Iranian oil industry', AMIRSADEGHI and FERRIER (eds), *Twentieth-century Iran*, *op.cit.* IX 6.9, and Laurence P ELWELL-SUTTON's 1955 *Persian oil: a study in power politics*, *op.cit.* IX 6.8. Journals which carry information and articles on Iranian oil affairs include *Middle East Economic Digest*, London, *Middle East Economic Survey*, Nicosia, *Petroleum Economist*, London, and *Petroleum Intelligence Weekly*, New York. An early account of oil operations in Iran is J W WILLIAMSON's *In a Persian oil field*, London 1927.

Economic and political implications of Iranian oil are discussed in many general works on petroleum. Some of these are produced by the oil companies themselves: an example is the BRITISH PETROLEUM COMPANY's *Our petroleum industry*, 5th edition, London 1977. International organizations, such as OPEC (Organization of Petroleum Exporting Countries) which was founded in 1960, produce a range of material not listed here (see OPEC Selected Documents, Annual Statistical Bulletin, etc.). Meanwhile, importing governments publish items such as

International petroleum cartel. The, Staff report to the Federal Trade Commission submitted to the Subcommittee on Monopoly of the Select Committee on Small Business, United States Senate, US Government Printing Office, Washington 1952; and

The international petroleum cartel, the Iranian consortium and US national security, prepared by Frank CHURCH for the Committee on Foreign Relations of the United States Senate, US Government Printing Office, Washington, DC 1974.

Some of the many other general works are

HARTSHORN, J E, *Oil companies and governments*, 2nd rev.ed., London 1967.

JACOBY, Neil H, *Multinational oil*, New York 1974.

MIKDASHI, Z, *The community of oil exporting countries - a study in govern-*

mental co-operation, London 1972.

O'CONNOR, Harvey, *World crisis in oil*, New York 1962.

ODELL, Peter R, *Oil and world power: a geographical interpretation*, 2nd ed., Penguin, Harmondsworth 1972.

PENROSE, E T, *The large international firm in developing countries: the international petroleum industry*, London 1968.

SAMPSON, Anthony, *The Seven Sisters: the great oil companies and the world they made*, London 1975.

Many of the titles listed under politics, economics, etc., in this *Guide* deal with Iranian oil. A sample listing of material of this varied type might include BANANI, *op.cit.* IX 5.1, BHARIER, *op.cit.* IX 6.5, CHUBIN and ZABIH, *op.cit.* 3.1.4, MILLSPAUGH, *op.cit.* IX 6.7, RAMAZANI, *op.cit.* IX 6.7, and AMUZEGAR and FEKRAT, *op.cit.* 4.1.

Among works on oil in a Middle Eastern context, with sections on Iran, are

HIRST, D, *Oil and public opinion in the Middle East*, London 1966.

ISSAWI, C, and M YEGANEH, *The economics of Middle East oil*, London 1963.

LANDIS, Lincoln, *Politics and oil: Moscow in the Middle East*, New York 1973.

LEEMAN, W, *The price of Middle East oil*, Cornell Univ. Press, Ithaca, New York 1962.

LENCZOWSKI, George, *Oil and state in the Middle East*, Ithaca, New York 1960.

LONGHURST, Henry, *Adventure in oil: the story of British Petroleum*, London 1959.

See re Iran, pp.15-152: general account.

LONGRIGG, Stephen H, *Oil in the Middle East: its discovery and development*, London 1968.

MIKDASHI, Z, *A financial analysis of Middle Eastern oil concessions, 1901-1965*, New York 1966.

MONROE, Elizabeth, *Britain's moment in the Middle East, 1914-1956*, London 1963.

MOSLEY, Leonard, *Power play: the tumultuous world of Middle East oil, 1890-1973*, London 1973.

SHWADRAN, Benjamin, *The Middle East, oil and the great powers*, New York 1955.

STOCKING, G W, *Middle East oil*, Penguin Books, London 1971.

TURNER, Louis, *Oil companies in the international system*, Royal Inst. International Affairs, London 1978.

An *Annual Report and Balance Sheet* series covers the development of the Anglo-Persian Oil Company (Anglo-Iranian Oil Company, later British Petroleum) from 1909 to 1954, since when - at least to 1978 - a similar *Annual Report* has been produced by the National Iranian Oil Company. The NIOC's Public Relations Office has released material - much of it in Persian, such as *The Iranian Oil Industry during the Pahlavi Dynasty*, 1972, and *Management Statistics* in the same year. Other public sources in Iran are the *Annual Report and Balance Sheet* of the Central Bank (Bānk-i Markazī-yi Īrān), the *Bulletin of the Iranian Institute of Petroleum*, and the *Annual Report of the Iranian Customs and Excise Office* (1910-1951).

Further titles on Iranian petroleum include

AMIRI, Kathleen B, *Oil and Iran: a systems analysis of policy and organization, 1973-74*, Ph.D. thesis, Univ. of Illinois 1976.

ASRARI, Reza, *The contribution of the oil industry to the economic development and social progress of Iran*, Ed.D. thesis, Univ. of Northern Colorado 1973.

BARTSCH, William H, 'The impact of the oil industry on the economy of Iran', Raymond F MIKESELL, *et al.* (ed), *Foreign investment in the petroleum and mineral industries: case studies of investor-host country relations*, Baltimore 1971 :237-63.

BECK, Peter J, 'The Anglo-Persian oil dispute 1932-33', *JCH* 9(4), 1974 :123-51.

CAREY, Jane Perry Clark, 'Iran and control of its oil resources', *Political Science Quarterly* 89(1), 1974 :147-74.

FĀTIḤ, Muṣṭafā, *Panjāh sāl-i naft-i Īrān*, *op.cit.* IX 6.8.

FERRIER, R W, *History of British Petroleum*, vol.I, Cambridge 1982.

FROOZAN, M, *et al.*, 'The development of the gas industry in Iran', *Taḥqīqāt-i iqtiṣādī* 7(19/20), 1970 :25-48.

GHORBAN, Nasri, *A study of the emergence, development and role of the national oil companies of Iran, Kuwait, and Saudi Arabia*, Ph.D. thesis, School of Oriental and African Studies, Univ. of London 1978.

MEGATELI, A, *Petroleum policies and national oil companies: a comparative study of investment policies with emphasis on exploration of Sonatrach(Algeria), NIOC(Iran), and Pemex(Mexico), 1970-1975*, Ph.D. thesis, Univ. of Texas, Austin 1973.

MELAMID, Alexander, 'Petroleum product distribution and the evolution of economic regions in Iran', *GR* 65(4), 1975 :510-25.

—— 'Satellization in Iranian crude-oil production', *GR* 63(2), 1973 :27-43.
On the concentration into central places of activities ancillary to crude-oil production and transportation.

MINISTRY OF FOREIGN AFFAIRS (Vizārat-i Umūr-i Khārija), *Taḥaqquq-i ḥākimīyat-i millī bar naft dar panjāh-sāl-i shāhanshāhi-i Pahlavī*, Tehran 1976.

History of the control of Iranian oil.

MOGHARI, Mohammad, *Impact of the oil technology on Iran, 1901-1951*, Committee on Technology and Social Change in Foreign Cultures, Iowa State Univ., Ames 1975.

MOTAMEN, Homa, *Expenditure of oil revenue, an optional control approach with application to the Iranian economy*, New York 1979.

NAKHAI, M, *Le pétrole en Iran*, Brussels 1938.

A historical survey.

NIẒĀM-MĀFĪ, Manṣūra, *The impact of oil on the Iranian economy*, Public Relations Office, National Iranian Oil Company, Tehran 1966.

RŪḤĀNĪ, Fu'ād, *Tārikh-i millī shudan-i ṣanᶜat-i naft-i Īrān*, *op.cit*. IX 6.8.

ṢAFARĪ, Ḥamīd, *Naft-i Īrān va impiriyālīsm-i naftkhvār*, Stassfurt 1973.

A 42-page Tūda publication on Iranian oil and imperialist policies.

STOBAUGH, Robert B, 'The evolution of Iranian oil policy, 1925-1975', LENCZOWSKI (ed), *Iran under the Pahlavis*, *op.cit*. IX 6.9, :201-52.

WILLIAMSON, J W, *In a Persian oilfield*, London 1927.

ZANGUENEH, A, *Le pétrole en Perse*, Paris 1933.

For works on the Anglo-Iranian oil dispute of 1951-53, see IX 6.8.

XV

EPILOGUE

The departure of the Shah from Iran in January 1979 and the return of Āyatallāh Khumainī shortly thereafter so completely changed the direction of political, social and economic trends that much of the preceding chapters, especially chapter XIV, that would in other circumstances have stood as an account of the contemporary situation, must now be regarded as history. For this reason, as well as because of the general uncertainty of the future, it seemed best to reserve a separate chapter to cover post-revolution developments.

1. *IRANIAN POST-PAHLAVĪ PUBLISHING*

More than three years after the establishment of the Islamic Republic the revolution is still going on in Iran. The new rulers are facing opposition of foreign powers, of their own counter-revolutionaries, as well as outright war with neighbouring Iraq. Although so far the Khumainī government has been successful on all three fronts, the material and ideological consequences of this struggle dominate Iranian life, including the publishing sector.

An unprecedented flood of political literature has come down on the Iranians since the overthrow of the Shah. Due to the lack of control of the central government, particularly during the early stage of the Islamic Republic, a broad spectrum of political ideologies offered solutions to and interpretations of the Islamic revolution. It is futile to speculate on the type of political system to be expected from groups which follow the leadership of Enver Khodzha or Che Guevara. Of course, Khumainī's idea of Islamic government cannot be equated with our notion of democracy either. The Imām made this quite clear in June 1980 when referring to Western-style university education; he has no use for a machinery that turns Muslims into communists. In general, post-Pahlavī Iran is a perpetuation of the political climate that prevailed among the former anti-Shah movement of the 1970s.

The central theme of most of the political literature is the proper interpretation of Islamic government as well as the struggle against imperialism. The Islamic government has launched a full scale publicity campaign in Persian and western languages to justify its policies in face of the vocal opposition. But with the achievement of the central aim of the anti-Shah movement, the opposition succumbed to increasing internal division. The factionalism of many parties has reached the point when it is no longer possible to consider the emerging entities as new parties; they are merely ideological cells that in many instances amount to no more than some hundred followers. By means of handbills, pamphlets, tracts, and tape recordings the various political groups accuse each other of opportunism as well as betrayal of the central committee of their respective party. A great deal of this political rhetoric attests to the euphoria prevalent among Iranians at this time. All positive manifestations of the Islamic revolution tend to be attributed to the popular movement, while all negative aspects are blamed on foreign imperialist influence. The ruling class, however, oversimplifies problems by considering all opposition as imperialist and counter-revolutionary now that the revolution has been achieved. Pro- and anti-government publications in Persian and western languages are listed in two bibliographies:

BEHN, W, *Islamic revolution or revolutionary Islam in Iran: publications from the overthrow of the Shah until his death*, Berlin 1980.

—— *Power and reaction in Iran*, Berlin 1981.

Additional material is listed in a work that covers mainly the history of the current political system.

—— *The Iranian opposition to the Shah: an annotated bibliography of publications from 1341/1962 to 1357/1979*, Wiesbaden 1979.

Five hundred of the important works relating to the anti-Shah movement and listed in these three bibliographies will be available in the forthcoming microfilm edition.

The Iranian opposition to the Shah: a documentary history, Zug 1982.

Three years after the establishment of the new government in Iran, the bibliographic control of commercial publications is still unreliable. The last issue of the Iranian national bibliography seems to have been published in the Pahlavī era. The only current bibliographic source has been *Āyanda*, the successor to *Rāhnamā-yi kitāb*, the journal of the Book Society of Persia; but only a fraction of the Iranian book production is listed: 328 and 292 titles for the Iranian years 1359 and 1360 respectively, against 2172 titles in the last complete issue of the *Iranian national bibliography* (1354/1975-76).

BEHN, W, 'Iranian publishing in the post-Pahlavi era', *Middle East Studies Association bulletin*, vol.15, no.1, July 1981 :10-13.

IMĀMĪ, K, 'Āyanda-i nashr-i kitāb dar Īrān', *Āyanda* V, nos.4-6, 1979 :191-203.

SEPEHRI, A, 'Publishing in Iran since the revolution', *MELA notes*, no.20, May 1980 :5-7.

'Rūznāma-hā, nashrīya-hā, majalla-hā-yi pīsh az qānūn-i matbūʿāt', *Āyanda* V, 10-12, Winter 1979 :917-21.

A list of about 250 periodicals published in Iran after the revolution and before the passing of the new Press Law.

The Iranian revolution was carried by the masses; it is therefore not surprising that the mass media in the form of periodical literature did and still do exert considerable influence. From the western vantage point it seems that revolutionary publishing is dominated by periodicals since no less than 475 new periodical titles have appeared during the first two years of the Islamic Republic Iran. This enormous number can be explained only by the necessity to respond quickly to current themes and events. It must be added, however, that the frequency is often quite irregular. The publishing history of some of these periodicals is a reflection of the political climate. As far as the content of the dissident periodicals is concerned, it is a serialized pamphleteering that started in the days of the dying Pahlavī dynasty.

BEHN, W, and W FLOOR, *Twenty years of Iranian power struggle: a bibliography of political periodicals from 1341/1962 to 1360/1981*, Berlin 1982.

Twenty-five revolutionary periodicals have been published in a micro-film edition (*Kār*, *Mardum*, *Mujāhid*, *Paikār*, *Ranjbar*, etc.).

The dissident press of revolutionary Iran up to 1359 (March 1981): selected periodicals with bibliographic description, comp. by W BEHN and W HÖFIG, Berlin 1981. 8 reels. 1st suppl., Berlin 1982.

2. *DOCUMENTS AND POLICY STATEMENTS*

The Draft Constitution of the Islamic Republic of Iran was published in the Iranian press in November 1979 (e.g. *Kaihān*, 17 November 1979, pp.1-4). A full translation of this was published in the *Foreign Broadcast Information Service*, and this was reproduced, with an introduction by Rouhollah K RAMAZANI, in the *Middle East Journal* 34(2), Spring 1980, pp.181-204. The Persian text, with a translation by Changiz VAFAI and notes and analysis by Nicholas A NIKAZMERAD and Gisbert H FLANZ, was published in April 1980, Dobbs Ferry, New York. Another translation by Hamid ALGAR was published in 1980, Berkeley, California.

A further document of interest is

The programme of the transitional government of the Democratic Islamic Republic of Iran, London 1981.

Among the more important of the theoretical writings that inspired the revolution are

KHUMAINĪ, Āyatallāh Sayyid Ruḥallāh Mūsavī, *Ḥukūmat-i Islāmī*, various editions, often without place or date. English tr. *Islamic government*, New York 1979. French tr. *Pour un gouvernement islamique*, tr. M KOTOBI and S SIMON, Paris 1979.

—— *Principes politiques, philosophiques, sociaux et religieux*, tr. J-M XAVIÈRE, Paris 1979. German and Swedish tr. 1980.

—— *Pensées politiques*, ed. and tr. Y A HENRY, Paris 1980.

—— *Selected messages and speeches*, Tehran 1980.

—— *Islam and revolution: writings and declarations of Imam Khomeini*, tr. Hamid ALGAR, Berkeley 1981.

Contains an 'authorized' translation of *Ḥukūmat-i Islāmī*.

—— *Khumeini speaks revolution*, tr. Mohiuddin AYYUBI, Karachi 1981.

Translation of six sermons and an interview.

—— *Kashf al-asrār*, Tehran 1942, repr. 1979.

—— *Mubāraza bā nafs yā jihād-i akbar*, Tehran 1978.

Zandagīnāma. Biyūgrāfī-yi pīshvā, Tehran 1978.

The official biography.

The principal works of ᶜAlī SHARĪᶜATĪ are the following:

SHARĪᶜATĪ, ᶜAlī, *Ārī chunīn būd barādar*, Tehran n.d., repr. Wilmette 1976.

—— *Dars-hā-yi Islām-shināsī*, Tehran 1971.

—— *Insān, Islām va maktab-hā-yi maghrib-zamīn*, Tehran ?, repr. 1976.

—— *Intiẓār, mazhab-i iᶜtirāż*, Tehran 1971.

—— *Mas'ūlīyat-i Shīᶜa būdan*, Tehran 1971.

—— *Shahādat*, Tehran 1972, repr. Wilmette 1977.

—— *Tashayyuᶜ-i ᶜAlavi va tashayyuᶜ-i Ṣafavī*, Tehran n.d.

All of the above works have been reprinted since the revolution.

—— *An approach to the understanding of Islam*, tr. Venus KAIVANTASH, Tehran 1979.

—— *Marxism and other western fallacies*, tr. R CAMPBELL, Berkeley, Cal. 1980.

—— *On the sociology of Islam*, tr. H ALGAR, Berkeley, Cal. 1980.

—— *Hajj*, tr. SOMAYYAH and YASER, Berkeley, Cal. 1981.

Other works by leaders of the revolution, past and present, include:

BANĪ ṢADR, Abu'l-ḥasan, *Uṣūl va żābiṭa-hā-yi ḥukūmat-i Islāmī*, Tehran 1979. English tr. M GHANOONPARVAR, *The fundamental principles and precepts of Islamic government*, Lexington, Kt. 1982.

—— *Quelle révolution pour Iran*, Paris 1980.

—— *Work and worker in Islam*, tr. Hasan MASHHADI, Tehran 1980.

BĀZARGĀN, Mahdī, *The inevitable victory*, tr. Mohammad YUSEFI, Bedford, Ohio 1978.

—— *Work and Islam*, Houston, Texas 1979.

JAZANĪ, Bizhan, *Capitalism and revolution in Iran*, London 1980.

3. *STUDIES AND ACCOUNTS OF THE REVOLUTION*

More than 80 works on the Islamic Republic have been published during the last two years in various languages. The complete repertory of these publications can be found in the monograph cumulation of J D PEARSON's Fifth Supplement to *Index Islamicus*, London, forthcoming in 1982. More selective listings and reviews are

HOOGLUND, Eric J, 'The Iranian revolution', *MEJ* 34(4), Autumn 1980 :485-89.

HUSSAIN, Asaf, 'A select bibliography of recent literature on the Islamic revolution', *The Muslim World Book Review*, vol.I, no.2, Winter 1981 :21-24.

A number of the publications listed in chapters IX and XIV of this *Guide* also contain brief analyses of the revolution, in some cases rather obviously tacked on to surveys largely completed before recent events. Among them may be cited ABRAHAMIAN (IX 6.9), AKHAVI (XIV 3.2.3), AMIRSADEGHI (IX 6.9), FISCHER (IX 6.9), GRAHAM (XIV 1.2), HALLIDAY (XIV 1.2), KATOUZIAN (IX 6.9), KAZEMI (XIV 1.4.1), KEDDIE (IX 6.9), RICHARD (VI 2.4), RUBIN (IX 6.9), and SAIKAL (IX 6.9).

Among other interesting or significant books may be mentioned (chosen to represent as many different points of view as possible):

ABD AL-RAHMAN (pseud.), *The betrayal of Iran*, n.p. 1979.

BEHRAWAN, Abdol Hossein (BIHRAVĀN, ᶜAbd al-ḥusain), *Iran: die programmierte Katastrophe. Anatomie eines Konfliktes*, Frankfurt 1980.

BINDER, Leonard, *Revolution in Iran*, American Academic Association for Peace in the Middle East, New York 1981.

BRIÈRE, C, and P BLANCHET, *Iran: la révolution au nom de Dieu*, Paris 1979.

DEHQANI-TAFTI, H B, *The hard awakening*, New York 1981.

Account of the revolution by the exiled Episcopal Bishop of Iran.

DREYFUSS, Robert, and Th. LEMARC, *Hostage to Khomeini*, New York 1980.

Economic consequences of the revolution in Iran. A compendium of papers submitted to the Joint Economic Committee, Congress of the United States, Washington, DC 1980.

ELWELL-SUTTON, L P, 'The Iranian revolution', *International Journal* 34(3), Toronto, Summer 1979 :391-407. Expanded version: Hossein AMIRSADEGHI (ed), *The security of the Persian Gulf*, *op.cit.* XIV 3.1.4, :231-54.

ENAYAT, Ḥamid, *Modern Islamic political thought*, London 1982.

GREUSSING, K (ed), *Religion und Politik in Iran*, Frankfurt a.M. 1981.

HOVEYDA, Fereydoun, *The fall of the Shah*, London 1980, tr. from the French (1979) by Roger LIDDELL.

JABBARI, A, and R OLSON, *Iran: essays on revolution in the making*, Lexington, Kt. 1981.

LEDEEN, Michael, and William LEWIS, *Debacle: the American failure in Iran*, New York 1981.

NAHAVAṆDI, Houchang, *Iran: deux rêves brisées*, Paris 1981.

NOBARI, Ali-Reza (ed), *Iran erupts: independence, news, and analysis of the Iranian national movement*, Stanford 1978.

PAHLAVĪ, Ashraf, *Visages dans un miroir: la soeur du Shah témoigne*, Paris 1980. English tr. *Faces in a mirror. Memoirs from exile*, Englewood Cliffs, NJ 1980.

PAHLAVĪ, Mohammad Reza, *Réponse à l'histoire*, Paris 1979. English tr. *The Shah's story*, London 1980. German tr. 1980.

SIDDIQUI, K, *The Islamic movement: issues and goals*, London 1981. Arabic tr., London 1981.

STEIN, A (ed), *Iran: neue Diktatur oder Frühling der Freiheit: 30 Interviews mit der Opposition*, Hamburg 1979.

Tell the American people: perspectives on the Iranian revolution, David H ALBERT (ed), Philadelphia 1980.

TERENZONI, T, and N VENTURI, *La repubblica Islamica dell'Iran, un ideale metafisico del XX secola*, Genoa 1980.

ZABIH, Sepehr, *Iran's revolutionary upheaval: an interpretative essay*, San Francisco 1979.

—— *Iran since the revolution*, London 1982.

Several periodicals provide additional information:

Iran Council Grapevine, six-monthly, Asia Society, New York.

Islamic Revolution: dimensions of the movement in Iran, monthly, Falls Church, Va. 1979-.

MERIP Reports, nos.75/76 (March/April 1979), 86 (March/April 1980), 87 (May 1980), 88 (June 1980), 98 (March 1981).

Articles and reports by Ervand ABRAHAMIAN, Fred HALLIDAY, Eric HOOGLUND, Lois BECK, and others.

ALEXANDER, Yonah (ed), *The United States and Iran*, *op.cit.* XIV 3.1.1. Includes documents on the hostages crisis.

Addendum

ABRAHAMIAN, Ervand, *Iran between two revolutions*, Princeton, NJ 1982.

INDEX